ESCHATOLOGY

ESCHATOLOGY

BIBLICAL, HISTORICAL, and PRACTICAL APPROACHES

A Volume in Honor of Craig A. Blaising

D. JEFFREY BINGHAM *and* GLENN R. KREIDER, *Editors*

Foreword by TIMOTHY GEORGE

CONTENTS

The New Testament

Part 3: The Doctrine of the Future in the History of Christian Thought

Part 4: The Doctrine of the Future and Christian Ministry

Contributing Authors

David L. Allen, Dean, School of Theology, Professor of Preaching, Southwestern Baptist Theological Seminary

J. Denny Autrey, Dean and Professor of Pastoral Ministries, Harvard School for Theological Studies, Southwestern Baptist Theological Seminary

Mark L. Bailey, President and Professor of Bible Exposition, Dallas Theological Seminary

D. Jeffrey Bingham, Associate Dean of Biblical and Theological Studies and Professor of Theology, Wheaton College

Stephen N. Blaising, Founder and President, Financial Dynamics, Inc., Dallas, TX

Daniel I. Block, Gunther H. Knoedler Professor of Old Testament, Wheaton College

Darrell L. Bock, Senior Research Professor of New Testament Studies, Executive Director of Cultural Engagement, Howard G. Hendricks Center for Christian Leadership and Cultural Engagement, Dallas Theological Seminary

J. Lanier Burns, Senior Professor of Systematic Theology, Research Professor of Theological Studies, Dallas Theological Seminary

David S. Dockery, President, Trinity International University

Eduard Friesen, Lecturer in Theology, Bibelseminar Bonn, Germany

Timothy George, Founding Dean of Beeson Divinity School and General Editor of the *Reformation Commentary on Scripture*

W. Edward Glenny, Professor New Testament and Greek and J. Edwin Hartill Chair of Biblical and Theological Studies, University of Northwestern, St. Paul

Nathan D. Holsteen, Associate Professor of Theological Studies, Dallas Theological Seminary

Steven L. James, Assistant Vice President for Academic Administration and Assistant Professor of Systematic Theology, Southwestern Baptist Theological Seminary

Friedhelm Jung, Professor of Systematic Theology, Southwestern Baptist Theological Seminary, Director of the Master of Arts Program, Bibelseminar Bonn, Germany

Kevin D. Kennedy, Associate Professor of Theology, Southwestern Baptist Theological Seminary

George L. Klein, Professor of Old Testament, Senior Associate Dean for the PhD Program in the School of Theology, Southwestern Baptist Theological Seminary

Glenn R. Kreider, Professor of Theological Studies, Dallas Theological Seminary

John D. Laing, Associate Professor of Systematic Theology and Philosophy, Harvard School for Theological Studies, Southwestern Baptist Theological Seminary (Houston)

Stefana Dan Laing, Assistant Librarian, Harvard School for Theological Studies, Southwestern Baptist Theological Seminary (Houston), Adjunct Professor of Theology, Houston Graduate School of Theology

Bryan M. Litfin, Professor of Theology, Moody Bible Institute

R. Albert Mohler, Jr., President of Southern Baptist Theological Seminary.

Paige Patterson, President, Professor of Theology, and L. R. Scarborough Chair of Evangelism, Southwestern Baptist Theological Seminary

Stephen O. Presley, Assistant Professor of Biblical Interpretation, Southwestern Baptist Theological Seminary

Mark F. Rooker, Professor of Old Testament and Hebrew, Southeastern Baptist Theological Seminary

Charles C. Ryrie, Professor Emeritus of Systematic Theology, Dallas Theological Seminary

Gregory S. Smith, Associate Vice President of Academic Administration and Associate Professor of Bible, Southwestern Baptist Theological Seminary

Stanley D. Toussaint, Senior Professor Emeritus of Bible Exposition, Dallas Theological Seminary

David L. Turner, Professor New Testament, Grand Rapids Theological Seminary

Jonathan P. Yates, Assistant Professor, Department of Theology and Religious Studies, Villanova University

FOREWORD

Timothy George

Although his own theology left much to be desired, Albert Schweitzer made an enduring contribution to modern biblical studies in his book *The Quest for the Historical Jesus*, published in 1906. The title of Schweitzer's study in German was *Geschichte der Leben-Jesu-Forschung*, which literally means "History of Life-of-Jesus-Research." Going back to the eighteenth century, Schweitzer reviewed the many attempts to reconstruct the story of Jesus and his message. Invariably, this "quest" produced a Jesus who looked very much like the liberal Protestant scholars who were writing about him—scholars who were happy with a social version of Christianity shorn of miracles and mystery.

However, as Schweitzer rightly saw, the documents of the New Testament presented a different sort of Messiah: one who, like his forerunner John the Baptist, preached a fiery message of coming judgment; one who said he had once seen Satan fall as lightning; one who declared that this world system and all of its pomp would be swept away when the "Son of man" comes in glory; one who spoke about budding fig trees and the signs of the end. Schweitzer brought back the sense of the apocalyptic and made it central both to Jesus's own self-understanding and to the message proclaimed by his first followers.

The disciples who accompanied Jesus to the Mount of Olives on his last earthly walk were told by heavenly messengers that "this Jesus, who was taken up from you into heaven, will come in the same way as you saw him go into heaven" (Acts 1:11, ESV). Meanwhile, Jesus's disciples were to go into all the world, empowered by the Holy Spirit, to bear a message of love and grace to all people, even as they waited for what the New Testament elsewhere calls "our blessed hope, the appearing of the glory of our great God and Savior Jesus Christ" (Titus 2:13, ESV). The first Aramaic-speaking Christians expressed this hope in a prayer: "*Maranatha*"—"Lord, come!"

But already, beginning in the New Testament period itself, various sources attacked and undermined this great expectation. The apostle Peter addressed the scoffers of his day who were saying, "Where is this 'coming' he promised?" He admonished the wavering believers both to wait for and to hasten by their godly living the coming of the day of God. For "the day of the Lord will come like a thief," he declared (2 Peter 3:4–13, NIV). This message is still urgently needed today. Although Gnosticism as a system of thought was rejected by the early church, its legacy can still be felt in the docetic eschatology of many who may affirm the soul's innate immortality but wonder why a visible parousia or bodily resurrection would be required, much less a millennial reign of Christ on earth.

In reaction to precisionist date-setters and time-keepers, some pastors have excised all references to the return of Christ from their preaching. Still others discount prophecy altogether in favor of a this-worldly, here-and-now commitment to social action and political theology. To this line of thought Karl Barth's words are worth noting: "The Christian hope does not lead us away from this life; it is rather the uncovering of the truth in which God sees our life. It is the conquest of death, but not of flight into the Beyond. The reality of this life is involved. Eschatology, rightly understood, is the most practical thing that can be thought."[1]

The essays in this book provide an overview of "the blessed hope" among the people of God, beginning with the Bible and continuing through the many challenges, reversals, and revivals of this hope in the course of Christian history. As such, this volume is an important contribution not only to historical theology but also to the church's thinking about eschatology today. Each contributor writes from an evangelical standpoint, though with differing perspectives on some matters. However, neither the tone nor the content of this book is sectarian. This is a book for the whole church—especially for the persecuted church, where the apocalyptic light has always shone brightest. The comfortable, culture-accommodated church of late modernity needs to engage seriously with the theme of this book. As T. A. Kantonen once reminded us: "The final scene in the drama of history is not the emergence of a utopia but the clash between Christ and Anti-Christ."[2]

It is appropriate that this volume is meant to honor the life and work of Professor Craig Blaising on the occasion of his sixty-fifth birthday. Throughout his distinguished career, Blaising has been both a diligent scholar of the academy

---

1. Karl Barth, *Dogmatics in Outline*, trans. G. T. Thomson (London: SCM Press, 1949), 154.
2. Cited in Donald G. Bloesch, *The Last Things: Resurrection, Judgment, Glory* (Downers Grove, IL: IVP Academic, 2005), 87.

and a faithful servant of the church. Blaising's election in 2005 as the president of the Evangelical Theological Society is an indication of the high esteem in which he is held by his colleagues and peers in the academy. Amidst his teaching and administrative responsibilities at three major seminaries (Dallas, Southern, and Southwestern), Blaising has written widely and deeply in the area of eschatology. His 1993 book *Progressive Dispensationalism*, cowritten with colleague Darrell Bock, was a landmark publication that continues to provide a paradigm for rethinking and restating a vital current of evangelical eschatology, one too often caricatured and misunderstood.

Two aspects of Blaising's overall approach deserve to be noted, namely his attention to *hermeneutics* and *development*. Unlike some historians of ideas who live in the clouds and never seem to land on earth, Blaising treats texts and their contexts with care and sensitivity. The right interpretation of any text, and especially the text of Scripture, involves complex issues of language, setting, nuance, and meaning. Blaising knows how important it is to attend to such matters, especially when treating controversial theological themes. Among evangelical scholars, Blaising has also been a pioneer in recovering a lively sense of the development of doctrine, both within the wider Christian tradition and in more recent theological construals. This has made his work of great value for all who wish to give expression to "the faith once delivered to the saints" and to do so in a way that is both coherent and compelling.

Craig Blaising's legacy is enshrined not only in his many learned writings but also in the several generations of students he has taught and guided in the faith. Those who have known him as a classroom teacher speak highly of his clarity and depth, his integrity and fairness, his gentlemanly deportment, and his personal and formative investment in their lives.

I am pleased to join with the editors and contributors of this volume in paying tribute to Craig Blaising at this milestone in his life and ministry. May the Lord see fit to adorn his church—and the Christian academy—with more Craig Blaisings!

BIOGRAPHY OF CRAIG ALAN BLAISING

Steven L. James

C raig Alan Blaising was born to Claude Lawrence Blaising and Mildred Helen Blaising in San Antonio, Texas, on September 28, 1949. Craig's father was a switchman and PBX installer at Southwestern Bell Telephone Company. His mother worked for the US Civil Service as a secretary. The oldest of three siblings, he has one brother, Stephen Neil Blaising, who was born on November 20, 1954. He also has a younger sister, Joy Dyanne Blaising, born on March 16, 1966.

In 1959, after hearing the gospel from Don Rose, associate pastor of Trinity Baptist Church in San Antonio, he placed his faith in Jesus Christ as his Savior and Lord and was baptized shortly thereafter. He was nine years old. Craig attended church regularly with his family and was active in Sunday school, Training Union, and various youth activities, including camps and retreats.

A youth choir trip in 1966 gave him the opportunity to participate in door-to-door witnessing. It was at that time that Craig sensed that God might be leading him into the Christian ministry. In his senior year of high school, he read the New Testament in its entirety for the first time through daily scheduled quiet times.

Following his graduation from Robert E. Lee High School (San Antonio) in 1976, he moved to Austin to attend the University of Texas. He went to college with the impression that the Lord might place him into full-time ministry, but he resolved to major in one of his primary interests, aerospace engineering.

At the University of Texas, Craig attended at Hyde Park Baptist Church and was involved in the Baptist Student Union. He was fundamentally and radically challenged by the Navigators to a life of Christian discipleship based on Scripture. Actively involving himself with the Navigators ministry and receiving encouragement from Navigators leaders, he devoted his senior year to praying about the possibility of full-time ministry. After several months, he was convinced that full-time ministry was the Lord's direction for his life.

Craig graduated from Texas in 1971 and chose to further his education by attending Dallas Theological Seminary (DTS), giving him the opportunity for a deeper grounding in Scripture, evangelical theology, and preparation for ministry. While a student at DTS from 1972–1976, the Lord directed his focus away from campus student ministries to teaching. Craig met Diane Sue Garrison in Dallas, and they were married on May 31, 1975 at Fellowship Bible Church, Dallas. After serving as the first Evangelical Bible Chair in the Department of Religion at the University of Texas at Arlington in 1978, Craig graduated with the ThM and he and Diane stayed in Dallas for him to begin the ThD degree, which he completed in 1979. Upon completion of the ThD, they journeyed to Scotland so that Dr. Blaising could begin PhD studies at the University of Aberdeen.

After completing residential studies at Aberdeen in 1980, Dr. Blaising joined the faculty of DTS. The Blaisings were blessed with a daughter, Emily Grace Blaising, on November 3, 1983, and then a son, Jonathan Craig Blaising, on February 16, 1987. Dr. Blaising graduated from Aberdeen with the PhD in 1988. Carrying both professorial and administrative responsibilities, he stayed at DTS for fifteen years until he was called to the faculty of the Southern Baptist Theological Seminary in Louisville, Kentucky, in 1995. He served at Southern in various roles, including the Joseph Emerson Brown Professor of Christian Theology.

In 2002 the Blaising family was called back to Texas, as Dr. Blaising was named executive vice president, provost, and professor of theology at Southwestern Baptist Theological Seminary in Fort Worth, the role that he has carried to the present. From 2002–2004, he also served Southwestern as dean of the School of Theology. Most recently, he has been appointed to the Jesse Hendley Chair of Biblical Theology at Southwestern.

Dr. Blaising was licensed to the ministry on May 17, 1972, at Trinity Baptist Church in San Antonio, and was ordained on August 28, 2005, at Travis Avenue Baptist Church in Fort Worth. He has served in a variety of ministerial roles such as Sunday school teacher, Wednesday night Bible teacher, youth discipleship teacher, and interim pastor. He has been a speaker internationally in churches, seminary and college chapel services, classrooms, and conferences. Currently, he teaches the Criswell Sunday school class at First Baptist Church in Dallas.

For nearly forty years, Dr. Blaising has served the Lord in teaching and administrative ministries in three seminaries. Teaching in the areas of systematic theology, historical theology, biblical theology, and spiritual formation, he has prepared thousands of students to boldly proclaim the inerrant and authoritative

Word of God through teaching and preaching. He has impacted his students in the classroom and those who have read his works or listened to him speak. In the classroom, Dr. Blaising exhibits the unique ability to articulate complex doctrines and concepts with precision and clarity. When he preaches and teaches, he makes the text of Scripture come alive.

In a brief biographical introduction, one can only summarize Dr. Blaising's contribution to the academy. After coediting *Dispensationalism, Israel and the Church: The Search for Definition* (1992) with Darrell Bock, he coauthored *Progressive Dispensationalism* with Dr. Bock (1993). Both are seminal works for the development of dispensational thought and have influenced wider evangelical discussions about the biblical covenants and hermeneutics. Several years before these works, Dr. Blaising laid the foundation for development within the tradition of dispensationalism by appealing to and noting the appropriateness of doctrinal development within Christian orthodoxy ["Developing Dispensationalism, Part 1: Doctrinal Development in Orthodoxy," *Bibliotheca Sacra* 145 (1998):133–40, and "Developing Dispensationalism, Part 2: Development of Dispensationalism by Contemporary Dispensationalists," *Bibliotheca Sacra* 145 (1988):254–80]. He is known as a patristic scholar and contributed to the Ancient Christian Commentary on Scripture, editing with Carmen Harden the volume on Psalms 1–50. He has contributed to two Zondervan works in the area of eschatology: *Three Views on the Millennium and Beyond* (1999) and *Three Views on the Rapture: Pretribulation, Prewrath, or Postribulation* (2010). In addition to *Bibliotheca Sacra*, Dr. Blaising has published articles in *The Criswell Theological Review, Journal of the Evangelical Theological Society, Pro Ecclesia, Southern Baptist Journal of Theology, Southwestern Journal of Theology, Wesleyan Theological Journal*, and others. He has written various entries in *The Encyclopedia of Early Christianity*, second edition (1997) and *The Evangelical Dictionary of Theology* (1984 and 2001). He has written numerous essays and presented papers across North America and in Europe. Dr. Blaising is currently working on several projects, including a volume on the subject of eschatology and what certainly will be his magnum opus, a systematic theology.

Dr. Blaising is well-known as an eminent scholar. He is active in the Evangelical Theological Society, the North American Patristics Society, the American Academy of Religion, and the Society for Biblical Literature. In 1986 he was chosen as the president of the Southwest Region of the Evangelical Theological Society and in 2005 served as the president of the society at the national level.

In addition to a broad contribution to evangelicalism, Dr. Blaising has influenced the denomination in which he is part. After being discouraged over the prospects for expositional preaching and teaching in Southern Baptist churches in the 1970s, he entered the Fellowship of Bible Churches and the teaching ministry of Dallas Theological Seminary. However, the conservative reformation which began in the Southern Baptist Convention in 1979 convinced him of the real possibility of an expositionally based theological ministry in the convention of churches in which he first heard the gospel and began to grow in Christ. During his tenure at two Southern Baptist seminaries, Dr. Blaising has worked to provide an environment in which the inerrant Scripture is taught. For the past thirteen years, Dr. Blaising has served as provost at Southwestern Seminary, leading the training of a whole generation of pastors, missionaries, educators, and other ministry leaders who currently serve the denomination in every part of the world.

EDUCATION

BS, University of Texas, Austin, 1971
ThM, Dallas Theological Seminary, 1976
ThD, Dallas Theological Seminary, 1979
PhD, University of Aberdeen, Scotland, 1988

ACADEMIC EXPERIENCE

Instructor, Dallas Theological Seminary Lay Institute, 1976–1977
Instructor, Evangelical Bible Chair, Department of Religion, University of Texas at Arlington, 1978
Assistant Professor of Systematic Theology, Dallas Theological Seminary, 1980–1985
Associate Professor of Systematic Theology, Dallas Theological Seminary, 1985–1989
Acting Department Chair, Systematic Theology, Dallas Theological Seminary, 1988–1989
Professor of Systematic Theology, Dallas Theological Seminary, 1989–1995
Visiting Professor of Historical Theology, Southern Baptist Theological Seminary, 1993–1994
Professor of Christian Theology, Southern Baptist Theological Seminary, 1995–1996
Department Chair, Christian Theology, Southern Baptist Theological Seminary, 1996–1999

Joseph Emerson Brown Professor of Christian Theology, Southern Baptist Theological Seminary, 1996–2001

Acting Director of Research Doctoral Studies and Associate Dean of the School of Theology, Southern Baptist Theological Seminary, 1997–1998

Associate Vice President for Doctoral Studies, Southern Baptist Theological Seminary, 1999–2001

Director of Advanced Master of Divinity Studies, Southern Baptist Theological Seminary, 2000–2001

Dean, School of Theology, Southwestern Baptist Theological Seminary, 2002–2004

Professor of Theology, Southwestern Baptist Theological Seminary, 2002–present

Executive Vice President and Provost, Southwestern Baptist Theological Seminary, 2002–present

Jesse Hendley Chair of Biblical Theology, Southwestern Baptist Theological Seminary, 2014–present

Honors

Engineering Fellows Program, University of Texas at Austin (1971)

Tau Beta Pi, Engineering Honor Society, University of Texas at Austin (1971)

Sigma Gamma Tau, Aerospace Engineering Honor Society, University of Texas at Austin (1971)

Graduated with Honors, University of Texas at Austin (1971)

Loraine Chafer Award in Systematic Theology, Dallas Theological Seminary (1976)

William M. Anderson Scholarship Award, Dallas Theological Seminary (1979)

Graduated with Honors, Dallas Theological Seminary (1976)

Who's Who Among Students in American Colleges and Universities (1977–1978)

Rotary Foundation Graduate Fellowship for Studies at the University of Aberdeen (1978–1979)

Outstanding Young Men in America (1982)

Who's Who in Theology and Science (1992)

Who's Who in Religion (1992–1993)

Who's Who in America (2000)

Fellow, The Research Institute of The Ethics and Religious Liberty Commission (elected 2002)

Fellow, The Institute for Theological Inquiry, Princeton Theological Seminary (2011–2012)

Memberships Held

American Academy of Religion
Evangelical Theological Society (President, 2005; Southwest Regional President, 1986–1987)
International Association for Patristic Studies
National Association of Scholars
North American Patristic Society
Society of Biblical Literature

History of Church Membership

Trinity Baptist Church, San Antonio, Texas (1959–1967)
Hyde Park Baptist Church, Austin, Texas (1967–1972)
Casa View Baptist Church, Dallas, Texas (1972–1973)
Fellowship Bible Church, Dallas, Texas (1973–1978)
Deeside Christian Fellowship, Aberdeen, Scotland (1978–1980)
Scofield Memorial Church, Dallas, Texas (1980–1983)
Faith Bible Church, DeSoto, Texas (1983–1988)
First Baptist Church, Dallas, Texas (1988–1993)
St. Matthews Baptist Church, Louisville, Kentucky (1993–1994)
First Baptist Church, Dallas, Texas (1994–1995)
Hurstbourne Baptist Church, Louisville, Kentucky (1996–2000)
Bethany Baptist Church, Louisville, Kentucky (2000–2002)
Travis Avenue Baptist Church, Fort Worth, Texas (2002–2012)
First Baptist Church, Dallas, Texas (2012–present)

Bibliography

Editor

With Carmen Hardin, "Psalms 1-50." In *Ancient Christian Commentary on Scripture*. Old Testament vol. 7. Downers Grove, IL: InterVarsity, 2008.

With Darrell L. Bock. *Dispensationalism, Israel and the Church: The Search for Definition*. Grand Rapids: Zondervan, 1992.

Books
With Darrell L. Bock. *Progressive Dispensationalism*. Grand Rapids: Baker, 1993.

Articles and Essays
"A Critique of Gentry and Wellum's, *Kingdom through Covenant*: A Hermeneutical–Theological Response," *The Master's Seminary Journal* 26 (2015): 111–27.

"Israel and Hermeneutics." Pages 151–67 in *The People, the Land and the Future of Israel: A Biblical Theology of Israel and the Jewish People*, edited by Darrell L. Bock and Mitch Glaser. Grand Rapids: Kregel, 2014.

"Premillennialism: A Progressive Dispensational Perspective," *Criswell Theological Review* 11 (2013): 63–70.

"A Response to Eastern Orthodoxy." Pages 54–66 in *Journeys of Faith: Evangelicalism, Eastern Orthodoxy, Catholicism, and Anglicanism*, edited by Robert L. Plummer. Grand Rapids: Zondervan, 2012.

"The Day of the Lord: Theme and Pattern in Biblical Theology," *Bibliotheca Sacra* 169 (2012): 3–19.

"The Day of the Lord and the Seventieth Week of Daniel," *Bibliotheca Sacra* 169 (2012): 131–42.

"The Day of the Lord and the Rapture," *Bibliotheca Sacra* 169 (2012): 259–70.

"The Day of the Lord Will Come: An Exposition of 2 Peter 3:1–18," *Bibliotheca Sacra* 169 (2012): 387–401.

"Prepared for Prayer: The Psalms in Early Christian Worship." Pages 51–64 in *Forgotten Songs: Reclaiming the Psalms for Christian Worship*, edited by Ray Van Neste and C. Richard Wells. Nashville: B & H Academic, 2012.

"The Kingdom That Comes with Jesus: Premillennialism and the Harmony of Scripture." Pages 141–59 in *The Return of Christ: A Premillennial Perspective; Reflections from the Acts 1:11 Conference*, edited by David L. Allen and Steve W. Lemke. Nashville: B & H Academic, 2011.

"A Case for the Pretribulational Rapture." Pages 25–73 in *Three Views on the Rapture: Pretribulation, Prewrath, or Postribulation*, edited by Alan Hultberg. Grand Rapids: Zondervan, 2010.

"Creedal Formation as Hermeneutical Development: A Re-Examination of the Nicene Creed," *Pro Ecclesia* 19 (2010): 371–88.

"New Creation, Eschatology, and Its Ethical Implications." Pages 7–24 in *Ethics and Eschatology: Papers Presented at the Annual Theological Conference of Emanuel University*, edited by Corneliu C. Simut. Oradea: Emanuel University Press, 2010.

"The Kingdom That Comes with Jesus: Premillennialism and the Harmony of Scripture, *Southern Baptist Journal of Theology* 14, no. 1 (2010): 4–13.

"The Future of Israel as a Theological Question." Pages 102–21 in *To the Jew First: The Case for Jewish Evangelism in Scripture and History*, edited by Darrell L. Bock and Mitch Glaser. Grand Rapids: Kregel, 2008.

"Faithfulness: A Prescription for Theology." Pages 201–16 in *Quo Vadis, Evangelicalism? Perspectives on the Past, Direction for the Future: Presidential Addresses from the First Fifty Years of the Journal of the Evangelical Theological Society*, edited by Andreas J. Kostenberger. Wheaton, Ill: Crossway, 2007.

"Faithfulness: A Prescription for Theology." *Journal of the Evangelical Theological Society* 49 (2006): 5–16.

"Dispensationalism." Pages 343–45 in *Evangelical Dictionary of Theology*. Edited by Walter A. Elwell. Second Edition. Grand Rapids/Carlisle, UK: Baker/Paternoster, 2001.

"William J. Abraham's *Canon and Criterion in Christian Theology: From the Fathers to Feminism.*" *Churchman* 115 (2001): 103–09.

"The Future of Israel as a Theological Question." *Journal of the Evangelical Theological Society* 44 (2001): 435–50.

"Premillennialism." Pages 155–227 in *Three Views on the Millennium and Beyond,* edited by Darrell L. Bock. Grand Rapids: Zondervan, 1999.

"Spiritual Formation in the Early Church." In *The Christian Educators Handbook on Spiritual Formation.* Edited by Kenneth O. Gangel and James C. Wilhoit. Wheaton, Ill: Victor, 1994.

"Changing Patterns in American Dispensational Theology." *Wesleyan Theological Journal* 29 (1994): 149–64.

"Contemporary Dispensationalism." *Southwestern Journal of Theology* 36 (1994): 5–13.

"Lewis Sperry Chafer." Pages 83–96 in *Handbook of Evangelical Theologians.* Edited by Walter A. Elwell. Grand Rapids: Baker, 1993.

"Developing Dispensationalism, Part 1: Doctrinal Development in Orthodoxy." *Bibliotheca Sacra* 145 (1988): 133–40.

"Developing Dispensationalism, Part 2: Development of Dispensationalism by Contemporary Dispensationalists." *Bibliotheca Sacra* 145 (1988): 254–80.

"Malachi." Pages 1573–89 in *The Bible Knowledge Commentary*. Edited by John F. Walvoord and Roy B. Zuck. Wheaton, Ill: Victor, 1985.

"Chalcedon and Christology: A 1530th Anniversary." *Bibliotheca Sacra* 138 (1981): 326–37.

"Gethsemane: A Prayer of Faith." *Journal of the Evangelical Theological Society* 22 (1979): 333–43.

Author of various entries in *The Encyclopedia of Early Christianity*, Second edition. (1997) and *The Evangelical Dictionary of Theology* (1984 and 2001).

Presentations and Addresses

Dr. Blaising has spoken at numerous chapel services, performed commencement addresses, and been involved in a multitude of theological forums that are not listed here. The following is a list of his major presentations and addresses throughout the last three decades.

"The Use of Matthew 10:24 in Early Christian Chiliasm." Society of Biblical Literature International Meeting, Buenos Aires, Argentina, 2015.

"A Critique of Gentry and Wellum, *Kingdom through Covenant*: A Hermeneutical and Theological Response." Evangelical Theological Society National Meeting, San Diego, 2014.

"Typology and the Nature of the Church." Evangelical Theological Society National Meeting, San Diego, 2014.

"The Coming Kingdom and Biblical Interpretation." Thy Kingdom Come Chosen People Ministries Conference, London, 2014.

"The People, the Land, and the Future of Israel and Hermeneutics." The People, the Land, and the Future of Israel Chosen People Ministries Conference, Calvary Baptist Church, New York, 2013.

"Early Christian Millennialism and the Intermediate State of the Dead: A Response to Charles Hill's Regnum Caelorum." Evangelical Theological Society National Meeting, Baltimore, 2013.

"ETS and Inerrancy: Reflections on the Pinnock, Sanders Membership Challenge." Evangelical Theological Society National Meeting, Baltimore, 2013.

"Eschatology and Exegesis in Early Christian Interpretation of the Apocalypse: A Re-examination of Charles Hill's Regnum Caelorum." Society of Biblical Literature International Meeting, St. Andrews, Scotland, 2013.

Day-Higginbotham Lecture Series, Southwestern Baptist Theological Seminary, 2013.

"Thy Kingdom Come: Promise, Prophecy, and the Coming of the Lord." Paschal Memorial Lectures, Baptist Missionary Association Theological Seminary, Jacksonville, TX, 2012.

"Beyond the Journey; Scripture and Salvation in Evangelicalism and Orthodoxy." Evangelical Theological Society National Meeting, Milwaukee, 2012.

"Does Evangelical Affirmation of the Canon Implicitly Support the Catholic Church's Authority?" Wheaton Theology Conference, Evangelicals Becoming Catholic: A Response, 2012.

Shepherds Theological Seminary Spring Colloquium, Cary, NC, 2012.

"The Millennium from a Progressive Dispensationalist Perspective." Future Kingdom: Perspectives on the Millennial Reign of Christ Conference, Criswell College, 2012.

"The Day of the Lord." The W.H. Griffith Thomas Memorial Lectureship, Dallas Theological Seminary, 2011.

"Classical, Traditional, Progressive: Validity of Labels in Distinguishing Types of Dispensationalism." Evangelical Theological Society National Meeting, San Francisco, 2011.

"Review of Jesus the Messiah: Tracing the Promises, Expectations, and Coming of Israel's King." Evangelical Theological Society National Meeting, Atlanta, 2010.

"Exegetical Foundations for Preaching the Psalms." Advanced Expository Preaching Workshop: Strategies for Preaching through the Psalms, Southwestern Baptist Theological Seminary, 2009.

"The Hermeneutics of Creedal Formulation: A Re-examination of the Nicene Creed." Evangelical Theological Society National Meeting, San Diego, 2008.

"Creedal Formulation as Hermeneutical Practice: A Re-examination of the Nicene Creed." Society of Biblical Literature International Meeting, Auckland, New Zealand, 2008.

"Faithfulness: A Prescription for Theology." Presidential Address, Evangelical Theological Society National Meeting, Valley Forge, PA, 2005.

"The Future of Israel as a Theological Question." Plenary Address, Evangelical Theological Society National Meeting, Nashville, 2000; also presented as "To the Jew First in the New Millennium." Chosen Peoples Ministry Conference, West Palm Beach, 2001.

"Response to William Abraham's Canon and Criterion." Evangelical Theological Society National Meeting, Nashville, 2000.

"Review of Recent Works on Theological Hermeneutics: Vanhoozer, Watson, and Wolterstorff." Evangelical Theological Society National Meeting, Boston, 1999.

"The Premillennial Eschatology of Jurgen Moltmann." Evangelical Theological Society National Meeting, Orlando, 1998.

"On Defining Dispensationalism: A Historical Response to Ryrie's Dispensationalism." Evangelical Theological Society National Meeting, Philadelphia, 1995.

"The Baptism of the Holy Spirit in the History of Redemption." Dispensationalism Study Group, Evangelical Theological Society National Meeting, Chicago, 1994.

"Progressive Dispensationalism." Evangelical Theological Society Southeast Regional Meeting, Louisville, 1994.

"Changing Patterns in American Dispensational Theology." Wesleyan Theological Society, Oklahoma City, 1993.

"Scripture, Tradition and Authority: An Evangelical Response to Emmanuel Clapsis." Society for the Study of Eastern Orthodoxy and Evangelicalism, Wheaton, Ill, 1992.

"Epigraphical Evidence for Montanist Regional Bishops Titled *Koinonoi*, A Response to Bill Tabernee." Seminar on the Development of Early Catholic Christianity, Fort Worth, 1992.

"The Kingdom of God in Progressive Dispensationalism." Evangelical Theological Society National Meeting, Kansas City, 1991.

"From Participation to Generation in *Contra Arianos* 1.15–16." Eleventh International Conference on Patristic Studies, Oxford, 1991.

"Water and Spirit Baptism According to Irenaeus of Lyons." Seminar of Development of Early Catholic Christianity, Dallas, 1991.

"Dispensationalism at the End of the Twentieth Century." American Academy of Religion National Meeting, New Orleans, 1990.

"Deification: An Athanasian View of Spirituality." Evangelical Theological Society National Meeting, Boston, 1987.

"Systematic Theology: Fourth Century Reflection on Twentieth Century Prospects." Presidential Address, Evangelical Theological Society Southwest Regional Meeting, San Antonio, 1987.

"Developing Dispensationalism." Dispensationalism Group Meeting, Evangelical Theological Society National Meeting, Atlanta, 1986.

"Preliminary Remarks on the Theological Method of Athanasius of Alexandria." Evangelical Theological Society National Meeting, Chicago, 1984.

PREFACE

Jeffrey Bingham and Glenn R. Kreider

O ur first encounters with Craig Blaising were in the classrooms of Dallas Theological Seminary. There he instructed us, mentored us, and formed us. He taught us to read critically, think theologically, and write purposefully. We knew nothing about theology before we were his pupils, and all we now comprehend and impart to others we do in poor imitation of him. We both point to an elective with him on "History, Hermeneutics, and Theological Method" as pivotal in setting the trajectory of our theological pilgrimages.

Both of us chose to do doctoral studies in theology at Dallas Theological Seminary because of Craig Blaising. In fact, we met in his seminar on hermeneutics and historiography and took several other seminars together. Blaising directed Bingham's dissertation on Irenaeus's use of Matthew.

This volume is a gift to Craig Blaising on the occasion of his sixty-fifth birthday. It comes not only from us but also from twenty-nine others united in deep affection and admiration for Craig. The contributors include former students, former teachers, colleagues, friends, presidents of the institutions at which he has faithfully served, and his brother. Each chapter testifies to the respect that each author holds for him.

Craig Blaising has made his greatest academic contributions in the areas of theological method, Athanasius of Alexandria, patristic biblical interpretation, John Wesley, dispensationalism, and eschatology. The wider Christian world knows him best for his work on the latter two; therefore, it was no difficult choice selecting the focus and form for this volume. Since he is a teacher at heart, the volume had to be an introductory, student-friendly textbook. Eschatology, the doctrine of the future, had to be its topic.

The book is divided into four parts. Each part provides information helpful to the student seeking to progress toward an evangelical, holistic, integrative, systematic perspective on the doctrine of the future. The first part, "The Doctrine of the Future and Its Foundations," is meant to orient the reader toward basic theological issues that undergird reflection on Christian faith claims concerning the future. Part 2, "The Doctrine of the Future in the Bible," introduces the reader to a biblical theology of the future. Here the purpose is to provide a thorough overview of how different portions of the canon each witness to the great Christian hope. Treatment of "The Doctrine of the Future in the History of Christian Thought" comprises the third section. How various theological systems and theologians have interpreted the biblical data is an important source for contemporary theological reflection. The volume concludes with a section on "The Doctrine of the Future and Christian Ministry." Christian reflection on any doctrine is not complete until it contemplates how to minister more effectively in light of that doctrine. Good theology is always practical.

We are deeply grateful to Tyson Guthrie, who has tirelessly contributed to the success of this volume with his editorial assistance. We also express our thanks to Dennis Hillman and Paul Hillman of Kregel Academic, and their editorial staff, for their professionalism and commitment in seeing this book through to publication.

Thank you, Craig, for a lifetime of service to the church and the academy. Thank you for a legacy of faithfulness and integrity. Thank you for pointing so many to the glorious gospel of the risen Savior. Thank you for encouraging so many students to pursue a life of gospel ministry. Thank you for demonstrating and exhorting us toward excellence. Thank you for teaching and modeling the hope of life everlasting. Thank you for mentoring so many to become more and more like the Lord Jesus Christ. We are grateful to God for you.

D. Jeffrey Bingham and Glenn R. Kreider
28 September 2014
65th Birthday of Craig A. Blaising
Feast of St. Exuperios, Bishop of Toulouse
Champion of the Poor; Curator of the Canon

Part 1

The Doctrine of the Future and Its Foundations

The Doctrine of the Future and Canonical Unity: Connecting the Future to the Past

D. Jeffrey Bingham

In an essay entitled "The Problem of Biblical Theology," ten years ago now, James D. G. Dunn questioned, as he reflected upon the nature of the two Testaments, "Does 'New' indicate movement onto a different plane of revelation, with 'Old' subordinated to a merely background role? Or is 'New' a new form of the 'Old', with each vital to a proper reception and understanding of the other?"[1] Further in the same work, along the same theme, he wrote, "The fundamental question of biblical theology is whether the diversity *between* the Testaments involves a discontinuity that decisively undermines claims to continuity."[2] Dunn, I think, has succinctly identified the problem of biblical theology. Do the differences between the Old and New Testaments, and we must recognize that there are many, dismiss the possibility of seeing theological continuity between them? In the middle of the second century, one biblical theologian had answered in the affirmative. He believed, to use Dunn's words, that "the diversity *between* the Testaments involves a discontinuity that decisively undermines claims to continuity."

Marcion: Dichotomy and Discontinuity

Marcion's Biography

Born in Sinope, on the Black Sea under the reign of Emperor Hadrian (117–138 CE), Marcion of Pontus was the son of Sinope's bishop.[3] Our sources

---

1. In *Out of Egypt: Biblical Theology and Biblical Interpretation* (ed. C. Bartholomew, M. Healy, K. Möller, and R. Parry; Grand Rapids: Zondervan, 2004, 174.
2. Dunn, "The Problem of Biblical Theology," 175 (italics original).
3. Epiphanius, *Panarion* 1.42.1.3; Hippolytus, *Refutation* 7.17; Pseudo-Tertullian, *Heresies* 6.2; Clement of Alexandria, *Stromata* 7.17.

tell us that though he was once committed to a celibate, hermitic life, Marcion fell into sexual sin with a virgin, was excommunicated by his own father, and eventually left Sinope for Rome, arriving there after the death Hyginus, bishop of Rome (138–142).[4] According to Irenaeus of Lyons and Tertullian, his influence was strongest under the ministry of Hyginus's successor, bishop Anicetus (ca.155–ca.166) and the reign of Roman Emperor, Antoninus Pius (138–162), although as Clement of Alexandria notes, he was already an old man, with the heretics Basilides and Valentinus being younger.[5] Justin Martyr (d. 165) writes that Marcion was teaching his error at the same time that Justin, in Rome, was composing his first *Apology* (ca. 153–155).

Prior to arriving in Rome, however, he traveled to Asia Minor. He had been a ship owner (*nauklerus*) in Sinope, perhaps part of a family business.[6] His hometown was known for the nautical and maritime trades, as the ships featured on the city's coins attest. Sinope provided the nautical setting and the required expertise and labor for shipbuilding, while the countryside was rich enough in timber to feed that industry.[7] We know that while in Asia Minor, Marcion failed to receive a warm welcome. One source suggests that the Ephesian church rejected him when he attempted to pass on his doctrine there.[8] Furthermore, he traveled to Hierapolis of Phrygia to meet bishop Papias (wrote ca. 130–140). He brought with him reference letters from Christians in Sinope.[9] This may suggest that there was a community in Sinope that was already open to or unconcerned about Marcion's views.[10] Papias, however, immediately disapproved of his teaching, believing that it was contrary to that of the church, particularly the writings

---

4. Epiphanius, *Panarion* 42.1.4–7; Pseudo-Tertullian, *Heresies* 6.2; Filastrius, *Different Heresies* 45.
5. Irenaeus, *Against Heresies* 3.4.3; Tertullian, *Against Marcion* 1.19; *Prescriptions* 30; Clement of Alexandria, *Stromata* 7.17.
6. Lionel Casson, *Ships and Seamanship in the Ancient World* (Baltimore: John Hopkins University, 1995), 314–16; cf. Sebastian Moll, *The Arch-Heretic Marcion* (Tübingen: Mohr Siebeck, 2010), 29–30.
7. David M. Robinson, *Ancient Sinope* (Chicago: University of Chicago, 1906), 18-19, 245, 261; Polyaenus, *Strategems* 7.21.2.5.
8. Filastrius, *Different Heresies* 45. It is difficult, however, to see John the Evangelist performing the excommunication. Cf. E. C. Blackman, *Marcion and His Influence* (London: SPCK, 1948), 2.
9. *Johannine Prologue* (Old Latin/Anti-Marcionite).
10. It is possible, I suppose, that these letters were from Christians in Pontus to Papias and were unconcerned with Marcion personally. Nevertheless, to trust Marcion as an emissary to Papias is tantamount to an endorsement.

of the Apostle John. In response, Papias excommunicated him.[11] We know, too, that Marcion came face to face with Polycarp, bishop of Smyrna (ca. 70–155).[12] This confrontation may have occurred during the same journey to Asia Minor, while Marcion was in Smyrna, or perhaps later in Rome, while Polycarp was visiting that city and restoring many who had been misled by Valentinus and Marcion.[13] On that occasion Marcion asked Polycarp if he knew him. Polycarp's reply was condemning: "I do know you, first born of Satan."

We see then, that prior to arriving in Rome, Marcion was already known for false teaching. He had already been excommunicated or rejected by two or three different bishops (his father, Papias, and Polycarp) in different cities (Sinope, Hierapolis, and possibly Smyrna and Ephesus).[14] The same was to happen to him in Rome. But in Rome he would separate from the apostolic church and plant his own.

According to Jerome, before he arrived in Rome, Marcion cautiously attempted to prepare the waters for his arrival by sending a woman as his emissary.[15] Given his reception in Asia Minor, such caution was not out of place. Marcion finally arrived in Rome after Cerdo and after the death of the Roman bishop Hyginus (ca. 142), probably around 144–145 on one of his own vessels.[16] He came well equipped with substantial wealth from his business as a sea merchant. Once there, perhaps in good faith, having already been sternly rebuked in both Sinope and Asia Minor, he presented himself to the church, made a

---

11. *Johannine Prologue* (Old Latin/Anti-Marcionite). I agree with F. F. Bruce that the best way to read the text is to suppose that the last *Iohanne* is an error. It should read *Papias*, so that Papias is the one who excommunicated Marcion, not John ("St John at Ephesus," *Bulletin of the John Rylands Library* 60 [1978]: 345-46). Perhaps this explains the anachronism in Filastrius, *Different Hesesies* 45 (cf. Moll, *The Arch-Heretic Marcion*, 56, n.53). D. de Bruyne ("Les plus anciens prologues latins des Evangiles," *Revue Benedictine* 40 [1928]: 193-214) argued that the action actually took place in Rome, that the one who excommunicated Marcion was a Roman ecclesiastical authority, and that John's name was substituted for that of the Roman authority. Blackman joins Harnack in reading the passage without reference to John and as a record of Marcion's rejection following Papias's denunciation of him (Blackman, *Marcion and His Influence*, 56).
12. Cf. Irenaeus, *Against Heresies* 3.4.3.
13. Cf. Blackman, *Marcion and His Influence*, 2.
14. Cf. Adolf von Harnack, *Marcion: das Evangelium vom fremden Gott* (Leipzig: J. C. Hinrich, 1924), 28. Unfortunately, the English translation does not include the appendices (Adolf von Harnack, *Marcion: The Gospel of the Alien God*, trans. J. E. Steely and L. D. Bierma (Durham: Labyrinth, 1990).
15. Jerome, *Ep.* 133.4.
16. Cf. Blackman, *Marcion and His Influence*, 2–3, n. 1; Moll, *The Arch-Heretic Marcion*, 31–41; Epiphanius, *Panarion* 42.1.7: Irenaeus, *Against Heresies* 1.27.1; 3.4.3.

generous contribution of 200,000 sesterces, and sought entrance into the fellowship from the Roman presbyters.[17] At some point, he tested the doctrine of the presbyters on the issue of the contrast between the Old and the New. They attempted to guide him into an acceptable view of the difference, but he rejected their interpretation. The presbyters, then, probably already aware of his view of the two gods and refusing to act contrary to his earlier excommunication from Sinope, refused his request for communion and returned his contribution.[18] In retaliation, he threatened to divide the church and form his own sect.[19] A blasphemous movement resulted that branched out from Rome to the whole world leading multitudes astray.[20]

Marcion's Thought: Novelty, Contradiction, and Dualism

We now turn our attention to some of the theological conceptions of Marcion, particularly those that relate to the issue of diversity between the Testaments. Adolf von Harnack, in his *History of Dogma*, summarized Marcion's issue this way:

> Completely carried away with the novelty, uniqueness and grandeur of the Pauline Gospel of the grace of God in Christ, Marcion felt that all other conceptions of the Gospel, and especially its union with the Old Testament religion, was opposed to, and a backsliding from the truth. He accordingly supposed that it was necessary to make the sharp antitheses of Paul, law and gospel, wrath and grace, works and faith, flesh and spirit,

---

17. Tertullian, *Against Marcion* 4.5; *Prescriptions* 30; Epiphanius, *Panarion* 42.1.7–3.2; Filastrius, *Different Heresies* 45. Marcion may have arrived in Rome in some sympathy with the faith of the Roman church. Tertullian indicates that perhaps some measure of faith was present when he first presented himself at Rome (*Against Marcion* 4.5) and a letter, by Marcion's own hand, apparently provided testimony to his once believing in accordance with the orthodox faith, a faith he later rejected (Tertullian, *On the Flesh of Christ* 2; *Against Marcion* 1.1; 4,4). Perhaps the most we can say is that he gave the impression of being a person of faith and at one point presented himself as such. Two hundred thousand sesterces was a great deal of money. It was equal to the annual income of a *ducenarius*, one of the highest-ranking imperial officials. With it Marcion could have purchased a house within the city of Rome, a manor in a Greek port city, or land sufficient for a midsize farm (See Peter Lampe, *From Paul to Valentinus: Christians at Rome in the First Two Centuries* [Minneapolis: Augsburg Fortress, 2003], 245).

18. Epiphanius, *Panarion* 42.1.7-3.2; Filastrius, *Different Heresies* 45; Tertullian, *Against Marcion* 4.5.

19. Epiphanius, *Panarion* 42.2.8.

20. Justin Martyr, *1 Apology* 26; Tertullian, *Against Marcion* 5.19; Epiphanius, *Panarion* 42.1.2.

sin and righteousness, death and life, that is the Pauline criticism of the Old Testament religion, the foundation of his religious views, and to refer them to two principles, the righteous
and wrathful god of the Old Testament, who is at the same
time identical with the creator of the world, and the God of
the Gospel, quite unknown before Christ, who is only love and
mercy.[21]

Our ancient sources support Harnack's summary. Tertullian tells us that
Marcion was deeply concerned with what he perceived to be the radical, utterly
unique novelty of Christ and the ministry and testament of grace that came with
him. In his theological enterprise, Tertullian says, Marcion was devoted to prov-
ing "the *newness* of the kindness of [his] *new* Christ."[22] Apparently, Marcion's
concept of the unity of redemptive history had been shattered by his vision of
the unique kindness that Christ had brought in his advent, a divine benevolence
unknown in the Old Testament. This thesis of such a radical dispensation of
grace necessitated, in his mind, a second deity, separate from the God of creation. So, in Marcionism, two gods existed. On the one hand there was the god
of the Old Testament, the god of the Jews, the creator of the universe. On the
other hand there was the Father of Jesus Christ who had no association with creation. With his thesis of novelty he corrupted the Church's faith. He discovered
in his Christ, Tertullian tells us, "a different dispensation of *sole* and unadulter-
ated benevolence, one opposite to the character to the Creator. He found it easy
to argue for a *new* and unknown deity that was only now revealed in its own
Christ. Consequently, with a little leaven he has soured with heretical acidity the
whole mass of the faith."[23]

Marcion's basic theological premise concerned a radical separation of the
Old Testament, "Law," from his conception of the apostolic testimony to the
good news of Christ and his teachings, "Gospel." Marcion's own writings, used
in the catechesis of his disciples prominently featured this premise. From this
premise of covenantal disharmony and contradiction, Marcion makes his move

---

21. Adolf Harnack, *History of Dogma* (trans. Neil Buchanan; 7 vols.; Boston: Little, Brown &
Co., 1896–1905), 1:269.
22. Tertullian, *Against Marcion* 4.10; trans. E. Evans, *Adversus Marcionem;* Oxford: Oxford University, 1972, 299. Emphasis added.
23. Tertullian, *Against Marcion* 1.2; trans. E. Evans, *Adversus Marcionem*, 7. Translation slightly
altered. Emphasis added. Cf. *Against Marcion* 1.19.

to conceive of two separate gods, one associated with each Testament, each component of Scripture—Law and Gospel, New and Old.[24] With Marcion, the church faced dispensational, theological, and scriptural dualism. It is obvious to Tertullian that neither Christ nor the teaching of the church ever entertained the notion of a god of the gospel who was distinct from the god of the law. Such a conception was Marcion's own invention, a doctrine that introduced rupture into redemptive history, rather than one that maintained the harmony and concord taught by Christ and the Church. Here are Tertullian's own words:

> The separation of Law and Gospel [Old Testament and the New Testament] is the primary and principal exploit of Marcion. His disciples cannot deny this, for it stands at the head of their document, the one by which they are inducted into and confirmed in this heresy. For such are Marcion's *Antitheses*, or Contrary Oppositions, which are designed to show the conflict and disagreement of the Gospel and the Law, so that from the diversity of principles between those two documents [Testaments] they may argue further for a diversity of gods. Therefore, since it is precisely this separation of Law and Gospel which has suggested a god of the Gospel, other than and in opposition to the God of the Law, it is evident that before that separation was made, the god of the Gospel was still unknown who has just recently come into our notice as a consequence of Marcion's argument for separation. And so he was not revealed by Christ, who came before this teaching of separation, but was invented by Marcion, who set up the separation in opposition to that peace between Gospel and Law which previously, from the appearance of Christ until the impudence of Marcion, had been kept unimpaired and unshaken by virtue of that [sound] reasoning which refused to contemplate any god of the Law

---

24. My concern in this essay is not to develop Marcion's concept of Scripture and canon, other than to emphasize that his dispensational dualism was linked with his concept of the division between the Old Testament and what became his collection of New Testament writings: selections from Paul's epistles and Luke's gospel. For introductions to these matters see Bruce M. Metzger, *The Canon of the New Testament: Its Origin, Development, and Significance* (Oxford: Clarendon, 1987), 90–99; F. F. Bruce, *Canon of Scripture* (Downers Grove, IL: InterVarsity, 1988), 134–44; Lee Martin McDonald, *The Biblical Canon: Its Origin, Transmission, and Authority* (Peabody, MA: Hendrickson, 2007), 324–33, 367–68.

and the Gospel other than that Creator against whom after so long a time, by a man of Pontus, separation has been let loose.[25]

And, "Certainly, the whole of the work that Marcion has done, including the preface of his *Antitheses,* he directs to the one purpose of setting up opposition between the Old Testament and the New, and thereby putting his Christ in separation from the Creator, as belonging to another god, and having no connection with the Law and the Prophets."[26]

Justin Martyr, in giving us our earliest descriptions of the heresy of Marcion, while he was still active in Rome, shows that the church's understanding of his teaching had not wavered in fifty years: "And there is Marcion, a man of Pontus, who is alive even now, and who is teaching his disciples to believe in some other god greater than the Creator. With the aid of the demons, he has caused many of every nation to speak blasphemies, and to deny that God is the maker of this universe, and to assert that some other being, greater than the Creator God, has done greater things."[27] And, "As we said before, the demons put forward Marcion of Pontus, who is even now teaching all to deny that God is the Maker of all things in heaven and on earth, and that the Christ predicted by the Prophets is his Son. He preaches another god besides the Creator of all, and likewise another son."[28]

Marcion's two gods, an idea that immediately conflicts with the monotheism of both Judaism and Christianity, have diverse properties, in addition to their relation to the origins of this world. The god of the Old Testament is hostile and condemnatory; the god of the New, merciful and gracious, full of charity. Irenaeus includes the following description in his catalog of early heresies as he relates Marcion to his mentor, Cerdo: "Marcion of Pontus succeeded him, and developed his doctrine. He advanced the most insolent blasphemy against the God proclaimed by the law and the prophets, declaring him to be the author of evil and one who delights in war. He was inconsistent

25. Tertullian, *Against Marcion* 1.19; trans. E. Evans, *Adversus Marcionem*, 49–51. Translation slightly altered.
26. Tertullian, *Against Marcion* 4.6; trans. E. Evans, *Adversus Marcionem*, 275. Translation slightly altered.
27. Justin Martyr, *1 Apology* 26. Some might contend that the Valentinian Ptolemy, in his *Letter to Flora,* actually provides our first description. This requires an early dating (ca. 150) for the letter (cf. Moll, *The Arch-Heretic Marcion*, 16–17, 48–49). If the letter can be dated that early, we find that Marcion associated the Creator of the universe with the devil (Epiphanius, *Panarion* 33.3.2). Such an early dating may be difficult to substantiate.
28. Justin Martyr, *1 Apology* 58.

and contradicted himself."[29] Likewise, Tertullian says: "For all that, we were aware that Marcion sets up unequal gods, the one a judge, fierce and warlike, the other mild and peaceable, solely kind and supremely good."[30] Hippolytus tells us that Marcion also characterized the two deities in a moral manner: The god of the gospel is good; the god of the law is evil.[31] Irenaeus says the same thing about Marcion's disciples: "Indeed, the followers of Marcion directly blaspheme the Creator by claiming that he is the Creator of evil things and holding an even more intolerable view of his origin. They say that by nature there exist two gods that are distinct from each other. One, by nature, is good; the other is evil."[32] In another place, Irenaeus varies his characterization of the natures of the two gods of Marcion and his disciples.[33] Though he continues to refer to the god of the gospel as "good," he now describes the god of law as "judicial." In Marcion's mind, he tells us, a god who is judicial is one who rebukes, one who is angry, and such attributes are not worthy of a supreme deity. To be judicial was to be evil. Marcion does not conceive of a deity who is both good and judicial, one who both saves and condemns.[34] Indeed, the followers of Marcion directly blaspheme the Creator, by claiming that he is the creator of evil things (although they hold to a more tolerable theory as to his origin, [and] maintaining that there are two beings, gods by nature, differing from each other—the one being good, but the other evil.

In addition to dualisms and divisions concerning dispensations, gods, and sacred writings, Marcion also held to a christological dualism. The Christ of the Father did not become incarnate. He merely came down from above, pouring

---

29. Irenaeus, *Against Heresies* 1.27.2 Critical edition used was *Irénée de Lyon: Contre les heresies, Livres 1–5*, ed. trans. and annot. A. Rousseau, L. Doutreleau, B. Hemmerdinger, and C. Mercier, Sources chrétiennes (SC) 263, 264 (Livre 1), 293, 294 (Livre 2), 210, 211 (Livre 3), 100.1, 100.2 (Livre 4), 152, 153 (Livre 5) (Paris: Cerf, 1979 (Livre 1), 1982 (Livre 2), 1974, 2002 (Livre 3), 1965 (Livre 4), 1969 (Livre 5). The idea that the god of the Law is the author of evil derives, at least in part, for Marcion, from his reading of Isa. 45:17 (*Against Marcion* 1.2)
30. Tertullian, *Against Marcion* 1.6; trans. E. Evans, *Adversus Marcionem*, 15.
31. *Refutation of All Heresies* 7.17.
32. Irenaeus, *Against Heresies* 3.12.12. Although most manuscripts read *tolerabiliorem* (tolerable); A. Rousseau in SC 210: 232 reads *intolerabiliorem* (intolerable) with Q and Erasmus (cf. *St. Irenaeus of Lyons: Against the Heresies, Book 3*, ACW 64, D. J. Unger and I. M. C. Steenberg, eds. and trans. [New York/Mahwah, N.J.: Paulist, 2012], 68, 154, n. 45). I have followed that reading. The point of the passage is a bit difficult to fully appreciate if one translates literally. I have taken certain liberties in an attempt to provide a rendering of the thought I believe Irenaeus wishes to convey.
33. Irenaeus, *Against Heresies* 3.25.3.
34. Irenaeus, *Against Heresies* 3.25. 2–3. This explanation of 3.25. 2–3 and the terminology of 3.12.12 seem to nullify Blackman's critique of Bousset (Blackman, *Marcion and His Influence*, 66–67).

himself forth from heaven as a "saving spirit."[35] He appeared, apparently, very suddenly, without witness or record, in Capernaum in Tiberius's fifteenth year.[36] He came to a creation that had been made by the god of the Old Testament, not one that he had created.[37] This of course, discounts the infancy narratives of the church's Gospels. His advent and passion—"phantasms" in docetic fashion—were in appearance only; he did not actually take on flesh and he did not actually die.[38]

Marcion's Book of Contradictions: The Anthitheses

Sadly, Marcion's own writings are no longer extant. We know of his book of *Antitheses* or *Contradictions* and a letter. *Antitheses* must be reconstructed, as much as possible, from the fragments preserved in Tertullian's *Against Marcion*, the *Adamantius Dialogue*, and perhaps an anonymous Syrian, *Exposition of the Gospel*, extant only in Armenian.[39] The *Antitheses* (or possibly his version of the gospel, a redaction of Luke's account) began with a line that conveys how wonderstruck Marcion was with the incomparable worth of the gospel: "O wealth of riches! Folly, power, and ecstasy!—seeing that there can be nothing to say about it, or to imagine about it, or to compare it to!"[40] It is this sense of amazement at the inauguration of the utterly unique gospel through the phantasmic advent of Christ that engenders Marcion's various dualisms. The dispensation of the gospel is totally

---

35. Tertullian, *Against Marcion* 1.19.
36. Tertullian, *Against Marcion* 1.19; 4.7.
37. Irenaeus, *Against Heresies* 3.11.2.
38. Tertullian, *Against Marcion* 3.8; 4.10; On the Flesh of Christ 1.1–4; Irenaeus, *Against Heresies* 4.33.2; Hippolytus, *Refutation of All Heresies* 10.15.
39. Once credited to Ephrem the Syrian, that connection now appears to be erroneous (Peter Bruns, "Ephrem der Syrer," in *Lexikon der antiken christlichen Literatur*, 3d. ed., 222); B. Outtier, "Une explication de l'Evangile attribuée à S. Ephrem," *Parole de l'Orient* 1 (1970): 385–408; David Bundy, "The Anti-Marcionite Commentary on the Lucan Parables (Pseudo-Ephrem A)," *Muséon* 103 (1990): 111–123.
40. Pseudo-Ephrem (A), *An Exposition of the Gospel* 1. See *Saint Ephrem, An Exposition of the Gospel*, Corpus Scriptorum Christianorum Orientalium 291–92, Scriptores armeniaci 5–6, ed. and trans. G. A. Egan (Leuven: Peeters, 1968), 1. The author or authors say that the passage occurs at the beginning of Marcion's Proevangelium, but that reference is unclear. It may refer to *Antitheses* or Marcion's Gospel (cf. J. Rendel Harris, "Marcion's Book of Contradictions," *Bulletin of the John Rylands Library* 6 [1921-22]: 299–300; Eric W. Scherbenske, *Canonizing Paul: Ancient Editorial Practice and the Corpus Paulinum* [Oxford: University Press, 2013], 80). Egan mistakenly attributes the text to Ephrem. For a response, see Ottier, "Une explication de l'Evangile attribuée à S. Ephrem." I have chosen to use the translation of F. C. Burkitt, "The Exordium of Marcion's Antitheses," *Journal of Theological Studies* 30 os (1929): 279–80. Burkitt demonstrates the presence of allusions to Rom. 11:33; 1 Cor. 1:18; and Luke 5:26 in the opening words. Cf. Harnack, *Marcion: das Evangelium vom fremden Gott*, 256, 355, who brings the passage to our attention and identifies it as the opening words of the *Antitheses*.

distinct from the previous dispensation of Law in substance. As the natures of the two gods are completely distinctive, so, too, are the covenants, the Testaments, and the dispensations. Rupture between natures, between substances, marks Marcion's understanding of history and of the divine. One period is not like the other, and Marcion's book, *Antitheses*, went to great lengths to demonstrate the discontinuity.

Tertullian describes the purpose and style of the *Antitheses* in this way: "For such are Marcion's *Antitheses,* or *Contrary Oppositions*, which are designed to show the conflict and disagreement of the gospel and the law, so that from the diversity of principles between those two documents they may argue further for a diversity of gods."[41]

The *Antitheses*, then, set forth apparent contradictions between Old and New Testament in order to demonstrate that they are set at odds and from there to claim the existence of two different deities. The structure of the text was along the lines of statements showing the god of the Old Testament saying such and such, but then, in apparent contradiction, showing that Christ had taught or done such and such. From Tertullian, the *Adamantius Dialogue*, and Theodoret of Cyrus, for instance, we know that one such pair alerted the reader to the ostensible conflict between the Creator's regulation concerning recompensing an eye for an eye and the teaching of the gracious Christ to turn the other cheek.[42] In another pair, Marcion sets in conflict the Law's command to love one's neighbor, and, apparently, according to him, to hate one's enemy [Matt 5:43-44], with Christ's teaching to love one's enemy.[43] In short, Marcion's *Antithesis* claimed a contrast between the cruel Creator and the merciful Christ by arranging what appeared to be incompatible sayings from each in the following format: the Law says this, but in his gospel the Lord says something else entirely.[44]

---

41. Tertullian, *Against Marcion* 1.19.
42. Tertullian, *Against Marcion* 4.16; *Adamantius Dialogue* 1.12; *Compendium of Heretical Accounts* 1.24. Theodoret actually credits the pairings to Cerdo, Marcion's predecessor, but they are helpful for our understanding of Marcion's *Antithesis*. There are other pairs. See Moll, *The Arch-Heretic Marcion*, 108–10.
43. Tertullian, *Against Marcion* 1.23; *Adamantius Dialogue* 1.15; *Compendium of Heretical Accounts* 1.24.
44. Cf. Moll, *The Arch-Heretic Marcion*, 111; J. Albert Harrill, *Paul the Apostle: His Life and Legacy in Their Roman Context* (New York: Cambridge University Press, 2012), 124–25. Whether the entire *Antitheses* was composed in this format, however, is unknown (cf. Scherbenske, *Canonizing Paul: Ancient Editorial Practice and the Corpus Paulinum*, 81). Scherbenske suggests that the *Antitheses* may have served as a preface to Marcion's gospel (*Canonizing Paul: Ancient Editorial Practice and the Corpus Paulinum*, 82), while Hans von Campenhausen believes it served as an introduction to his canon (*The Formation of the Christian Bible*, trans. J. A. Baker. [Philadelphia: Fortress, 1972], 161).

Marcion on History and Eschatology

The two concepts of history and eschatology are intimately related. Always, rupture in the one leads to rupture in the other. We have already seen Marcion's christological dualism in regard to Christ's incarnation and death. The same is true in regard to the second advent. In Marcion's perspective, one that reveals his abhorrence for the world, there are two Christs, and the difference he draws between them is as great as the chasm he digs between the two gods and the two dispensations. One Christ is the savior of the nations who comes in a docetic fashion and reveals the Father of the gospel. The other is associated with the Creator (Demiurge). The first one does not return to the creation to fulfill the hopes of Israel. It is not his to redeem. The Father's "Christ assumed absolutely nothing from the creation of the Demiurge."[45] It was Marcion's intention, due to the novelty of Christ's appearance, to divide this Christ from the messianic prophecies of the Old Testament and from the creation, its history, its future.[46] His conception of redemption, then, is radical. In Harnack's words, Christ "has redeemed us from the *creation* (and thus from ourselves) *and from its God*, in order to make us children of a new and alien God."[47] The other Christ, however, returns to the earth that he created in order to deliver his own creatures, his own people. Tertullian puts it this way:

> Marcion lays it down that there is one Christ who in the time of Tiberius was revealed by a god formerly unknown, for the salvation of all the nations; *and another Christ who is destined by God the Creator to come at some time still future for the reestablishment of the Jewish kingdom.* Between these he sets up a great and absolute opposition, such as that between justice and kindness, between law and gospel, between Judaism and Christianity.[48]

The Christ who returns, the Christ of the second advent, for Marcion and his disciples, is the son of Abraham and David, the one foretold by the

---

45. Harnack, *History of Dogma*, 1:277.
46. Tertullian, *Against Marcion* 3.2–3. Cf. Larry W. Hurtado, *Lord Jesus Christ: Devotion to Jesus in Earliest Christianity* (Grand Rapids: Eerdmans, 2003), 559; Blackman, *Marcion and His Influence*, 102.
47. Harnack, *Marcion: The Gospel of the Alien God*, 148, n.2. Emphasis original. Cf. Blackman, *Marcion and His Influence*, 106.
48. Tertullian, *Against Marcion* 4.6; trans. E. Evans, *Adversus Marcionem*, 275. Emphasis added.

Law and Prophets. He is not, however, the son of the Father. When one introduces contradiction into the history of redemption, when one hypothesizes a discontinuity that decisively undermines claims to continuity between the Testaments, when one discovers a second, new god, one must anoint a second Christ who cares nothing for the creation and does not come again in the clouds to redeem it.

ORTHODOXY: HARMONY AND DISCONTINUITY

The early church, the communities most proximate to his activity, did not accept Marcion and his thought. This was its consistent response. Papias, Polycarp, and the presbyters in Rome all rejected his teaching. Justin Martyr, Irenaeus, Hippolytus, Tertullian and Epiphanius wrote against his theses, including him among the heretics. Early, then, the church affirmed that its biblical theology and, hence, its eschatology, acknowledged a fundamental theological continuity between the Testaments. While recognizing differences between the Testaments, these differences, it insisted, did not undermine claims of continuity. They did not indicate contradictions, dichotomies, or antitheses.

We see the early church's confession regarding the continuity between the Testaments in a variety of ways in the latter part of the first century and throughout the second. Their commonality, however, is to be found in their confession of the common virtues promoted throughout Scripture, of the movement in sacred history from figure and anticipation to perfection, of Christ as the center point, fulfillment, and administrator of all redemptive history. Clement of Rome, for instance, teaches seamlessly on the virtues of humility and love from Christ, Paul, Abraham, Esther, David, and Moses.[49] Justin Martyr's *Dialogue with Trypho* appears, in its structure, to be the opposite of Marcion's *Antitheses*. Marcion was concerned to show the dichotomy between the Law and the Prophets and Christ. Justin, however, presents time and again the following refrain: The Old Testament predicted such and such, and Christ fulfills it either in his first or second advent.

One developed example of how early Christianity offered an alternative to Marcion, was Irenaeus of Lyons. In his *Against Heresies* 4.9–11, Irenaeus forms a thesis that the two economies of law and gospel are two stages of the same unified process ordered by one God: "Therefore, all things pertain to one and the same

---

49. *1 Clement* 16–18, 48–55.

substance, that is, from one and the same God."[50] To support his thesis he cites a word of the Lord from Matthew 13:52: "Therefore every scribe instructed in that which concerns the kingdom of heaven is like a master of a household who brings out of his treasure new things and old things."[51]

Reflecting on the text, he notes that the Lord did not teach "one [master] brought out the old things and another [master] the new things, but one and the same [master brought out both old and new]."[52] The one master is, of course, the Lord Christ who administers his household of sacred history. In his administration the Lord delivers to the Jews the Law (the old covenant), while to the church he gives appropriate precepts and his inheritance through the gospel (the new covenant).[53] Therefore, the same Lord administers both covenants, for there is only one treasure, one substance of sacred history.

Irenaeus further explains his thesis by commenting on Matthew 12:6: "For, the Lord says, 'There is here, more than the temple.'"[54] The "more," he associates with the new covenant. This, then, implies a "less" associated with the old covenant. But again, as with "new" and "old," Irenaeus explains that "more" and "less" do not apply to covenants that are uncommon or opposite, but to things that are of the same substance and have common properties. Such things to which the terms "more" or "less" apply differ only in quantity and size. "So," he says, "the grace of liberty [under the new covenant] is greater than the law of slavery."[55]

When Irenaeus thinks about the old covenant and law, he does not see a period of redemptive history incongruous with the new covenant and gospel, as Marcion did. The old covenant was an age of grace, as well, but it was a dispensation of less grace in terms of its geographical, ethnic boundaries (Israel and the Jews) and in terms of elements within its law that were external, figurative and prophetic. The new covenant is an age of greater grace because of the universal focus of the gospel, the internal changes it brings by the gift of the Holy Spirit, and its fulfillment of many prophetic expectations. So, there are discontinuities between the covenants, but one God and one Christ. Irenaeus explains the

---

50. Irenaeus, *Against Heresies* 4.9.1; translation influenced by the French in SC 100.2:477. See on *Against Heresies* 4.9.1–11.3, M.-F. Berrouard, "Servitude de la loi et liberté de l'evangile selon saint Irénée," *Lumière et Vie* 61 (1963): 41–48.
51. Irenaeus, *Against Heresies* 4.9.1; translation influenced by the French in SC 100.2:477.
52. Irenaeus, *Against Heresies* 4.9.1.
53. Cf. Irenaeus, *Against Heresies* 4.14.3–15.1.
54. Irenaeus, *Against Heresies* 4.9.2.
55. Cf. John 1:17; Irenaeus, *Against Heresies* 3.12.11.

discontinuities in terms of stages and degrees. The old covenant is one stage in one multi-stage, divinely orchestrated history of creation and redemption where earlier stages have "less" grace and later stages "more." The later dispensations expand upon the earlier.

Therefore, when we return to the topic of eschatology and the continuity of history, for Irenaeus the future dispensation introduces no utter rupture into the history of redemption, nor does it welcome a Christ other than the Father's. Eschatology, in his understanding, is the culmination and fulfillment of an entire history of expectation and salvation overseen by the one Creator and Father who governs it through his Son and Spirit. This Son returns in the end to judge and redeem both Jews and Gentiles and it is for this one and the same Son that the all creation waits:

> This is also made clear from the words of the Lord, who truly revealed himself as the Son of God to those of the circumcision. The Lord set himself forth as the one foretold as Christ by the prophets, the one who had restored liberty to men and the one who bestowed on them the inheritance of incorruption. The apostles taught the Gentiles that they should leave vain wood and stones, which they imagined to be gods, and worship the true God. He had created and made the entire human family and by means of his creation he nourished, increased, strengthened, and preserved them. The apostles also taught that they should look for his Son Jesus Christ, who redeemed us from apostasy with his own blood, so that we should be a sanctified people. Christ shall descend from heaven in his Father's power, and pass judgment upon all, and he shall freely give the good things of God to those who have kept his precepts. Christ, who will appear in these last times, the chief cornerstone, has gathered into one, and united those who were far off and those that were near, that is, the circumcision and the uncircumcision, by enlarging Japhet, and placing him in the dwelling of Shem.

Irenaeus's explanation is one way to account for the discontinuities between the Testaments without falling into the error of Marcionism. Of course, there are many others, but all, in some way, fit within the parameters drawn by Irenaeus.

Christian theologians persisted in treating the problem highlighted by Marcion because the issue of continuity and discontinuity in sacred history is the central issue in biblical theology. Augustine constructed an alternative. His solution to the apparently contradictory Testaments lay in his hermeneutic, one that by faith confessed the harmony between them and saw the New as the spiritual fullness anticipated in the earthly figures of the Old. Augustine's *Practices* is another text that sets Old Testament material side by side with that of the New in order to demonstrate the "togetherness" of the two, where Marcion had attempted to show them as incongruous. Michael Cameron describes Augustine's unifying hermeneutic this way:

> Side by side the two Testaments seem to feature wildly disparate economies of salvation, contradictory views of truth, asymmetrical ideas about God, conflicting visions of religious community, mutually exclusive templates of covenant, competing behavioral practices, and opposing forms of worship. But for Augustine, the savvy spiritual thinker knows that the earthy particularities of the Old anticipate the universal, deeply spiritual truths of the New, and that the two are mutually necessary and reciprocally enlightening. No two documents, he wrote, could be 'friendlier' (*amicus*; *Practices* 1.19.15).[56]

The same is true of Eastern Orthodoxy. Eugen Pentiuc summarizes the assumptions that underlie that tradition's perception of Scripture's unity: "(1) one and the same God as the author and ubiquitous figure of both testaments, and (2) Christ as the hermeneutical key to the unity of Scripture, shown in the relation of prophecy and fulfillment, anticipation and reality, and the complementarity between the two testaments."[57]

Furthermore, in Protestant history, Lutheranism's distinction between law and gospel, covenant theology and dispensationalism, are also carefully constructed Christian alternatives. Each offers a hermeneutical and theological model that accounts for discontinuities within redemptive history and revela-

---

56. Michael Cameron, *Christ Meets Me Everywhere: Augustine's Early Figurative Exegesis* (Oxford: Oxford University, 2012), 83.

57. Eugen J. Pentiuc, *The Old Testament in Eastern Orthodox Tradition* (Oxford: University Press, 2014), 61.

tion, with their own emphases and tendencies, without disparaging the unity inherent in the history of progressive revelation.[58] Each is an anti-Marcionite reply, although this has not always been recognized. Dispensationalism, especially, I fear, has been underappreciated as a contributing factor to the continuing demise of Marcionism. As a hermeneutic it has helped countless believers to divide the Scriptures and to make sense of its discontinuities without collapsing into theological dualism. In particular, John Walvoord, Dwight Pentecost, and Craig Blaising have been able to demonstrate continuity in redemptive history, while recognizing aspects of discontinuity, through treatment of the structure of biblical covenants and their relation to eschatology and Christology.[59]

Essential to any Christian eschatology is a Christian philosophy of salvation history and of progressive revelation. This philosophy must account for the differences between the Testaments and dispensations without wandering into the forbidden territory of dichotomy and contradiction. This philosophy must produce a hermeneutic that reads the differences only in linkage with the fundamental concepts of unity: One God, Creator and Father, one Christ, and one history with a common subject and objective throughout its parts. With such a philosophy and hermeneutic, we avoid doing dishonor, as Marcion did, to the one Lord Jesus Christ, the Son of God, both God and human.

Craig Blaising, in the tradition of the early theologians, has made clear the essential relationship between a Christian philosophy of history, a Christian hermeneutic, and a Christian doctrine of Christ and the future:

---

58. The Lutheran distinction is not a view of the discontinuity between Old and New Testaments. For Lutherans, law and gospel, or law and the promises, are the principle topics or doctrines of the entire Scripture, including both Old and New Testaments. See *Apology of the Augsburg Confession*, 4.5 and C. F. W. Walther, *The Proper Distinction Between Law and Gospel* (1929), Theses 1–4. For a helpful contemporary edition see *Law and Gospel: How to Read and Apply the Bible*, ed. C. P. Schaum (St. Louis: Concordia, 2010). On Covenant Theology and Dispensationalism see William VanGemeren, "Systems of Continuity" and John S. Feinberg, "Systems of Discontinuity," in John S. Feinberg, *Continuity and Discontinuity: Perspectives on the Relationship Between the Old and New Testaments, Essays in Honor of S. Lewis Johnson, Jr.* (Westchester: Crossway, 1988), 37–62; 63–86.

59. John F. Walvoord, *End Times* (Nashville: Word, 1998), 71-94. Dwight J. Pentecost, *Things to Come: A Study in Biblical Eschatology* (Grand Rapids: Zondervan, 1964), 65–128; Craig A. Blaising, "The Structure of the Biblical Covenants: The Covenants Prior to Christ," and "The Fulfillment of the Biblical Covenants through Jesus Christ," in Craig A. Blaising and Darrell L. Bock, *Progressive Dispensationalism* (Grand Rapids: Bridgepoint, 1993), 128–173; 174–210.

As God, [Christ] must also be interpreted in light of a history of redemption, as God has been revealed in the Old Testament. The New Testament carries this understanding of God forward, as we have also seen in the previous chapters. This means that He is that God who has made the covenant promises, who is expected to come in the eschatological age and rule the earth and all its peoples—taking away their guilt and bringing them into close and everlasting communion with Himself, blessing them with life, as He intended for them to live, forever.[60]

The fundamental question of biblical theology is, Does the diversity *between* the Testaments involve a discontinuity that decisively undermines claims to continuity? If Dunn has asked it, Blaising has answered it: No. Marcion was in error. The continuity of the Testaments is to be found in the one Christ to whom they both witness in their own inspired manner. They tell us of a Christ who is not outside of the creation, but who as Creator and Redeemer joins himself to it by manifesting himself progressively within history, within the dispensations, by becoming flesh on the earth and by returning to it in flesh, as promised, in order to raise and gather together his people, from all the dispensations, to the glory of God the Father. "[Christ] gives the dispensations their unity—a unity in historical development, not a static transcendental ahistorical unity—and He gives the redeemed their identity as the people(s) of God."[61]

---

60. Craig Blaising, "Theological and Ministerial Issues in Progressive Dispensationalism," in Blaising and Bock, *Progressive Dispensationalism*, 298.
61. Ibid., 301.

The Doctrine of the Future and the Concept of Hope

Stanley D. Toussaint

T he doctrine of the future is a significant subject and the concept of hope is fascinating.[1] Each of these is worthy of—and indeed has received—myriad book-length treatments. This article seeks to discuss both subjects and their relation to one another. To that end, hope will be discussed first, and then eschatology.

The Concept of Hope

A Definition

Someone once said, "Hope is a lovely breakfast, but a terrible dinner." Of course this is not a biblical concept of hope. "It seems no exaggeration to say that the OT breathes an atmosphere of hope throughout; but it is true that Hebrew seems to have no word which corresponds exactly to 'hope,' and no precise concept of hope in the sense of 'desire accompanied by expectation.' The words which most frequently express hope are *kawah,* 'to expect,' and *batah,* 'to trust or have confidence.'"[2] Burton Easton agrees there is no exact Hebrew word to describe the expectation of something good; instead he refers to some fifteen Hebrew words that are often given other translations than

---

1. It is a genuine and high honor for me to have a small part in this celebration of Craig Blaising's birthday. I have known Craig as a student in my classes, as a colleague on the faculty of Dallas Theological Seminary (his office was across the hall from mine), and above all a friend and beloved brother in the Lord. May the Lord continue to bless you and honor his name through both you and your lovely wife, Diane.
2. John L. McKenzie, *Dictionary of the Bible* (Milwaukee: The Bruce Publishing Co., 1965), 368.

"hope."[3] He goes on to say, "This lack of a specific word for hope has nothing to do with any undervaluation of the virtue among the Hebrews."[4] As will be seen in later paragraphs, hope existed in the hearts of OT believers.

The New Testament employs the verb form of the Greek noun *elpis*, which is *elpizo*. This verb only occurs five times in the Gospels, and the noun not at all. The only time *elpizo* is found in Matthew is 12:21, where it is a quotation of Isaiah 42:4 from the LXX. The word is not found in Mark. It occurs three times in Luke (6:34; 23:8; 24:21), and once in John's gospel (5:45). In Acts it is used twice (24:26; 26:7). The word occurs most often in the epistles, but, again, not at all in Revelation, but vocabulary is not the measure of importance. For example, in John's gospel hope is closely associated with faith.[5] In Revelation, it is communicated through the language of endurance. "The fact that *elpis* is not found in Revelation can cause astonishment only if we fail to see that it is included in the concept of *hupomone*."[6]

As defined above, for hope to be genuine it must contain both desire and expectancy; neither can be absent. One may desire to make a certain amount of money in a year, but if one does not expect to attain it, that is not hope. If one expects to have root canal surgery, but does not desire it, that is not hope. A believer in Christ has hope—desire with expectancy—because of God's program prophesied for the future.

Results of Hope

Hope is a basic Christian virtue; it is associated with faith and love in 1 Corinthians 13:13. These three virtues should characterize a believer living in the here and now. When a genuine Christian lives with hope as part of his daily life, certain benefits will accrue.

The first benefit is patient endurance (*hupomone*). In 1 Thessalonians 1:3 Paul writes, "constantly bearing in mind your work of faith and labor of love and steadfastness of hope in our Lord Jesus Christ in the presence of our God and Father."[7] Just as faith results in works and love produces labor, so hope results in endurance. History can document some amazing feats of perseverance

---

3. Burton Scott Easton, "Hope," *The International Standard Bible Encyclopedia*, vol. 3, ed. James Orr (Grand Rapids: Eerdmans, 1939), 1419.

4. Ibid.

5. Rudolf Bultmann, *"elpis, elpizo,"* *Theological Dictionary of the New Testament*, vol. 2, ed. Gerhard Kittel, trans. Geoffrey W. Bromiley (Grand Rapids: Eerdmans, 1964), 530.

6. Ibid.

7. All Scripture quotations are from the NASB.

because of hope. Many accounts could be given of faithful Christians who persisted in their faith despite horrible persecution because of hope. Hebrews 11:35–40 lists some of the faithful Old Testament saints who endured because of faith and hope.

A second product of hope is joy. In Romans 12:12 a simple phrase says it, "rejoicing in hope." Peter puts it this way, "To the degree that you share the sufferings of Christ, keep on rejoicing; so that also at the revelation of His glory, you may rejoice with exultation" (1 Peter 4:13). Both endurance and joy are seen in the Lord Jesus's example, "fixing our eyes on Jesus, the author and perfecter of our faith, who for the joy set before Him endured the cross, despising the shame" (Heb. 12:2).

Hope not only results in patient endurance and joy; it yields the fruit of assurance. The writer of Hebrews expresses his desire for the readers of that epistle by saying, "And we desire that each one of you show the same diligence so as to realize the full assurance of hope until the end" (Heb. 6:11). The noun translated "full assurance" is *plerophoria*. It has about it the idea of certainty and conviction—the same meaning it has in the rest of the NT (Col. 2:2; 1 Thess. 1:5; Heb. 10:22). The phrase "until the end" in Hebrews 6:11 "reiterates the eschatological emphasis of 3:14; it evokes the Parousia when hope will be fully realized (cf. 9:28)."[8] Assurance ultimately rests on God's sovereignty. He is in control and will bring all things to their ultimate goal.

Still another product of hope is purity. "Beloved, now we are children of God, and it has not appeared as yet what we will be. We know that when He appears, we will be like Him, because we will see Him as He is. And everyone who has this hope fixed on Him purifies himself, just as He is pure" (1 John 3:2–3). Interestingly, the words *agnos* (pure) and *elpis* (hope) occur only in this passage in all of John's writings.[9] This purity is an all-inclusive ethical purity. Marshall states, "The following verse shows that for John, purity meant purity from sins and mixed motives."[10] When one sees the results of hope, he realizes hope is a very *practical* virtue

---

8. William L. Lane, *Hebrews 1–8*, Word Biblical Commentary (Nashville: Thomas Nelson, 1991), 144.

9. Robert Morgenthaler, *Statistik des neutestament lichen Wortschatzes* (Zurich: Gotthelf-Verlag, 1958), 67, 94.

10. I. Howard Marshall, *The Epistle of John* (Grand Rapids: Eerdmans, 1978), 174. Cf. Rudolf Bultmann, *The Johannine Epistles*, R. Philip O'Hara, Lane C. McGaughy, and Robert W. Funk, trans. (Philadelphia: Fortress, 1973), 49.

HOPE IN THE BIBLE

Hope in the Old Testament

Adrianus Van der Born states, "in the OT hope (Hebrew *tigwah*) always refers to the expectation of a future good."[11] The first anticipation of a future good is found in Genesis 3:15, the well-known *protoevangelium*. After declaring the judgment on Satan of moving about "on your belly," God says he will put enmity between it and the "woman." Up to this point "the woman" is Eve. So Eve, who had been before attracted to the serpent, would now hate him. Furthermore, there would be "enmity between your seed and her seed." This looks at the ultimate struggle between Satan and Christ. "Seed" can be used not only of a number of progeny but also of a single individual (cf. Gen. 4:25; 21:12–13; Gal. 3:16; 4:4). Satan would bruise the heel of Christ (a painful but not a fatal strike), but the Lord Jesus would bruise or crush the head of the serpent, Satan (a fatal wound). In this prophecy, mankind was offered hope.

The Abrahamic Covenant. This is the grandfather of all of Israel's subsequent covenants and the hope of the world. It is repeated five times to Abraham in Genesis (Gen. 12:1–3; 13:14–17; 15:12–19; 17:3–14; 22:15–18); each strengthens the preceding promise and in some cases enlarges them (cf. 12:1–3 and 13:14–17). Isaac and Jacob have the promises confirmed to them (Gen. 26:3–5; 28:13–15; cf. Ps. 105:8–11). These commitments to Abraham, Isaac, and Jacob became the bases for the hope found in the rest of the Scriptures.

Even the doctrine of the resurrection of the body is grounded on the promises made to the patriarchs of Israel (Matt. 22:31–32; Mark 12:26; Luke 20:37). Many have contended that the present tense of "I am" in the Matthew passage argues for the resurrection of the dead. There are some problems with this. First, it does not prove a resurrection of physical bodies; it only substantiates the idea that Abraham, Isaac and Jacob are spiritually alive now. Furthermore, if the argument for the resurrection hinges on the present tense of "am" in Matthew 22:32, it is strange that it is not found in its parallels in Mark or Luke. Mark's omission may be explained by saying the "am" would be assumed. However, Luke says, "he calls the Lord the God of" (the Greek text simply states, "he says Lord the God"). The argument rather rests on the land promises made to each of these three patriarchs.

---

11. Adrianus van der Born, *Encyclopedic Dictionary of the Bible*, Louis F. Hartman, trans. (New York: McGraw Hill, 1963), 1024.

To all three God specifically promised the land saying, "to you and your seed" (cf. Gen. 13:15; 15:7 [Abraham]; 26:3 [Isaac]; 28:13 [Jacob]; cf. 1 Chron. 16:15–18). In order for these promises to be fulfilled, all three of these patriarchs have to be resurrected. The only land Abraham and Isaac owned when they died was a burial plot; Jacob owned the same burial plot and some land he purchased from the sons of Hamor near Shechem (Gen. 33:19). The Lord's dispute with the Sadducees is settled by the fact God must yet fulfill His promises to these patriarchs. This in turn is a defense of the concept of a future kingdom *on this earth.*

The Davidic Covenant. This covenant is first presented in the form of a promise to David that he would have an eternal house, kingdom, and throne (2 Sam. 2:16). These promises are also called a covenant, fortified with an oath (Ps. 89:3–4, 28–29, 34–37; 132:11). The eternality of David's kingdom and his throne still awaits a future fulfillment when the Lord Jesus returns to reign.

The New Covenant. This promise to Israel, mentioned in Jeremiah 31:31–34, declares that there will be a national conversion brought about by God sovereignly working in the hearts of the people of Israel (cf. Zech. 12:10–14; Rom. 11:26–27). This new covenant which supplants the Law of Moses (Heb. 8:6–13) is also called an "everlasting" covenant (Isa. 55:3; 61:8; Ezek. 16:60; 37:26).[12] In Ezekiel 36:24–32 the provisions of the new covenant are rehearsed, although it is named neither "the new covenant" nor "an everlasting covenant."

This new covenant is specifically promised to Israel, but the New Testament relates it to the church (2 Cor. 3:6; Heb. 8:6–13). Dispensationalists have discussed this connection for scores of years. It is clear the death of Christ is the basis of the covenant (Luke 22:20). It seems best to conclude the new covenant will be fulfilled for future Israel; but in the meantime some, but not all, of the provisions of the new covenant are given to the church.[13]

The prophet like Moses. When Moses approached the end of his life, he assured the generation of Jews alive at the time that God would raise up another prophet like him (Deut. 18:15; 18:18). It is correctly assumed that God would raise up another leader like Moses and that was Joshua (cf. Josh. 4:14). However, Deuteronomy 34:10 states, "Since then no prophet has risen in Israel like

---

12. In this verse, the covenant is also described as a "covenant of peace."
13. For instance, "all" do not know the Lord (Jer. 31:34).

Moses, whom the Lord knew face to face" (cf. Num. 12:6–8). Because God spoke to no one face to face as he did to Moses, the rabbis correctly anticipated the coming of a "new Moses" (cf. John 1:21, 25; 6:14; Acts 3:22).

The promises given by the prophets. The promises given by the prophets are so numerous that it is impossible to state them all here. Only a few samples will be given. These are prophecies that deal primarily with Israel, although many also concern Gentiles. Some illustrations are Isaiah 2:1–4; 11:6–16; 40:1–11; 44:1–8; 54:1–17; 60:1–22; Jer.16:14–15; 23:3–8; and 30:18–22. The pre-exilic prophets predicted great things from Israel, but so did the post-exilic prophets (Hag. 2:6–9, 20–23; Zech. 1:16–17; 2:1–13; 8:1–23; 10:1–12; 12:1–14; 14:1–21; Mal. 1:11; 3:17-18; and 4:5-6). This latter group serves to show the return to Israel from the Babylonian captivity was not the fulfillment of the pre-exilic prophecies.

The priest of the order of Melchizedek. The only New Testament book that refers to this priestly order is Hebrews (cf. 5:9–10; 6:20; 7:1–24). The historical Melchizedek is recorded in Genesis 14:18–20. The prophesied Melchizedek is foretold in Psalm 110:4, "The Lord has sworn and will not change His mind, Thou art a priest forever according to the order of Melchizedek." Just as the Law of Moses was a temporary necessity (Gal. 3:23–25; 4:1–5), so also was the Levitical priesthood. In Psalm 110:1, David looked ahead and saw a future descendant as his master. This offspring of David would be not only a greater king, but also a priest.

The predictions of a future prophet, the fulfillment of the Davidic covenant, and the prophecy of a coming priesthood present the Lord Jesus as a prophet, priest, and king! When this concept is joined with the promises of the OT prophets, it is no wonder the Jews lived in anticipation of the fulfillment of a great hope. This coming one would be their Savior and Messiah.

Hope in the New Testament

In the Gospels. The Synoptic Gospels were birthed in hope even though, as was previously noted, the vocabulary based on *elpis* is rare in those books of the Bible. All four of the Gospels begin the Lord's public ministry with John the Baptist's appearance in the wilderness at the Jordan River. In Matthew 3:2 John announces the nearness of the kingdom of heaven. When the people heard the message of the nearness of the kingdom, they were electrified with excitement.[14] Significantly, John did not explain the term; the people expected the fulfillment of the kingdom promise in the OT.[15]

John the Baptist, Jesus, and the Twelve all proclaimed the same message—the nearness of the kingdom (Matt. 3:2; 4:17; 10:7; Mark 1:15; Luke 10:9). The announcement was not to be given to Samaritans or Gentiles (Matt. 10:5–6). Why this restriction? The arrival of the kingdom is contingent upon Israel's repentance which will precede the kingdom's presence. The same contingency exists today. The world could see worldwide revival, but the kingdom will not arrive until the Jews turn to Jesus as the Messiah (cf. Matt. 23:39). As discussed earlier, God will sovereignly bring about this national repentance.

The Sermon on the Mount breathes with anticipation of the kingdom; it explains how the Lord's followers were to live during the interim of waiting for the kingdom's arrival. Likewise, the many miracles done by the Lord Jesus not only attest to who Jesus is, they also anticipate kingdom conditions (cf. Isa. 29:18; 33:24; 35:5–6; 65:17–20; Dan. 12:2). The religious authorities were forced to make a decision about Christ. Tragically they accused Jesus of performing his miracles by the power of Satan (Matt. 12:22–37; Mark 3:19–20).

This rejection on the part of the leaders of Israel was a harbinger of the nation's future refusal to accept Jesus as the Messiah. From this point on the kingdom is never proclaimed as "near." By using parables the Lord Jesus then taught a whole new age would precede the arrival of the kingdom (Matt. 13:1–53; Mark 4:1–34). John had said the judgment preceding the kingdom was near; now the Lord Jesus taught a period of time would elapse before that judgment. In this intercalation good and evil would coexist. Certainly this newly revealed age would not be the kingdom!

From this point on the Lord Jesus trained the Twelve for ministry. It is in this period of the Lord's ministry that opposition to Christ grew until the authorities ultimately brought about his crucifixion. Nevertheless, hope is not abandoned but encouraged and promoted. In Matthew 16:18, he stated he would build his church and Christ promised "the gates of Hades will not overpower" the church. The expression "gates of Hades" was a euphemism for

14. The verb is in the perfect tense and means "has drawn near;" it does not mean "here." The hearers were looking ahead to the coming of the kingdom predicted in the OT.
15. Matthew uses both "kingdom of heaven" and "kingdom of God"; the other evangelists use only "kingdom of God." Evidently the terms are used interchangeably. That neither John, Jesus, nor any of the apostles tell the people they were erroneous in this anticipation of an earthly kingdom is significant. If the Jewish population was in error, certainly someone would have corrected their error.

death.[16] This promise looked forward to the resurrection of the Lord Jesus and also the church. Soon after making this statement, the Lord was transfigured on a mountain in the presence of Peter, James, and John (Matt. 16:28–17:9; Mark 9:1–8; Luke 9:27–36). In all three Synoptics this event is introduced with the statement that some of the Twelve would see the kingdom and the Son of Man coming in his kingdom. In other words, the transfiguration was a confirmation of a future kingdom. This is precisely how Peter speaks of it in 2 Peter 1:16–18.

In a promise of Christ to the Twelve, Christ Jesus said, "Truly I say to you, that you who have followed Me, in the regeneration when the Son of Man will sit on His glorious throne, you also shall sit upon twelve thrones, judging the twelve tribes of Israel" (Matt. 19:28). The "regeneration" looks ahead to the rebirth of the world. At that time the Son of Man will sit on a glorious earthly throne with the Twelve who will rule over the twelve tribes of Israel. It is very difficult to explain this as referring to a purely spiritual kingdom.

Another item to be considered here is the Olivet Discourse (Matt. 24:1–25:46; Mark 13:1–37; Luke 21:5–36). These passages parallel the conclusion of this age as described by the parables of Matthew 13. In all three Synoptics the Lord predicted the complete destruction of the temple. Evidently the disciples thought of Zechariah 14, where the desolation of Jerusalem is followed by the coming of the Lord. They concluded, therefore, the coming destruction of Jerusalem would immediately precede the return of Jesus to deliver Israel. Their questions revolve around this concept. Therefore Jesus warned them that this was not necessarily so. The presence of false messiahs and wars does not mark the end. The beginning of the end times will be evidenced by massive wars, great earthquakes, famines, pestilence, and persecution. Evidently these will be on a scale never seen before in history (cf. Rev. 6:1–17; 8:1). The key sign will be the appearance of the "abomination of desolation" in the holy place. It is then that the Lord's followers must hurriedly seek refuge. Finally, the Son of Man will return and gather his own. In Matthew 25:31–46 the judgment of Gentiles is predicted. Preceding this judgment will be the assize of Jews who are physically alive at the end of the tribulation (Ezek. 20:33–40; Rom. 2:10).

Eschatology is also seen in the Lord's observance of the "last Passover." During this meal Christ Jesus looked ahead to the coming kingdom and anticipated a time of eating and drinking with his disciples (cf. Isa. 25:6; Matt. 26:29; Mark

---

16. R. T. France, *The Gospel According to Matthew* (Grand Rapids, Eerdmans, 1986), 255.

14:25; Luke 22:18). In addition, 1 Corinthians 11:26 is the basis for making the Lord's Table an ordinance for this age.

The first mention of the rapture is in the upper Room Discourse in John 14. In John 14:3 the Lord Jesus said, "If I go and prepare a place for you, I will come again and receive you to Myself, that where I am, there you may be also." This is only a quick glimpse of the rapture; the details of what Christ meant are stated by Paul at a later time.

In the Book of Acts. Acts begins with the post-resurrection ministry of the Lord to his apostles. For forty days he taught about the kingdom of God (Acts 1:3). When he said they soon would be baptized by the Holy Spirit, the disciples immediately assumed the Lord Jesus was proclaiming both the coming of the Holy Spirit and the arrival of the kingdom (Acts 1:6). Never does the Lord refute their view of the kingdom; he only says it was not for them to know "the times or epochs the Father has fixed" (Acts 1:7). The disciples assumed the kingdom would arrive soon.

In Acts 3 Peter promised the kingdom would arrive when Israel turned to God and accepted Jesus as the Messiah (cf. Acts 3:19–26).[17] That the early church in Jerusalem believed the arrival of the kingdom was near is evidenced by the selling of their real estate to share the proceeds with other believers. It is a basic principle of finance that one does not live from his assets, except in extreme circumstances. This practice is not duplicated later in the church.

In Acts 7:56 Stephen says, "Behold, I see the heavens opened up and the Son of Man standing at the right hand of God." The title "Son of Man" seems to be derived from Daniel 7:13–14, an undisputedly eschatological passage. Stephen recognized the Lord Jesus to be the coming ruler of the world.

In Acts 14 Paul and Barnabas assured the followers of Christ in Lystra, Iconium, and Antioch that there will be a future kingdom, but it is reached through "many tribulations" (Acts 14:22). The Jerusalem Council recorded in Acts 15 was convened to decide whether Gentiles who had accepted the gospel needed to be circumcised and required to observe the Law of Moses (Acts 15:5).

---

17. Acts 3:19 contains two purpose clauses. (1) When the people of Israel repent of their failure by recognizing who Jesus is (cf. Acts 2:30–36), their sins would be "wiped away." (2) The second purpose clause is based on the first. If Israel as a people would repent, "times of refreshing" would come and God would send Jesus the Messiah. The times of refreshing and the return of Christ are tied together. Ernest Haenchen states, "But the two promises are complementary statements about one and the same event." Ernest Haenchen, *The Acts of the Apostles*, B. Noble and G. Shinn, trans. (Oxford: Blackwell, n.d.), 208.

After testimonies by Peter, Paul and Barnabas, James settled the issue by quoting Amos 9:11–12. Amos was looking ahead to the kingdom, when the fallen tent of David will be restored. At that time Gentiles will be saved as Gentiles in the coming kingdom. Because God's method of justification is the same in all ages, Gentiles may be saved as Gentiles now.

In Paul's famous speech to the Athenian philosophers recorded in Acts 17, he pointed ahead to a fixed day of judgment with the resurrected Jesus as judge (Acts 17:31). This warning was an integral part of Paul's message. When Paul reasoned with the Jews in the synagogue at Ephesus, he discussed "the kingdom of God" (Acts 19:8). This would be the same kingdom the Lord was considering in Acts 1:3, a kingdom yet future but entered by grace. In Acts 20:25 the apostle refers to announcing "the kingdom" in his past ministry at Ephesus. Acts concludes with Paul proclaiming the same message (Acts 28:30). Entrance into this kingdom by faith was a great hope for the early church!

Paul's eschatology is clearly revealed in a statement he made before the council in Acts 23:6, "I am on trial for the hope and resurrection of the dead!" He made the same declaration in the presence of Felix (Acts 24:15) and before Festus and Agrippa (Acts 26:6–8).

In the Pauline Epistles. These letters are freighted with prophetic truths. Every epistle has some mention of the rapture, the second coming of the Lord Jesus, the great tribulation, the reign of Christ, future judgment, or eternity. The theme of the future so permeates the apostle's doctrine that it is impossible to list all the references. Only some specific eschatological subjects will be mentioned—the rapture of the church, the tribulation, the millennial kingdom, and eternity.

The next prophetic event to occur according to Paul's theology is the taking out of the church from the world. Before the last half of the tribulation, there must be the appearance of the "man of sin" (2 Thess. 2:3–12). In spite of this, Paul expected the Lord Jesus to come at any time. In 2 Corinthians 5:1–4 he states his desire to be clothed over (Greek *ependuo*) his present body.[18] This mortal body will be "swallowed up" by a heavenly body. It was Paul's desire to live until the rapture took place (Phil. 3:11). Evidently the Thessalonian church was expecting this to occur so soon that they were surprised and disappointed when

---

18. The only two occurrences of this verb in the NT are in 2 Corinthians 5:2 and 5:4. BDAG says it means "put on (in addition)." Bauer, Danker, Arndt, and Gingerich, *A Greek-English Lexicon of the New Testament and Early Christianity* (Chicago: University of Chicago, 2000), 284.

some of their brothers and sisters in Christ had died (1 Thess. 4:13). It is difficult to say that the early church did not have an expectation of the rapture.

Revelation 3:10 says believers will be kept from "the hour of testing, that which is about to come upon the world." The promise is to keep them from the *time* of the great tribulation, a promise that pertains to all the churches (cf. Rev. 3:13). The tribulation is a time when God will vent his wrath on the world system (Rev. 6:16–17), but 1 Thessalonians 1:10 says the Thessalonian believers were examples of genuine conversion and of waiting "for his Son . . . who rescues us from the wrath to come." After the rapture, the church, then in heaven, will be judged. Each believer will receive a reward for His good deeds. No sin will be brought up because these have been forgiven (Heb. 8:12). However, not all good deeds are rewardable. The key is *motive* (1 Cor. 4:5; cf. Matt. 6:1–18; Col. 3:23–24).

After the rapture the time theologians call "the tribulation" will occur on earth. The most pointed reference in Paul's epistles to this period is 2 Thessalonians 2:1–10. It begins with a word of assurance in verses 1–2. Evidently, false teachers were teaching the Thessalonian church that they were already in the tribulation period. This would make sense to that group of believers because they were being persecuted (1 Thess. 2:14). If Paul had taught a post-tribulational rapture, they would not have been "shaken up"; rather, they would have accepted the tribulation to be their fate. It may be assumed the Thessalonian church had been taught a pretribulation rapture.

However, two things must occur before the tribulation period can be said to be present. First, there must be "the apostasy" (2 Thess. 2:3). Second, this apostasy will be headed up by the "man of lawlessness" (2 Thess. 2:3), who will demand worship of himself as God (verse 4) by setting himself up as God in God's temple. These claims will be fortified by his ability to perform miracles (2 Thess. 2:9).[19] His appearance will be forestalled by the restraining work of the Holy Spirit.[20] The Spirit's being "taken out of the way" (verse 7) does not mean the Holy Spirit will be removed from the earth, because people will be saved during the great tribulation (Rev. 7:9–17). "The taking out of the way" refers to the removal of the restraining work by the Holy Spirit to prevent the appearance of the "man of sin" before his time.

---

19. The same three words used of miracles in 2 Thessalonians 2:9 describe the miracles of Christ in Acts 2:22. Miracles by themselves do not attest the truth; they must be confirmed by the Word of God and the witness of the Holy Spirit (cf. Deut. 13:1-3).
20. Space does not permit a defense of this position here. It can scarcely be human government because in the tribulation government will be super-strong (cf. Rev. 13:4–17).

The cataclysmic conclusion to the reign of the "man of sin" will be the return of Christ at the end of the tribulation. The Lord Jesus will slay or destroy the man of sin by the breath of his mouth. As powerful as the "man of sin" will be, the Lord Jesus will do away with him by "the breath of his mouth."

When the Lord Christ returns to bring the tribulation to a conclusion, he will judge those who are still alive at the end of the tribulation to determine who will enter the kingdom (2 Thess. 1:8; 1 Cor. 6:9–10; Eph. 5:5; cf. Ezek. 20:33–38; Matt. 25:32–46). The unsaved will be executed and the saved will enter the new age—that is, the promised kingdom.

The saved—some still in mortal bodies—and those who are resurrected or raptured, will reign with Christ. There will be degrees of reward indicated by one's position in the kingdom (1 Cor. 6:2–3; 9:24–27; 2 Cor. 1:26).

What is pointedly stated in the Apocalypse concerning the future of Satan (Rev. 20:1–3, 7–10) is implied by Paul in Romans 16:19: Satan will be "crushed" (cf. Gen. 3:15).

What is the relationship of the church to Israel's promises? It is clear the OT promises and covenants were made with Israel (Rom. 9:4–5). The church is not Israel. In 1 Corinthians 10:32 Paul refers to Jews, Greeks, and the church of God. A distinction is made between saved Jews and saved Gentiles by referring to "natural branches" and "wild olives" who are grafted in (Rom. 11:21, 17). The promises made to Israel will be fulfilled by Christ (cf. Matt. 19:28; Rom. 9:25–29; 11:26). Because the church is "in Christ," it will join with Israel in these future blessings and yet remain distinct from Israel. The blessings have been and will be extended to the church (cf. 1 Cor. 11:25; 2 Cor. 7:1; Rom. 1:17–24; Eph. 2:14–20). It cannot be argued, however, from Galatians 6:16 that the church is the new Israel. Paul wrote: "And those who will walk by this rule, peace and mercy be upon them, and upon the Israel of God."[21] Romans 11:26 refers to Israel being "saved" when the kingdom comes. Here "Israel" clearly means ethnic Israel because of verse 25, which refers to the hardening of Israel in this present age.[22]

The Lord's kingdom on earth will culminate with every living being recognizing Jesus as Lord of all (Eph. 1:10; Phil. 2:11; Col. 1:20). When everything has been subjected to Christ, the earthly kingdom will merge into eternity

---

21. S. Lewis Johnson, Jr., "Paul and 'the Israel of God': An Exegetical and Eschatological Case Study," *Essays in Honor of J. Dwight Pentecost*, ed. Stanley D. Toussaint and Charles H. Dyer (Chicago: Moody, 1986), 181–196.
22. C. E. B. Cranfield, *The Epistle to the Romans*, vol. 2 (Edinburgh: T & T Clark, 1979), 576–7.

(1 Cor. 15:28). In a very real sense Christ's earthly kingdom will be the "front porch" to eternity because many of the earthly promises will extend to the eternal state.

In the General Epistles. The book of Hebrews is filled with references to eschatology. The many quotations in the first chapter anticipate the coming kingdom climaxing in the conclusion of 1:14. The angels are "ministering spirits" who serve "those who will inherit salvation." The word "salvation" is a "hook word" that anticipates 2:3, the "so great a salvation." In other words, the salvation of 2:3 looks back to the prophesied salvation of 1:14 which, in the context of chapter 1, is the coming kingdom. This is confirmed by 2:5 which refers to "the world to come concerning which we are speaking." The usual meaning of "salvation" in Hebrews is eschatological. Hebrews 2:8 anticipates the day when Jesus, the ideal human, will subject everything under his feet (cf. v. 14). This was one purpose of God in creating humans (cf. Psalm 8:4–6; Gen. 1:28). The promised rest of Hebrews 3–4 looks ahead to the coming millennium and eternity. The Jews looked on the Sabbath day as a picture of the coming kingdom.

The quotation of Jeremiah 31:31–34 in Hebrews 8:8–12 supports what was stated above concerning the new covenant; namely, that it is clearly addressed to Israel and some of the provisions are yet to be fulfilled (cf. vv. 10:6–11). This is looking to the future repentance of Israel (Zech. 12:10) and the coming kingdom. In the meantime, one of the blessings of the new covenant has been extended to the church, namely no remembrance of sins (v. 12; cf. 10:17). Furthermore, OT saints were redeemed by Christ's death so that they "may receive the promise of the eternal inheritance" (9:16). In the words of Lewis Sperry Chafer, "The Old Testament saints were saved on credit and all the bills came due at Calvary."

In Hebrews 10:12–13 the Lord Jesus, of the order of Melchizedek, is now at the right hand of God "waiting . . . until His enemies be made a footstool for His feet." The kingdom has not yet come and the Lord Jesus is now awaiting that day. Chapter 10 anticipates not only the coming of Christ to reign, but also a terrible judgment of those who reject Christ (10:29–30). It seems from verse 29 that this is specifically the "unpardonable sin." This is a judgment of adversaries of the Lord Jesus (v. 27; cf. 9:27; 10:39a).

Chapter 11 of Hebrews proves the principle, "Your present faith determines your future hope." It also vindicates the theme of the chapter that faith brings approval from God. The chapter uses this as an *enclusio* (vv. 2, 39). Hebrews

11 is filled with eschatological hope and looks forward to the coming kingdom and eternity. The pronoun "us" in verse 40 is significant because it indicates the church will participate in the future promised kingdom (cf. Matt.19:28; Eph. 2:20). Hebrews 12 looks to a future shaking of "not only the earth, but also the heavens" (v. 26; cf. Hag. 2:6; Rev. 16:18–20). There was a destruction of the earth with a flood in Noah's day; 2 Peter 3:10 describes a destruction of the earth by fire. It is possible that this "shaking" refers to a climactic judgment at the end of the tribulation. In Hebrews 13:14 there is a reference to the city "which is to come," an evident allusion to the same city described in 11:10 and 12:22. This is the heavenly Jerusalem which will be here during the millennium and then go on into eternity.

James's epistle to the twelve tribes of the dispersion has several allusions to prophecy. In 1:12 he refers to the reward of "the crown of life" promised to "those who love Him." This implies a judgment of believers, just as Paul taught in 1 Corinthians 3:12–15. James 3:1 also anticipates this judgment as it pertains specifically to teachers. The futurity of God's kingdom on this earth is assumed in 2:5. Those who love him are heirs of that kingdom. Once again the judgment of believers is seen in 2:12 where James warns his readers they will be judged by the "law of liberty." He seems to be referring to the "righteousness of God" (1:20; cf. 1:27) achieved by the working of the Holy Spirit. In 5:7 James encourages his readers to be long-suffering (Greek *makrothumeo*) until the Parousia of the Lord. His Parousia has drawn near. In fact, the judge has taken his stand at the door (5:9).

The theme of 1 Peter is victoriously suffering for the cause of Christ, or for righteousness' sake, in the hope of glory. In chapter 1, Peter repeatedly refers to the believer's future hope (vv. 3, 4, 5, 7, 9, 10, 13, 21). First Peter 2:2 refers to this hope as "salvation." In 2:7–8 those who reject Christ are destined for judgment. In fact, these lost souls were "appointed" for "this doom" of stumbling because they disobeyed "the word." Chapter 3 says believers are to live like Christ to "inherit a blessing" (3:9). To fortify this promise, the apostle quotes Psalm 34:12–16a. What the psalmist says regarding temporal rewards, Peter employs in reference to future rewards at the judgment seat of Christ. This earthly blessing extends into eternity. Hope in this eternal blessing is to be so evident in a believer's life that unbelievers ask about it (3:15).

First Peter 4:7 says, "The end of all things is near." The same verb in the same tense was used to announce the nearness of the kingdom in the Gospels. This, of course, is a motivation to a godly life (vv. 7b–11). Verse 13 refers to the revelation" of Christ's glory, which most probably looks at the return of the Lord Jesus to establish his kingdom on the earth. In 5:1 and 2 Peter 1:16–18, Peter claims to have witnessed this glory personally in the transfiguration. The same passage (5:4) looks ahead to the judgment seat of Christ when faithful elders will receive an "unfading crown of glory" from the "Chief Shepherd." Peter goes on to say Christians will share with Christ in his "eternal glory" (5:10). Quite clearly, the revelation of Christ's glory when he returns to reign will be seen throughout eternity. Even when believers in Christ suffer for Christ or the cause of righteousness, they are to look forward to the hope of glory.

In 2 Peter the note of prophecy is struck loudly. A wonderful entrance into the future kingdom (1:11) is assured for those who will follow the ladder of virtues outlined in 1:5–8. The transfiguration was a guarantee and preview of the "power and coming" of the Lord Jesus (1:16–17). In 1:19–21 Peter assures his readers that the written word of prophecy is more sure than the experience of Peter, James, and John on the Mount of Transfiguration, because of the work of the Holy Spirit in moving these prophets to record prophecy. They did not simply interpret human events as they saw them. Second Peter predicts the coming of false prophets and apostasy. He used the judgments of the flood and Sodom and Gomorrah and the deliverances of Noah with his family and Lot to prove the point God is able both to judge and to deliver in the day of judgment. In fact, the lost are now enduring punishment in preparation for the final judgment (2 Peter 2:9). The coming of "the day of the Lord" is a theme of 2 Peter 3. When that occurs the elements of the earth and sky will be destroyed by fire. This destruction will take place at the end of the millennium in preparation for the new heavens and earth which will go into eternity (cf. Rev. 21:1).

The theme of eschatology is continued in 1 John. In 1 John 2:17—commonly translated "the world is passing away"—the idea of prophecy is often overlooked. This most certainly is a futuristic present and should be rendered "will pass away"; its lusts assuredly are not passing away now but they will. The presence of false teachers called "antichrists" (2:18, 22; 4:3; 2 John 7) presage the coming of the ultimate antichrist or "the man of sin" described in 2 Thessalonians 2 (cf. Rev. 13:1–10). The marvelous promise that believers will be like Christ is given in 1 John 3:2. Not only that, but in that day Christians will see him as he is! This is the hope that purifies (3:3). Confidence "in the day of judgment" is promised to those who fully walk in love; furthermore this confidence is buttressed by the believer's position in Christ. John assures his readers with the clause because "as He is, so also are we in this world" (4:17).

Jude also discusses some interesting prophetic facts. "And angels who did not keep their own domain [are now being] kept in eternal bonds under darkness (cf. 2 Peter 2:4; Greek *tartaroo* from *Tartaros*) for the judgment of the great day" (v. 6). Likewise, those who committed "gross immorality" in Sodom and Gomorrah are presently enduring "eternal fire" (v. 7). These are examples of false teachers who will experience deep darkness forever (v. 13). Enoch predicted this judgment will occur when the Lord comes (vv. 14–15). In the face of erroneous doctrines and deceptive teachers, God is able to preserve his own and present them blameless before himself (vv. 24–25). Significantly, security does not lead to license, but to worship!

In Revelation. It is impossible to discuss the Apocalypse in any detail in a closing portion of one chapter, but the theme is clear enough: Jesus is going to win, so Christians are to be encouraged. Revelation 1:19 provides a general outline for the book: "The things which you have seen" looks at the vision of Christ in chapter 1. Chapters 2 and 3 are represented by "the things that are." The consummation of the age, portrayed in chapters 4–22, is described by "the things which shall take place after these things."

After a description of the glorified Christ, John delegates a messenger to seven churches of western Asia Minor. These churches experienced failures and victories just like churches of today. Some have claimed that they portray a progression of church history. However, if they did, it would destroy the doctrine of imminency.

Chapters 5–6 represent a doxological highpoint in the NT. They demonstrate that ultimately there is worship of Jesus who alone is qualified to open the seven-sealed scroll. The scroll portrays the inheritance of the saints of all ages or it illustrates a title deed. The seals illustrate the tribulation the earth must experience before God's people enter that inheritance. Actually there are seven seals, seven trumpets, and seven bowls which are "telescoped"; that is, the last of a given series contains the entire subsequent series.[23]

In chapters 11–16, certain personages of the last half of the tribulation are portrayed. Revelation 14:6–17 is proleptic of the end of the tribulation and the judgment of the lost as well as a blessing on those who die in the Lord.

---

23. For a defense of this view see Merrill C. Tenney, *Interpreting Revelation* (Grand Rapids: Eerdmans, 1957), 35, 74–81; Robert L. Thomas, *Revelation 8–22, An Exegetical Commentary* (Chicago: Moody Press, 1995), 531–42.

In chapter 16 the final very rapid outpourings of the bowls of wrath are depicted; chapters 17 and 18 describe the judgment of Babylon; and chapter 19 portrays two events—the celebration of both the judgment of the "great harlot" and the preparation of the Lamb's bride, and a description of Christ's return to put down enemies at the end of the tribulation. The consignment of the beast and his false prophet to the lake of fire concludes the chapter. The millennium and its conclusion are described in chapter 20. Finally, in the same chapter there is the depiction of the great white throne judgment.

The last two chapters of Revelation look ahead to the eternal state of the new heaven and earth. An important part of this will be the Jerusalem from heaven, comprised of the redeemed of all ages. The conclusion of the book is the promise by Christ of his coming and a plea from his beloved disciple for it to happen soon, with a final benediction for believers (22:20–21).

Conclusion

When one begins to look at prophecy, he cannot help but marvel at God's sovereignty. He is in control. This logically leads to hope—a desire with expectancy for the Lord's return and all the accompanying blessings, too numerous to list.

THE DOCTRINE OF THE FUTURE
AND THE WEAKENING OF PROPHECY

Charles C. Ryrie

Prophecies are everywhere: radio and TV weather forecasts, Wall Street gains and losses, warnings of global warming dangers, and horoscopes in the daily papers predict what you can expect. Advertisers promise, "Guaranteed results when you buy this product!" And in December you can buy papers at the checkout aisles that predict what is going to happen next year. I once succeeded in reaching one of these "prophets" by phone. Her husband answered, and when I related to him that I wanted to know how his wife arrived at these predictions, he just laughed and said it was fun for her to do but actually was a joke (one that paid quite well). In light of this inundation of modern-day prophecy, several questions might be raised. What about prophecies in the Bible? Are they reliable? Were any of them false? How accurately can we expect yet unfulfilled prophecies to come to pass? What practical difference does all this make? Isn't it more important to live biblically than to be concerned with what may happen in the future?

SOME FACTS ABOUT PROPHETS
AND PROPHECY IN THE BIBLE

1. Who is a true biblical prophet? It is someone who announces God's will to people and/or predicts the future. Biblical prophets were sometimes reformers (Isa. 1), and sometimes predictors (Isa. 2:1–4). Bible teachers have often described the former role as "forth-telling," and the latter as "foretelling."

2. Some were wrong. The first untrue prophecy in the Bible was an-

nounced by Satan to Eve: "You surely will not die" (Gen. 3:4). But she did. (cf. Ezek. 13:1–8, Matt. 7:15, and Rev. 20:10).

3. In Old Testament times, false prophets were to be put to death by stoning (Deut. 13:5, 10). In New Testament times prophets were to be tested by other prophets (1 Cor. 14:29–32).

4. There are many true and accurate prophecies in the Bible. Many have been fulfilled; many are yet to be fulfilled.

THE WEAKENING OF PROPHECY

Past fulfillments provide strong evidence of the truth and accuracy of the Bible. Similarly, as to future prophecies there ought to be no question about the same certainty of their fulfillment. While many evangelicals would not deny that, in practice there seems to be a weakening of the existence and/or the accuracy of yet-to-be fulfilled prophecies. How such weakening is being accomplished is the subject of this essay.

Changing Traditional Dates

This approach insists or suggests that traditional dates for some biblical books must have been written later so that prophecies (according to the earlier, traditional dates) were actually histories recorded later, after the events happened. One such example concerns the prophecies in the book of Daniel. The traditional date for that book is the sixth century BCE. If so, then the prophecies in the book were true prophecies unfulfilled in Daniel's time but to be fulfilled after his time. Some were fulfilled by the time of the first coming of Christ (2:38–40), and some will not be fulfilled until the events surrounding his second coming occur (2:44; 7:24). Critics of the sixth-century-BCE date believe it was compiled by an unknown author about 165 BCE because it contains prophecies about post-Babylonian kings and wars which were accurately fulfilled and therefore could not have been prophesied but were written after the events occurred. That requires a later date since critics claim that these traditional prophecies are in reality historical records of events after they happened.

The date of the writing of the book of Revelation has traditionally been placed in the 90s. That means that the events described, especially in Revelation 4–19, would take place in the future, in relation to the time of writing. However, if the prophecies Christ spoke in Matthew 24–25—many of which are similar to those in Revelation 4–19—were fulfilled in the immediate future, then the date of the writing of Revelation would have to be moved from the 90s back to 64–66, so that those prophecies could be fulfilled by 70.

These are a few ways in which scholars have changed traditional dates to weaken and even eliminate true biblical prophecies.[1]

Embracing Preterism

Preterism is from the Latin and means "past." Preterism teaches that the prophecies in the book of Revelation were fulfilled by the time of the destruction of Jerusalem in 70. Preterists fall into one of three groups. (1) Mild preterism holds that the prophecies in Revelation were fulfilled in the first three centuries. (2) Extreme preterism includes all future prophecies having been fulfilled by 70, including those about the second coming of Christ and resurrections. (3) Moderate preterism sees the prophecies in Revelation 4–19 as fulfilled in 70, although some prophecies—like those related to Christ's second coming and future resurrections—are yet to be fulfilled in the future. Note that all three groups of preterists weaken the prophetic force of many passages by teaching that many passages that have traditionally been understood as yet-future have already been fulfilled.

Some evidence offered in favor of the preterist view includes the following: (1) Many internal struggles within Judaism during the years preceding Titus's destruction of Jerusalem in 70. The Roman soldiers, not a future person, were "an abomination leading to destruction" (Matt. 24:15). (2) Since the temple is mentioned in various prophecies, it was destroyed in 70, and there will be no temple in the future, then prophecies as those in Matthew 24 have to be fulfilled by 70. (3) Matthew 24:34 means that the generation living at the time Christ spoke these words would live to see their fulfillment. Thus, the prophecies would have to be fulfilled within about forty years of the time of Christ.

Admittedly preterism, especially the moderate form, does not deny that some prophecies will be fulfilled in the future, but it dismisses many as having already been fulfilled. This view eliminates some fulfillment and weakens the force of the entire body of biblical prophecy.[2]

---

1. For a survey of this view see J. C. Whitcomb, "Daniel," *The New Bible Dictionary* (Grand Rapids, Eerdmans, 1962), pp. 290–93.
2. For moderate preterism see R. C. Sproul, *The Last Days According to Jesus* (Grand Rapids, Baker, 2000), 158.

Using Genre–Dependent Hermeneutics

Genre is "a category of artistic, musical, or literary composition character-ized by a particular style, form or content."[3] Hermeneutics is the study of the principles of interpretation. Strictly speaking, it is not doing interpretation; it is ascertaining the principles which will be used in actually interpreting.

Genre-dependent hermeneutics results in a system of hermeneutics which is adapted from and affected by the genre of the material that is to be interpreted. For example, apocalyptic books in the Bible (especially Revela-tion) belong to a specific genre, which, in turn, requires a hermeneutic that reflects that genre. The genre of Revelation includes the use of many symbols which cannot be interpreted in the traditional, normal way but which need to be interpreted by a genre-driven hermeneutic which allows for nonliteral understanding and even multiple meanings. Numbers in apocalyptic litera-ture are not exact as 144,000 and one thousand, in Revelation chapters 7 and 20 respectively.

The recognition of different kinds of material in the Bible may help one's understanding of the text. However, when the meaning of the text is genre-dependent and includes a particular hermeneutic suitable to the particu-lar genre, then such an approach can weaken and even change the meaning and precision of prophecies in these apocalyptic books. Logically—and, with some writers, necessarily—every genre will need its own set of hermeneutical principles to use in interpreting the material of that particular genre. As a result, normal or literal interpretation is often jettisoned from the hermeneutic. When applied to prophetic passages they become nonliteral and weakened if not elimi-nated altogether. Even principles and symbols must be based on particulars. If a symbol does not relate to a literal truth, then it must be a symbol of another symbol, and that of another symbol, etc.

The overemphasis of genre leads to the need for special hermeneutics, which leads to nonspecific interpretation which leads to symbolic meanings.[4]

---

3. "Genre," *Merriam-Webster's Collegiate Dictionary*, 11th ed. (Springfield, MA: Merriam-Webster, Inc., 2003).

4. Robert H. Mounce, *The Book of Revelation* (Grand Rapids: Eerdmans, 1977), "Symbol-ism is . . . a matter of literary genre. Apocalyptic language has as one of its basic char-acteristics the cryptic and symbolic use of words and phrases." The fly leaf describes the book as taking a "position between and indefensible literalism an a highly imaginative subjectivism."

Banking on Chance

If one wants to downplay prophecy, why resort to any or all of the above more or less sophisticated ways? Wouldn't it be enough simply to depend on chance to account for the accuracy of prophecies? People have the notion that, given enough time, almost anything can happen by chance. That is easier to believe if one is thinking about a single prophecy only. But what about a group of prophecies that focus on a specific area of prophecy? Could a group of prophecies relating to an area of prophecy be fulfilled literally by chance? This can be answered by testing the detailed accuracy of prophecies fulfilled in the past.

An oft-used test case consists of the group of fulfilled prophecies concerning the first coming of Christ. One can think of several specific prophecies: Christ's birthplace as Bethlehem (Micah 5:2) predicted seven hundred years before; Christ would be announced by a forerunner (John the Baptist) predicted by Malachi (3:1) four hundred years before; many specific details about his ministry (Isa. 9:1; 11:2; 42:1); and specific details about his death and resurrection (Ps. 22:15, 18; 16:9–10). It is easy to find at least thirty predictions related to the first coming of Christ. It is not difficult to find more, even up to one hundred. Either these prophecies—and the Bible that recorded them—are true and accurate prophecies, or they happened by chance.

It is possible to test the reliability of the "chance" option. If you flip a coin twice, there are four possible results: it will land heads both times, tails both times, heads then tails, or tails then heads. Pick one—say, heads—both times. The chance of that happening is one out of four. Or to put it another way, if four people flipped the coin twice, one of them could be expected by chance to come up with two heads in a row. Four uninterrupted heads in a row would happen by chance one in sixteen times. If slightly more than a thousand people were all flipping coins a thousand times, the chances are that one of them would land heads ten times in a row. Twenty would happen once in a million flips. Thirty, once in a billion.

The point here is: If every person living at the first coming of Christ made predictions about him—statistically speaking—not one of them would have scored one hundred percent. Every living person would have been a false prophet. To successfully predict one hundred prophecies by chance is less than one in 1,000,000,000,000,000,000,000,000,000,000 (1×10^{30}). That fraction is so infinitesimally small that the mathematician would declare the chance of these prophecies being fulfilled is zero.

There are three conclusions we may draw from these statistics: (1) To use chance to account for biblical prophecies not only weakens the prophecies, it eliminates them. (2) We can check on the accuracy of past fulfilled prophecies, and when we do, we see that they were plainly, specifically, and accurately fulfilled. (3) We can be confident that yet unfulfilled future prophecies will also be fulfilled plainly, specifically, and accurately.

The study of biblical prophecy guarantees assurance of the truth of the Bible (2 Peter 1:19), gives hope that cleanses the believer (1 John 3:3), provides comfort in times of persecution and sorrow (2 Cor. 4:7, 14), and promotes worship of the living and true God (Rev. 7:9–12).

The Doctrine of the Future, the Doctrine of God, and Predictive Prophecy

John D. Laing and Stefana Dan Laing [1]

I am the first and I am the last.
There is no God but Me.
Who, like Me, can announce the future?
—Isaiah 44:6–7

A visit to New Orleans' Jackson Square provides a study in contrasts between two ways of knowing the future. Looking past the statue of General Andrew Jackson astride his rearing horse, one can see the façade of the Saint Louis Cathedral rises as a majestic backdrop. This church claims to be the United States' oldest Catholic cathedral in constant use. The congregation has been dispensing the Word of God to the city of New Orleans for nearly three centuries since its founding in 1720. Directly in front of the church, however, practically on its very doorstep, multiple tables and chairs are set up, representing another avenue people might pursue to find out what their future holds. Mediums, palm readers, tarot-card and tea-leaf readers, and prognosticators of all stripes advertise their own forecasting services. The church and its prophetic voice—as far as it faithfully speaks forth God's message through the Scriptures—represents a valid and divinely sanctioned method of accessing

---

1. We are privileged to contribute to this volume honoring our professor, mentor, and friend, Craig Blaising. We are profoundly grateful for his investment in our lives: professionally, as we studied Systematic Theology and Patristics under his teaching; vocationally, as he wisely advised us regarding the teaching ministry, emphasizing the importance of spiritual formation; and personally, as he blessed us on our wedding day with his homily extolling the wisdom and mystery of fierce love (Song 8:6–7), a precious and treasured memory.

God's plan for the future, while those out front represent avenues which are not only invalid but divinely proscribed.

To some degree, all people experience anxiety about the future and the unknown, and many seek their own ways of accessing that knowledge. This longing to know is a natural human desire, known by God and graciously provided for in God's Word. This chapter will address the reliability of the Bible to speak authoritatively concerning prophecy and future events, as its reliability is grounded in God's self-revelation, sovereignty, and omniscience. From Scripture, theology, and historical events, we will argue for the integrity of divine prediction and prophecy in matters pertaining to the future.

BIBLICAL FOUNDATIONS

The illustration above represents a situation which unfolded in Israel's history as well. In their distrust of God's covenant promises to Abraham, Moses, and David, Israel turned to other gods, the idols of the Canaanites, just as in the past they had served the gods of Egypt (Josh. 24:14–15). Although they had pledged to worship Yahweh alone, they eventually resorted to ascertaining their future in the same ways as the idolatrous nations surrounding them, by means of mediums, astrology, witchcraft, and necromancy, all divinely prohibited methods (Lev. 19:31; 2 Chron. 33:5–6; see also Ezek. 13:17–23). God instead spoke to them through the prophets, revealing himself and his plan, exhorting his people to trust him for the fulfillment of promises, and warning them of dire consequences for disobedience (on the model of the covenant blessings and curses of Deut. 27–31).

God's power and trustworthiness to know, reveal, and bring about the future constitutes a major theme in Isaiah 40–49, a portion of Scripture which will serve as a biblical foundation for our topic. Through Isaiah, God repeatedly confronted idols, as well as idolaters, for their emptiness and ineffectiveness. He declares his eternality saying, "I, Yahweh, am the first, and with the last—I am He" (Isa. 41:4). He challenged the idol-gods to accurately predict coming events: "Let them come and tell us what will happen. Tell us the past events, so that we may reflect on them and know the outcome, or tell us the future. Tell us the coming events, then we will know that you are gods. . . . Do something. . . look, you are nothing . . . your work is worthless" (Isa. 41:22–24). False gods (and their spokespersons) have no testimony about their fulfilled actions in the past nor do they possess the power to foretell the future, whereas the true and living and eternal God does both. He forecasts events well in advance: "The past events have indeed happened. Now I declare new events; I announce them to you before they occur" (Isa. 42:9). God invites Israel to prove him because the ability to predict, bring about, and shape the future—to speak something and bring it to pass—lies within his eternal and supreme power. Being transcendent and above the earth, he holds its past, present, and future in his hands, knowing the end from the beginning.

Understanding and interpreting prophetic predictions involves the spiritual state of the recipient/hearer. God admonished Israel, "Though seeing many things, you do not obey. Though his ears are open, he does not listen" (Isa. 42:20; also 42:23). These passages constitute a warning to those who witness revelations and fulfillments but refuse to acknowledge or recognize them as such because of their spiritual state: their hearts are "blind" and "deaf," although their physical faculties of sight and hearing are perfectly functional (see also 48:8). In this category we may include those who deny predictive prophecy and the supernatural dimension of biblical prophetic fulfillment.

Divine prediction is grounded in the nature of God as a living and active being; in his attributes of eternality, omniscience, omnipotence, and sovereignty; and in his love which is relational and redemptive. In contrast to the dead, deaf, and dumb idols, God is eternal and all-knowing with comprehensive knowledge of matters from their inception to their completion. He is also all-powerful and sovereign over the world, with the authority and right to fulfill his plans for all nations, both bringing about events and shaping their outcome. This God is a relational and loving Creator who actively works to forgive and redeem his creatures, and who has shown himself consistent throughout history in his providential plan of deliverance and restoration, a plan known as "salvation history." Naming himself "Yahweh," King, Redeemer, and Warrior ("Lord of Hosts"), he asserts, "I am the first and I am the last. There is no God but Me. Who, like Me, can announce the future?" (Isa. 44:6–7). God's self-proclamations are not empty boasts, but are in fact validated by the historical fulfillment of prophetic predictions (see below).

The Lord admonished Israel to recall his past works and fulfilled promises, specifically his work in the exodus and the constitution of Abraham's descendants as a nation and his special people, both fulfillments of his promises to Abraham, "My friend" (Isa. 41:8). Just as prophecies predicting the Babylonian exile as punishment for Israel's covenant-breaking were fulfilled, so in Isaiah God revealed his plan to return the exiles to their land. He states adamantly: "I declare the end from the beginning, and from long ago what is not yet done, saying, 'My plan will take place, and I will do all My will. I call a bird of prey from the east, a man for my purpose from a far country. Yes, I have spoken, so I will also bring it about. I have planned it; I will also do it" (Isa. 46:10–11). In this context, as God reveals that he will use Cyrus the Persian (r. 559–530 BC) to overthrow Babylon, judgment oracles against Babylon (also called Chaldea) follow in the text. "Daughter Chaldea" will experience "loss of children and widowhood" in a sudden calamity which she never anticipated, despite her "many sorceries and the potency of her spells"—that is, despite having what she thought were reliable means by which to forecast events (Isa. 47:9). Yahweh continues, "Devastation will happen to you [Babylon] suddenly and unexpectedly. So take your stand with your spells and your many sorceries . . . perhaps you will be able to succeed . . . you are worn out with your many consultations. So let them stand and save you—the astrologers, who observe the stars, who predict monthly what will happen to you" (Isa. 47:11–13). Incantations and non-covenantal methods of prediction utterly fail to give confidence and assurance in the face of God's irrevocable and unassailable intentions. "I declared the past events long ago; they came out of My mouth; I proclaimed them. Suddenly I acted, and they occurred" (Isa. 48:3). In order to overcome Israel's unbelief, God removes other explanations by fulfilling prophecies given long before, at an unexpected time. Prophecies do not always happen according to human understanding and expectation (the coming of the Messiah and his work of redemption being no exception). The text focuses on God's reliability and the fact that God has proven truthful in the past and can be trusted for future things.

The prophet's role was to speak the word of God to the king, nation, or people to reveal his will for their lives and how they should act. Prophecy sometimes included predictions, but always with a view to revealing something of God's will, plan, nature, or personality so that the hearers would respond appropriately in worshipful obedience. The true prophet was one who had stood in the council of God and received God's word directly, one who maintained a solid covenant relationship with the Lord and spoke faithfully the message entrusted by God. In effect, the prophet's words are God's words, and constitute direct revelation (e.g., Isa. 6:8–9; Jer. 1:7–9, 17–19; Ezek. 2:7–3:4).

THEOLOGICAL FOUNDATIONS

There are good theological reasons for believing that God knows the future and that the instances of predictive prophecy reported in the Bible are reliable. These theological reasons for our confidence should not be confused with apologetic reasons.[2] When we think theologically, we assume that God exists and has revealed himself. Christianity is a revealed religion, from God's acts in history, such as the miracles accompanying Israel's exodus from bondage in Egypt, to the spoken word of God by the prophets who proclaimed, "This is what the LORD says," insisting they only spoke the words God gave them (see Micaiah's response to King Ahab's attendant, 1 Kings 22:14); from the revelation of God in the person of Jesus Christ, who was the image of the invisible God (Col. 1:15), the radiance of his glory and the exact representation of his nature (Heb. 1:3), and who proclaimed that if you have seen him, you have seen the Father (John 14:9), to the written word of God, the Bible (2 Tim. 3:16). Theologians have typically divided revelation into two categories: general and special.

Divine Revelation

General revelation refers to the way God makes himself known through means available to all people, typically understood as observation of the created order, reflection upon the nature of God, or via the deliverances of the individual conscience.[3] The task of doing theology by means of general revelation is known as natural theology, and it is widely thought to produce substantial results.[4] Still,

---

2. Theological reasons are doctrinal and their purpose is to strengthen and clarify the faith of those who already believe, while apologetic reasons are meant to offer proof for unbelievers or to answer objections posed by skeptics. The former are primarily for the church, while the latter are primarily for the unchurched. Admittedly, there can be significant overlap, as theology may be used both apologetically and evangelistically, to clarify the substance of the Christian faith for skeptics who have misunderstandings and for unbelievers who have questions. Similarly, apologetic arguments can bolster the confidence of believers by providing answers to relevant questions in response to objections. For a helpful discussion of these issues, see James K. Beilby, *Thinking about Christian Apologetics* (Downers Grove, IL: InterVarsity, 2011), especially ch. 1.

3. Sometimes tracking the flow of human history is included here as well, since God is lord over history and the destinies of humans and/or nations (Job 12:23; Ps. 47:6–8; Isa. 10:5–13). The reality of this type of revelation is confirmed in the Bible. For example, the Psalmist notes that the heavens proclaim the glory of God (Ps. 19:1); and the apostle Paul claims that humans are without excuse for their unbelief, because God's nature and power are "clearly visible" in the creation (Rom. 1:20). Later in the same book, Paul speaks of those who have the Law of God (that is, the word of God in the Old Testament) in contrast with the Gentiles who do not have the Law, but who instinctively know the moral code and whose consciences confirm they have violated it (Rom. 2:12–16). The important point here is that the deliverances of the conscience with regard to sin (even of those who have never heard of the Bible or Christ) point to an inborn knowledge of God.

4. Natural theology can argue to the existence of God; most of the standard arguments for the existence of God are exercises in natural theology. For example, the so-called ontological argument,

numerous theologians are suspicious of this endeavor.[5] Special revelation refers to God's disclosure of himself and his ways to particular persons or at specific times. It can take many forms: visions and dreams from God, miraculous acts of God, appearances of God in space and time known as *theophanies*, and the word of God given orally or in writing. Prophecy is the primary oracular revelation, while the Bible is the primary written revelation; and the two together—the word of God—constitute by far the most common means by which God has revealed himself.

It has, until the relatively recent past, been axiomatic that Christians believed in biblical inerrancy, largely due to their conviction that the Bible is itself divine revelation. Although some question it, the vast majority of Christians (Catholic, Orthodox, and evangelical Protestant) still affirm this doctrine. Just as the prophets of old spoke God's own words, so also the authors of Scripture wrote God's words. In his letter to Timothy, Paul refers to Scripture as "God-breathed" (*theopneustos*, from *theos* "God," and *pneuma* "spirit" or "breath"; 2 Tim. 3:16). Theologians have sought to articulate this process of divine work upon the human authors of Scripture that allows us to speak of the Bible as God's Word, referring to it as *verbal-plenary inspiration*. Just as the prophets retained their mental faculties, so also the human authors were actively involved in the writing.

---

developed by Anselm of Canterbury, is based on the claim that if a person just thinks properly about the sort of being God is, he will have to admit that God exists and does so necessarily (couldn't not exist): the very statement, "God does not exist" is a contradiction. Anselm, *Proslogion* 2–3. Similarly, the cosmological argument, popularized in Christian circles by Thomas Aquinas, is grounded in one's observations of dependency relationships in the creation and the recognition that there could not be an infinite regress in those relationships. Thus, God is the First Cause, Prime Mover, and the like, the infinite, eternal Creator/Initiator of a finite, temporal creation. Thomas Aquinas, *Summa Theologica* 1.2.3. In addition to innate knowledge of God's existence and personal guilt, more can be said. For example, acknowledgement of one's guilt suggests a moral law and lawgiver, and these, along with rational reflection upon the nature of God (What sort of Being would be worthy of the ascription "God" and of worship?) can lead to the conclusion that God is holy and all good. Similar lines of reasoning can be used to arrive at a number of divine attributes: all-powerful, all-knowing, just, honest, truthful, loving, merciful, infinite, etc.

5. Their suspicion is due to two factors: First, they argue that the primary emphasis of Scripture is upon special revelation, even in Romans (ch. 1) the emphasis is upon the gospel. Second, they see it as an exercise in futility: Natural theology cannot lead to salvation, since it is unable to arrive at faith in Christ and is subject to the problem of the adverse effects of the Fall on the human mind. For example, it is generally well known that Karl Barth rejected the very prospect of natural theology, fearing that it sought to make a connection between God and humanity apart from Christ. Barth writes, "Only one thing cannot be granted to natural theology, namely, that it has a legitimate function in the sphere of the Church or that in this sphere it has any other destiny than to disappear." Karl Barth, *Church Dogmatics* II.I.26.2, trans. T. H. L. Parker, W. B. Johnson, Harold Knight, and J. L. M. Haire (Edinburgh: T & T Clark, 1957), 170.

Unlike dictation theories, which see the human authors as passive instruments in the hands of God, verbal-plenary inspiration emphasizes the active human authorship of the biblical books, and takes into account these authors' unique writing styles, word usage, and emphases.[6] As the Chicago Statement on Biblical Inerrancy says, "God in his work of inspiration utilized the distinctive personalities and literary styles of the writers whom he had chosen and prepared."[7] Thus, a proper understanding of biblical inspiration and inerrancy not only takes differences of genre into account, but also allows for phenomenological language (e.g., "four corners of the earth" does not mean the authors thought the earth is not spherical, Isa. 11:12), paraphrase, and even grammatical errors.[8]

Since the doctrine of inerrancy results directly from God's work in inspiration, and inspiration is the Holy Spirit's work upon the actual authors of Scripture and the prophets, inerrancy applies to the original writings or speech. How-

---

6. It was characteristic of pagan prophets to release control of their mental faculties in order to be controlled by the deity. In discussing pagan oracles, Sheppard and Herbrechtsmeier write, "The behavior of these divine spokesmen is often thought to have been ecstatic, frenzied, or abnormal in some way, which reflected their possession by the deity (and the absence of personal ego) at the time of transmission." Gerald T. Sheppard and William E. Herbrechtsmeier, "Prophecy: An Overview" in Mircea Eliade, ed. *The Encyclopedia of Religion* (New York: Simon & Schuster Macmillan, 1995), 12:8. See also Mircea Eliade, *Shamanism: Archaic Techniques of Ecstasy*, Willard R. Trask, trans. (Princeton, NJ: Princeton University Press, 1964). This release sometimes involved drug use. There is a somewhat spirited debate regarding the possibility of intoxication as a result of noxious fumes at the Delphic Oracle in ancient Greece. For a positive argument, see Henry A. Spiller, John R. Hale, and Jelle Zeilinga de Boer, "The Delphic Oracle: A Multidisciplinary Defense of the Gaseous Vent Theory" *Clinical Toxicology* 40:2 (2002): 189–96. For critical evaluations of their work, see J. Foster and Daryn Lehoux, "The Delphic Oracle and the Ethylene-Intoxication Hypothesis" *Clinical Toxicology* 45:1 (2007): 85–89; and Daryn Lehoux, "Drugs and the Delphic Oracle" *Classical World* 10:1 (2007): 41–56. In his confrontation with the prophets of Baal and Ashtoreth, Elijah notes the ecstatic nature of the pagan ritual in which they cut themselves and called out uncontrollably (1 Kings 18). By contrast, the depiction of prophecy in Israel was one in which the prophet retained control of his body, actions, and words. For instance, Ezekiel was instructed by God to refrain from mourning his wife's death as a sign-act for Israel (Ezek. 24:16–18). The obvious implication is that he could have mourned her because he had control of his emotions and actions.
7. *Chicago Statement on Biblical Inerrancy*, Article VIII.
8. B. B. Warfield, who arguably wrote more on the subject than any other evangelical scholar, writes, "No finding of traces of human influence in the style, wording or forms of statement or argumentation touches the question [of plenary inspiration]. The book is throughout the work of human writers and is filled with the signs of their handiwork . . . no objection touches the question, that is obtained by pressing the primary sense of phrases or idioms . . . no objection is valid which is gained by overlooking the prime question of the intentions and professions of the writer . . . if an author does not profess to report the exact words of a discourse or a document . . . then it is not opposed to his claim to inspiration that he does not give the exact words." Benjamin Breckinridge Warfield, *The Inspiration and Authority of the Bible* (Philadelphia: Presbyterian and Reformed, 1948), 437–38.

ever, it is important to note that this clarification is not meant to suggest that the Bibles we have today, which are the result of years of transmission through meticulous copying, have errors in them, as some critics have suggested.[9] Rather, it is simply to note the important theological basis for our confidence in the Scriptures, namely their divine origin and God's truthfulness, reliability, and steadfastness (Deut. 32:4; John 3:33; Rom. 3:4; Titus 1:2; Rev. 22:6). Since God inspired the prophets, their predictions were always true to the detail (Deut. 18:20–22), and since God inspired the authors of Scripture, their writings, including predictive prophecy, are true. Error speaks against divine inspiration.[10]

Theology Proper

Theological reflection on the nature of God is known as Theology Proper, and typically proceeds by examination of biblical passages that speak to divine attributes. It is common for professional theologians to divide the attributes into various groupings for ease of discussion, but often more confusion than clarity results.[11]

---

9. Most notably, Bart Ehrman has called the reliability of the Bible into question. See for example, Bart Ehrman, *Misquoting Jesus: The Story Behind Who Changed the Bible and Why* (San Francisco: HarperOne, 2007). For an evangelical response, see Daniel B. Wallace, *Revisiting the Corruption of the New Testament: Manuscript, Patristic, and Apocryphal Evidence* (Grand Rapids: Kregel, 2011); Steven B. Cowen and Terry L. Wilder, eds., *In Defense of the Bible: A Comprehensive Apologetic for the Authority of Scripture* (Nashville: Broadman & Holman, 2013); F. F. Bruce, *The Canon of Scripture* (Downers Grove, IL: IVP, 1988). See also Robert B. Stewart, ed., *The Reliability of the New Testament: Bart Ehrman and Daniel Wallace in Dialogue* (Philadelphia: Fortress, 2011).

10. In addition to accuracy, the prophet's message also had to cohere with the rest of God's word, most importantly it had to exhort people to worship and follow the true God (Deut. 13:1–5). So also, the principles of the Bible's consistency and its self-interpreting status (Scripture interprets Scripture) stand.

11. Some of the more common approaches have been to divide the attributes into natural (attributes which speak to God's nature) and moral (attributes which speak to God's values), or into absolute (those which refer to him in himself; his essence) and relative (those which refer to him in relation to the creation), or into communicable (those that have a corollary in creatures/humans) and incommunicable (those that are not found in creatures). The difficulty with all of these divisions is that there is always significant overlap between the two supposedly mutually exclusive categories. As Wayne Grudem, who makes use of the communicable/incommunicable distinction, rightly notes, "upon further reflection, we realize that this distinction, although helpful, is not perfect. That is because there is no attribute of God that is completely communicable, and there is no attribute of God that is completely incommunicable!" Wayne Grudem, *Systematic Theology* (Grand Rapids: Zondervan, 1994), 156. Similarly, Berkhof notes, "properly speaking, all the perfections of God are relative, indicating what he is in relation to the world." Louis Berkhof, *Systematic Theology*, 4th ed. (Grand Rapids: Eerdmans, 1993), 55. God's otherness (transcendence) means that he is in some sense unknowable, while his closeness (immanence) means that he can be known. Thomas Aquinas suggested that whenever we speak of God, we speak analogously because of this problem.

Thus, here we will simply note some of the best known attributes of God—holy, loving, just, merciful, pure, good, all-powerful (omnipotent), everywhere-present (omnipresent), transcendent, immanent, patient/long-suffering, infinite, creative, aesthetic, wrathful, and forgiving—and then focus on the three most relevant for the study of predictive prophecy: all-knowing (omniscient), eternal, and sovereign/providential.

Divine Omniscience

Probably the most obvious doctrine that impacts our understanding of predictive prophecy is divine *omniscience*, the claim that God knows all truth. Although there has been some debate over the *nature* of divine knowledge, the common sense understanding of omniscience as knowledge of all true propositions has enjoyed the majority opinion.[12] The class of true propositions typically includes those describing the future, and therefore, if God is omniscient, he possesses foreknowledge. Christian theologians have long maintained that God has knowledge of this sort. In fact, Augustine argued that foreknowledge is an essential attribute of God, and that Cicero's denial of divine foreknowledge was, in effect, a denial of God: "For one who is not prescient of all future things is not God."[13] However, in recent years, some theologians and philosophers have challenged the traditional view in favor of an understanding they call "the openness of God."[14] Basically, the model claims that God's dynamic loving relationship with his creation requires that he experience change and have limitations upon his knowledge and control not typically ascribed to him. In particular, the proponents argue that God cannot have knowledge of the future that would impede human freedom, which is necessary to a truly loving divine-human relationship.

---

12. Some theologians have objected to the idea that God's knowledge is propositional in form. William Alston argues that it is best to conceive of God as having immediate awareness of wholes, and thinks that propositional knowledge is all we can conceive of because of our limited capacities. William P. Alston, "Does God Have Beliefs?" *Religious Studies* 22 (1986): 287–306. However, just because God's way of knowing is different from ours does not mean that he cannot possess the same kind of knowledge; God could still have propositional knowledge, even if he doesn't need to know by means of propositions.

13. Augustine, *City of God* 5.9, in *Great Books of the Western World*, Marcus Dods, trans. (Chicago: Encyclopedia Britannica, 1990), 258.

14. In their influential and much-discussed book, theologians Clark Pinnock, Richard Rice, and John Sanders and philosophers William Hasker and David Basinger argued that many of the traditional attributes of God—immutability, impassibility, omniscience, omnipotence, sovereignty—were either misunderstood/misapplied or just wrong, and that a new understanding of God's nature and work was needed. Clark Pinnock, et al., *The Openness of God: A Biblical Challenge to the Traditional Understanding of God* (Downers Grove, IL: IVP, 1994).

Openness advocates argue for their perspective from various angles. First, they claim that the way the Bible depicts God as regretting his past actions (e.g., 1 Sam. 15:11, 35), changing his mind (e.g., Exod. 32:14), learning from history, and as realizing his own error in belief (e.g., Jer. 3:7; 32:35) suggests an openness view. For example, Greg Boyd appeals to the heartbreaking story of Israel's first king, Saul, rejected by God within a week of his anointing. He argues that since the Bible indicates that God's original intention was to bless Saul and his family for many generations (1 Sam. 13:13), and that God felt regret and sorrow for having made Saul king (1 Sam. 15:10, 35), God must not have known how poorly things would turn out. Genuine regret requires a lack of foresight: "Common sense tells us that we can only regret a decision we made if the decision resulted in an outcome other than what we expected or hoped for when the decision was made."[15] However, Boyd fails to address the fact that later in the same chapter when Samuel confronts Saul, he states that God "will not lie or have regret [concerning his judgment on Saul], *for he is not a man, that he should have regret*" (1 Sam. 15:29, emphasis added). It is unlikely that the author of First Samuel (or a later redactor/editor for that matter) would place such an obvious conflict of terminology in the very same chapter. He must have seen them as consistent and appealed to the range of meanings for the word "regret." The Hebrew root word, *naham*, refers to God's attitude (i.e., grief) about Saul's rebellion in two verses (10, 35), and to God's certitude in judgment in the other (29). Similar careful interpretive work can provide sound answers to the other examples given for the open view.

Second, it is common for open theists to argue that the traditional model of God is the result of the synthesis of pagan philosophy with Christianity, rather than of sound biblical exegesis.[16] As Pinnock writes,

> Theologians have to particularly face up to the influence of the pagan dogma of the absolute unchangeableness of God, which has placed severe limits upon how certain of his attributes are un-

---

15. Boyd writes, "Could God genuinely confess, 'I regret that I made Saul king' if he could in the same breath also proclaim, 'I was certain of what Saul would do when I made him king?' I do not see how. Could I genuinely regret, say, purchasing a car because it turned out to run poorly if in fact the car was running exactly as I knew it would when I purchased it?" Gregory A. Boyd, *God of the Possible* (Grand Rapids: Baker, 2000), 56.

16. Open theists are not the first to make this charge. Process theologians have complained of the Greek philosophical tradition's influence on Western theology for decades. See Charles Hartshorne, *Omnipotence and Other Theological Mistakes* (Albany, NY: SUNY Press, 1984).

derstood. It has created unnecessary difficulties and skewed our thinking. It forces us to think of God knowing a changing world in an unchanging way, as experiencing time as a simultaneous whole and not successively. Such tensions originate in the syncretism of biblical and Greek thought and arise out of the tension between Hellenistic and biblical ideas of divine perfection.[17]

Certainly many traditional Christian beliefs about God were also held by pagan philosophers like Socrates, Plato, Aristotle, and others. In fact, the early Christian apologist Justin Martyr referred to Socrates as a pre-Christian Christian.[18] However, a few brief points are in order. First, this charge is really the fallacy of guilt by association; just because pagans held to a theological view does not automatically make it false or unbiblical (Socrates argued in favor of monotheism).[19] Second, many traditional Christian beliefs distinguish themselves from paganism (e.g., doctrine of creation out of nothing). Third, the openness emphasis on change and dynamism as fundamental (over against permanence and stability) was also proclaimed by pre-Socratic pagan philosopher, Heraclitus. Thus, similarity to pagan beliefs is common to both views; the argument is a red herring.

Third, openness philosophers argue that there can be no true propositions about the future free actions of persons, and so God is omniscient without possessing foreknowledge (since human freedom is a given). As Hasker explains, "I cannot now change what God has always believed about what I will do, nor is it possible for me to act in a way that would contradict God's belief about me. So I have no free will—in this case, or in any other."[20] Philosophers, theist and

---

17. Clark H. Pinnock, *Most Moved Mover: A Theology of God's Openness* (Grand Rapids: Baker, 2001), 71. Pinnock cites E. Hatch, *The Influence of Greek Ideas and Usages Upon the Christian Church* (London: Williams and Norgate, 1890) as evidence of his claim. The bulk of Sanders' chapter in *The Openness of God* develops this argument as well. See Pinnock, et al, *The Openness of God*, 59–100.

18. Justin, *Apologia* II.10. See also II.13, where Justin also notes that Plato's teachings are very similar to those of Jesus.

19. Socrates also referenced the divine logos, which he saw as the rational ordering principle of the cosmos, and even spoke of it as the means by which God worked in the universe. Other Greek philosophers argued that the gods of the pantheon really represented different facets of the one true God.

20. William Hasker, *Metaphysics: Constructing a World View* (Downers Grove, IL: IVP, 1983), 52. Of course, Hasker believes we do have freedom, so he instead challenges the idea that God's past beliefs must be correct. See also his argument summarized in "A Philosophical Perspective" in Pinnock, et al., *The Openness of God*, particularly 147.

atheist, ancient and modern alike, have long wrestled with the problem of the compatibility of freedom and foreknowledge, and numerous answers have been given. For example, one ingenious reply notes the lack of a causal connection between the past proposition describing the event and the future event itself; the proposition's being true no more causes the later event than the event's occurrence causes the statement to be true. When the event happens, the proposition is *shown* to have been true. The point is that even seasoned philosophers do not agree on these contentious issues, so this challenge does not offer enough warrant for so radically adjusting our understanding of divine omniscience as rejecting foreknowledge.

Open theists do not think their model should be cause for concern. Sanders argues that, even if God can be mistaken in his beliefs about the future, there is no cause for alarm because God has the power, love, and wisdom "to continue working with his project until he brings it to the fulfillment he intends."[21] Bruce Ware rightly questions Sanders here, and argues that the examples of divine mistakes and regret offered by open theists undermine confidence in both the future and God's wisdom. He is worth quoting at length:

> If God is not sure that what he does is best, can we be sure
> that he really knows what he is doing? The simple fact is that a
> God who can only speculate regarding what much of the future
> holds, at times second-guesses his own plans, can get things
> wrong, can falsely anticipate what may happen next, and may
> even repent of his own past conduct is a God unworthy of de-
> votion, trust, and praise. What open theists have "gained" by
> their insistence on God as a risk-taker has been won at the ex-
> pense of God's full wisdom, knowledge, trustworthiness, maj-
> esty, sovereignty, and glory; and it leads inevitably to doubt,
> worry, and fear regarding the fulfillment of God's plans.[22]

So the openness model has challenged traditional views of omniscience, but the concerns it raises can be answered, and its own problems give good reason to reject it in favor of comprehensive divine foreknowledge.

---

21. John Sanders, *The God Who Risks: A Theology of Providence* (Downers Grove, IL: IVP, 1998), 133.
22. Bruce A. Ware, *God's Lesser Glory: The Diminished God of Open Theism* (Wheaton, IL: Cross-way, 2000), 159.

Divine Eternity

The doctrine of divine eternality (or eternity) is a function of God's infinity, and has historically claimed that God exists outside of time. That is, since God is infinite, he must be outside of time, at least if time is finite.[23] Christian theologians have long appealed to this aspect of God's nature/being in order to explain *how* God can know the future. From a timeless perspective, past, present, and future all appear simultaneously. Put differently, all of history exists immediately in eternity. Thus, Aquinas maintains that God knows all things, including future contingencies, because he sees all events as present to him in eternity. Aquinas likens God's perspective of creatures and events in time to an individual's observation of creatures and events on a road from a hilltop. He writes, "Things reduced to act in time are known by us successively in time, but by God are known in eternity, which is above time. Hence to us they cannot be certain . . . but they are certain to God alone, whose understanding is in eternity above time; just as he who goes along the road does not see those who come after him, although he who sees the whole road from a height sees at once all travelling by the way."[24]

Popular Christian author C. S. Lewis also appealed to divine eternity to explain how God's knowledge of the future can be reconciled with human freedom. He argues that God observes future free acts in eternity *as free*, and that this means that his foreknowledge does not conflict with our being free. He writes:

> Well, here once again, the difficulty comes from thinking that
> God is progressing along the Time-line like us: the only dif-

---

23. There is vigorous scholarly debate about this claim. After all, some have suggested that God could have *entered* time upon creating, and some have suggested that the biblical depiction of God as *personal* and *interactive* requires that he be temporal, while still others have suggested that there is a special kind of temporality related to God alone. For an interesting and engaging discussion of these issues, see Gregory E. Ganssle, ed. *God and Time: Four Views* (Downers Grove, IL: IVP, 2011). Still, if the connection between space and time noted in contemporary cosmology/physics is accepted, then it seems difficult to escape the conclusion that a time-bound God would also occupy space, but this would suggest pantheism (or panentheism), a position rejected by the Bible's clear distinction between God/Creator and creation.

24. Aquinas continues, "Hence what is known by us must be necessary, even as it is in itself; for what is future contingent in itself cannot be known by us. But what is known by God must be necessary according to the mode in which they are subject to the divine knowledge, as already stated (ANS. I), but not absolutely as considered in their own causes." Thomas Aquinas, *Summa Theologica* 1.14.13, trans. Fathers of the English Dominican Province, rev. Daniel J. Sullivan, in *Great Books of the Western World*, Robert Hutchins, ed. (Chicago: Encyclopedia Britannica, 1952), 88.

ference being that He can see ahead and we cannot. Well, if that were true, if God *foresaw* our acts, it would be very hard to understand how we could be free not to do them. But suppose God is outside and above the Time-line. In that case, what we call "tomorrow" is visible to Him in just the same way as what we call "today." All the days are "Now" for Him. He does not remember you doing things yesterday; He simply sees you doing them, because, though you have lost yesterday, He has not. He does not "foresee" you doing things tomorrow; He simply sees you doing them: because, though tomorrow is not yet there for you, it is for Him.[25]

So the doctrine of divine eternity may help explain how divine omniscience works with respect to the future and prophecy.

Divine Providence

The last doctrine that deserves comment here is divine sovereignty and providence. Sovereignty and providence go together because they refer to God's kingship and rule/governance over the entire universe and its history (Ps. 103:19). All Christians, no matter their theological position, affirm that God is in control and works all things according to the counsel of his will (Eph. 1:11). He is sovereign over the affairs of men (Job 12:23; Ps. 22:28; 75:6–7), over the natural order (Ps. 104:14–16; 135:6–7), and even over evil (Gen. 50:20; Ps. 17:13–14; 19:13; 2 Thess. 2:7–8). Nothing occurs apart from his will, understood as either causing or permitting, though the Bible always depicts his providence as concerned with salvation and the working out of his plan (Rom. 8:28).

Closely related to the doctrine of providence is the doctrine of creation. The Bible seems to link God's rightful rule over and claim upon the world to the fact that he created it: "The heavens are Yours; the earth also is Yours. The world and everything in it—You founded them. North and south—You created them" (Ps. 89:11–12a; cf. Isa. 43:1–7). The doctrine of creation has numerous implications for Christian theology, but the most important for consideration of the future and prophecy is the teleology it suggests. That is, God's creating humans in his own image (Gen. 1:26–27; cf. Col. 1:15, where Christ is described as the image of God) suggests an overarching plan behind its development, intricacy, and final

---

25. C. S. Lewis, *Mere Christianity* (New York: Macmillan, 1952), 133.

end or purpose (Greek *telos*). God's plan is revealed throughout the Bible as unfolding in human history, the nation of Israel, the church, and ultimately, the very universe itself, and the key to understanding it all is Christ (Eph. 2:10; Col. 1:16).

The apostle Peter makes it clear that salvation through Christ's shed blood on the cross and resurrection from the dead was planned by God prior to his creating or Adam's fall (1 Peter 1:20; cf. Rev. 13:8). Jesus said that the Scriptures testify about him (John 5:39; cf. Rom. 1:25–27, where Paul notes that the mystery of salvation in Christ was made known by the prophets) and on the road to Emmaus, he explained to the unnamed disciples how all the Scriptures refer to the Messiah and his sufferings (Luke 24:26–27). In fact, the primary way of reading the Old Testament by the early church was Christocentric. The apostolic preaching in Acts, the affirmations of Peter and Paul in their various epistles, and the close and substantive intertestamental exegesis in the book of Hebrews undergirds this idea. Writing about the interpretive method of the ancient church generally, Henri Crouzel confirms these theologians' view that "the Old Testament in its entirety is a prophecy of Christ, who is the key to it."[26] He continues, "For all the ante-Nicene Fathers the theophanies or appearances of God in the Old Testament . . . are regarded as appearances of the Son . . . Thus the Word [Christ] speaks in the Old Testament," which "speaks of him, prophesies about him, in its entirety and not simply in a few passages considered to be direct prophecies."[27] The second-century bishop Ignatius of Antioch stated that for him, the Old Testament (which he called "the archives" in a debate with opponents) consisted of "Jesus Christ, the inviolable archives are his cross and death and his resurrection and the faith which comes through him."[28] Later exegetes continued to interpret the Old Testament in this way, despite a few stubborn holdouts who held to a more literal-historical reading of the Old Testament.[29]

Interestingly, as we have seen above in the biblical material from Isaiah (42:18-20; 48:8), the church fathers also believed and taught that the Scriptures are completely reliable in their prophecies, and that anyone who labels the

---

26. Henri Crouzel, *Origen*, trans. A. S. Worrall (Edinburgh: T&T Clark, 1989), 64.
27. Ibid., 74.
28. Ignatius of Antioch, *Letter to the Philadelphians*, 9, in *The Apostolic Fathers*, ed. Michael Holmes, trans. J. B. Lightfoot and J. R. Harmer, 2nd ed (Grand Rapids: Baker, 1989), 108–109.
29. Theodore of Mopsuestia (ca. AD 350–428), a student of Diodore of Tarsus (ca. AD 330–390), refused to admit to more than two messianic psalms, but he was opposed exegetically by another representative of their school of thought—the so-called "Antiochene School"—the Bishop Theodoret of Cyrus (ca. AD 393–457) in his own Psalms commentary.

prophetic material obscure ought to engage in some spiritual self-examination. For example, in the Introduction to his *Commentary on Ezekiel*, the fifth-century bishop Theodoret of Cyrus explains that those who complain of a veiled and unclear meaning in the Scriptures lack spiritual maturity (2 Cor. 4:3). Furthermore, as Jesus explained to his disciples why he spoke in parables to the crowds, he cited Isaiah 6:9, indicating that many of his hearers were purposely unbelieving and would not be privy to the "mysteries of the kingdom" (Matt. 13:11; cf 13:10–15). Theodoret remarks, "Divine realities, therefore, are not obscure to everyone, only to those who are voluntarily blind. . . . Let no one, therefore, especially (Christians), adopt such a presumptuous attitude to the divine Spirit as to accuse his words of obscurity. Instead, in their longing to understand the sacred words, let them cry aloud with the divinely-inspired David, 'Unveil my eyes, and I shall grasp the marvels of your Law.'"[30]

PROVIDENCE AND COVENANT

When we speak of Christ being the subject of the whole Bible, we do not mean to say that each and every individual verse points to him, but rather that the intent behind the story is to point to Christ. In order to see how, some familiarity with the covenant structure of the Bible is necessary. There are several covenants (or agreements) between God and humanity recorded in the Bible, the most prominent being the Abrahamic, Mosaic, Davidic, and New. Each of these covenants plays a different role in God's redemptive plan for the cosmos. After humanity fell, the whole creation was subject to the power of death, but a plan for its restoration was already in motion, entailing God's special relationship with particular persons to point to the way of faith and ultimately to Christ. In the Abrahamic covenant, God promised Abraham numerous descendants who would live in a special land as a nation led by God (Gen. 12:1–3, 7; 15:4–8,18–20). Those covenant blessings were offered to Israel by means of the Mosaic covenant, wherein God gave regulations for living as his people, reflecting his holiness, justice, and mercy to the nations. The Levitical sacrificial system was meant to communicate these truths and point to both human sinfulness and divine mercy in Christ (Rom. 5:18–21; Gal. 3:19–26). The Abrahamic covenant further promised that all people would be blessed through Abraham, ultimately by salvation through

---

30. Theodoret, *Commentary on Ezekiel*, trans. Robert C. Hill (Brookline, MA: Holy Cross Orthodox Press, 2006), 28–29.

faith in his descendant, Christ (Rom. 4, esp. vv. 23–25; Gal. 3:7–9, 16). This becomes clear in the Davidic covenant, which represents a narrowing of the scope of the Abrahamic covenant, wherein a particular descendant from David will function as the righteous king of the earth, administering God's justice in the world with an everlasting rule (2 Sam. 7:12–16; cf. Isa. 9:6–7). The new covenant stands as the culmination of the biblical narrative and inaugurates the fulfillment of all the covenant promises; it provides that all peoples—Jews and Gentiles alike—may enter into relationship with God through Christ.[31] It is both superior to the old covenant (Mosaic; Heb. 3:3–6; 8:6–13; 9:11–15) and is its fulfillment (Matt. 5:17; Rom. 13:10; Eph. 1:10).

Most of the predictive prophecies in the Bible refer either to Christ or to the end. Many of the prophecies about Christ were fulfilled in his first coming: crushed the head of the serpent (Gen. 3:15), Immanuel, born of a virgin (Isa. 7:14; Matt. 1:22–23), born in Bethlehem (Micah 5:2; Matt. 2:1), of the tribe of Judah (Gen. 49:10; Heb. 7:14), son of David (2 Sam. 7:14; Matt. 21:9), healed the blind and deaf (Isa. 35:5-6; Matt. 11:5), suffered and died (Isa. 53; Ps. 22), rose from the dead (Ps. 16:10; Acts 2:30–31); while some await fulfillment at his second advent. The precision with which these prophecies were given and the accuracy of their fulfillment point to their divine origin. The study of the end of time, or *eschatology* (Greek *eschaton*, literally "end"), is somewhat contentious, but all Christians agree that there will be a return of Christ and some kind of cataclysmic reordering of the cosmos, where death will be destroyed and God will reign unchallenged (Rev. 22). Many of the predictive prophecies in the Bible include reference to this consummation of God's plan for the creation and in particular, humanity.

Of course, the point in noting God's providence and plan is to speak to the confidence we may have in the predictive prophecies recorded in Scripture. In addition to the Bible's inspiration and God's trustworthiness, omniscience, and eternity, we may also appeal to the fact that God is in control of the history of the universe, bringing all things into conformity with his plan. Thus, he knows the future with certainty because he is guiding the present to reach the future he desires and has proclaimed from the beginning (Isa. 46:10).

---

31. The book of Romans is particularly concerned with the relationship of Jews and Gentiles in the fledgling church, though Paul continuously dealt with the practical questions of Gentile entrance into the covenant promises through the church.

Historical Fulfillments

[I]t is worth noting that successful prophecy could be regarded as a form of miracle for which there could in principle be good evidence. If someone is reliably recorded as having prophesied at t_1 an event at t_2 which could not be predicted at t_1 on any natural grounds, and the event occurs at t_2, then at any later time t_3 we can assess the evidence for the claims both that the prophecy was made at t_1 and that its accuracy cannot be explained either causally (for example, on the ground that it brought about its own fulfillment) or as accidental, and hence, that it was probably miraculous.[32]

These words by noted atheist philosopher and critic of Christianity, John Mackie, speak to the importance of this chapter. Successful predictive prophecy adds strength to any claims about God's existence, the truth of the Bible, and a divine redemptive plan for humanity. Thus, it will be helpful to offer some examples of successful predictive prophecy and to answer some challenges to prophetic success.

Daniel's Four Kingdoms

In Daniel 2, the young exile Daniel interpreted a disturbing dream for the Babylonian king, Nebuchadnezzar. The dream involved a great statue composed of four metals, which Daniel interpreted as four great successive kingdoms. These are the Babylonians (gold, ca. 605–539 BC) and three subsequent kingdoms which Daniel did not name, but scholars agree they are historically accurate: Medo-Persians (silver, ca. 539–331 BC), Greeks (bronze, ca. 331–146 BC), and Romans (iron, ca. 509–27 BC).[33] Daniel foretold that "in the days of those kings" (meaning

---

32. J. L. Mackie, *The Miracle of Theism: Arguments for and against the Existence of God* (Oxford: Clarendon, 1982), 22–23.

33. These dates are approximate because there are periods of overlap in the existence of these kingdoms. For example, the Greeks as a culture existed long before Alexander the Great, but they were not a dominant world superpower as Alexander and his father, Phillip, made them, exporting Greek/Hellenistic influence from Macedon south to Egypt and eastward across the Middle East as far as India and Pakistan. Daniel aptly characterized this kingdom of bronze as one which will "rule the whole earth" (2:39). The Romans began as a nation ruled by kings, then moved to a more democratic, representative form of government, the Republic. This system was upset by the events following the assassination of Julius Caesar in 44 BC. In 27 BC, Augustus established the Principate, which basically brought back imperial rule. This nation described by Daniel as

the Romans, Dan. 2:44), God will set up his kingdom which would destroy the others, but itself be indestructible. Indeed, as Luke 2 recounts, Jesus was born in the days of "Caesar Augustus," thus inaugurating God's eternal kingdom in the midst of the Roman Empire. Daniel 7–12 parallels and elaborates on the basic theme of the successive kingdoms' rise and fall, focusing in detail on events in the life of Israel, which scholars identify as the period of the Maccabean Revolt (165 BC) against the oppression of the Greek-Syrian king, Antiochus IV Epiphanes. Disputes over Daniel's prophecies have arisen precisely because of the book's claims to predictive prophecy. In fact, issues of authorship and dating are key for Daniel because the answer to these questions "ultimately determines the interpretation of every aspect of this prophecy."[34] Was Daniel written in the sixth century BC as the Bible claims, or in the second century BC, as critical (liberal) scholars believe?[35] Are his predictions inspired prophecy, or is he reporting history after the fact? If the latter, then "Daniel" is a pseudo-prophet and fraud; but if the book truly records visions received in sixth-century Babylon, then the accuracy of Daniel's predictions is indeed astounding. Linguistic evidence based on the Hebrew and Aramaic vocabulary, including Persian and a few Greek loan words, support a sixth-century dating, and additional supporting evidence derives from manuscripts of Daniel found among the Dead Sea Scrolls at Qumran.[36] Jesus also confirmed the prophecy's authenticity, indicating that Daniel prophesied truthfully far into the future, to the time of the Messiah's second coming (Matt. 24:15–31). Even critical scholars must admit that all the linguistic or historical evidence they marshal against the

---

"strong as iron" which "crushes and shatters everything," would "smash all the others" (2:40). Additionally, the Romans constantly faced the problem of preserving the purity of their native stock of citizens, indicating that the empire was ethnically diverse, or as Daniel described the feet of the statue, partly of "fired clay and partly of iron—it will be a divided kingdom" (2:41–43). This mixture of Romans with foreigners contributed to the empire's weakening and eventual demise.

34. Stephen R. Miller, "Daniel," *New American Commentary* 18 (Nashville: Broadman & Holman, 1994), 23.

35. For example, John J. Collins maintains, "According to the consensus of modern critical scholarship, the stories about Daniel and his friends are legendary in character, and the hero himself most probably never existed." John J. Collins, *Daniel, Hermeneia* (Minneapolis: Augsburg Fortress, 1993), 1. His co-author and spouse concurs: "Daniel is not a reliable source of factual information about either the past or the future. This is apparent from the historical inaccuracies of the tales and the notorious problems of Darius the Mede and Nebuchadnezzar's madness, as well as from the unhistorical claim that the book recounts the visions of a Jew in the Exile. . . . The predictions of Daniel . . . are shaped by the literary conventions of the Hellenistic age, not by any deposit of revealed information. The time-bound character of the book cannot be evaded by vague statements that it is 'a true witness to the end of the age' that fail to explain how its witness is true." A. Y. Collins, in John D. Collins, *Daniel*, 123.

36. Miller, "Daniel," 39.

earlier dating could be subject to criticism itself and does not wholly preclude an earlier dating.[37] Also, archaeological evidence for other "historical inaccuracies" in Daniel (per A. Y. Collins) may not yet have surfaced. Until 1854, the only mention of "Belshazzar" as a Babylonian regent was in Daniel, and nowhere else in any other ancient documents. Critical scholars called this a historical inaccuracy that invalidated the truthfulness of Daniel's claims, but in excavations in Iraq in 1854, archaeologist J. G. Taylor unearthed four clay cylinders inscribed in cuneiform by Nabonidus (r. 556–539 BC), which mentioned Nabonidus's son and crown prince Belshazzar, thereby confirming the witness of Daniel.[38] The real problem seems to be a mistrust of prophetic claims to supernatural revelation of the future, as recognized by critical scholars themselves.[39]

Babylonian Exile and Return (Cyrus Prophecy)

Isaiah's prediction concerning the ascendancy of Cyrus the Persian is one of the most celebrated and incontestable prophecies in the Bible (Isa. 44:28–45:13). God affirms, "I am Yahweh . . . who says to Cyrus, My shepherd, he will fulfill all my pleasure" (Isa. 44:24, 28), and God further calls Cyrus "His anointed, whose right hand I have grasped" (Isa. 45:1). The Cyrus prophecy occurs as the culmination of a passage comforting Israel with promised restoration from the Babylonian exile through the agency of this future pagan monarch, an incredible and seemingly unlikely promise.

---

37. Kitchen writes (and other linguistic scholars also hold) that there are many loanwords from Old Persian in Daniel, especially administrative terms, which did not exist any longer by the Greek/ Hellenistic era, thus supporting an earlier rather than later date. K. A. Kitchen, "The Aramaic of Daniel" in D. J. Wiseman, et al., *Notes on Some Problems in the Book of Daniel* (London: Tyndale, 1965), 31–79. When the work was copied into Greek, those words were not understood by the Greek translators so they left them in just as they were. (Ibid., 43, 50). Collins, who holds to the later Maccabaean dating, writes that this observation weighs "against the theory that the whole book originated in the second century." John Collins, 19.
38. Alan Millard, "Daniel in Babylon: An Accurate Record?" in *Do Historical Matters Matter to Faith?*, ed. James H. Hoffmeier and Dennis Magary (Wheaton, IL: Crossway, 2012), 269–71.
39. J. A. Montgomery's commentary in the International Critical Commentary series breaks with the classic Maccabaean thesis, although he proposes a hybrid approach that is not exactly conservative (Preface, viii), but he warrants that predictive prophecy is valid, even on the terms of liberal scholars. "The (historian) naturally disowns the element of prediction in history, while the modern theologian deprecates it in prophecy. . . . However we may explain the fact, the majority of scholars who maintain the Macc. origin of [chapters] 7–12 regard them as composed before the triumph of the Maccabees in 165, and hence implicitly, if not explicitly, admit the historical fulfillment of their expectations." James Montgomery, *ICC Daniel* (Edinburgh: T&T Clark, 1927, 1950), 98.

> Who predicted this long ago?
> Who announced it from ancient times?
> Was it not I, Yahweh?
> There is no other God but Me,
> a righteous God and Savior;
> . . . Turn to Me and be saved,
> all the ends of the earth.
> . . . I am God, and there is no other.
> By Myself I have sworn;
> Truth has gone out from My mouth,
> a word that will not be revoked.
>   (Isaiah 45:21–23)

When Isaiah says "long ago," it is important to note just how long. This prophecy came forth between 740–700 BC, long before Cyrus's birth, before Babylon became a superpower, and around the time when the northern tribes of Israel were exiled by Assyria (722/21 BC). Critical scholarship beginning in the 1800s has contested that Isaiah was not written in the eighth century by one man; rather, they divide the book into two or three sections (chapters 1–39, 40–55, 56–66), claiming multiple authorship: The book was partly written by Isaiah and partly by disciples or later writers, these critics claim, explaining that there was a so-called school of Isaiah lasting two centuries. Isaiah of Jerusalem wrote the first part, an exilic prophet wrote the second part, while a post-exilic Jew wrote the third.

On this multiple authorship theory, no assumption whatsoever of predictive prophecy is necessary; as with the challenge to Daniel, a re-dating of the book removes any necessity of dealing with the supernatural.[40] However, as with Daniel, compelling reasons advocate for the earlier date and unified authorship. Literary tradition, theological consistency, and archaeological evidence all point to the book's unity. First, Isaiah's name not only opens the book, but also appears in several other places throughout the text. Also, Isaiah reiterates the theme of the "Holy One of Israel" throughout the book, not just in one section. Second, the New Testament

---

40. Conservative scholar G. W. Grogan states that "The case against the unity of the book usually begins with statements about the nature of biblical prophecy," showing that an anti-supernatural bias is at the heart of opposition to prophecy, although it does not exclusively drive criticism. Geoffrey W. Grogan, *Isaiah, Expositor's Bible Commentary, 6: Isaiah-Ezekiel* (Grand Rapids: Zondervan, 1986), 8, 11.

evidence is strong that first-century Judaism accepted Isaiah and circulated it as a unified whole. Jesus, the evangelists, and Paul quoted from all three sections of Isaiah, attributing it to the same author every time. Finally, Qumran scrolls of Isaiah containing the entire text show no breaks between the two or three supposed sections of the book. In fact, chapter 39 ends toward the end of a column of text, and chapter 40 commences immediately after, finishing out the column to the bottom and continuing at the top of the next column.[41]

Interpretive Considerations / Strategies

One of the strategies for dealing with apparent prophetic failure has been to claim that a judgment prophecy almost always includes an implied conditional: if the person or nation were to repent, God may show mercy after all.[42] The book of Jonah offers a clear example. God sent Jonah to Nineveh to preach God's judgment upon the city. Jonah instead tried to flee and was swallowed by a fish until he repented of his disobedience, eventually arriving in Nineveh to deliver the message. Upon hearing, the people conducted a city-wide fast and repented (Jonah 3:6–9), averting God's wrath and saving Nineveh. Irritated at God's manifest grace, Jonah explained that his anticipation of divine mercy was why he had fled (Jonah 4:1–2). Two important points surface: (1) Although the prophecy was given in definite terms ("God will destroy the city," Jonah 3:4), it included an unspoken element of mercy; and (2) Jonah's anticipation of God's mercy indicates that this element was a common feature of Old Testament prophecy.

---

41. Grogan, Isaiah, *Expositor's Bible Commentary,* 9–10; Nancy J. Eavenson, "Isaiah" in *Women's Evangelical Commentary on the Old Testament,* ed. Dorothy Kelly Patterson, et al. (Nashville: B&H, 2011), 1120–1281, referencing the Great Isaiah Scroll.

42. Sanders questions this move under a model that assumes comprehensive divine foreknowledge because there aren't any conditionals; the outcome is certain: "How can a conditional promise be genuine if God already foreknows the human response and so foreknows that he will, in fact, never fulfill the promise?" Sanders, *The God Who Risks,* 131. Sanders sees the typical application of the principle as suspect, wherein "failed" prophecies are claimed to be conditional, while "fulfilled" prophecies are not. He rightly notes that some fulfilled prophecies were also conditional. Still, Sanders fails to account for the human element in the recipient. It is likely that, if the prophecy were given in a conditional format, it would not be taken as seriously as when given in a definite format. Procrastination, even in repentance, is an all-too-common problem. These are theological arguments. Kaiser argues that biblically, the majority of Old Testament prophecies are conditional and follow the pattern of blessing/curse found in Leviticus 26 and Deuteronomy 28–32. Walter Kaiser and Moisés Silva, *Introduction to Biblical Hermeneutics: The Search for Meaning* (Grand Rapids: Zondervan 1994, rev. 2007), 2000.

A second strategy involves the recognition that some prophetic words refer to the immediate circumstances as well as future events. That is, some prophecies have a dual aspect, speaking to their own day while also awaiting fulfillment in the distant future. In some cases, there is an initial fulfillment at the time of the utterance and a final fulfillment in the future. Both events meet the conditions of the prophecy, but the future event is the more complete representation. In other cases, a single prophecy may include references to events both in the present and the distant future. This first form Kaiser refers to as "prophetic perspective" and explains, "It is the phenomenon of blending together both the near and distant aspects of the prediction in one and the same vision."[43]

One of the most popular messianic prophecies is found in the book of Isaiah. Ahaz ruled Judah (the southern kingdom) at the time, and he had recently turned away an assault on Jerusalem by Aram (modern Syria) and Israel (the northern kingdom) (Isa. 7:1), but he was still concerned about this alliance because he heard the kings wanted to supplant him with a puppet ruler who would do their bidding. Isaiah came to Ahaz with a word from God and told him he should not be afraid because both Aram and Israel would soon be destroyed by Assyria. To confirm the message, he offered a sign to Ahaz:

> Therefore, the Lord Himself will give you a sign: The virgin will conceive, have a son, and name him Immanuel. By the time he learns to reject what is bad and choose what is good, he will be eating butter and honey. For before the boy knows to reject what is bad and choose what is good, the land of the two kings you dread will be abandoned. The Lord will bring on you, your people, and the house of your father, such a time as has never been since Ephraim separated from Judah—the king of Assyria is coming (Isa. 7:14–17).

The Hebrew term referencing the soon-to-be-mother (*almah*) is ambiguous and can be translated as "young woman" or "virgin." This ambiguity lends itself well to dual fulfillment: an initial fulfillment during Ahaz's reign, and a final fulfillment in Mary's virginal conception. While scholars differ over the immediate identity of the woman and over Isaiah's knowledge of his prophecy's potential

---

43. Kaiser and Silva, *Introduction to Biblical Hermeneutics*, 195.

messianic nature, all agree that the context demands an initial fulfillment in Isaiah's day and that Matthew interprets it as ultimately fulfilled in Christ.[44]

The second form of prophecy, what Kaiser calls "sequential prophecies," can be seen in Jesus's own ministry.[45] When he visited the synagogue in his hometown of Nazareth, Jesus read from Isaiah to identify himself as messiah (Luke 4:16–21; Isa. 61:1–2a). Curiously, he ended his quote halfway through verse 2, omitting the references to God's vengeance, and instead emphasizing the good news of the Lord's favor. Many scholars have noted this selective quotation was intentional, addressing Christ's first advent, and they have argued that the rest of Isaiah's prophecy, with its focus on divine vengeance and Israel's restoration, speaks to Christ's second advent. Only the verses quoted were fulfilled during Jesus's earthly ministry.[46]

---

44. As Grogan writes, "Isaiah predicted the coming of a boy who would be a sign from God to his contemporaries and who would foreshadow Christ, in whom the terms of the prophecy—abstracted from its historical situation—would be fulfilled in fullest measure." Grogan, *Isaiah, Expositor's Bible Commentary,* 64. On the identity of the woman, some scholars think the mother was royal and the child, Hezekiah. J. Lindblom, *A Study on the Immanuel Section of Isaiah 7:1–9:6* (Lund: Geerup, 1958). Others believe it is a reference to Isaiah's wife and son. R. E. Clements, *Isaiah 1–39* (Grand Rapids: Eerdmans, 1980). The context certainly lends itself to this interpretation. The message to Ahaz seems to have been fulfilled in his own day and is recorded in the following chapter: "I was then intimate with the prophetess, and she conceived and gave birth to a son. . . . before the boy knows how to call out father or mother, the wealth of Damascus and the spoils of Samaria will be carried off to the king of Assyria. The Lord spoke to me again . . . the Lord will certainly bring against them the mighty rushing waters of the Euphrates River—the king of Assyria and all his glory. It will overflow its channels and spill over all its banks. It will pour into Judah, flood over it, and sweep through, reaching up to the neck; and its spreading streams will fill your entire land, Immanuel!" (Isa. 8:3–8). In verse 3, Isaiah references the birth of his son and uses his growth to date the invasion of Assyria. In verse 8, explicit reference is made to Immanuel, though here it is used to refer to Judah, the southern kingdom where David's descendants rule and currently seek God's righteousness.

45. Kaiser describes sequential prophecies: "The predictions contained within them place several events together in one prediction even though they will be fulfilled in a sequence and a series of acts perhaps stretching over several centuries." Kaiser and Silva, *Introduction to Biblical Hermeneutics,* 201.

46. Bock writes, "The remaining issue in Luke 4:19 is the omission of a reference to judgment [from Isaiah]. One of two explanations is possible. First, the omission may have been made to delay the allusion to judgment until Jesus's warnings in 4:24–27. . . . But another reason is more likely: the ultimate time of God's vengeance is not yet arrived in this coming of Jesus (9:51–56; 17:22–37; 21:5–37). The division of deliverance and judgment in God's plan, alluded to by the omission, is sorted out later in Luke. The omission represents part of the 'already-not yet' tension of NT eschatology, and a Gospel writer can discuss an issue from either side of the temporal perspective. Jesus's mission is placed initially in terms of hope, but it also brings an implication of judgment about which he will warn in 4:24–27." Darrell L. Bock, *Luke 1:1–9:50, Baker Exegetical Commentary on the New Testament* (Grand Rapids: Baker, 1994), 411.

Thus there are examples of successful prophetic prediction that even the most liberal scholars cannot explain away. In addition, there are legitimate interpretive strategies that may be employed, gaining their cues from the biblical text itself, that can explain instances where the prophet(s) seemed to "get it wrong" and is yet still confirmed as a true prophet of God. The examples given should inspire confidence in predictive prophecy.

CONCLUSION

Why, then, should we trust predictive Bible prophecies, or attempt to decipher them? At least four answers can be given. First, the Old Testament is full of prophecies, including many that were fulfilled within the Old Testament itself and its historical timeframe. For example, the multiplication of Abraham's offspring and their return to Canaan, the Assyrian exile, the destruction of Jerusalem and the Babylonian exile with many details, the return of exiles to Jerusalem under Cyrus, and many others. Second, the Old Testament's greatest and most consistent prophetic thread has to do with the promise of Messiah. These predictions—from Genesis to the last minor prophet—point to Christ, whose birth, life/ministry, and death were fulfilled in very specific ways which are beyond critics' ability to discount, and which constitute the ground of our faith and salvation. Third, Jesus himself spoke about the Old Testament writings which pointed to him (Luke 24), his advent, his atoning salvific work, and his gospel mission carried forward by disciples and the church generally. He confirmed the truth and accuracy of prophets like Daniel (Matt. 24:15), Jonah (Matt. 12:39), Isaiah (Mark 7:6, Luke 4:17, John 12:38), Jeremiah (Matt. 16:14), Moses (John 3:14; 5:46), and others, and the gospel writers as well as Paul carried forward this perspective of fulfilled messianic prophecy as a framework within which to understand the church's inception, growth, and global mission. Finally, Jesus's own teachings included exhortations to his followers to "interpret the signs of the times" (Matt. 16:3). He encouraged them—and by extension, us—to look for the fulfillment of things pertaining to God's historical redemptive plan coming to pass around them.

Part 2:

THE DOCTRINE OF THE
FUTURE IN THE BIBLE

The Old Testament

THE DOCTRINE OF THE FUTURE AND MOSES: "ALL ISRAEL SHALL BE SAVED"

Daniel I. Block

Y HWH, the God of Israel, planted the seed of humankind's eschatological hope in Genesis 3:15, when he predicted the ultimate triumph of the seed of the woman over the serpent who had seduced the first pair to revolt against God.[1] And with their revolt they had subjected not only the human race, but also the entire cosmos, to the fury of the Creator. Although some contend that the entire Pentateuch is driven by a vision of an eschatological Messiah, this understanding depends upon a strained reading of some specific texts and unfortunately negative readings of Israel's constitutional documents: the Decalogue (Exod. 20:2–17), the Covenant Document (Exod. 20:22–23:19), the Instructions on Holiness (Lev. 17–26), and the Deuteronomic Torah (Deut. 5–26, 28).[2] This is not to deny a significant eschatological thread in the Pentateuch—it is obviously there—but to caution against overlooking the "here-and-nowness" of the first major section of the Hebrew canon.

Since exploring the eschatology of the entire Pentateuch would require an entire volume, it is necessary to restrict our study to a specific segment of the Pentateuch, that is, the book of Deuteronomy. Although this book brings the narrative of Israel's earliest history to a close and concludes the biography of Moses, Deuteronomy consists largely of three embedded farewell

---

1. It is a great honor to devote this essay to my esteemed friend and former colleague, whose life and ministry have been characterized by grace and covenant righteousness. I am grateful to Michelle Knight and Jeffrey Bingham, who read earlier drafts of this paper and made helpful suggestions for its improvement.
2. See John H. Sailhamer, "The Messiah and the Hebrew Bible," *JETS* 44 (2001): 1–22; Sailhamer, *The Meaning of the Pentateuch: Revelation, Composition and Interpretation* (Downers Grove, IL: IVP, 2009), 236–46.

pastoral addresses by Moses (1:6–4:40; 5:1–26:19, 28:1–68; 29:2–30:20), a concluding national anthem dictated by YHWH (32:1–43),[3] and Moses's final benedictions for the tribes (33:1–29). In his addresses Moses offers the most systematic instruction of Yahwistic theology to be found in the Hebrew Scriptures.

Time in Deuteronomy

Among the remarkable features of Moses's speeches in Deuteronomy is the way he addresses the issue of time. On the one hand, his perspective is timeless. Even though most of the people standing before him had not yet been born, he suggests shockingly that they (1) lived in Egypt (29:16–17 [15–16]); (2) were enslaved by Pharaoh (6:21; 16:12; 24:18) (3) witnessed YHWH's signs and wonders (1:30; 4:34); (4) came out of Egypt (4:37; 16:1); (5) stood with Moses at Horeb/Sinai when YHWH established his covenant with Israel (4:33; 5:2–5); (6) worshiped the golden calf (9:7–21); and (7) provoked YHWH's wrath with their faithlessness at Massah, Taberah, and Kibroth-hattavah (9:22).[4] But Moses also insists that the covenant renewal rituals on the Plains of Moab that he has been supervising implicate all future generations as well (29:14–15 [13–14]).[5] We find a similar blurring of the ancestors. Sometimes the expression *'ābôt* refers specifically to the patriarchs (Abraham, Isaac, and Jacob; 1:8; 6:10; 9:5, 27; 29:13[12]; 30:20), but elsewhere the expression refers to the exodus generation (4:31; 5:3; 6:3[6]; 27:3; 29:25 [24]); 31:16), or even the ancestors of future generations who possessed the land (30:5, 9). This blurring of generations spills over into the covenants, so that the covenant YHWH made (*kārat*) with Abraham (Gen. 15, 17), established (*hēqîm*) with the exodus generation at Horeb (Gen.

---

3. On which see Daniel I. Block, "The Power of Song: Reflections on Ancient Israel's National Anthem (Deuteronomy 32)," in *How I Love Your Torah O LORD! Studies in the Book of Deuteronomy* (Eugene, OR: Cascade, 2011): 162–88.

4. Cf. Daniel I. Block, *Deuteronomy* (NIVAC; Grand Rapids: Zondervan, 2011), 154–55. In 29:16–17 he speaks of the present generation as having lived in Egypt.

5. In Deuteronomy Michael Fishbane's comment applies: "Sinai is . . . not a one-time event, but for all times; it is not only grounded in the historical past, but hovers in the living present. Sinai stands at the mythic core of religious memory, and the explication of its teachings is a sacred ritual for Judaism" (*Sacred Attunement: A Jewish Theology* [Chicago: University of Chicago Press, 2008], 49).

6. "Land flowing with milk and honey," never occurs in the Patriarchal stories, but first appears in YHWH's conversations with the exodus generation: Exod. 3:8, 17; 13:5; 33:3; Lev. 20:24; Num. 13:27; 14:8; 16:13–14.

17:7; Exod. 19:5–6; Deut. 8:18), and renewed with the present generation is one and the same.[7]

If Moses's speeches exude a kind of timelessness, this does not mean he is oblivious to present circumstances. On the contrary, his present addresses are largely driven by a very immediate pastoral concern (if not fear). He knows that Israel's next move is to cross the Jordan, but he also knows that since he will die shortly (31:2) he will not be able to cross over with them (1:37; 3:23–29; 4:21–22). Indeed, the narrator reminds readers that YHWH himself announced Moses's imminent death both to him and to Joshua in the "Appointment Tent" (31:14–16) and again after he had taught his people their anthem (32:48–52). The four concluding chapters may be interpreted as a single extended and complex death narrative.[8] This reality lends urgency to everything Moses says, for both he (31:24–29) and YHWH (31:16–21) fear that as soon as he is gone the Israelites will act corruptly by abandoning YHWH and breaking his covenant. The urgency in Moses's voice is reflected in the expression, *hayyôm hazzeh*, "this day," which he uses sixteen times.[9] Although Moses often deals with past and future events, with this phrase he keeps bringing his hearers back to the present moment of decision on the plains of Moab. Like the other sixty-one occurrences of the word, *hayyôm*, "today," in the Old Testament,[10] in Deuteronomy "this day" highlights the "emphatic contemporaneity" of the entire book.[11] Moses thereby insists that the Israelites are accountable both to the covenant to which they signed on at Horeb and his valedictory appeal, that is, "this Torah" (*hattôrâ hazzōʾt*), that Moses is setting before the people (4:8, 44; cf. 30:1, 10, 15, 19).[12] His primary concern is the fidelity of the present generation.

---

7. See further, Daniel I. Block, "Covenance: A Whole Bible Perspective," paper presented to the Evangelical Theological Society in Baltimore, MD, November 2013; Jerry Hwang, *The Rhetoric of Remembrance: An Investigation into the "Fathers" in Deuteronomy*, Siphrut 8 (Winona Lake, IN; Eisenbrauns, 2012), 232.

8. Bryan Cribb, *Speaking on the Brink of Sheol: Form and Message of Old Testament Death Stories* (Piscataway, NJ: Gorgias, 2009), 185–227.

9. Deut. 2:22, 25, 30; 3:14; 4:20, 38; 5:24; 6:24; 8:18; 10:8, 15; 11:4; 26:16; 27:9; 29:3, 27. The narrator uses the phrase in 32:48 and 34:6

10. For a listing of the remainder see Gary Millar, "Living at the Place of Decision: Time and Place in the Framework of Deuteronomy," in *Time and Place in Deuteronomy*, by J. G. McConville and J. G. Millar (JSOTSup 179; Sheffield: Sheffield Academic Press, 1994), 43, n. 61.

11. Gerhard von Rad, *The Problem of the Hexateuch and Other Studies* (London: SCM, 1966), 26.

12. The expression occurs fifteen times in the book: 1:5; 4:8; 17:18–19; 27:3, 8, 26; 28:58, 61; 29:29[28]; 31:9, 11–12, 24; 32:46.

HISTORY IN DEUTERONOMY

None of this should blur our vision for Moses's keen sense of history in Deuteronomy. In contrast to the canonical texts of other ancient peoples, Moses has a clear perception of Israel's past, and a clear sense of where the nation's history is going. We may summarize the key past events as follows:

1. In the beginning "God created humankind on the earth" (*bārā' 'ĕlōhîm 'ādām 'al hā 'āreṣ*; 4:32).[13]
2. YHWH identified the ancestors (Abraham, Isaac, Jacob) as the object of his love (*ḥāšaq, 'āhēb*) and chose (*bāḥ ar*) their descendants after them (4:37; 10:15).
3. YHWH swore to the ancestors that he would give the land of Canaan to them and their descendants (1:8, 35; 6:10, 18, 23; 7:13; 8:1; 9:5; 10:11; 11:9, 21; 26:3, 15; 28:11; 30:20; 31:20–21, 23; 34:4).
4. Their ancestors lived a precarious existence in the land, and ultimately their clan of seventy moved to Egypt (10:22; 26:5).
5. In the indeterminate past YHWH had dislodged the original populations of the regions south and east of the Dead Sea and given them to the Edomites, Moabites, and Ammonites, respectively (2:2–23).
6. Meanwhile in Egypt the clan of Jacob flourished and became a nation (*gôy*), great, mighty, and innumerable like the stars (10:22; 26:5), but there the Israelites observed the idolatry of the Egyptians (29:17–18 [16–17]) and at the end of their stay experienced brutal enslavement by Pharaoh (26:6).
7. By means of signs and wonders, YHWH punished the Egyptians, revealed himself to them and Israel, and rescued Israel from the bondage of Egypt (Deut. 4:34; 6:22; 7:19; 11:3; 26:8; 29:3; 34:11).
8. YHWH brought Israel to Horeb, where he established with them the covenant he had first made with Abraham (4:9–14) and revealed his will in the form of the Decalogue (4:13; 5:1–2) and the "ordinances and judgments" (*ḥuqqîm ûmišpāṭîm*).[14]

---

13. The word *bārā'* occurs only here in Deuteronomy.
14. This pair of expressions, which generally functions as shorthand for the Horeb revelation, occurs fourteen times: Deut. 4:1, 5, 8, 14, 45; 5:1, 31; 6:1, 20; 7:11; 11:32; 12:1; 26:16–17. Occasionally it is supplemented by *hā 'ēdût*, "the covenant stipulations (4:45; 6:17, 20). Although *ḥuqqîm* and *mišpāṭîm* may be used interchangeably, at root the former refers to divine decrees, while the latter refers to divine judgments concerning righteous covenantal conduct.

9. No sooner had the Israelites signed on to the covenant than they apostatized and worshiped the golden calf in place of YHWH. However, through the mediation of Moses, YHWH withdrew his threat to destroy them and renewed his covenant with them (9:1–10:11).

10. The Israelites left Sinai and experienced YHWH's remarkable care as they journeyed through the desert to the edge of the promised land (1:19, 30–33; 8:1–6, 15–16; 29:5–6 [4–5]; 32:10).

11. At Kadesh-Barnea the exodus generation faithlessly refused to enter the promised land, so YHWH sent them back into the desert for forty years, until that generation had died and been replaced by the current generation (1:20–29, 32–46; 2:1–2, 14–15).

The Israelite Covenantal Triangle

YHWH

People of Israel   **Land of Canaan**

12. Most recently, with divine support the Israelites had defeated the Transjordanian kingdoms of Sihon of Heshbon and Og of Bashan, whose land Moses had allotted to the tribes of Reuben, Gad, and a segment of Manasseh (1:4; 2:24–3:17; 4:46; 29:7–8 [6–7]).

Moses's historical memory is sharp, but he also has a keen sense of Israel's future, both immediate and long-range.

1. Once Moses has died, Joshua will take the reins and lead the people across the Jordan (1:38–39; 3:18–22, 28; 31:3–8, 23).

2. The first event to transpire across the river involves the ritual completion of the covenantal triangle binding the land to deity and nation on Mounts Gerizim and Ebal (11:29–32; 27:1–26).[15]

3. Thereafter the Israelites are to engage the Canaanites and occupy their

15. The covenantal bond between YHWH and Israel had been covenantally sealed at Sinai, and was being reinforced by the present rituals—on the Plains of Moab—that underlie the book of Deuteronomy. On the significance of the Gerizim and Ebal ceremony, see Daniel I. Block, "'What Do These Stones Mean?' The Riddle of Deuteronomy 27," *JETS* 56 (2013): 17–41.

land, which YHWH had sworn to the ancestors (6:10–11; 7:1–26; 8:7–10; 11:8–15, 21–25; 12:1; 17:14; 19:1; 30:20).

4. When the Israelites have rest from all their enemies, YHWH will choose a place to establish his name, to which all Israelites and aliens among them are invited for worship and fellowship with YHWH (12:5, 11, 14, 18, 21, 26; 14:23; 15:20; 16:2, 6–7, 11, 15–16; 17:8, 10; 18:6; 23:16; 26:2; 31:11).

5. If the Israelites demonstrate righteousness and are true to YHWH and his covenant, they will flourish and occupy the land in perpetuity (5:33; 7:12–16; 11:8–17; 22:7; 28:1–14; 31:20).

This is the hope. However, both Moses and YHWH present a more realistic view of the nation, repeatedly expressing doubts about Israel's future fidelity (5:29). Indeed they offer an alternative script, which exhibits strong marks of inevitability.

1. Once the Israelites are in the land, they will abandon YHWH and his covenant. At the end of his first address Moses seems to anticipate this as an event in the distant future (4:25), but by the time he finishes his addresses both he (31:27–29) and YHWH (31:14–20; 32:15–18) expect this to happen immediately upon Moses's decease.

2. YHWH will respond to this rebellion and ingratitude for the grace he had lavished on them through the centuries by withdrawing from them (31:17–18) and pouring on them his fury in the form of the severest of curses (4:25b–28; 11:16, 28; 28:15–68; 29:18–28; 30:1; 32:19-25), in effect destroying the covenantal triangle by driving Israel away from himself and from the land.

3. However, the judgment cannot be the last word. Ultimately the Israelites will come to their senses and turn back to YHWH (4:29–30; 30:1–3), and YHWH's compassion (4:31; 30:3; 32:36) will triumph over his fury (32:36–42). He will remember his [irrevocable and eternal] covenant (4:31), regather the people to their land (30:3–5), and circumcise their hearts so that they will love him with whole heart and being and walk in his ways. In effect, the covenantal triangle will be restored.

4. Israel will finally fulfill her mission to the world[16] as YHWH's people, chosen (bāḥar), treasured ('am sĕgullâ), holy ('am qādôš), and ad-

---

16. Gen. 12:3; 18:18; 22:18; 26:4; Exod. 19:4–6; Ps. 67.

opted as his sons (*bānîm*; 7:6; 14:1–2; 26:18–19). The nations will acknowledge not only the righteousness of YHWH's statutes, but also YHWH's nearness to them (4:5–8). Indeed they will recognize that Israel bears the name of YHWH (28:9–10) and that he has raised them high above all nations for [his] praise (*tĕhillâ*), fame (*šēm*), and honor (*tip'eret*; 26:19). Indeed, along with Israel, the nations and the angels will worship YHWH and celebrate his restoration of the people and their land (32:43).

Deuteronomy's Eschatological Language

With this survey of Deuteronomy's vision of Israel's past and her future we have established the context for considering the Mosaic eschatological vision. After a discussion of Moses's eschatological language, I will consider the features of Moses's eschatological vision, based on specific texts.

Although the Pentateuch as a whole is punctuated with eschatological vocabulary, to argue that "the Pentateuch was written primarily as a presentation of a future messianic hope centered in the tribe of Judah and grounded both in creation and covenant"[17] certainly overstates the case. It overlooks the fact that the books that make up the Pentateuch function as a sort of constitutional document, preserving a record both of divine grace that led to the establishment of Israel as YHWH's covenant people and of the divine revelation intended to guide the people in the fulfillment of his mission for them.[18] Although we find predictions that may legitimately be interpreted messianically, these are not only remarkably scarce,[19] but missing entirely from Deuteronomy.[20] The statements that most closely resemble Messianic

---

17. Sailhamer, "The Messiah and the Hebrew Bible," 18.
18. I include Moses's addresses in Deuteronomy as part of that revelation, inasmuch as both the narrator (1:1–5) and Moses (4:5, 14; 6:1) emphasize that his addresses were divinely inspired, and indeed canonical from the outset (4:2),
19. Gen. 3:15; 22:17b (Abraham's seed [singular] shall possess the gate of his enemies); 49:8–12; Num. 24:9, 17.
20. Contra prevailing opinion, represented, for example by Michel Rydelnik, *The Messianic Hope: Is the Hebrew Bible Messianic?* (Nashville: B&H, 2010), 54–59 (Kindle edition). I do not interpret Moses's prediction of "a prophet like me" as a prediction of an eschatological prophetic Messiah, but a succession of prophets who would continue like Moses to be God's mouthpieces for Israel. For brief discussion, see Daniel I. Block, "My Servant David: Ancient Israel's Vision of the Messiah," in *Israel's Messiah in the Bible and the Dead Sea Scrolls,* ed. R. S. Hess and M. D. Carroll R. (Grand Rapids: Baker, 2003), 26–32.

prediction occur in the Mosaic vision of kingship in Deuteronomy 17:14–20, which anticipates the [Davidic] Israelite king as the supreme embodiment of righteousness, as defined by the Torah. With hindsight we recognize that none of Israel's kings fulfilled this vision perfectly,[21] and that only Jesus, David's greatest son, did so (cf. Matt. 5:17). However, this perspective is possible only with hindsight; the original text lacks any hint of an eschatological or messianic significance.

When searching for eschatological texts, we look for distinctive vocabulary that speaks of "the last days," or "the end of the age."[22] The relevant expressions include *qēṣ/qāṣeh*, "end, extremity," and *'aḥărît*, "latter, afterward, outcome." The word *qāṣeh* occurs nine times in Deuteronomy, but usually with a geographic sense, referring either to the distant horizon, "the end of the heavens/sky" (4:32 [2x]; 30:4), or to "the end of the earth" (13:8 [2x]; 28:49 // *mērāḥôq*, "from far away"; 28:64 [2x]; 30:4). Only in 14:28 does it bear a chronological significance, but the sense is not eschatological: "at the end of [every] three years." The word *qēṣ* occurs only three times, always with a specifically defined chronological sense: "at the end of forty days and forty nights" (9:11); "at the end of seven years" (15:1; 31:10). Therefore, the *qēṣ/ qāṣeh* vocabulary of Deuteronomy provides no evidence of an eschatological perspective.[23]

Although the word, *'aḥărît* occurs less frequently than *qēṣ/qāṣeh* it offers slightly stronger evidence for an eschatological significance to Deuteronomy.[24] The word occurs six times,[25] always with a chronological meaning, though only two of these bear a possible eschatological significance.[26] According to

---

21. The historians single out David, Hezekiah, and Josiah as particularly virtuous, but all are flawed to a greater or lesser degree.
22. For discussion, see Gerald Klingbeil, "Looking at the End from the Beginning: Studying Eschatological Concepts in the Pentateuch," *JETS* 11 (2000): 174–87.
23. As does the evidence for this word in the rest of the Pentateuch; *qēṣ* and *qāṣeh* occur often, but never with an eschatological sense.
24. Cf. Klingbeil, "Eschatological Concepts." 178–83.
25. And four times in the preceding books, three in the context of Balaam's oracles: Gen. 49:1 (*bě'aḥărît hayyāmîm*, lit. "in the latter days"; Jacob's blessing of his sons concerns the distant future); Num. 23:10 (*'aḥărîtî*, "my end"; the suffix suggests one's personal destiny); Num. 24:14 (*bě'aḥărît hayyāmîm*, lit. "in the latter days"; as in Gen. 49:1, in this narrative introduction to an oracle, Balaam is about to speak of what Israel will do to Moab in the distant future); Num. 24:20 *'aḥărîtô*, "his end," speaking of Amalek's ultimate destruction (*'ōbēd*).
26. Deut. 8:16 (*bě'aḥărîtekā*, "in your end"), YHWH tested Israel for their "ultimate" good; 11:12 (*'ad 'aḥărît šānā*, "unto the end of the year"), in contrast to the beginning of the year (*mērē'šît haššānâ*).

4:30, when Israel is in distress (*ṣar*) because they have experienced YHWH's fury as described in vv. 25–27, "in the latter days" (*bě' aḥărît hayyāmîm*) they will return to YHWH their God and listen to his voice.[27]

The eschatological nature of these statements is not as obvious as scholars often assume. Admittedly, the Septuagint translates three of them with some form of εσχηατος (32:29 uses χρονος), but in the Greek rendering of Deuteronomy this word is used in a wide variety of contexts,[28] which cautions against premature identification of "the latter days" with "the end of the age" or "the end of time." This caution is reinforced by 31:29, which locates Israel's judgment "in the latter days." From Moses's perspective the fulfillment of this warning in 722 BCE and 586 BCE might have seemed like "the end of the days," but from our vantage it was not nearly the eschaton. Accordingly, initially we should interpret the expression no more specifically than "in the distant future."

Moses actually assumes a four-phased future for Israel: (1) the immediate future following his death (31:27–29); (2) several generations removed from the present after the Israelites have been in the land for some time and become spiritually lethargic (4:25);[29] (3) the distant future (*bě' aḥărît hayyāmîm*) when YHWH will have had enough of Israel's infidelity and he pours out his fury on them in the form of the covenant curses (31:29); (4) the period beyond the judgment (also *bě' aḥărît hayyāmî*) when Israel returns to YHWH and listens to his voice (4:29–31). To Moses these last two repre-

---

27. Whereas this text locates Israel's restoration after the judgment "in the latter days," 31:29 locates the judgment itself "in the latter days" (*bě' aḥărît hayyāmî*). Deut. 32:20 speaks of Israel's destiny in the wake of the judgment as "their end" (*'aḥărîtām*). In 32:29 a similar expression (*lě' aḥărîtām*, "with reference to their end") speaks of the destiny of Israel's enemies.

28. Of Israel's destinies (*'aḥărît* + suffix; 8:16; 32:20); in 32:29 the same expression is rendered *chronos*; simply for "afterward" (Heb *'aḥărōnâ*; 13:9 [10]; 17:7), "after" Moses's death (*'aḥărê môtî*; ; 31:27, 29); of the "latter" man (*hā'aḥărôn*; 24:3 [2x]); geographically of "the end of the earth" (*qaseh*; 24:89), and "the western sea" (*hā'aḥărôn*; 34:2).

29. Because the verb *nôšantem* is rare in the Old Testament, its meaning is unclear. It seems to be derived from a root meaning "old" (*yšn*) but it also sounds like a word meaning "to sleep" (*yāšēn*), which is occasionally associated with death (Job 3:13; Ps. 13:4). In the covenant curses of Lev. 26:10, the word describes old and stale grain. In either case, the word suggests a long time in the land, resulting either in lethargy or self-confidence (cf. Deut. 8:11–17). Moses seems to anticipate a waning of energy to keep alive the story of divine grace. How quickly this happened is demonstrated in the book of Judges (2:10–13). Moses would probably have been appalled that his own grandson Jonathan would be installed as the first priest of the pagan cult center at Dan (Judg. 18:30), on which see Daniel I. Block, *Judges, Ruth* (NAC; Nashville: Broadman & Holman, 1999), 512–13.

sented "the distant future";[30] only time would tell whether this would transpire at the end of the age, or even the climactic moment of cosmic history.
If we would speak of Moses's "eschatological vision," we should understand
that for him, Israel's distant future is firmly rooted in both Israel's past and
the nation's present.

The Features of Moses's Eschatological Vision

Deuteronomy describes the anticipated first phase of Israel's "distant future"
in detail in 28:15–68; 29:18–28; and 32:19–25. Since from our perspective
this phase has in fact been fulfilled in history, when considering the features of
Moses's "eschatological" vision, we must focus on those aspects of his vision
that have not been realized even in our time: phase 4 of the scheme outlined
on page 113. In exploring Moses's (and YHWH's) perspective of Israel's ultimate future, we may focus on three specific texts, the first two appearing in
prose at the end of Moses's first and third addresses (4:29–31; 30:1–10) and
the third in poetic form in the nation's anthem (32:36–43). Each text builds
on the preceding.

Deuteronomy 4:29–31

Moses's first "eschatological" statement is brief and focuses entirely on the restoration of divine human relations—without any reference to the land and its role
in the covenantal triangle. The geographic context is established by the words,
"there" (*šām*, v. 28a), that is, in the lands to which YHWH had scattered their
few survivors (v. 27) and where they have been serving senseless and insentient
humanly manufactured gods of wood and stone (v. 28). Three chronological
notes in verse 30 establish the chronological context: (1) "in the distant future"
(*bě'aḥărît hayyāmîm*, lit., "in the latter days"); (2) "when you experience the
distress" (*baṣṣar lěkā*); and (3) "when all these words "find" (*māṣā'*) you," that
is, the threats of 25b–28 have been fulfilled.

The definite article on "distress" and the expression "these things" indicate
that Moses had in mind not "trouble" in general, but a specific set of circum-

---

30. Jeffrey Tigay, *Deuteronomy*, Torah Commentary (Philadelphia: Jewish Publication Society,
    1996), 54; Peter C. Craigie, *The Book of Deuteronomy*, NICOT (Grand Rapids: Eerdmans,
    1976), 141.

stances. These are summarized in vv. 25b–28, which in style and vocabulary anticipate the detailed recitation of covenant curses in 28:15–68. The essential features are easily identified. The cause of their distress is the fury of YHWH their God, who has been provoked by "the evil" they have perpetrated with their idolatry, which violates the first and supreme command of the Decalogue: "you shall have no other gods besides me" (5:7–10).

Moses describes the distress that YHWH threatens to bring on his people in five dimensions: (1) The Israelites will certainly and quickly perish from the land they are about to cross into and possess. (2) Their dream of long life in the land will come to an end,[31] for they will be utterly destroyed.[32] (3) YHWH will scatter them among the peoples, and drive them to another place, like a shepherd drives his flock. (4) A few will survive[33] in the lands where YHWH has driven them. (5) In the lands where the worship of senseless gods is the norm, they will experience the futility of idolatry to the full (v. 28). Here Moses fails to mention the element that may have been most distressing of all: being abandoned by YHWH. Later, in 31:17–18 he will summarize the link between idolatry and trouble and the heart of the trouble itself: "On that day my fury with them will be ignited and I will abandon them; I will hide my face from them, and they will be destroyed. Many disasters (*rā'ôt*) and difficulties (*ṣārôt*) will find (*māṣā'*) them, and on that day they will ask, Have these disasters not found (*māṣā'*) us because our God is not with us?' And I will certainly hide my face on that day because of all the wickedness they have perpetrated, for they have turned to other gods."[34]

Obviously, the anticipated judgment would result in the complete disintegration of the covenant triangle: YHWH would abandon his people and his land, the land would be emptied of its people, and the Israelites would be driven

---

31. The motif of not prolonging their days occurs often in Deut. (4:40; 5:33; 11:9; 17:20; 22:7; 30:18; 32:47). It negates the desired purpose, "that their days may be lengthened" (5:16 [=Exod. 20:12]; 6:2; 25:15).

32. The emphatic constructions, *'ābōd tō'bēdûn,* "you shall certainly perish," and *hiššāmēd tiššāmēdûn,* "you shall certainly be destroyed," represent rhetorical hyperbole. As Moses himself will say (v. 27), there will be a few who survive in the lands where they are exiled.

33. Hebrew *nišar mĕtê mispār,* literally "be left men of number," that is, so few one may count them (Gen. 34:30; Jer 44:28; Ps 105:12). In Deuteronomy 26:5 and 28:62 Moses will use the stylistic variant *mĕtê mĕ'aṭ,* "a few men." Both expressions represent the reversal/opposite of what YHWH promises the patriarchs: descendants like the stars of the sky and sands of the seashore (Gen. 22:17), and descendants that are innumerable (*'ên mispār;* Gen. 41:49; cf. Deut. 10:22; 26:5).

34. Translation is author's own.

off to seek divine aid in a foreign land. However, if the punishment for covenantal infidelity threatened in verses 26–28 was certain, the same would apply
to the promise of hope in verses 29–31, which summarize Israel's ultimate destiny. Remarkably this first "eschatological" statement expresses no interest in the
role of the land in the covenantal triangle; the focus is entirely on restoring the
deity-people relationship. This is expressed from two sides.

On the one hand, Israel will experience a new disposition toward their God,
which is summarized with four verbs arranged in perfectly logical order (vv.
29–30). First, from the land of exile, the Israelites will seek YHWH their God.
"To seek" (*biqqēš*) YHWH does not mean to look for him as if he were lost, but
to seek him out, approach him humbly, and plead for a return of his favorable
attention. Second, they will find (*māṣā'*) YHWH, if they search for him with all
their heart/mind (*lēb*) and with their entire being (*nepeš*).[35] This added condition means the search for YHWH may be neither casual nor occasional, nor one
search among many. Moses demands that the people abandon all other searches
and seek YHWH alone. Third, they will return to YHWH. The verb *šûb* means
"to turn, to turn around," that is, to walk in the opposite direction, but is regularly rendered "to repent," that is, to turn around spiritually, to abandon one's
sinful course and "walk in the ways of YHWH." Fourth, the Israelites will listen to the voice of YHWH, which means not only obeying his commands,
but also receiving gladly his reminders of past and present graces, including the
words being preached presently by his spokesman Moses. Whereas the covenant
curses in chapter 28 conclude with words of distress,[36] without any ray of hope,
here Moses patterns his vision of Israel's "eschatological" future on Leviticus 26,
which means he cannot let Israel's story end with judgment. And it does not, for
Moses will return to this theme in his third address (30:1–10), and expound in
considerable detail how this will happen. Here he offers no clues why the Israelites in exile will experience such a dramatic change of heart.

If on one hand Israel will exhibit a new disposition toward YHWH, on the
other YHWH will respond by letting himself be found (v. 29) and resuming his
communication with them (v. 30). The promise that Israel will find YHWH if
they seek him wholeheartedly and that they will hear his voice again suggests
that the Deity who had abandoned his people will respond to their search with

---

35. Variations of this phrase recur frequently in Deuteronomy: 6:5; 10:12; 11:13; 13:3; 26:16;
    30:2, 6, 10. We hear echoes of the present statement in Jeremiah 29:13. In Daniel 9, the
    exiled Daniel models this focused search for YHWH. See also 2 Chronicles 7:14.
36. Deuteronomy 28:15–68 expounds and expands on 4:26–28.

renewed accessibility and renewed communication. Unlike the gods of wood and stone, he is responsive; indeed as Moses had declared at the beginning of this chapter, he will be near again to hear their calls to him and he will reveal himself once more (4:7–8).

Moses concludes this summary statement of Israel's "eschatological" hope by announcing three pillars on which this hope rests. First, Israel's hope rests on the compassionate character of God: "For YHWH your God is compassionate El." While the word *raḥûm* speaks of warm and tender affection, like the love of a mother toward a child,[37] the phrase *'ēl raḥûm* invites hearers/readers to remember Exodus 34:6–7, where this expression heads a list of seven extraordinary divine qualities. YHWH is merciful and gracious, slow to anger, abounding in steadfast love (*ḥesed*) and fidelity (*'ĕmet*), forgiving every kind of sin, while not leaving the guilty unpunished. As Daniel will plea in Daniel 9:18, given their history the Israelites have no reason to expect a favorable response from YHWH; but they may appeal to his great compassion (*raḥămîm*). Unlike the gods of wood and stone, YHWH is moved by the prayers of his people.

Second, YHWH will not abandon his people forever. From Moses's statement in verse 26, it had appeared that he would not withdraw his fury until he had "utterly destroyed" (*hiššāmēd tiššāmēdûn*) them. From what follows immediately this is obviously hyperbolic speech, for he speaks of a remnant of the population surviving in exile. Presumably the absolute statement refers to the covenant triangle relationship, which must be demolished before YHWH can start over with his people. In verse 31 Moses expresses YHWH's fidelity to Israel with two expressions: He will not "drop" (*hirpeh*) them, and he will not destroy (*hišḥît*) them. In everyday speech the first is used of relaxing the hands so that one drops what one is holding (cf. 2 Sam. 24:16 = 1 Chron. 21:15). Here it signifies "to abandon" or "to release" from the relationship. The second expression seems to answer the hopelessness created by verse 26. Because YHWH is gracious, he will not destroy (*hišḥît*) them totally. The Israelites may be determined to destroy themselves (v. 16 and 31:29 use the same verb, *hišḥît*), but YHWH's compassion prevents him from totally annihilating them. In effect, through the exile he saves the Israelites from themselves.

Third, though Israel may forget YHWH's covenant with them (v. 23), YHWH cannot forget his covenant with the ancestors. The last phrase, "cov-

---

37. It derives from the same root as *reḥem*, the word for "womb" (Isa. 49:15; Jer. 20:17). Cf. *HALOT*, 1216–18.

enant of your ancestors" (*bĕrît 'ăbōtêkā*), raises the question: Which covenant does Moses have in mind? Although most scholars assume the Abrahamic covenant,[38] the issues are not that simple. First scholars are recognizing increasingly that a dichotomy between the [supposedly unconditional] Abrahamic covenant and the [supposedly conditional] Israelite covenant is false. Since all covenants involve relationships, the health of such relationships is always conditional, depending upon the disposition and actions of each party toward the other.[39] Second, the covenant made at Horeb was anticipated in Genesis 17:7, and signified the establishment (*hēqîm*) with Abraham's descendants of the very covenant that YHWH had first made (*kārat*) with Abraham (Gen. 15:18). Third, although elsewhere we read of God's covenant "with" Abraham, outside this context "the covenant with the fathers," or "of the fathers" (*bĕrît 'ăbōtêkā*), never occurs.[40] Fourth, the argument based on Leviticus 26:42 is neutralized by verse 45, which, while referring to a "covenant with their predecessors" (*bĕrît ri 'šōnîm*) explicitly identifies them as those "whom I brought out of Egypt in the sight of the nations to be their God." Fifth, in Deuteronomy 4 generally and verses 9–31 particularly, the central issue is the covenant that YHWH made with Israel at Horeb.

On the other hand, there is no need to choose between the patriarchal covenant and the Israelite covenant; the distinct language is merely a matter of focus. Rather than emphasizing the land, which was the focus in the promise to the patriarchs, in verse 31 Moses's attention is on YHWH's

---

38. Thus Eugene Merrill, *Deuteronomy*, NAC (Nashville: B&H, 1994), 129; Moshe Weinfeld, *Deuteronomy 1–11: A New Translation with Introduction and Commentary*, AB 5 (New York: Doubleday, 1991), 210; A. D. H. Mayes, *Deuteronomy*, NCB (Grand Rapids: Eerdmans, 1981), 157. Three considerations may support this interpretation: (1) In previous occurrences of the expression, "which he swore to X," in Deuteronomy, the clause referred to YHWH's covenant promise of land to the patriarchs (1:8, 35), while the Sinai narratives never speak of YHWH "swearing" to Israel to keep the covenant; (2) biblical narratives frequently refer to the covenant with the patriarchs as God's covenant with Abraham, Isaac, and Jacob (Exod. 2:24; cf. 6:4; Lev. 26:42; 2 Kings 13:23; 1 Chron. 16:15–18 = Ps. 105:8–11); (3) the covenant curses in Leviticus 26 base Israel's hope for renewal on God's covenant with the patriarchs.

39. So also Walter Brueggemann, *Theology of the Old Testament: Testimony, Dispute, Advocacy* (Minneapolis: Fortress, 2013), 199; C. J. H. Wright, *Knowing Jesus through the Old Testament* (Downers Grove, IL: InterVarsity, 1995), 55–102.

40. The expression, "the covenant that I made with their/your ancestors" (*bĕrît 'ăšer kārattî 'et 'ăbôtām*) occurs in Jeremiah 31:32 and 34:13, but in both instances the ancestors are identified as the exodus generation.

relationship with his people: "He will neither fail *you* nor destroy *you*." Furthermore, the "return" spoken of in verses 29–31 is not to the land but to YHWH.[41] The issue in this chapter is much greater than land. Unlike the gods of the nations, who were primarily interested in territory and only secondarily concerned about people, YHWH's primary concern lies with his people and his relationship to them (cf. Gen. 17:7). The covenant he remembers is the one made with Abraham, extended to his descendants at Horeb, and confirmed with this generation in Moab. In Deuteronomy the covenant with the fathers and their descendants is one.[42] In the future YHWH may suspend the benefits of the covenant (4:25–28; cf. Lev. 26:14–39; Deut. 28:15–68), but this will not affect the covenant itself.[43] On the contrary, both the judgment and the restoration are written into the covenant. In the end, when the Israelites come to their spiritual senses and repent of their rebellion (Lev. 26:41; Deut. 4:30; 30:6–10), he will renew his covenant relationship with them.

DEUTERONOMY 30:1–10

Deuteronomy 30 represents the climax of the gospel Moses has proclaimed in this book. Much of the theological freight of this section is carried by key words. The most important of these is the root *šûb*, "to return, turn back," which occurs seven times, with some variation in meaning.[44] Since four of the seven involve Israel as the subject (vv. 1, 2, 8, 10) and three involve YHWH (vv. 3a, 3b, 9), Israel's future restoration obviously requires a change in the disposition of both parties.[45] The subthemes interwoven throughout this passage exhibit an exquisite chiastic arrangement:[46]

---

41. Cf. the references to the "land" that he swore to the ancestors in 1:8, 35; 6:10; 7:13; 10:11; 11:9, 21; 26:3; 28:11; 30:20; 31:20.
42. For full discussion, see Block, "Covenance," and Hwang, *Rhetoric of Remembrance*, 187–207, 302–8.
43. On the eternality of God's covenant with Israel, see note 80 below.
44. For a full study of the word, see W. L. Holladay, *The Root* šûb *in the Old Testament (with Particular References to Its Usage in Covenantal Contexts)* (Leiden: Brill, 1958).
45. The third occurrence of *šûb* involves the idiom, *šûb šěbût*, "to restore the fortunes" (v. 3a). For a more recent study of *šûb* in this context, see A. Frisch, "Repentance and Return— A Literary-Theological Study of Three Biblical Texts (Deut. 30:1–10; I Kings 8:46–51; II Chronicles 30:6–9)," in *Studies in Bible and Exegesis* 4, ed. B. Kasher, Y. Sefati, and M. Zipor (Ramat Gan: Bar-Ilan University, 1997), 129–48 [Hebrew].
46. Cf. Mayes, *Deuteronomy*, 289.

A   When you and your children return (v. 2a)
   B   and listen to his voice with all your heart and being (v. 2b)
      C   then YHWH will restore your fortunes and prosper you more than
         your ancestors (vv. 3–5)
         D   *YHWH will circumcise your heart and the heart of your offspring,*
         D' *so that you will love YHWH with all your heart and being, and*
            live (v. 6)[47]
      C' YHWH will delight in prospering you, as he took delight in your
         ancestors (vv. 8–9)
   B' if you obey the voice of the YHWH your God (v. 10a)
A' and if you turn to YHWH your God with all your heart and with all your
   soul (v. 10b).

This is a gloriously holistic text, announcing the full restoration of the triadic covenantal relationships. Based on syntactical and conceptual markers, the text breaks down into three readily identifiable segments each of which describes a specific feature of Israel's "eschatological" future: (1) The restoration of the bilateral relationship between YHWH and Israel (vv. 1–3); (2) The divine restoration of the trilateral covenant relationship (vv. 4–8); (3) The environmental proof of the restoration (vv. 9–10).

The Restoration of the Bilateral Relationship involving YHWH and Israel (vv. 1–3)

The way Moses begins suggests that verses 1–10 expand on his earlier summary statement in 4:29–30. He does not refer to "the latter days," but the clause, "when all these words have come upon you" pushes the events into the distant future. Although most translations render *kol haddĕbārîm hā'ēlleh* as "all these things," presumably the events predicted in 29:17–21[16–20],[48] his clarification, "the blessing and the curse," and the modifier, "which I have set before you" point back to the promises and threats of chapter 28.

Moses's description of the restoration of the bilateral relationship between deity and people divides into two parts: vv. 1b–2 highlights the change in Israel's

---

47. Verse 7 is omitted because it deals with what YHWH will do to the nations, rather than Israel, though these actions will ultimately be for Israel's benefit.
48. In Deuteronomy, and the Pentateuch as a whole, the expression always means "all these words." Gen. 20:8; 29:13; Exod. 19:7; 20:1; 24:8; Num. 16:31; Deut. 4:30; 12:28; 30:1; 32:45.

disposition toward YHWH, and v. 3 highlights YHWH's change in disposition toward Israel. Concerning the former, among all the nations where YHWH their God has banished them, they will (1) come to their senses,[49] (2) return (*šûb*) to YHWH their God,"[50] and finally listen to the voice of YHWH (cf. 4:30).[51] The coordinate expression, "with all your heart and with all your being" (vv. 2, 6, 10), picks up an oft-repeated refrain from 4:29[52] that highlights the completeness of the people's "repentance."

Additional echoes of 4:29–31 are heard in verse 3 as Moses shifts his attention to YHWH's changed attitude and actions. First, YHWH's *intentions* concerning Israel will change: He will restore their fortunes[53] by lifting the judgment and restoring the relationship between the people of Israel and their land. Second, YHWH's *disposition* toward his people will change: He will show compassion to them (*riḥam*, cf. 4:31), in response to Israel's listening to his voice and doing what is right in his sight (cf. 13:17 [18]). Third, YHWH's *orientation* regarding Israel will change: He will "turn around."[54] Here *šûb* expresses YHWH's fundamental reorientation: Instead of turning from Israel and operating as their enemy, he will turn toward them and act on their behalf. Fourth, YHWH's *treatment* of Israel will change: Whereas previously he had scattered them among the nations, now he will gather them (cf. 4:27; 28:64). While we hear nothing yet of the restoration of the people to the land, this divine action represents a necessary first step in the reversal of their uprooting (29:28 [27]).

---

49. In the clause rendered by NIV as "you take them to heart," the verb *hēšîb*, "to turn/bring x back," lacks an object. Assuming "all these words" (v. 1b) to be the object, in exile the Israelites will reverse their hardened disposition (cf. 29:19 [18]) and in effect recast as a confession what Moses had presented as a third-person interpretation in 29:25–28 [24–27].

50. A verbatim quotation from 4:30. The statement signifies a reversal of past faithless behavior that included "abandoning" YHWH (28:20) or his covenant (29:25), and turning aside from his way (9:12) or from him to serve other gods (11:16).

51. This clause serves as a refrain in the book: 4:30; 8:20; 9:23; 13:4, 18 [5, 19]; 15:5; 21:18, 20; 26:14, 17; 27:10; 28:1–2, 15, 45, 62; 30:2, 8, 10, 20.

52. See also Deuteronomy 6:5; 10:12–13: 11:13–15; 13:3 [4]; 26:16.

53. This is the first of twenty-five occurrences of the idiom *šûb šĕbût/šĕbît* in the Old Testament, and its only occurrence in Deuteronomy. In Job 42:10 the expression involved restoration of the beleaguered man's original good fortune.

54. When used of YHWH, the verb *šûb*, "to turn, return," reverses the hostile disposition reflected in expressions like, "he will turn away from you" (*wešûb me'aḥărêkā*, 23:14 [15]; 2 Chron. 30:8) and verbs of divine abandonment, like *'āzab*, or rejection, like *mā'as*, or abhorrence, like *gā'al*. The latter two occur in the Leviticus version of the covenant curses (Lev. 26:44).

The Restoration of the Trilateral Relationships involving YHWH, Israel, and the Land (vv. 4–8)

The syntax of verse 4 signals a shift in flow, though the repetition of the verb "to gather" suggests that verses 4–5 expand on the last clause in verse 3 and highlight the comprehensiveness of the restoration. Moses begins this paragraph by addressing the nation-land relationship of the triangle (vv. 4–5). His solution involves five elements, expressed with five verbs: He will gather (*qibbēṣ*) Israel, take (*lāqaḥ*) them,[55] "bring" (*hēbî'*) them to the land, ensure their well-being (*hēṭîb*),[56] and multiply (*hirbeh*) the population beyond anything their ancestors had known before the judgment.[57] Finally the physical and national ideals announced in the covenant with Abraham, and confirmed when the Israelites were incorporated in this covenant at Horeb, will be realized.

In verse 6 Moses addresses the heart of the problem: Israel's ruptured relationship with YHWH. Reintroducing a notion presented briefly in 10:16, where he had called upon the Israelites to circumcise their hearts, he now announces that YHWH will perform this spiritual surgery. The metaphor refers to removing all psychological, moral, and spiritual barriers to true devotion to YHWH, resulting in undivided love and obedience. This is not to say that this act happens here for the first time. There have always been individuals within Israel (like Abraham, Moses, Joshua, Caleb, David, the prophets), whose hearts were circumcised. What is new is that this will happen at the national scale: All Israel will be transformed from the inside out. While Moses observes that a positive disposition toward God is a prerequisite to restoration, he declares that permanent and total covenant commitment can be achieved neither by appealing to the people to get themselves right with YHWH nor by a mere return to the land. Apart from this divine surgery, national infidelity is not only inevitable, but also dangerous; it poses an ever-present threat to the current generation (5:29; 9:6, 13, 24; 13:2 [3]; 31:16–18, 27–29).

But Moses has already declared that however certain Israel's failure may be, just as certain is the conviction that alienation from YHWH and exile must end (cf. 4:28–31). YHWH will secure permanent and total devotion through

---

55. The verb "to take" is cryptic. The link with 4:20—the only other occurrence with YHWH as the subject and Israel as the object—suggests concrete affirmation of election; YHWH will claim Israel as his own possession once more.
56. YHWH's original delight, expressed concretely in the blessings of 28:1–14, will return.
57. For references to Israel prospering in the land and multiplication of the population, see also 6:3; 7:13; and 30:16.

circumcising the hearts of the generation he restores and their descendants in perpetuity. The goal of this surgery is simple but profound: "to love YHWH your God." As elsewhere "love" denotes commitment demonstrated in actions that serve the interests and pleasure of one's covenant partner (cf. 6:4–5). This could not be achieved by legislation; it required a radical new surgical removal of the symbols of the old affections.[58] This heart surgery will seal the complete restoration of the covenantal triangle.

After a brief passing notice that in that day YHWH will repair Israel's standing among the nations and impose the sanctions that his own people had experienced (29:22–28[21–27]) on those who served as his agents of punishment (v. 7), verse 8 describes concretely the evidence that the new day has arrived. YHWH's people will demonstrate a new orientation, a new receptiveness, and a new obedience in compliance with Moses's teaching.

The Environmental Proof of the Restoration (vv. 9–10)

Expanding on verse 5, in verses 9–10 Moses draws his hearers' attention back to YHWH, who causes the land to fulfill its role within the tripartite covenant relationship. In describing the physical evidences of this new order, he highlights Israel's special relationship with YHWH by what these two will do for each other. On the one hand YHWH will cause the Israelites to prosper in all they do. Echoing the blessing in 28:11, he cites three dimensions of this prosperity: in their own progeny, in the progeny of their livestock, and in the productivity of the ground. Reiterating his earlier promise, Moses declares that YHWH will "turn toward Israel"[59] with renewed delight over them (cf. 28:63). The promises made to the present generation (7:12–16; 8:11–13; 11:13–15; cf. 32:13–14) were not merely utopian dreams; they would one day be fully realized in all their physicality.

Moses concludes this section with one more reminder that although the triangular covenantal relationships will be fully restored, his people should not view these promises as unconditional predictions, overriding and trumping a rebellious disposition (v. 10). On the contrary, first, the Israelites must pay full attention to the voice of YHWH, which means ordering their conduct accord-

---

58. Since elsewhere Moses suggests this goal would be achieved through reading/hearing the Torah (17:19–20; 31:11–13), circumcising the heart is equivalent to implanting the Torah in peoples' hearts.

59. As in verses 3c and 8, NIV obscures the reference to reorientation by treating *yāšûb*, "he will return," as an adverb, "again."

ing to his commands and decrees as written in "this book of the Torah" (*bĕsēper hattôrâ hazzeh*), that is the transcript of Moses's addresses. Second, reversing the order of "hearing" and "returning" from verse 3, Moses declares that Israel must return to YHWH their God with all their heart/mind and their entire being. Introduced by the threefold occurrence of the particle *kî*, "because," Moses declares the grounds and the certainty of Israel's newfound prosperity: YHWH will bless Israel because he will delight in them (v. 9b), because they will listen to his voice (v. 10a), and because they will return to him (v. 10b).[60] It seems the missing element in Israel's history had not been the ability to keep the will of YHWH—as if it placed impossible demands on them—but the will to do so, an issue resolved in the circumcision of the heart.

In Deuteronomy 30:1–10 Moses reiterates and expounds on his vision of Israel's future, as summarized in 4:30–31 and envisioned in Leviticus 26:40–45. In the end, YHWH's mercy wins out over his fury and his eternal commitment to his people is confirmed. In this portrait of Israel's inevitable restoration, Moses has planted numerous seeds that will sprout and grow in later texts. In Jeremiah's announcement (Jer. 30:3) and in his vision of the new covenant (Jer. 31:27–37), we hear clear lexical and conceptual echoes of Deuteronomy 30:1–10.[61] Although Jeremiah does not use the language of heart circumcision here (cf. Jer. 4:4; 9:25–26 [24–25]), his understanding of the divine inscription of the Torah on the hearts of the people and his vision for all Israel participating in the new order fall within the same theological field. Like Moses, Jeremiah was fully aware that there are two Israels: (1) the Israel that claims status before God and before the nations by virtue of descent from Abraham, their identification with the exodus from Egypt through the annual celebration of the Passover, and their possession of the Torah (Paul's "Israel after the flesh," Rom. 4:1; 9:3, 5; Gal. 4:23, 29); (2) true spiritual Israel, for whom the *Shema* (Deut. 6:4–5) is the watchword, and who like Josiah turn to YHWH with their entire inner beings, their persons, and their resources (2 Kings 23:25); like Caleb, Rahab, and Ruth (who were Gentiles by blood), they have a different spirit and follow YHWH fully (cf. Num. 14:24; Deut. 1:36; Josh. 14:8); and

---

60. Cf. A. Aejmelaeus, "Function and Interpretation of *kî* in Biblical Hebrew," *JBL* 105:1986, 202–8. Contra McConville, *Deuteronomy*, 428, syntactically, the temporal interpretation seems too reliant on theological assumptions regarding Israel's incapacity to turn to YHWH prior to his circumcision of their heart in Deuteronomy 10:16.

61. "Restore [your] fortunes" (*šûb šĕbût*, cf. Deut. 30:3); "Bring [them] back to the land" (Jeremiah uses *hēšîb*; Deut. 30:5 uses *hēbî'*, "to bring"); the land (*hā'āreṣ*) associated with the ancestors ('*ābôt*; Deut. 30:5, "that your ancestors possessed"; Jer. 30:3, "that I gave their ancestors"); the verb, *yāraš*, "to possess," used of the land (cf. Deut. 30:5).

like David they trust YHWH fully (2 Sam. 22:2–51). Historically, times when the boundaries of these two Israels coalesced were rare. The contrast between the two may be portrayed graphically as follows:

The Two Israels
of the Past and Present   **The One Israel**
                                                                  of the Future

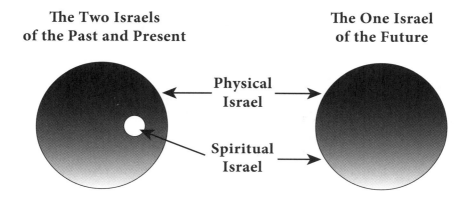

But the image envisioned here is different. As pictured on the right, Moses looks forward to a time when the boundaries of physical and spiritual Israel will be coterminous. All Israel will be circumcised of heart; all will love YHWH; all will listen to his voice and live according to the Torah of Moses; all will participate in YHWH's favor. Taking a page out of Moses's notebook, Jeremiah envisioned a future when the original Torah of YHWH would be internalized in the hearts of all Israel and all Israel would be freed to walk in the ways of YHWH.[62]

DEUTERONOMY 32:1–10

Although the poem inserted in chapter 32 is commonly identified as "the Song of Moses," it should really be called "the Song of YHWH,"[63] because YHWH

---

62. In context Jer. 31:27–40 is entirely parochial; only Israel is in view here. Ezekiel did not use the language of heart circumcision, but replaced this metaphor with that of a heart transplant. Echoing Moses's ambivalence in Deuteronomy, in one moment he calls on the Israelites to get themselves a new heart and a new spirit (Ezek. 18:31; cf. Deut. 10:16), and in the next speaks of YHWH transplanting the people's spirit and heart (Ezek. 11:19; 36:24–34; cf. Deut. 30:6). Like Moses, Ezekiel saw the proof of spiritual renewal to be obedience to the will of God.

63. "The song of Moses the servant of God, and the song of the Lamb" in Rev. 15:3 are often associated with this text, but the epithet may just as well refer to Exodus 15, which explicitly celebrates YHWH's deliverance of the Israelites from their tyrannical Egyptian overlords, which is paradigmatic of the salvation provided by the Lamb.

inspired it and apparently dictated it to Joshua and Moses in the Tent of Meeting (31:14–21). This is a complex composition, involving no fewer than four degrees of direct discourse.[64] Based on demarcations of the speeches and syntactical signals,[65] we may divide the song into sections and stanzas as follows:

A. The Exordium: A Call to Acknowledge the Perfections of YHWH (vv. 1–4)
B. The Recollection: A Call to Acknowledge the Imperfections of YHWH's People (vv. 5–18)
>   Stanza I: The Thesis Statement (vv. 5–6)
>   Stanza II: A Call to Remember YHWH's Grace (vv. 7–14)
>   Stanza III: Trampling Underfoot the Grace of YHWH (vv. 15–18)
C. The Confession: A Call to Recognize the Justice of YHWH (vv. 19–35)
>   Stanza I: YHWH's Justice in Dealing with His Own People (vv. 19–25)
>   Stanza II: YHWH's Justice in Dealing with Israel's Enemies (vv. 26–35)
D. The Gospel: A Call to Treasure the Compassion of YHWH (vv. 36–42)
E. The Coda: A Call to Celebrate the Deliverance of YHWH (v. 43)

This song presents a sophisticated poetic review of Israel's history from Moses's perspective: past (vv. 1–12) and future (vv. 13–43). With reference to Israel's anticipated future, the song speaks successively of (1) YHWH's blessing Israel with prosperity in the land (vv. 13–14), (2) Israel's revolt against their gracious God (vv. 15–18), (3) YHWH's outpouring of fury on his people (vv. 19–25), (4) YHWH's judgment on Israel's enemies (vv. 26–35), (5) YHWH's outpouring of restorative grace on his own people (vv. 36–42), and (6) the cosmic celebration of YHWH's full restoration of Israel and its land (v. 43). In accord with our previous observations, although "eschatological" vocabulary is missing, and verses 1–3 pertain to Israel's future from Moses's point of view (all having been fulfilled in the first millennium BCE), technically only verses 4–6 remain unfulfilled to

---

64. Cf. J. P. Fokkelman, *Major Poems of the Hebrew Bible, at the Interface of Prosody and Structural Analysis,* vol. 1, *Exod. 15, Deut. 32, and Job 3,* Studia Semitica Neerlandica (Assen, The Netherlands: Van Gorcum, 1998), 58–62.

65. Contra prevailing perceptions, the particle *kî* functions fundamentally as a discourse marker, which may function causally ("because," v. 20), or temporally ("when," v. 36c), though neither is certain. For full discussion, see Follingstad, *Deictic Viewpoint in Biblical Hebrew Text. (Dallas: SIL International, 2001)*

this time and relate to Israel's distant future. Therefore, they may be considered eschatological.

Israel is not the focus of verses 26–35, but like Ezekiel's oracles against the nations (Ezek. 25–32) and the oracle against Gog (Ezek. 38–39), this stanza offers hope for Israel, for here YHWH declares in unequivocal terms his determination to vanquish Israel's enemies. This stanza, which may be interpreted as a poetic commentary on 30:7, climaxes in a divine claim to the right to vengeance and retribution (*nāqām wĕšillēm*), followed by an announcement of the imminence of the day of their doom (*'ēd/'ătidōt*). However, the heart of the song's "eschatological" gospel occurs in 32:36–42, calling on Israel to treasure YHWH's amazing compassion.

This stanza opens with the voice of the poet, who announces the theme brilliantly:

> See, YHWH will champion the cause of his people
> and have compassion on his servants,
> when he sees that their power is gone
> and there is none remaining, neither ruler nor helper (v. 36).[66]

The first verb (*dîn*) involves a legal expression, meaning "to judge,"[67] but in cases involving the oppressed it means "to champion the cause of."[68] The second involves a hithpael of the root *nḥm*, "to be sorry, feel compassion" (cf. Ps 135:14; Num. 23:19).[69] While both YHWH and Moses deem Israel's future infidelity and judgment to be inevitable (Deut. 31:16–18, 20–21), already in 4:31 Moses had declared the present assertion of divine empathy to be rooted in YHWH's compassion (*raḥûm*). The second half of verse 36 sets the context of his change in disposition from the fury poured out in verses 19–25. The expression, "Their strength is gone" (lit. "Their hand evaporates"), contrasts Israel's powerlessness with the boast of the enemies (v. 27c). But the song adds a profound detail: YHWH sees! In contrast to the foreign gods (4:28) and reversing the hiding of his face earlier (v. 20), YHWH observes that the Israelites have expended their resources.

---

66. As translated by Block, "Power of Song," 183.
67. Often as an alternative to or correlative of *šāpaṭ* (e.g., Ps. 7:8[9]; 9:8[9]). In Deuteronomy 17:8 the cognate noun refers to a lawsuit or legal case too difficult for local courts to resolve.
68. So NJPS. Of God: Gen. 30:6; Ps. 54:1[3]; of human officials: Prov. 31:9; Jer. 5:28; 21:12; 22:16.
69. The niphal is used often to express God's sorrow or his change in disposition toward an object: Gen. 6:6–7; Exod. 32:12, 14; 1 Sam. 15:11, 29, 35 Jonah 3:9–10; 4:2.

In verses 37–38 YHWH's voice returns and carries on through verse 42. He begins by taunting the Israelites for having put their confidence in other gods. The rhetorical question (v. 37a) alludes to verses 15–18, ironically and sarcastically using the generic singular "rock." The gods the people have chosen are mere pebbles, in contrast to YHWH, the omnipotent and perfectly just Rock (v. 4). In verse 38 the mockery turns to idols themselves. Recognizing the importance of keeping gods satisfied, YHWH challenges the gods they have chosen to come to their aid by asking where the gods who accepted their devotees' sacrifices and libations are. The triad of action verbs reinforces the sarcasm: "Let them rise up and help you; let them be your protection." These expressions all play on the reference to the gods as "rock" in verse 37.

The unparalleled heaping up of attention-grabbing expressions in verse 39 signals the climax—"See! Now! Note! I! I am he!"[70]—and focuses hearers' attention on YHWH, who declares self-assuredly, "There is no God beside me." Whether we interpret *'immādî* as "with me" or "besides me," he alone controls the events of history; no one shares status or rank with him.[71] The remainder of verse 39 and verses 40–42 elaborate on YHWH's exclusive control over the fates and fortunes of human beings. If Israel has suffered, this has indeed been the work of YHWH, but the switch to an imperfect verb turns this statement into a promise: YHWH will certainly heal (*'erpâ*) his people. The last line of verse 39 emphasizes that when he acts on Israel's behalf, no outside power—neither divine nor human—can stop him.

The final strophe (vv. 40–42) seals Israel's future. With a dramatic non-verbal gesture and an emphatic verbal declaration, YHWH assures Israel that he will deal with their enemies once and for all. The idiom "to lift the hand to heaven," followed by the oath formula, suggests a legal gesture of raising the hand in association with swearing an oath.[72] By adding "forever" to the oath (*ḥay 'ānōkî lě'ōlām*) the certainty of YHWH's defeat of the enemy equals that of his oath to Abraham in Genesis 22:16.

Verses 41 and 42 reinforce the substance of the divinely sworn affidavit, beginning with a reference to the context: when YHWH, the divine warrior, prepares his weapons for battle. The first line speaks literally of sharpening "the lightning of my sword." But YHWH's weapons of war are also weapons of judg-

---

70. *rě'û 'attâ kî 'ănî hû'*. Cf. 1 Chron 28:10, *rě'ēh 'attâ kî*, "See! Now! Note!"
71. The use of *'ănî hû*, "I [alone] am he," in Isaiah confirms this: Isa. 41:4; 43:9–13; 43:25; 46:3–4; 48:12; 51:12; 52:6.
72. For further attestation and bibliography of the idiom, see Block, *Deuteronomy*, 766.

ment. Alluding back to verse 35, YHWH declares that he will repay his enemies, personally wielding the sword he had placed in the hands of Israel's enemies (v. 25). In verse 42 the picture turns grotesque, portraying YHWH's sword and arrows as carnivorous beasts that cannot get enough of human blood and human flesh.[73]

Israel's anthem ends on a festive note, with a coda appealing to the nations and the host of heaven to join in the celebration of YHWH's gracious acts on behalf of Israel (v. 43). The reading is problematic, and scholars disagree in their assessment of the textual evidence for this verse, but the arguments for the eight-line reading of LXX are persuasive and serve as the base for our comments:[74]

> Rejoice, O heavens with him,
> and bow down to him, all sons of God.
> Rejoice, O nations, with his people.
> And let all the messengers of God strengthen themselves.
> See, the blood of his sons he will avenge;
> and avenge and take vengeance on his enemies.
> He will pay back those who hate him,
> and atone for the land of his people.

The switch from first person forms in verse 42 to third person in verse 43 signals a shift in speaker from YHWH (vv. 37–42) to the poet. Lexical features keep the attention focused squarely on YHWH.[75] The way the coda refers to Israel reinforces this interpretation. Given the complete collapse of the relationship between deity and nation in verses 15–25, that the nation should be referred to as "his sons" (*bānāyw*)[76] and "his people" (*ʿammô*) alone is cause for celebration, for it declares that the promise of verse 36a–b has been fulfilled.

The first four lines focus on the addressees, which consist of two categories: the heavenly host, identified as "the heavens" (*haššāmayim*), "all sons of God"

---

73. While the notion of arrows drinking occurs only here, the image of a sword devouring its victims is common in the Old Testament (2 Sam. 2:26; 11:25; Isa. 1:20; 34:5–6; Jer. 46:10; etc.), and elsewhere (*ANET*, 540, ll. 635–36).

74. For discussion of and bibliography on the complex text-critical issues involved, see Block, "Song of Power," 184, and "Excursus B: Text-Critical Issues in Deuteronomy 32:43," 185–88.

75. The object of praise is not named, but YHWH is referred to at least twelve times, eight explicitly by means of pronominal suffixes on nouns, and four implicitly in third-person singular verbs, to which we should add the phrases, "sons of *God*," and "messengers of *God*."

76. MT reads *ʿăbādāyw*, "his servants," as in verse 36.

(*kol běnê 'ělōhîm*), and "envoys of God" (*mal'akê 'elōhîm*), on the one hand, and the "nations" (*gôyim*), on the other. The last reference is especially significant, for it has the nations celebrating together *with* (*'et*) "his people." Apparently this indicates the realization of YHWH's goal declared in 26:19, "He will set you high above all nations that he has made, for [his] praise, fame, and honor, and that you might be a people holy to YHWH your God, as he promised."

The last four lines shift the focus from the celebrants to the targets and beneficiaries of YHWH's action. The middle pair of four lines arranged chiastically echo verse 41c–d and function as a shorthand expression for YHWH's fuller declaration of his defeat of his adversaries in verses 39–42. The statement is remarkable, for Israel's enemies have become YHWH's adversaries. The outside lines identify the beneficiaries of YHWH's actions. To be sure YHWH will defeat his enemies, but in doing so he will avenge the blood of his sons and make atonement for his land and his people.[77] The need for the land's atonement was created by human blood violently shed (Num. 35:30–34) and unburied corpses (Deut. 21:23) that defile the land—the effects of the slaughter of the Israelites (32:43c; cf. 25).

Viewed as a whole, verse 43 presents the hosts of heaven and the nations with three reasons to celebrate and pay homage to YHWH: (1) YHWH has restored his relationship with Israel; (2) YHWH has taken vengeance on Israel's (and his own) enemies; (3) YHWH has made atonement for the land. In so doing he has reversed the earlier dissolution of the tripartite relationship involving deity-nation-people that was precipitated by Israel's idolatry. This is cause for celebration not only by the Israelite beneficiaries of the divine action—as in this song—but also by the hosts of heaven and the nations; indeed, the entire universe rejoices.

CONCLUSION

On this magnificent note we reach the climax of Deuteronomy's eschatological vision. The remarkable correspondence between Moses's anticipation of Israel's immediate future and the way events actually transpired up to the fall of Judah to Babylon gives readers confidence that the nation's ultimate destiny following the judgment will also follow the basic contours that the book establishes. Rooted in the covenant that YHWH made with Abraham (Gen. 15, 17), established with their descendants at Horeb (Deut. 4:9–24), and confirmed with the

---

77. The verb *kipper*, "to atone for, to cleanse," occurs elsewhere in Deuteronomy only in 21:8.

present generation on the Plains of Moab (cf. 26:16–19; 29:10–13 [9–12]), the basic elements of Israel's eschatological hope were established. If the covenant secured the tripartite relationship involving YHWH, Israel, and the land he promised them, and if the nation's punishment involved the total disintegration of this triangular association, then the restoration must involve the reconstitution of this triangle. This would require the following critical elements: (1) the preservation of the physical seed of Abraham as an identifiable ethnic people, who would embody before the nations the transforming power of divine grace; (2) a change in YHWH's disposition so that he would look again on his people with compassion; (3) the return of Israel to the promised land.

Although many assume that the destruction of Judah and the deportation of its population in 586 BCE signaled the end of YHWH's covenant with Israel, and called for a new dispensation involving a spiritual people of God, this interpretation is unwarranted on several counts. First, as noted earlier, YHWH's covenant with Abraham and his descendants was repeatedly declared to be eternal, that is, irrevocable (*lĕ'ōlām*).[78] However, the same kind of language is used of the Israelite covenant.[79] Second, as Daniel recognizes in his penitential prayer (9:7–14), both the curse for persistent infidelity (Lev. 26:14–39; Deut. 28:15–68) and the promise of ultimate restoration (Lev. 26:40–45; Deut. 4:29–31; 30:1–10) were written into the covenant. YHWH would have betrayed his covenant if he had not abandoned his people and brought in first the Assyrians and then the Babylonians

---

78. The eternality of the covenant made with Abraham is highlighted repeatedly in the Patriarchal Narratives with expressions like *bĕrît 'ōlām* (Gen. 17:7, 13, 19; cf. 9:16) and assurances that specific promises have eternal force "to your seed forever" (*'ad 'ōlām*; Gen. 13:15; 17:8; 48:4; Exod. 32:13; Ps. 105:8–10; 1 Chron. 16:15).

79. Exod. 31:16–17 speaks of an eternal/irrevocable covenant for their generations (*lĕdōrōtām bĕrît 'ōlām*), with the seventh-day Sabbath functioning as a sign forever (*'ôt hî' lĕ'ōlām*); Lev. 24:8 characterizes the covenant established at Horeb as an "everlasting covenant" (*bĕrît 'ōlām*; so also Isa 24:4–5); in Judges 2:1 YHWH declares he will never break his covenant with Israel; Psalm 111:5 declares YHWH will remember his covenant forever (*lĕ'ōlām*; cf. also v. 9); in Isaiah 54:4–10, YHWH speaks of his eternal *hesed*, places his covenant with Israel in the same irrevocable category as the cosmic covenant, and declares that "my covenant of peace" (*bĕrît šĕlômî*) will never be removed; Jeremiah 31:35–37 declares that YHWH's commitment to Israel is as firm and irrevocable as the fixed order of the universe. Like the Isaiah text, here Jeremiah attaches the certainty of the cosmic order (as guaranteed in the cosmic covenant) to the Israelite covenant. Ezekiel characterizes YHWH's future "covenant of peace" (*bĕrît šālôm*) as an "eternal/irrevocable covenant" (*bĕrît 'ōlām*, 16:60; 37:26). This is the covenant that he remembers "from the days of your youth" (i.e., at Sinai), whose features in 34:25–30 deliberately echo the blessings built into the Israelite covenant in Lev. 26:4–13. For discussion, see Daniel I. Block, *The Book of Ezekiel Chapters 25–48*, NICOT (Grand Rapids: Eerdmans, 1998), 303–306.

to destroy what remained of Israel's attachment to the land. Third, in fulfillment of Jeremiah's prediction (2 Chron. 36:22–23; Ezra 1:1; cf. Jer. 25:12; 29:10), and in response to Daniel's prayer (Dan. 9:1–2, 20–23), the restoration of the remnant community in Jerusalem in the Persian era served as a deposit of Israel's ultimate full restoration.[80] However, this was only a partial (*mĕ'aṭ*) fulfillment; in contrast to the Mosaic and prophetic visions, (1) the population was small and numerable (Ezra 2; Neh. 7); (2) they occupied only a small portion of the promised land in the vicinity of Jerusalem; (3) although YHWH's blessing was on the community initially, his temple was a mere shadow of the original (Hag. 2).[81] Since this community represented only a fraction of the restoration celebrated in Deut. 32:43, and in any case would be totally destroyed again in 70 CE, this was not the fulfillment Moses and YHWH had in mind in Deuteronomy.

Even so, the irrevocable divine covenantal commitments remain (Rom. 9–11), and Paul looks forward to the day when "all Israel will be saved" and the ideals of his covenant will finally be realized. Although Paul's vision of Israel's future is refracted through the lens of Jeremiah 31:31–40, the roots of this hope were established centuries earlier in the Torah of Moses and in Israel's national anthem.

---

80. The prayer of confession in Nehemiah 9:5–37 is laced with references to the covenant and assesses the present circumstances of the post-exilic community in the light of the covenant.
81. Although not explicitly part of the Mosaic vision, the Davidic line was preserved, but the representative (Zerubbabel) was merely a governor, rather than a king ruling from David's throne.

THE DOCTRINE OF THE FUTURE
IN THE HISTORICAL BOOKS

Gregory Smith

A t first glance, one might not think to look into the Old Testament historical books (Joshua–Esther) for information regarding Israel's future. History, after all, focuses on the past and involves an author—the historian, who records the details of the past regarding people, places, and events. Students of the Bible know that biblical authors recorded more than just history. Biblical historians evaluated past events theologically, and did so in a way that addressed the issues of their day.[1] They evaluated the turning points of Israel's history such as the failed monarchy, the exilic experience, and the return from exile. Their evaluation addressed the theological concerns specific to their respective audiences.[2] For example, the pre-exilic Jews asked a different set of questions than the post-exilic Jews who returned to the land after the seventy years of Babylonian captivity. While both groups shared a common historical experience of the past, it is the unique differences in how this shared history is reported and evaluated for both the exilic and post-exilic communities that are of interest here. In fact, how some of those differences reveal the historian's concern for Israel's *future* will be discussed. Central to this historical concern is the Davidic covenant and its offer of hope for Israel's *distant future*.

---

1. For an excellent discussion of the relationship of history and theology in the biblical context, see Eugene H. Merrill, "Old Testament History: A Theological Perspective," in *The New International Dictionary of Old Testament Theology and Exegesis*, ed. Willem VanGemeren (Grand Rapids: Zondervan, 1999), 68–85.
2. For the purposes of our discussion, we will refer to the author of Samuel-Kings as the "Historian" and the author of 1–2 Chronicles as the "Chronicler." The Historian's purpose is the evaluation of the monarchy for the audience who is in exile. The Chronicler evaluates the same historical period, but for the group returning after seventy years in Babylon.

The way ahead first explores the broader contexts for both of the Bible's primary historical texts, Samuel-Kings and 1–2 Chronicles. Of particular interest is the Davidic covenant's relationship with the former promises of the Abrahamic and Mosaic covenants on the issue of conditionality.[3] David's personal response to Nathan's oracle will also be explored for the way that it addresses the past, present, and future. Of particular interest is the unique emphasis placed on the Davidic covenant and its promises for Israel's future.[4] The biblical historians understood that despite her failure, Israel's future was secured on the basis of divine promises made to and through Abraham, Moses, and David and would be ultimately realized in the restored Israel—Israel's *distant future*.

David's *Distant Future* in Its Historical Context

Israel's salvation history is intertwined with the themes of promise and fulfillment. On the backdrop of these promises is the reality of Israel's failed monarchy. This theme emerges as the center of gravity for the historical and theological evaluation found in the books of Joshua through Esther. Israel's early spiritual failure during this time is attributed to the pagan influence of unconquered nations (see Josh. 10:40–43; 11:16–23; 21:43–45; also Judg. 1:27–36).[5] Judges offers specific theological assessment and suggests that unconquered nations became the means of testing and refining Israel's covenant fidelity during the four-hundred-year settlement period (Judg. 2:21–23).[6] Judges also offers the first clue that Israel's monarchy will provide no immediate relief to the spiritual chaos recorded in the book (Judg.

---

3. The potential objection that the Hebrew term for "covenant" does not appear in the context of 2 Samuel 7 or 1 Chronicles 17 is easily solved. See discussion in Craig A. Blaising and Darrell L. Bock, *Progressive Dispensationalism* (Wheaton, IL: BridgePoint, 1993), 162–65; *1 Samuel–2 Kings*, ed. Tremper Longman and David E. Garland, The Expositor's Bible Commentary, vol. 3, rev. ed. (Grand Rapids: Zondervan, 2009), 397. See also Michael V. Fox, "*Ṭôb* as Covenant Terminology," *Bulletin of the American Schools of Oriental Research*, no. 209 (1973): 41–42.
4. The Davidic covenant and its promises have great implications for Israel's future. The epicenter of the debate concerns the issue of whether the covenant promises are fulfilled in Christ's present rule or in his future rule in the millennial kingdom. For an excellent overview of this topic, see John F. Walvoord, "The Fulfillment of the Davidic Covenant," *Bibliotheca Sacra* 102, no. 406 (1945): 156.
5. See an excellent summary of this scholarly discussion in Terrance A. Clarke, "Complete v. Incomplete Conquest: A Re-Examination of Three Passages in Joshua," *Tyndale Bulletin* 61, no. 1 (2010): 89–104; Daniel Isaac Block, *Judges, Ruth*, The New American Commentary, vol. 6 (Nashville: Broadman & Holman, 1999), 105–9.
6. See Gregory Smith, *The Testing of God's Sons: The Refining of Faith as a Biblical Theme* (Nashville: B&H Academic, 2014), 103, 125.

17:6; 21:25).[7] Moreover, it will be the wrong *kind* of king in Israel that will actually aggravate the problem—Israel's first king represents the antithesis of the *kind* of king Israel needs, in contrast to the king prescribed by Deuteronomy 17:14–20 (cf. 1 Sam. 8:1–22).[8] Out of the spiritual chaos created by Saul, God instructs Samuel to appoint David as Israel's first true earthly king. It is no surprise that *this* king, the one who sought after the very heart of God, responds with humility to the promises delivered by the prophet Nathan. In the central text of the covenant, David proclaims, "Who am I, O Lord God, and what is my house, that You have brought me this far? And yet this was insignificant in Your eyes, O Lord God, for You have spoken also of the house of Your servant concerning the *distant future*. And this is the custom of man, O Lord God" (2 Sam. 7:18–19, emphasis mine).[9]

Nathan's oracle to David constituted the center of gravity for the historical conversation regarding Israel's eschatological future. After King David, just a handful of Israel's kings receive positive evaluation in the historical assessment of Samuel-Kings. Aside from the few attempts at spiritual reform from kings such as Hezekiah and Josiah, the threat of religious syncretism finally takes over and robs Israel of her spiritual vitality. In response, Yahweh acts on covenant grounds against his own people. In 722 BCE, Israel becomes exiled at the hands of the Assyrians. Just over a century later, the Babylonians will destroy the city of Jerusalem and the temple of the Lord. While Israel's monarchy ends in dismal failure, is it possible that the unconditional covenant promises of God failed as well? What about David's acknowledgment of the "distant future" in response to the promises made to him? The preliminary answer is that Israel's future has everything to do with the promises of her past. While the prophetic books offer a more fully developed theology of this future, it is significant that Israel's historical books also contribute to this message of hope. In order to gain clarity on this historical perspective, it will be helpful first to explore the issue of conditionality in the covenantal promises that relate to the question of Israel's future. Any future for Israel must be understood in light of the nature of the promises that God has made to his people.

---

7. Block suggests that the author is already aware of the fractures in the monarchies of both northern and southern kingdoms based on the criteria of Deuteronomy 17:14–20. See Block, *Judges, Ruth*, 483.
8. Of course, at any time in her history, Israel's true king is God. Any earthly king, by Moses's description, should only be a conduit toward that reality. After 520 years of failure after failure, Israel's prophets will return emphasis to the covenantal idea of God as King.
9. All Scriptural references will be taken from the New American Standard Bible, unless otherwise noted.

CONDITIONALITY AND THE COVENANTS

The question of conditionality in the covenant promises is significant to the historical evaluation of Israel's failed monarchy and any question of a future monarchy in Israel. The scholarly discussion of the conditionality or unconditionality of Israel's covenant promises is expansive.[10] Recent discoveries into the types of covenants or treaties most common in the ancient world have informed the discussion. Most agree that biblical authors were influenced by these ancient covenant forms in their writing. First, the land grant represented just one category of unconditional covenant agreement in the ancient world.[11] Scholars assign the Abrahamic and Davidic covenants and Jeremiah's new covenant to this unconditional category.[12] Second, the suzerain-vassal treaty represented a conditional agreement between two covenant members in the ancient world.[13] Scholars typically assign the Mosaic covenant to this category.[14] The categories of conditional and unconditional that emerge from this discussion offer significant implications for Israel's failed monarchy, as well as any promised hope for the future, because future fulfillment is typically only thought of in terms of unconditionality. Covenant failure in both Israel (north) and Judah (south) included both king and kingdom.[15] Scholars recognize the difference in emphasis between the books of Samuel-Kings and 1–2 Chronicles in how this failure is presented.[16]

---

10. For an excellent evaluation of the current positions, see Walter C. Kaiser, "The Blessing of David: The Charter for Humanity," in *Law and the Prophets* (Phillipsburg, NJ: Presbyterian and Reformed Publishing, 1974), 305–8.
11. Bruce K. Waltke, "The Phenomenon of Conditionality within Unconditional Covenants," in *Israel's Apostasy and Restoration*, ed. Avraham Gileadi (Grand Rapids: Baker, 1988), 124. See also David Noel Freedman, "Divine Commitment and Human Obligation, the Covenant Theme," *Interpretation* 18, no. 4 (1964): 420; Michael A. Grisanti, "The Davidic Covenant," *Master's Seminary Journal* 10, no. 2 (1999): 234. For a full discussion on the concept of the land grant, see Moshe Weinfeld, "*Berît*—Covenant vs. Obligation," *Biblica* 56, no. 1 (1975): 120–28; Moshe Weinfeld, "The Covenant of Grant in the Old Testament and in the Ancient Near East," *Journal of the American Oriental Society* 90, no. 2 (1970): 184–203.
12. Grisanti, "The Davidic Covenant," 234.
13. Ibid., 235.
14. Weinfeld, "Covenant of Grant," 185.
15. Israel's kings are evaluated on the criteria of Deuteronomy 17:14–20. The breakdown in spiritual leadership from the top down leads to the religious syncretism that causes the slow fade over time. For example, 2 Kings 17:7–23 offers a spiritual evaluation of both Israel and Judah and reason for the exiles. The details of Judah's spiritual decay are expressed in the context of the reform efforts of King Josiah in 2 Kings 23:4-14.
16. Scholars disagree over the authorship of Kings. See Eugene H. Merrill, Mark F. Rooker, and Michael A. Grisanti, *The World and the Word: An Introduction to the Old Testament* (Nashville: B&H Academic, 2011), 324–25. Of course, the vantage point of each author and his

In 1–2 Chronicles, for example, large portions of the negative assessment of Israel's history included in Samuel-Kings is noticeably absent. The much brighter evaluation of Chronicles includes a special interest in the Davidic covenant and its future focus.[17] On this point, Gary Knoppers comments regarding the Chronicler, "His composition results in a much tidier, optimistic, and flattering account of Israel's experience under David than that offered in Samuel-Kings."[18] However, on the conditional promises that defined Israel's national status at Sinai, and on the eve of Israel's national failure, how can such historical optimism be justified? Against the general tendency to assign rigid conditionality or unconditionality to the covenant promises, some scholars recognize the fact that all of Israel's covenants share aspects of both. Their consensus is that even amidst Israel's failure and the conditional aspects of the Sinai covenant, the promises of both Abrahamic and Mosaic covenants cannot be annulled.[19] Bruce Waltke, for example, investigates the often overlooked aspects of conditionality within the category of grant and observes similar aspects of conditionality within the Abrahamic covenant.[20] Waltke concludes, "Through conditional on human obligations, YHWH's grants to the patriarchs are unilateral because they do not depend on Israel's pledge to fulfill obligations. The irrevocable oaths to the patriarchs, qualified to extend only to a loyal progeny, logically entails that YHWH must sovereignly and graciously elect Abraham's seed. Without these attributes and activity, the promises would fail."[21]

---

intended audience has shifted. For the author of Kings, the audience was exilic. For Chronicles, the audience was post-exilic. Knoppers recognizes that the Chronicler's "reworking of the Davidic promises was deliberate and carefully planned." See Gary N. Knoppers, "Changing History: Nathan's Oracle and the Structure of the Davidic Monarchy in Chronicles," in *Shai Le-Sarah Japhet* (Jerusalem: Bialik Institute, 2007), 103–8.

17. William Dumbrell points out that it is the end of the Hebrew canon, in Chronicles, that puts emphasis on the "second exodus theology of Isaiah 40–55" and the new covenant. He suggests that the Chronicler sets this eschatological hope, against the failed Ezra-Nehemiah reforms, in the future fulfillment of God's program for Israel implicitly found in the covenant at Sinai. See William J. Dumbrell, "The Prospect of Unconditionality in the Sinaitic Covenant," in *Israel's Apostasy and Restoration*, 142–43.

18. Knoppers, *Changing History*, 119. Knoppers suggests that the Chronicler's theological bias intended to support the new temple and the priests who served in it during the Second Temple period.

19. Bruce Waltke points out that David's failure, for example, comes immediately after the high point of Nathan's oracle, similar to Noah's failure placed immediately after the details of covenant in the context of Genesis 8. In both contexts, Waltke comments, "By this arrangement, he (the author) subtly instructs us that the beneficiaries' darkest crimes do not annul the covenants of divine commitment." See Waltke, "Phenomenon of Conditionality," 131.

20. See ibid., 128–30.

21. Ibid., 130.

Other scholars recognize the unconditional aspects of both Abrahamic and Mosaic covenants as they relate to the Davidic covenant. William Dumbrell identifies in the Sinai covenant a clear eschatological focus for Israel. He suggests that in contrast to Israel's failure to meet the demands of Sinai during the time of the monarchy, and in light of the failure of the Ezra-Nehemiah reforms, the Chronicler concludes with a message of hope on the future fulfillment of the promises made there. At Sinai, Dumbrell points out, unconditionality exists in the fact that divine commitment to Israel is made before the expectation of human response. First, Exodus 19 describes the salvation activity of the Lord with the image of an eagle carrying the nation away to safety (v. 4). Dumbrell observes that the conditional language of verse 5 refers not to the covenant stipulations soon to be announced at Sinai, but to the stipulations of the Abrahamic covenant previously enacted.[22] On this observation, the election language of Exodus 19:5—specifically, the Hebrew designation of "special treasure"—extends the promise made to Abraham's seed in Genesis 12:1–3 to the covenant community at Sinai. David recognizes the implications of this. His reference to the "distant future" builds on the extended promise that God has established a people for himself—forever (2 Sam. 7:19, 24).[23] Regarding Israel's designation as the "special treasure" of the Lord, Dumbrell explains that this status "not only indicates the fact of choice, but the implications of choice. Israel is now the Lord's 'royal property.'"[24] Israel's valued status as "special treasure" extends from the Lord's kingship—the fulfillment of this fact carries with it future implications for Israel. Israel's status will one day be on display before the nations of the world. The unconditionality of this declaration, combined with the fact of Yahweh as king, ensures the future preservation and final fulfillment of the status of "special treasure" for Israel.

---

22. Dumbrell ("Prospect of Unconditionality," 144) argues that until this point in the text, the only covenant that has been referred to is the Abrahamic covenant (Exod. 6:1–8). In addition, he observes that the phrase "keep my covenant" as used in the Hebrew Bible always occurs where human obedience is commanded in response to a divine commitment previously given (Gen. 17:9–10; 1 Kings 11:11; Ezek. 17:14; Pss. 78:10; 103:18; 132:12). See also Kaiser, "The Blessing of David," 307–8.

23. Dumbrell argues that God's election of Israel also has the world in view. On God's declaration of *special treasure,* Exodus 19:5 also affirms that this declaration is set in the affirmation that the entire cosmos is divine property (Exod. 19:5). See Dumbrell, "Prospect of Unconditionality," 146. The implication of this for Israel's future is that in *that* day, when God will rule as King, Israel will be on display as God's סגלה, "special treasure," for the entire world to see.

24. Ibid., 145. See excellent discussion of this term in Daniel Isaac Block, *How I Love Your Torah, O Lord!: Studies in the Book of Deuteronomy* (Eugene, OR: Cascade Books, 2011), 152–53; Daniel Isaac Block, *The Gospel According to Moses: Theological and Ethical Reflections on the Book of Deuteronomy* (Eugene, OR: Cascade Books, 2012), 245–46.

History demonstrates that against Israel's struggle to maintain this status remains the divine commitment to preserve it. Against the failure of Israel's human kings (highlighted in Samuel-Kings) and the shortcomings of the post-exilic community (highlighted in Ezra-Nehemiah) is found the contrasting hope for a future day when the Lord will fulfill his promises—this will be the Chronicler's eschatological emphasis. Dumbrell calls this the "eschatological goal" of Yahweh's redemption of Israel.[25] Dumbrell's observations raise the question of *when* in Israel's salvation history these unconditional promises will be fulfilled.

NATHAN'S ORACLE

These observations regarding the conditionality of the Abrahamic and Mosaic covenants together raise questions concerning the Davidic covenant. Against the failed monarchy (from the vantage point of the historian) how is it that the Davidic covenant can look back to these prior promises and establish hope for the anticipated future fulfillment of those same promises?[26] This will constitute the primary thrust of the discussion ahead.

For the exiles in Babylon, the historical reminders of the promises made to King David would have come as a breath of fresh air.[27] Nathan's oracle to David maintains the covenantal link to prior divine promises despite Israel's recent failure. Central to the covenant is the divine promise of the establishment of David's name (2 Sam. 7:9; 1 Chron. 17:8). This promise extends to David that which was first promised to Abraham (Gen. 12:2).[28] Included in the idea of "name" is the broader idea of one's reputation.[29] Thus, Yahweh commits to establish David's reputation above his enemies and amongst all the kings of the earth (2 Sam. 7:9b; 1 Chron. 17:8b). Similarly, Psalm 18:37–50 celebrates in

---

25. Dumbrell, "Prospect of Unconditionality," 146.
26. The vantage point of the historical books, Samuel-Kings, probably rests in the midst of the exiles in Babylon. Combined with the prophetic ministry of the prophet Ezekiel, these historical books served to remind the exiles of their sinful past, the reason for the exile, and in the case of the Davidic covenant, hope for the future.
27. The prophet Ezekiel returns to Nathan's oracle as a means of encouraging the faithful remnant (Ezek. 34:24; 37:24–28; Jer. 30:9; 33:14–26). Ezekiel's emphasis on the shepherd role for this returning Davidic king is also made the focus of praise (Ezek. 37:24; cf. Ps. 78:70–72).
28. For a summary of the scholarly debate, see Grisanti, "The Davidic Covenant," 237n17.
29. See Block, *No Other Gods*, 237–71. For example, the prophet Malachi raises concern for the profaning of the *name* of Yahweh in the way the post-exilic community abuses their privilege of bringing tithes and offerings to the temple. Thus, Yahweh's name and reputation amongst the nations is essentially linked to the corporate obedience of his people (Mal. 1:11–14; see also Isa. 12:4–5; Jer. 10:6–7; cf. Deut. 12:5).

song Yahweh's defeat of the enemies of David, and in response, David celebrates the name of Yahweh and declares, "I will give thanks to You among the nations, O Lord, and I will sing praises to Your name" (v. 49). In the immediate context, this promise comes on the eve of David's defeat of the Philistines and the return of the ark of the covenant to Jerusalem.[30] In response, David recognizes that it is not his name that will be made great, but the name of Yahweh (2 Sam. 7:23, 26). Thus, in the future—the *distant* future—Yahweh's name will be established among the nations through the establishment of the name of one from the line of David.

Yahweh also promises a place for his people to be planted and live in peace (2 Sam. 7:10; cf. 1 Chron. 17:9; Gen. 12:1b; 15:18; Deut. 11:22–32; Josh. 1:4ff.). While Abraham's promise of land was made unconditionally, Deuteronomy 11:22–24 attaches conditionality to Israel's remaining in the land as a function of their demonstrated obedience. Should Israel adopt the paganism practiced by those nations originally driven out, Yahweh claims his covenant obligation to also drive Israel out from that place (Deut. 28:63–65). Thus, the promise of exile establishes the potential for the experienced loss of both place and rest. During the reign of King David, Israel dwells in the land with relative security. The vantage point of the author, however, has seen the history of spiritual decay and failure. His audience is experiencing this loss of place in exile firsthand. As the faithful remnant emerges from exile, their anticipation will be for a *future* place. The Chronicler will bring hope for a future place to this post-exilic audience.

Related to this promise of place is the promise of rest from enemies (2 Sam. 7:11; see also 1 Chron. 17:10). While some suggest that this promise was fulfilled during the time of King David at his defeat of Israel's enemies, as reported in 2 Samuel 7:1ff., others have suggested that this promise must await fulfillment at some time in Israel's eschatological future.[31] On the direct relationship between place and rest more needs to be said as it relates to the future.

---

30. Another clear example of the establishment of David's *name* is in 2 Sam. 8:13 (cf. 1 Chron. 8:12; see also 1 Sam. 18:30) where David makes for himself a *name* upon his victory over his enemies. *Expositor's Bible Commentary*, 385.

31. The immediate fulfillment evident in Israel's history is the relative relief that David brings for Israel by subduing some of her enemies. This reverses the cycle of four hundred years of oppression at the hands of Israel's enemies during the period of the Judges. See ibid., 386; Grisanti, "The Davidic Covenant," 238; Dennis J. McCarthy, "2 Samuel 7 and the Structure of the Deuteronomic History," *Journal of Biblical Literature* 84, no. 2 (1965): 133; Wolfgang Roth, "Deuteronomic Rest Theology: A Redaction-Critical Study," *Biblical Research* 21 (1976): 8; R. P. Gordon, *1 & 2 Samuel: A Commentary* (Exeter: Paternoster, 1986), 74.

Future Implications of *Place* and *Rest*

Two significant implications for the Davidic covenant emerge from implications that relate to the relationship of place and rest. First, Israel's designation as *segulah* and the fulfillment of the implications of this designated status—kingdom *of priests* and a *holy nation*—will take place in a specific *future* place: the tabernacle at the time of the day of the Lord (cf. Zeph. 3:14–20; Ezek. 39:25–29; 47:1–12). Regarding this earthly tabernacle (temple), designed or patterned after the heavenly reality (Exod. 25:9), Dumbrell comments, "As a copy of the heavenly, the tabernacle seeks to replicate the heavenly dwelling. Put summarily, the tabernacle is the earthly palace of the heavenly king, and the gradations of approach within the tabernacle—the manner of its service, the vestments of its officials, etc.—all underscore this point."[32] It is significant that Exodus 25–31 and the details of the tabernacle fall in close proximity to Exodus 19:5–6 and the Lord's designation of Israel as his *segulah*. This suggests that Yahweh's primary means for preserving Israel's designated status as special treasure links to the tabernacle and its role in Israel. Regarding the eschatological significance of this link, Dumbrell comments, "Like Abram, Israel was called outside of the land that would be hers. Like Abram, Israel would be a great nation (*gôy*), occupying a 'promised land.' Like Abram, the world would find its sauce of blessing in this Israel. . . . The strand of covenant theology that began with Abram continues with Sinai. It will add kingship to its ambit with 2 Samuel 7. Its direct unconditionality, because it is divinely imposed and sustained, will emerge in Jeremiah 31:31–34."[33]

Thus, it is the Davidic covenant that anticipates the fulfillment of the promise of "place." The Lord proclaims in 2 Samuel 7:10, "I will also appoint a *place* for My people Israel and will plant them, that they may live in their own place and not be disturbed again, nor will the wicked afflict them any more as formerly" (emphasis mine, cf. 1 Chron. 17:9). The Lord's sovereign and unconditional divine concern for his *segulah* anticipates a future fulfillment (even amidst the failed monarchy and destroyed temple) and permeates the promises of Nathan's oracle. For example, the establishment of this future place for God's people also extends rest for the faithful. Dumbrell observes that this rest extends from God's rule as King and the proper response of

---

32. Dumbrell, "Prospect of Unconditionality," 149.
33. Ibid., 153.

the faithful remnant to that divine rule.[34] It is significant that the theological foundation for rest stems from the commands for the Sabbath day of rest set forth in Exodus 20:11 and the charge to maintain the Sabbath in Exodus 35:1–2. Each of these commands resides in the context of the temple building instructions for Israel. This relationship of rest and tabernacle also stems from the completion of God's creation activity and his divine resting on the seventh day (Gen. 2:1–3). Genesis establishes the fact of God as both Creator and King, sitting on his throne at the completion of his work and sovereignly ruling over all that he has made—this is the picture of rest (v. 4). Thus, *future* rest for the faithful remnant extends from the Lord's divine rule as King and the establishment of his kingdom. Not surprisingly, this idea emerges as a central theme in the Davidic covenant. David recognizes the unconditionality of this promise and its relationship with Israel's declared status as the special treasure of Yahweh in 1 Chronicles 17:22, "For Your people Israel You made Your own people forever, and You, O LORD, became their God." Thus, the Sinai covenant and its unconditionality establish the foundation for David's confidence in a future for the nation.[35]

Nathan's oracle continues to declare that the Lord will make David a house (2 Sam. 7:11b). Scholars question whether this promise anticipates the house of God and the idea of a future temple, or if Nathan's promise relates to the future dynasty of King David. The immediate context of the promise suggests the idea of dynasty on two points. First, the terms "house" and "kingdom" are juxtaposed in verse 16, "And your *house* and your *kingdom* shall endure before Me forever; your throne shall be established forever" (emphasis mine). Second, the context of the promise qualifies its duration as a "forever" house (v. 16), and again in David's request that Yahweh confirm and bless his house "forever" (v. 25, 29). David acknowledges that the fulfillment of the promise of this house must be in the "distant future" (v. 19).[36] Thus, while the immediate house of verse 13 suggests the temple to be built by a son of David, verse 11b suggests that it will be Yahweh himself who builds this future "forever" house for David. The combination of this house, located at a

---

34. Ibid., 150. Zephaniah 3:13–17 portrays promised rest to the remnant on the Day of the Lord as an extension of his rule as King. On that day, the reality of this fact will be a focus of great rejoicing (v. 14; see also Isa. 11:1–11; 2 Sam. 7:7; Ps. 78:71).

35. See Roth, "Deuteronomic Rest Theology: A Redaction-Critical Study," 8–9, 14. See also *Expositor's Bible Commentary*, 386; Kaiser, "The Blessing of David," 304–5.

36. Grisanti, "The Davidic Covenant," 239.

particular place and at a particular time in the future, will have tremendous implications for Israel's future in the discussion ahead.[37]

Nathan's oracle also extends a future for David's dynasty through the promise of a perpetual descendant or "seed" (v. 12).[38] The scholarly discussion on the idea of "seed" focuses on the question of whether the term refers to the coming Messiah (singular), or to the entire Davidic line that extends to the future Messiah (plural). This second option finds support in other contexts that link "seed" to the entire Davidic line, such as Psalms 89:4, "I will establish your seed forever and build up your throne to all generations" (see also Ps. 89:29, 36). The close proximity of "seed," "house," and "kingdom" in 1 Samuel 7:11–12 also supports this interpretation. In addition, it is one from this seed who will build the house, and it is to him that the Lord promises to establish an "eternal kingdom" (v. 13).[39] While these texts connect the Davidic dynasty to the plural sense of the term "seed," it is Paul who makes the point in Galatians 3:16, 29 that Christ fulfills the promised "seed" in its singular sense. Thus, there is a sense that both are true with regards to future fulfillment.[40]

Finally, Nathan's oracle extends the fullness of covenant relationship to David. The language of suzerain/vassal relationship permeates the promise of 2 Samuel 7:14, "I will be a father to him and he will be a son to Me" (cf. Exod. 4:22).[41] The grace of covenant relationship extends indefinitely to David in the future (2 Sam. 7:15) and is reaffirmed in the forever promise of an enduring house, kingdom and throne (v. 16). In his prayerful response, David recognizes the future implications of these promises for both himself and the faithful remnant of God on the foundation of what Yahweh declared to Israel at Sinai (v. 23). David recognizes Israel's unique role as the center of his salvific activity, and thus the Lord's showcase to the nations. David's words in verse 24 suggest that Israel's status as special treasure, first expressed at Sinai, will also find future fulfillment. He makes this clear

---

37. See William J. Dumbrell, "The Davidic Covenant," *Reformed Theological Review* 39, no. 2 (1980): 40; 46–47; *Expositor's Bible Commentary*, 386.
38. Cf. Gen. 17:7, 8, 9, 10, 19; 13:15; 24:7 all refer to "seed" and not "seeds." See *Expositor's Bible Commentary*, 387.
39. While the idea of the monarchy in Israel was anticipated in earlier texts (cf. Gen. 17:6, 16; 35:11), the basic idea that Israel's king would not replace Yahweh as king was also early (cf. Deut. 17:14–20; see also 1 Chron. 28:5; 2 Chron. 9:8; 13:8). Other texts will suggest that the future Davidic king as the "Lord's anointed" (1 Sam. 24:6; 2 Sam. 19:21) or with reference to the "horn of His anointed" (1 Sam. 2:10; 1 Sam. 16:13; Ps. 89:24; 132:17; Ezek. 29:21). See ibid., 384ff.
40. Grisanti, "The Davidic Covenant," 239.
41. Ibid., 241n40.

in his acknowledgement of the full implications of Nathan's oracle, "For You have established for Yourself Your people Israel as Your own people forever, and You, O LORD, have become their God" (v. 24; cf. Exod. 19:1–5).[42] The Davidic covenant establishes a clear message, that despite present circumstances, the Lord has not completely fulfilled all that he has promised.

DAVID'S RESPONSE TO THE ORACLE

David responds to the oracle with a focus on the present (vv. 18–21; 1 Chron. 17:16–19). David's acknowledgement of Yahweh as "sovereign" five times in this context parallels Abraham's similar acknowledgement in Genesis 15:2, 8. Clearly, David sees his role as king as a vassal of Yahweh and addresses himself as the "servant" of Yahweh ten times in this context.[43] David's question, "Who am I, O Lord God, and what is my house, that You have brought me this far?" has clear covenantal implications (v. 18b). David's immediate acknowledgement addresses his own question—whatever Yahweh has done thus far is small in comparison to the anticipated "more" that will come in the distant future (v. 19).[44] The Chronicler's version of this same verse in 1 Chronicles 17:17 adds additional emphasis to the future implications of the Davidic covenant. Consistent with his strategy of highlighting the positive aspects of the history already told in Samuel-Kings, the Chronicler adds an additional word to his account not found in 2 Samuel 7:19.[45] The Chronicler writes, "And this was a small thing in your eyes, O God; but You have spoken about Your servant's house regarding a

---

42. God also promised that he would be Israel's God and that they would be to him a people (2 Sam. 7:23, 24; cf. Gen. 17:7, 8; 28:21; Exod. 6:7; 29:45; Lev. 11:45; 22:33; 25:38; 26:12, 44, 45; Num. 15:41; Deut. 4:20; 29:12–13). This builds on the unconditional declaration at Sinai. See *Expositor's Bible Commentary*, 395–96. There will be a day, a future day, when Israel will be the "kingdom of priests" and the "royal nation" that God had always intended them to be. This may have an eschatological fulfillment in those prophetic texts that suggest that the nations will come to Zion to see Israel as a showcase to the world.

43. See Fox, "*Tôb* as Covenant Terminology," 41–42; Abraham Malamat, "Organs of Statecraft in the Israelite Monarchy," *Biblical Archaeologist* 28, no. 2 (1965): 64; *Expositor's Bible Commentary*, 397.

44. *Expositor's Bible Commentary*, 395. Kaiser suggests that David's full awareness of the Messianic implications of Nathan's oracle should be captured in the stronger translation "charter of humanity" for 2 Samuel 7:19 and 1 Chronicles 17:17. The strength of this implication is also found in David's reflection in 2 Samuel 23:2–5 and Psalm 110. See Kaiser, "The Blessing of David," 318; Dumbrell, "The Davidic Covenant," 46.

45. Eugene Merrill recognizes both the David covenant and the temple as major themes of the Chronicler. See Merrill, Rooker, and Grisanti, *The World and the Word*, 339–41.

distant future, and You see me as a charter for humanity, the ascent, O LORD God (1 Chron. 17:17; cf. 2 Sam. 7:19, Translation mine)."[46] The Chronicler adds the word המעלה, "the ascent," to his edition of 2 Samuel 7:19. Regarding the possibility of a textual variant, no clear scholarly consensus has emerged.[47] Scholars follow the general rule that the Masoretic text offers the best solution and that textual variants, in some cases, can emerge to reflect the author's theological intentions.[48] In the case of the Chronicler, the additional Hebrew term המעלה, "the ascent," is not beyond his overall strategy of omitting the negative and even adding positive aspects of Israel's history for the overall purpose of amplifying good news for the returned exiles.[49] Thus, the Chronicler's theological

---

46. Kaiser evaluates the interpretive options for the Hebrew term, תורה, and argues that the "this" of 2 Samuel 7:19 "refers to the content of the promise, more specifically, the 'seed' of Abraham, Israel, and David, which is to live and reign forever and be the Lord's channel of blessing to all the nations of the earth, the law in this context is a principle by which all mankind is to be blessed." He suggests the translation "charter" of humanity for the idea in context. See Kaiser, "The Blessing of David," 314. Regarding the root, מעלה, English translations range from "future generations" (ESV), "the most exalted" (NIV), "high degree" (NASB) and "high rank" (NRSV). 2 Samuel 7:19 does not have this term. With the definite article, this feminine singular noun is most commonly used in the sense of the stairs of the temple (for example, Ezek. 40:6), but also serves to designate the "ascent" to the Pilgrim feasts and the songs to be sung by the pilgrims as they journey to Jerusalem (for example, the Psalms of Ascent, Pss. 120–134; 84:6). This sense of מעלה as "ascent" best fits the theological context and agenda of the Chronicler. See also BDB, 752. Our translation understands the term המעלה functioning syntactically as a nominative absolute, where the idea of "the ascent" offers the comment or explanation for the pronoun זאת.

47. S. R. Driver concludes that no "satisfactory emendation of the passage has been proposed." See S. R. Driver, *Notes on the Hebrew Text and the Topography of the Books of Samuel: With an Introduction on Hebrew Palaeography and the Ancient Versions and Facsimiles of Inscriptions and Maps*, 2d ed. (Oxford: Clarendon Press, 1913), 277. Sara Japhet points out the syntactical and interpretive challenges of verse 17 and comments, "It would seem that in spite of all difficulties, the text may be understood basically as it stands, as reflected by the literal translations of NEB, 'and now thou lookest upon me as a man already embarked on a high career', or JPS, 'you regard me as a man of distinction'." See Sara Japhet, *I & Ii Chronicles: A Commentary*, 1st American ed., The Old Testament Library (Louisville: Westminster/John Knox Press, 1993), 339. In other contexts, this term describes both a "step" and is the term translated "ascent" for each of the Psalms of Ascent (Ps. 120–134). See *Expositor's Bible Commentary*, 398. With regards to the translation of the Hebrew המעלה, Kaiser suggests that it be translated as an attributive adjective with the basic idea of "bringing up" or "raising," following the same idea in the context of Ezekiel 19:3. See Kaiser, "The Blessing of David," 316. See also Gary N. Knoppers, *I Chronicles: A New Translation with Introduction and Commentary*, 1st ed., The Anchor Bible, vol. 12–12A (New York: Doubleday, 2004), 678.

48. Socrates also referenced the divine *logos*, which he saw as the rational ordering principle of the cosmos, and even spoke of it as the means by which God worked in the universe. Other Greek philosophers argued that the gods of the pantheon really represented different facets of the one true God.

49. The classic example of the Chronicler's omission is his avoidance of the event of David and

reason for omitting the second half of the Cyrus decree in 2 Chronicles 36:23 shares the same theological reason for adding the term המעלה in 1 Chronicles 17:17—both the omission and the addition of the Chronicler in this case focus on the same Hebrew root, עלה, "to go up."[50] Scholars recognize the Chronicler's overall program of encouragement for the returned exiles.[51] It is significant that the Chronicler leaves behind his most significant word of encouragement in the very last word of the Hebrew canon![52] In his intentionally shorter version of the Cyrus decree, he writes, "Thus says Cyrus king of Persia, 'The LORD, the God of heaven, has given me all the kingdoms of the earth, and He has appointed me to build Him a house in Jerusalem, which is in Judah. Whoever there is among you of all His people, may the LORD his God be with him, and *let him go up!*'" (2 Chron. 36:23, emphasis mine).

Here, the very last word of the Hebrew canon links back to the very place where the promise of David's *future* house was first made—the promise of 1 Chronicles 17:17 offers the object or event to which 2 Chronicles 36:23 issues the invitation. As was observed, 1 Chronicles 17:17 reveals David's response to the long-reaching implications of Nathan's oracle—the *future* fulfillment of the

---

Bathsheba—2 Samuel 11:1 and 1 Chronicles 20:1 begin the same, but the Chronicler omits the entire section that focuses on David and Bathsheba (2 Sam. 11:2–12:30). The sense is that the Chronicler is not repeating "bad news" for the Babylonian exiles, who need not a reminder of the past, but hope and encouragement for the future.

50. Second Chronicles 36:23 ends with the *waw* + *Qal* Imperfect 3ms (jussive) from the root עלה. First Chronicles 17:17 includes the Hebrew feminine singular noun form, מעלה, built from this same Hebrew root עלה. Michael Avioz assigns some of the differences between 2 Samuel 7 and 1 Chronicles 17 to the Chronicler's work to revise, shorten and even expand the sources he used according to his own theological agenda. See Michael Avioz, "Nathan's Prophecy in II Sam. 7 and in I Chron. 17: Text, Context, and Meaning," *Zeitschrift für die alttestamentliche Wissenschaft* 116, no. 4 (2004).

51. Eugene Merrill develops the idea of Israel's future restoration in the second exodus or pilgrimage to Zion. He identifies the psalms that focus on King David's returning of the ark to Zion as: Psalms 46, 48, 76, 84, 87, 122. Psalms 84 and 122 served as encouragement for the exiles in their pilgrimage from Babylon back to Zion. Merrill points out, particularly, the language of Psalm 122:4 and the language of "go up" that refers to the journey to Zion. See Eugene H. Merrill, "Pilgrimage and Procession: Motifs of Israel's Return," in *Israel's Apostasy and Restoration*, 264–65.

52. Stephen Dempster makes the excellent observation that Israel's exile continues even after she has returned to the land, thus, the exile will not end until the Messiah comes. He comments, "Thus Chronicles concludes with the urging an exiled Judah to return home and build the temple, this temple that will one day stand at the centre of world geography and be located on the highest mountain, this temple that is inextricably tied to the dynasty of David." See Stephen G. Dempster, *Dominion and Dynasty: A Biblical Theology of the Hebrew Bible*, New Studies in Biblical Theology, vol. 15, ed. D. A. Carson (Downers Grove, IL: InterVarsity, 2003), 224–25.

promised house for one from the line of David. However, the Chronicler's reference to the Cyrus decree leaves out the text that focuses on the immediate house rebuilt by the post-exilic community. Thus, it is the Chronicler's strategy that focuses attention away from the post-exilic house and onto yet another house—a *future* house for a *future* Davidic king.[53] He does this by bringing attention back to the original Davidic promise. For the Chronicler, the invitation "let him go up" directs Israel's future Davidic king and Israel's future faithful remnant to participate in the activities surrounding this future house. This promised future house is prominently featured in the context of the Davidic covenant and David's response (2 Sam. 7:11, 19; cf. 1 Chron. 17:10, 17). For the Chronicler, God's intentions for his faithful remnant will find future fulfillment and will not end with the temple of the post-exilic period. In the future, there will be something far greater![54]

David's emphasis on the greatness of God and his future work is brought out in 2 Samuel 7:22–24 as he reflects on God's greatness, or incomparability, in the events of Israel's past. David's prayer echoes Hannah's prayer in its description of the incomparability of the Lord (v. 22; cf. 1 Sam. 2:2).[55] David further extends the theme of the incomparability of Yahweh to the demonstration of God's redemption of Israel out of Egypt (v. 23; cf. Deut. 7:8; 9:26; 13:5; 15:15; 21:8; 24:18; Neh. 1:10; Jer. 31:11), the establishment of his name amongst his people (v. 23), and the accomplishment of great and awesome things for the land and people (v. 23; cf. Deut. 10:21; 7:21; 10:17; Neh. 9:32; Ps. 99:3; 106:22; 145:6; Dan. 9:4; Joel 2:31).[56] In a climactic fashion, David grounds the incomparability of Nathan's present oracle to Israel's defining moment at Mount Sinai, where he acknowledges that it was there that God established Israel as his people "forever" (v. 24). The former promise of "I will be your God and you will

---

53. We find this same perspective in the prophet Haggai. After his rebuke of the stalled efforts and rebuilding (Hag. 1:2–15), Haggai encourages the builders to continue their efforts, not because their temple will in any way outdo the grandeur of Solomon's temple, but because their temple reflects the eternal reality of the temple that is yet to come (Hag. 2:1–9; cf. Exod. 25:8–9; Heb. 8:5). Thus, both Haggai and the Chronicler offer this same voice of encouragement, that is, it is not about *this* temple, but about the one yet to come.

54. *Expositor's Bible Commentary*, 396. On this future emphasis, Dumbrell comments, "Davidic kingship proved to be a political disappointment. It disappeared with the exile and the post-exilic attempts at its revival were desultory. But 2 Sam. 7 had clearly laid bare the shape of the future, realizable only as the case proved, under 'great David's greater Son.'" Dumbrell, "The Davidic Covenant," 47.

55. *Expositor's Bible Commentary*, 396.

56. Ibid.

be my people" is now transformed into the firm declaration for Israel's future, "You, O LORD, have become their God" (v. 24; cf. Gen. 17:7–8; 28:21; Exod. 6:7; 29:45; Lev. 11:45; 22:33; 25:38; 26:12, 45; Num. 15:41; Deut. 26:17; 29:13).[57]

Finally, David focuses on the future implications of Nathan's oracle (cf. 2 Sam. 7:25-29). This emphasis on the future builds on the establishment of the people of God "forever" (v. 24) and the establishment of the Davidic dynasty "forever" (v. 25, 26, 29 [2x]; also v. 13). David recognizes the permanence of these promises in the fact that these *words* were *spoken* and *promised* by the LORD (vv. 25, 28, 29).[58] Thus, the future establishment of David's house extends from the recognition of the great *name* of Yahweh (v. 26; cf. v. 16).[59] Additional covenant emphasis stems from the multiple references of David as "servant" (vv. 25, 26, 27[2x], 28, 29) and the affirmation of the *good* that will come to David through his servant role (v. 28).[60] This covenant good extends forever as a blessing to the Davidic king.[61]

IMPLICATIONS: THE VANTAGE POINT OF THE CHRONICLER

While the books of Samuel-Kings develop the theme of the failed monarchy, the question raised by Judges 21:25 (cf. 17:6; 18:1; 19:1) regarding the *kind* of king that would bring rest for the nation has finally been addressed—only a future Davidic king will emerge and establish a kingdom (and temple) out of the chaos. As was previously discussed, it is the Chronicler who brings a unique emphasis to Israel's future as it relates to king, kingdom, and temple. Like the books of Samuel-Kings, Ezra and Nehemiah illustrate the spiritual

---

57. Ibid., 397. See also Avraham Gileadi, "The Davidic Covenant: A Theological Basis for Corporate Protection," in *Israel's Apostasy and Restoration*, 160.

58. *Expositor's Bible Commentary*, 397. See also 1 Kings 6:12; 8:24–26. The Hebrew דבר is often used to convey the sense of "promise."

59. Here is the idea of "Let him go up" as an invitation to this future Davidic king. He is the one who will sit on that throne and rule. It is incredible to think that David may very well be recognizing the answer to his own question, "Who am I?" with the acknowledgement that *he* is the one who will sit on that throne.

60. *Expositor's Bible Commentary*, 397.

61. The emphasis on "bless" in verse 29 (3x) connects with the promise to Abraham that all the nations of the earth would be blessed through him. Could this be the fulfilling of this promise in the extension of healing to the nations? For a fuller discussion of "good" in the context of covenant relationship, see Smith, *Testing of God's Sons*, 78–84.

decline that begins for the returned exiles. The Chronicler, however, reveals hints of an eschatological concern in his historical recasting of Israel's history. William Dumbrell, for example, recognizes that the end of the Hebrew cannon, which closes with the Cyrus decree and its emphasis on the temple rebuilding, also anticipates a future and second exodus "return" and new covenant for Israel.[62] As we have already pointed out, this emphasis comes with the very last word. On this point, the Chronicler's invitation to "go up" echoes the prophetic voice of Isaiah 2:3,

> And many peoples will come and say,
> "Come, *let us go up* to the mountain of the LORD,
> *to the house* of the God of Jacob;
> That He may teach us concerning His ways
> And that we may walk in His paths."
> For the law will go forth from Zion
> And the word of the LORD from Jerusalem (emphasis mine, cf. Mic 4:2; Jer 31:6).

David's questions, "Who am I?" and "What is this house?" in 2 Samuel 7:18 (cf. 1 Chron. 17:16) are thus answered by the Chronicler. By adding the word, המעלה, "the ascent" in 1 Chronicles 17:17, the Chronicler brings attention to the invitation "Let him go up" and the location of *where* the faithful are to journey—it is to the house of the Lord promised in the Davidic covenant (2 Chron. 36:23b; 1 Chron. 17:7; cf. Isa. 2:3; Mic. 4:2). With this emphasis, the Chronicler encourages his post-exilic audience with a view to their future (2 Sam. 7:19; 1 Chron. 17:17). This future will occur regardless of any earthly king or dynasty, as it anticipates the time when God will again rule as King and establish peace for his people.[63] The Chronicler's last word redirects Israel's attention beyond the Cyrus decree and its immediate agenda—the

---

62. Dumbrell, "Prospect of Unconditionality," 143.
63. William J. Dumbrell, "The Purpose of the Books of Chronicles," *Journal of the Evangelical Theological Society* 27, no. 3 (1984): 265-66. This same emphasis was shared by the seventh-century prophets Nahum, Habakkuk, and Zephaniah, by the absence of a clearly developed messianic focus. In light of the failed kings, such as Manasseh, these prophets looked forward to the day when God would return and rule as King (e.g. Zeph. 3:8–11, 14–20; Hab. 3:1–7). See O. Palmer Robertson, *The Books of Nahum, Habakkuk, and Zephaniah*, New International Commentary on the Old Testament (Grand Rapids: Eerdmans, 1990), 17–20.

rebuilt temple—onto what God has promised for Israel's future. Dumbrell concludes, "It is thus the burden of the Chronicler that the disappointments of the postexilic period must not be permitted to cloud the hopes that the prophetic movement of the exilic and postexilic periods had promoted. God would never withdraw from his Abrahamic commitments. Once again the promised land would be Israel's. The kingdom of God would come, and the theocracy would be established."[64]

Not *this* house, says the Chronicler, but a *future* house, where the promises to God's "special treasure," his "kingdom of priests" and "holy nation," would fully be realized (Exod. 19:4–5). Here, we find the Chronicler's last word as a clear invitation for faithful Israel to return and ascend to Zion—not this temple, but the future temple, not this king, but the future king—to a restored Jerusalem, where God would again rule over his people.[65]

Conclusions and Implications for Future Israel

The Davidic covenant anticipates a coming king who will one day, in a distant future, establish his temple, throne, and rule over his people and extend blessing to the nations.[66] Even amidst the failed monarchy, the Chronicler places

---

64. Dumbrell, "The Purpose of the Books of Chronicles," 266.
65. This invitation also invites the nations to Zion and the temple, where the LORD's healing will be extended to the nations, as fulfillment of the original promise of blessings to the nations through Abraham (Gen. 12:1–3). First, the prophet Jeremiah describes the restoration of God's people and announces for Yahweh, "For I will restore (lit. *cause to go up*) you to health, and I will heal you of your wounds" (Jer. 30:17). While one should not bring full theological import into a new context on the occurrence of a single term, it is worth noting here the proximity of the same Hebrew root with the idea of healing. Yahweh identifies himself as "healer" in Exodus 15:26, after turning the waters at Meribah. The divine activity of healing becomes evident in the prophetic texts such as Ezekiel 47 and Ezekiel's vision of the future temple. There, the water that is described as merely trickling from the south side of the temple becomes a river (v. 5), that also supplies life to trees on either side (v.7), and brings not only healing to the salt waters of the sea (v. 8), but also healing and life to all living things wherever the river goes (vv. 9–12). This same image of the temple is given more specific development in Revelations. There, as an extension of God himself, and the Lamb of God, sitting on the throne, the water that flows extends life and healing for the nations goes forth as an extension of the rule of God as King and in fulfillment of the promise made to Abraham (Rev. 22:1–2). On the point, the Chronicler also echoes the post-exilic prophets Zechariah and Haggai. Haggai will encourage the temple rebuilding on the fact that the future temple will involve the nations "going up" to participate in all that the LORD has for them (2:6–9; cf. Zech. 14:14, 16–21).
66. Psalm 72 assigns the unique role of the king as the mediator of covenant blessing to the

emphasis on the fact that what was promised to David is not fulfilled in the post-exilic temple and in any king who would sit on its throne. This fulfillment will take place in a future temple. His last word invites a very specific future king to "go up" and sit, rule, and establish his kingdom.

This emphasis of the Chronicler shares in the prophetic voice and the prophetic call to repentance and salvation.[67] For example, the prophets Micah and Isaiah repeat this open invitation in parallel passages that invite the faithful remnant to Zion and experience the promised restoration of the nations on the day of Yahweh. Micah 4:1–2 confidently proclaims, "And it will come about in the *last days* that the mountain of the house of the LORD will be established as the chief of the mountains. It will be raised above the hills, and the peoples will stream to it. Many nations will come and say, 'Come and *let us go up to the mountain of the LORD* and to the house of the God of Jacob, that He may teach us about His ways and that we may walk in in His paths.' For from Zion will go forth the law, even the word of the LORD from Jerusalem" (emphasis mine; see also Isaiah 2:2–4).[68]

---

nations. Craig Blaising recognizes the relationship between the Davidic and Abrahamic covenants on this point and comments, "On the one hand the Davidic covenant is *part* of the blessing of the Abrahamic covenant. A blessed king from the line of David is one way in which the promise to bless descendants of Abraham will manifest itself. On the other hand, the Davidic covenant provides the *means* by which the Abrahamic blessing will be fulfilled for all descendants. The blessings for the many will be mediated by the rulership of the one, the king." See Blaising and Bock, *Progressive Dispensationalism*, 166–68.

67. Eugene Merrill offers an excellent discussion that traces the theme of "pilgrimage to Zion" in the prophetic texts. For example, Amos addresses Israel's future restoration as a new exodus (Amos 9:7) that will involve a remnant that will be gathered from all the nations (9:9). Similarly, Hosea speaks of the LORD bringing his people back to the land (Hos. 2:18–19) and the remnant that will come from all destinations north (Assyria) and south (Egypt) (11:1). Micah speaks of the ascent to Zion (Mic. 4:1–8), the city of the coming king (v. 2), that also will involve a procession from all points on the earth (7:12–13). Jeremiah also speaks of the pilgrimage of the remnant of Israel and the nations to Zion (3:14–17). To the exiles, Ezekiel refers to the return to Jerusalem in terms of a new exodus (20:33–39). In contrast to this prophetic hope, Merrill points out that the post-exilic prophets Haggai and Zechariah did not regard their immediate situation as the fulfillment of this Zion expectation (see, for example, Hag. 1:7–8; Zech. 1:16–17; 2:8–13). Finally, Isaiah, more than any of the other prophets, brings together the two themes of pilgrimage and second exodus (see for example 11:1–16; 41:17–20; 42:14–17; 43:1–7; 51:9–11; 56:6–7). See Merrill, "Pilgrimage and Procession," 266–69. Delbert Hillers recognizes that the Hebrew verb, עלה, "go up," in Micah 4:2 is the common term used in pilgrimage to Jerusalem contexts (cf. Ps. 24:3; 122:4; Isa. 2:3; Jer. 31:6). See Delbert R. Hillers, Loren R. Fisher, and Paul D. Hanson, *Micah: A Commentary on the Book of the Prophet Micah*, Hermeneia (Philadelphia: Fortress, 1984), 50; John H. Walton, "Psalms: A Cantata about the Davidic Covenant," *Journal of the Evangelical Theological Society* 34, no. 1 (1991): 21–31.

68. The witness of the nations to God as ruler over his people is also found in Deut. 4:32–38;

This invitation announces the day of the Lord to the nations as well; they are invited to experience the benefits of this day at the house of the Lord promised in the Davidic covenant (Mic. 4:1; Isa. 2:2). At the house of the Lord, the nations will be streaming (Heb: נהר) up the mountain.[69] Thus, by *going up* to this mountain, Yahweh extends the blessings of covenant relationship as they receive the instruction of Torah (Mic. 4:2b; Isa. 2:3b). David recognizes the significance of the activity of this distant future as it relates to both his house, and the idea that it (the promise) is a custom (Heb. תורה=Torah) of humanity (2 Sam. 7:19; 2 Chron. 17:17).[70] Thus, the fulfillment of the Davidic covenant involves significant global implications. As an extension of the rule of the Lord, the nations will experience peace and rest (Mic. 4:3–5; Isa. 2:4). The Chronicler's last word encourages the future remnant, both Jew and Gentile, to wait on the Lord and wait for his day to come, where he will establish rule, extend blessing, offer healing to the nations, and restore peace to the faithful remnant.[71] No earthly king, dynasty, or temple built by human hands offers this kind of hope. Beyond any potential for human failure, these future promises are true and will happen because they are essentially linked to the very nature and character of God himself.

Israel's eschatological hope—David's *distant future*—rests in the fulfillment of God's promises to the remnant. As salvation history has shown, this remnant emerges out of the ruins of a failed monarchy and a post-exilic period that also saw Israel's spiritual decline. It is the combined Abrahamic and Mosaic covenant affirmations that set the agenda for this remnant to emerge—as a future eschatological reality.[72] Nathan's oracle to David acknowledges that

---

7:6–9; cf. 2 Sam. 7:23–25. This fulfillment also links to the prophetic concern for the "name" or reputation of Yahweh amongst the nations (Isa. 12:4–5; Jer. 10:6–7; Mal. 1:11–14; cf. Deut. 12:5).

69. Normal rivers flow downward in elevation. In this unusual scene, the river flows up the mountain, which brings emphasis to the human heart (and willful effort) involved in responding to the invitation to "go up." I thank my colleague, Steven James, the administrative and research assistant for Dr. Craig Blaising, for this insight.

70. See discussion in Kaiser, *The Blessing of David*, 313–14.

71. Dempster comments, "As the Jews make their way up to the temple, spurred on by the Psalms of Ascent (Pss. 120–134), the people from the nations will grab the hems of their robes, saying, 'Let us go with you, because we have heard that God is with you' (Zech. 8:23). The goal of the canon is clearly the great house of God, which is as inclusive as the globe." Dempster, *Dominion and Dynasty*, 227.

72. Walter Moberly recognizes the aspects of conditionality and unconditionality in the demonstrated faith of Abraham in light of the unconditional promises made to him. He comments, "Abraham by his obedience has not qualified to be the recipient of blessing, because the prom-

the fulfillment of these promises will come for the remnant in the *distant future*.[73] In alignment with the prophets, the Chronicler emphasizes that this fulfillment parallels the activity of the return to Zion. At Zion, the Davidic promise of rest will be experienced by a remnant, comprised of both Jew and Gentile, who will worship together, shoulder to shoulder, as the true "kingdom of priests" (2 Sam. 7:10; Exod. 19:6).[74] It is in the new heaven and new

---

ise of blessing had been given to him already. Rather, the existing promise is reaffirmed but its terms of reference are altered. A promise which previously was grounded solely in the will and purpose of Yahweh is transformed so that it is now grounded *both* in the will of Yahweh *and* in the obedience of Abraham. It is not that the divine promise has become contingent upon Abraham's obedience, but that Abraham's obedience has been incorporated into the divine promise. Henceforth Israel owes its existence not just to Yahweh but also to Abraham." See R. W. L. Moberly, "The Earliest Commentary on the Akedah," *Vetus testamentum* 38, no. 3 (1988): 318.

73. Zephaniah comments on the exact makeup of this eschatological remnant in 3:9, "For then I will give to the people purified lips, that all of them may call on the name of the LORD, to serve Him *shoulder to shoulder*" (emphasis mine). In his context, Zephaniah announces that on the day of the LORD, the nations and kingdoms would be assembled for the purpose of witnessing the testimony of the LORD against Judah, then receive the judgment that is due them (v. 8). Then verse 9 announces that this transformed remnant from the nations emerges and joins with the remnant of Israel to participate in activities of declaring the name of Yahweh, bringing offerings, and experiencing the fullness of a restored physical body (vv. 9–11; cf. Acts 2:11). This day of the Lord is marked by the return of God as King over his remnant (v. 15, 17), where he will establish the promised rest for his people (v. 15; cf. Isa. 11:1–11) and re-establish this newly formed remnant as the divine סגלה (vv 15–17; cf. Exod. 19:4; Deut. 4:20; 7:6; 14:2; 26:18; 1 Peter 2:9). O. Palmer Robertson comments, "God's ancient people of Israel join with converts from the world's distant climes. They call on the name of the Lord with lips purified by the Holy Spirit, serving him with a single shoulder. This community of the new covenant, heir to all the blessings prefigured in the old, have all shame removed and all pride purged. They manifest the sensitive moral character of a people who will do not evil, who will not lie. They live in safety with no one to terrify them. The records of the new covenant attest to the fulfillment of all these promises, while at the same time pointing to an ultimate consummation in the future. Only then, in that Day, shall a completed restoration be enjoyed to the fullest." See Robertson, *The Books of Nahum, Habakkuk, and Zephaniah*, 326–33.

74. Regarding the question of the relationship of Israel to the church, we appreciate Kaiser's emphasis on the "oneness" of God's future plan. He builds his argument on three significant pillars. First, the church is grafted into Israel and not vice versa. Second, Jeremiah's new covenant was promised to the restored Israel, not the church. Finally, God's concern has been for the faithful remnant from the beginning of humanity. In their concluding response, Darrell Bock and Craig Blaising recognize this *oneness* in the manner in which both Jew and Gentile are included in the "regenerating, renewing, Christ-uniting ministry of the Holy Spirit" at the time of the established millennial kingdom. This work of the Spirit, as a fulfillment of the one new covenant, extends forward and culminates in the future glorification of the faithful remnant. See Darrell L. Bock and Craig A. Blaising, eds., *Dispensationalism, Israel and the Church: The Search for Definition* (Grand Rapids: Zondervan, 1992), 361, 383–84. See also Dumbrell, "Prospect of Unconditionality," 153.

earth where one from David's seed will rule forever.[75] Thus, the promises to
Israel of land, blessing, life, and peace, are fulfilled with the return of Christ
to rule and establish his kingdom in the millennium—the reality of one program of God for one people—the faithful remnant.[76]

---

75. While Solomon's line (seed) is cut off at the time of the captivity, in the genealogies of Matthew
and Luke, it is clear that while the legal lineage came to Christ through Joseph (his legal father
came through Solomon's heirs), the actual seed of David came through Nathan and then to Mary.
This line never sat on a throne. Thus, the failed kingship did not lead to a failure of this promise
of the Davidic covenant. See Walvoord, "The Fulfillment of the Davidic Covenant," 160.

76. Ibid., 162. Walter Kaiser acknowledges the Progressive Dispensational affirmation of the "one
people and one program of God" emphasis that appreciates the continuity of the covenants.
Kaiser maintains that "the content of each of the covenants and promises in the Scripture was
both retained and progressively enriched, enlarged, and incorporated into a body of foundational truths that carried the main burden of the whole message and plan of the Bible." He
continues, "It did all of this without jettisoning God's promises to the ancient nation of Israel
or barring the door for the Gentile inclusion while grafting all believers, Jew and Gentile, into
the same olive tree." Walter C. Kaiser, *The Promise-Plan of God: A Biblical Theology of the Old
and New Testaments* (Grand Rapids: Zondervan, 2008), 30–31.

The Doctrine of the Future in the Psalms: Reflections on the Struggle of Waiting

George L. Klein

From the time of the fall in Genesis 3, humanity has recognized that creation, as exquisite as it is, is flawed by sin, guilt, injustice, suffering, and death.[1] The apostle Paul clearly affirms the point when he wrote, "We know that the whole creation has been groaning together in the pains of childbirth until now" (Rom. 8:22).[2] Such powerful disjunction between what creation is and what God intended it to be brings manifold sorrow to all who live in this sin-marred world. For the faithful, those who place their hope in God, the pain and chaos of life in such a tortured world moves them to long for the Lord to intervene and to save. The yearning of all believers seeks focus in a blurry world, peace in the place of turmoil, justice to supplant evil, and righteousness to displace sin. This waiting for God's future salvation also seeks assurance that the suffering and sacrifice of one's present circumstances will not be in vain. Faith seeks to know that God will re-inaugurate righteousness as he originally intended, not just in the creation at large, but also in the unique situations each believer faces in life. Thus, hope in God does not merely concern itself with the general and more abstract idea of a new perfect and righteous world.

---

1. It is a pleasure to present this essay in honor of Craig Blaising in gratitude for his lifelong commitment to the pursuit of systematic theology and his contributions to theological education. In recognition of Dr. Blaising's concern for eschatology, this study will examine the eschatological perspectives of the psalmists, giving particular attention to their hope in God for deliverance. Special thanks to Ethan Jones, a gifted Old Testament scholar in his own right, whose research assistance and thoughtful conversations proved helpful in the preparation of this essay. Also, Dr. Paul Hoskins, a New Testament scholar with notable Hebrew exegetical skills, offered numerous helpful suggestions to this essay.
2. All Scripture quotations are taken from the ESV unless otherwise noted.

As believers wait on God's deliverance, it is important for them to know that the Lord will right the wrongs in the lives of the faithful worshipers of the Lord and reward the sacrifices for faithfulness' sake, at least in some future context. At the heart of this concern lies the character of God himself. Believers, individually and collectively, must remember that the Lord is holy and just, wise and providential, attentive and loving, as the Creator restores his handiwork to the state he intended for it. Hence, one critical component of creation's groaning is its desire to see the Creator's purposes carried to complete fruition.

The believer's focus on this future restoration seems to adopt different emphases as the conditions of the believing community vary. In periods of comparative calm and stability, the people of God tend to focus more on the larger issues of how the Lord will restore his creation and right the wrongs which presently permeate creation. When God's people face affliction and crisis, the perspective tends to concern itself more with the individual deliverance of each believer. In these times of social and political confusion, the individual need becomes a poignant cry for the believer to see the Lord's deliverance.[3]

It is this individual perspective that typifies the majority of psalms, which lament and look to God for future blessing. A multitude of psalmists, some prominent in Old Testament history, many unnamed, cry out to their Lord for him to save. Just as in real life in any other epoch, the book of Psalms infrequently tells the story of the psalmist's deliverance after waiting upon God. While the psalmists' hope in God was undiminished as they waited on him, these examples of the faithful nonetheless stood steadfast in the midst of immeasurable tension and crisis as they waited for God.

A variety of terms convey ideas of waiting or hoping in the Old Testament. One of the more prominent, *qawah*, appears to convey waiting, or "eagerly looking for someone or thing."[4] For example, this well-known verb occurs in Isaiah 40:31:

> But they who wait for the LORD shall renew their strength;
> they shall mount up with wings like eagles.

Psalm 25:5 illustrates a similar usage of *qawah* in the Psalter:

---

3. Brian E. Daley, *The Hope of the Early Church: A Handbook of Patristic Eschatology* (Cambridge: Cambridge University Press, 1991), 1-3.
4. Koehler-Baumgartner, *Hebrew and Aramaic Lexicon of the Old Testament* (*HALOT*) (Leiden: Brill, 2002), s.v., "*qwh*."

Lead me in your truth and teach me,
for you are the God of my salvation;
for you I wait all the day long.

While *qawah* represents the better known of the words for waiting and hoping, other terms merit mention. The word *chakah* expresses ideas of waiting, but appears less frequently than either *qawah* or *yahal*, and only occurs twice in the Psalter (Pss. 33:20; 106:13).[5] A rarer word, *sibber*, also signifies waiting or hoping, and can be found in Psalms 104:27, 119:166, and 145:15. A nominal derivative from *sibber* occurs in Psalms 119:116 and 146:5.[6] A somewhat less prominent term, *yahal*, generally translated "to wait" or "to hope in," falls within the semantic field of *qawah*. Similar terms will receive the primary attention below.

This study aims to explore the semantic range of *yahal*, probing its Old Testament usage as well as that of its various nominal derivatives, giving priority to the Psalms. While a few nominal forms which are semantically and morphologically related to *yahal* exist, primary attention will rest on verbal examples based on the comparative frequency of the verbs. The occurrences of *yahal*, both non-theological and theological, will be examined, beginning with important examples outside of the book of Psalms. Some instances of waiting will describe a present hope without any certainty of a future resolution. Two passages which illustrate this somewhat dismal outlook occur in Job 29:23 and Proverbs 13:12 ("hope deferred makes the heart sick"). The theological use of *yahal* outside the Psalter can be best seen in Lamentations 3, where waiting on the Lord portrays a quiet, patient hope in the surety of God's Word and his deliverance.

Next, the primary examples of *yahal* in Psalms will be considered. Finally, we will examine the primary examples of *yahal* in Psalms, reflecting on the theological significance of hoping in God from the Psalms' perspective. The use of *yahal* in the book of Psalms stresses looking to the Lord for strength and deliverance in trial (Psalm 31) and possessing such confidence in God that the believer remains silent before his Deliverer (Psalm 37). However, the Psalter also depicts believers' struggles with the tension between trusting in a faithful God and the absence of an actual deliverance from trials and sorrow (Ps. 42–43). We will see that *yahal* describes waiting on God's Word (Ps. 119) and waiting on forgiveness for sin (Ps. 130). Woven through each of these themes, one sees the connecting

---

5. Koehler-Baumgartner, *HALOT*, s.v., "*ḥkh*."
6. Koehler-Baumgartner, *HALOT*, s.v., "*śbr*."

thread of God's faithful love. We now turn to view these aspects of waiting on the Lord in greater detail.

HOPE AND WAITING OUTSIDE OF THE PSALTER

The term *yahal* is widely distributed over the Old Testament, from Genesis to 1 Samuel and 2 Kings and from Job to Isaiah, Lamentations, Ezekiel, and Micah. However, the preponderance of examples emerges in the Psalter. When combining the verbal and the few nominal forms, *yahal* appears some forty-eight times in the Old Testament.[7] Among these, some forty occurrences are verbal. Although *yahal* occurs with some frequency in the Old Testament, it is not attested in any of the other Semitic languages. Perhaps more surprising still, *yahal* and its derivative words do not appear in the rabbinic writings which were prepared and collected in the early centuries of the Christian era.[8] Despite the relative prominence of the word *yahal* in the Old Testament, particularly in the book of Psalms, conveying the concept of "waiting" and "hoping" in the Lord, sources for exploring the significance of this term are exclusively biblical.

Before beginning an examination of the usage of *yahal* in the Hebrew Old Testament, it is illustrative to review how the Greek versions of the Old Testament translated *yahal,* since this gives insight into how ancient translators understood the term. Although this topic merits more significant discussion than possible here, an overview of Hatch and Redpath indicates that *yahal* was translated by various Greek terms.[9] The following words translate *yahal* in the Greek versions, *dialeipeo* ("intervals [of time]," "intermittent"); *elpizeo* ("to look for");

---

7. Solomon Mandelkern, *Veteris Testamenti: Hebraicae atque Chaldaicae* (Tel Aviv: Sumptibus Schocken Hierosolymis, 1978), s.v. "*yahal.*" Niphal: Gen. 8:12; Ezek. 19:5; Piel: Job 6:11; 13:15; 14:14; 29:21, 23; 30:26; Ps. 31:24 (Heb. 25); Ps. 33:18, 22; 69:3 (Heb. 4); 71:14; 119:43, 49, 74, 81, 114, 147; Ps. 130:7; 131:3; 147:11; Isa. 42:4; 51:5; Ezek. 13:6; Mic. 5:7 (Heb. 6); and Hiphil: 1 Sam. 10:8; 2 Kings 6:33; Job 32:11, 16; Ps. 37:7; 38:15 (Heb. 16); 42:5 (Heb. 6), 11 (Heb. 12); 43:5; 130:5 (Heb. 6); Lam. 3:21, 24; Mic. 7:7. The noun *tohelet* ("hope") appears in: Job 41:1; Ps. 39:8; Prov. 10:28; 11:7; 13:12; Lam. 3:18. It must be added that in numerous other passages scholars have emended the Hebrew text, positing additional examples of *yahal.* These examples have not been included in this study, but the issue of forms which scholars emend, plus the uncertainty of the Hebrew root lying behind several Old Testament passages, makes the precise number of occurrences slightly fluid.

8. Marcus Jastrow, *A Dictionary of the Targumim, the Talmud Babli and Yerushalmi, and the Midrashic Literature* (New York: G. P. Putnam's Sons, 1903).

9. Edwin Hatch and Henry A. Redpath, *A Concordance to the Septuagint,* 2nd reprint ed. (Grand Rapids: Baker, 1998).

epelpizo ("to buoy with hope," "to hope in"); and *upomeno* ("to await," "to abide," "to stand firm").[10] These Greek words translating their Hebrew precursor reflect a conservative, and at times somewhat literal, philosophy of translation in the Greek Bible.[11] These Greek terms translating *yahal* focus on a future hope, and these words in the Greek Old Testament understand hope in God as equivalent to "thoughts of trust and refuge in God."[12] To look at the manner in which the Greek Old Testament connects the idea of hope in God with trust, a survey of the Hebrew words translated by *elpizeo* reveals that around half of the examples translate the Hebrew verb *batah*, "to trust."[13]

The examples of *yahal* in the Hebrew Old Testament are distributed fairly evenly between non-theological and theological uses. This distribution proves helpful since non-theological uses of Hebrew words typically lend insight into the usage of the term. Perhaps the simplest example of the Old Testament usage of *yahal* outside of Psalms appears in Genesis 8:12, where Noah "waited another seven days." Likewise, Ezekiel 19:5 speaks of Israel figuratively, stating, "when she saw that she waited in vain." For both of these examples, *yahal* serves to express the idea of "remaining" or "tarrying." A similar usage in Job appears where the younger man respectfully waits on his elder to conclude his discourse. Job 29:21 states, "Men listened to me and waited and kept silence." A later passage in Job employs the same function of *yahal*, "I waited for your words" (32:11; see also verse 16). In Job 29:21, 23, and Micah 5:7 (Heb. 6) a human stands as the object of waiting or hoping. The idea of merely waiting in these examples changes to something more nuanced elsewhere in Job.

In Job 29:23 one reads, "They waited for me as for the rain," adding a new dimension to waiting, where waiting becomes "intensified to an expectation."[14] In Job 29:23 the perspective shifts from simply remaining, a state which may or may not convey the prospect of anything in the future, to waiting for some thing which is believed will occur. The nominal form of the lexeme *tohelet* ("hope") illustrates

---

10. Henry George Liddell and Robert Scott, *A Greek English Lexicon*, reprint ed. (Oxford: Clarendon, 1968), s.v. "*dialeipeō*," "*elpizō*," "*epelpizō*," "*úpomenō*."
11. Anneli Aejmelaeus, "Characterizing Criteria for the Characterization of the Septuagint Translators: Experimenting on the Greek Psalter," in *The Old Greek Psalter: Studies in Honour of Albert Pietersma*, ed. R. J. V. Hiebert, C. E. Cox, and P. J. Gentry, (Sheffield: Sheffield Academic Press, 2001), 54–73.
12. Walther Zimmerli, *Man and His Hope in the Old Testament* (Naperville, IL: Alec R. Allenson, 1971), 9.
13. Hatch and Redpath, s.v. "*elpizō*."
14. Ernst Jenni and Claus Westermann, *Theological Lexicon of the Old Testament*, trans. M. E. Biddle (Peabody, MA: Hendrickson, 1997), II:540.

the same point. For example, Proverbs 13:12 declares, "Hope deferred makes the heart sick, but a desire fulfilled is a tree of life." This shift of meaning from simple waiting to waiting with *expectation* will prove important later, particularly with the theological uses of *yahal*. Waiting can either be problematic or positive, destructive or constructive, depending on the object of hope and the likelihood of a beneficial outcome to the dilemma (see Ezek. 19:5).

Ezekiel 13:6 serves as a transition from the non-theological uses of *yahal* adding, "They claim, 'This is the LORD's declaration,' when the LORD did not send them, yet they wait for the fulfillment of their message" (HCSB). Verse 6 describes the false prophets' erroneous belief that the Lord would accomplish their declarations on their behalf.

Lamentations 3 may be the best known passage, certainly among those outside of the Psalter, which incorporates *yahal* into the teaching on hope in God.

> But this I call to mind, and therefore I have hope (*yahal*):
> The steadfast love of the LORD never ceases;
>   his mercies never come to an end;
> they are new every morning; great is your faithfulness.
> "The LORD is my portion," says my soul,
>   "therefore I will hope (*yahal*) in him."
> —Lamentations 3:21–24

Jenni and Westermann describe Lamentations 3 as "a fugue on the theme of waiting upon God, a considered development of the confession of confidence."[15] Further, this waiting on God, this hope, resides in a penitential prayer; that is, a prayer where the worshiper humbly confesses sin and implores the Lord to forgive and to restore. A plea for God's mercy rests upon the Lord's graciousness and his faithfulness to his covenant with his people.[16]

Other examples of *yahal* in the Old Testament generally speak of waiting on God or his word. An overview of these passages reveals waiting on *the LORD* (Pss. 31:24 [Heb. 25]; 33:22; 37:7; 38:15 [Heb. 16]; 42:5 [Heb. 6], 11 [Heb. 12]; 43:5; 69:3 [Heb. 4]; 71:14; 119:43, 49, 74, 81, 114, 147; 130:5, 7; 131:3; Lam. 3:24; Mic. 7:7); *the word of the LORD* (Pss. 119:74, 81, 114, 147; 130:5; Ezek.

15. Ibid., II:541.
16. See Heath Thomas, "'I Will Hope in Him': Theology and Hope in Lamentations," in *A God of Faithfulness: Essays in Honour of J. Gordon McConville on His 60th Birthday* ed. J. A. Grant, A. Lo, and G. J. Wenham (New York: T&T Clark, 2011), especially 204–208.

13:6); *the judgments of the* LORD (Ps. 119:43); *the law* (Isa. 42:4); *the* LORD*'s (covenantal) loyal love* (Pss. 33:18; 147:11); *the arm of the* LORD (Isa. 51:5); and *the deliverance of the* LORD (Lam. 3:26).[17]

HOPE AND WAITING IN THE PSALMS

Predictably, the psalms that contain *yahal* bear essential similarities to one another. These psalms generally belong to the lament genre, although some psalms do not exhibit the classical structure of a lament. Nonetheless, these psalms all echo the poignant cry of the psalmist as he bemoans his circumstances and affirms his confidence in the Lord to bring deliverance. Only representative examples of the Psalter's utilization of *yahal* will follow.

To begin, the Davidic Psalm 31 portrays faithful worshipers of the Lord as those who steadfastly look to their God for strength and deliverance from trial. "Be strong, and let your heart take courage, all you who wait for the LORD" (Ps. 31:24 [Heb. 25]). The Hebrew word translated "you who wait" is one of the few participles derived from the verb *yahal*. The significance of this grammatical feature in verse 24 (Heb. 25) is its timelessness, as is the case with participles generally in biblical Hebrew. The absence of any time limitations on this use of the term underscores the patient trust in God's ultimate salvation which characterizes those who have faith in the Lord. For example, Psalm 31 pictures the faithful who waited on the Lord in the past, look to him in the present, and wait for his deliverance in the future. This internal, spiritual demeanor differentiates those who place actual faith in the Lord from those who do not exercise faith, people who merely express verbal claims to hope in the Lord without genuine faith.

A variety of passages in the Psalms express the psalmist's faith in the Lord. For instance, "Let your steadfast love, O LORD, be upon us, even as we hope in you" (Ps. 33:22). This psalm exhorts the fellow worshipers to sing a "new song" to their God, and is one of several psalms which focus on offering the praise of a fresh song to the Lord.[18]

One of the most effective tools to analyze any word in Old Testament poetry is to examine the words that the biblical author pairs with the term under consideration. Consequently, the union of paired terms provides much greater clarity into

---

17. Christoph Barth, *Theological Dictionary of the Old Testament*, ed. G. J. Botterweck and H. Ringgren (Grand Rapids: Eerdmans, 1990), VI:51.
18. Richard D. Patterson, "Singing the New Song: An Examination of Psalms 33, 96, 98, and 149," *Bibliotheca Sacra* 164 (October–December 2007): 416–434.

the meaning of either term individually. Essentially, the word pair enters into a paired or binary relationship with one another. Psalm 37:7 declares, "Be still before the LORD and wait patiently for him." Paired with *yahal*, another word typically translated "be still" (*damam*) follows. Being silent before God represents a submissive attitude toward the Lord and a determination to trust him rather than to attempt to take matters into one's own hands. Accordingly, being silent before God and waiting on him present two very similar concepts.[19] Moreover, this attitude of patience and silence stands in opposition to attitudes of apprehension and vexation.[20]

The importance of the relationship between the themes of silence and waiting becomes particularly clear in Job 29 which marries the concepts of listening attentively, silence (*damam*), and waiting (*yahal*). The interrelationship between these ideas plainly emerges in Job 29:11, "Men *listened to* me and *waited* and *kept silence* for my counsel." Likewise, in Psalm 37 the psalmist faces the problem of envy, agitation, anger, and injustice resulting from the prosperity of the evildoers and the comparative suffering of the righteous worshiper. Expressions of fretting and anger represent polar opposites to faith since these attitudes contradict faith, silence, and waiting. Thus, truly to trust in God, according to Psalm 37, means "to be still" and "to wait" before the Lord.[21]

Similar themes follow in Psalm 38:15 (Heb. 16), "But for you, O LORD, do I wait; it is you, O Lord my God, who will answer." Verse 15 (Heb. 16) stands in contrast to the disrespect and opposition the psalmist faced from his peers. The psalmist's persecution at the hands of his neighbors starkly contrasts with the faithfulness of God. Repeatedly in Psalm 38 the writer focuses on the source of his salvation. He calls directly to the Lord in 38:1 (Heb. 2), 9 (Heb. 10), 15 (Heb. 16), 21 (Heb. 23), 22 (Heb. 23). Most notably, though, the psalmist focuses on the personal dimension of his commitment to the Lord, addressing him as "my God" in 38:15 (Heb. 16), 21 (Heb. 22). The psalmist also addresses the Lord as "my Savior" (38:22 [Heb. 23]).

One of the most notable occurrences of *yahal* appears in Psalms 42–43. Although separated into two psalms, it is highly likely that these two psalms were originally a single composition. The primary reason for this claim is the identical, repeated refrain occurring twice in Psalm 42 and once at the end of Psalm 43. The presence of a heading to Psalm 42, which also begins Book 2 of

---

19. Bruce K. Waltke and James M. Houston, *The Psalms as Christian Worship* (Grand Rapids: Eerdmans, 2010), 236. See also, Barth, *Theological Dictionary of the Old Testament*, VI:53.
20. John Goldingay, *Psalms, Volume 1: Psalms 1-41* (Grand Rapids: Baker, 2006), 521–522.
21. Hans-Joachim Kraus, *Psalms 1–59*, trans. H. C. Oswald (Minneapolis: Augsburg, 1988), 405.

the Psalter, and the absence of a heading for Psalm 43 lends credence to the view that Psalms 42–43 were originally unified texts.[22] Accordingly, these two psalms will be viewed as a unity below.

The poignant refrain of Psalm 42–43 reads:

> Why are you cast down, O my soul,
>> and why are you in turmoil within me?
> Hope in God; for I shall again praise him,
>> my salvation and my God
> (Ps. 42:5 [Heb. 6], 11 [Heb. 12]; 43:5).

We will examine this refrain, since it includes *yahal* in all three occurrences.

In a compressed fashion, Psalm 42–43 conveys the tension between the absence of God and faithful waiting on him. In Psalm 42–43 God seems absent to the psalmist. Note the repeated question, "Where is your God?" (42:3 [Heb. 4], 10 [Heb. 11]). Nonetheless, Psalm 42–43 mentions the Lord by name some twenty-five times, not counting the numerous other pronominal references to God.[23] Despite all appearances to the contrary, the Lord remains quite present in the life of the psalmist.[24] This said, the affirmation of God's presence is an affirmation of faith, not an assertion based on any wondrous acts of salvation that had already been performed on behalf of the psalmist, since the longed-for deliverance from the Lord has not manifested itself at the time the psalmist wrote. The declaration, "I shall again praise him" conveys a future hope for salvation since the psalmist remains mired in his painful circumstances, all the while lamenting his sorrows.

Psalm 42–43 races from extremes of drought to torrent, from depression to exultation, from the absence of God (or at least the fear of having been abandoned by the Lord) to praising God for bringing the psalmist's salvation and for being his personal God ("my God"). Brown summarizes the extreme emotions experienced by the psalmist, stating that this psalm "is a pilgrimage that

---

22. Luis Alonso-Schökel, "The Poetic Structure of Psalm 42–43," *Journal for the Study of the Old Testament* 1 (1976), 4-11.

23. John Goldingay, *Psalms, Volume II: Psalms 42–89* (Grand Rapids: Baker, 2007), 33–34. See Hans-Joachim Kraus, *Theology of the Psalms* (Minneapolis: Fortress, 1992), 197–198, for a helpful treatment of the influence of Psalm 42–43 on the gospel accounts.

24. Reinhard Feldmeier and Hermann Spieckermann, *God of the Living: A Biblical Theology*, trans. M. E. Biddle (Waco, TX: Baylor University Press, 2011), 501–502. Also, William P. Brown, "Thirsting for God in the Classroom: A Meditation on Psalm 42:1–8," *Teaching Theology and Religion* 6 (2003), 187–188.

oscillates between the poles of lament and praise."[25] Psalm 63:1 offers a fitting commentary on the psalmist's expectant hope in the Lord, "O God, you are my God; earnestly I seek you; my soul thirsts for you; my flesh faints for you, as in a dry and weary land where there is no water."

However, Psalm 42–43 chooses not to dwell on lament or the circumstances leading to the plea for God's intervention. Rather, Psalm 42–43 boldly declares that the Lord himself should represent the object of the deepest yearning from the heart of the faithful, not God's deliverance or anything else mortals might hope the Lord would provide. Thus, the believer's longing should be none other than the Lord himself.

During his time of travail in Gethsemane, Jesus echoes the words of Psalm 42:5-6 in Mark 14:34 and John 12:27. Just as the psalmist in Psalm 42–43 exercises profound faith in his God, however absent momentarily, likewise, Jesus placed even greater faith in his Father when he faced his hour of greatest trial.

As seen in Psalm 42–43, the psalmist's wait for God typically does not reflect the peacefulness and joy resulting from the Lord's most recent deliverance. Frequently, the psalmist encounters just the opposite. For example, "I am weary with my crying out; my throat is parched. My eyes grow dim with waiting (*yahal*) for my God" (Ps. 69:3 [Heb. 4]). Psalm 69 presents circumstances which are more than mere disappointments. Instead, the faithful psalmist finds himself in grave danger as he finds himself sinking (figuratively) to his neck and suffers the light and life of his eyes growing dim.[26]

Our study now turns to the magisterial Psalm 119 where the term *yahal* appears six times (vv. 43, 49, 74, 81, 114, and 147). Predicatably, all occurrences focus in some sense on waiting on the word of the Lord. Specifically, Psalm 119 presents the object of the psalmist's hope as "your rules" (v. 43), "your word" (vv. 49, 74, 81, 114), and "your words" (v. 147).

Psalm 119:43 adds an important dimension to hoping in God generally, and in the Lord's word specifically, stating, "And take not the word of truth utterly out of my mouth, for my hope is in your rules." Here the object of deliverance is God's "word of truth," emphasizing the faithfulness and the trustworthiness of the divine word. Certainly, the word of the Lord stands solidly for the psalmist because of the true God upon whom the true word rests.

---

25. William P. Brown, "Psalms 42 and 43," in *Psalms for Preaching and Worship*, ed. R. E. Van Harn and B. A. Strawn (Grand Rapids: Eerdmans, 2009), 154.
26. Frank-Lothar Hossfeld and Erich Zenger, *Psalms 2*, trans. L. M. Maloney (Minneapolis: Fortress, 2005), 177.

The affirmation of hope and confidence in God's word is not a dispassionate declaration. Rather, the psalmist appears to find himself in an unspecified distressing situation, and in response he hopes in God for deliverance.[27] The translation of the final word in the Hebrew text, *lemishpateka*, differs significantly among translations. The word is rendered variously as "your rules," "your laws," and "your judgments." When applied to God, *mishpat* routinely speaks of the Lord's justice or judgment, the fulfillment of God's will, or divine uprightness (Gen. 18:25; Deut. 32:4; Job 40:8; Ps. 33:5; 37:28; 111:7; 119:149; and others). The emphasis of Psalm 119:43 lies on God's integrity and faithfulness to save his faithful ones, not on rules he has established. The psalmist fervently believes that God will deliver him, based on the Lord's faithfulness and truthfulness. Moreover, the psalmist vows not to keep God's future salvation to himself, promising to speak of it, even before kings (Ps. 119:46).

The remaining passages in Psalm 119 all center on the Lord's word as the focus of waiting (verses 49, 74, 81, 114). Psalm 119:49 deviates somewhat from the other verses in the psalm examining waiting by focusing both on God's past word to the psalmist which brought him safely to his present circumstances, as well as the future assurances from the Lord, "in which you have made me hope," on which the psalmist's future confidence rests. Thus, the psalmist envisions the time when the Lord gave his word to him, but remains in his present circumstances waiting for God's promised deliverance to occur. This tension fills the life of the psalmist, just as it does in the lives of all believers throughout history.[28] The focus of this stanza in Psalm 119 is to "remember." Remembering the Lord's faithfulness is the primary duty, but in times of such stress it is particularly difficult.

We see a similar progression from reflection on God's past faithfulness to confidence in the Lord for future, yet unseen, salvation in many other places in the Bible. For instance, in Psalm 119:73 the psalmist proclaims his trust in God after remembering that the Lord had created him, "Your hands have made and fashioned me; give me understanding that I may learn your commandments." God created him and made him able to recognize the Lord and to believe in his word. See Psalm 139:13–17 for a similar progression from

---

27. Frank-Lothar Hossfeld and Erich Zenger, *Psalms 3*, trans. L. M. Maloney (Minneapolis: Fortress, 2011), 270. See also John Goldingay, *Psalms, Volume III: Psalms 90–150* (Grand Rapids: Baker, 2008), 400.

28. Goldingay, *Psalms III*, 402. See Hossfeld and Zenger, *Psalms 3*, 271.

recognition of God's creative activity in the believer's life to expressed faith in the Lord.[29]

Psalm 119:81, 114, and 147 all emphasize the Lord's word, stating, "I hope in your word." Verse 114 stands in a stanza (vv. 113–120) that employs military metaphors to portray the danger in which the psalmist finds himself. He prays for the Lord to strengthen him so he can stand firm against all who oppose God's word by disobeying its message.[30] It is possible that the psalmist begins by reviewing the Lord's past acts of salvation for him, translating verse 114 with a past tense verb, "You have been my hiding place and my shield." This past salvation would lend confidence to the psalmist as he faces his present crisis.[31] Viewing verse 114 as a retrospective on a past deliverance is uncertain, and the stanza reads more consistently translating all of the verbs as with a present tense. Viewing the action as present is more likely since it is more consistent with the perspective of the psalm as a whole.

To summarize this section, the Bible presents past accounts of the Lord's great miracles in creation not just for information's sake. Rather, these wonders exist to teach the faithful of all generations that God deserves complete trust. The truth of God's trustworthiness and faithfulness presents more than an abstract claim about the Lord. Rather, the truth represents a bold and demanding command that all the faithful should wait confidently upon their God.

Among the diverse psalms incorporating *yahal*, Psalm 130 may be the most prominent. This penitential psalm is so named because in it the psalmist cries out to God for deliverance, not because of some external situation, but due to the weight of his own sin—transgressions which he confesses to the Lord. The early church classified Psalm 130 as one of the seven "Penitential Psalms" to be read during seasons of confession (also Pss. 6, 32, 38, 51, 102, 143). Psalm 130 has also received the title *De Profundis* ("Out of the Depths"), because of its importance in the individual and collective worship of Christians.[32] The depths of sorrow for sin in Psalm 130:1, "Out of the depths I cry to you, O Lord," also link Psalm 130 with both Micah 7:19 and Jonah 2:4.[33]

---

29. Hossfeld and Zenger, *Psalms 3*, 274. Also, Hans-Joachim Kraus, *Psalms 60–150*, trans. H. C. Oswald (Minneapolis: Fortress, 1993), 417–418.
30. Hossfeld and Zenger, *Psalms 3*, 278–279.
31. Goldingay, *Psalms III*, 423–424.
32. James Limburg, "*De Profundis*: Psalms 130 and 131," *Currents in Theology and Mission* 26 (1999), 117–122.
33. Harry P. Nasuti, "Plumbing the Depths: Genre Ambiguity and Theological Creativity in the Interpretation of Psalm 130," in *The Idea of Biblical Interpretation: Essays in Honor of James L. Kugel*, ed. H. Najman and J. H. Newman (Leiden: Brill, 2004), 110–124.

The lament then in Psalm 130 is for sin, and the prayer focuses on forgiveness and restoration. The brokenness faced by the psalmist grows out of the broken relationship with his God. Psalm 130:3 states, "If you, O Lord, should mark iniquities, O Lord, who could stand?" Thus, verse 3 extends the effects of sin to all humanity, broadening the understanding of sin well beyond focusing on sins which one might be able to avoid. Some have noted that Psalm 130 moves beyond other penitential psalms, uniquely focusing not on a particular sin committed by a specific individual, but lamenting the sad fact of all human sinfulness.[34] Help in such dire circumstances must come only from the Lord. Psalm 130:4 states, "But with you there is forgiveness." Verse 7 opens by affirming, "with the Lord there is steadfast love." This "steadfast love" (*hesed*) describes God's absolutely faithful covenantal commitment to his people. The same verse concludes, "with him (God) is plentiful redemption." Forgiveness, steadfast love, and redemption stand as one in both Old and New Testaments as the foundation for a relationship with God.[35] Wonderful as salvation promises to be for the psalmist, it is not enough for him to celebrate privately. The lament of the individual (v. 1) becomes an exhortation for the whole community to hope in God (v. 7), believing that the Lord will redeem all of their iniquities (v. 8).[36]

Psalm 130 served as the basis for one of Luther's most famous hymns, "From Depths of Woe I Cry to Thee." The third stanza powerfully summarizes the theological message of Psalm 130:7:

> Therefore my hope is in the Lord
> And not in mine own merit;
> It rests upon His faithful Word
> To them of contrite spirit
> That He is merciful and just;
> This is my comfort and my trust.
> His help I wait with patience.[37]

---

34. Ibid., 98–99.
35. See the helpful treatment of these themes in Keith F. Nickle, "Psalm 130," *Interpretation* 33 (1979) 176–181.
36. Limburg, "Psalms 130 and 131," 120; Kraus, *Psalms 60–150*, 468.
37. Martin Luther, "From Depths of Woe I Cry to Thee," hymn 329, *The Lutheran Hymnal*, trans. C. Winkwirth (St Louis: Concordia, 1941). Friedrich Beisser treats the topic of Luther's eschatological interpretations in *Hoffnun und Vollendung* (Gütersloher: Gerd Mohn, 1993), 19–76. See Nasuti for a useful overview of the use of Psalm 130 in Christian tradition, "Plumbing the Depths," 110–120.

Psalm 147:11 revisits the theme of the Lord's steadfast love, similar to Psalm 130:7, proclaiming, "but the LORD takes pleasure in those who fear him, in those who hope in his steadfast love." God's steadfast love, characterized by broken hearts and sincere contrition (147:3, 6), offers the only basis for standing before the Lord. Any other human advantage such as power or prestige means nothing to God (147:10).[38]

Previously in this study, the terms the psalmist paired with *yahal* provided clarity into the meaning of waiting on the Lord. Psalm 147:11 offers a unique insight by pairing waiting on the Lord with "those who fear him." Kraus states the point particularly well, noting, "The fear of God is interpreted by the parallelism in verse 11 as constant waiting for Yahweh's gracious attention and salvific faithfulness . . . a complete disregard of all inherent, controllable powers and expectation and openness for the creative activity of God."[39] Psalm 33:18 reflects the same image, "Behold, the eye of the LORD is on those who fear him, on those who hope in his steadfast love." The pairing of waiting on God with one of the preeminent requirements of the faithful in the Old Testament, fearing the Lord, underscores the importance of the faithful attitude of patiently waiting on God. The people of God in all ages should not place their trust in horses, a feared military weapon in the psalmist's day, or in any other human device, but should emphatically accept the Lord as King. Note the trajectory of thought between Psalm 146:3 to Psalm 149:4–5, reminding the faithful not to trust in humans (146:3), but to remember that the LORD blesses "the humble with salvation" (149:4).[40]

THEOLOGICAL REFLECTION

Waiting on the Lord surely represents one of the prominent motifs in the book of Psalms, even in the entire Old Testament. The biblical text presents God as worthy of trust, a Lord who is almighty yet also gracious, loving, and willing to deliver his people. This focus on God himself stands as one of the main points to recognize since, somewhat surprisingly, the biblical authors who describe waiting on the Lord frequently make no specific reference to what they want God to do on their behalf. Indeed, it is the Lord their God who is the focus of their hope

---

38. Kraus, *Psalms 60–150*, 557.
39. Ibid.
40. Hossfeld and Zenger, *Psalms 3*, 625.

and the aim of their waiting.[41] Psalm 131:3 illustrates this point well, "O Israel, hope in the Lord from this time forth and forevermore" (see also Pss. 33:22; 37:7; 38:15 [Heb. 16]; 42:5 [Heb. 6], 11 [Heb. 12]; 43:5; 69:3; 71:14; 130:7; 131:3; 147:11; also Job 13:15; Isa. 51:5; Lam. 3:21, 24; Mic. 7:7). The key point of the eschatology of Psalms is the reminder that the Lord alone can serve as Refuge for those who place their hope in him.[42] Accordingly, the Psalms never allow the focus to shift solely to the human need, for the Lord always remains the focus. One of the greatest lessons is to understand that the ultimate objective is to give honor and praise to God, a message Psalm 71 makes quite clear. The ESV translates Psalm 71:14:

> But I will hope continually
> and will praise you yet more and more.

The final half of the couplet might be better understood as a purpose clause indicating the purpose of the continual hoping. So understood, the second half of verse 14 would read, "so that I may praise you more and more."

In the Psalter, hoping in the Lord and waiting on him does not portray idealism or mere optimism. Rather, the psalmists focus on the character of God himself. Because the Lord is faithful, because he always extends his loyal love (*hesed*) to those who wait for him, he can be trusted with present and future crises. Referring to Psalm 130, Limburg asks how can the desperate plea in verse 1, "Out of the depths I cry to you, O Lord!" become the confident assertion in verse 5, "I wait for the Lord, my soul waits, and in his word I hope." The answer lies with the recognition of the Lord's loyal love, which never lets go of his people.[43]

Psalm 131:3 continues the admonition to all Israel to "hope in the Lord," with one very significant difference. In Psalm 131, the idea of hope in the Lord is dramatically extended. In Psalm 130, Israel must hope in the Lord for redemption from her iniquities. This immediate hope for an imminent salvation shifts in Psalm 131:3 to a perspective which can be legitimately called eschatological,

41. Barth, *Theological Dictionary of the Old Testament*, VI:54; Feldmeier and Spieckermann, *God of the Living*, 501–502.
42. Note Psalms 1–2, despite the absence of the language of "waiting." Mark J. Whiting, "Psalms 1 and 2 as a Hermeneutical Lens for Reading the Psalter," *Evangelical Quarterly* 85 (2013), 255–256.
43. Limburg, "Psalms 130 and 131," 120–121. See Robert B. Chisholm, Jr., "A Theology of the Psalms," *A Biblical Theology of the Old Testament*, ed. R. B. Zuck (Chicago: Moody, 1991), 278–281, 283–288.

since verse 3 projects the time of waiting forever. Some add that this eschatological hope may include the anticipation of personal resurrection, largely based on inferences from texts like Psalm 131:3. Additionally, the usage of the Hebrew word *sheol*, found elsewhere in the Old Testament, seems to describe the future place of the unbelieving dead.[44]

This extension of time seen in Psalm 131:3 proves both disquieting and quieting. The idea is disquieting since for the original audience the trials of the Persian era so painfully seen in Ezra and Nehemiah would not see an immediate resolution. Physically and politically, Israel's prospects would not be bright, and verse 3 does little to alleviate this crisis. But the psalmist's exhortation is profoundly quieting since it addresses the spiritual needs of all believers, ancient and modern, commanding them to hope in the Lord forever.[45] Psalms 121:8 and 125:1–2 make similar points about the permanent protection the Lord will grant his people.

One must also acknowledge that Psalm 131 commands hope in the Lord. Further, this command is directed to the entire people of God. The Psalms never present waiting on God as less than the duty of the individual believer and of the community of faith collectively. It is never appropriate for individual hope to remain private—it must also inform and instruct others to hope in God. When the community of faith gathers, the emphasis is always on waiting for the Lord (Pss. 130:7; 131:3).[46] The people of God who actively place their hope in the Lord should rejoice that "there are no days outside of God's providential care."[47]

The real tensions between turmoil and peace, suffering and blessing, as well as despair and hope, all permeate life. Most importantly, God expects that his people will bring these troubles to him. The Lord also desires to answer his people's needs according to his own loyal love for them.[48] Proverbs 30:8b–9 states a similar tension in the life of the faithful, "give me neither poverty nor riches; feed me with the food that is needful for me, lest I be full and deny you and say, 'Who is the LORD?' or lest I be poor and steal and profane the name of my God."

---

44. Philip S. Johnston, "Psalm 49: A Personal Eschatology," in *Eschatology in Bible & Theology*, ed. K. E. Brower, and M. W. Elliott (Downers Grove, IL: InterVarsity, 1997), 73–84; Michael J. Gruenthaner, "The Future Life in the Psalms," *Catholic Biblical Quarterly* 2 (1940), 57–63.
45. Goldingay, *Psalms III*, 538. See Hossfeld and Zenger, *Psalms 3*, 447.
46. Kraus, *Theology of the Psalms*, 71.
47. Carolyn Pressler, "Certainty, Ambiguity, and Trust: Knowledge of God in Psalm 139," in *A God So Near: Essays on Old Testament Theology in Honor of Patrick D. Miller*, ed. B. A. Strawn and N. R. Bowen (Winona Lake, IN: Eisenbrauns, 2003), 97.
48. Michael A. Smith, "Psalms 42 & 130—Hope for the Hopeless," *Review and Expositor* 91 (1994), 77–80.

Although a separate topic, the royal psalms contribute significantly to the idea of waiting on the Lord, adding content to the hope that the Psalms offer about the future promises from God. The high point of the royal psalms is the Davidic King who will rule with righteousness and mercy over the creation, not just Abraham's descendants (Psalms 2; 72; 89; 110; 132; see 2 Samuel 7).[49]

One of the most insightful comments about waiting on God comes from the pen of Zimmerli, who writes, "'Hope' is not in the first place a situation of tension toward the future, a wish or the indication of a goal that one awaits with tension—it is above all, and the Septuagint emphasizes this very strongly, a situation of surrender and trust, which naturally cannot be realized in a vacuum, but which requires one who stands over against us and calls us to trust."[50] This hope focuses on the future, on the Lord's actions on behalf of the worshiper, given freely because of God's grace.[51] Hope is based on trust in the Lord and remains staunchly convinced that the future will disclose a good ending. It is most striking to note the degree of certainty with which the psalmists envision the hope that the Lord will offer to those who wait for him, despite the present trials they might face.[52]

The importance of waiting exclusively on the Lord permeates the book of Psalms. Feldmeier and Spieckermann summarize the overarching message clearly: "Hope is longing for the God whose love as the center and substance of life has the specific form that his people always need: salvation from the entanglements of life, whether self-made or maliciously devised by others. In the Psalms, hope, like love (*hesed*) and salvation, is a concentrated theological expression of what shapes human life in relation to God: founded by love, saved by love, desire for the fullness of love. This love is never an idea but always the same thing: God."[53]

---

49. Horst Dietrich Preuss, *Old Testament Theology, Volume II*, trans. L. G. Perdue (Louisville: Westminster John Knox, 1992), 34–38. See David A. Hubbard, "Hope in the Old Testament," *Tyndale Bulletin* 34 (1983), 39–42. A significant body of scholarly literature concludes that the placement of royal psalms in the book of Psalms reflects an eschatological message. See recent contributions by David C. Mitchell, "LORD, Remember David: G. H. Wilson and the Message of the Psalter," *Vetus Testamentum* 66 (2006), 526–548; Jinkyu Kim, "The Strategic Arrangement of Royal Psalms in Books IV–V," *Westminster Theological Journal* 70 (2008), 143–157.
50. Zimmerli, *Man and His Hope*, 8.
51. Ibid., 24.
52. Ibid., 37.
53. Feldmeier and Spieckermann, "Hope and Comfort," 498–499.

Conclusion

The Old Testament never views waiting on the Lord as the result of weakness or resignation to fate. Waiting is not mere silence, believing that circumstances will surely improve, naïve optimism, as it were. Waiting on God is not fatalism. Waiting on the Lord means never surrendering to grief or disappointment, never yielding to fatigue, never giving up.[54] Further, waiting is not a passive state. In contrast, waiting is confidence in God, seeing the Lord as gracious, full of loyal love (*hesed*), and willing to save, for waiting on the Lord is full of tension and exhausts both body and heart. Psalm 69:3 states this point plainly, "I am weary with my crying out; my throat is parched. My eyes grow dim with waiting for my God." The tears and weeping verse 3 describes show that the life of faith, of hoping in the Lord, is not an easy path.[55]

This essay began by recalling Paul's words in Romans 8, in which he observes that the entirety of creation has been "groaning" from the moment it was changed by disobedience to God. Paul's ensuing remarks on hope, waiting, and deliverance in Romans 8 bring this study to a fitting close: "And not only the creation, but we ourselves, who have the firstfruits of the Spirit, groan inwardly as we wait eagerly for adoption as sons, the redemption of our bodies. For in this hope we were saved. Now hope that is seen is not hope. For who hopes for what he sees? But if we hope for what we do not see, we wait for it with patience" (Rom. 8:23–25).[56]

---

54. Kraus, *Theology of the Psalms*, 158.
55. Ibid.
56. See Feldmeier and Spieckermann, "Hope and Comfort," 510–516 for an overview of New Testament development of the hope and waiting. Note also 1 Thessalonians 1:9–10.

The Doctrine of the Future in the Prophets

Mark F. Rooker

T he prophetic books comprise the largest section of the Bible.[1] In Jewish tradition the prophetic division includes the Former Prophets (Joshua–Kings) and the Latter Prophets (Isaiah, Jeremiah, Ezekiel, and the Twelve). The Former Prophets have much to say about individual prophets but seldom conveys messages from them (e.g., Elijah and Elisha); the Latter Prophets contain much of the individual prophetic messages but say virtually nothing about them as individuals.

What Is Prophecy?

For many people today the notion of prophecy conjures up the idea of gazing into a crystal ball to get a glimpse of the future. While it is true that prophets did predict future events, these oracles originated from the prophets addressing contemporary problems, often of an extremely critical nature. The overarching concern of the prophets was Israel's faithfulness to her covenant responsibilities as prescribed in the Mosaic Law. The prophets' preoccupation with this concern has rightly led to their being designated as covenant-enforcement mediators.[2] The prophets repeatedly confronted the Israelites with

---

1. The Jews commonly divided the Old Testament into three sections: the Law, the Prophets, and the Writings (see Luke 24:44). English Bibles following the Septuagint (the Greek translation of the Hebrew Bible) divide the Prophets into the Historical Books and the Prophetic Books, each of approximate equal length. The Historical and Prophetical Book sections are each separately of more length than any other major section of the entire Bible.
2. G. Fee and D. Stuart, *How to Read the Bible for All Its Worth*, 2nd ed. (Grand Rapids: Zondervan, 1993), 174. Elijah should be viewed as the first covenant-enforcer, accusing the nation of covenant violations (1 Kings 18:21).

the law, particularly its blessings and curses (Lev. 26; Deut. 26–28).[3] Whereas judgment was based on Israel's disobedience, the oracles of hope were the result of God's grace and faithfulness to his promise in the Abrahamic covenant.

THE ROLE OF THE PROPHET

Four terms are used in the Old Testament to designate a man or a woman who performed prophetic activity. These terms are *nābî'*, "prophet," *iš 'Elōhîm* ("man of God"), and *rō'eh* and *hōzeh,* which are both translated "seer." Some have argued that each of these terms reveals a distinctive role.[4] However, the terms often appear interchangeable (see 1 Kings 16:7, 12 with 1 Chron. 29:29; 2 Chron. 19:2; Isa. 29:10; 30:10). First Samuel 1:9 indicates that the term *nābî'* became the predominant designation at least by Samuel's time (eleventh century BCE).

Nābî' occurs more than three hundred times in the Old Testament and is cognate to the Semitic (Akkadian) verb *nabûm* "to call." Based on this parallel scholars have concluded that the Hebrew prophet was one who had been "called by God." The prophet was one who was commissioned to speak on God's behalf, not unlike a modern-day ambassador representing his homeland.[5] The prescription for carrying out the role of a prophet is found in Deuteronomy 18:15–22:[5]

> The LORD your God will raise up for you a prophet like me from among you, from your brothers—it is to him you shall listen— just as you desired of the LORD your God at Horeb on the day of the assembly, when you said, 'Let me not hear again the voice of the LORD my God or see this great fire any more, lest I die.' And the LORD said to me, 'They are right in what they have spoken. I will raise up for them a prophet like you from among their brothers. And I will put my words in his mouth, and he shall speak to them all that I command him. And whoever will not listen to my words that he shall speak in my name, I myself will require it of

---

3. For a listing of pentateuchal curses which occur in prophetic literature, see Douglas Stuart, *Hosea-Jonah,* WBC (Waco, TX: Word, 1987), xxxiii–xlii.

4. See D. L. Petersen, *The Roles of Israel's Prophets,* JSOT Sup (Sheffield: JSOT Press, 1981).

5. The term *nābî'* ("prophet"), first occurs in Genesis 20:7, in connection with Abimelech's recognition that Abraham was capable of interceding with God on his behalf. Although this intercessory role of a prophet is not absent from the rest of the Old Testament (Exod. 32:10–33; 33:12–23; 1 Sam 12:19; 1 Kings 18:36–37; 2 Kings 19:4 = 2 Chron. 32:20; Jer. 4:4; Hab. 3:1–19), it does not seem to be a dominant function of the prophet in the Bible.

him. (20) But the prophet who presumes to speak a word in my name that I have not commanded him to speak, or who speaks in the name of other gods, that same prophet shall die.' (21) And if you say in your heart, 'How may we know the word that the LORD has not spoken?'—(22) when a prophet speaks in the name of the LORD, if the word does not come to pass or come true, that is a word that the LORD has not spoken; the prophet has spoken it presumptuously. You need not be afraid of him. [6]

The importance of Deuteronomy chapter 18 for the role and function of a prophet cannot be overestimated. Deuteronomy 18:22 is the criterion for distinguishing true prophecy from false prophecy. The prophet is first and foremost, according to this key passage, one who can successfully predict the future.[7]

Although Moses was Israel's unique prophet (Exod. 33:11; Num. 12:6–8; Deut. 34:10–12), he became the prototype for later prophets who would address the nation with the word of God. The biblical prophets, like Moses, did not volunteer to serve God, they did not seek an office or position, but they were called from various stations in life for the sole purpose to proclaim God's word.[8] Their main task, as with Moses, was to announce God's message. As Deuteronomy 18:18b states, "I will put My words in his [the prophet's] mouth." The prophets were people who enjoyed access to privileged information—"things into which angels long to look" (1 Peter 1:10–12). As Lindblom states, "The prophet is not in himself a politician, a social reformer, a thinker, or a philosopher; nor is he in the first place a poet, even though he often puts his sayings in a poetical form. The special gift of a prophet is his ability to experience the divine in an original way and to receive revelations from the divine world. The prophet belongs entirely to his God; his paramount task is to listen to and obey his God. In every respect he has given himself up to his God and stands unreservedly at His disposal."[9] The manner in which a prophet may receive God's message (the way the Lord puts his words in the prophet's mouth) might happen in various ways or in various forms. But a genuine prophet received the word through divine revelation. Visions and auditions might come to them

---

6. All Scripture quotations are taken from the ESV unless otherwise noted.
7. J. F. Sawyer, *Prophecy and the Prophets of the Old Testament* (Oxford: Oxford Univ. Press, 1987), 23.
8. N. Habel, "The Form and Significance of the Call Narratives," *ZAW* 77 (1965): 297–323.
9. J. Lindblom, *Prophecy in Ancient Israel* (Philadelphia: Fortress, 1962), 1.

suddenly and without premeditation (Num. 12:6–18). This communication of God's truth to the prophets explains the frequent occurrence of phrases such as "Thus says the Lord," "The word of the Lord came to" (1 Sam. 15:10; 2 Sam. 24:11; 1 Kings 19:9; Jonah 1:1; Hag. 1:1; 2:1,20; Zech. 7:1, 8; 8:1), "The spirit of God came on" or a slight variation thereof (Num. 11:24–30; Judg. 6:34; 1 Sam. 10:10; Isa. 61:1; Ezek. 11:5), and "The hand of God was on" (or a slight variation thereof; Jer. 15:17; Ezek. 33:22; 37:1) at the beginning of a prophetic announcement. The phrase "The word of the Lord" occurs 221 times in the prophetic writings.[10]

And yet it certainly bears repeating that the characteristic feature of the prophet's message is its actuality, its expectation of something soon to happen.[11] Thus fulfilled prediction is the characteristic feature of biblical prophecy. Note how certain prophecies from the book of Isaiah are fulfilled in the New Testament.[12]

- John the Baptist (Isa. 40:3; Matt. 3:3; Luke 3:4–6; John 1:23)
- Virgin birth (Isa. 7:14; Matt. 1:23; Luke 1:34)
- Teaching in parables (Isa. 6:9–10; 29:13; Matt. 13:13–15; 15:7–9; John 12:39–40; Acts 28:24–27)
- Suffering Servant (Isa. 53:1; John 12:38; Acts 8:27–33)
- Mission to the Gentiles (Isa. 9:1–2; Matt. 4:13–16)
- Servant of the Lord (Isa. 61:1–3; Luke 4:14–21)
- Avoidance of fame (Isa. 42:1–4; Matt. 12:15–21)
- Enthronement of God (Isa. 6:1–3; John 12:41)
- Incorporation of Gentiles (Isa. 11:10; 65:1; Rom. 10:20; 15:12)
- Remnant for Israel (Isa. 1:9; 10:22; Rom. 9:27–29)
- Renewal of paradise regained (Isa. 65:16–66:24; Rom. 8:18–25; Rev. 21–22)

Similarly, on ten occasions Matthew introduced Old Testament prophecies with the formula "this took place to fulfill what the Lord had spoken by the prophet," or words synonymous with this (1:22; 2:15; 2:17; 2:23; 4:14; 8:17; 12:17; 13:35; 21:4; and 27:9).

---

10. What Eliphaz described in his speech in Job 4:12–17 is often cited as an illustration of the prophet's reception of divine revelation.
11. Gerhard von Rad, *The Message of the Prophets* (London: SCM, 1968), 91.
12. See Eugene H. Merrill, Mark F. Rooker, and Michael A. Grisanti, *The World and the Word: An Introduction to the Old Testament* (Nashville: B&H Publishing, 2011), 376.

The New Testament writers were not unique in reading the Prophetic literature in this way. An early illustration of a prophetic oracle being understood and read as predicting the future may be found in Daniel 9:1–2, where Daniel reflects on Jeremiah's prophecy that "seventy years" would pass before the end of the desolations of Jerusalem (Jer. 25:11–12). The former Galilean General Josephus understood that the prophet Daniel foresaw not only the Maccabean age but also the Roman empire in Palestine, that is, events of Josephus's own time (first century CE; *Ant.* 9:276). Another example of reading the prophets in this way may be aptly observed in the Dead Sea Scrolls where for example almost any passage in the Habakkuk commentary (1QpHab) demonstrates the community's conviction that ancient prophecies referred to events that recently occurred or were about to occur in the immediate future.[13]

EXPRESSIONS OF PREDICTIVE PROPHECY

The futuristic announcements "the days are coming" (Jer. 23:5; 49:2) and "in that day" are the two prominent phrases in the prophetic literature. The latter expression occurs over one hundred times in the Prophetic Books (e.g., Isa. 19:16, 18, 19, 23, 24; Hos. 2:16) with no less than fifteen of these in Zechariah 12–14.[14]

Two kinds or forms of prophetic oracles specifically deal with the future. One is the judgment speech, with its standardized form of accusation and announcement (e.g., Ezek. 25:15–17). The second, the salvation oracle, can include various positive themes including descriptions of a state of well-being (Jer. 31:23–25). Future events were also envisioned and conveyed through symbolic actions or sign acts. For example, the future reunification of Israel and Judah was illustrated in Ezekiel by the use of two sticks joined together (Ezek. 37:15–23).

The Day of the Lord
The day of the Lord/the day of Yahweh signifies a time when the Lord supernaturally intervenes in the course of human history. This expression has often

---

13. See John Barton, *Oracles of God: Perceptions of Ancient Prophecy in Israel after the Exile* (London: Darton, Longman & Todd, 1986), 180–182. Some argue indeed that the Old Testament ends on an eschatological and messianic note (Mal. 4:5–6). This is only true of the Septuagint (Greek translation of Hebrew Bible), followed by the English Bible arrangement. The last book of the Old Testament in the Hebrew Bible is 2 Chronicles. For the argument that the end of 2 Chronicles also ends on a predictive messianic note, see John H. Sailhamer, "The Messiah and the Hebrew Bible," *JETS* 44, no. 1 (2001) 12.
14. E. A. Martens, *DOTP*, "Eschatology," 178.

been regarded as the very heart of the prophetic eschatology. According to German Old Testament theologian Gerhard von Rad, sixteen chapters in the prophetic literature refer to the day of Yahweh (Isa. 2:12; 13:6, 9; 22:5; 34:8; Jer. 46:10; Ezek. 7:10; 13:5; 30:3; Joel 1:15; 2:1, 11; 3:4 [2:31]; 4:14 [3:14]; Amos 5:18–20; Obad. 15; Zeph. 1:7, 8, 14–18; Zech. 14:1).[15]

The prophets frequently motivated the people to action by proclaiming that the day of the Lord was near (Isa. 13:6; Ezek. 30:3; Joel 1:15; 2:1; 3:14 [Heb. 4:14]; Obad. 15; Zeph. 1:7, 14).[16] In the day of the Lord God would judge unrighteousness and bring blessing and security for the faithful (Amos 9:13–15). This anticipation of deliverance was the primary component for the development of eschatology that focuses on the future saving action of God.

Isaiah 13:9–16 addresses the subject of the punishment of the day of the Lord:

> Behold, the day of the LORD comes, cruel, with wrath and fierce anger, to make the land a desolation and to destroy its sinners from it. For the stars of the heavens and their constellations will not give their light; the sun will be dark at its rising, and the moon will not shed its light. I will punish the world for its evil, and the wicked for their iniquity; I will put an end to the pomp of the arrogant, and lay low the pompous pride of the ruthless. I will make people more rare than fine gold, and mankind than the gold of Ophir. Therefore I will make the heavens tremble, and the earth will be shaken out of its place, at the wrath of the LORD of hosts in the day of his fierce anger. And like a hunted gazelle, or like sheep with none to gather them, each will turn to his own people, and each will flee to his own land. Whoever is found will be thrust through, and whoever is caught will fall by the sword. Their infants will be dashed in pieces before their eyes; their houses will be plundered and their wives ravished.

The picture is one of terror on the part of the people confronted by the Lord: terrifying images are taken from war (Isa. 13:15–16), strange astronomical

---

15. Von Rad, *The Message of the Prophets*, 95.
16. This announcement may have served a previous role in summoning men to battle. For war terminology used in the Prophets, see H. Barstad, "No Prophets? Recent Developments in Biblical Prophetic Research and Ancient Near Eastern Prophecy," *JSOT* 57 (1993) 54 n.43.

phenomena (Isa. 13:10–11), and the heavens and the earth will be thrown off course (Isa. 13:13).[17]

The day of the Lord as a time of God's visitation occurred most often as God's special judgment in the Old Testament against unfaithful Israel as well as against the nations who violated universal ethical values (e.g. Amos 1–2). In this sense they have been fulfilled. The day of the Lord also applies to a time in the future when once again God will intervene to judge those who are in rebellion and violation of his standards but will reward a faithful remnant. The judgment announced on Gog and Magog in Ezekiel 38–39, for example, differs from that of the judgment oracles against the nations in Ezekiel 25–32. The invasion of the land by Gog, the foe from the north (38:15; 39:2), moves beyond the simple judgment theme on a nation to an eschatological scheme that goes beyond Israel's contemporary experience and represents God's future judgment on all nations that oppose Israel.

Thus the day of the Lord is a time of God's visitation in judgment, but it is also the inauguration of a wonderful new age in which there will be no more wars (Isa. 2:4; cf. 11:6–9),[18] a paradisiacal prosperity and security for Israel (Joel 3:18-20; cf. Isa. 35:1–10) and for the world (e.g. Amos 9:13–15). This means that this present age will come to an end; there will be a complete break in history; and a new heaven and a new earth will be brought into being (e.g., Isa. 65–66; Rev. 21–22). Yahweh will be exalted on that day, and his rulership will be recognized (Isa. 2:11b).[19]

Already/Not Yet Fulfillment of Prophecy

The notion that a *prophecy* of the Old Testament may not be fulfilled in its details all at once is a rather well-known feature in Old Testament prophecy. But the Old Testament prophetic *text* was commonly understood as a single whole. We find this feature in Jesus's inauguration of the kingdom in his first advent, which will be culminated at the second advent. A specific historical illustration of this phenomenon occurred when Jesus entered the synagogue early in his ministry in Nazareth and began to read from Isaiah 61. After Jesus read from Isaiah 61:1–2a, he stopped the reading and announced that "Today this Scripture has been fulfilled in your hearing" (Luke 4:21). What is of interest is that Jesus purposely stopped before reading Isaiah 6:2b: "and the day of vengeance of our God." It is significant

---

17. Practically every verse in Ezekiel 7 makes some reference to the day of the Lord.
18. Although until that day, there will be wars and rumors of wars (Matt. 24:6).
19. Martens, "Eschatology," 181; Sawyer, *Prophecy and the Prophets of the Old Testament,* 60.

that Jesus did not claim the fulfillment of this day of the Lord announcement but only the content of Isaiah 61:1–2a, which pertained to his ministry in the first advent. While the Isaiah 61 passage appears to be one package unit, we discover that the fulfillment of this prophecy will come in two stages—in the first advent, which Jesus already announced had been fulfilled, and the second advent when he will return in judgment, as depicted in the book of Revelation. This concept can perhaps be visualized by the following diagram of two concentric circles.

Understanding Prophetic Texts

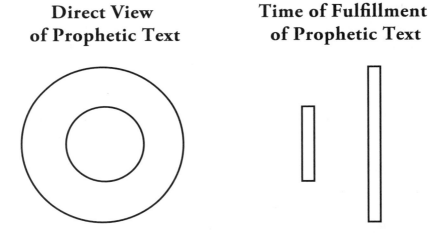

**Direct View
of Prophetic Text**   **Time of Fulfillment
of Prophetic Text**

Looking at the two circles directly head-on (on the left), they seem to belong together and for the sake of illustration it can be said that they represent two parts of a prophetic message that appear to occur at exactly the same time. But if we look at the same circles from the side (on the right), we see that they are separated. This would illustrate that while they look like one package, their fulfillment occurs in two different stages separated in time.

Having now surveyed some of the features of the Prophetic Books and prophetic prophecy we will now turn to address the doctrine of the future in the Prophets by examining what the biblical prophets say about three major areas of human and earthly existence. These areas include the future of Israel, the future of the world, and the future of mankind.[20]

---

20. Many of the passages examined may actually refer to two or even all three of these categories,

The Future of Israel in the Prophets

Future Blessing for Israel

While the book of Jeremiah focuses on the subject of the coming doom of Israel and Judah that is to be administrated by the Babylonians (e.g., Jer. 4:4–8; 6:1–8), the prophet also describes a future golden age that will include dispersed exiles returning to live again in the promised land (Isa. 43:5–7; Jer. 24:4–7; Ezek. 11:16–21), a rebuilt temple in Jerusalem where God will once again dwell in the midst of his people (e.g., Ezek. 40–48), and the restoration of worship places and practices (Jer. 31:6, 10–14). Israel will be restored as a garden (Isa. 51:3; 61:11; Jer. 31:12). Thus a face-value reading of these texts as well the promise of Jeremiah 31:36 would seem to indicate that Israel's continued existence is as certain as the continued orderly function of the solar system. Even though many exiles returned in 539 BCE and Jerusalem's walls were rebuilt (Neh. 6:15), and a temple was completed in (516 BCE), this can only be understood as a partial fulfillment of the greater blessings that the nation of Israel will receive.[21]

Isaiah 2:1–7; Micah 4:1–5

Another way to look at the future role of Israel in the coming age has to do with the central role the city of Jerusalem will play for future worshipers. The opening oracle in Isaiah 2:1–3 and Micah 4:1–2 states that in the future Mount Zion is to be elevated above all other mountains of the world, and the Lord will be worshiped as supreme over any divine or political rival.[22] The nations recognize the supremacy of Yahweh and go up to Jerusalem for instruction. Isaiah 60–62 states that people from other nations will help rebuild Zion and the restored mourners will be comforted (Isa. 60:1–3, 8–10; 61:2–4). This future centrality of Jerusalem is the focus of Zechariah 8:1–8:

> And the word of the LORD of hosts came, saying, "Thus says the LORD of hosts: I am jealous for Zion with great jealousy, and I am jealous for her with great wrath. Thus says the LORD: I have returned to Zion and will dwell in the midst of Jerusalem, and Jerusalem shall be called the faithful city, and the mountain of

---

but it is still important to examine them separately to shed specific light on the passages that highlight what will take place in the future with regard to these classifications.

21. See Martens, "Eschatology," 180.
22. Ps. 48:1–2 [Heb. 2–3] refers to Yahweh as the great king over the mountains.

the Lord of hosts, the holy mountain. Thus says the Lord of hosts: Old men and old women shall again sit in the streets of Jerusalem, each with staff in hand because of great age. And the streets of the city shall be full of boys and girls playing in its streets. Thus says the Lord of hosts: If it is marvelous in the sight of the remnant of this people in those days, should it also be marvelous in my sight, declares the Lord of hosts? Thus says the Lord of hosts: Behold, I will save my people from the east country and from the west country, and I will bring them to dwell in the midst of Jerusalem. And they shall be my people, and I will be their God, in faithfulness and in righteousness.

The worship of the Lord in Jerusalem will be an occasion of momentous and unspeakable joy in the coming age. We see in this text, particularly from the standpoint of the return from exile, that God will still yet restore his people to their land in the last days. God's people will be restored to the promised land (esp. Zech. 8:7–8). The future restoration of the Israelites to their land is a common theme in the prophets (Isa. 27:13; 35:10; 51:11; 60:4; 66:20; Jer. 3:14; 32:37; Ezek. 20:33–44; 37:26; Joel 3:20; Mic. 4:6–7,10; Zeph. 3:20; Zech. 2:7; 8:7–8).[23] Even though the nations of the world will oppose Israel in the coming days, Israel will ultimately be victorious over her enemies (Isa. 34:8; Joel 3:1–21; Obad. 16; Mic. 4:11–13; Zech. 1:14–15; 12:2–9; 14:1–3, 12–19).

God's Plan for the Nations

Several of the writing prophets devote a great amount of space to the subject of the future of the foreign nations (Isa. 13–23; Jer. 46–51; Ezek. 25–32; Amos 1–2). Two books from the Twelve (the Minor Prophets)—Nahum with reference to Assyria, and Obadiah with reference to Edom—focus their oracles entirely on a single foreign nation. The theme of the book of Jonah has to do with God's right to his concern for a foreign nation (Ninevah, capital of Assyria) other than Israel (Jonah 4). There is good news ahead for certain nations as, for example, in Egypt (Isa. 19:24–25 and Jer. 46:25–26) and Assyria (cf. Isa. 56:7–7). There will also be restoration for Ammon (Jer. 49:6)

---

23. Since the exiles had already returned from Babylon at the time of Zechariah's writing, the promise that Israelites will be brought back to their homeland remains a future promise (e.g., Zech. 10:10).

and Elam (Jer. 49:39). Foreigners will be able to serve in God's ministry (Isa. 66:18–21). Even though Ezekiel paints a scene in which nations will gather in war against the nation of Israel (Ezek. 38–39), the survivors of this conflict will become worshipers of the God of Israel (Zech. 14:16).[24]

The teaching of the Prophetic Books about the relationship of Israel with the nations could be summarized as follows:[25]

- God will use foreign nations to punish Jerusalem for her sins and to purge her of her evil (Isa. 28:21).
- God will suddenly step in to rescue Jerusalem from the foreign nations gathered against it (Isa. 29:1–8; 31:4–5; cf. 10:5–15).
- The Mount of Olives will be split in two and living waters will flow out of Jerusalem (Zech. 14:4–5).
- Jerusalem will be exalted as the only high mountain in the region, and the city and all her surviving inhabitants will dwell in security (Isa. 2:1–7; Mic. 4:1–5).
- Israel will be established as the special place for the worship of all nations (Zech. 14:16).
- Those survivors of the nations who came up against Jerusalem will make a yearly pilgrimage to Jerusalem to worship the real King, the Lord of hosts, and celebrate the feast of booths (Zech. 14:16).

The same tradition seems to lie behind Joel's vision of God's summoning of the nations to the valley of Jehoshaphat for judgment (Joel 3 [Heb. 4]. God calls the nations to the land of Israel, to the valley of Jehoshaphat, for war. But just as in Ezekiel and Zechariah, God intervenes, roaring from Zion and thundering from Jerusalem, becoming a refuge for his people (Joel 3:16 [Heb. 4:16]). He accomplishes this by destroying the enemies of Israel. As a result Jerusalem will be secure and the enemies of Israel will be destroyed. The city will become the dwelling place of the Lord and as in Ezekiel 47 and Zechariah 14:8, a stream will come forth from the house of the Lord to water the land.

---

24. Martens, "Eschatology," 181.
25. See J. J. M. Roberts, "The End of War in the Zion Tradition: The Imperialistic Background of an Old Testament Vision of Worldwide Peace," in *Character Ethics and the Old Testament: Moral Dimensions of Scripture,* M. Daniel Carroll R. and Jacqueline E. Lapsley, eds. (Louisville, London: Westminster John Knox, 2007), 124–125.

The theme of the nations coming to Jerusalem to worship the Lord is harmonious with the New Testament as well.[26] This is particularly evident in Romans 9–11 and Romans 15 where Paul profusely cites the prophetic word in support for his argument for the conversion of the Gentiles.[27] The Christian movement could point indisputably to the inclusion of Gentiles in its ranks as evidence that this expectation was being fulfilled. It is around this issue that Paul assembles predictive prophecies that are coming true in his own work.[28]

THE FUTURE OF THE WORLD IN THE PROPHETS

When we read the Prophets, or any other place in the Bible for that matter, we are impressed by the perennial rebellion of the Israelites and the general depravity of man in general. We take away a perspective that all is not right with God's creation. That was clearly the thinking of the prophet Jeremiah as we have noted. To describe the potential outcome of the Israelites' disobedience and idolatry, Jeremiah 4:23 uses a familiar phrase to describe a world teetering on the edge of annihilation: "without form and void" (*tōhû wābōhû* from Genesis 1:2a). Jeremiah says that due to Israel's rebellion the world is on the brink of reverting back to the time before the completion of the six-day process of creation. The behavior of the Israelites has undone what God has created. Similarly, the book of Zephaniah opens with a judgment announcement for all creation (Zeph. 1:2–3). God announces universal judgment on the world whereby everything will be swept away. Using language similar to that found in the flood account in Genesis (Gen. 6–7), Zephaniah announced that all life will be destroyed on the earth (Zeph. 1:2–3; cf. the seismic changes in Zech. 14:3–10 [see Isa. 24–27; Joel 2:3–31]). The series of beings listed in Zephaniah 1:3—man, beasts, birds, and fish—is in reverse order to their creation in Genesis 1:20–26 and constitutes an allusion to the biblical flood. The reversal of the order of the created beings probably indicates that God's act of judgment is an act of "anti-creation" (see Hos. 4:1–3).[29]

---

26. If we combined all the passages in the prophetic literature that addressed the nations, the length of that volume would be longer than the New Testament.
27. It was a tradition in Judaism that the gathering in of the Gentiles was part of the overall complex of events that constituted the last days (see E. P. Sanders, *Jesus and Judaism* [London: SCM Press, 1985], 217).
28. Barton, *Oracles of God*, 190–91.
29. J. Kselman, "Zephaniah, Book of," in *ABD* 6:1078.

The visitation on the day of the Lord will include a judgment that is world-wide in scope (Zeph. 1:18b).[30]

But the day of the Lord will also include God's intervention on behalf of his people. The massive change in nature can only come about by the work of Almighty God. God must transform nature itself, to make the produce of the land abundant and to banish hunger forever (Ezek. 36:30, 35).[31] In it barren regions trees will abound, and deserts will flourish (Ezek. 36:30; cf Isa. 41:18–20; 51:3; 55:12–13). Forests will be a safe place (Ezek. 34:25; cf. Isa. 29:17). As a symbol of divine blessing, fish will teem in a river described as flowing eastward from the temple to the Dead Sea in a new topography (Ezek. 47:9).[32]

Ezekiel 36:13–38 contains an excellent summation of the comprehensiveness of Old Testament eschatology, particularly what it says in reference to God's creation. The following chart illustrates the profound changes that will ensue in the coming age.

EZEKIEL 36:13–38	
Fertility and agriculture	8–9, 11, 29–30, 34–35
Return and occupation of land	10, 12, 24, 28
No more reproach for land	13–15
Israel's sin and basis for restoration	16–23
Cleansing	25, 29
New heart and spirit	26–27
Repentance	31–32
Nations will know	36
Population increase	37–38

---

30. Martens, "Eschatology," 183.
31. See Donald E. Gowan, *Eschatology in the Old Testament*, 2nd ed. (Edinburgh: T&T Clark, 2000), 2.
32. Martens, "Eschatology," 183.

In this future age there will be no more human infirmity (Isa. 35:5–6a); no more hunger (Ezek. 36:30); and no more war (Mic. 4:3). Other passages address the transformation in speaking about an abundant fertility (Isa. 4:2; Joel 2:23; 3:17–18), a new natural order where there will be no harm to living things (Isa. 11:6–9; 65:25) and a new earth (Isa. 35:1–10; 65:17–18; Ezek. 47:1–12; Zech. 14:4–8, 10).[33]

The prophet Isaiah in particular addresses the future in the terms of a new heaven and new earth (Isa. 65:17–25; 66:18–23). Similar phrases link the new-earth prediction (Isa. 66:25) to the prophecy of the future reign of Messiah (Isa. 11:6–9). Promises of blessing on the land of Israel along with the future glory of Jerusalem harmonize with these promises of blessing on the earth.[34] In this new world, people aged one hundred will be considered young (Isa. 65:20) and the whole earth will be full of the knowledge of God.[35]

The new creation is to be conceptualized not as a restoration, but rather as a transmutation of one order of existence into another. That transmutation still keeps a focus on the earth, even if it is a new earth. The "place" of heaven is the new earth in the larger salvation story, including the Old Testament.[36]

THE FUTURE OF MANKIND IN THE PROPHETS

The Future of God's People

According to the prophetic record, there will be in the future a transformation of God's people that has not been experienced since the fall of Adam and Eve. This transformation will be possible as God will provide a forgiveness of sins that had not been known in any previous stage. This eschatological forgiveness is referenced in such prophetic passages as Isaiah 33:24; 40:2; Zechariah 13:1.[37] Ezekiel 20:40–44 is a particularly significant passage that illustrates this point, as well as other themes associated with the day of the Lord:

---

33. This transformation of nature is also seen in such Old Testament prophetic texts as Isa. 11:6–9, quoted in part in Isa. 35:5–6, 43:20, and 65:25; Isa. 60:19–20; Ezek. 34:25, 28; Ezek. 47; Hos. 2:18, 21–23a; and Zech. 14:8, 10–15 (see Gowan, *Eschatology in the Old Testament*, 10, 102–104, 113–117).
34. This parallels the promises given in the covenant with Noah (the earth) and Abraham (the land of Israel).
35. Martens, "Eschatology," 184.
36. Ibid.
37. Repentance is associated with forgiveness in Isa. 59:20; Jer. 29:10–14; Ezek. 16:59–62.

For on my holy mountain, the mountain height of Israel,
declares the Lord GOD, there all the house of Israel, all of
them, shall serve me in the land. There I will accept them,
and there I will require your contributions and the choic-
est of your gifts, with all your sacred offerings. As a pleasing aroma I will accept you, when I bring you out from the
peoples and gather you out of the countries where you have
been scattered. And I will manifest my holiness among you
in the sight of the nations. And you shall know that I am the
LORD, when I bring you into the land of Israel, the country
that I swore to give to your fathers. And there you shall remember your ways and all your deeds with which you have
defiled yourselves, and you shall loathe yourselves for all the
evils that you have committed. And you shall know that I
am the LORD, when I deal with you for my name's sake, not
according to your evil ways, nor according to your corrupt
deeds, O house of Israel, declares the Lord GOD.

According to Jeremiah 33:8 sin and guilt will be erased in this coming era. This
makeover of the people of God in the future will require an act of God and will
result in transformation and obedience. This is stated in the promise of Jeremiah
32:39–40:

I will give them one heart and one way, that they may fear me
forever, for their own good and the good of their children after
them. I will make with them an everlasting covenant, that I will
not turn away from doing good to them. And I will put the fear
of me in their hearts, that they may not turn from me.[38]

This new covenant, God said, will supersede the old (Mosaic) covenant in that it
will guarantee obedience to the law as being written on the heart. "And I will give
you a new heart, and a new spirit I will put within you. And I will remove the heart
of stone from your flesh and give you a heart of flesh. And I will put my Spirit
within you, and cause you to walk in my statutes and be careful to obey my rules"
(Ezek. 36:26–27). The possibility that as in the past they will be unable to obey

---

38. See also Isa 30:20–21; 33:24; 35:5–6; 59:21; 65:20; Jer 33:6; 50:5; Joel 3:17.

the law is not considered an option for the people of the city of the future (Zech. 8:16–17). The restoration will vindicate the Lord's name (Ezek. 36:22–23), and this restoration of the nation will be like a resurrection from the dead (Ezek. 37).

The Future of All Humanity[39]

Given the vast amount of literature that is found in the Old Testament (almost eighty percent of the entire Bible), it is somewhat surprising that we find very little about what happens to an individual after death. The Old Testament does affirm, however, the belief in bodily resurrection. One of the clearer statements comes in Isaiah 26:19: "Your dead shall live; their bodies shall rise. You who dwell in the dust, awake and sing for joy! For your dew is a dew of light, and the earth will give birth to the dead." The previous chapter of Isaiah is also clear on this issue as the prophet addresses the hope of what will transpire in the coming age: "He will swallow up death forever; and the Lord GOD will wipe away tears from all faces, and the reproach of his people he will take away from all the earth, for the LORD has spoken" (Isa. 25:8). Perhaps the most familiar Old Testament prophetic passage on resurrection is located in Ezekiel 37 regarding the reviving of the dead dry bones. The vision of Ezekiel about dead bones coming to life is about the restoration of Israel (Ezek. 37:1–14), but it affirms and underlines a belief in the truth of a bodily resurrection of the dead. Martha affirms her belief in the resurrection of Lazarus, a theological truth that undoubtedly was informed by her understanding of the Old Testament (John 11:24).

Daniel's statement is often believed to be the most explicit Old Testament statement about the resurrection: "And many of those who sleep in the dust of the earth shall awake, some to everlasting life, and some to shame and everlasting contempt" (Dan. 12:2). Thus, as in the New Testament, two destinies are projected, one positive and the other negative. A positive description of that future is found in the pictorial of the new Jerusalem (Isa. 65:17–25), which apparently serves as the backdrop for John's vision (Rev. 21). But negatively, it is said of those who rebelled against God in the last verse of the book of Isaiah that "their worm shall not die, their fire shall not be quenched" (Isa. 66:24 [cf. Jesus's description of Gehenna in Mark 9:48]).[40]

There can be no doubt that the prophets assume a future judgment, for retribution is part of present and end-time reality (Isa. 63:1–6; Ezek. 38-39; Hab.

---

39. For a fuller treatment consult Martens, "Eschatology," 182–83.
40. See Martens, "Eschatology," 182.

2:6–8; Zech. 14). "The day," as we have seen, is one of the Lord's wrath and destruction (Zeph. 1:14–16). See Ecclesiastes 12:14, which provides specificity to Daniel's statement with the description "the court sat in judgment, and the books were opened" (Dan. 7:10c).[41]

CONCLUSION

According to the prophets, the future kingdom that God will establish upon this earth will be everlasting in its duration. We have seen this truth in such passages as Daniel 2:34–35, 44; Isaiah 2:2–4; and Micah 4:1–8. What the prophets also predict is that this kingdom will be composed of both Jews and Gentiles.

Consistent with the prophetic testimony is the fact that the New Testament does not nullify the role of national Israel in the future. There is no thought in the New Testament that Israel as a national entity has disappeared from God's eschatological plan, as Jesus preaches the kingdom of Israel (Acts 1:3, 6–7, 3:19–21 [cf. 3:18–26]).[42] However, with the coming of Christ in the first advent, the new covenant has been inaugurated. This new covenant, which promised a united house of Judah and house of Israel, was initiated in the New Testament at the Last Supper, when Jesus said, "This cup is the new covenant established by My blood" (Luke 22:20, HCSB; see 1 Cor. 11:25). The church is now experiencing the benefits of the new covenant (the forgiveness of sin, Jer. 31:34)—a fulfillment that illustrates the already/not yet pattern. But other aspects of the new covenant, particularly those promises given to the nation of Israel, will not be realized until the second coming of Christ. With that event the unconditional promises to Abraham will be realized (Jer. 31:35–37; Gen. 12:3b), and the creation itself will be released from its groaning at the revelation of the children of God (Rom. 8:21).

But curiously, death still remains a feature in some of the prophetic texts of the new world order (Isa. 65:20). By contrast, Isaiah 25, on the other hand, predicts a reign of God in which death will be abolished. Similarly, some passages predict conditions for the eschatological kingdom in which sin is present while others exclude it altogether. For example, Zechariah 14 plainly states that when the Lord comes in the day of the Lord, when he descends to the earth and

41. Martens, "Eschatology, 182–83.
42. See Craig A. Blaising, "A Premillennial Response to Robert B. Strimple," in *Three Views on the Millennium and Beyond*, ed. Darrell L. Bock (Grand Rapids: Zondervan, 1999), 145–46.

proceeds to reign from Jerusalem, he will require the nations to worship him and will punish those who refuse to do so (Zech. 14:16–19). The repetition of phrases between Isaiah 11 and 65 also seems to relate both of these passages to the same eschatological conditions, and those conditions point to a situation prior to the final dealing with sin and death. Daniel 9:24, on the other hand, expects that when the kingdom comes, sin will come to an end. It is conceivable that the differences in these descriptions point to two different phases of the eschatological kingdom, one before and one following the final judgment on sin.[43] The structure of the oracle in Isaiah 24–25 indicates some kind of intermediate situation between the coming of God in the day of the Lord and the everlasting reign in which sin and death are done away completely. This intermediate set of conditions points to a millennial kingdom which will transpire prior to the new world conditions in which the everlasting reign will be fulfilled. This millennial kingdom is best interpreted as a future phase or stage of that eschatological kingdom in the age to come.[44]

Taken together, the large number of prophecies about Israel, the nations, and the cosmos convey a message about a God who is sovereign over the individual, the faith community, and the nations. God determines the fate of all nations (Joel 3:1–21). He is the universal sovereign over the natural world (Zech. 10:1–2), as well as over all political structures (Dan. 4:34–35; 6:25–28; 7:13–14, 23–27).[45] The Lord knows the end from the beginning (Isa. 41:22). Fulfilled prophecy demonstrates without a doubt that God is an omnipotent, all-powerful sovereign. As a consequence in the final disposition of all things, righteousness will prevail. In the last judgment God will deal fully and finally with evil, for judgment will fall on the wicked, and the world will be set right, and that on a cosmic scale.[46]

Fulfilled prophecy also demonstrates that Jesus Christ is the one essential factor upon which all Old Testament prophecy depends.[47] In Romans Paul speaks of "the gospel of God, which he promised beforehand through *his prophets* in the holy Scriptures concerning his Son" (Rom. 1:1–3, emphasis mine). Two special Isianic oracles in eighth century prophecy about a future Davidic king share a vision of peace (see also Isa. 2 and Mic. 4). In Isaiah 9:5–6, this ruler is named

---

43. Craig A. Blaising, "Premillennialism," in *Three Views on the Millennium and Beyond,* 202.
44. Ibid., 197.
45. This is illustrated in the book of Jonah where all of nature responds positively to God's sovereignty except for God's prophet. Merrill, Rooker, and Grisanti, *The World and the Word,* 451.
46. Martens, "Eschatology, 184.
47. See Barton, *Oracles of God,* 186.

"the prince of peace" and under his rule there "will be no end to peace" as he establishes his rule in "justice and righteousness." In Isaiah 11:3–4, this ruler will judge and arbitrate (the same two verbs used in Isa. 2:4) in righteousness and equity, and the result will be an idyllic, peaceable kingdom, for the knowledge of Yahweh will fill the earth (Isa. 11:5–9). The rule of the righteous King is a common ideal theme in the prophets (Isa. 11:9; 44:28; Jer. 33:16; Zech. 4:5–10; 6:12–13; 9:9–10).

This promise of a new Davidic line is found in Jeremiah (23:1–6; 33:14–16) and Ezekiel (34:23–24; 37:24–28); as well as in Haggai 2:20–23 and Zechariah 4:6–14; 6:9–14. Additional messianic expectations are found in Zechariah (12:7–8; 13:1) and remained a vibrant hope into New Testament times.

The stone in Daniel 2 is the Messiah, Jesus Christ, who will bring in the coming kingdom. In Jesus that kingdom has been inaugurated, but the world still awaits the full establishment of the kingdom of God.

Jesus will bring peace and justice to this troubled world, and the end of conflict. In his reign the world will be transformed, and every knee shall bow and recognize his supremacy (Phil 2: 10). All people will worship him "from every tribe and language and people and nation" (Rev. 5:9). "The establishment of God's rule, his Kingdom, is the central hope of the prophets."[48]

---

48. G. E. Ladd, *The Last Things: An Eschatology for Laymen* (Grand Rapids: Eerdmans, 1978), 43.

The New Testament

The Doctrine of the Future
in the Synoptic Gospels

Darrell L. Bock

S ome people think that looking into the future is like trying to gaze into a crystal ball; but when one is dealing with revelation, one is not looking into a future that is hazy. Rather, one is catching a glimpse of God's promised activity that completes and fulfills promises he has made and already begun to fulfill. This is especially the case when one looks at the Synoptic Gospels and what Jesus said about the future. So we consider how Jesus spoke about what is yet to come. We divide our discussion into four parts, the first three focus on the program of God for the world: sayings about the future, parables about the future, the Olivet Discourse, concluded by a summary on what the future holds for individuals. We will keep an eye on how each synoptic gospel addresses these issues as we proceed, for different gospels have distinct contributions to make to our topic.

One word needs to be said about the term "eschatology" and the timing of the future before we survey the texts. In the New Testament, eschatology applies to everything tied to Jesus's first and second comings. He is seen as the fulfillment of promises God made in the Old Testament. Texts like Luke 7:28, 10:24, and 16:16 point to Jesus' first coming as a break point in God's program, as we move from promise into initial realization.[1] This means that

---

1. Darrell L. Bock, *Jesus according to Scripture* (Grand Rapids: Baker, 2002), 565–93. The discussion on the kingdom in Jesus's teaching shows this emphasis, as do texts like Acts 2:14–40 and Hebrews 1:1-2. Also Craig L. Blaising and Darrell L. Bock, *Progressive Dispensationalism* (Wheaton, IL: Victor Books, 1993), 232–83. The chart on page 254 points to the kingdom present in the person of the King during Jesus's ministry, the kingdom in mystery form in heaven with kingdom citizens on earth in the present era, and the kingdom in its fullness after the day of the Lord in the era to come. Benefits of forgiveness and the Spirit bestowed after Jesus's death inaugurate the new covenant, starting with Acts 2. Robert Saucy, *The Case for Progressive Dispensationalism* (Grand Rapids: Zondevan, 1993), 81–110.

the promise of realization and the future starts with Jesus's first coming in the New Testament, as depicted in the Gospels.

In this essay we will consider events that are not merely future to the time of the writing of the New Testament but in the future for readers today. Nonetheless, one should be sensitive to the fact that eschatology in the New Testament is not just about future events for us, but touched on many events tied to Jesus's presence on earth.

Sayings about the Future

Consummation Soon, Yet with Seeming Delay

The first set of texts about the future that we will consider introduce a tension tied to teaching about the future in the NT. The future consummation is both soon and yet long enough away that the faith of some will waver. Numerous texts push on this tension.

In the Olivet Discourse, when Jesus notes the signs that accompany the destruction of the temple as well as the return, he observes that certain things will happen before the end. Wars and rumors of wars precede these events (Mark 13:7). In addition, the gospel must go out into all the world before the end (Mark 13:10). Paul shows in Colossians 1:6 that the penetration of the gospel into all the world is something he can contend is already taking place in his day, so one should be careful not to overextend this image. Still these texts show that certain events were seen as preceding the consummation of promise.

Delay is also seen in a remark Jesus makes to the disciples in Luke 17:22. He tells them they will long to see the days of the Son of Man (a reference to the consummation) and yet they will not see it. Later he tells them his suffering must come first (Luke 17:25). Yet another hint of delay in consummation comes in Luke 19:11, where Jesus tells a parable of accountability because the disciples thought the kingdom of God would come immediately. This text looks at the kingdom's coming in consummation in contrast to other texts that say it is here already (Matt. 12:28; Luke 11:20; 17:21). It is important to note that kingdom texts in the gospels come with one of two time periods in mind. Some portray it as here, looking to its inauguration with Jesus, while others look to its coming in fullness and consummation.

A text that argues for a coming soon, but also with this note of a delay long enough to trouble some is found in Luke 18:8. Here Jesus says justice will come speedily for the disciples, since the coming of the kingdom is seen as the vindication of the righteous; but he goes on to ask if the Son of Man will find faith on earth when he comes.

All of these texts show that Jesus pointed to what would come in the future but refused to specify a time when it would take place. In one passage he even notes that the timing is known to the Father alone (Matt. 24:36; Mark 13:32)—something also affirmed in Acts 1:6–7 as being the Father's business.[2] The stress in Scripture is not on trying to figure out exactly when these events will take place, but to keep a watchful eye on them, keeping ready, while doing what God has called his people to do until he returns.

Three other texts are often brought into this discussion. Matthew 10:23 has the disciples still sharing with all the towns and villages of Israel when the Son of Man comes. On the surface, this looks like a prediction of a soon return of the Son of Man, even in the disciples' lifetime, but this fails to see the disciples as representative of all who share the gospel and has to ignore other texts, like those just noted, where some time passing before the end is assumed. Matthew 16:28, Mark 9:1, and Luke 9:27 predict that some of the disciples will see the kingdom of God in power, but this looks like a text that points to the transfiguration as a preview of the end and not the end itself. The most discussed of the three texts pointing to a soon return are the parallel accounts of Mark 13:30, Matthew 24:34, and Luke 21:32 ("this generation will not pass away until all of these things take place"). These texts are a part of the Olivet Discourse. On the surface it looks like a prediction of the return within the generation of the disciples. However one of three other readings is more likely. The first is that the events of the end once they start in earnest take no longer than a generation from start to finish. In other words, once the events of the end start, as opposed to the events that simply precede the end, everything will come to a close quickly. Another possibility is the exact reverse reading. The events leading to the destruction of the temple in 70 CE take place within this generation as precursors and guarantees of the end, like buds on a fig tree that will bloom in full one day.[3] A third option is that "generation" points not to time but an ethical condition and is shorthand for "this evil generation." In that case, Jesus makes the point that the end will bring judgment to those who are evil and represents a vindication of the

---

2. On the Acts text and the issue of the future for Israel there, Darrell L. Bock, *Acts* (Grand Rapids: Baker, 2007), 62.

3. For this view, which I very slightly prefer for this difficult text, see David Turner, *The Gospel of Matthew* in Cornerstone Biblical Commentary (Carol Stream, IL: Tyndale House, 2005), 318; also Robert Stein, *Mark* (Grand Rapids: Baker, 2008), 619.

saints—an idea that is core to the idea of the return and consummation, as the next subsection will show.

Return Means Judgment

Jesus's future return means judgment. Luke 13:1–5 and several texts in Matthew make this point. Luke 13 has Jesus note that if one does not repent, then one will perish in the future. Matthew 13 has a series of kingdom parables that anticipate a separation of the righteous and wicked in a judgment to come at the end (Matt. 13:30, 48). Matthew 12:41–42 sees a judgment coming for cities in Israel that reject the Messiah. Matthew 25:31–46 has the parables of the sheep and the goats that make the same point. The picture of the cosmic chaos in the Olivet Discourse (Matt. 24:29–30; Mark 13:24–25; Luke 21:25–27) points to the day of the Lord imagery of the OT (sun and moon, Isa. 13:10; see also Ezek. 32:7; Joel 2:10; 2:31; 3:15; stars, Judg. 5:5; Ps. 18:7; 114:7; Amos 8:9; 9:5; Mic. 1:4; Nah. 1:5; Hab. 3:6).[4]

These texts indicate that a major feature of the future is to establish righteousness and vindicate those who have responded to God. The parables about the future we consider in the next section add detail to this emphasis. Justice comes in the future and accountability to God exists now, because of what is taught about the future. The absence of eschatology in one's thinking means the creation makes less sense and lacks a sustained moral rationale for the presence of evil, since there is no resolution to its presence.

Tribulation until the End

Matthew 10:17–22 makes the point that those who faithfully carry the message of God will experience tribulation until the return. The mention of enduring to the end makes this point. Similar imagery shows up in the Olivet Discourse (Mark 13:9–13; Luke 21:12–19). There is no hint that this opposition stops before the return by the way the discourse unfolds. Acts 14:22 says much the same thing when it says we must enter into the kingdom of God through much persecution. Jesus's teaching that the disciple must be willing to carry the cross also is making this point (Matt. 16:24; Mark 8:34; Luke 9:23). So the disciple needs to be prepared for rejection and suffering.[5] Following Jesus is no elixir to difficulty.

---

4. William Lane, *The Gospel according to Mark* (Grand Rapids: Eerdmans, 1974), 475.
5. For this theme in Luke's gospel and Acts which mirrors the other synoptics, Scott Cunningham, *"Through Many Tribulations": The Theology of Persecution in Luke-Acts* (Sheffield: Sheffield Academic Press, 1997).

The Future Points to Our Resurrection

The dispute Jesus had with the Sadducees over resurrection shows that the resurrection is something Jesus affirmed about the future. This text does not teach immortality of the soul alone, nor does it affirm reincarnation. Resurrection means a fresh kind of existence like the angels have, where former earthly relationships like marriage do not apply. All the passages on this event make this point and show Jesus affirming resurrection as being something taught as early as Exodus 3:6 (Matt. 22:22–33; Mark 12:18–27; Luke 20:27–40). Death is banished by this resurrection, as people do not die again (Luke 20:36)

A Future for Israel When She Repents

An important text in terms of the nation of Israel is a saying Jesus utters about the house of Israel being desolate until she says, "Blessed is he who comes in the name of the Lord" (Matt. 23:37–39; Luke 13:34–35).[6] Jesus cites the affirmation of Psalm 118:26 as a counter to the current judgment Israel is under for rejecting the sent Messiah. The desolate house is language from Jeremiah and points to an exilic-like judgment that is in place until the nation's response changes. The remark foresees a day in the future when the nation will turn—something Romans 11 also affirms.[7]

The Future Is about the "Renewal"

Matthew 19:28 calls the era to come the "regeneration" or "renewal" when the disciples will rule over Israel. This looks to foresee a standard kingdom rule in the age to come. The disciples will share in this kingdom to come.[8]

The Synoptic Gospels' sayings on the future cover an array of ideas that point to vindication, hope, and the establishment of righteousness. These are given more details in parables that discuss what will happen in the future.

PARABLES ABOUT THE FUTURE

The parables that treat the future can be divided up into those associated with

---

6. On this sequence of "until" texts in Luke-Acts, "The Restoration of Israel in Luke-Acts," in *Introduction to Messianic Judaism*, ed. David Rudolph and Joel Willets (Grand Rapids: Zondervan, 2013), 168–77. Acts 3:18–22 should be added to two Lucan texts (Luke 13:35 and 21:20–23).
7. Detail on this important theme appears in Darrell L Bock, *A Theology of Luke and Acts* (Grand Rapids: Zondervan, 2013), 279–89.
8. Turner, *Matthew*, 253, 255.

the Olivet Discourse and those that are distinct from it. A few parables Jesus taught are in both contexts but make the same point.

Luke 12:35–48: The Wedding Feast and the Abusive Steward

The key theme about the future in the Synoptics is not to give a chronicle of events or calendar; it is to call for faithfulness because of the accountability that is tied to the return. This is seen very evidently in the sequence of two parables we get in Luke 12.

The first, in 12:35–40, is to be awake and ready for the time of the return. Jesus compares it to a master who returns from a distant wedding at an unannounced hour. One is "to be dressed for service and keep one's lamps burning." This is a picture of readiness. When the master knocks, the servant is ready to open the door and welcome the master back. It is the alert servant who is blessed. One is to be ready, because the hour of the return of the Son of Man is not known.

The second image elaborates on this scene with the issue of different responses to the stewardship the servant has in the interim. Four scenarios are presented but one is stressed. The one who is obedient and faithful will be rewarded (12:43–44). The one who does the opposite of what is asked will be "cut into pieces" and placed with the unfaithful—a picture of rejection because the response shows an utter lack of faith (12:45–46). This is the most shocking image, the one that catches one's attention. There are two other types of disobedience that are disciplined with different levels of beating. The one who knows but fails to do gets a severe beating (12:47) The one who acts out of ignorance gets a light beating (12:48a). The passage closes with a summary in 12:48b. Of the one who has been given much, much is required. So the passage emphasizes the accountability one has before God before the consummation.

Luke 18:1–8: The Prayer for Justice

Our survey has shown that the future is about vindication of the saints and the establishment of righteousness. One parable Jesus tells underscores this point. It urges disciples to pray at all times and not lose heart (18:1). The point is made using the picture of a widow seeking justice from a judge who does not care for people. She badgers the judge until he responds (18:3–5). That is the picture of how disciples are to seek God out in praying for the establishment of justice and vindication on earth. Jesus then gives assurance that God will vindicate his own speedily, but with a long enough delay that when the Son of Man comes, he may not find faith (18:6–8).[9] So we see the future means hope, not just for individual salvation, but for the world at large. Justice comes into the world with the return, and at that time God brings vindication to those allied to God who have been wronged.

Matthew 25:14–30 and Luke 19:11–29: Accountability for Stewardship

This parable shows up in two forms that make much the same point. Luke 19:11 tells us the parable is told because the disciples thought the kingdom was coming as Jesus was approaching Jerusalem. Matthew situates his version in the Olivet Discourse in Jerusalem. The point is that the kingdom in fullness is not coming when Jesus gets to Jerusalem. Instead there is a stewardship for those associated with Jesus. They have a responsibility to carry out that stewardship until he returns.

In the parables, each disciple is given resources (ten, five, and one mina in Luke; five, two, and one talent in Matthew). They are to use those gifts to make a profit. This is a picture of ministry capability and using one's efforts for the kingdom. In both versions the first two disciples make a profit and are commended for their labor. In each version the third disciple does nothing with what they have received, having hidden it. In that third case in each version, the disciple is rebuked and has what he had taken from him, ending up with nothing. This is stated most emphatically as the one who "has nothing even what he has is taken from him." This is a way to state that this disciple had and has absolutely nothing. It raises the category of the "odd person out," a theme common in many of Jesus's parables about the end and judgment. The disciple stated he did not regard the master positively and therefore did nothing with what he had received. The parable as a whole is about accountability until the return. It warns that those who "associate" with Jesus but really do not regard him well may have nothing. They really do nothing in response to their exposure to him and will end up with nothing. They do not have anything that could be called faith in Jesus. They end up on the outside looking in. The opportunity to be a part of the kingdom and future blessing means that one has a faith that has regard for the King to whom one is accountable.

---

9. Darrell L. Bock, *Luke 9:51–24:53* (Grand Rapids: Baker, 1996), 1451–56.

Matthew 25:1–13: Always Be Ready

In Matthew 25:1–13 Jesus tells another "odd person out" parable in the Olivet Discourse that stresses being ready, as one does not know when the Son of Man will return. This parable is about ten virgins. Five take extra oil with them for their lamps, while five do not. When the time comes to be escorted to the wedding, the five wise virgins with oil have enough to be able to go to the wedding. The five foolish virgins who lacked oil do not. When the groom arrived for the entourage, five could go; the others had to get oil, only to be locked out of the celebration by the time they bought their oil and returned. The shut door comes with the remark that he did not know them. This parable precedes the parable of the talents in Matthew and sets the stage for the accountability that the parable of the talents pictures. The wise virgins are responsive to the future by being ready for it. This reflects knowing the one who is to come, having a faith in the one to come. The closing exhortation in the parable of the ten virgins gives its application: Stay alert, because you do not know the day or the hour.

Putting these two parables together points to how one should think about the future. The future is a time for celebration as it represents the vindication of the saints and the establishment of righteousness. One indicates faith and readiness for this future time to come in a faith that is responsive to God's current call. That response of faith makes use of the talents God offers by grace. Those who know God are alert and responsive, using the amount of gifts God has given and bearing fruit. This is one way they show their readiness for what is to come. They join in and participate responsively to the program of God. Others do nothing with the opportunity. In fact they really do not know the One who has made this opportunity available. They end up the "odd persons out."

So how we see the future and respond to it now is a litmus test for our hearts before God. The future is that important. It motivates us to act in faith and engenders hope. It keeps us accountable.

Matthew 25:31–46: Another Picture of Accountability for How We Treat Those of the Faith

The third of the Matthean Olivet parables shows how judgment in the end will separate people, with that judgment tied to how people of faith are treated. People of the nations will be separated into two groups, sheep and goats. The sheep inherit the kingdom. The parable says they do so because they treated "one of these brothers and sisters of mine" with care when they had a core need of being hungry, thirsty, naked, or in prison. The goats are sent into eternal fire for failing to respond to such needs.

The parable pictures the judgment at the end. It also suggests in its juxtaposition with the earlier parables that a faith that trusts God shows itself in compassion for those who belong to God (1 John 3:17). To love God and trust him is to be moved to love others (1 John 4:19). Faith works. It understands that grace as a gift is appreciated in a way that leads into responsiveness. That responsiveness honors God by honoring and caring about those who are his. Faith has an ethic of compassion and care that shows one has learned from grace how to be like God and his care (Matt. 18:23–35). This understanding about the future shows how a future hope can have a purifying impact (1 John 3:3). Appreciating the future encourages us to live in a way that is grateful to God. Such appreciation responds to what he has asked of us in gifting us with the opportunity of experiencing life in the context of forgiveness, enabling us to live well and flourish.

THE OLIVET DISCOURSE AND THE FUTURE

Setting the Context: A Pattern Prophecy

Jesus's most focused discussion of the future is found in the Olivet Discourse (Matt. 24–25; Mark 13; Luke 21:5–36). This is a complicated discourse because we have it in three versions and it addresses two events at the same time that mirror each other. Those events are the destruction of the temple in 70 CE and the events tied to the end times. The destruction is seen as a precursor and reflection of the end. This kind of multiple event mirroring is known as typology, or pattern prophecy; it is where one event sets a pattern for another that comes later. If one does not appreciate this mirrored or layered structure in this discourse, it becomes very confusing to read the text, especially in its various versions.

Some, in failing to see the layers, force us to choose between 70 CE and the end for the discourse as a whole. Some argue the passage is only about 70 CE and the destruction of Jerusalem. They point to the opening remarks of Jesus that led to the disciples asking about when these things would be. Jesus is predicting the temple's destruction when he says not one stone will be left on another of the temple the disciples are admiring. Others say that Jesus is discussing the end when he refers to the Son of Man and the gathering of the saints. Not only that, but the question in Matthew explicitly points to and asks about the end. So which approach is correct?

The better answer is not to force a choice, but to see both as correct because a patterned fulfillment is being presented. One set of events mirrors and points to

the other in a patterned fulfillment.[10] Such patterns are common in Jewish interpretation of the period. One can speak of the exodus or a new exodus. One can
speak of the day of the Lord and mean Joel's locust plague as a picture of the
end-time judgment. One can see Eden as a picture of the new heaven and earth.
The antichrist can be Antiochus Epiphanes, a Roman emperor, or the figure of
the end. Patterns for looking at the future using the past, present, or near future
are common in the Bible. That is what is happening here. This means that a
writer can present the text focusing on the pattern itself in its double layering.
One can emphasize the near setting that sets the pattern or look to its end result
in the completion of the pattern. Our contention is that Mark simply presents
the pattern, while Matthew focuses on the end time and Luke focuses on the
nearer event that sets the pattern. Matthew's unique reference to the end in the
opening question shows his focus. Luke's reference to the destruction of the city
and his lack of reference to the abomination of desolation shows his near view
focus. With this interpretive observation in place, we can now consider how
Jesus presents what lies ahead.

Jesus begins his discourse with a series of events he says come before the
end, as either the beginning of birth pangs or things that are not yet the end.
These include messianic claimants, wars and rumors of wars, earthquakes, and
famines. It is a chaotic period. In a passage unique to Luke that gives us some
timing for these events, Luke 21:11 introduces the idea that before the above
list comes a period of persecution of believers. The exhortation in this section
is to be faithful and to not worry as to what should be said; the Spirit will help
in replying. One can see by the way Jesus covers this material that his goal is
not to give a sequence of events or a calendar but to describe in general terms
the conditions that lead to both the destruction and the end. In fact, Jesus is
reassuring the disciples that no matter how chaotic things get and seem, God's
plan is unfolding. Disciples can trust in God and remain faithful, even in the
midst of great pressure. That pressure will start immediately for the disciples
and will remain until he returns. Those who follow Jesus need to understand
that and always be prepared for rejection and persecution.

Luke's version discusses next how the city itself is surrounded, referring to
its desolation. He discusses how the city will be trampled down until the days
of the Gentiles are complete. This anticipates how the city will be completely

---

10. For Matthew and Mark, Turner, *Matthew,* 305-22 and Darrell L. Bock, *Mark* in Cornerstone
    Commentary (Carol Stream, IL: Tyndale, 2005), 515-24.

overrun in 70 CE. It looks to the short-term image. In Matthew and Mark we have a discussion instead of the abomination of desolation, a specific sacrilege by the antichrist standing in the Holy Place at the end, as Daniel 9:27 foretold. In both eras, the temple is under great duress. One event mirrors the other. In one, the temple is destroyed. In the other, the city will be rescued.

Then comes the discussion of the return at the end as the Son of Man rides the clouds and comes with glory to gather the elect. He will carry out the judgment that many of the passages we have noted already promised would take place. Jesus's picture of the future does not go into much detail. He simply presents the end as an act of divine vindication that includes a judgment of the wicked and the gathering of the righteous. Other New Testament texts give more detail to this basic structure.

When it comes to what to do with this information regarding what will precede the end, Jesus has one core application: Keep watch, for no one but the Father knows exactly when this will happen. Keeping watch and being ready fit the themes we saw in some of the parables Jesus tells about the end. When the end of the discourse tells the disciples not to engage in dissipation, the point calls for application of what the future should lead us to do: to live in a sober way and not ignore the return of the Lord. The picture is of disciples living and carrying out the mission the parables also describe.

What this overview of the Olivet Discourse shows is how its themes also fit the themes about the future we already saw elsewhere. The end will be chaotic. The call is to keep watch and be faithful. Judgment and accountability come at the end. God has a program, and the chaos does not mean things are out of control, so be ready and keep watch. The Synoptic Gospels use the future to encourage followers to be faithful and trust that God has a plan. The future will result in the vindication of the righteous in the end. A judgment comes that separates the righteous and the wicked. So be an ally of God, be accountable to God in your stewardship of your calling to walk with him, and trust in the One he has sent as you carry out the mission God has given you.

The Future of the Individual

With the judgment coming at the end, the Synoptics also discuss the fate of the individual in death and in judgment. We close our discussion looking at those passages.

Accountability

One theme in many of these texts involves our accountability to God. This is usually seen as negative and tied to the judgment of the wicked or other types of failure. Yet Luke 14:14 looks to a positive example, where acts of compassion and kindness are rewarded as God sees us when we care for the poor, crippled, lame, and blind. The text says the all-seeing God will reward those who care for such people in need.

Instant Sense of Blessing

Another key passage within this more individualized theme describes the sense of immediate presence those who die have with God. The key passage here is Luke 23:42–43. Here the thief on the cross who has defended Jesus asks to be remembered when Jesus comes into his kingdom. The expectation the thief likely had in making the request is that when the resurrection comes he would be included among the righteous, because Jewish vindication expected righteousness to be established with the resurrection at the end of history (Dan. 12:1–2). Jesus's answer gives the thief more than he asked for. Jesus replies that today the thief will be with his Christ in paradise. There is no other detail here. Nonetheless what this shows is that there is a sense for the righteous of being blessed once we have died.

Knowing Him Is Crucial

It is significant to observe what is highlighted in two of the texts looking at a negative judgment: those excluded do not know God. Matthew 7:21–23 is an important text for this theme. Jesus teaches in the Sermon on the Mount that not everyone who says "Lord, Lord" will survive the judgment. As they are being excluded, the protest comes: "Did we not prophesy in your name, cast out demons and do other miraculous deeds?" The remark is short and crisp: "I never knew you. Go away from me you lawbreakers."

Matthew 25:12 makes the same point to the foolish virgins, in the parable of the ten virgins. When they are refused entry, the explanation is, "I tell you the truth, I do not know you." Though this example is a picture in a parable, it makes the point clearly enough, functioning in effect as an application of the parable.

The man cut up into pieces in Luke 12:46 is another example of the odd person out. These are folks who have a connection or association with Jesus, but who lack a genuine faith connection to him. This is why the language is about not knowing him. Superficial association with Jesus does not survive the accountability that comes with future judgment.

The Image of Outer Darkness

Rejection in judgment is a serious thing about the future. This is why the place people end up is called "outer darkness" (Matt. 8:12; 22:13; 25:30).[11] God is light. His people are in the light, as Jesus as Messiah functions as light (Matt. 4:16; Luke 1:78–89). Those who are in outer darkness are seen as being as far removed from the light as is possible. That is why there is weeping and gnashing of teeth there. So this is an image that depicts a total lack of connection to God. It is a figure that points to an absence of faith and knowledge of him. It shows the result that comes from that lack of faith.

The Image of Hell as a Place of Torment

Numerous texts picture the residence of those judged negatively as a place of terrible torment. Luke 16:23 describes hell as a place of torment for the rich man who ended up there. It is characterized as a place of unquenchable fire (Mark 9:43, 48). Matthew 10:28 speaks of the one who can destroy both body and soul—a picture of the God who judges. Matthew 13:4, 50 speak of being tossed into the fiery furnace—a picture of a place of terrible torment. Matthew 25:41 describes a place of eternal fire. These images depict an unending torment that is the result of being permanently separated from a God they now know exists.[12]

What we see in these more individualized texts is that the future is a place of blessing or rejection, a time of accountability to God. The idea that we are completely independent beings is not a biblical one. Having been made in the image of God, we are accountable to our Creator, who knows what we are doing with our lives. Part of the point of being so vivid with what the punishment of the future holds is to remind us of that accountability, warning us to take our connection to God and our response to him very seriously.

Conclusion

For those who respond to God with faith the future is full of blessing and vindication. This is why the future is considered a blessed hope or the great hope to come. The future is about the vindication of God and his program. It is the time

---

11. Craig Keener, *The Gospel of Matthew: A Socio-Rhetorical Commentary* (Grand Rapids: Eerdmans, 2009), 269.
12. Leon Morris, *Matthew* (Grand Rapids: Eerdmans, 1992), 263; and Grant Osborne, *Matthew* (Grand Rapids: Zondervan, 2010), 397.

when righteousness and peace are established, as the saints also are gathered into permanent blessing. Jesus focuses on the core themes associated with the future and gives little detail to it. In the future God will be shown faithful to those who know him and are his. They will share in the peace God's program brings when all in the world are held accountable for how life has been lived. That is what the future looks like, from Jesus's teaching in the Synoptic Gospels.

THE DOCTRINE OF THE FUTURE
IN JOHN'S WRITINGS

David L. Turner

Gleaning a *doctrine* of the future from the exegesis of a historical corpus of narrative, epistolary, and apocalyptic writings is a difficult, even tenuous task.[1] Doctrinal formulation seeks prescriptive and universal conclusions, while exegesis is a process that necessarily has descriptive and local concerns. In the present study I will present an exegetically based biblical theology *en route* to doctrine—not a formal, comprehensive statement which purports to have arrived at that destination. John's gospel will be the focus, although attention will be drawn to the letters and the Apocalypse. Certain themes in the letters are clearly related to the gospel. The Apocalypse presents many issues that cannot be discussed in the space allotted to this study, issues which have frequently been addressed elsewhere.[2]

---

1. It is a privilege to participate in a project that honors Craig Blaising. I have enjoyed being acquainted with Craig since first working with him and others years ago on what has come to be known as progressive dispensationalism. Craig's interest in the church's ongoing engagement with Scripture as it gradually develops its doctrinal standards has stimulated and guided my own interest in the relationship of biblical exegesis to systematic theology, especially as it pertains to the biblical theology of Israel and the church. (See his "Doctrinal Development in Orthodoxy," and "Development of Dispensationalism by Contemporary Dispensationalists," in *Bibliotheca Sacra* 145 (1988): 133–40, 254–80.

2. See the better commentaries and S. Gregg, *Revelation: Four Views, A Parallel Commentary* (Nashville: Nelson, 1999); C. M. Pate, ed. *Four Views on the Book of Revelation* (Grand Rapids: Zondervan, 1998); and C. M. Pate, *Reading Revelation: A Comparison of Four Interpretive Translations of the Apocalypse* (Grand Rapids: Kregel, 2009). In my view, the Apocalypse should be approached eclectically. At least three of the common approaches to the book have merit. Preterism anchors the book in its first-century CE context. Idealism focuses on Christ's glorious victory as both center and goal of redemptive history. Futurism engages the content of the church's hope. It is difficult to find value in the historicist (continuous historical) approach to the book.

It is argued here that John's teaching about the future is less prominent and relevant than his teaching about the present. John's interest is not so much to project *what will be* as it is to describe *what is* in light of what will be. What *is* anticipates what *will be*; what will be has already begun. Jesus's followers have already been "raised" by his word to eternal life. Their "resurrection" betokens the resurrection of humankind in the last day. The hour is coming, yet now is.

HISTORICAL ASSUMPTIONS

The working assumptions of this study should be identified. Neither the gospel, the letters, or the Apocalypse of John specify that John the apostle, the beloved disciple, is their author. Nevertheless, a strong case can be made for the view that the apostle John wrote all five works, or at least was the source of the traditions transmitted by his immediate followers. Views of this sort remain common among conservative scholars.[3] Be that as it may, the theological continuity of this corpus is more relevant to the present study than its authorship.

How the gospel, letters, and Apocalypse of John came to be is not clear. One might posit the composition, circulation, and reception of the gospel as the setting for the letters and ultimately the Apocalypse. An opposite scenario is also plausible, one in which the letters reflect the developing Johannine teaching which later comes to its full expression in narrative and apocalyptic denouement. Whatever the historical relationship between gospel and letters, the Apocalypse may plausibly be taken to represent a later stage of Johannine teaching, one which envisions the victory of Jesus that has already been narrated in the gospel and applied in the specific situations represented in the letters.[4]

---

3. For this study I am assuming the theological unity of the gospel, letters, and Apocalypse of John. It is also plausible that that this corpus comes ultimately from the same apostolic author, John the son of Zebedee, the beloved disciple (Matt. 10:2; Mark 3:17; John 13:23; 18:15–16[?]; 19:26–27; 20:2–4, 8; 21:7, 20, 23–24; Acts 1:13; 3:1, 11; 4:13; 8:14; Rev. 1:1, 4, 9; 22:8). See further C. L. Blomberg, *The Historical Reliability of John's Gospel* (Downers Grove, IL: InterVarsity, 2001); C. E. Hill, *The Johannine Corpus in the Early Church* (Oxford: University Press, 2004); D. M. Smith, *Johannine Christianity: Essays on Its Setting, Sources, and Theology* (Columbia: University of South Carolina Press, 1984).

4. After noting the inherent difficulties, L. T. Johnson presents a plausible reconstruction in *The Writings of the New Testament: An Interpretation* rev. ed. (Minneapolis: Fortress, 1999), 521–23, 559–69, 579–81. Johnson suggests that the varied reception of John's gospel leads to three letters being sent as a packet carried by Demetrius to a single community. Third John commends Gaius's fidelity, exposes Diotrephes's opposition, and endorses Demetrius. Second John is to be read to the church as a cover letter or introduction to 1 John. First John is a homily exhorting faithfulness

Future, Realized, or Inaugurated Eschatology?

The most basic question facing a study of the future in the Johannine writings is whether the future is addressed at all.[5] Ladd bluntly stated that "the most superficial comparison of the Synoptics and John leaves one with the impression that the Johannine Jesus is little interested in eschatology."[6] Stephen Smalley's comment is more nuanced: "the fourth evangelist has little to say about the 'last things' as such, and is much more concerned about the—to him—vital inter-relation between time and eternity."[7] Certain Johannine teachings stress the present realization of things typically understood as yet to come. For example:

- Jesus the Messiah has already come to reveal God and establish authentic worship (John 1:14–18; 4:21–26; 1 John 4:2; 5:6).
- Jesus has overcome the world; his work of redemption is finished (John 16:23; 17:4; 19:30; 1 John 2:8; 3:5; cf. Rev. 1:5; 3:21; 5:5). Believers in Jesus have already overcome the evil one (1 John 2:13–14; 4:4; 5:4–5; cf. Rev. 12:10–11).

---

to the elder's tradition. Although the genre and style of the Apocalypse present many difficulties, the book's authorship, geography, and theology link it to the other Johannine writings.

5. Although A. J. Köstenberger affirms that "John's eschatology is one of the most distinctive features of his theology," he takes only three pages to survey the topic. See *A Theology of John's Gospel and Letters* (Grand Rapids: Zondervan, 2009), 295–98. More thorough and helpful discussions include R. E. Brown, *An Introduction to the Gospel of John*, ed. F. J. Moloney, (New York: Doubleday, 2003), 234–48; J. T. Carroll, "Present and Future in Fourth Gospel Eschatology," *Biblical Theology Bulletin* 19 (1989): 63–69; W. R. Cook, "Eschatology in John's Gospel," *Criswell Theological Review* 3 (1988): 79–99; W. J. Dumbrell, "Johannine Eschatology" in *The Search for Order: Biblical Eschatology in Focus* (Grand Rapids: Baker, 1994), 235–58; L. R. Helyer, *The Witness of Jesus, Paul, and John* (Downers Grove, IL: InterVarsity, 2008), 344–77; R. Kysar, *The Fourth Evangelist and His Gospel* (Minneapolis: Augsburg, 1975), 207–14; R. Kysar, *John: The Maverick Gospel* (Atlanta: John Knox, 1976), 84–110; G. E. Ladd, *A Theology of the New Testament*, ed. D. A. Hagner, rev. ed. (Grand Rapids: Eerdmans, 1993), 334–44; M. Pamment, "Eschatology and the Fourth Gospel," *Journal for the Study of the New Testament* 15 (1982): 81–85; D. R. Sime and J. Yates, "Eschatology in the Gospel of John," in *The Last Things*, ed. W. B. West and J. P. Lewis (Austin: Sweet, 1972), 124–139. The most extensive study is J. Frey, *Die johanneische Eschatologie*, 3 vols., WUNT 96, 110, 117 (Tübingen: Mohr-Siebeck, 1997–2000). A related comprehensive bibliography is presented by S. E. Porter and A. K. Gabriel in *Johannine Writings and Apocalyptic: An Annotated Bibliography* (Leiden: Brill, 2013).

6. G. E. Ladd, *Theology of the New Testament*, 334. Contrasting John to the Synoptics, Ladd notes John's emphasis on present eternal life rather than the inbreaking kingdom of God and on the coming of the Spirit rather than the apocalyptic Parousia of Christ.

7. S. Smalley, *John: Evangelist and Interpreter* (Exeter: Paternoster, 1978), 235.

- The "hour" of resurrection is already here: Dead people are hearing the Son of God's voice and coming to life (John 5:25–29).
- Satan, the prince of this world, has already been judged (John 12:31; 16:11; 1 John 3:8; cf. Rev. 12:7–10).
- Believers in Jesus already have eternal life;[8] unbelievers are already under judgment (John 3:18, 36; 1 John 5:12–13, 19).
- Antichrists are already in the world (1 John 2:18, 22; 4:3; 2 John 7).

And yet John does speak univocally about the future:

- Jesus will go to prepare a place for his disciples and then come for them (John 14:1–3, 18, 28; 21:22–23; cf. 1 John 2:28; 3:2–3; Rev. 1:7; 2:5, 15, 25; 3:3, 11; 16:15; 19:11–16; 22:7, 12, 20).
- Jesus's enemies may be permitted to overcome his people for a time (Rev. 6:2; 11:7; 12:11; 13:7), but ultimately Jesus will overcome them (Rev. 17:14).
- The hour of resurrection is coming: all people will be raised, either to life or to judgment (John 5:28–29; 6:39–40, 44, 54; cf. Rev. 11:15–18; 20:4–6).
- Current antichrists demonstrate the reality of the future antichrist (1 John 2:18; 4:3).
- It is the last hour (1 John 2:18), and believers in Jesus may anticipate judgment day with confidence (1 John 4:17).

The complexity of John's teaching in this area has led scholars such as C. H. Dodd and Rudolf Bultmann to argue that the "future" in John should be taken as having already been fully realized in the present time. Dodd argued that the delay of Christ's coming led early Christians to sublimate a primitive futuristic apocalyptic eschatology into a nuanced mystical sense of Christ's indwelling through the Spirit.[9] Bultmann's demythologizing existentialist agenda resulted in his denial of all things miraculous, including an apocalyptic end of the world. He understood eschatology as authentic personal existence

---

8. D. E. Aune stated that eternal life is "the primary mode of expressing realized eschatology within the Fourth Gospel." See "The Present Realization of Eschatological Salvation in the Fourth Gospel," in *The Cultic Setting of Realized Eschatology in Early Christianity*. NovTSup 28 (Leiden: Brill, 1972), 82.

9. See, e.g., *The Apostolic Preaching and Its Developments* (London: Hodder & Stoughton, 1936), 155, 170–74; *The Coming of Christ* (Cambridge: University Press, 1954), 6–7.

and attributed futuristic texts in John to later interpolation.[10] The more recent work of von Wahlde handles things similarly by arguing for three editions of the Fourth Gospel which progressively develop eschatology from (1) possession of eternal life by the believing community to (2) spiritual existence of believers beyond death to (3) future physical resurrection of believers at a future time of reckoning.[11]

An opposite view is typically expressed by traditional dispensationalists, for whom God's reign is entirely future. Charles Ryrie downplayed the role of the gospel and letters in the study of Johannine eschatology, stating that "Johannine eschatology is found mainly in the Apocalypse."[12] This statement assumes a strictly futuristic approach. John Walvoord acknowledged that the kingdom of God was present in some sense during Jesus's first advent, but went on to say that "the hopes and promises and expectations associated with his coming did not take place—the eschatology which included them was not realized."[13] Walvoord's view of a promised advent without even the least realization of promised eschatological blessings is starkly futuristic. Similarly, A. J. McClain's treatment of John 5:25–29 separates the present "hour" of spiritual regeneration from the eschatological "hour" of physical resurrection so strictly that one wonders why Jesus would describe the former in terms of the latter.[14] In the larger context of NT theology, this sort of futurism has affinities with what has been called consistent eschatology.[15]

---

10. Bultmann internalized eschatology, viewing faith itself as eschatological existence. See *Theology of the New Testament*. 2 vols., ET, trans. K. Grobel, (London: SCM, 1955), 2.75–92. D. E. Holwerda counters Bultmann's approach in *The Holy Spirit and Eschatology in the Gospel of John: A Critique of Rudolf Bultmann's Present Eschatology* (Amsterdam: Vrije Universiteit, 1959). Utilizing the theological concept of perichoresis (inter-penetration), J. Moltmann critiques Bultmann's (and many others') bifurcation of present and future while arguing for an eschatology in motion—those who are in the risen Christ (cf. John 15:5) are in a sort of ante-room intertwined with and moving toward God's future kingdom. See "God in the World—the World in God: Perichoresis in Trinity and Eschatology," in *The Gospel of John and Christian Theology*, ed. R. Bauckham and C. Mosser, (Grand Rapids: Eerdmans, 2008), 378–81.

11. U. C. von Wahlde, *The Gospel and Letters of John*, 3 vols. (Grand Rapids: Eerdmans, 2010), 3.459–74; 490–93.

12. Charles C. Ryrie, *Biblical Theology of the New Testament* (Chicago: Moody, 1959), 345. Despite Ryrie's question-begging futurism and lack of engagement with other views, his discussion includes passing references to John 5:24–29; 8:51; 14:1–3; 1 John 2:18; 3:14; 2 John 7 (347–52, 356).

13. John F. Walvoord, "Realized Eschatology," *Bibliotheca Sacra* 127 (1970): 322–23.

14. A. J. McClain, *The Greatness of the Kingdom* (Chicago: Moody, 1968), 489.

15. Consistent eschatology describes the futuristic eschatology of the German scholar Johannes Weiss (1863–1914). See his *Jesus' Proclamation of the Kingdom of God*, trans. and ed. R. H.

New Testament scholarship by and large across the theological spectrum has resisted both of these "all or nothing" approaches, viewing the realized and futuristic aspects of New Testament eschatology as complementary and correlative, not contradictory and corrective. The differences between John's focus on eternal life and that of the Synoptics on the kingdom of God are commonly understood not as disparate teachings but as distinct emphases. W. F. Howard argued that the Johannine teaching on Jesus as the exegesis of God's glory (John 1:14–18) requires an ultimate full manifestation of that glory.[16] C. F. D. Moule believed that John's emphasis on personal or individual eschatology led him to a realized emphasis.[17] Speaking about John 3:17, Rudolf Schnackenburg stated that no one grasped the significance of Jesus's eschatological revelation better than John, and that John's emphasis on present judgment does not deny the future judgment, which perfects the saving action of God in the present.[18] David Aune traced the realized or mystical aspects of Johannine eschatology to a cultic setting.[19] W. G. Kümmel spoke of the substantive necessity of hope in the promised future consummation as a part of the divine saving act which led to present reality of salvation in John.[20] C. K. Barrett acknowledges the Johannine emphasis on the present but insists that John retains a measure of last-day apocalypticism in texts like John 6:39, 40, 44, 53.[21] Leonhard Goppelt linked present and future in the Fourth Gospel by viewing the latter as the ultimate, concrete, visible manifestation of the former.[22] D. Moody Smith remarks that in John salvation is not only a present reality, and that "by virtue of its presence the future is already a matter of assurance rather than hope."[23] Frank Thielman

---

Hiers and D. L. Holland (Philadelphia: Fortress, 1971). The editors' introduction (1–51) helpfully surveys the development of various eschatological views.

16. W. F. Howard, *Christianity According to St. John* (London: Duckworth, 1946), 106–28.

17. C. F. D. Moule, "The Individualism of the Fourth Gospel," *Novum Testamentum* 5 (1962): 174.

18. Rudolf Schnackenburg, *Present and Future* (Notre Dame: University of Notre Dame, 1966), 15.

19. Aune, *Cultic Setting*, 45–135.

20. W. G. Kümmel, *The Theology of the New Testament*, J. Steely, trans. (Nashville: Abingdon, 1973), 294–95.

21. C. K. Barrett, *The Gospel of John and Judaism*, D. M. Smith, ed. (Philadelphia: Fortress, 1975), 73–74. Barrett affirmed that it is methodologically false to dissolve the coexistence of present and future eschatology in John by source or redaction theories. In an explanatory footnote (91) acknowledging redactional activity in John, Barrett bluntly stated, "The redactor was a theologian, not a fool."

22. Leonhard Goppelt, *Theology of the New Testament*, 2 vols., trans. J. Alsup (Grand Rapids: Eerdmans, 1982–83), 2.303–05. Goppelt argued that Jesus's teaching in John 5:28 ran counter to the overly realized eschatology encountered by Paul in 1 Cor. 4:8; 15:12–19; 2 Tim. 2:18.

23. D. Moody Smith, *The Theology of the Gospel of John* (Cambridge: Cambridge University Press,

describes John's emphasis on the present as "unusual" in the New Testament, yet he takes John's corresponding emphasis on the necessity of perseverance during persecution as evidence that future eschatology is a theological necessity for John.[24] Thomas Schreiner begins his treatment of New Testament theology by utilizing already/not yet language as a fundamental characteristic of the kingdom of God.[25] Craig Koester describes the coming of Jesus as a "rift in time," which decisively changes the world by transforming the relationship of future hopes and present realities.[26] G. K. Beale's overarching approach to New Testament biblical theology is based on God's action in Christ to inaugurate the renewal of creation as a whole, concluding with a discussion of the relationship between inaugurated and consummated eschatological realities.[27]

It seems clear, then, that John portrays God's glorious reign neither as fully realized nor fully future, but as both partially realized in the present and yet to be fully experienced in the future. New Testament theologians commonly speak of both the ethical/vertical present fulfillment of future realities and the eschatological/horizontal future consummation of those realities.[28] In describing the Johannine teaching, the term "inaugurated" is more appropriate than the term "realized."[29] Strictly futurist eschatology truncates the Johannine stress on the powerful impact of Christ's life, death, and resurrection and his sending the Spirit to empower his people to do his work (John 20:21–23; 1 John 2:8, 13–14, 20, 27). Strictly realized eschatology truncates biblical teaching about what God will do to finish what he has begun in Christ. Johannine eschatology links the "already" to the "not yet" in that the eschatological life already experienced by followers of Jesus abides in them by the Spirit

1995), 150. Smith notably comments that "John sees the eschatological drama as already farther along than does Paul" (151).

24. Frank Thielman, *Theology of the New Testament* (Grand Rapids: Zondervan, 2005), 172–79. Thielman understands the Fourth Gospel to have accepted, affirmed, and yet modified traditional Jewish eschatology. The modification consists in the reversal of the order of resurrection and eternal life.

25. Thomas Schreiner, *New Testament Theology: Magnifying God in Christ* (Grand Rapids: Baker, 2008), 41–116. Schreiner's treatment of John focuses on eternal life (84–90), and concludes by stating, "The future resurrection, in fact, is secured by the gift of life now."

26. Craig R. Koester, *The Word of Life: A Theology of John's Gospel* (Grand Rapids: Eerdmans, 2008), 175–86.

27. G. K. Beale, *A New Testament Biblical Theology* (Grand Rapids: Baker, 2011). For discussions of Johannine theology, see 131–36; 203–7; 234–37; 332–34; 569–72.

28. E.g., W. Hall Harris, "A Theology of John's Writings," in *A Biblical Theology of the New Testament*, ed. Roy B. Zuck, (Chicago: Moody, 1994), 233–34; Ladd, *Theology of the New Testament*, 259–72, 338–39.

29. J. Jeremias spoke of *sich realisierende eschatologie*, "eschatology in process of realization." See *The Parables of Jesus*, 3rd rev. ed. (London: SCM, 1972), 229 n. 3.

and empowers them for the troubles that are ahead (John 15:18–16:11; 16:20–22, 32–33; 17:14; 21:18). Further, the teaching about eternal life as a present reality assumes the future consummation and is based on it.[30]

When one applies this approach to the already/not yet bullet points laid out above, a remarkable theological perspective emerges:

- Jesus has come from the Father to reveal God and establish authentic worship. He will go to the Father to prepare a place for his followers and then return to earth to consummate his relationship with them.

- Jesus has finished the Father's work and overcome the world and its prince. His followers share in this victory through faith. Yet they will experience troubles and will even be overcome temporarily by Jesus's enemies before they share in his ultimate vindication and victory.

- Jesus's message is already raising people from the death of alienation from God into the life of fellowship with him. The present possession of this life assures believers of its permanence in the future.[31] One day Jesus will resurrect all humans for reward or punishment.

From this general perspective one may profitably examine Johannine themes which portray the future. Selecting such themes for a short study such as this requires difficult methodological choices. One might profitably survey John's teachings topically, as does W. R. Cook, who treats "death," "eternal life," "resurrection," "heaven," "judgment," and "Christ's return."[32] Due to space limitations, the remainder of this study will engage only a few highly relevant Johannine themes: the coming-yet-here "hour," the kingdom of God, the coming of Jesus, and the renewal of creation.

Selected Eschatological Themes

The "Hour" That Is Coming Yet Already Here

Although the word "hour" occurs around twenty-five times in the Fourth Gospel, the saying "the hour is coming, and is now" (John 4:23; 5:25) requires

---

30. C. S. Keener, *The Gospel of John: A Commentary*, 2 vols. (Peabody, MA: Hendrickson, 2003), 1.323.
31. D. Moody Smith, *The Theology of the Gospel of John* (Cambridge: Cambridge University Press, 1995), 149–50.
32. Cook, "Eschatology in John's Gospel," 87–98.

special attention.[33] In its two occurrences this striking expression epitomizes "the presence of the future," the present fulfillment of prophetic promises as precursor to their ultimate apocalyptic consummation.[34]

Jesus's conversation with the Samaritan women led to his teaching about an authentic messianic worship in Spirit and truth, a worship which transcended historic rivalries (John 4:21–25). The woman insightfully perceived Jesus's prophetic identity and alluded to the historic divide between Samaritan worship on Mount Gerizim and Jewish worship in Jerusalem (4:20). Jesus candidly affirmed the centrality of Jerusalem in redemptive history to that point, but noted the present movement of God which prioritized *manner* of worship over *place* of worship (John 4:21). Jesus was speaking not of the rejection of the Jews and Jerusalem but of the messianic renewal of the Jewish people and of Jewish worship. In keeping with God's promise to Abraham (Gen. 12:1–3), the Jerusalem temple was to be a house of prayer for all nations—Jews, Samaritans, and all humanity (cf. John 2:17, citing Ps. 69:9). The Samaritans' coming to faith in Jesus (John 4:39–42) showed that God's plan to reach all humanity was already coming to pass (cf. John 1:9; 3:16; 10:14–16; 12:32; 1 John 2:2; 4:14; Rev. 5:9–10; 7:9-12; 12:5; 14:6–7; 21:3, 24–26; 22:2). The hour of authentic spiritual worship was already being realized through Jesus the Messiah (John 4:23–25).

On Jesus's second trip to Jerusalem, his healing of a paralyzed man on the Sabbath led to conflict with the authorities just as his clearing the temple had led to conflict on his previous trip (John 5:1–5; cf. 2:13–20). Jesus defended

---

33. Commonly *hora* is an indicator of the time of day (1:39; 4:6, 52; 19:14), of a particular moment of time (11:9; 16:21; 19:27), or of a short period of time (*pros horan*; 5:35). At other times the word refers to the culminating events in Jerusalem leading to the cross. This "hour" is "not yet" in some contexts (2:4; 7:30; 8:20) but it "has come" in others (12:23, 27; 13:1; 17:1). As the "hour" of Jesus's death draws near, he speaks to his disciples of a coming "hour" when he will speak plainly to them about the Father (16:25). He also warns them of a coming "hour" when their association with him will lead to persecution (16:2, 4). In 16:32 this hour of persecution "is coming and in fact has come." In 1 John 2:18 the presence of anti-christian teachers indicates that "it is the last hour." The Apocalypse tends to use the word "hour" to describe the time of Christ's return and the judgment associated with it (Rev. 3:3, 10; 14:7, 15; 18:10, 17, 19). S. Mihalios argues that "the hour" in Johannine literature is tied to Daniel's presentation of end-time tribulation and resurrection. See *The Danielic Eschatological Hour in the Johannine Literature* (Edinburgh: Clark, 2012).
34. I am indebted to George E. Ladd not only for this terminology but also for stimulating much of my thinking about NT eschatology. See *The Presence of the Future* (Grand Rapids: Eerdmans, 1974). Unfortunately for the present study, Ladd dealt rather sparingly with the Fourth Gospel in this book.

his actions by linking his Sabbath "work" with the Father's constant activity, affirming that his own actions simply mirrored those of the Father and that the Father had entrusted to him the work of raising the dead to life and judging them (John 5:16–23). Such language would typically refer to the future resurrection and judgment at the last day, but Jesus explains it is already occurring. He is already giving life to whom he will. Those who receive him have already passed from death to life, experiencing a "resurrection" that removes them from condemnation at the last day (5:23–24). In this sense the "hour" of eschatological judgment is already present in that "dead" people living life apart from God are hearing Jesus's life-giving message and receiving eternal life (5:25–27). This present "hour" of ethical-spiritual inner renewal should not be surprising to Jesus's audience, since it augurs the future hour of physical resurrection when all in the tombs will be raised to life or condemnation (5:28-29; cf. Rev. 20:11–15).[35]

Jesus's conversation with Martha about the death of Lazarus (John 11:17–27) is best understood in light of this teaching about the coming-yet-present hour. Jesus intentionally arrives in Bethany after Lazarus's death, and promises Lazarus's sister Martha that her brother will rise again. Martha affirms her belief in the ultimate resurrection of her brother "on the last day" (cf. John 6:39–40, 54). Jesus acknowledges Martha's belief (11:25b), but emphasizes a more profound truth—his messianic identity as giver of resurrection life (11:25a) means that those who believe in him already have life and will never die. Their vital, dynamic relationship with God transcends the grave.[36] Lazarus's coming out of his tomb demonstrates what Jesus has already taught (John 5:21–29). It also anticipates the empty tomb of Jesus, the dawn of the coming day.

The striking expression "the hour is coming, yet is now" (John 4:21, 23; 5:25, 28) does not minimize the reality of God's future redemptive work so

---

35. Brodie's helpful discussion of this passage includes the idea of "grading." Brodie shows how the healing of an isolated case, the official's son (4:46–54), followed by that of the invalid among many other chronically ill people at the pool of Bethesda (5:2–9), leads up to Jesus's words in 5:25–29 about life and death. See T. L. Brodie, *The Gospel according to John* (New York: Oxford University Press, 1993), 248–50.

36. J. Ashton believes that futuristic eschatology and the physical resurrection of the dead are of little interest to John even though these concepts are most likely the origin of John's teaching about eternal life in the present. In John's mind, the resurrection of Jesus fused present and future. See John Ashton, *Understanding the Fourth Gospel* (New York: Oxford University Press, 2007), 405.

much as it maximizes the present availability of the life to be fully experienced at Christ's coming. The genuine though partial present fulfillment of salvation is predicated on the assumed reality of future eschatological consummation.

The Kingdom of God

Although the kingdom of God is not frequently mentioned in the Fourth Gospel,[37] it is nevertheless a key to understanding the future in John's teaching. Jesus has come from above, from heaven, as the agent of God's authority on earth (1:14, 51; 3:13, 31; 6:31 [Exod. 16:4], 33, 38, 41–42, 46–51, 58; 19:11). Jesus's words to Nicodemus speak of spiritual rebirth (John 3:3–8) as a necessity for participating in the kingdom.[38] Despite his learning, Nicodemus is boggled by this statement. Given his background, he likely thought of "kingdom" in terms of the prophets' promises of God's future blessings on Israel, restoring them to his favor in the land promised to them, judging their enemies, and bringing them everlasting *shalom*. Jesus's words do not appear to challenge Nicodemus's assumptions about the kingdom itself so much as to challenge his nationalistic assumptions about entering it.[39] Since Jesus's kingdom is not from this world (18:33-38), transformational supernatural birth and resulting insight are required to experience it (cf. 1: 12–13; 3:3–10; 6:14–15, 26–32; 10:26; 17:6–9).[40] All of this is consistent with the view that the kingdom of God transcends the present ministry of Jesus and will have a future consummation.

---

37. "Kingdom" is found only in 3:3, 5; 18:36. Yet Jesus is portrayed as a king several times. Nathaniel refers to Jesus as king of Israel (1:49). Jesus's miraculous feeding of the multitudes results in their seeking to make him king (6:15). Jesus is proclaimed king as he enters Jerusalem on Palm Sunday (12:13, 15; cf. Ps. 118:26; Zech. 9:9). Jesus as king plays a prominent role in John's passion narrative (18:33–38; 19:1–3, 8–22). Cf. Rev. 1:6, 9; 5:10; 11:15–17; 12:10; 16:10; 17:14; 19:6, 16; 20:4, 6; 22:5.
38. "Seeing" (1 John 3:2–3; Rev. 22:4; cf. Matt. 5:8; Heb. 12:14) and entering (cf. Mark 9:43–47) the kingdom would likely be understood futuristically by Nicodemus in terms of resurrection, final judgment, and fully experiencing God's reign on earth.
39. Commentators regularly cite *mSanh* 10:1, which says that all Israel have a portion in the world to come and cites Isa. 60:21 in support. See D. A. Carson *The Gospel according to John* (Leicester/Grand Rapids: InterVarsity/Eerdmans, 1991), 188–89. Yet the following mishnahs in the tractate list many exceptions to this apparent universality. M. A. Elliott argues for the prevalence of remnant theology over nationalistic election in *The Survivors of Israel* (Grand Rapids: Eerdmans, 2000). See 654–57 for his comments on studies of the Fourth Gospel.
40. It seems likely that Jesus's words depend on the prophetic tradition exemplified in Ezek. 36:25–27. Cf. Ps. 51:10; *Jub.* 1:20–21; 4Q393, f. 1–2, 2.5–6; 1 John 2:29; 3:9; 4:7; 5:1, 4, 18; Titus 3:5–6; 1 Pet. 1:3, 23; See further C. S. Keener, *The Gospel of John: A Commentary*, 2 vols. (Peabody, MA: Hendrickson, 2003), 1.542–44.

The Coming of Jesus

John's narrative highlights that Jesus has already come as God's messianic king.[41] Jesus's promises of a future "coming" (cf. 21:22–23; 1 John 2:28–3:3)[42] are emphasized primarily in the discourse found in John 13:31–16:33, bracketed by foot washing (13:1–30) and prayer (17:1–26). These promised comings present ambiguities leading to much scholarly discussion. Only a brief summary is possible here. Jesus's promise to come again to his disciples after going to prepare a place for them (14:1–6; cf. 21:22–23) is best understood as a reference to his future coming as eschatological messianic King, leading to the disciples' being taken to dwell with him.[43] This promise appears to be alluded to in 14:28–29; 16:28. Jesus's promise to manifest himself to the disciples so that they will see him and not be orphaned (14:18–21) most likely refers to the post-resurrection appearances narrated later in the gospel (20:11–21:23) (cf. 14:28; 21:22–23). This promise seems to be alluded to in 16:16–24. Jesus's promise to come with the Father and abide with those who love him and keep his word (14:22–23) probably should be taken with the passages that promise the coming of the Counselor-Spirit (14:15–17, 25–26; 15:26–27; 16:7–15). As the Father sent the Spirit to equip Jesus for his ministry, so Jesus bestows the Spirit on his disciples after the resurrection to equip them to continue his ministry (20:22–23). The Spirit's christocentric ministry is both retrospective and prospective—he causes the disciples to remember what Jesus has taught, and he teaches them about things to come and convicts the world through their ministries. Thus the Helper's ministry continues the post-resurrection appearances of Jesus beyond the scope of the Fourth Gospel's narrative.[44]

Both the post-resurrection "comings" of Jesus and his proximate "coming" to the disciples with the Father through the Spirit enable the disciples to carry on

---

41. A cursory tracing of *erchomai* leads to John 1:9, 15, 27, 30; 3:2, 19, 31; 4:25–26, 42; 5:43; 6:14; 7:27–28, 31, 41–42; 8:14, 42; 9:39; 10:10; 11:27; 12:13 [Ps. 118:26], 15 [Zech. 9:9], 46–47; 15:22; 16:28; 18:37; cf. 1 John 5:6; 2 John 7; Rev. 5:7.

42. Of course, the "coming" of Jesus is heavily featured in the Apocalypse. See Rev. 1:7; 2:5, 7, 16, 25; 3:3, 11; 16:15; 19:11–16; 22:7, 12, 20; cf. Dan. 7:13; Rev. 6:17; 11:15–18; 12:5, 10–12; 17:13; 19:6–8; 20:11–15.

43. Against many scholars who stress that Jesus will take believers to himself and who understand the "place" mentioned by Jesus in 14:2 as a metaphor for Christian community in the Spirit. See, e.g., R. H. Gundry, "In My Father's House Are Many *Monai* (John 14:2)," *Zeitschrift für die neutestamentliche Wissenschaft* 58 (1967): 68–72.

44. Most likely the "seven spirits of God" in the Apocalypse (Rev. 1:4; 3:1; 4:5; 5:6; cf. Zech. 4:2) should be viewed as the christocentric fullness of the Holy Spirit's future ministry. See G. K. Beale, *The Book of Revelation*, NIGTC (Grand Rapids: Eerdmans, 1999), pp. 189–90.

Jesus's ministry despite all the troubles to come before his ultimate "coming." Accordingly, the upper room discourse turns out to be not so much a farewell address as it is an exhortation that Jesus's disciples continue his ministry as they experience his ongoing transformed presence through the Helper-Spirit he will send.

The Renewal of Creation

A somewhat neglected example of John's theology of the coming hour which is already here is found in the prologue, John 1:1–18. This majestic text presents the Word/*Logos* not only as the preexistent, *asarkos* Creator but also as the incarnate, *ensarkos* revealer of God. John 1:1–3 presents the Word as the original Creator of everything. John 1:4–5 presents the Word as revealer in a fashion that validates a latent Johannine new creation theology. This is seen in the extensive use of light and darkness language to portray the life available through faith in the *Logos* (1:12–13) and the death which remains for those who do not believe (cf. 3:16–21). John's portrayal of the *logos* as life and light underscores the *logos ensarkos* as renewer of creation. John's teaching on the Word as revealer, more clearly emphasized in John 1:14–18, draws on Moses's experience of God in Exodus 33:7–34:9, especially 34:6. What is commonly understood to be explicitly communicated by Paul in epistolary argument (Rom. 5:12–21; 8:18–23; 2 Cor. 4:3–7; 5:17; cf. Matt. 19:28) is also communicated by the author of the Fourth Gospel, albeit implicitly in narrative artistry.

Commentaries tend to make isolated observations about the creation overtones of various details of John 1, but extended treatments of the theme are relatively uncommon.[45] Certain commentaries and studies find seven days in John 1:19, which are viewed as echoing Genesis 1.[46] Other studies find evidence of a paradise motif in John 20:15's reference to a garden (cf. Rev. 2:7; 22:1–2, 14,

---

45. Studies of creation renewal in John include J. K. Brown, "Creation's Renewal in the Gospel of John," *Catholic Biblical Quarterly* 72 (2010): 275–90; C. Carmichael, *The Story of Creation: Its Origin and Its Interpretation in Philo and the Fourth Gospel* (Ithaca, NY: Cornell University, 1996); J. DuRand, "The Creation Motif in the Fourth Gospel," in *Theology and Christology in the Fourth Gospel,* ed. G. Van Belle, et al. (Leuven: Leuven University, 2005); M. Endo, *Creation and Christology: A Study of the Johannine Prologue in Light of Early Jewish Creation Accounts,* WUNT 2/145 (Tübingen: Mohr-Siebeck, 2002); J. Painter, "Earth Made Whole: John's Rereading of Genesis," in *Word, Theology, and Community in John,* ed. J. Painter, et al. (St Louis: Chalice, 2002); "Theology, Eschatology, and the Prologue of John," *Scottish Journal of Theology* 46 (1993): 27–42; W. Phythian-Adams, "The New Creation in John," *Church Quarterly Review* 144(1947): 52–75.

46. T. Barrosse, "The Seven Days of New Creation in St. John's Gospel," *CBQ* 21 (1959): 507–16. Cf. T. Phillips, "'The Third Fifth Day?' John 2:1 in Context," *ExpTim* 115 (2004): 328–31.

19).[47] John 20:22 may be an allusion to Genesis 2:7. All in all, the association of the reality of life in the Word with the metaphor of light in John 8:12 is especially significant for the understanding of John 1:4–5 as a new creation text.

First John also associates light and life. Those who claim to be in the light while living in the darkness demonstrate that they are not part of the new creation (1 John 1:4–7). The present encroachment of God's light upon Satan's darkness is a metaphorical presentation of ethical dualism and progressive creation renewal (1 John 2:8–11). First John 2:13–14 evokes Genesis 1:1 and John 1:1 by referring to believers as those who know "him who is from the beginning" (cf. 1 John 1:1, ESV), whose speech brought light into existence.

John's Apocalypse also contributes to the Johannine theology of Jesus and creation renewal. It is likely that the description of Jesus as the "beginning of the creation of God" (Rev. 3:14, ESV) has reference to Jesus as the exalted head over creation's renewal.[48] Jesus is opposed by Satan, described as the old serpent in reference to his deception of Adam and Eve (Rev. 12:9; 20:2). The praise given to the enthroned Creator in Revelation 4:11 is paired with the praise given to the slain Lamb in 5:9–10. At the end of the throne room scene the enthroned One and the Lamb receive the same praise, culminating in eternal dominion over creation. In Revelation 10:6 an angel swears by the God who created everything in heaven, earth, and the sea that judgment is to be delayed no longer. God's role as protological Creator entitles him to be eschatological purifier of the creation. Similarly, in Revelation 14:7, those who live on earth are urged to worship the God who made heaven and earth as Babylon is about to fall under the wrath of God. God's agent of judgment is his Logos (Rev. 19:13). Ultimately, the fall of wicked city Babylon prepares the way for the descent of the holy city New Jerusalem as all things in heaven and earth are made new (Rev. 3:12; 21:1; cf. 2 Peter 3:13). This language harks back to Isaiah 65:17–66:2. Several features of the New Jerusalem remind the attentive reader of Genesis 1–3, among them the end of death and all the pain related to it, the availability of the water and tree of life, and the presence of unending divine light. God's presence is fully mediated to his

---

47. N. Wyatt, "'Supposing Him to Be the Gardener' (John 20;15): A Study of the Paradise Motif in John," *ZNW* 81(1990): 21–38. Cf. J. Suggit, "Jesus the Gardener: The Atonement in the Fourth Gospel as Recreation," *Neot* 33 (1999): 161–68.
48. As argued by G. Beale, *The Book of Revelation* NIGTC (Grand Rapids: Eerdmans, 1999), pp. 297-301. In this understanding the exalted Jesus is the inaugurator of the new creation (cf. 2 Cor. 5:15, 17). Beale thinks that Colossians 1:15–18 alludes to both the original creation and to a new cosmic beginning through Christ's resurrection.

people, since the Lord God Almighty and the Lamb are its temple (21:4–6, 23–25; 22:1–5). [49]

Conclusion

John clearly emphasizes what has come to be known as inaugurated eschatology, "the presence of the future," more than the future itself. This is seen particularly in Jesus's teaching that the presence of the coming hour means that authentic worship is no longer a matter of geography and that believers already experience unending life in communion with God. Along the same lines, Jesus teaches the necessity of present spiritual transformation for participation in the coming kingdom of God. He must go to the Father and come again in order for that eschatological participation to be realized, but in the meantime he will appear to the disciples after his resurrection and will send the Spirit as his proxy to be their Helper. His overarching goal in all this is nothing less that the renewal of the world—a new heaven and a new earth in which God dwells with his people in a new Jerusalem.

The differences between John and the Synoptic Gospels on the future should not be overly pressed. Both unarguably teach, as Ashton puts it, that "the place that people will occupy in the life to come is entirely determined by moral decisions made in the present life." [50] In Ashton's view, John's emphasis on the immediate consequences of belief (life) and unbelief (death/judgment) "de-eschatologizes [final] judgement," [51] but it is more true to John's thought to say that John "eschatologizes" present life, underlining the urgency of belief in Jesus and the reality of true fellowship with God through him.

As Paul taught in 1 Corinthians 11:24–26, believers come to the Table not to ponder the future, but to remember and proclaim the past (the Lord's death) with a view to the future (until he comes). The decisive, foundational significance of Christ's work in the past necessarily renders the coming denoument absolutely essential yet in a sense anticlimactic. The glories of the future only amount to an unfolding of the infinite value of Jesus having already finished the work given him by the Father. Ashton's words merit thought: "[T]he nature of Christian belief entails some reduction in the importance attached to [futurist]

49. David L. Turner, "The New Jerusalem in Rev. 21:1–22:5: Consummation of a Biblical Continuum," in *Dispensationalism, Israel and the Church: The Search for Definition*, ed. Craig A. Blaising and Darrell L. Bock (Grand Rapids: Zondervan, 1992), 264–92.
50. Ashton, *Understanding the Fourth Gospel*, 409.
51. Ibid., 409.

eschatological expectation of any kind. For by far the most crucial revolution in man's relationship with God has been achieved by Christ: without some conviction of this kind the Gospel would be relatively small beer."[52]

- "The Lion of the tribe of Judah, the Root of David, has conquered" (Rev. 5:5; cf. John 16:33).
- "Worthy is the Lamb who was slain to receive power and wealth and wisdom and might and honor and glory and blessing!" (Rev. 5:12; cf. John 17).
- "Come, Lord Jesus!" (Rev. 22:20; cf. John 14:3).

The hour is coming, yet is now.

---

52. Ibid., 410.

THE DOCTRINE OF THE FUTURE IN PAUL'S WRITINGS

W. Edward Glenny

This essay is an introduction to Paul's doctrine of the future, or his eschatology.[1] Paul's understanding of the future provided the structure for his understanding of the person and work of Christ, and in turn his understanding of the person and work of Christ came to inform his view of history and the future. For Paul "the end[s] of the ages" had arrived in the climactic events of the death and resurrection of Jesus Christ, and those events determine the future.[2] In this introductory survey of Paul's eschatology, we will attempt to demonstrate how Paul's understanding of the future flows out of and is based upon this core belief that the ends of the ages had arrived in Christ.

Before we go any further, we should explain what we mean by a few terms. First, when we speak about doctrine with respect to Paul, we need to remember that Paul did not write theology books. He wrote occasional documents, which we call letters, to churches and Christian leaders addressing topics that were relevant to them. His letters contain theological truths, but technically speaking theology, or doctrine, is the result of the study and organization of the theological truths found in his letters. This paper is an attempt to organize and summarize his teaching concerning the future. Second, the "doctrine of the future," as

---

1. It is a pleasure to present this essay to Dr. Craig Blaising. Through his writings and interactions with me, he has had a great influence on my life, for which I am grateful.

2. "Now these things happened to them as an example, but they were written down for our instruction, on whom the end of the ages has come" (1 Cor. 10:11, ESV). Interestingly the phrase at the end of this verse could be more literally rendered "the ends (pl.) of the ages has come." Few English Bibles render it correctly; one happy exception is the Holman Christian Standard Bible. All citations from Scripture in this paper are from the English Standard Version, unless otherwise noted.

it is being used in this essay, could be called eschatology, or the doctrine of last things. However, as I will seek to demonstrate in this essay, for Paul "last things" are not limited to what is far off in the future. Third, I should clarify what I mean by "Paul's writings." The material in this essay is based only on the writings of the apostle Paul that have come down to us in the Christian Scriptures, and all thirteen letters traditionally attributed to Paul were considered in the research for this paper.[3]

We will address Paul's view of the future in three parts: the inauguration of the future in this age, the intermediate state of Christians who die, and the events of the end of this age and the age to come. However, before we embark upon our survey of Paul's view of the future we must summarize his understanding of the structure of reality and temporal history.[4]

The Structure of Paul's View of the Future

Paul's eschatological perspective came primarily from his Jewish heritage and its division of temporal history into two ages, this age and the age to come.[5] Jewish two-age theology, sometimes called temporal dualism or apocalyptic dualism, was based on Old Testament passages like Isaiah 65:17 where the prophet writes, "For behold, I create new heavens and a new earth, and the former things shall not be remembered or come into mind."[6] The division of history into two ages is also a common theme in other Jewish writings from the time of the New Testament like 4 Esdras 7:112–113, which says, "This present world is not the end; the full glory does not remain in it. . . . But the Day of Judgment will be the end of this age and the beginning of the immortal age to come, in which corruption has passed away" (NRSV).[7]

According to this Jewish two-age worldview, the present age since the fall of Adam and Eve is characterized by death, sin, evil, suffering, and disease; by con-

---

3. A convenient place to find support for the Pauline authorship of the thirteen books traditionally attributed to him is D. A. Carson and Douglas J. Moo, *An Introduction to the New Testament*, 2nd ed. (Grand Rapids, Zondervan, 2005).
4. Paul's understanding of history or reality is the center of all of his theology; see George Eldon Ladd, *A Theology of the New Testament*, rev. ed. (Grand Rapids: Eerdmans, 1993), 550–551.
5. L. J. Kreitzer, "Eschatology," in *Dictionary of Paul and His Letters*, ed. Gerald F. Hawthorne, Ralph P. Martin, and Daniel G. Reid (Downers Grove, IL: InterVarsity Press, 1993), 255.
6. Other Old Testament passages that refer to the structure of reality using the two-age paradigm are Daniel 2, 7; Joel 2–3; and Zechariah 7–14.
7. See also 4 Esdras 2:36, 39; 4:27; 6:9; 7:50; 8:1; 9:18–19; 2 Enoch 66:6; and 2 Baruch 15:7; 44:8–15.

trast, the age to come, the kingdom of God, offers life, righteousness, joy, and glory. The present age is going to give way to the coming age, or the kingdom of God, after a time of tribulation and religious apostasy. The age to come, which involves the Lord's direct intervention to judge and bless, was sometimes called the day of the Lord by the Old Testament prophets. Saul the Pharisee would have believed he was living in the present evil age and was waiting for the coming age, which would be ushered in at the advent of the Messiah and the arrival of God's kingdom.[8]

However, if Jewish two-age theology was the background and basic structure for Paul's eschatology, it was not the essence of it. Paul significantly adapted his Jewish eschatological viewpoint after he met the resurrected and glorified Christ on the road to Damascus and witnessed the glory reflected in the brilliant "light" that radiated from Christ (Acts 9:3; 22:6; 26:13). Through this experience and the guidance of the Holy Spirit in his life, Paul realized that Jesus, whose followers he was persecuting, is the Messiah. He is the resurrected and ascended Son of God, and the general resurrection that was to occur at the end of this age according to the Jewish two-age scheme has already broken into history in the coming of the Christ and his resurrection from the dead.[9] However, although the eschatological age has arrived in the death and resurrection of Jesus and the subsequent sending of the Spirit, the consummation of redemption is not yet accomplished and awaits Christ's return. At the Messiah's return he will establish the promised and long awaited messianic kingdom and completely defeat God's enemies, including the last enemy, death (1 Cor. 15:25–26, 54–55). Thus, Christians live in a time of overlap of the two ages. On one hand the eschatological age has been inaugurated, and on the other hand, it has not been totally realized yet. One age is beginning, and the other is passing away (1 Cor. 7:31). This time of overlap of the two ages is often called the time of the "already" and the "not yet." In a famous illustration of "already" and "not yet," Oscar Cullmann compares the first advent of Christ and the victory he won through his death

---

8. The language of "this age" and "the age to come" is reflected most clearly in Paul's letters in Ephesians 1:21 where he describes the rule of Christ over all creation "not only in this age but also in the one to come." That such a dualistic understanding of history was the basic structure of his beliefs as a Christian is also supported by his reference to the two-age idiom in other passages (Ladd, *A Theology of the New Testament*, 402–403). See also the phrases "the wisdom of this age" and "the rulers of this age" in 1 Corinthians 2:6 (also 1:20; 2:8; 3:18); "the present evil age" in Galatians 1:4 (also Eph. 5:16; 6:13); "the course [age] of this world" in Ephesians 2:2, which is contrasted with "the coming ages" in 2:7; and "the god of this world [age]" in 2 Corinthians 4:4.

9. C. Marvin Pate, *The End of the Ages Has Come* (Grand Rapids: Zondervan, 1995), 20–21.

and resurrection to D-day, which was the beginning of the end of World War II, and he likens the Parousia, or second advent of Christ, to V-day, the conclusion of that war.[10] Being a Christian is like living between D-day and V-day; the decisive battle has already been won at the cross, and the arrival of the promised gift of the Spirit marks the inauguration of the age to come in the here and now, but complete salvation and subjugation of Satan have not yet been realized and thus Christians await the "not yet," the return of Christ.

There is strong evidence in the New Testament that early Christians understood that the eschatological age had arrived with the coming of Christ. Some were so confident in the present reality of the age to come that they had overreacted to it and had an over realized view of Christian existence. For example, in 2 Timothy 2:18 Paul warns about those who "have swerved from the truth, saying that the resurrection has already happened." Also Paul's reference to the Corinthians thinking they were already kings and reigning (1 Cor. 4:8) and to their belief that there is not a resurrection from the dead in the future (1 Cor. 15:12), suggests an over realized perspective. They apparently thought they had already been resurrected in some sense.[11]

Having laid the foundation for the study of the doctrine of the future in Paul with our overview of the structure of his eschatology, we are now prepared to survey the various topics that constitute Paul's doctrine of the future. We will divide our discussion into three main categories, attempting to follow the chronology of future events as they fit into the structure of Paul's eschatology. First, since for Paul and the other New Testament authors the eschatological future has broken into this present age through the Christ events, we will provide a brief overview of some specific elements of the "already" aspect of Paul's doctrine of the future, the elements of the age to come that have already begun to unfold in this age. Then we will briefly consider the intermediate state, the fate of Christians who die before the resurrection. And finally we will examine the events connected with the end of this age and the age to come.

---

10. D-day is a military term for the day a military attack or operation is to be initiated; the term is commonly used for June 6, 1944, the day the Allies crossed the English channel to invade Europe in WWII and established a beachhead in Europe. V-day (or VE-day) stands for Victory in Europe Day, the day the Allies accepted the Nazis unconditional surrender at the end of WWII (May 8, 1945). See Oscar Cullmann, *Christ and Time*, trans. F. V. Filson (Philadelphia: Westminster, 1950), 84.
11. See Kreitzer, "Eschatology," 257. Also the reference in 2 Thessalonians 2:2 to the belief among the Thessalonians that the day of the Lord had already arrived suggests an over-realized understanding of Christian existence on their part.

The "Already" and Paul's Doctrine of the Future

Since Christians are people on whom "the ends of the ages has come" (1 Cor. 10:11), they are people who are already in the present experiencing the inauguration of future events that have broken into this age. All of the aspects of the "already" that we will review in this section are closely related to the person and work of Christ. They are the appearance of the Messiah, the kingdom of God (or Christ), the resurrection of Jesus, the judgment, and the giving of the Spirit.[12]

Jesus Is the Messiah

For Paul and the other New Testament authors, the appearance of the Messiah was regarded as an eschatological event and "an indisputable sign that the age to come had arrived."[13] His experience on the Damascus Road convinced Paul that Jesus was the Christ, the promised Jewish Messiah. One important reference to the messiahship of Jesus in Paul's letters is in Romans 9:5. Here Paul is clear that Jesus is the Christ, the Messiah, "whose coming is in the stream of the redemptive history of Israel, the covenants, the Law, and the promises."[14] He fulfilled the prophets (Rom. 1:2) and his death and resurrection were "in accordance with the Scriptures" (1 Cor. 15:3). Paul also believed that Christ was going to return to earth in glory with his mighty angels to judge the living and the dead and to consummate his kingdom reign (2 Tim. 4:1; 2 Thess. 1:5–7).

The Kingdom

Paul refers to two aspects of Christ's kingdom. He speaks of a present dimension of the Messiah's reign (Col. 1:13; 4:11), which seems to be primarily his exercise of his lordship over believers in his church (Eph. 1:20–23), although the kingdom is not to be equated with the church.[15] The present stage of the

---

12. Other subjects could be added to this list of aspects of the already in Paul, such as growing ungodliness and apostasy, which is discussed below in the section on the day of the Lord.

13. Kreitzer, "Eschatology," 256. All one has to do to prove this is to survey the prophecies fulfilled by Jesus, according to the New Testament authors.

14. Ladd, *Theology*, 449. Romans 9:5 is one of the few places Paul uses Christ as a title, meaning Messiah; other occurrences of the word Christ that are sometimes thought to be titular are 1 Corinthians 10:4, and 2 Corinthians 4:4; 5:10.

15. The sphere of Christ's kingdom reign is larger than the church, and all in the church may not be included in the kingdom.

Messiah's kingdom is concerned principally with spiritual things, such as "righteousness and peace and joy in the Holy Spirit," and it is not defined by the practices of this age, such as eating and drinking, which are passing away (Rom. 14:17; 1 Cor. 7:29–31). Paul also addresses the future dimension of the Messiah's reign in several passages, which I will discuss later (1 Cor. 6:9–10; 15:50; Gal. 5:21; Eph. 5:5; 1 Thess. 2:12; 2 Thess. 1:5).[16]

The Resurrection

The resurrection of Jesus from the dead is the "key event which guarantees or authenticates" his messiahship.[17] According to Romans 1:4 he "was declared to be the Son of God in power according to the Spirit of holiness by his resurrection from the dead." Furthermore, Jesus's resurrection demonstrates how the eschatological age, the age to come, has broken into and overlaps with the present; Christ is the firstfruits from the dead (1 Cor. 15:20, 23; cf. Col. 1:18), and his resurrection guarantees the future resurrection of those who believe in him (see also 1 Cor. 15:12, 20–22). The resurrection life of the age to come has begun in Christ, and Christians partake of that life in this age. The "newness of life" they experience is a result of them sharing in Christ's resurrection (Rom. 6:4–5). But the full realization of resurrection life for Christians, involving a resurrection body, awaits the consummation. It is not too much to say that the resurrection of Jesus is the "fundamental eschatological event that marks the onset of the new age";[18] by virtue of his resurrection and exaltation, Christ defeated and brought under his authority all forces in the universe (Eph. 1:18–22; Phil. 1:19; Col. 1:20), including death (2 Tim. 1:10).

The Judgment

The end-time judgment of God has also impinged on this age. Foundational to Paul's teaching concerning the Christian life is the truth that believers in Christ have died with him and been raised from the dead with him and are now seated with him in heaven (Col. 3:1–4; Eph. 2:4–7; Rom. 6:1–14). The death and resurrection of the Christ and his enthronement as Lord at the right hand of God in heaven are the basis for the justification of believers. Because Christ has already accomplished their salvation, the day of judgment verdict concerning their salvation has already been declared (Rom. 2:13–16; 8:31–34; Gal. 5:5);

---

16. See Pate, *The End of Ages*, 230, for a chart of the references to the kingdom of God (Christ) in Paul.
17. Kreitzer, "Eschatology," 256.
18. Sigurd Grindheim, *Introducing Biblical Theology* (London: Bloomsbury, 2013), 218–9.

they have already been justified or declared righteous by God on the basis of the work of Christ in which they participate and of which they receive the benefits. Since Christ has been raised from the dead, to be "in Christ," or in the Jewish Messiah, is the beginning of the "new creation," or is itself part of God's "new creation" (2 Cor. 5:17), which was promised in the Scriptures.[19] There are also a few verses in Paul's writings that suggest unbelievers are already in this present age beginning to experience God's final verdict concerning their unbelief and opposition to God (Rom. 1:18; 1 Thess. 2:16).

The Spirit

Another aspect of the inauguration of the eschatological age in the present is the end time outpouring of the Spirit of God on Christians. The Spirit is related to all of the other elements included in the "already" aspect of salvation. The main characteristic by which the Messiah could be recognized was the presence of the Spirit on him (Isa. 11:1–3; 42:1; 61:1). The resurrection of Christ brought into being the coming age, the age of the Spirit (Rom. 1:4), and in 1 Corinthians 15:45 the resurrected Christ is described as "a life-giving Spirit" (see also 2 Cor. 3:6). As Lord and Christ at the right hand of God, Jesus now pours out the end-time gift of the Spirit on his followers, both Jews and Gentiles, in fulfillment of God's promises to Abraham and as part of the blessings of the new covenant, which he administers (Gal. 3:14; 2 Cor. 3:3–8). Thus, life in the Spirit is an eschatological reality, and the presence of the Spirit in all God's people in this age is the initial fulfillment of the end-time pouring out of the Spirit prophesied in Joel 2:28–32 (see Acts 2:16–36; Rom. 8:9–17). Life in the Spirit is the kind of life that characterizes life in the kingdom of God (Rom. 14:17), and the pouring out of the Spirit signals that the kingdom of God has been inaugurated.

Paul could not be clearer that the Christian's experience of the Spirit in this age is an eschatological blessing, a taste of the age to come; but this taste is not the full realization of the blessing. He calls the Spirit the "firstfruits" of the full realization of adoption as God's children and redemption of the body (Rom. 8:23).[20] The Spirit is the "guarantee" God gives to believers of their ultimate redemption in the age to come (2 Cor. 1:22; 5:5; Eph. 1:13–14). Paul also connects the Spirit with

---

19. On the promised new creation see Isaiah 43:18–19; 65:17–25; 66:22–23.
20. Compare 1 Corinthians 15:20, where the resurrected Christ is called "the firstfruit of those who have fallen asleep." Other verses that connect the Spirit with the believer's adoption include Romans 8:15 and Galatians 4:5–6.

the future inheritance of believers; it is only those who have the Spirit that will inherit the kingdom of God (1 Cor. 6:9–11; 15:50; Gal. 5:16–24).[21]

THE INTERMEDIATE STATE

Christians in this age are already sharers in the life of the world to come through their union with Christ and the presence of the Spirit in their lives, but they are also still in mortal bodies and subject to death. What happens to believers who die before the end of the age and the final resurrection? The most important passage addressing this topic in the Bible is in Paul's second letter to the Corinthians (5:1–10).[22]

In the context of 2 Corinthians 5:1–10 Paul is explaining that in the midst of weakness, suffering, and death, Paul and other believers persevere in life and ministry because they know "that he who raised the Lord Jesus will raise us also with Jesus and bring us . . . into his presence" (4:14). Then in 5:1–10 Paul addresses the wasting away of the body, which he calls the "earthly tent," and what happens to believers who die before the return of Jesus, since it is at that time that Christians will be raised from the dead and receive their resurrection bodies. Paul is confident that believers "have . . . a house not made with hands, eternal in the heavens," which refers to the resurrection body, and they long to live in that mode of existence (5:1–2). They long for their immortal, resurrection life, so they will not be left in an intermediate state, "naked" and "unclothed" (5:3–4), and the Holy Spirit is their guarantee that the Lord has prepared them to receive glorious resurrection bodies (5:5). Because they are in Christ and the Spirit dwells in them, believers can always live and minister with courage, even though they are in their physical bodies and away from the Lord (5:6–7). But they "would rather be away from the body and at home with the Lord" (5:8), which is a reference to the intermediate state between their physical bodies and resurrection bodies.

Paul prefers the intermediate state over this life (Phil 1:21, 23), because it is to be with the Lord. But it does not yet involve putting on the resurrection body. Paul's confidence that the intermediate state of Christians is superior to this life is apparently based on their "in Christ" relationship (Rom. 6:1–11).

---

21. For a development of these and other end time events that could be connected with the "not yet," see Pate, *The End of Ages*, 225–236.
22. Paul also addresses a form of this question in 1 Thessalonians 4:13–18.

He knows that nothing can separate them from Christ (Rom. 8:35–39), and therefore when they die he is confident they will be "with Christ" (Phil 1:23). His confidence that Christians will be with Christ is because of the impinging of the age to come on this age. But Christians must await the "not yet"—the age to come—to receive their resurrection bodies. Thus, the intermediate state that Christians experience if they die before the return of Christ and the resurrection of their bodies is life with Christ as a disembodied spirit, awaiting the resurrection. Such a disembodied existence is not what Paul ultimately wishes for, but he knows that it involves being present with the Lord, which is far better than life in the earthly tent.

Events at the End of the Present Age and in the Age to Come

The events that are the topics in this section make up the "not yet" of Paul's eschatology. Thus, these are things that may have already begun to be realized in some way in "this age" through the work of Christ, but they have not been totally realized and are part of "the age to come" (Eph. 1:21).

The Day of the Lord

A good place to begin our discussion of end time events in Paul's writings is with the day of the Lord, or the day of Christ.[23] In the Old Testament the phrase "day of the Lord" refers to a time at the end of this present age when God directly intervenes in the affairs of the world to judge and bless (Isa. 2:1–12; Amos 5:18).[24] Man is presently having his day, but the time is coming when God will directly intervene in the affairs of the world to have his day; this is day of the Lord. It does not involve one single day or event, but it is a series of events over a period of time that results in the climactic accomplishment of God's plan in the world (1 Cor. 5:5; 1 Thess. 5:2; 2 Thess. 2:2; cf. Acts 2:20). The day of the Lord will conclude this present evil age and usher in the age to come; it will come unexpectedly and with hostile intent for unbelievers (2 Thess. 5:1–3).

---

23. The day of the Lord, or a similar phrase, is found in 1 Cor. 5:5; 1 Thess. 5:2; 2 Thess. 2:2, and the day of Christ, or a similar phrase, is found in 1 Cor. 1:8; 5:5; 2 Cor. 1:14; Phil. 1:6, 10; 2:16; 2 Thess. 1:10; 2 Tim. 1:18; see also "the day" in 1 Thess. 5:4; 1 Cor. 3:13; and "that day" in 2 Tim. 1:12, 18; 4:8.

24. See also J. D. Barker, "The Day of the Lord" in *Dictionary of the Old Testament Prophets,* ed. Mark J. Boda and J. Gordon McConville (Downers Grove, IL: InterVarsity, 2012), 132–143.

The phrase "the day of Christ" elevates Christ to the same status as Yahweh.[25] It is the same basic concept as the day of the Lord, although the contexts where it occurs focus on the return of Christ and the judgment when he returns (1 Cor. 1:8 "Day of Lord Jesus"; 1 Cor. 5:5 "Day of Lord Jesus Christ"; 2 Cor. 1:14 "Day of Lord Jesus"; Phil. 1:6 "Day of Lord Jesus," Phil. 1:10 and 16 "Day of Christ").[26] Paul also refers to the day of the Lord as "that day" (1 Thess. 5:4; 2 Thess. 1:10; 2 Tim. 1:12, 18; 4:8; 1 Cor. 3:13 has "the Day"), and with the possible exception of 1 Thessalonians 5:4 and 2 Thessalonians 1:10, this phrase also refers to the day of judgment, apparently after the return of Christ.[27] Thus, the day of the Lord, the day of Christ, and other related phrases in Paul refer primarily to the return of Christ and the judgment that will follow, which are the main aspects that pertain to Christians; however, the meaning of the day of the Lord may be broader in some passages, as seems to be required in 1 Thessalonians 5:2 and 2 Thessalonians 2:2. Paul's important information about that day in these two verses indicates that it must include events preceding the return of Christ to reign, which are apparently the judgment or darkness connected with the day of the Lord in the Prophets. In 1 Thessalonians 5:1–3 Paul warns that the day of the Lord will come unexpectedly as a thief in the night, and with the hostile intent of a thief for those who are in spiritual darkness.[28]

In his second letter to the Thessalonians (2:1–3) Paul addresses their concern that the day of the Lord had already arrived, and in this context he connects it with "the coming of our Lord Jesus Christ and our being gathered together to him" (2:1). Thus, it appears that in 2 Thessalonians 2:1–12 Paul is correcting misunderstandings related to his teaching of the coming of Christ and the day of the Lord in 1 Thessalonians 4:13–5:11.[29] The Thessalonians are shaken,

25. Pate, *The End of the Ages*, 235.
26. This also seems to be the understanding of the day of the Lord in the quotation from Joel 2 in Acts 2:20, since in that context "the sun will be turned to darkness and the moon to blood before the Day of the Lord."
27. It is clearly connected with Christ's return in 2 Thessalonians 1:10.
28. In 5:4–8 Paul qualifies the description of the coming of the day of the Lord as a "thief in the night," explaining that Christians are in the light and for them it will not come as a thief in the night with evil intent, as it will come upon those in darkness; but for believers it will involve salvation (5:9–11). However, the fact that the day of the Lord comes unexpectedly applies to all, believers and unbelievers alike.
29. In 2 Thessalonians 2:1 "the coming of our Lord Jesus Christ and our being gathered together to him" is apparently the same event described in 1 Thessalonians 4:13–18; the same word for "coming" is used (and it is not used in 2 Thessalonians 1:6–10), and the compound noun "gathering together" in 2 Thessalonians 2:1 is related to the simple verb "bring" in 1 Thessalonians 4:14. The language in 2 Thessalonians 2:1 suggests that in 2 Thessalonians 2 Paul is clarifying things concerning the teaching in 1 Thessalonians 4.

thinking they have missed this gathering together unto Christ and are in the day of the Lord, or they are wildly excited thinking that they are in the day of the Lord and that the return of Christ is coming soon.[30] Paul corrects their false ideas, teaching that the day of the Lord is not present unless there has been first "the rebellion" and the revelation of the "man of sin."

The meaning of the verb *enistēmi*, commonly rendered "has come" in the phrase "the day of the Lord has come" at the end of 2 Thessalonians 2:2, is very important for determining the time of the day of the Lord.[31] This verb occurs five other times in Paul, and four of those times it is in the perfect tense, as it is in 2 Thessalonians 2:2. Every other time the verb occurs in the perfect tense in Paul's writings it means "to be present" (Rom. 8:38; 1 Cor. 3:22; 1 Cor. 7:26; Gal. 1:4), and it should probably also be understood that way in 2 Thessalonians 2:2.[32] Furthermore, the way *enistēmi* is translated in 2 Thessalonians 2:2 affects the meaning of 2:3, because the clause containing this verb from 2:2 must be supplied in the second clause of 2:3 to make sense of that verse.[33] I would render the second clause of 2:3 "For that day is not present unless. . . ." This is a different sense than "the day will not come unless," as in the English Standard Version.[34] My point is that in 2:3 Paul is not teaching what comes before the day of the Lord but rather what indicates that it is present. Paul is saying that they will know it "is present" if "the rebellion" comes and "the man of lawlessness is revealed." These would be the "first" indications people on this earth have that the day of the Lord has arrived.[35] In the remainder of the context Paul explains the

---

30. Pretribulational premillennialists sometimes suggest the first of these scenarios, and posttribulational premillennialists and others who only understand there to be one stage of Christ's return sometimes suggest the second.

31. In ESV the verb is translated "has come"; NIV renders it "has already come" and NRSV renders it "is already come."

32. See BDAG, 337. The other occurrence of this verb in Paul is in 2 Timothy 3:1 where it is in the future tense and refers to future time ("will come" in ESV). This verb should be supplied in the second clause of 2:3 also, as the English versions do.

33. A literal rendering of the second clause of 2:3, without the implied words from the end of 2:2, would be something like "for unless the rebellion comes first. . . ." If the understood words from the end of 2:2 are supplied it reads like modern English versions (i.e., ESV: "For [that day will not come] unless the rebellion comes first").

34. The NIV has "until" instead of "unless" which accentuates the problem.

35. First Thessalonians 2:3 could mean that the "apostasy" and the revelation of the "man of lawlessness" must come before the day of the Lord ("first"), or it could mean that the "apostasy" and revelation of the "man of lawlessness" are indications of the presence of the day of the Lord and if they do not see these signs ("first") they know they are not in that day. I am arguing for the latter interpretation, and the fact that the day of the Lord comes like a thief in the night (1 Thess. 5:1–3) supports the latter interpretation.

revelation of the man of lawlessness, which parodies the revelation of Christ. It will be with signs and wonders and other specific events (2:4–10), and after this lawless one has been revealed and has opposed God and his people for a time, even setting himself up as God in the temple of God, Jesus will slay him at his return (2:8).

The concept of an end-time figure who would oppose God and his people goes back to the Old Testament and may find its roots in figures like the king of Tyre in Ezekiel 28:1–19 and Gog in Ezekiel 38–39.[36] Christians often call this man of lawlessness the man of sin, or antichrist. Although the "mystery of lawlessness is already at work" in this age, it is being restrained until the Lord's time for the "man of lawlessness," the antichrist figure, to be revealed (2:7–8).[37] Thus, 2 Thessalonians 2 teaches that the coming of this figure at the end of the age, shortly before Christ returns, fulfills the antichrist spirit of this age and is a parody of Christ's coming.

"The rebellion," or apostasy that is connected with the coming of the lawless one at the end of the age in 2 Thessalonians 2:3, is apparently the fulfillment of what Paul has in mind in 1 Timothy 4:1 when he writes that "The Spirit expressly says that in later times some will depart from the faith devoting themselves to deceitful spirits and teachings of demons." The phrase "in later times" in 1 Timothy 4:1, which corresponds to "in the last days" in 2 Timothy 3:1, probably refers to this age from the resurrection of Christ until his triumphant return. In the 2 Timothy 3:1 passage Paul writes that "in the last days there will come times of difficulty" for God's people, and he writes elsewhere in 2 Timothy that there will be "more and more ungodliness" (2:16) and "evil people and impostors will go on from bad to worse" (3:12) in this age.[38] These verses

---

36. See Pate, *The End of the Ages*, 225–226, for other suggestions for the roots of the antichrist figure in the Old Testament. The lawless figure in 2 Thessalonians 2 has several parallels with the little horn figure in Daniel 7 and the willful king from the north in Daniel 11:21-45. These figures assign themselves divine status (Dan. 7:8; 11:35–36; 2 Thess. 2:4); desecrate the temple (Dan. 11:31; 2 Thess. 2:4); are described as "lawless" (Dan. 11:32; 2 Thess. 2:3); will be destroyed by the Lord (Dan. 7:11; 2 Thess. 2:8); and are revealed in their time, apparently according to God's purposes for them (Dan. 11:35; 2 Thess. 2:6).

37. See 1 John 2:18; 4:3; Matt. 24:5, 23-24/Mark 13:6, 21–22 for descriptions of the spirit of antichrist and false Christs before the revelation of the figure who fulfills this pattern. The identification of the restrainer in 2 Thessalonians 2:6–7 is greatly debated. Some suggestions are the Holy Spirit, human government, a divinely ordained period of time, Paul, a spiritual being like the angel Gabriel, and the need for the gospel to be proclaimed throughout the world. The fact that the words that describe this restraining force are in the neuter gender in 2:6 and the masculine in 2:7 increases the difficulty of identifying it (him).

38. Second Timothy 3:1–9 describes the godlessness of the last days, which includes false teachers and opposition to the truth.

indicate that ungodliness and sin will increase in this age, and that difficult days are ahead for God's people, especially at the end of the age. There is also a biblical tradition that there will be tribulation at the end of this age (Dan. 12:1; Jer. 30:7; Revelation), and Paul's language supports this tradition. In 2 Thessalonians 2 he connects "the rebellion" at the end of the age with the day of the Lord and the revelation of the man of lawlessness.

The Return of Jesus

Arguably the most important end-time event in Paul's writings is the coming of Jesus.[39] Paul employs three different nouns to describe the future coming of Jesus Christ: *Parousia* means "arrival" or "presence";[40] *epiphaneia*, which Paul uses to refer to Christ's first and second comings, means "appearance";[41] and *apokalupsis* means "revelation" or "disclosure."[42] A study of the passages where these words are used to describe the future coming of Christ to earth indicates that his coming in the future is the occasion when the authority and glory of the resurrected Christ will be revealed to all and, as Lord of all, he will exercise his rule over all creation. The exercise of his rule will involve his judgment of people, evil angels, and Satan, resulting in the rewarding of his servants and the punishment of his enemies. There is debate about whether the references to the Lord's future return all refer to the same coming, or whether the Lord's future coming involves two stages. Many premillennialists believe the verses describing Christ's future coming will be fulfilled in two stages: the rapture and the second coming. Amillennialists, postmillennialists, and historic premillenialists believe that the verses describing Christ's return all refer to the same event—namely, his return at the end of this age to usher in the eternal state. An important passage that premillennialists believe describes the first stage of Christ's future return is 1 Thessalonians 4:13–18, which refers to the Lord catching up living and dead Christians to meet him in the air to

39. Kreitzer, "Eschatology," 260, comments that Paul never uses the phrases "the Second Coming" or "the Second Advent" to refer to Christ's return (but note the language of Heb. 9:28).

40. BDAG, 780–781. It was used as a technical term to describe the manifestation of a hidden divinity by the revelation of its power and for the visit of a ruler to a province. See 1 Cor. 15:23; 1 Thess. 2:19; 3:13; 4:15; 5:23; 2 Thess. 2:1.

41. BDAG, 385. See 2 Timothy 1:10, referring to Christ's incarnation, and 2 Thess. 2:8; 1 Tim. 6:14; 4:1, 8; and Titus 2:13, referring to Christ's future coming.

42. BDAG, 112. See 1 Cor. 1:7; 2 Thess. 1:7. Other passages use verb forms related to these three nouns to describe the Lord's future coming; see Kreitzer, "Eschatology," 259–260 for other references to the Lord's return.

remain with him.[43] Premillennialists who believe in the rapture also hold that after or in conjunction with that event Christ will return to reign over his millennial kingdom on earth.[44]

The Resurrection

Paul connects the future resurrection of believers with the return of Christ (1 Cor. 15:23) and the new creation (Rom. 8:18–23). In 1 Corinthians 15:23 Paul writes that at his return Christ will make alive all who belong to him. Paul is also clear in 15:50–53 that believers must follow Christ in putting on an incorruptible body, and that will take place instantaneously at the last trumpet when Christ returns. Exactly when this resurrection takes place is viewed differently by different systems of interpretation: Amillennialists and postmillennialists place it at the one return of Christ; premillennialists believe that the resurrection of Christians is at the time of the rapture, and that the resurrection of other believers is at the second coming of Christ.

It is important to realize that existence in the resurrection body will differ greatly from the disembodied intermediate state we discussed above. The resurrection body described in 1 Corinthians 15 will be like Christ's resurrection body described in the gospel accounts. After he was resurrected from the dead, Christ appeared in bodily form to many witnesses, including Paul (1 Cor. 15:5–8). The resurrected Christ, whom Paul met on the road to Damascus, is the firstfruits of our resurrection (15:20, 22), and we will bear the image of his resurrected body (15:49). There is an ontological continuity between the original physical body and the resurrection body.[45] But the resurrection body will not be the old, natural body, which Paul describes as "flesh and blood"; that body will be "changed" into an imperishable body to function in the spiritual realm (15:50–53). Often in 1 Corinthians 15 the resurrected body is characterized as "spiritual" (15:44–46), which does not mean it is immaterial but rather that the Holy Spirit animates and empowers it. It will also be incorruptible, glorious, powerful, and immortal (15:42–43, 53–54).

---

43. Some premillennialists also believe there are other passages that speak of Christ's return at the rapture, such as 1 Corinthians 15:51–52.
44. Premillennialists who believe in the rapture are divided over its timing. See the discussion of the three main views in Richard R. Reiter, et al., *The Rapture: Pre-, Mid-, or Post- Tribulational?* (Grand Rapids: Zondervan, 1984).
45. Paul likens it to the relationship between a seed and a plant in 1 Corinthians 15:35–41.

The Reign of Christ

Earlier in this study we referred to the future dimension of the Messiah's kingdom reign (1 Cor. 6:9–10; 15:50; Gal. 5:21; Eph. 5:5; 1 Thess. 2:12; 2 Thess. 1:5).[46] The future kingdom is the glorious inheritance of believers (1 Cor. 6:9-11; Gal. 5:21; Eph. 5:5; 1 Thess. 2:12), for which they presently suffer (2 Thess. 1:5). The descriptions of the kingdom in 1 Corinthians 15 confirm its close connection with the resurrection of Christ and the defeat of death. In 15:22–28 the resurrection of Christ is one stage in the subjection to God of the entire universe, and that complete subjection is accomplished in three stages through the reign of Christ. The three stages are distinguished by the repetition of "then" in our English versions of 1 Corinthians 15:22–26.[47]

> (For as in Adam all die, so also in Christ shall all be made alive. But each in his own order: Christ the firstfruits, then at his coming those who belong to Christ. Then comes the end, when he delivers the kingdom to God the Father after destroying every rule and every authority and power. For he must reign until he has put all his enemies under his feet. The last enemy to be destroyed is death.

The first stage of Christ's subjugation of the universe is his resurrection from the dead (15:23a). The second stage, marked by "then" in 15:23b, is at his coming when those who belong to him will be made alive with him. And the third stage ("then" in 15:24) is after Christ has destroyed every rule and authority and power, including death, when he will deliver the kingdom to God so that the Father might be all in all. It is important here to note that just as there is an interval between the first two stages—the resurrection of Christ and the resurrection of those in Christ which occurs when he returns to reign—in the same way an interval is implied between the second and third stages while he reigns over all between the time of his return and the time he delivers the kingdom to God. This passage fits nicely into a premillennial scheme, in which at his second coming Christ establishes his kingdom on earth and reigns until he has subjected all other authorities to his rule, and then at the end he delivers

---

46. See Pate, *The End of the Ages*, 230, for a chart of the references to the kingdom of God (and Christ) in Paul.
47. In the Greek there are two words rendered "then."

the rule to the Father for the consummation, or eternity.[48] This passage is more difficult for amillennialists, because it strongly implies that Christ reigns for a period of time after his return to earth and the resurrection of believers before he "delivers the kingdom to God the Father." For amillennialists the coming of Christ and resurrection of believers is not separated from the time Christ delivers the kingdom to the Father.[49]

Paul also addresses the future kingdom in 1 Corinthians 15:50–56. In this passage he teaches that only believers who have incorruptible resurrection bodies will be able to share in the inheritance of the kingdom, for "the perishable cannot inherit the imperishable" (15:50).[50] Living and dead believers will inherit the kingdom at the time of the last trumpet when Christ returns, and the time of this inheritance should be connected with the second stage of events in 15:22–26 discussed above.[51]

For Paul the coming fullness of the kingdom, which believers can share, is one of the main reasons to be faithful in Christian ministry. When he charges Timothy to fulfill his ministry in 2 Timothy 4:1, he charges him before God and Christ Jesus, who will be his judge; however, Paul also charges Timothy in view of Jesus's future appearing and kingdom. For Paul, the return of Christ to judge and to rule in his kingdom is the ultimate reality and should be Timothy's focus to encourage and motivate him in his ministry.

The Salvation of "All Israel"

Another end-time event connected with the return of Christ is the salvation of "all Israel," predicted by Paul in Romans 11:25–27. This promise is near the end of a context in which Paul addresses the issue of Israel's rejection of Christ and the impact that issue has on the relationship of Jews and Gentiles in the church at Rome (Rom. 9–11). In that context Paul argues that the Jewish nation's rejection of Jesus Christ does not mean that the promises God made to the Jewish people have failed

---

48. Michael F. Bird, *A Bird's Eye View of Paul* (Nottingham: Intervarsity Press, 2008), 125, proposes that in this passage Paul "implies a messianic or millennial reign of Christ upon the earth."

49. See Robert B. Strimple, "Amillennialism" in *Three Views on the Millennium and Beyond,* ed. Darrell L. Bock (Grand Rapids: Zondervan, 1999), 108–112.

50. The Greek verb translated "inherit" twice in 15:50 in English versions means "acquire, obtain, come into possession of" (BDAG, 547), perishable bodies cannot possess the kingdom of God.

51. See the discussion in the previous paragraph of the different ways different schools of interpretation would understand this.

(9:6). Those promises never involved the salvation of every Jewish person (9:6–33), and there is still a remnant of Israelites, of which Paul is one (11:1–6). Furthermore, the nation of Israel was hardened and stumbled for a time so that salvation might come to the Gentiles. Jews, the natural branches in God's olive tree, have been removed from the tree, and Gentiles, who are wild branches, have now been grafted in. The Gentile Christians should not become proud of their position in God's olive tree, because God in his kindness has grafted them in and he can also graft in again the natural branches if they turn from their unbelief (11:17–24).[52] Another reason the Gentiles should not become proud is because their salvation and reconciliation to God is a result of the Jews' present rejection of Christ. But Paul emphasizes that if the Jews' present rejection led to riches for the Gentiles, much greater riches will result from their future "acceptance" and "full inclusion" (11:12, 14).[53]

Paul is clear that the partial hardening that has happened to Israel is "until the fullness of the Gentiles has come in" (11:25), and then that hardening will be reversed and "all Israel will be saved" (11:26). The salvation of "all Israel" in 11:25–27 must involve more than the present remnant, and it is reasonable to understand it to refer to "the nation generally."[54]

There are many controversial details concerning the salvation of "all Israel" in Romans 9–11. But I believe the context supports reading it as a reference to the salvation of a large number of Jews at the end of the age. And such a restoration of Israel is in keeping with the promises to the nation in the Old Testament. As Michael Bird contends, "For God's faithfulness to be vindicated and for Christians to have a true sense of assurance in God's saving righteousness, there needs to be a fitting end to God's dealings with Israel, or else God's own character is jeopardized and brought into question."[55]

---

52. The olive tree is probably to be understood as God's covenant program of salvation, which requires faith and loyalty in the covenant partner. The blessings resulting from the grafting of Gentiles into God's olive tree are perhaps what Paul is referring to in Romans 15:27, where he speaks of Gentiles sharing in the Jews' "spiritual blessings."

53. In 11:15 Paul connects the future "acceptance" of his fellow Jews with "life from the dead." Douglas Moo, *The Epistle to the Romans*, NICNT (Grand Rapids: Eerdmans, 1996), 694–696, gives three considerations that favor understanding "life from the dead" as a reference to "the general resurrection that will take place after the return of Christ in glory, or to blessed life that will follow that resurrection" (694). He comments, "A standard apocalyptic pattern featured the restoration of Israel as the event that would bring in the eschatological consummation" (696); this pattern is also found in Acts 3:19–20.

54. Moo, *Romans*, 722; he further defines the phrase as "the corporate entity of the nation as it exists at a particular point in time" (723). In Romans 9–11 "Israel" always refers to ethnic, national Israel, with the exception of 9:6b where it refers to the elect within the nation.

55. Bird, *A Bird's Eye View*, 119.

According to the time references in 11:25–26 it must be after the full salvation of Gentiles that "all Israel will be saved" (11:26). This suggests that the salvation of Israel Paul refers to in Romans 11:25–27 is at the end of the age. In Romans 11:26b–27 Paul supports his statements concerning Israel's salvation with Scripture from Isaiah 59:20–21a and 27:9, and his use of these Scriptures also indicates the salvation of "all Israel" is connected to the return of Christ.[56] Important for our purposes is the change Paul makes that differs from all known manuscripts in the first line of the Scripture quotation. Instead of the phrase "to Zion" as in the Hebrew or "for the sake of Zion," as in the LXX, Paul writes that "The Deliverer will come from Zion" to banish ungodliness in Jacob in fulfillment of his covenant.[57] "The Deliverer" in Romans must be Jesus Christ, who will take away Jacob's sins (11:27b), and the fact that he comes to Jacob "from Zion" is best understood as a reference to Christ coming from the heavenly Jerusalem to earth to save his people, Israel.[58] The connection of the restoration of Israel with the resurrection, or "life from the dead" in Romans 11:15, is also consistent with the end-time salvation of Israel at the time of the return of Christ.[59]

The Final Judgment

Paul did not abandon the standard Jewish belief that God would judge all men and women (Rom. 2:1–11; 14:10–12). For him, the final judgment comes at the end of the age and is closely associated with the return of Christ (2 Thess. 1:5–10; 1 Thess. 3:13; 5:23), apparently taking place in conjunction with it or shortly thereafter. The day of judgment is a day of revelation of God's wrath (Rom. 2:5, 8; Rom. 5:9).[60] God will judge all people by their works (Rom. 2:6; Eph. 6:8).[61] There will be rewards for the righteous and

---

56. The first three lines of Paul's quotation in Rom. 11:26b–27a come from Isaiah 59:20–21a, and the clause in Romans 11:27b is from Isaiah 27:9; he appears to be using a text similar to the LXX.

57. The covenant could be the Abrahamic or the new; it appears elsewhere that Paul understands them to be related (note the connection of the new covenant gift of the Spirit with the blessings of Abraham in Galatians 3:14).

58. The heavenly Jerusalem is called Zion in Hebrews 12:22, and probably that is also the meaning of Zion in the quotation from Isaiah 28:16 in 1 Peter 2:6 and Romans 9:33.

59. We discussed above the connection in Paul between the resurrection and the return of Christ. See also n. 54.

60. Wrath is a common theme in Paul's writings. The phrase "the wrath of God" occurs three times (Rom. 1:18; Eph. 5:6; Col. 3:6). Promises of deliverance from God's wrath are often used to defend a pretribulational rapture (see 1 Thess. 1:10 and 5:9).

61. Judgment in the New Testament is always according to works (see Rev. 20:12–13); this does not mean that people are saved by means of their good works, but it indicates that saving faith and good works are inseparably connected (see Gal. 5:6; Phil. 2:12–13).

punishment for the wicked (2 Thess. 1:5-10). All believers will receive an inheritance from the Lord (Col. 3:24), but the wicked will be consigned to eternal, conscious suffering (2 Thess. 1:9).

Twice Paul refers to the "judgment seat." In Romans 14:10 he refers to "the judgment seat of God," and in 2 Corinthians 5:10 he speaks of "the judgment seat of Christ." Such variation between judgment by God and judgment by Christ is common in Paul's writings; it probably reflects the truth that "God judges the secrets of men [humankind] by Christ Jesus" (Rom. 2:16). In 1 Corinthians 3:12–15 Paul describes the judgment of those who are "God's fellow workers" (3:9), apparently a reference to Christians who are involved in the work of God. The fire of the day of judgment will reveal the character of their work; if their work survives they will receive reward, and if their work is burned up they will be saved but without reward.[62] Paul also refers to the future judgment of Satan and his angels (Rom. 16:20; 1 Cor. 15:24),[63] the destruction of the "man of lawlessness," which will occur at the coming of Christ (2 Thess. 2:8), and the participation of God's people with Christ in the final judgment (1 Cor. 6:2–3).

New Creation

In Romans 8 Paul describes the groaning of creation, waiting for the day when it will be set free from the bondage to corruption (8:19–22). Along with creation believers await their full adoption as children of God, the redemption of their bodies, which is also part of the new creation (8:23). As discussed above, the new creation has already invaded this age through the work of Christ, and by virtue of their "in Christ" relationship, Christians are already "new creation" (2 Cor. 5:17; Gal. 6:15). The "firstfruits of the Spirit" is their guarantee that the work of the redemption of their bodies will be completed. Thus, they long for the day of Christ's return when the whole creation will be redeemed from the effects of sin, and the curse that came upon all creation through the sin of Adam will be finally and completely removed by Christ.

---

62. Some premillennialists understand this judgment to be a special judgment, the judgment seat of Christ (see 2 Cor. 5:10), for believers who are raptured, which occurs before the general judgment at the end of the age.

63. Christ's future victory over evil angels is the conclusion of the victory he has already won on the cross (Eph. 4:8; Col. 2:15).

SUMMARY

In Ephesians 1:9–10 Paul writes that God's purpose in his administration of all the epochs of history is to unite all things under one head in Christ the Messiah.[64] This verse speaks of God's control of all the ages of history to bring "the heavens and the earth" to his goal for them, and God is going to accomplish that "in Christ." The phrase "in Christ" is one of Paul's favorites, and he teaches elsewhere that if anyone is "in Christ" the new creation has arrived (2 Cor. 5:17), since to be "in Christ" is to share in his resurrection life. Thus, to unite all things "in Christ" and under his headship involves the application to creation of the redemption that Christ provided and the renewal of all creation. The "fullness of times" when God does this is at the culmination or end of all the ages or epochs of history.[65] And this uniting of all things in the Messiah must involve Christ's rule over all, which Paul also describes in 1 Corinthians 15:20–26.[66] Paul explains that by his death, resurrection, and exaltation, Christ is beginning to bring all things under his headship in this age (see Eph. 1:7, 20–22; 2:6–7), but all the universe has not yet been brought together under Christ's rule (Eph. 2:2; 6:11–13). He must return to liberate creation from its bondage to corruption (Rom. 8:18–23), to restore Israel (Rom. 11:25–27), and to subjugate all other powers and authorities in the universe, including death (1 Cor. 15:20–26). For Paul, the ages of history are moving to their culmination under the rule of Jesus Christ, who will bring all into subjection, and then he will give everything to the Father so that he may be all in all forevermore.[67]

---

64. Harold Hoehner, *Ephesians: An Exegetical Commentary* (Grand Rapids: Baker, 2002), 216, offers the following translation of 1:10: "in the administration of the fullness of times, to unite under one head all things in Christ, the things in heaven and the things on earth in him." "Christ" actually has an article with it in Ephesians 1:10, and it could be understood as a title, "the Messiah."

65. Compare the phrase "fullness of times" in Ephesians 1:10, apparently referring to the ages or epochs of history, with the similar phrase "fullness of time" in Galatians 4:4, referring to the time when God sent Jesus into this world.

66. See the discussion of this passage above.

67. See Hoehner, *Ephesians*, 216–225 for more detail on Ephesians 1:10. Interpreters argue about the length of Christ's rule when he returns. But I believe the most straightforward way to read Paul is to understand the rule of Christ to continue on this earth when he returns in what is called the millennium. Thus, he will redeem creation and rule over the restored creation with resurrected believers (Rom. 8:18–23); he will also restore Israel and rule over the nations of the earth, including Israel, in fulfillment of promises in the Old Testament; and he will subdue all authorities in the universe and continue to reign over them until he totally destroys death at the end of his reign, at which time he will turn the kingdom over to God the Father (see the earlier discussion on 1 Cor. 15:20–26).

The Doctrine of the Future in Hebrews and the General Epistles

David L. Allen

"What is going to happen in the end times here on earth and in heaven?" is a question that fascinates everyone. Fortunately, we are not left in the dark on the issue, since God has revealed many things about the future in the Bible. On many occasions in the four Gospels, Jesus spoke of the future. Paul talked about the future often in his thirteen letters. The last book of the Bible, Revelation, is a virtual Mount Everest of future prophecy and the consummation of all things.

But what of Hebrews and those letters in our New Testament called the General Epistles, namely James–Jude? Most Christians are less familiar with these letters tucked away in the back of the New Testament. Do they tell us anything about what is going to happen in the future? Indeed, they do. Eschatology plays a significant role in each of them.[1]

It is important to recognize that the concept of the end times for the biblical authors was not limited to the events that would occur at the end of history as we know it. Rather, the end times, or "latter days," actually were inaugurated with the life, death, and resurrection of Christ. Notice how the author of Hebrews puts it in Hebrews 1:1–2: "In many manners and many modes of old times God spoke to the fathers by the prophets, but in these last days He has spoken to us in His Son [Jesus]." John speaks, in 1 John, of his readers living

---

1. For helpful surveys of the eschatology of Hebrews and the general epistles, consult Donald Guthrie, *New Testament Theology* (Downers Grove, IL: InterVarsity, 1981), 810–12; 840–43; 863–66; 882–85. A more recent treatment that is also excellent is *Dictionary of the Later New Testament & Its Developments*, ed. Ralph Martin & David Peters (Downers Grove, IL: InterVarsity, 1997). Look under individual headings for Hebrews and the general epistles, then check subjects such as "heaven," "judgment," "second coming of Christ," etc.

in the "last hour." This does not preclude for these authors, however, a series of end-time events leading to the climax of history such as one finds in Revelation.

The general pattern of eschatology one finds in the Gospels, Acts, and the Pauline Epistles is continued in Hebrews and the General Epistles. In this chapter, I shall begin with Hebrews and work through James; 1 and 2 Peter; 1, 2, and 3 John; and Jude, summarizing the eschatological teaching of these letters.

Hebrews

The prologue to Hebrews, 1:1–4, immediately employs eschatological language. God has now spoken with finality through the life, death, resurrection, and ascension of Jesus, and this occurs "in these last days" (1:2). His incarnation commences the beginning of the end times. One of the main themes of Hebrews is how Christ is the fulfillment of Old Testament prophecy and the one who inaugurates the new covenant through his death on the cross, resurrection, ascension, and heavenly exaltation. These events have cosmic consequences for all creation.

Psalm 110:1 and the Future in Hebrews

Psalm 110:1 is the most frequently quoted verse in the entire New Testament. It is a key messianic and eschatological promise which began to be fulfilled at the resurrection, ascension, and exaltation of Jesus at the right hand of God in heaven; will be further consummated when Christ rules from David's throne on earth during the millennial reign (Rev. 20:1–6); and finally consummated with Christ's reign through all eternity as King of kings and Lord of lords.[2] It should come as no surprise, then, that the author of Hebrews builds his entire argument around Psalm 110:1: "The LORD says to my Lord, 'Sit at My right hand until I make Your enemies a footstool for Your feet'" (NASB). Psalm 110:1 is directly quoted only once in Hebrews (1:13), but the author alludes to it on five occasions (1:3; 8:1; 10:12–13; 12:2).

The author of Hebrews builds on his exposition of Psalm 110:1 in 2:1–18, most particularly in Hebrews 2:5–9. The author speaks of "the world to come" in 2:5. The "until" of Hebrews 1:13 anticipates the "not yet" of Hebrews 2:8— "We do not yet see everything subject unto him." Jesus, by virtue of the incarna-

---

2. See D. M. Hay, *Glory at the Right Hand: Psalm 110 in Early Christianity*, Society of Biblical Literature Monograph Series 18 (Nashville: Abingdon, 1973), for how Psalm 110:1 is used in Hebrews.

tion, is made for a short time "lower than the angels." But after his resurrection, he ascended back to heaven and seated himself at the right hand of God, as Psalm 110:1 states. That the Son sits at the right hand of God implies kingship, enthronement, authority, supremacy, and superior dignity. Yet God has "not yet" subjected all things under his feet.[3] That will occur in the end times with the second coming of Jesus.

Here we see an important concept introduced by Jesus himself in the Gospels with respect to the future and the end times. The biblical authors talk about how the kingdom of God has already broken into this present time (the "already"), and yet there is an aspect of it that awaits God's final consummation in the future (the "not yet").[4] This is an important concept of eschatology which can be seen throughout the New Testament.

Hebrews 2:10 speaks of Christ's goal to "bring many sons to glory," a statement of how God plans to complete the salvation of his people eschatologically through Christ. The solidarity of Christ with those who are believers in Christ assures them of final victory and strengthens them to remain faithful in this life despite hardship and persecutions.

The Concept of Present and Future "Rest" in Hebrews

The author of Hebrews not only approaches eschatology from the twin foci of "already/not yet," he also develops something of a two-dimensional eschatology. First, there is a horizontal, or temporal, dimension that speaks of final salvation as a future event in time and history. There is a sense in which salvation is in three tenses: past, present, and future. You have been saved (justification); you are being saved (sanctification); and you will be saved (glorification). Final salvation is the ultimate focus of the author of Hebrews.

Second, there is a spatial dimension in that the "heavenly temple" of Hebrews 9–10, however interpreted, is a reality. This spatial dimension is described by the author in Hebrews 4 as "rest" which Christians are said to enter. The nature of this rest is twofold. It is a present reality and yet a future goal—something which Christians possess now in this life (4:3), and yet is something that we are to "be diligent to enter" (4:1, 9).

---

3. See David L. Allen, *Hebrews*, New American Commentary, vol. 35 (Nashville: B&H, 2010), 201–212.
4. See the helpful summary of this notion in Hebrews in Buist Fanning, "A Theology of Hebrews," in *A Biblical Theology of the New Testament*, ed. Roy Zuck (Chicago: Moody, 1994), 403–05.

Hebrews 4:1–4:11 is in line with other New Testament authors who consistently take the perspective that the age to come has somehow already begun with the advent of Christ, and thus the two overlap. Sometimes this view of the two ages is presented in linear and historical terms (horizontally) and sometimes in more spatial terms such as heaven and earth (vertically). For the author of Hebrews, the last days began with the first coming of Jesus (1:1–2) and culminate in the second coming (9:23–28).

The author of Hebrews makes use of typology to explain to his readers this notion of "rest." The primary biblical background is the exodus generation on their way through the wilderness toward the promised land of Canaan. Because of their sin, most of the people of the exodus generation (those twenty years of age and older) failed to enter the promised land (Num. 14) as a result of God's judgment. God did not permit them to enter because of their unbelief and disobedience. The typological parallel is not only between the earthly land of Canaan as "rest" in the past and the heavenly "rest" in the future. Rather, the true typology is that between the two communities—his own and the exodus generation—both of which were confronted by the same word of God.

The key chapter in Hebrews addressing the concept of rest is Hebrews 4.[5] Verses 10–11 conclude: "So there remains a Sabbath rest for the people of God. For the one who has entered His rest has himself also rested from his works, as God did from His. Therefore let us be diligent to enter that rest, so that no one will fall, through following the same example of disobedience" (NASB). Looking at Hebrews 4:1–11 as a whole, there are five possible meanings of the concept of "rest": (1) God's creation rest (Gen. 2:2); (2) Israel's rest in Canaan (Joshua; Psalm 95); (3) the Christian's spiritual rest (victory through obedience); (4) millennial rest (Heb. 4:9); (5) heavenly rest.[6] It is clear that even within the context

---

5. Exactly what the author of Hebrews means by "rest" in Hebrews 4 is a matter of debate. The two significant works on the subject are Jon Laansma, *"I Will Give You Rest": The Rest Motif in the New Testament with Special Reference to Mt 11 and Heb 3–4* (Tübingen: Mohr Siebeck, 1997); and Judith Wray, *Rest as a Theological Metaphor in the Epistle to the Hebrews and the Gospel of Truth: Early Christian Homiletics of Rest*, SBLDS 166 (Atlanta: Scholars Press, 1998). See also Allen, *Hebrews*, 270–82; 290–97.

6. Hebrews 4:9 is in the future tense but since it is unlikely the reference is to heaven, it is possibly a reference to the millennium, when resurrected believers will reign with Christ and assist in the governance of the world. One possible interpretation is that the unfaithful Christian who suffers loss at the judgment seat of Christ, though clearly not loss of salvation, will not rule with Christ during the millennium: Mark 10:24–31; 2 Corinthians 5:10; 2 Timothy 2:11–13; Revelation 2:25–27. This ties in with the warning in Hebrews 6:4–6 and pressing on to maturity as Hebrews 6:1 enjoins. Christian fruitfulness or barrenness will be revealed at the judgment seat (Hebrews 6:7–8; John 15:6; 1 Corinthians 3:9–15; 2 Corinthians 5:10–11).

of these eleven verses, several of the above meanings can be discerned. No doubt (1) and (2) are used. It is likely that (3) is also used. Some premillennialists would see a reference to (4) in light of Hebrews 2:5, while many interpreters would view the concept of "rest" in a primarily futuristic way as in (5). Clearly options (1) and (2) apply neither to the readers of the epistle nor to Christians today. The difficulty is discerning which of the final three options are in focus by the author. Given what he says in these eleven verses, it is difficult to choose between a strictly present or a strictly future meaning. Choosing one over the other leaves something unexplained in the verses. The best approach is to see these verses as referring to both.[7] Such a dualism is not unknown in the New Testament. It is reflective of the "already/not yet" tension that pervades the sayings of Jesus in the Gospels as well as what one finds in Paul's epistles.

It is difficult to limit the "rest" to a location or specific point in time. Genesis 2:2, as used by the author, indicates that God's rest is open-ended. The "rest" must be seen as a present reality and not only as a reality at death or in the eschaton. How could the readers seem to have fallen short of the rest now if it lies entirely in the future? In that case, all Christians would be "short" of it. Thus, it seems best to understand the "rest" to have a threefold dimension: the present time, a state entered at death, and that which is experienced by the believer at the eschaton. The already/not yet eschatology of the author makes this interpretation likely.

The Concept of Future Inheritance in Hebrews

In conjunction with this rest, Hebrews often speaks of our "inheritance" which will be consummated in the future, final salvation (Heb. 6:11–12, 17–18, 9:15, 10:23, 11:39).

Christians will receive the inheritance of all God's promises in the future consummation of all things (Heb. 11:9–16; 13:14). This inheritance is eternal since at the time of the Christians' reception of it, God's presence is fully realized and enjoyed by his people in heaven (Heb. 12:14).

In Hebrews 6:13–20, the author speaks of those of us who, like Abraham, through faith and endurance "inherit the promises." In Hebrews 1:2, Jesus is said to be the "heir of all things." Through Christ, Christians receive promises from God which we inherit and which will be completely fulfilled in the end times. Those who inherit these promises are said to have a "hope" which is "an

---

7. See Allen, *Hebrews*, 292–95.

anchor for the soul" (6:19). Jesus is the eschatological hope of final salvation for all believers. When the Bible speaks of our hope in Christ, one should not understand any of the uncertainty connoted by the English word "hope." In Scripture, the word "hope," when applied to what we as believers possess through our relationship in Christ, is a settled certainty and confident expectation based on the promises of God.[8] We have a hope because we know God, who cannot lie, will fulfill all the promises he has made to us in Christ Jesus. We are joint-heirs with Christ.

This reception of a future inheritance is spoken of many places in Hebrews (cf. 9:15; 10:36; 11:14, 16; 13:14). According to 10:36–39, Christians are to endure suffering because, though they have not yet received all the fulfillment of God's promise, they will indeed receive it in the future. The quotation of Habakkuk 2:3–4 in Hebrews 10:37–38 is introduced in a catchy way in Greek; literally "yet a little how much, how much!"[9] The phrase serves to encourage us that our wait for the return of Jesus will not be unrewarded: He will return. Until then, endurance by faith is the order of the day. This exhortation for the righteous one to live by faith is given in the context of the imminence of the second coming of Jesus and hearkens back to 9:28, where Christ is said to appear a second time to those who are eagerly awaiting his return.

In Hebrews 11, the author lists a number of great men and women in biblical history, all of whom bear testimony to God's faithfulness by means of their faith. The author concludes Hebrews 11:39–40 with these words: "And all these, having gained approval through their faith, did not receive what was promised, because God had provided something better for us, so that apart from us they would not be made perfect" (NASB). This is a statement about what God intends to do in the future when Christ comes and all believers are united together in heaven with Christ. We have not yet reached perfection, but the day is coming when God will see to it that we do.

Hebrews 11:40 speaks of "something better" which "God had provided" for Christians. Although the identification of "something better" is not explicitly stated in the text, contextually it clearly involves the salvation brought to all believers in Christ in the future. Throughout Hebrews, "perfection" is used in the sense of completion and fulfillment. Thus, for the author of Hebrews, Jesus has ushered in the "end" of biblical history in the sense of completion. "Perfec-

8. Ibid., 401.
9. Ibid., 532.

tion" here has an eschatological focus, and refers to entrance into the promised eternal inheritance.[10]

The reason the readers of Hebrews could endure persecution was because they kept an eschatological eye toward God's future promises; they knew they had "better and lasting possessions." Their heavenly "possessions" are described as being "better" and "lasting." Their eschatological reward is "better"—a favorite word of the author in this epistle where heavenly realities are far superior to earthly ones.

The Atonement and the Future in Hebrews

The author of Hebrews views Christ's atonement as an event which takes place "at the consummation of the ages" (9:26; 10:10, 12, 14). The author of Hebrews quotes Jeremiah 31:31–33 concerning God's inauguration of a "new covenant." Jeremiah and Hebrews both link this event to the end times. Jesus's atonement on the cross was not only accomplished in the past, but also has something to do with the future (Hebrews 9:8, 23).

Christ came the first time to make an atonement for sin at the cross. But according to Hebrews 9:28, he is coming back to earth a second time and we are to watch for Christ's second coming: "And unto them that look for him shall he appear a second time without sin unto salvation" (KJV). Hebrews 10:25 informs Christians that we should be all the more diligent to draw near, hold fast, and stir one another up to good deeds at the present time, because "the day is approaching." This reference to the "day" speaks of Christ's second coming, and may be a direct reference to the Old Testament concept of the "day of the Lord," which is always in context a day of judgment. Hebrews 10:37 states: "For yet a very little while, He who is coming will come, and will not delay" (NASB). Hebrews 10:31, too, speaks of future judgment when Christ returns (see also 6:2 and 12:23).

The Future Heavenly Zion and New Jerusalem in Hebrews

According to Hebrews 12:22–24, Christians are under the new covenant, not the old Mosaic covenant given at Sinai. The author says we have come to Mount Zion. Such language indicates that Christians have entered a permanent, eternal relationship with God through Jesus Christ and the salvation he has provided. The references "Mount Zion," "city of the living God," and "heavenly Jerusalem" are all in apposition to one another and refer to the

---

10. Ibid., 567.

same place. What exactly is meant by these references? In Judaism, "Zion" referred to the hill in Jerusalem where the temple stood. The name covers not only the temple hill, but all of Jerusalem as well. It was the place where Israel gathered for worship and where one hoped to see God manifested in his glory. Significant for Hebrews, Psalm 110:1–4 speaks of Zion as the place where the Messiah—the one seated at God's right hand—would rule.

The Old Testament prophets sometimes speak of a restoration of the Davidic kingdom in a religious/political sense under the shorthand of "Zion."[11] For example, Amos 9:11 predicts that Yahweh will "raise up the fallen booth of David," which is a reference to the "booth" or "tent" pitched at Zion. Isaiah 16:1–5 exhorts the people of Israel to bring sacrifices "to the mount of daughter Zion" (NASB), followed by a promise that "a judge will sit on it in faithfulness in the tent of David" (NASB). Later, in Isaiah 66:8, Zion gives birth to sons who are taken not only from Israel, but from all the nations (66:20–21). References to Zion in the prophets hearken back specifically to David's reign as the "golden age" that will one day be re-established. Old Testament promises of a restored Zion are promises inaugurated in the new covenant by the Son of David, Jesus.[12]

The "city of God" is a major theme developed under a variety of metaphors. By extension, the author is using these references in a spiritual sense to refer to a heavenly state and to the spiritual place of God's presence and his people's home. This word in Greek translated "joyful assembly" was used in the Greco-Roman world for civic festivals and athletic competitions. The term was also used in the Septuagint to speak of Israel's festivals.[13]

The "assembly" or "congregation" refers to all believers who are either on earth or who are on earth and in heaven in the future. The assembly is made up of the "firstborn," referring to the readers as well as all believers, living or dead. This reference hearkens back to Hebrews 2:12 where the author quoted Psalm 22:22, "I will tell of Your name to my brethren, in the midst of the assembly I will praises You." The readers have also come to "God, the judge of all men." They have also come to the "spirits of righteous people made perfect" (Heb. 12:23) The use of this surprising phrase probably indicates the spirit apart

---

11. An excellent historical overview of Zion symbolism in the Old Testament and Second Temple Judaism is Kiwoong Son, *Zion Symbolism in Hebrews: Hebrews 12:18–24 as a Hermeneutical Key to the Epistle* (Milton Keynes, UK: Paternoster, 2005), 29–74. Also very helpful is I. P. Leithart, "Where Was Ancient Zion?" *Tyndale Bulletin* 53.2 (2002): 161–175. See also Allen, *Hebrews*, 590–91.
12. Leithart, "Where Was Ancient Zion?" 174–75.
13. Allen, *Hebrews*, 592.

from the body awaiting the final resurrection. That these "righteous people" have been "made perfect" means they have died and reached the state of having been perfected by Christ's atonement. Note that the use of the perfect tense implies permanence. The reference is to both Old Testament and New Testament saints. These saints have had their names "written" in heaven, which carries the sense of "enrolled" or "registered."[14] Hebrews 13:14 says: "here we do not have a lasting city, but we are seeking the city which is to come" (NASB).

The Future "Shaking" of All Creation in Hebrews 12:25–29

The author warns his readers not to refuse God who is speaking, informing us that God has promised, "Yet once more I will shake not only the earth, but also the heaven" (NASB). This expression, "Yet once more," denotes the removing of those things which can be shaken, as of created things, so that those things which cannot be shaken may remain. Such terminology once again is future in orientation and speaks of the eschatological judgment which God will bring on the earth when Christ returns.

The author quotes Haggai 2:6, slightly altering it by inserting "not only" and "but also." By this reference, the author intends to intimate a future time of eschatological judgment, as is indicated by verse 27, where the author interprets the meaning of the quotation as indicating the removing of what can be shaken. The phrase "things that can be shaken" are said to be "created things" and refers to the material universe. The purpose of this "removing" is stated in the following clause "so that those things which cannot be shaken may remain." God's kingdom is immutable and possesses eternal stability. Following this final eschatological judgment expressed by the "shaking," God will accomplish salvation's final eschatological consummation with the new heaven and earth.[15]

The author makes use of the term "kingdom" in verse 28, which refers to the kingdom of God. This indicates that verses 22–24 are descriptive of the kingdom of God, a kingdom which believers are a part of presently. The author's language in verses 22–28 illustrates the "already/not yet" tension that exists in the New Testament and Hebrews with respect to kingdom eschatology. There is a sense in which the kingdom is now, and Christians are a part of it. Yet future dimensions remain to be unfolded, such as final eschatological judgment, pictured here by the reference to Haggai 2:6 and the shaking of all things. A key point

14. Ibid.
15. Ibid., 596.

in this section is the author's use of the perfect tense, indicating that his readers "have come" to this kingdom and are by implication experiencing it now (v. 22).

Thus, "Zion" was the center of God's redemptive activity in the past; it is the center of God's present redemptive activity and reign of Christ in heaven; and it will be the center of eschatological judgment and restoration in the future as well.

Summary

We have seen that Hebrews contains many passages that speak directly to the future. Some speak of future judgment, others of future inheritance and rewards. Christians are exhorted to persevere in this life amidst trials and tribulations. We are to "press on to maturity" (Heb. 6:1) and "run with endurance the race that is set before us, fixing our eyes on Jesus" (Heb. 12:1–2, NASB). He will bring us home to heaven. The author of Hebrews teaches us that suffering in this life must be viewed from an eschatological perspective, which not only informs how Christians view suffering, but also is that which gives them strength to endure it. This is the focus of Hebrews 12:2–3 in speaking about Jesus's suffering and how we are to look to him in our own suffering. The future reward serves as a present incentive to endure and remain faithful whatever the cost. Only in the eschaton will suffering itself be overcome by Christ's victory. The fulfillment of God's promises to his people is independent of whatever external circumstances they may experience. Suffering and adversity cannot and will not hinder God from making good on all his promises. Discipline will last only a short time, and then God's people will receive what he has promised (10:35–36).

JAMES

There is less material directly related to the future in James than in Hebrews.[16] The key focus in James is on the imminence of the coming of the Lord and the judgment that comes for those who don't know Him.[17]

In James 2:5, within the context of the problem of showing favoritism in the church to those who are wealthy, James states: "Did not God chose the poor

---

16. Peter Davids, *Commentary on James*, New International Greek Text Commentary (Grand Rapids: Eerdmans, 1982), 39: "Eschatology is not the burden of the book; it is the context of the book."

17. For a brief summary of James's eschatology, consult Andrew Chester and Ralph Martin, *The Theology of the Letters of James, Peter, and Jude*, New Testament Theology (Cambridge: CUP, 1994), 16–20; and Davids, *James*, 38–39.

of this world to be rich in faith and heirs of the kingdom which He promised to those who love him?" (NASB). Here is the first reference to the "kingdom" in James. We know from the rest of Scripture that the concept of the kingdom of God has present and future connotations, commensurate with the "already/not yet" eschatology of the entire New Testament.

Other than this passage, all of the direct references to the future in James occur in chapter 5. In James 5:1–3, again addressing the rich, James states: "Come now, you rich, weep and howl for your miseries that are coming upon you! . . . It is in the last days that you have stored up your treasure!" (NASB). James declares that self-ish use of temporal goods will bring judgment. The wealthy who forget God think they are "treasured up" for old age, when in reality they have treasured up for eternal damnation. Their wealth will become, as it were, fire that will burn them in the end. The "last days" have already begun, but the unwary wealthy man is unaware of the danger he is in. His future judgment will come sooner than he expects.

The most significant passage pertaining to the future occurs in 5:7–9: "Therefore be patient, brethren, until the coming of the Lord. . . . strengthen your hearts, for the coming of the Lord is near. . . . behold, the Judge is stand-ing right at the door" (NASB). Here James states three propositions concerning the future: (1) the Lord is coming, and Christians should wait patiently for his return; (2) the second coming of Jesus is imminent; and (3) when Jesus comes, he will function as a judge of believers as well as unbelievers, though the context of James 5:9 is on Christ's judgment of believers. James states that Christians should not grumble against one another, lest you be judged.

Belief and behavior must match, according to James. The picture of an im-minent return of Christ as the eschatological judge who is "standing at the door" is certainly a sobering image. The faithful will be rewarded and the unfaithful will be judged in the future when the Lord returns. Though no details of the second com-ing of Christ are given by James, the event is no less certain, and Christians should pay close heed to how they live, in light of the imminent second coming of Christ.

1 & 2 Peter

These letters by the Apostle Peter speak frequently of future events, and in some distinctive ways.[18] In 1 Peter 1:3, Christians have been born again "unto a living

---

18. For a brief summary of eschatology in 1 Peter consult Karen Jobes, *1 Peter,* Baker Exegetical Commentary on the New Testament (Grand Rapids: Baker, 2005), 49–51. For a summary of

hope." This hope is further linked to the resurrection of Christ which is itself linked to the end times in 1 Peter 1:20–21 where speaking of Jesus, Peter writes: "chosen before the foundation of the world but was revealed at the end of the times for you." Note the reference to "end of the times," signifying again that with the advent of Christ, the "end times" actually began. Like Hebrews, Peter speaks of "an inheritance incorruptible, and undefiled, and unfading, reserved in heaven for you" (1:4). Christians have an inheritance reserved in heaven for a future time of reception and this inheritance is described by Peter as sin-proof, time-proof, and death-proof. Believers are guarded by the power of God, through faith, "unto a salvation ready to be revealed in the last time" (1:5). Here Peter speaks of salvation in the future tense. It is a present possession, but it is a full and final salvation to be received in heaven in the future. In 1:7, 13, Peter speaks of the second coming of Christ as "the revelation of Jesus Christ." "Revelation" is one of the key Greek words used in reference to the second coming of Jesus.

Peter clearly weds together the present reality of Christians amidst persecution and suffering with their guaranteed future hope. For Peter, "Christian ethics must be grounded on a rightly conceived eschatology."[19] Faith must be tested, and its genuineness will be revealed in the future in which Christ comes again. Like Hebrews and James, Peter affirms the "already/not yet" aspect of eschatology.

Peter summons Christians to godly living that is partially motivated by the imminence of end-time judgment (1 Peter 4:1–11). In 4:5–7, Peter speaks of those "who shall give account to him who is ready to judge the living and the dead . . . but the end of all things is at hand." The living and the dead, believers and unbelievers, must one day give an account to Christ who will be the impartial judge. When this judgment will take place is left unspecified, but contextually it must be at some point after the second coming of Christ. In 4:13, Peter speaks of Christ's glory being revealed, which is also a reference to the future event of the second coming of Christ. In 4:17–18 we learn that there is a day coming "when God will judge all according to their works."[20] This day is still in the future, and presumably will occur at some point after the second coming of Christ.

In 1 Peter 5:1, reference is made to "glory about to be revealed," and in verse 4 those who shepherd the church of God in a way pleasing to the Father will receive "an unfading crown of glory." These phrases indicate a future time of

---

eschatology in 2 Peter, consult Chester and Martin, *The Theology of the Letters of James, Peter, and Jude*, 155–58.

19. Jobes, *1 Peter*, 49.

20. Jobes has an excellent, concise discussion of this passage in her *1 Peter*, 290–295.

fulfillment. Those who are "in Christ" have been called into "eternal glory" according to 5:10. This status and standing for believers is true in the present time but will receive final consummation at the second coming of Christ.

Turning to 2 Peter, we find many references to future events. We are told in 1:11 that the messianic kingdom, inaugurated by Christ at his first coming, will be established. This kingdom is "eternal," and God promises that believers will have (future tense) their entrance into this kingdom supplied to them by God.

Second Peter 2:3 and 3:7 speak of the final judgment which is to come in the future. In 2 Peter 3:3-4, we are told that "in the last days" false teachers will query "where is the promise of his coming?" Peter continues to teach that "the present heavens and earth are being reserved for fire, kept for the day of judgment and destruction of ungodly men" (3:7). This "day of judgment" is best understood as a future, literal judgment, though some interpret it figuratively.[21] What is important to note is how Peter attributes the delay of the return of Christ to the earth as a demonstration of God's mercy that people not perish, but that all come to repentance. In light of this coming judgment, believers in Christ should live holy lives and be found faithful when the day of judgment comes.

Second Peter 3:10 states that "the day of the Lord will come as a thief in the night, in which the heavens will pass away with a great noise, and the elements will melt with fervent heat: both the earth and the works that are in it will be burned up"[22] (NKJV). Here is a dramatic picture of future judgment that affects "the heavens and the earth" (NKJV). On the basis of this coming judgment, Peter exhorts his readers to holy living in 3:11. In 3:12, he states that Christians should be "looking for and hastening the coming of the day of God" (NKJV). In 3:13, Christians are informed that they should also look for a future "new heavens and a new earth in which righteousness dwells" (NKJV). This would appear to be a statement about an earthly kingdom and may reference the millennial reign of Christ. Second Peter 3:13 is based on prophecies in Isaiah 65:17 and 66:22-24. The latter is especially interesting because it speaks of "all flesh shall go forth and look upon the corpses of men who have transgressed against Me" (NKJV). Isaiah seems to be describing events on the "new earth."

21. Joseph Mayor, *The Epistles of Jude and II Peter: Greek Text with Introduction, Notes, and Comments* (Grand Rapids: Baker, 1979), 154.
22. For an overview of the concept of "The Day of the Lord" in Scripture, consult Richard Mayhue, "The Bible's Watchword: Day of the Lord," *The Master's Seminary Journal* 22.1 (Spring 2011), 65–88. See also Craig Blaising and Darrell Bock, *Progressive Dispensationalism* (Grand Rapids: Baker Academic, 2000), 262–64.

In both 1 and 2 Peter, one finds a link between holy living and the second coming of Christ, along with future judgment. Ethics and eschatology are integrally linked.

1–3 John

Though there is less about eschatology in John's letters than the Petrine epistles, the concept of the future is clearly intimated in several ways. John makes repeated reference to the antichrist beginning in 1 John 2:18. He considers false teachers to be "little antichrists," whose presence in the church is a sign of the end times. The antichrist is a satanic world dictator who will arise on the scene during the days of tribulation outlined in Revelation 4–19. This individual will appear in the days of the return of Christ. The presence of the "many antichrists" in John's day indicates that it is the "last hour."[23]

In 1 John 2:28, Christians are commanded to abide in Christ, "that when He appears, we may have confidence and not be ashamed before Him at his coming" (NKJV). Here is a direct reference to the imminent second coming of Christ.

The most important eschatological passage in the letter is 1 John 3:1–3: "See how great a love the Father has bestowed on us, that we would be called children of God; and such we are. For this reason the world does not know us, because it did not know Him. Beloved, now we are children of God, and it has not appeared as yet what we will be. We know that when He appears, we will be like Him, because we will see Him just as He is. And everyone who has this hope fixed on Him purifies himself, just as He is pure" (NASB). Our future inheritance awaits the return of Christ, but there is a real sense in which we share in that inheritance now: We are children of God.

Here, once again, is the "already/not yet" tension in New Testament eschatology.[24] John affirms that Christians are "now" the children of God. He also states that it has "not yet" appeared what we shall be in the future. The present is the prophet of the future. Now we are limited to speak in the language of earth; on that day in the future, we will learn the vocabulary of heaven. With respect to our future state, John affirms both our ignorance and our knowledge. He affirms our ignorance, inasmuch as "it does not yet appear what we shall be"; he affirms

---

23. See G. K. Beale, "The Old Testament background of the 'last hour' in 1 John 2,18," *Biblica* 92 (2) 2011, 231–254, for a helpful discussion on this important concept in 1 John.
24. See the discussion in Judith Lieu, *The Theology of the Johannine Epistles*, in New Testament Theology (Cambridge: Cambridge University Press, 1991), 73, 88–89.

our knowledge, since we have the ground of assurance that "when He appears, we will be like Him." What does this mean? The word in Greek for "like" here connotes the notion of similarity in characteristics. At least three things will be true of Christians at this future point. First, we will possess a resurrected body (Phil. 3:21). Second, we will possess a purified character. There will be no sin in heaven. Third, we will possess a satisfied heart. As the psalmist said in Psalm 17:15: "As for me, I shall behold Your face in righteousness; I will be satisfied with Your likeness when I awake" (NASB).

John concludes in verse 3 by stating "everyone who has this hope in Him purifies himself, just as He [Christ] is pure." Like Hebrews, James, and 1 and 2 Peter, John connects ethical living to eschatology. The future guides the present.

John's final statement in his letter about the future is found in 1 John 4:17 and concerns how our love, when it is perfected, prepares us to "have boldness in the day of judgment" (NKJV).

JUDE

The one-chapter letter of Jude is probably the least known of the general epistles. For some, it seems to occupy a dark corner of the New Testament. Jude speaks of fallen angels, apostates, and future judgment.

Jude refers to fallen angels in verse 6, whom God "has reserved in everlasting chains under darkness for the judgment of the great day" (NKJV). Jude speaks in verse 7 of "Sodom and Gomorrah, and the cities around them in a similar manner as these . . . are set forth as an example, suffering the vengeance of eternal fire" (NKJV). These are stark images of eternal judgment. In Jude 14–15, he speaks of the second coming of Christ: "Behold, the Lord comes with ten thousands of His saints, to execute judgment on all, to convict all who are ungodly among them of all their ungodly deeds" (NKJV). In Jude 18 we learn there will be "mockers in the last times" (NKJV),. identifying again that with the first coming of Christ, the "last days" are said to have been inaugurated.[25] In Jude 21, Christians are to be "looking for the mercy of our Lord Jesus Christ unto eternal life" (NKJV). This is a statement referring to the second coming of Christ and the fact

---

25. Jude quotes the non-canonical book 1 Enoch here as the source of the prophecy about the second coming of Christ. One of the best accessible discussions of the issues this raises is found in Thomas Schreiner, *1, 2 Peter, Jude*, New American Commentary (Nashville: B&H, 2003), 468–473. Schreiner concluded that Jude "probably cited a part of *1 Enoch* that he considered to be a genuine prophecy" (469).

that when he comes, he will bring mercy and eternal life to those who are his. Jude concludes in verse 24 with a statement that God's people will one day stand in the immediate presence of God and his glory throughout eternity.

CONCLUSION

Hebrews and the general epistles share a similar concept of the future. The following common elements may be observed: an "already/not yet" dualism; the second coming of Christ; judgment on unbelievers and fallen angels; a future "inheritance" and "rest" for believers; a millennial reign of Christ, destruction of the heavens and the earth; new heavens and a new earth; and Christ's eternal reign with his saints. The biblical authors use these future events to exhort and encourage Christians to be faithful and holy as they live in the present.

Part 3:

THE DOCTRINE OF THE FUTURE IN THE HISTORY OF CHRISTIAN THOUGHT

The Doctrine of the Future in the Apostolic Fathers, Justin Martyr, and Irenaeus of Lyons

Stephen O. Presley

The Christian community of the post-apostolic age continued the fervent evangelistic and apologetic efforts initiated by the apostles. As they proclaimed the gospel, they, like the apostles, also waited expectantly for the Lord to return and establish the kingdom of God. This expectation of the Christian hope was not worked out in any systematic fashion, at least not the way it would be in the later tradition, but forged through the fires of persecution or defended before Roman officials. From this perspective, the Christian thinkers of the early church sustained a vibrant spiritual life rooted in a devotion to the Christian hope that is far from "unreflective."[1] The following chapter will summarize the essential elements of the doctrine of the future in the second century, including the second coming, resurrection of the dead, the final judgment, the millennial kingdom, and the formation of the new heavens and the new earth. For these early Christians, these events formed the fitting conclusion to the work of Christ expressed in other aspects of their theological frameworks.

In general, the historical context of the second century presented certain challenges for the early church that influenced its eschatology in different ways. These challenges included various incidents of persecution, the continued delay of the Lord's return, and heretical views, including a realized eschatology that, among other things, rejected the hope of a bodily resurrection. These issues were already present in embryonic forms in the writings of the New Testament, but

---

1. J. N. D. Kelly, *Early Christian Doctrines* (New York: HarperCollins, 1978), 462.

they continued to develop in the second century.[2] First of all, by the turn of the second century the church had already experienced a number of periods of severe persecution including the persecutions under Nero, Domitian, and Trajan. Likewise, the community of Lyons where Irenaeus ministered also experienced persecution during the reign of Marcus Aurelius.[3] The account of the martyrs of Lyons and Vienne, preserved in a letter possibly written by Irenaeus, paints a stirring portrait of the faith and hope of the early Christians facing persecution and death.[4] These episodes compelled Christians to give attention to their doctrine of the future and the cosmic struggle against sin, death, and the devil. Thus, the connection between martyrdom, persecution, and eschatology is well attested in the early church.

Second, the early Christian community was also slowly coming to terms with the delay of the Parousia. Like the writers of the New Testament, early Christians expected the Lord to return at any moment. The longer the Lord tarried, the more consideration they had to give to the issues of managing the church.[5] In this sense, the second century is characterized by a tension between the prevailing expectation of the Lord's return, and the emerging demands of the Christian community. These Christians were not overly concerned by the Lord's delay, but the pressing matters of the community demanded their attention.

---

2. For example, the Christian community in Thessalonica questioned Paul about the eschatological hope in the face of persecution, while the letters to Timothy described some incipient forms of early gnostic beliefs filtering into the church. See 1 Thess. 4:13–5:11, 2 Thess. 2:1–12, 1 Tim. 1:4, and 1 Tim. 6:20. Similarly, the letters of John and Paul ardently defended the bodily resurrection and rejected those who denied it. See 1 John 1:1–3, 1 John 4:1–3, 2 John 1:7, Col. 2:8–12, and 1 Cor. 15:12–18. The nature and label of Gnosticism is highly debated, especially within the Pauline corpus, but Irenaeus begins his refutation of gnosis with an allusion to 1 Timothy 1:4 and also traces Gnosticism back to the teachings of Simon Magnus in Acts 8. *Haer.* 1.23.2. Unless otherwise noted, all translations of Irenaeus's *Against Heresies* are adapted from *Ante-Nicene Fathers Volume 1: The Apostolic Fathers, Justin Martyr, Irenaeus*, trans. Alexander Roberts and James Donaldson (Peabody, MA: Hendrickson, 2004).
3. There is a long tradition that links martyrdom, persecution, and eschatology. For example, the book of Revelation was comforting for those who were martyred in Irenaeus's community of Lyon and Vienne in the late second century. See D. Jeffrey Bingham, "The Apocalypse, Christ, and the Martyrs of Gaul," in *The Shadow of the Incarnation: Essays on Jesus Christ in the Early Church in Honor of Brian E. Daley, S.J.*, ed. Peter W. Martens (Notre Dame, IN: University of Notre Dame Press, 2008), 11–28.
4. Eusebius preserved the account of the martyrs who died in the severe persecution in 177 titled, "The Letter of the Churches of Vienne and Lyons to the Churches of Asia and Phrygia," *Hist. Eccl.* 5.1.1–2.8. Translations of Eusebius are taken from *Eusebius' Ecclesiastical History*, trans. C. F. Cruse. (Peabody, MA: Hendrickson, 1998).
5. Leslie W. Barnard, "Justin Martyr's Eschatology," *Vigiliae Christianae* 19, (1965): 86–98, 89.

Third, the early Christian community struggled against various heretical and sectarian communities that affirmed a realized eschatology. These groups were often docetic or gnostic in their theological orientation and assumed creation was the product of a lesser, incompetent god. This framework was informed by Greek philosophy and often more concerned with protology than eschatology.[6] They rejected any association with the material world and viewed salvation as an escape from the trappings of the physical body. In contrast, the polemical theology of the early church continually affirmed the importance of a futurist eschatology, including the hope of bodily resurrection and the new creation. Therefore, within this setting of persecutions, developing forms of church governance, and emerging heresies, the theologians of the second century set forth their doctrine of the future.

DOCTRINE OF THE FUTURE IN THE APOSTOLIC FATHERS

The first group of Christian thinkers to follow the apostles was an eclectic group of writers and thinkers known as the apostolic fathers.[7] These theologians reportedly had immediate connections back to the teachings of the apostles. Polycarp, for example, was a disciple of the apostle John, while Clement of Rome served as bishop in Rome after the apostle Peter. The dates of their works span the first half of the second century, and most are either letters or sermons. Some texts, such as *1 Clement* or the *Didache*, are concerned with pressing issues of church polity and governance and, as a result, contain only minimal references to eschatology. Other texts, such as *2 Clement* and the writings of the Shepherd of Hermas, contain concentrated discussions of eschatology.[8] Therefore, drawing together these references, it is possible to develop an integrative look at the basic contours of eschatology in these early Christian documents including the timing and nature of the second coming, the resurrection from the dead, the final judgment, a temporary earthly reign of Christ, and the inauguration of the new creation.

---

6. Hennie Stander, "The Eschatology of the Theologians of the Second Century," in *Eschatology of the New Testament and some related documents*, ed. Jan G. van der Watt (Tübingen: Mohr Siebeck, 2011), 583–84.

7. This collection includes the following texts: the letters of Ignatius, *1–2 Clement*, *Martyrdom of Polycarp*, the *Didache*, *Letter of Diognetus*, the writings of the Shepherd of Hermas, and *Epistle of Barnabas*.

8. For a survey of the eschatological message of each writer individually, see Brian Daley, *The Hope of the Early Church: A Handbook of Patristic Eschatology* (Baker: Grand Rapids, 2002), 9–19.

First, the Christians of the early church anticipated the Lord's return at any moment. They viewed themselves as strangers and aliens in the present world and sought to persuade others of the importance of repentance and maintaining moral and doctrinal purity until the coming of the Lord.[9] For example, *2 Clement*, an early Christian sermon, stresses the immediacy of the Lord's return and implores readers to come to repent and continue in purity while they are still in this world, since there is no opportunity to repent after death.[10] The author even suggests waiting "from hour to hour" for the future kingdom.[11] Ignatius also emphasizes the imminence of the Lord's return, saying plainly, "[t]hese are the last times."[12] The *Epistle of Barnabas* adds, "The day is near when everything will perish together with the evil one, 'The Lord, and his reward, is near.'"[13] Like the others, *Barnabas* also implores the reader to give attention to their lives and to live soberly and modestly as they await the coming of the Lord.

At the same time there was a growing realization among the apostolic fathers that the Lord's return might be delayed longer than expected. They acknowledged that the timing of the Lord's return remained uncertain and there was no speculation about specific dates or predictions. *First Clement* compares the Lord's return to the growth of a tree and remarks that it takes time for the tree to mature.[14] The Shepherd of Hermas also compares the advancement of the church to the construction of a building and indicates that the Lord will eventually return to inspect the building when it is finally complete.[15] Even *2 Clement* acknowledges that though they wait daily, the faithful do not know the day of the Lord's appearing.[16]

As the community waits expectantly for the coming of the Lord, they also draw on the Lord's predictions of a time of tribulation in the Olivet Discourse to encourage the faithful to be watchful of the deceiver who will come and lead many astray. The *Didache* warns that lawlessness will increase before "the deceiver of the world will appear as a son of God and 'will perform signs and wonders,' and the earth will be delivered into his hands."[17] Similarly, the *Epistle*

---

9. *Diogn.* 5.1–17 and *2 Clem.* 8.1–6. Unless otherwise noted, all translations of the Apostolic Fathers are taken from *The Apostolic Fathers: Greek Texts and English Translations*, ed. Michael W. Holmes (Grand Rapids: Baker, 1999).
10. *2 Clem.* 8.1–2.
11. *2 Clem.* 12.1.
12. Ign. *Eph.* 11.1.
13. *Barn.* 21.3.
14. *1 Clem.* 23.4–5.
15. Herm. *Sim,* 9.5.1.
16. *2 Clem.* 12.1–2.
17. *Did.* 16.4–5.

of Barnabas cautions to keep from sin, otherwise the "evil ruler" will gain power and restrict some from entering into the kingdom of God.[18] They do not describe the reign of the antichrist in any great detail, but the allusions indicate a future time of tribulation where many will be deceived.

Whenever the Lord returns he will come in glory and power to resurrect his people from the dead. This resurrection includes both the righteous, who are raised to eternal blessing, and the wicked, who are raised to eternal punishment. They regularly point to Christ's resurrection as the paradigm for the future resurrection and reject any view, such as Docetism, that denies the bodily resurrection.[19] *First Clement* states, "Let us consider, dear friends, how the Master points out to us the coming resurrection of which he made the Lord Jesus Christ the first fruits when he raised him from the dead."[20] These apostolic fathers are also emphatic that the resurrection includes restoration of the same flesh. *Second Clement* says, "Let none of you say that this flesh is not judged and does not rise again."[21] For Ignatius, who was facing the prospect of martyrdom as he penned his letters, resurrection was a central aspect of his hope.[22] *First Clement* even uses several images and metaphors from nature as proofs or signs of the coming resurrection, including night transforming into day, dry seeds transforming into living plants, and the imagery of the phoenix rising from the ashes.[23] The images from nature are regular reminders of the future hope of the resurrection.

Alongside descriptions of resurrection they consistently warn of the impending judgment of sin, death and the devil.[24] The apostolic saying that God will come again to "judge the living and the dead" is common in the second century.[25] The *Epistle of Barnabas* describes this separation of the righteous and wicked, saying, "The Lord will judge the world without partiality. Each person will receive according to what he has done: if he is good, his righteousness will precede him; if he is evil, the wages of doing evil will go before him."[26] Even Polycarp, when he was threatened with death, responded passionately to his executors, "You do not

---

18. *Barn.* 4.13.
19. *1 Clem.* 24.1, Ign. *Smyrn.* 3.1–3, Ign. *Trall.* 9.1–2, and *Barn.* 5.6–7. These references often point to the resurrection appearances of Christ such as Luke 24:33–42.
20. *1 Clem.* 24.1.
21. *2 Clem.* 9.1.
22. Daley, *Hope of the Early Church*, 13. See also Ign. *Eph.* 11.1-2 and Ign. *Rom.* 4.2–3.
23. *1 Clem.* 34.3–5 and *1 Clem.* 35.1–4.
24. *Diogn.* 7.5, *2 Clem.* 17.4–7, and *1 Clem.* 35.2–3.
25. Pol. *Phil* 2.1, *2 Clem.* 1.1, and *Barn.* 7.2. See also Acts 10:42, Rom. 14:9–12, 2 Tim. 4:1, and 1 Peter 4:5.
26. *Barn.* 4.12. See also *Barn.* 21.1.

know the first of the coming judgment and everlasting punishment that is laid up for the impious."[27] The apocalyptic text of Shepherd of Hermas uses a parable of the trees in season to contrast the present condition and the coming judgment.[28] The present world is like the winter for the righteous, when all the trees are leafless and indistinguishable, but the summer is coming when only the trees that are budding will be revealed. The sinners, whose trees do not produce leaves, will be "burned because they sinned and did not repent."[29] This contrast between the righteous and the wicked is a theme that pervades many of these passages relating to the judgment, so there is a consistent teaching that the reprobate will be subject to eternal punishment. Ignatius, for example, echoing the words of 1 Corinthians 6:9–10, reports that those who are corrupt and immoral will not inherit the kingdom of God and instead go to the "unquenchable fire."[30] Barnabas also considers this judgment of the wicked to entail "eternal death and punishment."[31] For many, such as Clement, this judgment is cosmic in its scope. The author writes, "But you know that 'the day' of judgment is already 'coming as a blazing furnace,' and 'some of the heavens will dissolve,' and the whole earth will dissolve."[32]

The righteous, on the other hand, will experience everlasting joy and immortality in the kingdom of God.[33] The concept of the kingdom of God in the second century includes early forms of millennialism (or chiliasm), or "the belief that after Jesus comes, he will establish and rule over a kingdom on this earth for a millennium, that is, for a thousand years."[34] The roots of millennialism are well attested in the second century, making millennialism the prevailing view of eschatology in the early centuries of the church.[35] Amillennialism, as it would develop later in the tradition, is never defended by orthodox Christians in the

---

27. *Mart. Poly.* 11.2. See also *1 Clem.* 28.1–3 and *2 Clem.* 18.1–2.
28. Herm. *Sim* 3.1–4.8.
29. Herm. *Sim* 4.4.
30. Ign. *Eph.* 16.2.
31. *Barn.* 20.1.
32. *2 Clem.* 16.3. See also Malachi 4:1 and Isaiah 34:4.
33. *1 Clem.* 34.3-7.
34. Craig Blaising, "Premillennialism," in *Three Views on the Millennium and Beyond*, ed. Darrell Bock (Grand Rapids: Zondervan, 1999), 157. In his study of patristic millennialism, Hill defines the term similarly: "the belief in a temporary earthly Messianic Kingdom to be realized sometime in the future." Charles Hill, *Regnum Caelorum: Patterns of Millennial Thought in Early Christianity* (Grand Rapids: Eerdmans, 2001), 5.
35. Craig Blaising, "Early Christian Millennialism and the Intermediate State: A Response to Charles Hill's *Regnum Caelorum*" (paper presented at The Seminar on Early Catholic Christianity, Southwestern Baptist Theological Seminary, April 11, 2013), 1–2. See also Hill, *Regnum Caelorum*, 2–3.

second century.[36] Millennialism is explicit in the writings of Papias, and some elements of it have been detected in Polycarp, Ignatius, and Hermas. All of these have some association with Asia Minor and the apostle John, who first described the millennial kingdom in Revelation 20.[37] Polycarp's views on the millennium come down to us through Irenaeus, who received them via Papias, a "hearer of John, and a companion of Polycarp."[38] Though Polycarp does not detail the millennial kingdom, he refers to it indirectly when he describes how believers will "also reign with him [Christ]" if they persevere in their faith.[39] Papias, however, is the key figure for early Christian millennialism. Irenaeus reports that Papias related the teaching of the Lord and the apostle John on the fecundity and blessing of the intermediate earthly kingdom, saying:

> The days will come, in which vines will grow, each having ten thousand branches, and in each branch ten thousand twigs, and in each true twig ten thousand shoots, and in each one of the shoots ten thousand grapes, and every grape when pressed will give five and twenty metretes of wine. And when any one of the saints will take hold of a cluster, another will cry out, 'I am a better cluster, take me; bless the Lord through me.' In like manner the Lord declared that a grain of wheat will produce ten thousand ears, and that every ear should have ten thousand grains, and every grain will yield ten pounds of clear, pure, fine flour; and that all other fruit bearing trees and seeds and grass will produce in similar proportions; and that all animals feeding on the productions of the earth, should become peaceful and harmonious among each other, and be in perfect subjection to man.[40]

---

36. Given the evidence and extant literature, this is clearly the case despite the arguments of Hill, who attempted to detect the presence of orthodox non-chiliasm in the early church. Blaising has argued persuasively that Hill's analysis, especially regarding the non-chiliasts mentioned in Irenaeus, is rather unconvincing. Blaising, "Early Christian Millennialism," 20–21.
37. Larry V. Crutchfield, "The Apostle John and Asia Minor as a Source of Premillennialism in the Early Church Fathers," *Journal of the Evangelical Theological Society* 31.4 (1988): 411–427, 419.
38. *Haer.* 5.33.4.
39. Pol. *Phil.* 5. Hill is not convinced this refers to the millennial kingdom, but given the circumstantial evidence offered through Irenaeus, it seems highly probable. Hill, *Regnum Caelorum*, 91. See also Crutchfield, "The Apostle John," 418–22. Similarly, the millennialism of Ignatius is rather tenuous as well, though it is interesting that his eschatological references are concentrated in letters associated with Polycarp. Ibid., 417–18.
40. *Haer.* 5.33.3.

For Papias, the millennial kingdom is a temporary period of earthly abundance and peace for God's people and a time of preparation for the eternal kingdom. Papias also reports that Judas questioned the Lord about the reliability of this future restoration and the Lord simply responded, "'Those who shall come to these times shall see them.'"[41] *Barnabas* also adds another aspect to these millennial views when he interprets the days of creation in Genesis eschatologically, or what Daniélou calls "paradisal millennialism," as a week of ages.[42] This reading interprets the days of creation with Psalm 90:4 (2 Peter 3:8), "a day for the Lord is as one thousand years" as six sequential thousand-year periods or ages that trace out the trajectory of salvation history from creation to new creation.

Finally, these early fathers exhort the faithful to persevere through trials and tribulations in order to receive the blessing of the new creation. The Shepherd of Hermas praises those who "patiently endure the coming great tribulation."[43] *Second Clement* exhorts the reader to righteousness saying, "Therefore let us love one another, that we all may enter into the kingdom of God" and then later adds, "if we do what is right in God' sight, we will enter into his kingdom and receive the promises which 'ear has not heard nor eye seen nor the heart of man imagined.'"[44] This blessed state is the prize for the righteous who "rejoice in an eternity untouched by sorrow."[45] The inauguration of a new creation will involve a cosmic reordering, where heaven and earth will perish by fire and be purified to be ready to receive God's people.[46]

Doctrine of the Future in Justin Martyr

Following the apostolic fathers, in the middle of the second century, several Christian theologians began writing careful defenses of the Christian faith for various Roman and Jewish authorities. These thinkers utilize many of the resources of Greco-Roman philosophy to defend the right for Christians to worship freely without fear of persecution. The most prolific apologist is Justin Martyr, who composed two apologies addressed to the Emperor Antonius Pius, and a theological

---

41. *Haer.* 5.33.4.
42. Jean Daniélou, *The Theology of Jewish Christianity*, trans. John A. Baker (London: Darton, Longman & Todd, and Philadelphia: Westminster Press, 1964), 393, 399. Daley, *Hope of the Early Church*, 11. *Barn.* 15.1–8.
43. Herm. *Vis.* 2.2.7.
44. *2 Clem.* 9.6, *2 Clem* 11.7.
45. *2 Clem.* 19.4.
46. *2 Clem.* 16.3, See also Herm. *Vis.* 4.3.1–5.

debate with a Jew named Trypho over Christ's messianic identity. Some scholars, such as Goodenough, have remarked that Justin's eschatology is "completely un-critical," but Goodenough's criticism goes too far.[47] Like the Apostolic Fathers, the genre of Justin's writings did not require a more systematic treatment of his doctrine of the future. Instead, Justin's eschatology is filtered into the stream of his apologetic and exegetical debates, so his treatments are often brief and unde-veloped. Nevertheless, drawing these references together, it is possible to paint a coherent portrait of Justin's views of eschatology.

To begin with, one curious aspect of Justin's eschatology is the apparent lack of concern about the delay in the Lord's second coming. Justin never addresses the issue and even indicates that the Lord's delay may be part of a larger plan of redemption that includes even some not yet born.[48] This concern is also implicit in Justin's apologetic arguments that petition the emperor for the right to worship freely. This indicates that the delay of the Parousia did not cause any kind of "radi-cal re-formation of Christian doctrine and practice."[49] At the same time, Justin, like the apostolic fathers, warns that the faithful should be vigilant for the "Man of Lawlessness" (Dan. 7:25) who will rise up, reign for three and a half years, and "utter bold and blasphemous words against the Most High."[50]

Immediately following the reign of the antichrist, Justin argues, the Son of God will come again in glory to judge the living and the dead.[51] He consistently emphasizes the twofold advent of the Lord and uses the term "Parousia" no less than twenty-nine times.[52] The manifestation of the Lord's return initiates a series of events that he describes in summary form saying: "He [The Son of God] will come from heaven with glory with His angelic host; when also He will raise the bodies of all the people who have lived, and will clothe the worthy with incorruption, but will send those of the wicked, eternally conscious, into eternal fire with the wicked demons."[53] His summary contains all the standard aspects of orthodox eschatology. Christ will come again in glory, raise the faithful to

---

47. Erwin R. Goodenough, *The Theology of Justin Martyr* (Jena: Frommannsche Buchhandlung. 1923), 291.

48. *1 Apol.* 28. Translations of Justin's works are taken from *St. Justin Martyr: Dialogue with Try-pho*, trans. Thomas Falls (Washington DC: The Catholic University of America Press, 2003) and *St. Justin Martyr The First and Second Apologies*, trans. Leslie W. Barnard, ACW no. 56 (New York: Paulist Press, 1997).

49. Barnard, "Justin Martyr's Eschatology," 89.

50. *Dial.* 32.3.

51. *Dial.* 40.4, *Dial* 45.4.

52. Barnard, "Justin Martyr's Eschatology," 87.

53. *1 Apol.* 52.

incorruption, and the wicked to eternal punishment. Justin joins this section with a series of prophecies taken from the Old Testament that describe the nature of these events in more detail.[54] Some scholars have argued that the works appear inconsistent, but Justin's presentation is shaped by the genre of his two extant writings.[55] In the context of his *Apologies* Justin clarifies that the Christian expectation of the future kingdom is not a "human kingdom," like other nation states, but a kingdom that is founded and ruled by *God*.[56] This is an important distinction, since a Roman emperor would no doubt have grave concerns about references to other kingdoms. At the same time, Justin argues against his Jewish interlocutor that Christ is the messianic King who will come again to establish this kingdom of God.[57] Both Justin and Trypho, however, agree that "Jerusalem shall be rebuilt" and that the people of God shall inherit the land of Canaan once again.[58] Referring to the earthly millennial kingdom, Justin writes that the apostle John received "revelation and foretold that the followers of Christ would dwell in Jerusalem for a thousand years, and that afterwards the universal and, in short, everlasting resurrection and judgment would take place."[59] Like Papias, Justin describes the blessing and prosperity of the millennial kingdom, but in this context appeals to the words of Isaiah 65:17–25 to depict the nature of the restored Jerusalem and earthly fecundity of the millennial kingdom.

At the conclusion of the millennial kingdom there will be a general resurrection, where God will raise up the wicked to judgment along with the Devil and his angels and the faithful to incorruption and blessing. For those who consider this impossible, he simply appeals to the words of the Lord in Matthew 10:28, "the things that are impossible with men are possible with God."[60] At the same time, Justin provides the rational defense of the resurrection appealing to the logic of the uniformity of nature. Though it might seem impossible, a fully

---

54. Justin's citations include a complex assortment of prophetic passages drawn mostly from Isaiah, Ezekiel, and Zechariah.

55. Stander, "Eschatology in the Second Century Theologians," 590–91. See also Barnard, "Justin Martyr's Eschatology," 93–4; Hill, *Regnum Caelorum*, 23–4. There is also some debate surrounding the degree to which Justin is influenced by the events of the Bar Kochba revolt, and how this event shaped the *Dialogue* as a whole. See Barnard, ibid., 94-95 and Hill, ibid., 27.

56. *1 Apol.* 11.

57. *Dial.* 80.5.

58. *Dial.* 80.1.

59. *Dial.* 81.4. In the same context Justin cites Genesis 2:17, Psalm 90:4 (2 Peter 3:8), and Isaiah 65:17–25, which are other key passages in the discussion of the millennial kingdom.

60. *1 Apol.* 19. See also *Haer.* 5.5.2. He also appeals to Jewish and Greek philosophers to argue that resurrection is a concept already present in their writings. *1 Apol.* 20–21.

developed human person grows from a tiny human seed, so also is it not too difficult for God to raise the body that is sown into the ground. The future resurrection also serves Justin's apologetic. His appeals to the emperor for freedom to worship are coupled with warnings that ultimately, martyred Christians suffer nothing, while those who persecute them will suffer eternally.

At the time of the general resurrection, the reprobate will be punished for his deeds in an eternal fire.[61] Justin appeals to the authority of the Lord's words to fear God alone who is able to cast the body and soul into Gehenna.[62] He follows the Jewish tradition received in the New Testament that identifies the location of Gehenna near Jerusalem as the site of punishment for the wicked. Throughout both his writings, Justin is consistent that the punishment for the wicked is everlasting fire and torment.[63] For the faithful, on the other hand, the blessing of the new creation is a reward for faithfulness in this life and those who have lived in obedience to Christ.[64] He gives special attention to the Joshua-Christ typology, so that just as Joshua established the kingdom of Israel in the conquest, so also Christ will establish the new creation and give the people an "inheritance for eternity."[65] The faithful will put on incorruption and live eternally in fellowship with God free from all "suffering, corruption, sorrow, and death."[66]

Doctrine of the Future in Irenaeus

Finally, the full flowering second-century theology is expressed in the writings of Irenaeus of Lyons. Irenaeus was born in Asia Minor, but he eventually made his way to Lyons where he served as bishop of a community that was under severe persecution. His extant writings include an extensive apologetic work called *Against Heresies* and a shorter catechetical manual entitled *Demonstration of the Apostolic Preaching*. Irenaeus's primary contribution is the defense of orthodoxy against the rise of various gnostic sects that challenged many of the basic tenants of the faith including their eschatology. While the references to his doctrine of eschatology are scattered throughout his writing, the concluding chapters of *Against Heresies* provide a general framework of his eschatology.[67] A

---

61. *1 Apol.* 17.
62. *1 Apol.* 19.
63. *1 Apol.* 12, *1 Apol.* 16–7, *1 Apol.* 57, *2 Apol.* 1, *2 Apol.* 7, *Dial.* 45.4.
64. *1Apol.* 10, *1 Apol.* 12, *1 Apol.* 14, *1 Apol.* 16–7, *1 Apol.* 52, *1 Apol.* 57, *2 Apol.*, *Dial.* 117.3.
65. *Dial.* 113.4. See also *Dial.* 75.2 and *Dial.* 139.2.
66. *Dial.* 45.4.
67. *Haer.* 5.25–36.

distinguishing feature of Irenaeus's view of eschatology is the way it serves his larger vision of the scriptures as one continuous narrative of salvation history.[68] For Irenaeus, the opening events in creation are connected to a broader understanding of the *telos* of history and to his doctrine of recapitulation. These connections are also evident in his summaries of the rule of faith.[69] From this perspective, Irenaeus's millennialism (or chiliasm) is a fitting conclusion to God's ultimate work of salvation that brings "humanity from its Edenic state of infancy to the true maturity of God-likeness."[70]

As the faithful wait for the Lord's return, Irenaeus, like the apostolic fathers and Justin, points to the antichrist as the key figure who signals that the return of the Lord is nearing.[71] Irenaeus argues that the antichrist is a person that comes "recapitulating in himself the apostasy of the devil" and persuading people that "he himself is God."[72] He also ponders the symbolism of the number of the name of the antichrist (666) and reasons that the number was given so that the faithful would be watchful, yet his actual name was not recorded because his wickedness will be so exceedingly great. At the conclusion of the six-thousand-year period, the antichrist will assume power for a period of three and a half years and enact the abomination of desolation (Matt. 24:15, Dan. 9:27), which will be a significant time of persecution for the people of God.[73]

After the reign of the antichrist, several events ensue that constitute the basic framework for Irenaeus's eschatology, including the second coming, the resurrection, judgment, the earthly millennial kingdom, and the inauguration of the new creation. He summarizes these events saying, "But when this Antichrist shall have devastated all things in this world, he will reign for three years and six months, and sit in the temple of Jerusalem; and then the Lord will come from heaven in the clouds, in the glory of the Father, sending this man and those who follow him into the lake of fire; but bringing in for the righteous the times of the kingdom that is, the rest, the hallowed seventh day."[74]

---

68. Daley, *Hope in the Early Church*, 29.
69. *Haer.* 1.10.1 and *Haer.* 1.22.1.
70. Christopher R. Smith, "Chiliasm and Recapitulation in the Theology of Irenaeus," *Vigiliae Christianae* 48.4. (1994): 313–331, 329.
71. *Haer.* 5.25.1–30.4.
72. *Haer.* 5.25.1.
73. *Haer.* 5.25.2–4.
74. *Haer.* 5.30.4. The treatment of eschatology in the rule of faith reveals the importance of these issues in his debates with the gnostics. There are a number of biblical citation and allusions in this passage including: Matt. 18:8; 25:41; John 14:15; 15:10; Rom. 2:5; Eph. 1:9–10; 4:12; 6:12; Phil. 2:10–11; Col. 1:15; and Titus 1:8.

After the reign of the antichrist, the Lord will return in the clouds to resurrect and to judge. This general resurrection, prior to the millennial kingdom, is either a resurrection to judgment or resurrection to blessing. Irenaeus warns his opponents that even if they reject God in this life, "they will surely rise again in the flesh in order to acknowledge the power of Him who raises them from the dead."[75] Christ comes to separate and, at long last, judge the devil and his angels, the heretics, and anyone who perseveres in disobedience. When Christ comes again, he will cast all of those who opposed God's will and works into the lake of fire.[76] Irenaeus frequently conjoins Matthew 25:41 with the blessing of the righteous in Matthew 25:33–34, which contributes to the basic confession of the church's faith regarding judgment.[77] For Irenaeus, God's judgment is based upon humanity's free will and the choices of good or evil.

In response to his gnostic interlocutors, Irenaeus goes to great lengths to defend the bodily resurrection.[78] The living resurrected body reveals the glory and righteous work of God.[79] He argues logically that the same body that participated in sin and death must be raised to new life in and participate in righteousness. In Irenaeus's words, "In these same members, therefore, in which we used to serve sin, and bring fourth unto death, does He wish us to be obedient unto righteousness, that we may bring forth fruit unto life."[80] The framework for the resurrected body is, once again, the resurrected body of Christ that anticipates the nature of the future resurrection.[81]

In terms of the future bodily resurrection, Irenaeus conceives of two separate events including the resurrection of the just and a general resurrection. The general resurrection includes the heretics and the reprobate, who are judged along with the devil and his angels. The resurrection of the just, on the other hand, is bodily resurrection to new life in the kingdom of God. The just who are raised to new life will not die, but neither is their immortality static. Even in the new creation they

---

75. *Haer.* 1.22.1.
76. *Haer.* 5.27.1.
77. *Haer.* 5.28.2, *Haer.* 5.30.4. D. Jeffrey Bingham, *Irenaeus's Use of Matthew's Gospel in Adversus Haereses*, Traditio Exegetica Graeca (Louvin: Peeters, 1998), 288–89.
78. The gnostics even appeal to a number of Pauline texts to support their rejection of the bodily resurrection, and much of *Haer.* 5 is concerned with refuting the gnostic reading of these select Pauline texts, such as 1 Corinthians 15:50 and Romans 8:8. Bertrand provides a good summary of this debate as it relates to eschatology. Dominique Bertrand, "L'eschatologie de saint Irénée," Théophilyon XVI-1 (2011): 113–148, 117–122, 126–27.
79. *Haer.* 4.20.7.
80. *Haer.* 5.14.4.
81. *Haer.* 5.14.3.

will continue to grow and to learn as they become ever increasingly accustomed to their immortality. In addition to those who are resurrected, Irenaeus argues, those who are alive are "translated" into the kingdom like Enoch and Elijah.[82] Like Justin, Irenaeus also defends the resurrection by appealing to God's work in creation in Genesis 1–2. He reasons that it is no more difficult for God to resurrect humanity from the dust of the earth than it was for God to create humanity in the first creation. He also depicts the beauty of the resurrected body by comparing it to imagery of gold and silver and saying that the resurrected body will be so glorious that "the King Himself will have pleasure in your beauty."[83]

Following the resurrection, the Lord will establish a temporary earthly kingdom where the faithful will experience all the blessings promised to Abraham. Irenaeus follows the millennial tradition of Polycarp and Papias.[84] Irenaeus argues that it is fitting for the resurrection and earthly kingdom to come prior to judgment, so that "the creation itself, being restored to its primeval condition, should without restraint be under the dominion of the righteous."[85] Irenaeus interprets the earthly kingdom in a literal sense, including imagery of the animals coexisting peacefully and abundant produce.[86] He rejects the allegorical interpretation of these eschatological texts employed by the gnostics because they deny any expectation of an earthly kingdom.[87] Like those in the *Epistle of Barnabas*, Irenaeus's millennial views are also related to a view of "paradisal millennialism" and an intertextual reading of Genesis 2:2–3, Psalm 90:4 (2 Peter 3:8), and Revelation 13:18 that interprets the days of creation as six one-thousand-year periods leading up to the inauguration of the eschatological Sabbath.[88] The true Sabbath of the righteous is when "they shall not be engaged in any earthy occupation; but shall have a table at

---

82. *Haer.* 5.5.2.
83. *Haer.* 4.39.2. Psalm 45:11.
84. *Haer.* 5.33.4. Eusebius rejects the views of Papias and Irenaeus, saying, "he [Papias] said there would be a millennium after the resurrection and that there would be a corporeal reign of Christ on this very earth." Eusebius reports that Papias received it from an "unwritten tradition." *Hist. Eccl.* 3.39.11–12. This view, however, was affirmed by Hippolytus, who composed an entire work on the antichrist, entitled *On Antichrist*, and a commentary on the book of Daniel, entitled *Exposition of Daniel*, which is the oldest extant Christian commentary. In these works, he cites various apocalyptic and eschatological texts arguing that not all the prophecies of Daniel had been fulfilled.
85. *Haer.* 5.32.1.
86. *Haer.* 5.35.2. Blaising describes the importance of Irenaeus's literal reading of Revelation within the history of early Christian thought. Blaising, "Premillennialism," 164, 166, 170, and 188n.52.
87. *Haer.* 5.35.1–2.
88. *Haer.* 5.28.3. *AH* 5.33.1–3. See Daniélou, *The Theology of Jewish Christianity*, 393, 399.

hand prepared for them by God, supplying them with all sorts of dishes."[89] Against the gnostics, Irenaeus argues that salvation is not an instantaneous event of the soul's escape, but an extended progressive development whereby God directs his people toward sanctification and glorification.[90]

The earthly kingdom, at last, gives way to the new heavens and the new earth. Irenaeus is clear that the creation itself is not annihilated, but the form of the earth in which sin and death had previously reigned passes away. He describes this transition, saying, "But when this present fashion of things passes away, and man has been renewed, and flourishes in an incorruptible state, so as to preclude the possibility of becoming old, then there shall be the new heavens and the new earth, in which the new man shall remain continually, always holding fresh converse with God."[91] In the new heavens and the new earth, he also argues for a level of gradation. Those who are most worthy are taken to heaven, while others dwell in paradise, and still others dwell in the city of God. In each case there remains the potential for progression toward the presence of God and the divine likeness. The eschatological state of the redeemed, therefore, is not a static condition, like it is for the gnostics, but a further opportunity to grow and conform to the divine likeness.

Conclusion

In conclusion, the doctrine of the future in the second century is characterized by several developments that extend the apostolic testimony in different ways. First, their doctrine of the future is forged in the face of persecution and theological disputes with various heretical sects. These occasions allow the early Christians to clarify the church's convictions about the end times. In general, the delay of the Lord coming does not appear to be a significant issue even given the various episodes of persecution. In spite of the Lord's delay, the church remains confident that God will complete the work of salvation, even as they deal with the pressing issues of their developing ecclesiology.

Second, the second-century thinkers continued to develop the basic elements of the church's conviction of the end times, including the expectation of the second advent, the bodily resurrection, the judgment of wicked and the

---

89. *Haer.* 5.33.2.
90. Bertrand, "L'eschatologie," 134.
91. *Haer.* 5.36.1.

devil, the future earthly millennial kingdom, and the inauguration of the new heavens and the new earth. The hope of the Lord's return gave them confidence in the face of persecution, and reminded them that God's judgment was coming for all those who rejected God. With the rise of Gnosticism, there is a significant emphasis placed on the bodily resurrection and the earthly millennial kingdom. These Christians fully expected that God would resurrect the body to live in a temporary earthly kingdom.

Finally, these early Christians rarely considered their doctrine of the future without tying it closely to other aspects of their theological framework. The condemnation of sin, death, and the devil, the resurrection from the dead, and the kingdom of God were the culmination and conclusion of God's work in salvation history. Their views on the earthly millennium in particular offered a fitting conclusion to a broader view of salvation history and the hope of a bodily resurrection that enjoys all the blessings of an earthly kingdom ruled by God alone. Clearly, these early fathers of the church ministered through a robust theology of hope in the coming of the Lord and the completion of their salvation.

THE DOCTRINE OF THE FUTURE
IN ORIGEN AND ATHANASIUS

Bryan M. Litfin

ack in my high school days, I traveled to Knoxville, Tennessee, on an educational field trip for aspiring journalists. On the way home to Memphis after the conference, our teacher—perhaps unnerved at the prospect of driving a van full of rowdy youth—made a wrong turn at a fork in the highway. Instead of taking I-40 west to Memphis, she headed down I-75 to Chattanooga. We had nearly crossed into the state of Georgia before any of us noticed the error. Although we were glad for an extension to our road trip, the teacher was frustrated by the delay. In the end, though, we arrived in Memphis without any further problems.

Sometimes the highway of theology can be a little like this. We can be traveling down a well-established trajectory, unaware that a wrong turn has begun to take us off course. At first, the divergence from the original path is hardly noticeable. Perhaps we are even headed more or less in the right direction. Yet, in time, it will become apparent that the destination city is not correct. We're going to end up somewhere we did not intend. Only the willingness to choose a different road will get us pointed in the right direction again.

The ancient church's search for a doctrine of the future was one of those times when creative route-finding became necessary. The brilliant thinker Origen of Alexandria advanced Christian eschatology several miles ahead. He was a theological pioneer, a bold innovator who ventured into unexplored territory as he blazed a new trail. Yet somewhere along the way, he got lost in the wilderness, and the historical church did not see fit to follow him. Origen's excessive speculations about the end times did not become standard theology in the Christian tradition. Fortunately, his many successors in the faith—including the great Alexandrian bishop

Athanasius—were able to rediscover a theological path that the church as a whole could follow. In this way, the thinkers of ancient Christianity forged a viable eschatology that is still with us today.

ALEXANDRIA: ANCIENT BEACON OF LEARNING

If Harvard and Yale are the best universities in America, and Oxford and Cambridge represent the height of British learning, it was Alexandria, Egypt, where every scholar of the ancient world wanted to go. The city was founded in 332 BCE by its namesake, the powerful Greek conqueror Alexander the Great. Situated with harbors on the Mediterranean and a lake that connected the city to the Nile and the Far East, Alexandria was perfectly positioned to thrive as a hub of commerce and trade. Yet it wasn't only the exchange of merchandise that made the city famous; it was also the exchange of ideas. The Greek kings who took control after Alexander's death established a house of learning near the royal palace, which included a temple to the nine goddesses of inspiration known as the Muses. This religious and academic complex, from which we get the word "museum," eventually included a repository of scrolls for the scholars who studied there and dined over genteel conversation. Such was the genesis of the great Library of Alexandria. Since Alexandria was a prominent seaport, the accumulated knowledge of the world was quick to come flooding in. Just as the marvelous lighthouse in the city's harbor guided the ships to safety, so the renowned library served as a beacon to the leading intellectuals of the day.

What did all those ancient scholars study? During the four centuries before the birth of Christ, and continuing into the first several centuries of the ancient church, the writings of Plato provided the primary underpinnings of the philosophical task. It should come as no surprise that Platonism saturated the academic climate at Alexandria, but it is perhaps more remarkable that it also became the foremost philosophy of the early Christians. Though the present chapter is not the place for a detailed treatment of Greek intellectualism, a few important points should be discussed because they helped shape the ancient church's eschatology, as expressed by figures like Origen or Athanasius.

The famous philosopher Plato lived approximately 429–347 BCE, long before the Christian religion had gotten its start. Plato looked around his world and saw that every physical object was in a state of change. Objects were always moving, decaying, eroding, etc. "Everything changes and nothing holds still," an earlier philosopher had said, and Plato agreed. So how, he wondered, can anything of lasting value be learned from the material world, which is always shifting under our feet? Plato decided that the path to truth must lie elsewhere. He reasoned that timeless and immutable "forms" or "ideas" must give unifying coherence to all physical things. Take beauty, for example. Why are a sunset, an attractive woman, a stately building, and a perfectly played harp all considered "beautiful"? Surely there must be some overarching concept of beauty that we recognize in these particularly beautiful things. Yet in our ever-changing world, the red dusk always turns to darkness, the bloom of youth fades, the work of the hand crumbles, and the harp goes out of tune. Even so, beauty itself persists as an ideal from one generation to the next. Plato could only conclude that there must be a timeless and abiding form of beauty (and many other forms as well) existing in a higher realm than ours. Thinking about these heavenly forms is the way to understand ultimate reality.

Perhaps you have already sensed from this description the problem that would plague the later followers of Plato, the ones who made his philosophy the most popular "-ism" of the day. If the forms are in one realm and matter is in another, what connects the two? How do the timeless forms give shape to their physical copies? Or to be more specific, what is the means by which Beauty lends itself to such disparate things as the sun, a woman, a building, and an audible note? Plato himself wasn't clear about how earthly things "participate" in the heavenly forms. Over time, this thorny problem gave rise to the hypothesis of intermediaries. The more distant and rarified the forms became in Greek thought—and the more lowly and inferior matter became, as result—so all the more acutely did the ancient Platonists feel the need for gradations or stepping stones to connect the two worlds.

By the dawn of the first century CE, the great philosophical question was how the superior and inferior worlds could be bridged. The ancient church apologists were quick to suggest the solution to this dilemma could be found in Jesus Christ, who came down from heaven as a man so he could bring us back to God. This seemed like the perfect convergence of biblical revelation and Greek wisdom. Jesus of Nazareth was the solution the Greeks had been waiting for all along. He was the great mediator between the divine and human realms (John 1:14; 1 Tim. 2:5). Based on this line of thinking, Christian Platonism became the intellectual vehicle in which the Alexandrian church fathers decided to ride as they traveled down the road of theology.

CHRISTIANITY ON THE NILE

Before we take a look at the eschatology of the Alexandrians, it will be worth our while to consider how Christianity first came to this great city in the Nile delta. Strangely, the earliest known figures in Alexandria who were interested in the life and thought of Jesus were actually of gnostic persuasion. The religious philosophers Basilides and Valentinus taught a mystical version of Christianity in second-century Alexandria—a version very much at odds with the original proclamation of Jesus's followers in Jerusalem. Although the early church fathers interacted with and sometimes even appreciated aspects of Gnosticism, they roundly criticized teachers like Basilides and Valentinus as heretics. So when do we encounter believers of more orthodox belief in the city? Other than figures from New Testament times about whom we know little, such as Mark or Apollos (Acts 18:24–25), the first known church father from Alexandria was a late second-century teacher named Pantaenus. Though he too is shrouded in mystery, one important thing stands out about him: He seems to have been the master of an Alexandrian "school" for Christians.

The precise nature of the Alexandrian school is a matter of scholarly debate. We must keep in mind that schools in the ancient world did not include foundational charters, permanent buildings, formal degrees, and the ongoing perpetuation of the same curriculum. Rather, schools were centered on the authority of respected teachers. If enough famous scholars began to congregate in the same place, the informal school began to attract students from across the empire. At Alexandria, the presence of the museum and library had fostered the city's reputation for academic excellence. It is not surprising, then, that the intellectual Christians of Alexandria such as Pantaenus, Clement, and Origen would instruct students and constitute something that could rightly be called a school. By Origen's day, this school appears to have been used by the bishop to instruct new believers in basic Christian doctrine, a process known as "catechesis." For this reason, it has come to be called the Catechetical School.

In the ancient church, the basic function of catechesis was to teach converts—most of whom were steeped in paganism—the fundamental tenets of the Christian faith. The appointed time for this instruction was prior to baptism. To ensure unity across a wide area, the teachers used a basic creed called the Rule of Faith. Though different cities had slightly different wording for their creeds, the essential contours were the same. Anyone who has ever recited the Apostles' Creed will be familiar with the shape of the early church's catechetical instruction, for that creed emerged from the Rule of Faith as taught in Rome. And just as the ancient Roman creed can be reconstructed, so too we can recover the one used in Egypt. Early Christian belief about future things always included four basic doctrines: the second coming of Jesus Christ at the end of the world, the bodily resurrection of the dead, final judgment before Christ's throne, and humanity's eternal destiny of blessing or punishment based upon that judgment. As a catechist in the school of Alexandria, Origen would have believed these things too. Yet when we take a closer look at Origen's doctrine of the future, we discover he had some additional beliefs that took him into places other Christians were unwilling to go. It is time now to meet one of the most brilliant—and problematic—fathers of the ancient church.

Origen: A Diamond in the Rough

Origen of Alexandria (185–254 CE) was known in ancient times by the nickname "Adamantius." The word means "undefeated" in Greek, and by analogy it referred to the diamond, a gem so hard it cannot be scratched. This was the kind of man Origen was: Hardened by the practice of self-discipline for many years, he was impervious to the torture inflicted upon him at the end of his life for his Christian faith. Yet diamonds are known not only for their hardness but also for their beauty. This, too, could be said to characterize Origen. His thought patterns were deep, wise, and complex. Like a diamond, Origen's scholarly contributions are beautiful and precious to the church. However, as we have already noted, some aspects of his theology were unacceptable to other Christians. Just as gems need to be sanded and polished over time, so Origen's eschatology needed the burnishing that further theological reflection would provide.

Above all, Origen was an intellectual. Sometimes this word signifies a hard-hearted person who operates by cold rationality instead of warm human emotions. Christian intellectuals can be viewed as "ivory-tower academics" whose spiritual lives are dry and shriveled. This certainly was *not* the case with Origen. Even as a boy, he demonstrated an intense love for God, asking profound theological questions that his father for Leonides, struggled to answer. Leonides used to sneak into his son's room at night and kiss his beloved boy, amazed that God had considered him worthy to parent such a pure soul. Later, when Origen was sixteen, Leonides faced the ultimate test of persecution and was martyred for the name of Jesus. Origen so passionately wanted to join his father in death that he intended to run to the jail and declare his Christian faith. However, Origen's mother hid his clothing so he could not go outside, preventing the murder of her son by this desperate ploy. And so Origen did not die as a teenager—but now he faced the challenge of providing food and shelter for his widowed mother and six brothers.

To pay the bills, Origen resorted to what he did best: academics. He took a lowly job as a teacher of Greek literature. Yet it wasn't long before Alexandria's bishop took note of the promising young man. Seeing his potential, Bishop Demetrius put Origen in charge of the church's catechesis. In this way Origen became affiliated with the so-called Catechetical School of Alexandria. But once again, let us recall that "schools" in the ancient world were not exactly like colleges and universities today. Instead of imagining Origen as a stern professor lecturing in front of a chalkboard, we should think of him more like an extremely smart spiritual mentor. He was a magnetic figure, a man who earned a following based on admiration and respect. His disciples gravitated to him for his godliness as much as for his mind. And that is just the point: In third-century Alexandria, a robust intellectualism wasn't contrary to devotion—it was the fruit of it. Therefore, when we call Origen a "Christian intellectual," we are honoring him as someone who directed his mind toward the deepest thoughts about the God of the universe.

Perfection, Fall, Return

Like all of Origen's theology, his doctrine of the future is fundamentally intellectual in outlook. He does not highlight the bodily delights Christians will experience, much less a physical place where believers will someday dwell. Rather, Origen focuses his eschatology on what we will *think about* at the consummation of all things. The mind of the Christian will once again be able to meditate upon the vision of God. Heaven will be an eternal, unbroken act of contemplating God's splendor. And if you are now saying to yourself, "That doesn't sound like much fun to me!" Origen would be quick to reply, "That is because your earthbound laziness has prevented you from understanding the incredible beauty of who God really is!"

Origen's theology of the future cannot be understood apart from the past and the present. That is to say, his eschatology is inextricably linked to his cosmology, his anthropology, his soteriology, and even his angelology. How the world was created and organized, how humans function in body and soul, how we are saved by Jesus Christ, and how angels and demons came to be—all of these areas of doctrine are interconnected in Origen's thought. The great Alexandrian was one of the most systematic thinkers among the ancient church fathers. We might even say he was the first to write a textbook of systematic theology—his famous four-volume work, *On First Principles*. In this book Origen lays out a sweeping vision of God's activity from initial creation to final consummation. And to do so, he draws equally from the text of Scripture and the Platonic philosophy that was so important in his day.

To establish a Christian theology of creation, Origen picks up where Plato left off. Recall that the world above is always remote in Platonic thought, a realm of immaterial and unchanging essence. Plato had argued that in order to create the physical world, an intermediary being must have gazed at the eternal forms and molded the world by what he saw there. In similar fashion, Origen suggests that while God himself is utterly transcendent and distant from all physical things, the Son of God served as an agent of creation at his Father's command—a notion that can be found in John 1:1–3 and Colossians 1:15–16. Thus, just as we would expect, the insights of Greek philosophy are confirmed by the written revelation of God.

Origen develops his cosmological system out of these fundamental principles. In eternity past, before there was a universe or even time, God brought forth his beloved Son. But God also created what are usually described as "intelligences." These disembodied minds were engaged in contemplation of God's majestic beauty, which is an act of warm love and devotion. Yet these intelligences possessed free will. Rather than continue to love God perfectly, the intelligences chose to turn away from him. Origen understands this failure as a cooling of desire, resulting in the intelligences becoming lesser beings called "souls," for Origen believed the Greek word for soul (*psyche*) was related to *psychesthai*, to cool off or freeze. He writes, "As therefore God is 'fire' (Heb. 12:29) and the angels 'a flame of fire' (Heb. 1:7) and the saints are all 'fervent in spirit' (Rom. 12:11), so on the contrary those who have fallen away from the love of God must undoubtedly be said to have cooled in their affection for him and to have become cold. For the Lord also says, 'Because iniquity has multiplied, the love of the many shall grow cold'" (Matt. 24:12).[1] This unholy chilling took place to varying degrees. Some beings cooled very much and became the devil and his demons (and as Origen points out, we observe in the natural world that snakes

---

1. *Princ.* 2.8.3, translated in G.W. Butterworth, *Origen: On First Principles* (Gloucester, MA: Peter Smith, 1973), 123.

are indeed cold-blooded). Other beings didn't cool as much in their worship, so they became human souls. The higher astronomical bodies—the sun, moon, and stars—cooled less than humans and so didn't fall all the way to the earth. And the beings that cooled the least are the angels, who are heavenly spirits still in close fellowship with the immaterial God.

This, then, is the plight of humankind: Our souls have fallen away from the vision of God and are trapped in physical bodies, whose urges distract us from our highest good. Sin is our failure to gaze upon God's majesty in wonder and worship. Although the rational part of us, the inner soul, desires in some long-forgotten way to contemplate God once more, the preoccupations of daily life and the constant demands of our lustful bodies prevent us from worshiping properly.

However, not everyone is equally far from God. Among the fallen souls of the human race we discover a kind of gradation. Some people live in a fleshly way, pursuing whatever actions the body dictates. Origen only had to look around the decadent city of Alexandria to find plenty of examples among the pagans. In contrast, many Christians had rejected this path and were followers of Christ; yet they, too, were often materialistic and worldly. They didn't pursue the hard work of detaching themselves from their passions so they could truly gaze upon God. Only the most committed Christians would be granted this blessing. After all, didn't Jesus say, "Blessed are the pure in heart, for they shall see God" (Matt. 5:8, NASB)? The vision of God restored to its bright splendor—that is the goal of Christian sanctification. The process is begun in this world, and completed in the next.

But how, exactly? What means has God provided to restore the soul's proper affections? Knowing we could not achieve salvation on our own, God sent his Son, the eternal Logos (or Word, John 1:1), to illumine the path to divinity. The Logos united himself to the one soul that hadn't cooled off in its love: the soul that indwelt Jesus of Nazareth. By this merciful and mysterious act of incarnation, the world above was joined to the lowly world of material things. Now, at last, there was someone in our midst who could call us back to our original blessed state. Through the inspired Gospels, as well as his ongoing ministry in our lives, Christ the Logos teaches virtue to our souls. The one who is "at the Father's side" (John 1:18) educates us in the knowledge (*gnosis*) of our Father God.

In his emphasis on virtuous knowledge, Origen captures a basic insight of the gnostics, yet without their heretical mythology and full-blown prejudice against physical matter. Origen's "educational" model of salvation is unlike Gnosticism because it insists on the importance of the cross and the empty tomb. Human beings are captive to the devil, who is lower than us and far more evil. The wicked serpent has enslaved the human race. As a remedy for this tragic development, Christ offers himself as a ransom-price to the Father, and to the devil as well, paying for sin and purchasing us back from our enslaver. The victory of the resurrection enables all people to participate in the living Logos. Through our free will, we can share in the wisdom the Logos has to offer. We can choose the path to holiness, gradually learning to discard our attachments to the flesh. As we train our eyes to look at Jesus, we begin to look at the One from whom he was sent. This is exactly what the end of the world holds for believers: the vision of God. Salvation on earth simply allows us to start upon that road earlier, at least to the degree that we are willing to take up such a high calling. The Christian's holy life is but practice for heaven.

New Trails and Dead Ends

With his grand Platonic scheme of perfection, fall, and return, Origen interpreted the big picture of eschatology in intellectual terms. Yet this doesn't mean he wasn't a traditional theologian. As a catechist in the school of Alexandria, Origen accepted the basic creedal doctrines of Christianity about the end times. Jesus Christ will return at his second coming to reward the righteous and defeat his enemies. Then there will be a final judgment, just as Christians have always believed (Matt. 25:31–46; John 5:28–29; 2 Cor. 5:10; Rev. 20:11–15). "The end of the world and the consummation will come when every soul shall be visited with the penalties due for its sins," Origen writes. "This time, when everyone shall pay what he owes, is known to God alone."[2] Yet Origen goes on to say, "We believe, however, that the goodness of God through Christ will restore his entire creation to one end, even his enemies being conquered and subdued."[3] This statement reminds us that God's cosmic purpose for the future is to restore things to the way they were at the outset—the great return to original perfection that the Christian Platonists had always emphasized.

---

2. *Princ.* 1.6.1 (Butterworth, 52). In describing his understanding of the creed, Origen affirms that the soul "will be rewarded according to its deserts after its departure from this world; for it will either obtain an inheritance of eternal life and blessedness, if its deeds shall warrant this, or it must be given over to the eternal fire and torments, if the guilt of its crimes shall so determine. Further, there will be a time for the resurrection of the dead, when this body, which is now 'sown in corruption,' shall 'rise in incorruption,' and that which is 'sown in dishonour' shall 'rise in glory' (1 Cor. 15:42–43)" (*First Principles* 1.Preface.5; Butterworth, 4).
3. *Princ.* 1.6.1 (Butterworth, 52).

At this point, perhaps you are remembering that in Origen's system, humans did not originally have physical bodies but were disembodied "intelligences." Since we are going to return to our original state, does that mean we will become pure minds once again? Or to put it more bluntly, did Origen reject the vital Christian doctrine of bodily resurrection? It depends on how one defines a "body." Origen suspects we will have bodies, but on the authority of the apostle Paul's description of "spiritual bodies" in 1 Corinthians 15:44, he assumes they won't be exactly like the earthly bodies that now weigh down the soul. Our future heavenly bodies will be "exceedingly refined and pure and splendid," and as such, they will be "a fitting habitation" for souls contemplating the exalted and majestic God for all eternity.[4] Although Origen considered these to be true human bodies, many of the later church fathers criticized him for describing the spiritual body in such sublime terms that it wasn't a physical body at all. To the critics, Origen's views sounded too much like the doctrines of the gnostic sects.

But one area in which almost all of church tradition has accepted the Origenistic perspective is his symbolic view of the thousand-year reign of Christ. Prior to Origen, some Bible interpreters understood Revelation 20 to teach a literal millennium during which Jesus would reign on earth. These believers, known as "chiliasts" from the Greek word *chilias* (one thousand), held that Christ would set up an earthly kingdom at his second coming to bless the faithful. The list of known chiliasts includes many important church fathers such as Papias, Justin Martyr, Irenaeus, Tertullian, and Lactantius. In fact, according to one detailed investigation of this topic, only four anonymous Christian texts and one known writer prior to the third century CE can definitely be called non-chiliast.[5] There is no doubt that literal millennialism was a common view in some parts of the ancient church.

Although there were other early writers who harbored skepticism about the doctrine of a thousand-year reign, it was Origen who first made a clear and forceful case against Christian millennialism. "Now some men," he writes, "who reject the labour of thinking and seek after the outward and literal meaning of the law, or rather give way to their own desires and lusts, disciples of the mere letter, consider that the promises of the future are to be looked for in the form

---

4.   *Princ.* 3.6.4 (Butterworth, 249–250).

5.   Charles E. Hill, *Regnum Caelorum: Patterns of Millennial Thought in Early Christianity* (Grand Rapids: Eerdmans, 2001), 271–272. The four anonymous texts are Shepherd of Hermas, *2 Clement, Epistle of the Apostles*, and *Apocalypse of Peter*; and the known writer is Clement of Alexandria.

of pleasure and bodily luxury."[6] Revelation 20 must instead be interpreted not as a time of physical eating and drinking, but as a symbol of the soul eternally feasting upon Christ, the bread of life.

Origen's heavy influence on later Greek writers assured that the Eastern Christian tradition would take a symbolic view of the millennium; and indeed, that is still the general position of the Orthodox Church today. However, Origen's views might not have taken hold in the Western tradition had they not been mediated by the preeminent father of the church, Augustine of Hippo. Though Augustine did hold to chiliasm for a time, he later changed to the symbolic view of Origen. Roman Catholicism has taught that view ever since, and so do most Protestant denominations today. The doctrine of a literal millennium wasn't held by any significant group of Christians until it began to be restored by some Anabaptists and Moravians in the 1500s, followed by the German Pietists of the 1600s. Though its popularity skyrocketed with the rise of dispensationalism in the 1800s, it remains a minority view in the contemporary church. Here is an area where Origen's doctrine of the future was highly influential on later Christians.

The exact opposite must be said about Origen's view of hell. Instead of being picked up by subsequent generations of theologians, it was criticized by nearly everyone and ended up causing Origen to be declared a heretic. Recall that Origen thought of the Christian life, or the process of sanctification, as "educational." Christ the Logos instructs the soul in virtue as we progress toward a more intimate relationship with God. Any attachment to the physical world blocks our vision like a speck of dirt in our spiritual eyes. Influenced by Platonist philosophy (though not without biblical support as well), Origen insisted the universe must end up where it started: with all of God's creatures—and indeed, the very cosmos itself (Eph. 1:10; Col. 1:19–20)—restored to harmony with the Creator. To bring this about, Origen thought of hell as God's remedial work on still-resistant sinners. Instead of literal fire and brimstone, hell is the purging, cleansing fire of God's own presence, a spiritual fire by which he purifies fallen souls from every worldly concern (1 Cor. 3:12–15). But if that is the case, asked Origen's critics, doesn't it indicate hell must be finite in duration?

The doctrine of an educational hell that leads sinners back into fellowship with God is known as *apokatastasis* or the "restoration of all things," a word mentioned only once in Scripture at Acts 3:21. The main biblical evidence for this doctrine is 1 Corinthians 15:24–28, which promises all evildoers will eventually

---

6. *Princ.* 2.11.2 (Butterworth, 147).

be obedient to Jesus. But does obedience mean full relational restoration? Since Origen is inconsistent in what he writes, modern scholars debate whether he believed in some type of universalism. A particularly thorny issue is the salvation of the devil. In *On First Principles,* Origen appears to entertain the possibility that demons could turn back to God.[7] Yet elsewhere he writes, "For that one who is said to have fallen from heaven, there will not be any conversion at the end of the age."[8] When accused during his lifetime of teaching the salvation of the devil, Origen denied it, claiming other people had misrepresented his position. "They declare that I hold … the devil is to be saved, a thing which no man can say even if he has taken leave of his senses and is manifestly insane."[9] However, even if Origen didn't teach the universal salvation of the devil or unbelievers, he certainly said enough controversial things to get himself in trouble.

At two different times after his death, once in the 390s and again in the mid-500s, the theologians of the ancient church became so concerned about certain aspects of Origen's thought that an "Origenist Controversy" developed. Various issues were on the table each time, such as Origen's doctrine of the Trinity, the value of the human body and sexuality, and how to practice the monastic life; but the topics that concern us here are the nature of resurrection bodies and the final destiny of all creatures. As we have already noted, these issues were problematic in Origen's eschatology because their heavily Platonic orientation seemed to diverge from scriptural teaching. The great scholar of Alexandria had drawn from his immense learning to help the church find a new way forward—but was it the right road?

Unfortunately, as time went on and the complicated church politics played out, Origen's views began to be exaggerated or subjected to the standards of later generations. In the end, a church council called by Emperor Justinian in 553 condemned several Origenistic ideas as heretical. This was somewhat unfair, since Origen's later followers had developed his thought in objectionable ways and went beyond what the master himself had stated. Nevertheless, we have

---

7. *Princ.* 1.6.3 (Butterworth, 56–57). There are complex manuscript issues here which make scholars uncertain about what Origen actually wrote. But he seems to suggest that at least some of the less evil demons could ascend to higher ranks and eventually find salvation.

8. *Commentary on Romans* 8.9.4, translated in Thomas P. Scheck, *Origen: Commentary on the Epistle to the Romans Books 1–5* (Washington, DC: Catholic University of America Press, 2001), 168.

9. Rufinus, *Concerning the Adulteration of the Works of Origen*, translated in Philip Schaff, et al., *Nicene and Post Nicene Fathers*, 2nd ser., vol. 3 (New York: Christian Literature Publishing Company, 1892), 423.

to acknowledge that Origen often ventured into new theological territory. He was willing to say things that had never before been expressed. While this can sometimes be fruitful, it can also lead to heresy. Thus, when it comes to certain aspects of Origen's eschatology, his speculative trailblazing finally hit a dead end within the church. It was up to his successors to determine how to navigate a better theological route.

Athanasius: Finding the Road Again

When Origen died from grievous injuries sustained in torture, the ancient church lost a precious jewel in its crown. Yet within fifty years of that loss, a new hero was born in the same city: Athanasius of Alexandria, one of the greatest theologians the Christian faith has ever produced. Athanasius was born around the turn of the fourth century, a pivotal moment in church history when persecution gave way to imperial favor. By the time he was a teenager, the empire that had once executed Christian leaders was instead offering them positions of rank and influence. Suddenly the rescue of Jesus's second coming seemed less urgent. End-times theology waned as the fourth-century church fathers leapt at the chance to investigate other pressing questions of doctrine.

As the bishop of the Roman Empire's third greatest city, Athanasius found himself embroiled in theological debates that had taken on political overtones. In particular, Athanasius is most often celebrated for defending the doctrine of the Trinity in the form that would become the orthodox consensus to this day. Yet despite his important contributions to Trinitarianism, the doctrine of the future did not go unmentioned in his writings. This great church father picked up several important strands of Origen's eschatology; but to his credit he freely discarded others. In so doing, Athanasius found a way forward the whole church could accept.

Athanasius rejected the exceptionally Platonic details of Origen's cosmology. He basically ignored Origen's theory that fallen "intelligences" had existed prior to their embodiment—an aberrant view that mainline Christian theology has never seen fit to embrace. Athanasius also held more traditional views than Origen about the second coming, future bodily resurrection, and final judgment. He believed resurrection bodies will be made of actual human flesh, as opposed to bodies so "spiritual" one has to wonder if they're even real. When Jesus Christ returns to the world in true flesh just as he came the first time, he will raise the dead into physical bodies capable of standing before his divine judgment seat. The righteous will enter a glorious new life while the wicked will be condemned to suffer in hell forever.[10] Although Athanasius shared Origen's opinion that Christ's kingdom will be spiritual instead of a pleasurable thousand-year reign on earth, he generally took a more physical view of future events than did his famous Alexandrian predecessor.

Even so, while Athanasius wasn't burdened by Origen's excessive speculations about the end times, his underlying eschatology was thoroughly Origenist in its shape. Along with many other church fathers, Athanasius carried forward an appropriately Platonic form of biblical eschatology that treats God's awe-inspiring glory as humanity's highest hope and greatest good. The perfection/fall/return cosmology that can be found in Plato is not entirely foreign to a Christian way of thinking. As Origen had realized and Athanasius agreed, this was an area where Greek philosophy dovetailed with Scripture. We humans need to overcome our fallen existence and find the way back to the worshipful life for which we were made. Only a mediator from above can deliver us from the worldly obsessions that so easily entangle us. Having tumbled so low, a spiritual ascent is required for our salvation. The beatific vision is attainable only after earthly concerns have been purged away—which is a difficult task for any Christian, requiring great moral effort. Such spirituality is known as "ascetic." We cannot grasp the eschatology of the Alexandrian fathers without understanding this concept.

Asceticism (from the Greek word for self-discipline, *askesis*) means learning to deny fleshly appetites so the soul can commune with God unhindered. As we have already seen, Origen suggested the believer's journey back to God begins in this life and continues in the next. Therefore, asceticism should characterize every Christian's life in anticipation of the future existence when the blessed will be freed from their bodily burdens. By the time Athanasius came on the theological scene about a century after Origen's heyday, the Christian ascetic movement was in full swing. In fact, Athanasius was one of its chief sponsors, for he wrote a book about a monk of the Egyptian desert that would have a lasting influence on the entire ascetic tradition. In the *Life of Antony* we meet a man who has already traveled far down the path of holiness. The noble monk Antony is depicted as a sojourner moving step by step toward his final destination of union with God. It is good, Antony says, for tempted monks to consider the future day of judgment when all sins will be revealed. Likewise the prudent monk should consider the heavenly rewards God has in store for his followers.

---

10. *On the Incarnation* 56. Anonymous translator, *St. Athanasius: On the Incarnation* (Crestwood, NY: St. Vladimir's Seminary Press, 1996), 95-96.

"Let us not consider, when we look at the world, that we have given up things of some greatness," Antony advises, "for even the entire earth is itself quite small in relation to all of heaven."[11] We can take nothing with us after death, so why not detach ourselves from material possessions and focus on lasting Christian virtues instead? Such insights from the saintly Antony reflect Athanasius's own doctrine of the future as well.

All this talk about striving for virtue and journeying to heaven might make us suppose the Alexandrian fathers believed in works salvation, as if humans can attain eternal life by their own merits. Nothing could be further from the truth. The constant focus of the ancient Christians was the person and work of Jesus Christ. Yet the precise nature of his salvation was often understood in different ways. Origen had explained salvation as the restoration of an intellectual relationship between God and humans, thereby setting his eschatology into the framework of Greek philosophy. Athanasius continued the important theme of cosmic restoration, not by rejecting its Platonic mode of expression, but by subordinating it to what the Bible has to say about Christ's incarnation. Whereas for Origen, the Logos took on a body so he could educate mankind about the right way to go, for Athanasius the Logos became flesh so he could conquer sin on the cross and join believers to his own resurrection life. This wasn't something Origen would have denied, of course. Yet it was Athanasius's lasting contribution to eschatology that he restored the historical work of Jesus Christ as the cornerstone of our final restoration.

As can be seen especially in his book *On the Incarnation*, Athanasius celebrated the real flesh of the incarnate Jesus—a true human who was born of a woman to save a lost human race. "[T]aking a body like our own, because all our bodies were liable to the corruption of death, He surrendered His body to death in place of all, and offered it to the Father. This he did out of sheer love for us."[12] Salvation consists of the glorious God stooping low to rescue his creatures, joining them in their frailty, taking on the limitations of fleshly existence. And what is the greatest limitation of all? It is death, the ever-present enemy of the human race, the evil power that if left unchecked will shatter our communal existence and launch us into non-being. Therefore, the God-Man took death into his own self. He faced it, embraced it, endured it—then destroyed it by the

---

11. *Life of Antony* 17. Robert C. Gregg, *Athanasius: The Life of Antony and the Letter to Marcellinus* (New York: Paulist Press, 1980), 44.
12. *Inc.* 8.

power of his resurrection. In so doing, our gracious Savior opened the way for humans to ascend back into relationship with God. The future is bright for those joined to Christ.

Alexandria's Lasting Contribution

For both of the great Alexandrian theologians described in this chapter, eschatology is a restoration of the world to its original perfection. Yet Athanasius appreciated (in ways Origen did not) that Christian salvation is eminently *physical*. Our bodies matter to the Creator God, so we can expect them to be eschatologically transformed along with our souls. Athanasius derived this point from his profound understanding of the incarnation. The heavenly Logos was, in a great mystery, made flesh in our midst. Drawing from previous thinkers such as Irenaeus of Lyon, Athanasius claimed it is our intimate union with the Incarnate One—the man Jesus of Nazareth who is simultaneously the Son of God—that brings about human salvation. With his clear understanding that the Logos assumed flesh, Athanasius perceived that the salvation of our bodies is just as much a part of our final destiny as the exaltation of our souls. We will not end up as mystical spirits encased in pseudo-bodies contemplating God in a purely intellectual fashion. Rather, we will be real persons, raised anew into bodies of flesh, identifiable as ourselves yet no longer plagued by sin. When the final trumpet sounds, the graves of believers will break open and our loved ones will come forth with a shout. The sting of death will be gone, its supposed victory overturned in defeat. And we know all this because of Jesus Christ. His resurrection was bodily, just like ours will be. He himself is the firstfruits of our salvation. The empty tomb is the guarantee that our faithful God will raise us up in both body and soul.

The overarching trajectory of Alexandrian eschatology reminds us that our final goal and highest good is the direct and unobstructed presence of God—Father, Son, and Holy Spirit in full communion with us. Worshipful contemplation of the Lord is all that will ultimately satisfy the human race. We were created for such a relationship, and we long for its restoration. Yet while Origen expressed this perspective more thoughtfully and elegantly than any Christian before him, he remained, unfortunately, too indebted to his cultural situation to accept just how *physically* the Scriptures speak about our eternal hope. A few decades later, Athanasius found himself in a better position to view the theological landscape through the lens of the incarnation. With the God-Man always squarely in his sights, the bishop of Alexandria helped locate a viable theological road for later generations to follow. Believers of every age have recognized that the Christian life is an arduous journey. The pilgrimage to Mount Zion is hard. Even so, it should never be pursued without hope, for Christ our Savior has come to us in grace. And although we now, like the ancients before us, can only look through a glass darkly, we know the day is coming when we shall see our God face to face.

THE DOCTRINE OF THE FUTURE IN AUGUSTINE

Jonathan P. Yates

> The forgiveness of sins in this life is chiefly because of the future
> judgment ... everything that is done in the sacraments of salva-
> tion is concerned more with the hope of good things to come
> than with retaining or gaining good things in the present.
> —Augustine, *Enchiridion*, 66[1]

Augustine of Hippo (354–430)—a title assigned after he was ordained bishop of Hippo Regius, an important (and relatively wealthy) port city in late antique Roman North Africa, probably in 396—is the single most important and influential post-biblical Christian theologian in the western tradition. In more historical terms, this sentiment has been expressed by noting that "from the Middle Ages to the present, Augustine has remained the most prominent and most widely studied author in western Christianity, second only to biblical authors such as Paul."[2] More impressive, if also more sweeping, are the words of the late Sir Henry Chadwick, a scholar of Augustine renowned for his English translation of *Confessions*, who once labeled Augustine as "the greatest single mind and influence in Christian history."[3]

---

1. For this translation, see *WSA* I/8, 312. *WSA* is an abbreviation for the series *The Works of Saint Augustine: A Translation for the 21st Century*, ed. J. E. Rotelle (New York: New City Press, 1990 ff.).
2. H. R. Drobner, "Studying Augustine: An Overview of Recent Research," in *Augustine and His Critics: Essays in Honour of Gerald Bonner*, ed. R. Dodaro and G. Lawless (London and New York: Routledge, 2000), 17.
3. H. Chadwick, s.v. "Augustine," *A Dictionary of Biblical Interpretation*, ed. R. J. Coggins and J. L. Houlden (London: SCM Press, 1990).

To these profound assessments many more could easily be added. But the point is probably clear that, when it comes to western theology and to discussions of the development of Christian doctrine—including Christian eschatology[4]—Augustine is the proverbial elephant in the room. You can pretend he is not there, or that his existence is irrelevant, but in practice, this pretense is exceedingly hard to sustain.

To this should also be added that we know more about Augustine's life and have more words from Augustine's pen than we know or have from any other figure of the premodern period.[5] Scholars have reckoned that, even if we limit ourselves to those texts of Augustine's that have been preserved (and it is certain that many, including multiple thousands of his sermons, have been lost), we possess approximately 5.5 million of his own words! To put that into perspective, it has also been reckoned that, if you count up all the words in all the works that survive from the pen of Shakespeare, that is, from his (at least) thirty-seven plays and all of his poetry, we still have approximately *nine times more* material from Augustine than we have from Shakespeare. It is no wonder that Isidore of Seville, a Spanish bishop who died approximately two hundred years after Augustine, could feel justified in writing "the one who claims to have read all of Augustine, he is a liar."[6]

In light of the enormity of Augustine's influence and literary output, what follows will necessarily be a selective overview of his thinking about time, about God's plan for his created order, and about God's plan for the future of humanity as reflected in a few of his most influential writings.

---

4. Cf. B. Daley, *The Hope of the Early Church: A Handbook of Patristic Eschatology*, rev. ed. (Peabody, MA: Hendrickson Publishers, 2003), 131: "Without a doubt the theologian who has most influenced the development of Latin eschatology . . . [is] Augustine of Hippo. . . . In Augustine's reinterpretation of early Christian hope for the world and the individual, the Western Church found a balanced, sober, yet profoundly inviting theological structure for articulating its own expectations."

5. To give but two examples, (1) while in his forties and soon after he became a bishop, Augustine penned his *Confessions*, a thirteen-book masterpiece that includes a significant amount of autobiographical data that most scholars see as generally reliable and (2) very shortly after his death in 430, his longtime friend and fellow North African bishop, Possidius, composed a *uita* or "life" of Augustine that also includes much information that would otherwise remain unknown.

6. Isidore's original Latin is: "Mentitur qui te totam legisse fatetur." Note that, when taken in context, Isidore seems to have been referring to the difficulty of *obtaining* Augustine's works, not just to reading them all. Nevertheless, the quotation indicates that Isidore knew how prolific an author Augustine had been. For more on this, see J. Kelley, "Carolingian Era, Late," ed. Allan D. Fitzgerald, ed. *Augustine through the Ages An Encyclopedia* (Grand Rapids: Eerdmans, 1999).

Augustine on Time, History, and Eternity

Augustine was a man profoundly concerned with time and history, both of which he regarded as parts of God's creation.[7] In fact, it is impossible to understand Augustine's vision of the future without understanding something about his thinking about time, since "the key to understanding Augustine's eschatological hope is to understand the sharp, metaphysically grounded distinction he draws between time and eternity—between human existence now in history . . . and the final existence we long for . . . united in stable knowledge and love with God, our source and our goal."[8]

Although it is not a philosophical exercise in the strict sense, Book 11 of *Confessions* is an important "go-to" text for understanding Augustine's thinking about time.[9] In Book 11, Augustine investigates time for both theological and exegetical ends: It is theological because "the discussion of time serves as an exploration of the mystery of the Incarnation"; it is exegetical because it is devoted to the interpretation of Genesis 1:1. Indeed, for Augustine Genesis 1:1's "In the beginning (*in principio*) God created the heavens and the earth" should be read primarily as claiming that it was in and through Christ, the principle (*principium*) and beginning and source of all that exists, that God, the Creator of all things, created the heavens and the earth.[10]

Also important for understanding Augustine's view on time is the fact that, for profound theological reasons, he thought time, generally speaking,

---

7. See, e.g., *conf.* 11.13.15: "You are the originator and creator of all ages," "You have made time itself" and 11.14.17: "you made time itself. No times are coeternal with you since you are permanent. If they were permanent, they would not be times." For these translations, see Augustine, *Confessions*, trans. H. Chadwick (Oxford: Oxford University Press, 1991), 229–230. Note that throughout this chapter references to the works of Augustine are abbreviated according to the system developed by the *Augustinus-Lexikon*. The *A-L* abbreviations list is available at: http://www.augustinus.de/bwo/dcms/sites/bistum/extern/zfa/lexikon/Werkever-zeichnisAL3.pdf. For a helpful discussion of *conf.* 11, see R. P. Kennedy, "Book Eleven: The *Confessions* as Eschatological Narrative," in *A Reader's Companion to Augustine's Confessions*, ed. K. Paffenroth and R.P. Kennedy (Louisville, KY: Westminster John Knox Press, 2003), 167–183.

8. Daley, *The Hope of the Early Church*, 131–32.

9. Cf. Augustine, *Confessions*, 230 and n.19.

10. Cf. *conf.* 11.3.5-9.11, especially 11.8.10-11.9.11, and 11.30.40. In fact, for Augustine, because of its dual nature as both human and divine, the Bible provides a helpful illustration of how time and eternity are both crucial parts of God's plan. See Kennedy, "Book Eleven: The *Confessions* as Eschatological Narrative," 183: "The very fact that the words of Scripture are both temporal and yet the perfect expression of God's eternal will shows that the incomparability between time and eternity does not imply any opposition between them."

must be linear rather than cyclical.[11] In other words, for Augustine, time has a distinct beginning and a distinct end; no individual period of time—whether long or short—would ever be repeated.[12] Certainly not the least of his reasons for this view is his aforementioned conviction regarding the centrality of the Incarnation for the Christian faith.[13] For Augustine, "the coming of Christ was also the ultimate refutation of any theory of cycles within human history, which would necessarily imply that . . . Christ would have to die over and over."[14] Moreover, in Augustine's view, any type of cyclical history "would be the very antithesis of the hope and the promise [of Christianity] if . . . the saints could look forward only to losing it all and beginning the whole wretched cycle [of human history] over again."[15]

Although Augustine readily concedes that, by convention, we measure time by the movement of bodies and especially by that of the heavenly ones, he is adamant that this is not the best way to understand time.[16] Augustine reasoned that "past and future do not exist in external things,"[17] but only within us, because it is we who recall something that is past or expect something that we think will come to be. Strictly speaking, the past no longer exists except in our memories and the future does not yet exist except in our "premeditations."[18] Even more importantly, Augustine reasoned that just

---

11. Daley, *The Hope of the Early Church*, 150. This is not to say that Augustine did not realize that some aspects of human history were repeatable. He even seems to have believed that certain negative events that were prophesied in apocalyptic books like Revelation might be repeated as a way of teaching the faithful not to love this life and the present world too much. See K. Pollmann, "Moulding the Present: Apocalyptic as Hermeneutics in *City of God* 21–22," in *History, Apocalypse, and the Secular Imagination: New Essays on Augustine's City of God*, ed. M. Vessey, K. Pollmann, and A. Fitzgerald (Bowling Green, OH: Philosophy Documentation Center, 1999), 179.

12. Ibid., 132: "For Augustine, the eschaton is not simply the end of this present age and the beginning of a new one, but the end of history itself and the beginning of the 'eternal Sabbath,' when God, who is beyond all time and temporal succession, will 'rest in us.'"

13. J. Pelikan, *The Mystery of Continuity: Time and History, Memory and Eternity in the Thought of Saint Augustine*, The Richard Lectures for 1984–85 (Charlottesville: The University Press of Virginia, 1986), 39: Augustine "learned . . . to cherish time and history as the locus of the incarnation of the eternal Son of God within the temporal process."

14. Ibid., *The Mystery of Continuity*, 49, citing from *ciu.* 12.13.

15. Ibid., 50. Cf. Daley, *The Hope of the Early Church*, 150: "the only genuine meaning of human history is to be found in God's eternity."

16. *Conf.* 11.23.29–11.24.31. Cf. Augustine, *Confessions*, 237 and n.25: "Time is not identical with the units by which we ordinarily measure it."

17. *Conf.* 11.20.26. See Augustine, *Confessions*, 235; cf. Kennedy, "Book Eleven: The *Confessions* as Eschatological Narrative," 178.

18. See *conf.* 11.18.23: Augustine's word here is "praemeditatio." Cf. Augustine, *Confessions*, 234.

measuring time would ultimately be unsatisfying since "external, physical time cannot provide a meaningful account of time; it has no significance because it is simply the tendency of things to undergo change."[19]

Given that Augustine has put so much effort into thinking about time, it should come as no surprise that he also was concerned with eternity. Most people generally assume that eternity is simply time without end. Augustine would disagree with this since, in his view, the two concepts were distinct by their very nature. For Augustine, eternity is not just time without end; rather, it is "a total freedom from duration, extension or sequence; it is the utterly simple, unchanging present of God's being."[20] Indeed, in Augustine's view, "the difference between the continuity of eternity in God and the continuity of time lay in this, that, since it was a creature, 'time does not exist without some movement and transition, while in eternity there is no change.'"[21]

Augustine's "Unsystematic System"

Augustine was not a systematic theologian; that is, he never attempted to account for all the major doctrines of Christianity within one framework. On the contrary, Augustine was first and foremost a pastor, a priest, and a bishop, who often wrote in order to think and to help others understand what to confess.[22] Moreover, much of what he wrote was in response to a particular question that had been posed to him or an issue that had arisen either inside or outside the life and faith of the church. This fact, however, does not mean that his thought, even at the "big picture" level, is incoherent. The more one reads Augustine, the more one can appreciate just how well the vast majority of what he writes does come together to form an "unsystematic system" and how even his eschatological thinking is grounded in it. Although abbreviated, what follows is intended as an introduction to that "system."

Although it is often assumed that Augustine invented the doctrine of original sin—that is, the doctrine that when Adam (and Eve) sinned in the

---

19. Kennedy, "Book Eleven: The *Confessions* as Eschatological Narrative," 178.
20. Daley, *The Hope of the Early Church*, 132.
21. Pelikan, *The Mystery of Continuity*, 38, quoting *ciu.* 11.6. Cf. also *conf.* 9.10.24 where true wisdom is said to lack "past and future ... since it is eternal." See Augustine, *Confessions*, 171.
22. For an example with eschatological overtones, see *ep.* 92 (*WSA* II/1, 371–4). Augustine addressed this letter to Italica, a recent widow. In it, he offers her consolation for her loss but does so by reminding her of her hope in the next life. This letter also demonstrates a stage in Augustine's thinking about what it means to "see" God, a topic discussed in greater detail below.

Garden of Eden, that sin alienated Adam, Eve, and all of their naturally born descendants, not to mention the created order,[23] from God—this is not exactly the case. As several studies have shown (and as Augustine himself claimed with at least some plausibility), the assertions that would comprise the doctrine of original sin—even if their implications had never been fully worked out—existed before Augustine (re-)joined the church. What Augustine did do, more than anyone who preceded him, was to clarify and work out this fundamental doctrine's implications. To use a metaphor, Augustine took many more or less stable "bricks" that he found in the Bible, in the writings of Christians who had gone before him, and within the Christianity with which he was catechized, and assembled them into an impressive and profound new "building." It must also be remembered that, as noted above, Augustine was serving as a pastor and bishop for the majority of the time that he was developing his theology and that these positions allowed him both in-depth and daily exposure to the reality of human sin and imperfection. Suffice it to say that Augustine's belief in the doctrine of original sin, in many ways, provided the basis for his most influential theological views and, by extension, his vision for the future.[24]

For Augustine, all naturally born human beings enter the world as part of what he, using vocabulary from Romans 9, labeled as the "already condemned mass or lump (the *massa damnata*)." This made sense because, for Augustine, when Adam sinned we all were, in a sense, in Adam; we were all part of the "lump of clay" that Adam, who himself had been made from the earth (cf. Gen. 2:7), represented as the father of all human beings. Therefore, when Adam chose to sin and, as a result, both alienated himself from God and altered his "very good" (cf. Gen. 1:31) nature for the worse, he also alienated all of us—that is, all of Adam's naturally born descendants—from God,

---

23. Cf., e.g., Rom. 8:21–23.
24. For Augustine's theology of the creation and fall of humanity, see Books 12–14 of *ciu.*, which, as M. Ludlow, "Augustine on the Last Things" in *T&T Clark Companion to Augustine and Modern Theology*, ed. C. C. Pecknold and T. Toom (London: Bloomsbury, 2013), 92, notes, "are crucial for understanding [his] eschatology." Augustine's theology of the creation and fall is crucial precisely because, in Augustine's mature thinking, both the existence and inheritance of original sin has left humanity incapable of determining a positive eschatological destiny without gratuitous grace in general and without the gratuitous graces of election and perseverance unto salvation in particular. In a word, for Augustine, humanity in its current state is impotent before God and unable even to initiate—much less carry out—the process of salvation.

and altered all of our natures for the worse.[25] In short, "as we come from Adam's flesh, we share Adam's fate."[26]

For Augustine, it follows from this that we stand in need of being saved from both sin and its consequent guilt. Crucially, it is Augustine's answer as to exactly how and how frequently this happens that points us toward the central idea of his teaching about salvation and the future of the human race. For Augustine, any human being who is saved from her naturally born status as part of the *massa damnata* is saved precisely because God took the initiative to apply the grace that Christ merited through his life, passion, death, and resurrection to her status before God. It is no exaggeration to say that Augustine was completely enthralled by the idea of God's grace and the fact that, whenever it is dispensed, it is God who does the dispensing.[27] Augustine never tired of writing that God's grace, which he understood as God's unmerited favor, is not true grace unless it has been freely given by God.[28] For Augustine, then, because we are powerless to escape this inherited condemnation on our own, salvation can only come to us as recipients of God's fully gratuitous grace. That is, God must take the initiative and apply his grace to us in a way that frees us both from the guilt of sin that we inherited from Adam and from the guilt of all the sins that we have committed during the time we lived in our alienated state, while also beginning to heal and to restore our sin-damaged nature.

An obvious question that follows from this is: Does God supply this absolutely necessary grace to everyone? Augustine does not think so. For him, those who receive grace, a group that Augustine will label as "the elect," will be saved by God's grace precisely because he elected or chose them for salvation in eternity

---

25. J. Bowlin, "Hell and the Dilemmas of Intractable Alienation" in *Augustine's City of God: A Critical Guide*, ed. J. Wetzel (Cambridge/New York: Cambridge University Press, 2012), 196: "As Adam's nature changed when grace was withdrawn, it's that changed nature that we inherit. As God would not have created us disobedient to ourselves and thus prone to moral weakness, this inheritance must come as punishment for the sins of Adam that we share as kin, first in origin and now in consequence."

26. Ibid., 196.

27. Not surprisingly—and especially from the late 390s—Augustine routinely described his own faith and relationship to God in these terms. To cite just a few examples, note *conf.* 5.7.13's "How can salvation be obtained except through your hand remaking what you once made?," which appears in the midst of Augustine's discussion of how God was providentially at work to compel him to leave Africa for Italy, and *conf.* 11.2.4's "By [Christ] you sought us when we were not seeking you." See Augustine, *Confessions*, 80 and 223 respectively.

28. For Augustine "the term grace ... refers to that divine operation in angels and humans through which they are moved to know and love God." See C. E. Fitzgerad, ed., *Augustine through the Ages: An Encyclopedia* (Grand Rapids: Eerdmans, 1999), s.v. "grace" by J. Patout Burns.

past.[29] Augustine rejected out of hand the view that God's electing was a result of his foreknowledge—that is, his decision to look down the corridors of time and see who would respond in faith to the message of the gospel and, as a result of their faith, go on to live well and obediently.[30] Those who do not receive grace live out their days as part of the *massa* and, as a result, die in the alienation that Adam's sin and their own subsequent sinful choices has generated for them. Augustine is equally insistent that the reason why God elected some and left others to their own devices is, from the limits of the human perspective, unfathomable.[31]

Augustine states very clearly that he does not know how many human beings will be saved by God.[32] He does, however, say that, given the gravity and seriousness of the problem of sin and his own empirical observation of humanity, he expects the saved to be only a very small number of the immense hoard who had lived before him and who would eventually be born.[33] Also important is that, for Augustine, there really is no such thing as what some call "assurance of salvation." That is, Augustine did not believe that it was ever possible to know with certainty that anyone, even oneself, was actually saved.[34] He saw this as both arrogant and dangerous precisely because it could, and usually would, breed pride.[35]

However, in practical terms, Augustine is just like most of us. It is easy to find passages in his works in which he speaks of this or that person, especially

---

29. Augustine sometimes described the elect in terms of their citizenship in "the city of God" which is "the elect city, the predestined remnant, chosen by God from eternity and for eternity." Throughout history, God's grace and mercy have always been the unique means of entry into that domain "from its very first member, Abel, who was 'the stranger in this world, the citizen of the City of God, predestined by grace, elected by grace, by grace a stranger below, and by grace a citizen above.'" See Pelikan, *The Mystery of Continuity*, 44, quoting from *ciu.* 17.5 and 15.1.

30. This should not be read as if Augustine denied that God possessed foreknowledge. On the contrary Augustine repeatedly affirmed God's ability to foreknow. See, e.g., *ciu.* 5.9–10 in Augustine, *Concerning the City of God against the Pagans*, trans. H. Bettenson (London/New York: Penguin Books, 2003), 190–95: "To acknowledge the existence of God, while denying him any prescience of events, is the most obvious madness" (cf. 190).

31. Augustine frequently cites Rom. 11:33 in support of exactly this sentiment.

32. *Simpl.* 1.2.22. For an English trans. see *Augustine Earlier Writings*, Library of Christian Classics 6, ed. J.H.S. Burleigh (London: SCM Press, 1953), 405–6. For the claim that the number is certain from God's perspective, see *corrept.* 13.39 (*WSA* I/26, 136).

33. *Ciu.* 21.12 is particularly clear: "Now there are many more condemned by vengeance than are released by mercy; and the reason for this is that it should in this way be made plain what was the due of all mankind." See Augustine, *Concerning the City of God against the Pagans*, 989. See also *corrept.* 10.28 (*WSA* I/26, 128), *ep.*190.12 (*WSA* II/3, 268) and *s.* 111.3 (*WSA* III/4, 143).

34. See, e.g., *perseu.* 22.62 (*WSA* I/26, 233) and *corrept.* 13.40 (*WSA* I/26, 137).

35. See, e.g., *corrept.* 13.40 (*WSA* I/26, 137).

if the person in question had been an apostle, a saint, a martyr, or some combination of the three, as actually having been saved. Augustine can also come very close to numbering himself among the elect, even though he was still alive and, according to his own definition, could not yet know with certainty that he would persevere all the way to the end.[36]

Augustine on the Resurrection and the Resurrected Body

For Augustine, everyone who has ever lived will be resurrected from the dead and, indeed, "the resurrection of the dead is the very center of eschatological transformation, the dividing line between time and eternity."[37] To this principle, there will be no exceptions nor will the lifespan of the person in question be important. Even stillborn infants, abortions, and fetuses who die in the womb will be resurrected: "It seems to me to be too presumptuous to say that fetuses that are cut out and removed from the womb, lest by remaining there dead they might also kill their mothers, have never been alive. Now once a person begins to live, from that moment he is already able to die; and I cannot find a reason why a dead person, however death has happened to him, should be excluded from the resurrection of the dead."[38] Given the antipathy or, at best, ambivalence that many ancient intellectuals (especially those of a "Platonist" persuasion who stressed the non-material nature of ultimate reality) had for the ever-changing and illness-prone physical body, it is helpful to be reminded just how radical the Christian assertion that the physical body would be resurrected was in that context.[39]

---

36. Briefly put, because no human being could know that she or anyone else was certainly among the elect, Augustine's doctrine of "perseverance" asserted that the claim that an individual was one of the elect could only be made with plausibility after that individual had died "in Christ." In other words, to be saved one had to persevere "in faith in him" until the moment of death. This was both a sign that one was among the elect and a sign that one had received what Augustine referred to as the gratuitously given gift or grace of perseverance. For Augustine's explanations of this important term, see, e.g., *ciu.* 21.25; *perseu.* 1.1; 6.10; 14.35; and 17.41. At the same time, it is precisely because the identity of the elect is unknown that we should pray for this gift to be given to ourselves and to others. See *perseu.* 2.3 and 7.15.

37. Fitzgerald, *Augustine through the Ages: An Encyclopedia*, s.v. "Resurrection" by B. E. Daley.

38. *Ench.* 86 (*WSA* I/8, 324). See also *ciu.* 22.12–21; and cf. D. Hunter, "Augustine on the Body," in *A Companion to Augustine*, ed. M. Vessey (Chichester, West Sussex/Malden, MA: Wiley-Blackwell, 2012), 362.

39. This antipathy or "ridicule" was well known to Augustine. In *ciu.* 22.11–12, for example, he addresses it head-on.

While Augustine seems to have initially wanted to spiritualize the Christian doctrine of the resurrection, by ca. 400, "he began to emphasize that it was the same body that was buried that would be raised again."[40] More impressively, by the time he penned the last books of *The City of God* in the 420s, he "had come to conceive of salvation not as a flight from the body, but rather as an intensification of bodily experience made possible by the incorruptible union of body and soul."[41] As we will see below, it is this idea of an ultimately "incorruptible union" between the body and soul that, for Augustine, went a long way toward explaining how hell could include both psychological and physical pain and why heaven would be populated by the elect in resurrected bodies.[42]

For Augustine, at the resurrection all physical defects, for example, all babies that are born "seriously deformed," all "Siamese twins," and all persons who "are said to be physically deformed because they have an extra part to their bodies or one missing or some major deformity," will not rise in the condition in which they were born but "rather . . . with their nature healed and rectified"; indeed, everyone, even those who will rise only to be "punished with the devil and his angels," "will be restored to a normal human form by the resurrection so that each soul will have its own body" and so that everyone "will have complete human bodies."[43] Better still, in Augustine's view, all bodies will be restored "to the stature of the full maturity of Christ," that is, to the condition that obtains when one is in the prime of life, or about thirty years of age.[44] The one possible exception to this principle is the bodies of the true martyrs. Just as was the case with Christ when he appeared to his disciples in a resurrected body but with his wounds intact,[45] Augustine speculated that the scars and wounds of the genuine martyrs would still be present on their resurrected bodies precisely because they

40. D. Hunter, "Augustine on the Body," 361. However, in keeping with his figurative exegesis of Rev. 20:1–6, Augustine spiritualized his interpretation of the "first resurrection" (cf. Rev. 20:5–6), claiming that it stood for the "dying and rising" that happened when one is baptized. Cf. Rom. 6:3–5 and Col. 2:12.

41. Ibid.

42. Ibid.: "Both eternal pain and eternal happiness required a body that would no longer be subject to corruption and death." Eternal happiness was conceived as possible precisely because Augustine's view of "the risen body was based on a reversal of the effects of original sin" including a re-harmonization of the relationship between the soul and the body. Similarly, the eternal pain will be possible and, indeed, "made endless by the enforced unity of body and soul." Cf. *ciu.* 21.3.

43. *Ench.* 92 and 87 (*WSA* I/8, 326 and 324).

44. Cf. D. Hunter, "Augustine on the Body," 362, citing from *ciu.* 22.15.

45. Cf., e.g., John 20:24–29.

would not be defects: "For in those wounds there will be no deformity, but only dignity, and the beauty of their valor will shine out, a beauty in the body and yet not of the body."[46]

Closely connected to this is the fact that all of us trim our hair and must regularly cut our nails. We also lose hair when we bathe and our skin cells are constantly dying or otherwise being rubbed off. Do all of these things constitute a genuine part of us?[47] If the hair of the typical human being grows at a rate of one-half an inch per month, then it grows about six inches per year. Now consider a man who never goes bald and who lives to be one hundred years old: By the time he is one hundred, he will have generated approximately fifty feet of hair from his head. When this man is raised from the dead, will he rise with all that hair reattached? Although not usually discussed today, the relative novelty of the claim that, like Christ, everyone would rise from the dead at some point in the future necessitated that the earliest Christians think such problems through. Augustine asserts that the "earthly material that becomes a corpse on the departure of the soul will not be restored at the resurrection in such a way that those substances that seep away . . . will necessarily return to the same part of the body as they were in before. Otherwise if all the hair were to receive back what has been removed by frequent cutting, and the nails all that has been removed so often from them by paring, anybody who thought about it would form a picture of extreme and unsuitable ugliness, and be led to disbelief in the resurrection of the flesh."[48]

In sum, for Augustine, speculating about the exact nature of the resurrected body may well be both interesting and worthwhile, but the controlling principle that must never be left out of the mix is that God, "the one who was able to make what he willed even out of nothing," will reconstitute our bodies in a way that is both "suitable" and "decorous"; indeed, all resurrected bodies will be "beautiful."[49]

---

46. *Ciu.* 22.19 and 22.30. See Augustine, *Concerning the City of God against the Pagans*, 1062, 1088. Augustine reckoned that those who had been beheaded or lost a limb as they suffered for Christ would have those losses restored for the sake of beauty and symmetry. They would, however, receive scars at the site of the loss so that all would know what had happened. Also helpful here is how pithily he expressed this idea in some of his sermons: the martyrs' "torments (*tormenta*)" would become that which gave them magnificence and honor, that is, their "*ornamenta.*" See *s.* 280.5 (*WSA* III/8, 75) and *s.* 328.6 (*WSA* III/9, 179).

47. Cf. also Luke 21:18: "Yet not a hair of your head will perish."

48. *Ench.* 88 (*WSA* I/8, 324–5).

49. *Ench.* 89–90 (*WSA* I/8, 325).

AUGUSTINE ON CHRIST'S RETURN
AND THE MILLENNIUM

One of the most significant aspects of Augustine's vision of the future is his skepticism regarding our ability to know much about how or when it would unfold. That is, while Augustine very clearly confessed his belief in the existence of predictive prophecy and in such prophesied events as the return of Christ and the last judgment, he did not believe that it was possible for us to speak about these or other future events in detail, much less to determine exactly when they are going to occur. From Augustine's perspective, both eschatology in general and the apocalyptic events described in Revelation in particular "escape our powers of prediction precisely because they form the frontier between time and eternity."[50] Augustine preached sermons in which he advocates this position early in his career. The following, which is from his *Exposition of Psalm 6*, dates from about 391:

> People believe that [Christ's] coming, reckoning the years from Adam, will be after seven thousand years. This means that seven thousand years pass like seven days, and then that time comes like the eighth day. But the Lord himself said, "It is not for you to know the times or seasons which the Father has appointed by his own authority" (cf. Acts 1:7), and "No one knows the day, or the hour: no angel, no power, nor even the Son, but the Father alone" (cf. Mark 13:32). There is also that other statement, that the day of the Lord comes like a thief (cf. 1 Thess. 5:2; 2 Peter 3:10). These all show quite clearly that nobody should arrogate to himself knowledge of that time, simply by counting up the years.[51]

---

50. Daley, *The Hope of the Early Church*, 136. While never doubting its canonicity, Augustine changed his attitude toward Revelation as he grew older. The turning point seems to have been at or before 400 and to have followed his initial exposure to the exegetical practice of a North African lay person of the previous generation named Tyconius. Tyconius provided Augustine with a principle-based way to interpret Revelation allegorically. In short, although Augustine did not follow Tyconius blindly, Tyconius's approach made that difficult text accessible to Augustine. Cf. P.B. Harvey, Jr., "Approaching the Apocalypse: Augustine, Tyconius and John's Revelation," *Augustinian Studies* 30/2 (1999): 133–152. Cf. Augustine, *Confessions*, 222 and n.5: "Echoes of the Apocalypse of John pervade books XI–XIII [of *Confessions*]."

51. *En. Ps.* 6.1 (*WSA* III/15, 104).

Toward the end of his life, Augustine can be found offering similar advice to a friend who had prompted him about how to balance expectant hope for Christ's return with the appropriate amount of caution. This is one area in which Augustine apparently did not mind being what we would call an agnostic:

> Hence, one who says that the Lord will come sooner says what is more desirable but is in danger if mistaken. . . . But the one who says that the Lord will come later, and yet believes, hopes, and loves his coming, even if he is mistaken about his slowness, is of course mistaken, though happily so. . . . But the one who admits that he does not know which of these is true hopes for the former, endures the latter, and is mistaken in nothing, because he does not either affirm or deny any of them. I beg you not to look down on me for being such a person.[52]

In addition to the timing of Christ's return, Augustine also had doubts about traditional claims regarding the nature of Christ's kingdom and the prevalent belief that it would last for exactly one thousand years.[53] A late and important passage which makes this clear is *The City of God* 20.7–9. Here Augustine offers an extended figurative commentary on several of the details of Revelation 20:1–6. In Chapter 9, Augustine explicitly says that the "thousand years" denotes not literally one thousand years but "the period beginning with Christ's first coming" and includes all the years of the Christian era, however long it will last.[54] This, in turn, means that, for Augustine, the millennium is also "an allegorical representation of the historical church in its present state,"[55] even though he is equally clear that one

---

52. *Ep.* 199.13.54 (*WSA* II/3, 353–54).
53. While it is possible to find "traces . . . of older millenaristic ideas" in some of Augustine's earliest surviving works, by ca. 400 "even the residual echoes of millenaristic ideas . . . finally disappear." See R. Markus, *Saeculum: History and Society in the Thought of St Augustine* (Cambridge: Cambridge University Press, 1970), 19–20.
54. Cf. Markus, *Saeculum*, 19–21: Augustine's "attack on [millennial thinking] displays one of the fundamental themes of his reflection on history: that since the coming of Christ, until the end of the world, all history is homogeneous, that it cannot be mapped out in terms of a pattern drawn from sacred history, that it can no longer contain decisive turning-points endowed with a significance in sacred history." J.K. Coyle has gone so far as to conclude that "no evidence suggests that Augustine ever subscribed to a literal thousand-year reign on earth—millennialism in the strictest sense." See his "Augustine's 'millennialism' reconsidered," *Augustinus* 38 (1993): 155–164, here 164.
55. K. Pollmann, "Moulding the Present: Apocalyptic as Hermeneutics in *City of God* 21–22," 168.

should not equate the church with God's kingdom on earth. Augustine offered several reasons for this latter position, not the least of which is his belief that the church is currently a "thoroughly mixed" body whose membership includes both some of the elect and some of the non-elect.

AUGUSTINE ON DEATH, HELL, AND PURGATORY

That Augustine's nickname, "The Teacher of Grace," applies to his teaching on the means of salvation is perhaps not a surprise; that it also forms the foundation of his thinking about humanity's eternal destiny might be: "while wicked angels and humans remain in eternal punishment, [all the elect] will know more fully the good that grace has conferred on them ... for nobody is set free except by an underserved mercy, and nobody is damned except by a judgment he deserves."[56]

For Augustine, to die is to be immediately disembodied and just as immediately to be judged, even though this judgment is both distinct from and a mere precursor to the final judgment. All the dead remain disembodied until the resurrection that precedes the final judgment: their souls "are kept in hidden places of rest or of punishment depending on what each soul deserves because of the lot they won for themselves while they lived in the flesh."[57]

For Augustine, the reality of an eternal hell cannot be denied.[58] More particularly, he taught that the hell to which unbelievers will be assigned after the final judgment is to be equated with the "second death" that is mentioned repeatedly in Revelation.[59] This death, which is also the equivalent of eternal

---

56. *Ench.* 94 (*WSA* I/8, 327).
57. See, e.g., *ench.* 109 (*WSA* I/8, 335) and *praed. sanct.*12.24 (*WSA* I/26, 168–9).
58. *Ench.* 113 (*WSA* I/8, 328). Cf. Daley, *The Hope of the Early Church*, 149: "For Augustine ... the aspect of damnation that needed the most elaborate defense was not its materiality but its eternity: not only before skeptical pagans, but also before some of our 'tender-hearted [fellow Christians].'" As G. Keith, "Patristic Views on Hell—Part 2," *The Evangelical Quarterly* 71/4 (1999): 299, has pointed out, Augustine often argued for hell's eternity for "pastoral reasons" since he thought that the "fear of Hell actually helped many to make a first step toward true piety." Cf. 291–92: "the doctrine of Hell ... was not ... a matter for debate or even pious speculation.... To deny it, or even to suggest that Hell was a threat which would never ... materialise, was to impugn God's veracity."
59. For Augustine, the "first death" is the "death" that occurs when sin separates one from God. Moreover, physical death is the unnatural and violent separation of the soul from the body and is itself a punishment for sin. Cf. Daley, *The Hope of the Early Church*, 136. This view places Augustine in opposition to both Platonic philosophy and some earlier Christian thinkers including Ambrose of Milan, the bishop who baptized him. See J. Cavadini, "Ambrose and Augustine *De Bono Mortis*," in *The Limits of Ancient Christianity: Essays on Late Antique*

damnation, is "experienced by sinners in a reunited soul and body that will never be annihilated."[60]

Augustine also held that the punishment of hell will be perfectly commensurate with one's deeds in this life (cf. 2 Cor. 5:10). That is, the fewer sins one has committed, the lighter one's punishment: "the gentlest punishment of all will be for those who have added no further sin to the original sin they have contracted [from Adam]; and as for those who have added further sins, the smaller each person's wickedness here, the more bearable will be his damnation there."[61]

With regard to purgatory, Augustine is ambivalent; as a result, the language he uses when discussing related issues is not always clear.[62] Nevertheless, in several texts he does endorse the ancient tradition of praying for the dead—even as he rejects the idea that one should pray for everyone who has passed away.[63] For example, in *Confessions* Book 9 Augustine prayed for his deceased mother Monica just before urging his readers to pray both for her and for his father, Patrick, who had died while Augustine was still a teenager.[64] Then, approximately twenty years later and in a work intended to instruct new believers, Augustine asserted that "the customs of the Church in praying for the dead are not contrary to the mind of the apostle (cf. 2 Cor. 5:10); for even the possibility of benefitting from them was won by each person while living in the body."[65]

Moreover, in that same work he seems to indicate that he thought something very like purgatory might be possible for some. Basing himself on passages such as 1 Corinthians 3:12–15, Augustine suggested that "it [is not] beyond belief that … after this life … some of the faithful are saved by a purifying fire,

---

Thought and Culture in Honor of R.A. Markus, W.E. Klingshirn and M. Vessey, eds. (Ann Arbor: The University of Michigan Press, 1999), 232–249, especially 237–243.

60. Daley, *The Hope of the Early Church*, 136.
61. *Ench.* 93 (*WSA* I/8, 327). Similarly and somewhat (in-)famously, Augustine consistently claimed that unbaptized babies who died before they became in any way accountable for their thoughts, desires, attitudes, or actions would be in hell but their punishment "would be the lightest punishment possible." See, e.g., *pecc. mer.* 1.16.21 (*WSA* I/23, 45).
62. Indeed, it is somewhat anachronistic to speak of the doctrine of purgatory in Augustine since "what in Augustine were only tentative ideas were elaborated into a full-scale doctrine of Purgatory" only well after his death. Cf. Keith, "Patristic Views on Hell—Part 2," 298. For a summary of Augustine on what would become purgatory, including the observation that his views on it have "long been debated," see Daley, *The Hope of the Early Church*, 140–41.
63. On the contrary, he held that if someone died (1) unbaptized, (2) unrepentant, (3) immersed in serious sin, or (4) after deserting the faith, she was permanently lost and, thus, could not be helped by the prayers of the faithful. See Keith, "Patristic Views on Hell—Part 2," 297 and cf. *ciu.* 21.19 and 21.24–25.
64. *Conf.* 9.13.35–37.
65. *Ench.* 110 (*WSA* I/8, 336).

more or less quickly depending on whether they have loved perishable good things more or less."[66] A few years later, in the next-to-last book of *The City of God*, he did more than simply suggest; there he affirmed that "not all men who endure temporal pains after death come into ... eternal punishments, which are to come after [the final] judgment. Some, in fact, will receive forgiveness in the world to come for what is not forgiven in this ... so that they may not be punished with the eternal chastisement of the world to come."[67]

AUGUSTINE ON "SEEING" GOD[68]

Like many philosophical thinkers before him, both Christian and non-Christian, Augustine believed that "the ultimate human happiness consists in an intellectual vision of God."[69]

Soon after his conversion in 386, Augustine began to seriously consider both what the Bible meant when it asserted that some human beings such as Moses had been given glimpses of God in this life and what the Bible (as well as other Christians) meant when they asserted that, in the future, the saved would see God or Christ "face to face" (cf. 1 Cor. 13:12) or "as he really is" (cf. 1 John 3:2).[70]

In a letter from the middle of his career, "Augustine scornfully rejects as [demented] the notion that human beings will ever be able to see the essence of God with their bodily eyes, in this world or in eternity."[71] This was for several reasons, but the most basic was that Augustine firmly believed that God did not possess a material body that, by definition, would confine him to one place. This was also an idea that he was not slow to preach to his people: "God cannot be seen in a place, because he is not a body; because he is everywhere, because he is

---

66. See *ench.* 69 (*WSA* I/8, 315). For a detailed exegesis of 2 Cor. 3:12–15 by Augustine, see *ciu.* 21.26.

67. *Ciu.* 21.13. See Augustine, *Concerning the City of God against the Pagans*, 991.

68. Although it would later become entrenched in the tradition, Augustine never uses the exact phrase "Beatific Vision (*uisio beatifica*)" in his discussions of the phenomenon of "seeing" God.

69. Fitzgerald, ed., *Augustine through the Ages: An Encyclopedia*, s.v. "*Videndo deo, de*" by F. van Fleteren. Cf. Daley, *The Hope of the Early Church*, 145: For Augustine, the direct contemplative vision of God is "the very heart of the eternal beatitude of the saints."

70. Cf., e.g., Exodus 33:18–23 as well as Augustine's own visionary experience while with his mother in Ostia as recounted in *conf.* 9.10.23–25.

71. Daley, *The Hope of the Early Church*, 145 referring to *ep.* 147, which was written probably in 413.

not less in one part, and more in another. Let us hold on to this with the utmost firmness."[72]

Interestingly, by the end of his life Augustine had worked out a position that was more conciliatory but that did not fundamentally compromise his earlier statements. This position allowed him to assert that humans cannot see God without God's help, that, in this life, even fleeting glimpses of God are exceedingly rare, and that the saved would in fact "see" God, but would do so in a new way and with an intellectual or spiritual vision, not with a corporeal or physical one (cf. 1 Cor. 15:53).[73] In other words, the mature Augustine "does not doubt that with their physical eyes [the blessed] will see God Incarnate . . . [they] will see God by seeing the inward reality of each others' [sic] souls—that is the love that other souls have for God . . . [they] will see the qualities of souls expressed physically."[74]

Conclusion: Augustine on Heaven

For Augustine, the good that the future holds for the person of faith is good for one simple reason: It has its basis in God, the One who is both eternally outside and the unique source of time, of history, and of all that is good.

Although he was reluctant to explain exactly how, Augustine was supremely confident that all of time and all of history are directed toward bringing about all the goodness that God, the Creator of all, who is perfectly good and perfectly immutable both in his essence and in his will, intends. Just as it all began, *in principio*, with God the Father creating in and through the soon-to-be-incarnated Son, so also will it all end with all of the redeemed offering the triune God praise for his perfectly executed plan.

More specifically, Augustine's vision of the future is grounded in the gospel of Christ and, specifically, in God's plan to identify with us and with our sin-laden plight through the miracle of the incarnation. Those who, by the predestinating and electing grace of God, have placed their faith, hope, and love in Christ

---

72. See *s.* 277.18 (*WSA* III/8, 45).
73. On the rarity of glimpses of God in this life, see Fitzgerald, ed., *Augustine through the Ages: An Encyclopedia*, s.v. "*Videndo deo, de*" by F. van Fleteren. On the way in which the saved would see God, cf. D. Hunter, "Augustine on the Body," 363, who, basing himself on *ciu.* 22.29, notes that "Augustine was convinced that the resurrected saints would see God *in* the body" but "was not willing to forgo the possibility that in the resurrection physical eyes might have their proper function even in the apprehension of God" (italics in original).
74. P. Burnell, *The Augustinian Person* (Washington DC: Catholic University of America Press, 2005), 167.

will come to a good end and will abide with the triune God forever in heaven. It is there that they will spiritually "see" God forever and will have even the ability of sinning—not to mention dying—removed from them.[75] Those who, by the selfish pursuit of the desires of their own sin-hardened hearts, have placed their faith, hope, and love in themselves will come to a bad end and will abide apart from the triune God forever. They will be aware of their plight and will suffer eternal torment, but will never be allowed to glimpse God in any sense. This, in short, is the difference between heaven and hell for Augustine.

In heaven, believers will finally experience the true life that was their goal all along, whether they knew exactly what to expect there or not. In heaven, the elect not only will see and love God, but will also become ever more like him (cf. 1 John 3:2).

Given both the power and beauty of much of what he wrote, it would be unjust to end a discussion of Augustine's vision of the future without letting the Bishop of Hippo speak for himself. Both of the following excerpts, which come from the final chapter of the twenty-second and last book of *The City of God*, that "great and arduous work,"[76] include some of the most moving and hopeful of all the 5.5 million words that posterity has preserved. Here Augustine speculates about what believers can expect when all is consummated in God.

> The reward of virtue will be God himself, who gave the virtue, together with the promise of himself, the best and greatest of all possible promises. . . . He will be the goal of all our longings; and we shall see him for ever; we shall love him without satiety; we shall praise him without wearying. This will be the duty, the delight, the activity of all, shared by all who share the life of eternity.[77]

Then, a few paragraphs later, he concludes both that chapter and the whole book by reminding his readers that,

> The important thing is that the seventh [epoch] will be our Sabbath, whose end will not be an evening, but the Lord's day,

---

75. Cf. *corrept.* 12.33 (*WSA* I/26,132). See also *ench.* 111 (*WSA* I/8, 337).
76. Cf. *ciu.* 1.praef. The original Latin is "magnum opus et arduum."
77. *Ciu.* 22.30. See Augustine, *Concerning the City of God against the Pagans*, 1088.

an eighth day, as it were, which is to last forever, a day conse-
crated by the resurrection of Christ, foreshadowing the eternal
rest not only of the spirit but of the body also. There we shall be
still and see; we shall see and we shall love; we shall love and we
shall praise. Behold what will be, in the end, without end! For
what is our end but to reach that kingdom which has no end?[78]

Capturing such a vision for the future in ink and on paper is a big part of
what has made Augustine the single most important and influential post-biblical
Christian theologian in the western tradition. Indeed, given that he has provided
that tradition with so much over the course of the 1,600 years since his death,
it is hard to see how anyone's theological education—including their eschatological education—could be called complete without knowing what he thought,
taught, and believed.

---

78. *Ciu.* 22.30. See Augustine, *Concerning the City of God against the Pagans*, 1091.

The Doctrine of the Future in John Calvin

Nathan D. Holsteen

Introduction

"Quousque, Domine!" (How long, O Lord?) were John Calvin's last words.[1] They are clearly words of hope—hope that transcends the grave. Just as clearly, then, Calvin's theology was to him a theology of hope. But just how did Calvin arrive at his understanding of the Biblical teaching on the last things? How did he determine his eschatological views?

This chapter will suggest that Calvin's understanding of eschatology was largely inherited from the teaching of the Roman Catholic church of his day and was modified significantly by the emphases of the Reformation—leaving him with an eschatology that some find understated.[2] This suggestion explains the shape of Calvin's eschatology, as well as the relative paucity of material on the subject within Calvin's works.

Problem

The major obstacle in finding a holistic understanding of Calvin's eschatology is the lack of anything like a systematic treatment of the last things from Calvin's pen. The observations are well-known: There is no summary of eschatology in the *Institutes;* there is no commentary on the Revelation of Jesus Christ (even though Calvin wrote a commentary on every other book in the

---

1. See Donald K. McKim, ed., *The Cambridge Companion to John Calvin* (Cambridge: Cambridge University Press, 2004), 23.
2. For example, Holwerda states: "Calvin has never been famous for his eschatology." David E. Holwerda, "Eschatology and History: A Look at Calvin's Eschatological Vision," in *Exploring the Heritage of John Calvin,* ed. David E. Holwerda (Grand Rapids: Baker, 1976), 110.

New Testament); there is no condensed discussion of eschatology in any of his theological works.

It is not fair, however, to suggest that Calvin avoided the topic entirely. Instead, it is best to say that Calvin dealt with eschatological themes as they arose in his pursuit of other goals. Quistorp, one of the most celebrated scholars to have wrestled with Calvin's eschatology, says, "We do not find in Luther and Calvin any coherent system of eschatology, but rather they treat the last things from time to time at relevant points in their scriptural exegesis and preaching and in their exposition of the creed."[3]

This *ad hoc* treatment of eschatology in Calvin's work occasions a predictable result: There are significant gaps in Calvin's eschatological discussion. There is very little, for example, on the future form of the kingdom. There is very little on the new heavens and the new earth. There is next to nothing on the rapture.[4]

The image of Calvin's eschatology as something of a patchwork quilt is further bolstered by examining the contents of the *Institutes*. The *Institutes* similarly do not provide a complete eschatology, at least in accordance with modern expectations. It is not too much of a stretch to say that there is but one chapter devoted explicitly to a topic that is clearly eschatological: Book 3, Chapter xxv.[5] These observations lead Quistorp to the same conclusion suggested here: "[Luther and Calvin] never succeeded in attaining any conclusive and independent formulation of Christian eschatology."[6]

So we have come face to face with the most significant problem to be tackled in addressing Calvin's eschatology, and already there are some valuable hints that

---

3. Heinrich Quistorp, *Calvin's Doctrine of the Last Things*, trans. Harold Knight (London: Lutterworth Press, 1955), 12. We will come back to Quistorp's suggestion that there is a connection between biblical exegesis and the shape of Calvin's eschatology later.

4. Even when Calvin discusses 1 Thessalonians 4:17—the passage that gives rise to the term *rapture*—he does not offer much by way of clarification. This is probably to be expected, as Calvin seems to view the rapture as another facet of the singular event known as the second coming. One of the most striking aspects of Calvin's commentary on 1 Thessalonians 4:17 is the explicit connection he makes between that passage and the creedal expectation of judgment at Christ's coming. Calvin writes, "The Apostle unquestionably had nothing farther in view here than to give some taste of the magnificence and venerable appearance of the Judge, until we shall behold it fully. With this taste it becomes us in the mean time to rest satisfied." John Calvin and John Pringle, *Commentaries on the Epistles of Paul the Apostle to the Philippians, Colossians, and Thessalonians* (Bellingham, WA: Logos Bible Software, 2010), 283.

5. III.xxv is a chapter titled, "The Final Resurrection."

6. Quistorp, *Calvin's Doctrine of the Last Things*, 11. As we have already noticed, Holwerda's more recent work on Calvin's eschatology echoes the same sentiment in its opening words (Holwerda, "Eschatology and History: A Look at Calvin's Eschatological Vision," 110).

will aid us in our assessment. First, any conclusions to which we ultimately come must be able to explain adequately the patchwork nature of Calvin's treatment of eschatology. If it does not do so, it fails to address the most significant datum on the topic. Second, the patchwork nature of Calvin's eschatology need not dissuade us from attempting to find a coherent and holistic understanding. It is *not* the case that Calvin abandoned eschatology entirely. Calvin *did* have an eschatology; it was simply, as Quistorp suggested, dependent and somewhat inconclusive.

Solution: The Context of Calvin's Eschatology

One of the most fruitful approaches in analyzing a system of doctrine (or a part of a system, for that matter) is found in the question, "How does this fit?"[7] I would suggest that our first line of attack in attempting to understand Calvin's eschatology is to ask "How does it fit?" with respect to several contexts: first, with respect to the historical context; second, with respect to the context of Calvin's theological method; and third, with respect to the context of Calvin's overall theology. It is to a consideration of these contexts that we now turn.

The Context in History

The first context that will help us understand Calvin's eschatology is the historical context. Without a doubt, the dominant figure in this context is the monolith of sixteenth-century Roman Catholicism. It is the backdrop for every discussion of reformation. The Reformation was, after all, a movement that insisted that the doctrine and practices of the Church of Rome ought to be *re-formed.* The great church historian of Scotland, William Cunningham, says it well: "There are two leading aspects in which the Reformation, viewed as a whole, may be regarded. . . . In the first aspect it was a great revolt against the see of Rome, and against the authority of the church and of churchmen in religious matters, combined with an assertion of the exclusive authority of the Bible, and of the right of all men to examine and interpret it for themselves."[8]

---

7. Even as I write these words, I am compelled to acknowledge a debt. There is much about my approach to theological analysis that exists primarily because of the teaching of Craig Blaising. He taught me to ask this question, and others like it. In my files I have notes from a course I took on *Prolegomena and Bibliology,* taught by Craig Blaising at Dallas Theological Seminary in the fall term of 1987. Lecture 4 on "Field Argumentation and System Justification" shaped the way I think about the task of theology. I guess you could say that I am significantly "Blaisingian."

8. William Cunningham, *The Reformers and the Theology of the Reformation,* vol.1 in Collected Works of the Rev. William Cunningham (Edinburgh: T&T Clark, 1862), 2.

As a result, it is not a mistake to evaluate the teaching of the reformers against the backdrop of the teaching of Rome. As a matter of fact, such an evaluation is often the best place to start. One *ought* to consider the reformers to be Catholic wherever they do not distinguish their views from Rome.[9] This attitude seems implicit in Calvin's thought. For example, in describing the need for reformation at the Diet at Spires, Calvin explains to the Emperor Charles V, "I here profess to plead in defense, both of sound doctrine and of the Church."[10] Calvin was not out to destroy the Roman church in its entirety; he was out to set straight its doctrines and practices (as the remainder of *The Necessity of Reforming the Church* makes clear).

It should come as no surprise, then, to suggest that there are huge similarities between Calvin's eschatology and the eschatology of Rome. There are a number of ways to make this point; my favorite is to compare what Calvin and Rome taught their churches. In other words, a comparison of catechisms turns out to be impressively instructive. My intent in the paragraphs that follow is to investigate *The Catechism of the Church of Geneva* (authored by John Calvin himself) and *The Catechism of the Council of Trent* (a catechism arising from the Catholic council held from 1545 to 1563).

By asking several questions about the nature and form of the kingdom of God, one primary insight will arise. We will find a significant agreement on the broad outlines of eschatology.

What Is the Nature of the Kingdom?

The first question that demands to be asked is about the nature of the kingdom. When two different views of eschatology answer the question, "What is the nature of the kingdom?" differently, those eschatologies will necessarily diverge

---

9. This observation is substantiated in some rather surprising places. One such place is in Calvin's *Acts of the Council of Trent with the Antidote*. In a book devoted to correcting the errors taught by the Council of Trent (a Roman Catholic council that re-established Roman Catholic doctrine in response to the Reformation), Calvin encounters two heads of teaching (see the section "On the Sixth Session of the Council of Trent") about which he says simply, "The third and fourth heads I do not touch." Calvin did not find anything in the third and fourth heads that he considered worth refutation or correction. He simply passed right on by. Here we have an interesting point concerning Calvin's view of the extent of the atonement. But that's a discussion for another day.

10. John Calvin, *The Necessity of Reforming the Church*, in *Calvin's Tracts Relating to the Reformation*, trans. Henry Beveridge (Edinburgh: Printed for the Calvin Translation Society, 1864), 1:124.

in fundamental ways. This is because one's understanding of the nature of the kingdom, or what the kingdom looks like, will provide the basic shape of one's understanding of the Christian's future hope. A case in point: If one understands the kingdom to be spiritual with no hint of a physical aspect, then there is no room for a physical, earthly kingdom in God's future fulfillment of his promises.

So what does Calvin's catechism say about the nature of the kingdom of God? The catechism of Geneva says: "It is spiritual, as it is governed by the word and Spirit of God; which bring with them righteousness and life."[11] It is worth noting the emphasis on the spiritual nature of the kingdom in Calvin's thought. That emphasis is certainly articulated here, precisely because Calvin does not even mention any physical or earthly ramifications of this spiritual kingdom. He will, and we will attend to those ramifications later. But for now, it is critical that we observe the fundamentally *spiritual* nature of the kingdom of God for Calvin.

The Catechism of Trent, on the other hand, describes the nature of the kingdom in this way: "This kingdom of Christ is spiritual and eternal, begun on earth, but perfected in heaven: and, indeed, he discharges by his admirable providence the duties of King towards his Church, governing and protecting her against the open violence and covert designs of her enemies, imparting to her not only holiness and righteousness, but also power and strength to persevere."[12]

The similarity between the two is obvious. The basic nature of the kingdom of God is spiritual.

It is true, the Catechism of Trent goes much further in this instance, spelling out several ways in which the spiritual kingdom is manifested in the physical realm. But this is not necessarily an area of disagreement between Calvin and Rome; it is rather a difference of expression in the articulation of the kingdom's basic nature. The reason for this difference of expression will become more clear as we continue to investigate Calvin's eschatology.

What Are the Components of the Kingdom?

This question is not one that might arise naturally in the mind of a modern reader, but it is a question that is forced upon the reader by both catechisms. Both catechisms include a section in which the catechumen is led through a discussion of the Lord's Prayer, and when the catechumen arrives at the phrase "Thy

---

11. John Calvin, *The Catechism of the Church of Geneva,* trans. Elijah Waterman (Hartford, CT: Sheldon & Goodwin, 1815), 17.
12. *The Catechism of the Council of Trent,* trans. J. Donovan (Baltimore: Lucas Brothers, 1829), 35.

kingdom come," he is asked to answer several questions about the kingdom. In this section, both catechisms follow a very similar sequence of concepts.

As it turns out, this question will help us see how both Calvin and Rome begin to develop their understanding of the nature of the kingdom. The catechism of Geneva says: "It consists chiefly in two things; that he governs his elect, by his Spirit; and that he destroys the reprobate."[13]

This declaration adds much to our understanding of Calvin's view of the kingdom. It is, as we have already seen, spiritual in essence. But that is clearly not the end of the story. The spiritual kingdom is seen in things that happen in the physical world—namely, God's government of those who are his, and God's destruction of the reprobate.

We also catch a glimpse of a concept that is significant for Calvin: the truth of God's predestination. Here in a discussion of the components of the kingdom of God, we find Calvin responding in terms of the body of the elect and the body of the reprobate. Our immediate inference is that predestination informs Calvin's understanding of the kingdom. God's kingdom is nothing more (and nothing less) than his government of those he has chosen, along with his destruction of those predestined for destruction (the reprobate).

Further, whatever we see in this world that demonstrates God's spiritual government of his elect—or God's destruction of the reprobate—ought to be considered the physical manifestation of a kingdom that is essentially spiritual.

So what does the Catechism of Trent say about the components of the kingdom of God? It says: "The words 'kingdom of God,' ordinarily signify not only that power which he possesses over all men, and over universal creation, a sense in which they frequently occur in Scripture, but, also, his providence which rules and governs the world. . . . By 'the kingdom of God' is also understood that special providence by which God protects, and watches over pious and holy men."[14]

Once again, the similarity between Calvin and Rome is obvious. Even though Rome admitted up front that the kingdom is both spiritual and earthly (and that insistence clearly shows up again here), the common element is unmistakable. God's government is central to both definitions. Here, God's government is acknowledged over all creation, then identified in his government over the world, and ultimately focused on his providential care over those in the church ("pious and holy men").

---

13. Calvin, *The Catechism of the Church of Geneva*, 75.
14. *The Catechism of the Council of Trent*, 346.

What Does "Thy Kingdom Come" Mean?

The third question we need to ask of Calvin and Rome drives a little closer to the heart of the issue. When we ask "What does 'Thy kingdom come' mean?" we are asking something about the respondent's hope for the future. To put it another way, if you tell me what you expect to see when God's kingdom comes, I will know something fundamental about your Christian hope.

So how does Calvin answer this question? The catechism of Geneva says: "That the Lord would daily increase the number of believers; that he would enrich them constantly with fresh gifts of his Spirit, until they shall be perfected. Moreover, that he would render his truth more luminous, and his righteousness more manifest, by scattering the darkness of Satan, and abolishing all iniquity."[15] Calvin's response here is entirely in line with his previous discussion of the kingdom of God. The kingdom is spiritual in essence, and that essence is clearly affirmed here. The coming of the kingdom (which has apparently already happened) is something for which every believer ought to continue to pray. And what we pray for is this: an increase in the number of believers (note that this can only happen by God's act, and it is a spiritual act), the spiritual enrichment of believers, and the continued work of God to exalt righteousness and abolish sinfulness. For Calvin, the coming of the kingdom has already happened, and progressively happens as God *grows* his kingdom. It is a spiritual kingdom with physically observable manifestations. Hesselink confirms our observation here, claiming that "for the most part, Calvin identifies the kingdom with the church, which obviously has both visible and invisible dimensions."[16]

Rome's answer to this question is also instructive: "that the kingdom of Christ, that is, his Church, may be enlarged; that Jews and infidels may embrace the faith of Christ, and the knowledge of the true God; that schismatics and heretics may return to soundness of mind, and to the communion of the Church of God, which they have deserted."[17] The physical nature of the kingdom of God is becoming more and more pronounced as we continue to observe the catechism of Trent. While the kingdom of God is spiritual in essence, that essence, according to Rome, is manifested in something that is entirely visible. To say it another way, the church *is* the kingdom, and the church *is* the visible communion of the Roman church. Those who have departed from communion with Rome have departed from communion with the true church, and thus have

---

15. Calvin, *The Catechism of the Church of Geneva*, 75.
16. I. J. Hesselink, "Calvin on the Kingdom of Christ," in *Religion without Ulterior Motive*, ed. E. A. J. G. van der Borght (Leiden: Brill, 2006), 145.
17. *The Catechism of the Council of Trent*, 347.

placed themselves outside the kingdom. As a result, to pray that God's kingdom might come is to pray that the communion of Rome might be enlarged, and to pray that those who have left might return to communion with Rome.

It is noticeable once again that the kingdom has, apparently, already come. The church of Rome is here, and it *is* the kingdom. But even though the kingdom has come, we pray that it may come in more fullness.

In What Sense Has the Kingdom Already Come?

The idea that the kingdom has already come is common to both Rome and Calvin, as we have seen. But in what sense has the kingdom already come? Both catechisms offer a degree of clarification. The Catechism of Geneva states: "[Because God is already performing the things listed in the citation above] the kingdom of God may be said to be begun. We pray, therefore, that it may be continually increased and enlarged, until it shall be advanced to its highest glory; which we trust will be accomplished at the last day, when all creatures being reduced to subjection, God shall be exalted and shine forth; and thus he shall be all in all."[18] Calvin's catechism clarifies what we have already observed: God's activity of exalting righteousness and abolishing sinfulness is an unmistakable sign that the kingdom has already come. But now we find out that there is more. There is another stage of the kingdom's coming that will only be revealed at the last day, when all creatures will be in subjection and God will be all in all.

This distinction is a significant characteristic of Calvin's teaching and explains why some scholars call Calvin's view a "two-kingdoms eschatology."[19] The kingdom is already present, but there is an equal emphasis on the form of the kingdom that has not yet come—the kingdom that will only come at Christ's second coming.

What is most interesting about this (and also about Bolt's essay) is that few scholars have taken the time to set Calvin's views accurately against the backdrop of Roman Catholic teaching. When we consult the Catechism of Trent, a strange congruity emerges:

> By the words "kingdom of God" is also meant that kingdom of his glory, of which Christ our Lord says in St. Matthew: "Come ye blessed of my Father, possess the kingdom which was prepared

---

18. Calvin, *The Catechism of the Church of Geneva*, 76.
19. One example is a fine essay by John Bolt. See John Bolt, "'A Pearl and a Leaven': John Calvin's Critical Two-Kingdoms Eschatology" in *John Calvin and Evangelical Theology: Legacy and Prospect,* ed. Sung Wook Chung (Milton Keynes: Paternoster, 2009).

for you from the beginning of the world." This kingdom the thief, acknowledging his crimes, begged of him in these words: "Lord, remember me, when thou comest into thy kingdom." . . . But the kingdom of grace must precede that of glory. . . . Whilst we are clothed with this frail mortal flesh . . . we often stumble and fall; but when the light of the kingdom of glory, which is perfect, shall have shone upon us, we shall stand for ever firm and immoveable. Then shall every imperfection be eradicated.[20]

There is, in the Roman Catholic thought of Calvin's day, the very same distinction between the present form of the kingdom, and the future form of the kingdom. The timing of the future kingdom is even the same: when all things are set straight. The Catechism of Trent calls the present form of the kingdom "the kingdom of grace," and the future form of the kingdom is termed "the kingdom of glory."

Summary of the Historical Context

Given the comparison between the eschatology of Rome (seen in the teaching of the Catechism of the Council of Trent) and Calvin's eschatology (seen in the Catechism of the Church of Geneva), it seems reasonable to suggest that the overall shape of Calvin's eschatology was inherited from Rome. Augustine provided the basic outline, and this outline was followed by Thomas Aquinas, the bishops gathered at Trent, and also by Calvin.[21]

This is not to say that every aspect of Calvin's eschatology was derived from Rome; we will see later that Calvin's theological method and its resulting emphases were quite different from Rome. But the point nevertheless remains:

---

20. *The Catechism of the Council of Trent*, 346–47.
21. This suggestion is not as audacious as it might appear at first. John Bolt suggests something similar when he writes, "it is hard to present Calvin faithfully as a 'revolutionary' thinker whose joining of history and eschatology provides a vision for establishing the kingdom of Christ on earth. Calvin is an Augustinian on this score, while Moltmann's eschatology of hope is part of a tradition of challenge to Augustine. Instead of seeing the kingdom of God as a spiritual reality manifested primarily in the church, as Augustine did, Moltmann joins a long line of theologians of messianic eschatology or historicizing eschatology that was present in the early church, [and was] repudiated by Augustine." (Bolt, "'A Pearl and a Leaven': John Calvin's Critical Two-Kingdoms Eschatology," 257). So in this critical and formative aspect of eschatology, Calvin followed Augustine, and so did Thomas Aquinas. It is worth mentioning in this regard that the bishops gathered at the Council of Trent followed Aquinas too. According to Pope Leo XIII, the bishops gathered at the Council of Trent "made it part of the order of conclave to lay upon the altar, together with sacred Scripture and the decrees of the Supreme Pontiffs, the Summa of Thomas Aquinas" (see Pope Leo XIII, *Aeterni Patris,* encyclical, 22).

the basic shape of Calvin's eschatology was derived from Rome. This basic shape includes the spiritual nature of the kingdom, an articulation of how the spiritual manifests itself in the physical, the two stages of kingdom fulfillment, and the timing of the ultimate form of the kingdom.

THE CONTEXT OF CALVIN'S THEOLOGICAL METHOD

The second context that will help us understand Calvin's eschatology is the context of his own theological method. To say this another way, we are now asking how a consideration of Calvin's theological method might clarify aspects of his eschatological thought.

Perhaps the most dominant characteristic of Calvin's theological method is found in his overarching devotion to the authority of Scripture. Beyond this, however, it must be mentioned that in the reading of Scripture, Calvin advocated the use of a literal hermeneutic. These two aspects of Calvin's theological thinking do indeed offer a helpful perspective on his eschatological thought.

First, it is virtually a commonplace that Calvin's theology is predicated on the unrivalled authority of Scripture. Very near the beginning of the *Institutes,* Calvin teaches that true doctrine cannot be adjudged apart from Scripture. "If we turn aside from the Word," Calvin writes, "though we may strive with strenuous haste, yet, since we have got off the track, we shall never reach the goal."[22] And then, to make his position clear, Calvin contradicts the teaching of the Roman church: "But a most pernicious error widely prevails that Scripture has only so much weight as is conceded to it by the consent of the church. As if the eternal and inviolable truth of God depended upon the decision of men!"[23] Indeed, Calvin's own words lay the foundation of his theological method. The authority of Scripture is to be the starting point and also the measuring stick of sound doctrine.[24]

---

22. Calvin, *Institutes,* I.vi.3 [1:73]. John Calvin, *Institutes of the Christian Religion,* vol. 1, The Library of Christian Classics, vol. XX, ed. John T. McNeill; trans. Ford Lewis Battles (Philadelphia: The Westminster Press, 1960), 73. The traditional form of reference is Book I, Chapter vi, Section 3. Hereinafter, references to the *Institutes* will list both the traditional book, chapter, and section numbers, as well as the page number from the above edition in brackets.
23. Calvin, *Institutes,* I.vii.1 [1:75].
24. This foundational assertion is substantiated by the most highly regarded Calvin scholars. See, for example, Wilhelm Niesel, *The Theology of Calvin,* trans. Harold Knight (Philadelphia: Westminster Press, 1956), 25. Another example is François Wendel, *Calvin: The Origins and Development of His Religious Thought,* trans. Philip Mairet (London: Wm. Collins, Sons & Co., 1965), 153.

Beyond the unrivalled authority of Scripture, however, there is another compelling question that determines the direction of Calvin's theological method. Namely, how is Scripture to be read? While a number of responses to this question could be offered, it appears that the most compelling answer is this: Calvin was clearly devoted to the primacy of the *sensus literalis* in his exegesis.[25] Calvin read Scripture *literally.* Now this does not mean, of course, that Calvin eschewed all figures of speech in reading Scripture; that is far from the truth. Instead, Calvin read Scripture in accordance with its historical and grammatical contexts. As Torrance has observed, "It has often been remarked that Calvin's exegesis is astonishingly 'modern', a judgment that is being reinforced by the new translations of his commentaries. The reason for this lies partly in the fact that he assimilated as much as he could the best scholarship of the humanists, and shared with them their determination to be faithful to the grammatical sense, and to bring out the genuine, straightforward meaning of what was written from its own context in text and history."[26]

The possible implications of this rather simple observation are significant. No one, for example, knows precisely how to explain the fact that Calvin never wrote a commentary on the Revelation of Jesus Christ, even though he wrote commentaries on every other book in the New Testament. I too would number myself in that crowd. I do not know precisely how to explain this. But recognizing Calvin's commitment to a literal hermeneutic provides one possible explanation. The plentiful figures of speech in the text of Revelation brought Calvin pause for two reasons. First, the figures created grave difficulty in interpretation; and second, the book of Revelation created no significant change in the basic shape of his eschatology.[27] Indeed, it might be argued that precisely *because of* Calvin's failure to apply his normal hermeneutic to the text of Revelation, he ensured that Revelation created no ripples in his eschatology.[28]

---

25. See, for example, Richard Burnett, "John Calvin and the *Sensus Literalis,*" in *John Calvin and the Interpretation of Scripture: Calvin Studies X and XI,* ed. Charles Raynal (Grand Rapids: CRC Product Services, 2006), 331–42.

26. Thomas F. Torrance, *The Hermeneutics of John Calvin,* (Edinburgh: Scottish Academic Press, 1988), 72.

27. Quistorp hints at the tension visible when Calvin wrestles with various passages in the Revelation of Jesus Christ. Though Calvin's overall hermeneutical approach is founded in literalism, his reading of Revelation often reveals plainly a spiritualizing hermeneutic. See Quistorp, *Calvin's Doctrine of the Last Things,* 160–61.

28. Quistorp's final assessment of Calvin's treatment of millennialism (see Quistorp, *Calvin's Doctrine of the Last Things,* 162) seems to suggest just such a conclusion.

The Context of Calvin's Theology

The third context that will help us assess Calvin's view of eschatology is the context of his own overall theology. In other words, evaluating the major emphases of his theology will help us determine how his eschatology fits into the whole picture. And finally we encounter an aspect of Calvin's thought that has occasioned great unanimity among scholars. This unanimity arises precisely because Calvin speaks again and again about one of the central emphases in his theology, and he does so in a variety of situations. That central emphasis is soteriological.

In a word, Calvin's entire theology is soteriological. While this is not true in every respect, it seems reasonably complete. At one point in my doctoral studies, my adviser assigned to me the task of determining the overarching theme of Calvin's theology. While I did not then—nor do I now—claim that my conclusion is beyond dispute, I decided that Calvin's theology condenses to this one thought: *God's benevolent fatherhood is applied, in all its richness, by the Spirit to all who are in Christ by faith.*

While this observation is open to debate, it does exemplify one thing: Many readers of Calvin find his work to be fundamentally focused on soteriology. But for some scholars, this assertion is too ambiguous. More specificity is needed, and some say we find that specificity in Calvin's own words: "[Justification by faith] is the main hinge on which religion turns, so that we devote the greater attention and care to it."[29] In this way, some suggest that the dominant theme in Calvin's theology is not only soteriological, but specifically related to the doctrine of justification by faith. This suggestion is certainly defensible, for elsewhere Calvin states, "[justification by faith] is the principle of the whole doctrine of salvation and the foundation of all religion."[30]

It is no accident then that Quistorp's work, one of the most respected studies of Calvin's eschatology, begins with these two sentences: "The theology of

---

29. Calvin, *Institutes,* III.xi.1 [1:726].
30. John Calvin, "Sermon on Luke 1:5–10," in *Ioannis Calvini Opera Quae Supersunt Omnia,* vol. 46:23. The passage reads, "Il nous faut sortir de nous-mesmes: c'est à dire, il faut que nous soyons vuides de toute fiance de ce que nous cuidons apporter à Dieu, et que nous cherchions nostre iustice en Iesus Christ, voire ceste iustice de la foy, dont il est parlé tant souvent en l'Escriture saincte. Et c'est le principe de toute la doctrine de salut, et le fondement de toute religion." In English, this reads, "It is necessary that we remove from ourselves, that is to say, it is necessary that we be empty of all confidence in that which we think to bring to God, and that we find our righteousness in Christ, even that righteousness of faith, of which so much of Holy Scripture speaks. And that is the principle of the whole doctrine of salvation, and the foundation of all religion [translation mine]."

the reformers is not primarily concerned with questions of eschatology (we are thinking especially of Luther and Calvin). Their chief concern is with the problem of justification and the matters immediately relevant to it."[31]

While it is beyond the scope of this essay to deal more fully with the role of justification by faith in the overall theology of John Calvin, it seems reliable enough to offer one general conclusion: The doctrine of justification by faith is significant enough in Calvin's theology to ask how it might affect our understanding of Calvin's eschatology.

Thankfully, T. F. Torrance offers some guidance in this regard. Torrance implicitly acknowledges that the difference between Calvin's eschatology and the eschatology of the Roman church in his day has primarily to do with the nature of man's incorporation into the body of Christ, the church (note here that man's incorporation into the body of Christ is a soteriological question). Torrance writes, "Apart from this setting Calvin's mature teaching about eschatology cannot be understood, but in this setting it is very clear that eschatology is the analogical transposition of Christology to the whole understanding of the Church."[32]

To unpack this further, one must note that Calvin's understanding of man's incorporation into the body of Christ revolves around the concept of union with Christ—something accomplished by God on the basis of faith and linked inextricably with justification by faith. The Roman church, however, understood man's incorporation into the body of Christ as something more visible. If a man is visibly related to the Roman church, he is incorporated into the body of Christ. Even though the church does include those who are not saved, the church is still to be identified with the kingdom of God.[33]

And now we see a compelling reason for considering this third context: the context of Calvin's overall theology. A theology focused on soteriology—and even more specifically, the doctrine of justification by faith—necessarily affects one's understanding of union with Christ. In turn, one's understanding of union with Christ affects one's understanding of the nature of the church. Then, one's

---

31. Quistorp, *Calvin's Doctrine of the Last Things*, 11.

32. T. F. Torrance, *Kingdom and Church: A Study in the Theology of the Reformation* (Fair Lawn, NJ: Essential Books, 1956), 101.

33. The Catechism of Trent has a particularly poignant statement regarding the mixed nature of the church. "But it is a melancholy truth, that, in the church of God, there are to be found those 'who profess they know God, but in their works deny him;' whose conduct is a reproach to the faith which they glory to profess; who, by sinning, become the dwelling-place of the devil, where he exercises uncontrolled dominion" (*The Catechism of the Council of Trent*, 347-48).

understanding of the nature of the church affects one's understanding of the nature of the kingdom. Finally, one's understanding of the nature of the kingdom affects the specific form of one's eschatology.

Calvin's overall theology, focused as it is on the doctrine of justification by faith, stamps Calvin's eschatology in its own image.

CONSEQUENCE: CALVIN'S ESCHATOLOGY SUMMARIZED

We have considered Calvin's eschatology in the light of three different contexts: historical, methodological, and theological. In each case, we found elements in the context that helped us understand Calvin's eschatology from some particular standpoint. What remains to do is to put all of these pieces in place so that a coherent overall picture might emerge.

Re-Tooled by the Theological Emphases of the Reformation

The first aspect of this summary acknowledges the historical, methodological, and theological contexts by offering a suggestion that ties all of them together. It seems reasonable to propose that Calvin's eschatology is founded upon the Augustinian tradition as handed down to Aquinas and affirmed by the Roman church of Calvin's day. Thus, Calvin's basic eschatology was amillenarian in structure, affirming that the kingdom is spiritual in nature. Further, the kingdom, while present in the church, anticipates an ultimate form that is yet future. That ultimate form of the kingdom will be ushered in when God brings in eternal perfection at the second coming of Christ.

But the emphases of the Reformation brought significant change to the details of Calvin's eschatology. The reformation emphasis on *sola Scriptura* brought a rejection of purgatory and a greater emphasis on exegesis of Scripture as the foundation of the theological task. Building on this foundation, Calvin finds an eschatology that is fundamentally the same as Rome, and yet differs in surprising ways.

Consequences for Ecclesiology

The second aspect of this summary investigates the logical consequences of the first. Namely, the reformation emphasis on justification by faith immediately changed Calvin's perspective on union with Christ. A saint is no longer defined by his or her relationship with the Roman church—he or she is defined by his relationship with Jesus Christ. Those chosen by God for salvation are united with Christ by faith, and thus are part of the true church. In this way, the soteriological (and justificational) emphases of the reformation created a new vision of ecclesiology.

Now certainly there are significant differences in Calvin's perspective on the church when compared to Rome's. This, indeed, is one of the significant aspects of the theology of the Reformation. For the reformers in general, and for Calvin in particular, the church is, in its essence, invisible. This is because the nature of the church grows out of the doctrine of justification. For Calvin, the nature of the church is defined by the gracious act of God in Christ. The church is, quite simply, the elect. For Rome, the church is something categorically different. It is a *visible* society.

This distinction in ecclesiology leads directly to a distinction in eschatology. While the *shape* of Calvin's eschatology is thus the same as Rome's, the details differ in direct response to Calvin's understanding of the church.

Effect on Eschatology

The final step in the summary of Calvin's eschatology is to observe how changes in ecclesiology result in changes to eschatology. This is because the nature of the church shapes the nature of the kingdom, and the nature of the kingdom shapes the whole of eschatology.

For this reason, it might benefit us to consider again Calvin's definition of the kingdom: "It is spiritual, as it is governed by the word and Spirit of God; which bring with them righteousness and life."[34] But the spiritual nature of the kingdom is not the end of the story. No, that spiritual kingdom is seen physically in the church. This becomes clear when Calvin states:

> But even though the definition of this Kingdom was put before us previously, I now briefly repeat it: God reigns where men, both by denial of themselves and by contempt of the world and of earthly life, pledge themselves to his righteousness in order to aspire to a heavenly life. Thus there are two parts to this Kingdom: first, that God by the power of his Spirit correct all the desires of the flesh which by squadrons war against him; second, that he shape all our thoughts in obedience to his rule.[35]

---

34. Calvin, *The Catechism of the Church of Geneva,* 17.
35. Calvin, *Institutes,* III.xx.42 [2:905]. It is interesting to note that the Catechism of Trent and the *Institutes* both provide the above cited definitions of the kingdom in the context of commentary on the phrase in the Lord's Prayer, "Thy kingdom come."

The same tension between invisible and visible is echoed in Calvin's ecclesiology. In a famed passage from the *Institutes,* Calvin writes:

> I have observed that the Scriptures speak of the Church in
> two ways. Sometimes when they speak of the Church they
> mean the Church as it really is before God—the Church into
> which none are admitted but those who by the gift of adop-
> tion are sons of God, and by the sanctification of the Spirit
> true members of Christ. In this case it not only comprehends
> the saints who dwell on the earth, but all the elect who have
> existed from the beginning of the world. Often, too, by the
> name of Church is designated the whole body of mankind
> scattered throughout the world, who profess to worship one
> God and Christ, who by baptism are initiated into the faith;
> by partaking of the Lord's Supper profess unity in true doc-
> trine and charity, agree in holding the word of the Lord,
> and observe the ministry which Christ has appointed for the
> preaching of it. In this Church there is a very large mixture
> of hypocrites, who have nothing of Christ but the name and
> outward appearance: of ambitious avaricious, envious, evil-
> speaking men, some also of impure lives, who are tolerated
> for a time, either because their guilt cannot be legally estab-
> lished, or because due strictness of discipline is not always
> observed. Hence, as it is necessary to believe the invisible
> Church, which is manifest to the eye of God only, so we are
> also enjoined to regard this Church which is so called with
> reference to man, and to cultivate its communion.[36]

The consequence of this is that Calvin never truly developed a unique eschatology. One may arrive at a reasonably accurate summary of Calvin's eschatology
by following a very simple recipe: start with the eschatology of the sixteenth-
century Roman church, and redefine the church as the body "into which none
are admitted but those who by the gift of adoption are sons of God, and by the
sanctification of the Spirit true members of Christ."[37] In other words, reshape the

---

36. Calvin, *Institutes,* IV.i.7 [2:1021].
37. Ibid.

understanding of the church by pinning it to the doctrine of justification by faith (and thus, union with Christ), and the change is complete.[38]

The basic *shape* of Calvin's eschatology is therefore similar to the basic shape of Roman eschatology: The church *is* the kingdom, but not yet in its ultimate form. The details have been reworked to accommodate the doctrine of justification by faith and its consequent, the nature of the church as essentially invisible.

CONCLUSION

This chapter has argued that the major problem arising from Calvin's eschatology—or rather, the lack of any complete or systematic explanation of eschatology from Calvin—is resolvable when one considers the contexts that gave it form. By considering the broader context of the Reformation and its stance with respect to Roman Catholic teaching, we found a way of grappling with the overall shape of Calvin's eschatology, which is largely Augustinian. By examining the context of Calvin's theological method, we found an explanation for some of the silence in the Calvin *corpus*; there are places we would expect Calvin to speak on eschatological questions, and he simply passes over such discussion. By investigating the theological emphases of the Reformation, we found a chain of implications that connects the soteriological claims of the Reformation with the nature of the kingdom in Calvin's eschatology, thus explaining its uniqueness in the face of what is primarily a Roman eschatology.

And so we see that Calvin, though clearly a child of his time, was willing to let his theological emphases work their way through his entire theological system, giving new impetus to time-tested patterns of eschatological thinking.

---

38. Note that this simple recipe also explains (as hinted earlier) Calvin's rejection of purgatory. Since union with Christ is accomplished in the divine work of justification and does not depend on the work of man, there is no place in Calvin's thought for the doctrine of purgatory.

THE DOCTRINE OF THE FUTURE
IN ANABAPTIST THOUGHT

Paige Patterson

O ne of the anomalies of the sixteenth-century Reformation is that prisons of the period might host at once both the most violent and the most passive of all men. The now belligerent and pacifistic Anabaptists were certainly capable of being a nuisance to the sacral state and church as demonstrated by George Blaurock, the blue-coated evangelist, and his uninvited open challenge to the astonished pastor of the parish church in Zollikon.[1] This apparent devotion to public confrontation and debate, coupled with the abortive effort by Jan Matthys and Jan of Leyden to establish the millennium in Münster, created the perfect storm for uncritical commoners as well as for Romans, Lutherans, and Reformed. The Schwärmer were simply viewed as dangerous.

Although Luther labored to extricate himself from liability for the Peasants' War, he did carry considerable responsibility for its outbreak. Some of this was the unavoidable concomitant of the Reformation; however, the vituperation of some of the Wittenberger's writings was also referenced by the peasants. Luther might even have lent more support, but his perspective was broad enough that he knew the odds against long-term peasant victory. Besides, much of the leadership of the movement frightened him, and he feared that the revolt would capsize his own more modest revolution, placing Rome back in full control. As Luther anticipated, the results of the Peasants' War were gruesome beyond comprehension. Will Durant estimates the demise of 130,000, and the barbarity of their deaths turned all of Europe pale.[2]

---

1. William R. Estep, *The Anabaptist Story* (Nashville: Broadman, 1963), 32.
2. Will Durant, *The Reformation: A History of European Civilization from Wyclif to Calvin: 1300–*

When you add to this the apocalyptic threat of the Turks in the east, an emerging picture of the social and religious restiveness poses an enigma for contemporary minds to grasp. In the midst of this confusion, the four distinct branches of the Reformation became reality. The Lutheran phase, centered in Wittenberg, was followed by the Zwinglian reform in Zürich, the Calvinistic reform in Geneva, and ultimately the English reformation in that island nation. Although here it may also owe its origin to the Zwinglian circle in Zürich, the Radical Reformation (as opposed to the Magisterial Reformation) was from its onset much more mobile. This scenario was partly due to its doctrine of two kingdoms, which had the effect of leaving it neither armed nor supported by civil weaponry. But their doctrine of nonresistance precluded the use of such, had it been available. Consequently, long tenures were out of the question.

Only Luther, of the major early Reformers, thought apocalyptically. And Luther was not bound to eschatological reflection as were the Radicals. Durant, in a typical overreach, observes, "All the Anabaptist groups were inspired by the Apocalypse and the confident expectation of Christ's early return to the earth; many believers professed to know the day and hour of His coming. Then all the ungodly—in this case all but Anabaptists—would be swept away by the sword of the Lord, and the elect would live in glory in a terrestrial paradise without laws or marriage, and abounding in all good things. So hopeful men steeled themselves against toil and monogamy."[3]

Granted the overstatement, Durant was certainly correct to posit the Radical Reformers as an apocalyptic people. Colwell observes, "Beyond the historical research pursued by Mennonites, Baptists, and perhaps Brethren . . . the Anabaptists remain liable to dismissal with a passing censorious reference to polygamy and violence of Münster."[4] Colwell concludes,

> Who were the Anabaptists anyway? We are not referring to a single 'stream' or 'movement' but to a series of separate and largely

---

1564, The Story of Civilization, vol. 6 (New York: MJF Books, 1985), 392. While Claus-Peter Clasen (Anabaptism, A Social History, 1525–1618 [Ithaca, NY: Cornell University Press, 1972]) insists that Anabaptism had no substantive relationship to the Peasants' War, James M. Stayer argues that a substantial connection exists at least indirectly (The German Peasants' War and Anabaptist Community of Goods, McGill-Queen's Studies in the History of Religion 6 [Montreal & Kingston: McGill-Queen's University Press, 1991], 3).

3. Durant, The Reformation, 396.
4. John E. Colwell, "A Radical Church? A Reappraisal of Anabaptist Ecclesiology," Tyndale Historical Theology Lecture, 1985, Tyndale Bulletin 38 (1987): 119.

independent groups some of which began to merge in the course of time; to an amalgam of differing strands in which the heterodox and the orthodox occasionally appear strangely blurred. That which survives of their own writings may be less than representative, is indicative of considerable difference of emphasis and sometimes exposes a lack of opportunity for detached and rigorous academic theological reflection on the part of the various writers.[5]

Colwell goes on to identify the essence of Anabaptism as ecclesiastical in nature—namely, the concept of a redeemed church, a conclusion advanced by many. Colwell also suggests that this redeemed church was informed by an eschatological commitment to two kingdoms.[6] While admitting that the terminology is anachronistic, Colwell says that, "While therefore it is probably unhelpful to define this expectation as a form of non-dispensationalist premillennialism it is nonetheless distinguishable from the 'spiritualist' group in its affirmation of an expectation for the restitution of the contemporary church and distinguishable from the 'church-kingdom' group, the magisterial reformers and the mediaeval church in its recognition of the limitations of this expectation in the present."[7]

To summarize, the Anabaptists believed that they were living in the last days. Christ would return to establish his kingdom and punish the wicked. They can be forgiven for believing that they were living through the tribulation. Although these positions are not constant among the Radicals, this view represents the anticipation of most.

One additional factor influenced Anabaptist eschatology. The Radicals were biblical literalists except in their interpretation of the Lord's Supper. On this last subject, they mirrored Zwingli far more closely than the Romans or Luther. They were confident that Jesus never intended that his actual body and blood were present in the elements of the Supper. Beyond this, the Anabaptists read their Bibles in a straightforward manner. Graeme Chatfield notes the following concerning Hubmaier:

> In common with the evangelical Reformers, Hubmaier holds
> to the formal principle of *sola scriptura*. Primarily, Scripture is

---

5. Ibid.
6. Ibid., 124. Colwell goes on to point to Thomas Muntzer as resembling the amillennial or postmillennial eschatology of the magisterial reformers.
7. Ibid., 127.

considered to be the only authority by which matters of faith and practice in the church are to be judged. Other possible sources of authority, such as the church fathers, councils, decretals, and the tradition of the church, are to be accepted as authoritative only in so far as they can be demonstrated to agree with Scripture. Hubmaier maintains this opinion of the authority of Scripture consistently throughout his writings, varying it only in his final writing, the *Vienna Testimony*. Even in this final writing the concession he makes in agreeing to postpone his teaching on baptism and the Lord's Supper until the matter has been discussed by a General Council, or has been examined by representatives of Ferdinand of Austria, is qualified by the formal principle that the examination takes place only according to Scripture. Even in his extreme need to modify his position so that it would be favorably viewed by the Catholic Austrian authorities, Hubmaier continues to challenge them on this fundamental premise on which the work of all the Reformers was built.[8]

This high view of the reliability of Scripture is discernible at every turn in the works of Hubmaier and other Anabaptists. Hubmaier says, "All of which cannot take place more fittingly nor properly than through the proclamation of the clear Word of God as written in both Testaments. For in all divisive questions and controversies only Scripture, canonized and sanctified by God himself, should and must be the judge, no one else: or heaven and earth must fall."[9]

As a result of this perspective regarding the Bible, when Scripture speaks of a millennium, of great tribulation, of hell, or of heaven, the Radical response was to receive that witness. The chiliasm of the Anabaptists was then generally the rule, even if the details of the end times were not so carefully enumerated.

ESCHATOLOGY IN MAJOR ANABAPTIST THEOLOGIANS

The three major writing Anabaptists were Balthasar Hubmaier, Pilgram Marpeck, and Menno Simons. Simons (1496–1561) wrote against the "blasphemy" of Jan of

---

8. Graeme R. Chatfield, *Balthasar Hubmaier and the Clarity of Scripture: A Critical Reformation Issue* (Eugene, OR: Pickwick Publications, 2013), 360.

9. H. Wayne Pipkin and John H. Yoder, trans. and eds., *Balthasar Hubmaier: Theologian of Anabaptism*, Classics of the Radical Reformation 5 (Scottdale, PA: Herald Press, 1989), 23.

Leyden. Remonstrating with John about his use of the sword, Simons affirms that Babylon will be punished but not by Christians, who should use only the sword of the word of God. Of that final intervention of Christ, Simons states:

> This Scripture clearly testifies that the Lord Christ must first come again before all His enemies are punished. And how Christ will come again He Himself testifies, saying, For the Son of man shall come in the glory of his Father, with his angels; and then he shall reward every man according to his works. Again, For as the lightning cometh out of the east, and shineth even unto the west, so shall also the coming of the Son of man be. And then shall appear the sign of the Son of man in heaven: and then shall all the tribes of the earth mourn, and they shall see the Son of man coming in the clouds of heaven, with power and great glory. The two angels also testified how Christ would come again, saying, Ye men of Galilee, why stand ye gazing up into heaven? This same Jesus, which is taken up from you into heaven, shall so come in like manner as ye have seen him go into heaven. From this it is plain to everybody how Christ shall come. Therefore when ye shall see Christ come in this manner you may rest assured that all the enemies of God will be punished. And do not suppose that it will be so before His return, for you will find yourself mistaken unless God's Word be false, a thing that is impossible. Luke says that the Lord had received the kingdom.[10]

Simons insists that the judgments on "the whore of Babylon" and on wicked men do not come until Christ returns. Working through the various parables of Jesus, he insists that Christians are the "good seed" and not the reapers. Only the Lord Jesus will be revealed from heaven and take vengeance. Further, in this life the wheat and tares grow together. Only Christ is adequate to separate them.[11]

In addition to Simon's well-known opposition to the use of the sword (a common but not universal theme among the Radicals), this treatise makes several things abundantly clear. Christians are not to anticipate a prolongation of

---

10. John Christian Wenger, ed., *The Complete Writings of Menno Simons c.1496–1561*, trans. Leonard Verduin (Scottdale, PA: Herald Press, 1956), 47.
11. Ibid., 48–49.

the present situation. They are to suffer after the example of Christ in the present age. At the conclusion of this age, Christ will return just as prophesied by the angels at His ascension. He will come to punish and eliminate the wicked from the earth. Apparently, Simons anticipated an earthly manifestation of the kingdom of God. In *Foundation of Christian Doctrine*, he says:

> We write the truth in Christ and lie not, that as to the spirit we acknowledge no king either in heaven above or upon the earth beneath, other than the only, eternal, and true king David in the spirit, Christ Jesus, who is Lord of lords and King of kings.
>
> And if anyone declares himself king in the kingdom and dominion of Christ, as John of Leiden did at Münster, he with Adonijah shall not go unpunished, for the true Solomon, Christ Jesus Himself, must possess the kingdom and sit eternally upon the throne of David.[12]

By the same token, Simons was certain that the church at Rome was not merely the Babylonian whore but also the antichrist. Among his most severe words were those reserved for Rome, second only to Jan of Leyden. For example, he opined that:

> On the other hand, the church of Antichrist is begotten of deceiving seduction through the spirit of error. Paul says, "Now the Spirit speaketh expressly, that in the latter times some shall depart from the faith, giving heed to seducing spirits, and doctrines of devils; speaking lies in hypocrisy." Yes, reader, what else has the church of Christ laid low and the church of Antichrist raised up again, if not the vile, false doctrines of the learned ones, the many mutually contradictory councils, decretals, statues, doctrines, and commandments of men? What is it that blinds the Germanic peoples today? What keeps them in their ungodliness, if not the frivolous doctrine of the preachers, the miserable infant baptism, the unscriptural, idolatrous Supper, and the neglect of the Lord's ordinance of the ban as practiced by the apostles?[13]

---

12. Ibid., 199.
13. Ibid., 737.

Confidence that the eternal destinies of heaven and hell await the human family completes the eschatology of Menno. While his concerns were primarily for the church, and though he was continually reacting against the abuses of errant chiliasm, his theology is still determined by hope for the intervention of Christ at the terminus of the age.

The same theses are traceable in Hubmaier's writings, but his eschatology is more prominent and somewhat more developed. Tragically, the eschaton arrived for Hubmaier in 1528 in Vienna, where he was burned. With his penchant for writing and amid heavy pastoral duties, a few more years might have made a significant difference with the only Anabaptist theologian who held a terminal degree. Hubmaier—after a colorful career as a Catholic priest, which included study with John Eck, the most astute debater of the era—was well prepared both to contemplate the issues and to debate with the most learned of the day. Taking a page from his mentor's book, he referred to Eck as the "elephant of Ingolstadt" and to himself as the "fly of Friedberg." Hubmaier was baptized in April of 1525, with the mysterious Wilhelm Reublin officiating. Three years later, on March 10, 1528, his voice was silenced and his pen laid to rest. Prodigious writing, as well as what would today be called a megachurch in Nikolsburg, capped a remarkable career.

Hubmaier's general eschatology is encapsulated in the following brief statement from his 1527 masterpiece, *On the Sword*: "At some distant day this Christ, her Bridegroom, will come again in corporeal and visible form, in his glory and majesty, and will take again in person his kingdom, until he shall deliver it up to his Heavenly Father, as Paul writes (I Cor. 15:24), until God shall be all in all. Even that is the secret (mystery) in Christ and his church, according to the contents of the letter to the Ephesians."[14]

In a treatise of equal importance entitled *On the Christian Ban*, Hubmaier develops his doctrine of church discipline. This tract, prepared in the early period of his Nikolsberg pastorate, probably encountered difficulties that Hubmaier could not have imagined, given the rapid growth of the congregation. In developing the concept of "authority," he promises:

---

14. D. Balthasar Huebmör von Fridberg, "On the Sword: A Christian Exposition of the Scriptures, Earnestly Announced by Certain Brothers as against Magistracy (That Is, That Christians Should Not Sit in Judgment, nor Bear the Sword)," in *Anabaptist Beginnings (1523-1533): A Source Book*, Bibliotheca Humanistica & Reformatorica Vol. 15, ed. William R. Estep, Jr. (Nieuwkoop, Netherlands: B. de Graaf, 1976), 114.

After his resurrection, just as he was to ascend into heaven, Christ assigned all his authority to the holy Christian church and hung the promised keys at her side, that she should use the same for the loosing and binding of sins according to his command in his bodily absence, until his second bodily coming. John 20:23; Matt. 16:19. Then with a battle cry and the voice of the archangel and with the trumpet of God he will come down again from heaven; the dead in Christ will first rise, 1 Thess. 4:16f. After them we who live and survive will at the same time with them be seized up into the clouds to meet the Lord in the air. There and then the church will return her authority and keys to Christ her spouse, for her authority will have come to an end, since she is no longer on earth. Now she is with Christ in the air and will be with him forever. Thus her power is given to her only on earth as Christ precisely spoke to her.[15]

Here, citing 1 Thessalonians 4:16, Hubmaier anticipates a coming of Christ at the end of the age. The dead rise, and all believers who have survived will be "seized up" and will return to Christ the keys of the kingdom bestowed by Christ on his bride in Matthew 16:18ff. The judgment of all "the living and the dead" follows.

A more detailed analysis of the end times comes in his *Apologia*, which is a direct result of his discussion with Faber in 1527. Nothing is in his hand, and the one surviving copy seems to have belonged to Faber. However, its accuracy is not seriously questioned. Two instructive articles occur—the thirteenth on purgatory, and the fourteenth on the last day.

On the basis of 1 Corinthians 3:10, Hubmaier rejects the existence of purgatory. First, if purgatory exists, it negates the idea of full forgiveness in Christ. Second, in all of Scripture there is no mention of such a place. Finally, judgment is for the lost who will have no chance after death.[16]

Regarding the last days Hubmaier notes that God has given numerous signs whereby one can posit an imminent conclusion to this age. However, he cautions that this information is insufficient to assign a precise day. Citing Mark

---

15. Hubmaier, "On the Christian Ban," in *Balthasar Hubmaier: Theologian of Anabaptism*, 415.
16. Ibid., 541.

13:32, he warns against establishing a date for the return of Christ. Based on these remarks, Hubmaier recalls his rebuke of Hans Hut:

> Out of these words I have always and everywhere formulated the article as it is stated above, but said that the day of the Lord is closer than we know; therefore we should persist in daily contemplation, righteousness and the fear of God.

> I was also very severe against Johann Hutt and his followers [because] they gave simple folk the idea of a definite time for the last day, namely now at this very next Pentecost, and thereby induced them to sell their possessions and property, forsake wife and child, house and farm, thus depriving the simpleminded of work in order to persuade them to run after him. This seductive error arose out of a serious misunderstanding of the Scripture which indicates the four years that Daniel calls "a time, two times, and half a time," Dan. 12:7. John in Revelation 13:5 calls the time forty-two weeks, which weeks constitute three and one-half years; this will be the period when the Antichrist (whom Paul calls a man of sin and a son of perdition, 2 Thess. 2:3), will become active and reign, and at the close of the period God will destroy him with the breath of his mouth without moving his hand, Isa. 11:4, Dan. 8. Out of these three and one-half years, which are solar and Danielic years, the ignorant Hutt made ordinary years. This is a great error. A solar year is the time in which the sun runs its own course of a circle once, with a little left over. Therefore leap years were inserted, so that an ordinary year makes just one day of a solar year. It follows from this that where Hutt teaches about three and one-half years, as found in Daniel, or about forty-two weeks in Revelation, understanding them as three and one-half ordinary years, which in a correct understanding and truth of the Scriptures is three and one-half sun years, which make 1,277 ordinary years, his reckoning has erred to that extent, as I unambiguously told him openly and earnestly rebuked him for exciting and misleading the simple populace without basis in the truth, as I can testify by the theses that I made against him. Indeed, I could speak even more profoundly

and clearly about the judgment day, by his Word, but for the sake of brevity I cannot do it at this time. Thus, I conclude with Christ: "Take heed, watch and pray; for you know neither the day nor the hour," Mark 13:32; Matt. 25:13. "Behold," says James, "the Judge is already standing at the door," James 5:9.[17]

Beyond these references, passing acknowledgment of Scripture contains information on the end times. But Hubmaier was a busy pastor with a thriving church, pressured constantly by those who wished to see him dead. He simply never had time to work out his eschatology. Pilgram Marpeck, on the other hand, lived until about 1556, allowing him about thirty years as an Anabaptist if, indeed, he was baptized as an Anabaptist in 1527. To be sure, some of that time was spent on the run or in obscurity, but the longer period should provide more information about his theology, including eschatology. We are indebted to the work of Walter Klaassen and William Klassen, who provided not only an assessment of Marpeck's life but also a translation of his works. But even here, there is little guidance. Klaassen and Klassen remark concerning this apocalyptic spirit of the age:

> The sixteenth century was a time when the apocalyptic imagination was in full flower. Scholar J. J. Collins observes that the legacy of such apocalyptic literature includes "a powerful rhetoric for denouncing the deficiencies of this world" and a conviction that the world as now constituted is not the end. Above all, he says, apocalypses show the strength of the human imagination "to construct a symbolic world where the integrity of values can be maintained in the face of social and political powerlessness and even of the threat of death." Marpeck's *Exposé of the Babylonian Whore* in all these respects was a classic expression of the literature of end times.[18]

Fortunately, one of Marpeck's brief tracts came to light in the 1950s. The provenance of this work, using the shortened title *Exposé of the Babylonian Whore*, is

---

17. Ibid., 542–43.
18. Walter Klaassen and William Klassen, *Marpeck: A Life of Dissent and Conformity* (Scottdale, PA and Waterloo, ON: Herald Press, 2008), 162. They cite John J. Collins, *The Apocalyptic Imagination: An Introduction to the Jewish Apocalyptic Literature* (Grand Rapids: Eerdmans, 1998), 215.

not certain, but most scholars suggest that Marpeck is the author. In this tract, Marpeck avers that both auditors and author are living in the last times. Marpeck expects this time to usher in the return of Christ. He observes, "The time has now come, according to the word of the Lord in Matthew 24[:11–12]. It says that temptations so difficult will come that it is possible that even the elect would not escape them unless the days were shortened. Lord, come; cut them short soon for the sake of your chosen ones. May your will be done soon."[19]

Marpeck sees a stern judgment of God on the horizon and sees the coming of that day as a surprise. The "red Roman Whore" is the culprit he wishes to expose.[20] Surprisingly, Luther is conjoined with Rome in the mind of Marpeck:

> They presented infant baptism and the pope's idolatry [the mass or Lord's Supper], over which they quarreled, and prattled about receiving it in both kinds *sub utraque specie* [in both kinds, the bread and the wine], as the most important matters on which their salvation depended, and so filled the whole world with their contentions and writings. Thus Satan could carry out his seductions so much the better. In Martin Luther's eyes all who eat and drink both the body and blood of Christ, regardless of whether they are adulterers or prostitutes, gluttons or drunkards, gamblers, murderers, betrayers, tyrants, deceivers, or whatever else are all a good community of his kind of godliness. Even as, in Luther's view, the body of Christ is in the bread and the blood in the chalice, his faithful ones and disciples are transformed into the nature and essence of Christ.[21]

Finally, Marpeck turns to the parable of the wheat and tares to illustrate his point:

> Listen to Christ's interpretation of the parable when the disciples ask him about its meaning, and let these nay-sayers themselves judge whether Christ committed the sword of secular Authority

---

19. Pilgram Marpeck, "Exposé of the Babylonian Whore," trans. and introduction by Walter Klaassen, in *Later Writings by Pilgram Marpeck and His Circle, Vol. 1: The Exposé, A Dialogue, and Marpeck's Response to Caspar Schwenckfeld*, trans. Walter Klaassen, Werner Packull, and John Rempel (Scottdale, PA: Herald Press, 1999), 24.
20. Ibid., 24–25.
21. Ibid., 26.

to his own, or whether he commanded them to gather in the weeds before the End of the world. Jesus answered his disciples: "The one who sows the good seed is the Son of Man; the field is the world, and the good seed are the children of the kingdom; the weeds are the children of the evil one, and the enemy who sowed them . . . is the devil; the harvest is the end of the age, and the reapers are angels. Just as the weeds are collected and burned up with fire, so will it be at the end of the age. The Son of Man will send his angels, and they will collect out of his kingdom all causes of sin and all evildoers, and they will throw them into the furnace of fire where there will be weeping and gnashing of teeth. Then the righteous will shine like the sun in the kingdom of their Father. Let anyone with ears listen!" [Matt. 13:37–43].[22]

In all of this, Marpeck takes issue with the Protestant theologians who made the field to be the church. Marpeck notes that the parable says, "The field is the world." No violence is to be used to uproot the tares. That is alone the work of the reapers at the time of the coming of Christ.

Some might conclude from this brief survey of the most prolific of Anabaptist theologians that eschatology was a sidebar. Abraham Friesen, however, points to two eschatologies at work among the Radicals. He notes the chiliasm of the Münsterites and of Thomas Müntzer as one strand, but also notes the rejection of all such positions by the majority of a peaceful Anabaptist/Mennonite point of view, which rejected all of chiliasm with its violent provocations.[23] Friesen even speculates that the volatile form of millennialism was not "home grown" but imported from no less than Augustine.[24]

Friesen also cites the 1522 sermon on Luke 21, delivered by Luther, in which he quoted the following from Lactantius:

When the last end shall begin to approach to the world, wickedness will increase; all kinds of vices and frauds will become frequent; justice will perish; faith, peace, mercy, modesty, truth, will have no existence; violence and daring will abound;

---

22. Ibid., 40.
23. Abraham Friesen, *Reformers, Radicals, Revolutionaries: Anabaptism in the Context of the Reformation Conflict* (Elkhart, IN: Institute of Mennonite Studies, 2012), 147–48.
24. Ibid., 150.

no one will have anything, unless it is acquired by the hand, and defended by the hand. If there shall be any good men, they will be esteemed as a prey and a laughing stock. No one will exhibit filial affection to parents, no one will pity an infant or an old man; avarice and lust will corrupt all things. There will be slaughter and bloodshed. There will be wars, and those not only between foreign and neighboring states, but also intestine wars. States will carry on wars among themselves, every sex and age will handle arms. . . . Cities and towns will be destroyed, at one time by fire and the sword, at another by repeated earthquakes; now by inundation of waters, now by pestilence and famine. The earth will produce nothing, being barren either through excessive cold or heat.[25]

Friesen concludes that such enthusiasm for the time of God's ultimate intervention captivated Anabaptist thinking for decades. Some Anabaptists, however, simply viewed it as the inevitable course of a sinful world, which included the suffering of the true church.[26]

Klaassen and Klassen argue that there emerged a clear difference in this tractate between Luther and Marpeck:

At first blush, Marpeck's separation of the spiritual and secular powers into independent spheres looks very Lutheran. There is every reason to believe that to a considerable degree Luther was his teacher. He was almost certainly deeply influenced by his Rattenberg priest, Stefan Castenbaur, who for several years promulgated Luther's early views on the separation of church and state. . . . But the difference between Marpeck and Luther was as important as the similarity. Luther taught that in the best case, God gave the authority of the sword to believing Christians and that in this capacity they were authorized—indeed mandated—to kill with the sword should the necessity arise. Marpeck argued in the Exposé that no Christian has been

---

25. Ibid., 147. Friesen quotes from "Epitome of the Divine Institutes," in *The Ante-Nicene Fathers*, 7:253. Luther's sermon is found in Martin Luther *Sämmtliche Schriften*, ed. Johann Georg Walch (St. Louis: Concordia Publishing House, 1880), 11:56–57.
26. Friesen, *Reformers, Radicals, Revolutionaries*, 150.

given a killing sword because it is contrary to the command
and example of Christ.[27]

Robert Friedmann agrees with Friesen, describing the two responses among
the Radical Reformers as "violent eschatology" in comparison with a "quiet eschatology." Citing a study by Paul Althaus, he suggests that the chiliasm of the
Anabaptists propelled the missionary enthusiasm of the "quiet" Anabaptists. The
coming kingdom of Christ was the focus that motivated the extraordinary missionary efforts of the earliest Anabaptists and later the Hutterites.[28]

Friedmann also chronicles a decisive change in Hans Hut. At first belonging to the more aggressive chiliasts, he moderated considerably under the
influence of Hans Denck. He further suggests that the kingdom, and not just
personal salvation, was in the forefront of Anabaptist thinking. Further, he
cites the influence of Petrus Olivi's *Postil on the Apocalypse,* written 1295–96,
as a book of substantial influence on the Hutterites. Olivi was a leader among
the Spiritual Franciscans.[29] This informed the sense of the imminent coming
of the kingdom.

The Radical Radicals

No assessment would be complete without some attention to the more developed eschatologies that have served to jaundice much of the world against
the Radical Reformation. Much more directly influenced by apocalyptic
thinking were the writings of Peter Riedemann, Hans Hut, and David Joris.
Riedemann (1506–1556), in his *Confession of Faith* (1543–45), takes a frequent
Anabaptist theme, positing a *descensus ad inferos.* He writes:

> In order that he might fulfill all things, we confess that Christ
> went down to the lowest parts of the earth, that is, to the place
> of captivity where those are kept who formerly did not believe
> the word spoken to them. Christ proclaimed to those spirits that
> the word of salvation had now been sent. God had previously
> planned this word of salvation and had promised it to humanity,

27. Klaassen and Klassen, *Marpeck,* 159.
28. Robert Friedmann, *The Theology of Anabaptism: An Interpretation,* Studies in Anabaptist and
    Mennonite History 15 (Scottdale, PA: Herald Press, 1973), 103.
29. Ibid., 111.

so that all who believed it in their hearts should be set free. Now, in accordance with the Father's promise, Christ through his death had destroyed the power of death, hell, and the devil, which for so long had betrayed humans and led them astray.[30]

Riedemann also anticipated a literal return of Christ from heaven. Christ's return will be terrifying with flaming fire and will take vengeance on the ungodly. This will occur with the sounding of the last trumpet. The dead in Christ will rise out of their graves because sentence has already been passed, and those who believe are saved. Those who have not believed are lost. Here, Riedemann interestingly appeals to books of judgment in Daniel:

> As Daniel says, "The court sat, and the books were opened." After him, John testifies that the dead were judged from what was written in these books and sentenced according to their works. So we truly believe that all our words and deeds, good or evil, are recorded before God and his Son as though written in a book. When the time comes, God will open his secret book and show to each all their deeds. Paul says, "The day of the Lord will clarify all things, and then each will know why he is to be blessed or condemned."[31]

Riedemann posits an incorruptible resurrected body followed by judgment before "the terrible judge." At that time, the judge appoints each man to his deserved reward. Actually, eternal life begins at the moment of true faith but takes on additional significance in the eschaton. The believer, who until that moment has walked by faith, will then see Christ as he is. The "insignificant body" of the believer will be transfigured and become like the glorified body of Christ.[32]

The city of Strasbourg was, for much of the time, the most tolerant city in the Reformation. Consequently, there is no surprise that Lutherans, Anabaptists, spiritualists, and chiliasts flocked to Strasbourg. While this created

---

30. John J. Friesen, ed. and trans., *Peter Riedemann's Hutterite Confession of Faith: Translation of the 1565 German Edition of* Confession of Our Religion, Teaching, and Faith by the Brothers Who Are Known as the Hutterites, Classics of the Radical Reformation 9 (Scottdale, PA: Herald Press, 1999), 70–71.

31. Ibid., 72–73.

32. Ibid., 82–83.

almost infinite difficulties for the city council, the various strands of Reformation thought experienced greater opportunity to develop and commit to writing their perspectives. Melchior Hoffman arrived in the city around April of 1529. Having imbibed the spirit of the Reformation, the story of his life in Strasbourg is a tale of uncertainty and shifting doctrine and emphasis.

Awaiting the fiery preacher in Strasbourg were the Strasbourg Prophets, Lienhard and Ursula Jost. Although Lienhard was confined for some time to the "madhouse" in Strasbourg, the two had considerable impact on Hoffman, who eventually declared himself the "second Elijah." Klaus Deppermann analyzes the situation in the city as follows:

> The sectarian movement in Strasbourg became increasingly powerful between 1529 and 1534. Hoffman's preaching gave it an apocalyptic tone, with the result that the evangelical preachers feared a general uprising. Hoffman's highest hopes related to the Imperial City itself; he believed that Strasbourg was called to be the "heavenly Jerusalem," the centre of a world-wide renewal. 144,000 "apostolic messengers" would go out from its gates to prepare the earth and to receive the Son of God.[33]

Hoffman pursued his reform, counting on the city council to support his efforts. Instead, he was imprisoned "for life." Deppermann notes that the anticipated "revolt of the Melchiorites actually took place in Münster,"[34] while referring to such programs as Münster and Strasbourg—together with the abortive efforts of Thomas Müntzer and the Zwickau prophets—as postmillennial. That is precisely what they were. Each was an effort to establish the kingdom of God into which Christ would surely come.

Whether Hoffman would have taken his revolution in Strasbourg as far as Jan of Leyden did in Münster is conjecture. What can be said is that for all of Hoffman's vulnerability to such ill-fated chiliasm, and even though he was much too susceptible to prophets like the Josts, his spirit was more irenic than that of most such chiliastic leaders. Though a fiery and influential preacher, he

---

33. Klaus Deppermann, *Melchior Hoffman: Social Unrest and Apocalyptic Visions in the Age of Reformation*, ed. Benjamin Drewery; trans. Malcolm Wren (Edinburgh: T. & T. Clark, 1987), 161.

34. Ibid.

nevertheless heard the voices of the Reformers Zell, Hedio, Bucer, and Capito, and was especially influenced by the far more pacifistic thought of Hans Denck and other Anabaptists.

When interrogated, Hoffman defended the revolution in Münster: "In Münster they have a prophet by the name of John Mathis who claims that he is one of the witnesses of God. Münster will not be oppressed. We will have three kings here before this city. We wait for it every hour."[35] Like almost all Reformers and Anabaptists, Hoffman saw Rome as Babylon. The true Jerusalem could never become a reality until Babylon was overthrown.[36] The sense of the prophetic direction of the Holy Spirit through visions, dreams, and other ecstatic experiences prompted a certain impatience about waiting for the direct intervention of Christ.

CONCLUSION

Hoffman and the chiliasts influenced the development of Anabaptism in two ways. First, inspired preaching fused with apocalyptic hope in an era of persecution was solace to the soul and energy for the spirit of mission. More thoughtful Anabaptists were too biblically versed to succumb to the programmatic chiliasm of Müntzer, Jan of Leyden, or even Hoffman. Even those like Hubmaier who were not strictly pacifists were alarmed by these human efforts to establish by force the kingdom on earth. But they were, like Martin Luther, cognizant of the desperation of the day and saw that the intervention of God was the only possible solution.

On the other hand, most Anabaptists understood that their ecclesiology took center stage with eschatology remaining a hope without a timetable. This included the essential of a new birth for every man prior to baptism. As a responsible member of the body of Christ, each of the redeemed must enter the mission tasks. As a part of this assignment, a robust doctrine of the inevitability and purpose of God in human suffering informed their theology.

There can be no doubt that for most Anabaptists, persecution, including dislocation from their families and even martyrdom, was made bearable by the sense of the imminent return of Christ. The details they left to God, but they believed themselves to be in the last days. They were prepared to live for Christ and proclaim his message of a church made up of twice-born men.

---

35. Walter Klaassen, ed., *Anabaptism in Outline: Selected Primary Sources*, Classics of the Radical Reformation 3 (Scottdale, PA: Herald Press, 1981), 329.
36. Ibid., 328.

And, if necessary, as was often the case, they were prepared to die for Christ. After all, Jesus had done this for them. The kingdom of Christ would follow, and every injustice would be set right. They were a biblical people possessed of an eschatological hope on an informed mission to bring Christ to all men.

Regarding the eschatology of the Radical Reformation, consider the judgment of George Huntston Williams:

> We have also found the idea of the return of a combined Golden Age, Paradise, and primitive Church in varying strengths and permutations in Balthasar Hubmaier, John Hut, Melchior Hofmann, Menno Simons, Dirk Philips, Jacob Hutter, Michael Servetus, Camillo Renato, William Postel, and George Schomann.

> A more generalized millennialism, based upon a harmonization of scriptural and apocryphal prophecies, reinforced by various medieval prognostications, was the most common eschatology, because it was always amorphously amenable to fresh calculations in the light of current signs and developments. Whether as a provisional paradise or garden enclosed, as the harbinger of the third Age of the Spirit or of Christ, as the outpost of the Fifth Monarchy of Christ the King, or as the gateway to the millennium, the churches of the Radical Reformation were sustained and emboldened by the conviction that they and their often charismatic leaders were the instruments of the Lord of history in the latter days.[37]

---

37. George Huntston Williams, *The Radical Reformation*, 3rd ed., Sixteenth Century Essays & Studies 15 (Kirksville, MO: Sixteenth Century Journal Publishers, 1992), 1304–5.

THE DOCTRINE OF THE FUTURE
IN JONATHAN EDWARDS

Glenn R. Kreider

Accourding to Charles Ryrie, "Only dispensationalism presents a properly optimistic philosophy of history. Furthermore, the charts notwith-
standing, the dispensational pattern does not form a repetitive cyclical
picture, but rather an ascending spiral."[1] He further explains, "Dispensationalism reveals the outworking of God's plan in the historical process in a progressive
revelation of His glory. It magnifies the grace of God, for it recognizes that true
progress can come only through God's gracious intervention in human society.
If there were not 'cyclical' interventions, then the course of history would be
only downward and entirely pessimistic."[2] Ryrie's claim stands in stark opposition to the widely reported charge that dispensationalism is pessimistic, that its
belief in the pretribulational rapture and premillennial return of Christ give it
a negative, defeatist, pessimistic, and gloomy outlook on life.[3] But, surely Ryrie

---

1. Charles C. Ryrie, *Dispensationalism Today* (Chicago: Moody Press, 1965), 42. This citation is
   from my dog-eared and well-marked copy that I read and annotated for the course 414 Issues
   in Dispensation Theology with Craig Blaising in spring 1988.
2. Ryrie, *Dispensationalism Today*, 43. Every time I teach eschatology I am reminded of my in-
   debtedness to Craig Blaising for teaching me the story of redemption in 406 Eschatology in
   summer 1989.
3. Gerry Breshears and Mark Driscoll, *Vintage Church* (Wheaton, IL: Crossway Books,
   2008), 61, claim that dispensationalism is "a gloomy, pessimistic underrealized eschatology that thinks we can't make a difference in the world as the church by the power of the
   gospel." Gary M. Burge writes, "Dispensationalism embraced a pessimistic view of history,
   thinking that the world was coming to its end and that the judgment day was near. And
   as a result, it became sectarian, separating itself from mainstream society, calling sinners
   to repent and be saved from the inevitable catastrophe of the human story." Burge, "Why
   I'm Not a Christian Zionist, Academically Speaking," http://www.christianzionism.org/
   Article/Burge02.pdf (accessed April 15, 2014). For a different view, see Robert L. Thomas,

has overstated the case when he implies that only dispensationalism is optimistic.[4] Rather, Christian eschatology, the message of hope that one day God will complete his work of redemption, is necessarily optimistic. The apostle Peter expressed it this way: "Blessed be the God and Father of our Lord Jesus Christ! According to his great mercy, he has caused us to be born again to a living hope through the resurrection of Jesus Christ from the dead, to an inheritance that is imperishable, undefiled, and unfading, kept in heaven for you, who by God's power are being guarded through faith for a salvation ready to be revealed in the last time" (1 Peter 1:3–5, ESV). And this optimistic ethos is true regardless of positions on the millennium.

This essay assesses the eschatology of Jonathan Edwards. Edwards was a millennialist; he believed in a future one-thousand-year period of time in history during which Christ and his followers would rule over the earth.[5] But there is much more to his view of the future than the hope of the millennium. Edwards, the eighteenth-century New England pastor, held to an optimistic view of history because of his view of redemption, which he explicates throughout his ministry, particularly in the sermon series "A History of the Work of Redemption." McClymond and McDermott identify the thesis of this work: "He devoted his 1739 sermon series on the history of redemption to expounding the thesis that God was directing the movement of every atom in the universe toward his predetermined end."[6] Further, they claim that Edwards's eschatology permeates everything he wrote: "All his thought was eschatological in a generalized sense."[7] They explain:

> For many thinkers in the Reformed tradition, eschatology was a theological appendage. But for Edwards eschatology was both central and integral to his thought. His philosophy of history presumed that God directed every atom in the universe to-

---

"Dispensationalism's Role in the Public Square," *The Masters Seminary Journal* 20 (Spring 2009): 19–40.

4. Ryrie goes beyond implication when he claims that since it "obviously does not have any goal within temporal history, [covenant theology] is therefore pessimistic." Charles C. Ryrie, *Dispensationalism*, rev. ed. (Chicago: Moody Press, 2007), 21.

5. C. C. Goen, "A New Departure in Eschatology," *Church History* 28 (1959): 25–40, argued that Edwards was responsible for the development of postmillennial thought in American theology. See also the summary in Christopher B. Holdsworth, "The Eschatology of Jonathan Edwards," *Reformation and Revival* 5 (1996): 119–48.

6. Michael J. McClymond and Gerald R. McDermott, *The Theology of Jonathan Edwards* (New York: Oxford University Press, 2012), 566.

7. Ibid., 566.

ward a cosmic conclusion. His biblical typology suggested that all of nature and history teems with types of future, end-time realities. Eschatology spilled over into Edwards's private life, providing delight and solace during his years of pastoral difficulty in Northampton and Stockbridge. Though unusual for the eighteenth-century, his eschatologically-driven theology may be better appreciated and understood today, when both biblical and systematic theologians have rediscovered the role of the future in Christian reflection.[8]

The History of the Work of Redemption

The Sermon Series

Edwards delivered this series of thirty sermons in 1739, between March and August, to his church in Northampton.[9] The text for the sermons is Isaiah 51:8: "For the moth shall eat them up like a garment, and the worm shall eat them like wool: But my righteousness shall be for ever, and my salvation from generation to generation."[10] From this text Edwards develops the doctrine: "The Work of Redemption is a work that God carries on from the fall of man until the end of the world."[11] In typical Puritan sermonic style, the text is explained, the doctrine developed and defended, and then applied.[12] This is true of each sermon and of the series as a whole. John F. Wilson explains, "The thirty edifying lectures had a narrative and theological unity so pervasive that, when they were finally published, their editor was able easily to strip away such sermonic characteristics as repetition of text and doctrine and reiteration of the argument. In so doing, he revealed the sustained treatise, organized by rationally ordered and largely chronological subdivisions, that we know as *A History of the Work of Redemption*."[13]

---

8. Ibid., 579.
9. John F. Wilson, "Editor's Introduction," in Jonathan Edwards, *History of the Work of Redemption*, vol. 9, Works of Jonathan Edwards, ed. John F. Wilson (New Haven, CT: Yale University Press, 1989), 5. [Hereafter cited as *HWR*.]
10. Ibid., 9.
11. Ibid., 9.
12. On Edwards's sermonic form, see Wilson H. Kimnach, "General Introduction to the Sermons: Jonathan Edwards' Art of Prophesying," in Jonathan Edwards, *Sermons and Discourses 1720–1723*, vol. 10, Works of Jonathan Edwards, ed. Wilson H. Kimnach (New Haven, CT: Yale University Press, 1992), 3–261.
13. Wilson, "Editor's Introduction," 9. The sermon series was published posthumously in 1774.

Edwards divides the history of the work of redemption into three major periods: "The first reaching from the fall of man to Christ's incarnation, the second from Christ's incarnation till his resurrection, or the whole time of Christ's humiliation, the third from thence to the end of the world."[14] For each of these periods, Edwards develops a proposition:

> I. That [from] the fall of man till the incarnation of Christ, God was doing those things that were preparatory to Christ's coming, and working out redemption and were forerunners and earnests of it.

> II. That the time from Christ's incarnation till his resurrection was spent in procuring or purchasing redemption.

> III. That the space of time from the resurrection of Christ to the end of the world is all taken up in bringing about or accomplishing the great effect or success of that purchase. In a particular consideration of these three propositions the great truth taught in the doctrine may perhaps appear in a clear light and we may see how the Work of Redemption is carried on from the fall [of man to the end of the world].[15]

These three stages of the history of the work of redemption are chronologically successive, but they are also redemptively progressive. Each stage builds on the previous one and each is grounded in the work of Christ. Of particular interest for this essay is the third stage, from the resurrection of Christ until the end of the age—the culmination of God's plan of redemption of his people.

The Third Stage of the History of the Work of Redemption

The Four Stages of the Kingdom

The third stage in the history of the work of redemption, according to Edwards, accomplishes the establishment of the "kingdom of heaven and kingdom

---

14. Edwards, *HWR*, 127.
15. Ibid., 128.

of God. . . . This kingdom began soon after Christ's resurrection, and was accomplished in various steps from that time to the end of the world."[16] Thus, rather than coming in one cataclysmic event, the kingdom comes successively in stages.

Edwards explicates his view of the kingdom in a bit more detail as he observes several things about its coming. First, there are "four successive great events, each of which is in Scripture called 'Christ's coming in his kingdom.'"[17] The first of these is the destruction of Jerusalem in 70 CE (cf. Matt. 16:28, 24:27–31). The second "was accomplished in Constantine's time in the destruction of the heathen Roman empire" (Rev. 6:12–17).[18] The third is the destruction of the antichrist (Dan. 7) and the last is the final judgment, "which is the event principally signified in Scripture by Christ's coming in his kingdom" (Matt. 25:31–46).[19]

Second, Edwards continues, "I would observe that each of the three former of these is a lively image and type of the fourth and last, viz. Christ coming to the final judgment, as the principal dispensations of providence before Christ's final coming were types of kingdoms first coming like it, as Christ's last coming to judgment is accompanied with a resurrection of the dead, and so is each of the three foregoing with a spiritual resurrection."[20] Thus, each of the first three comings is a type of the final return of Christ and the resurrection of the dead.

Third, Edwards continues, "I would observe that each of those four great dispensations that are represented as Christ's coming in his kingdom are but so many steps and degrees of accomplishment of one event. They aren't the setting up of so many distinct kingdoms of Christ; they are all of them only several degrees of accomplishment of that one event."[21] Thus, there are not four comings of Christ; there is one coming that occurs in four stages: "I would observe that as there are several stages of the accomplishment of the kingdom of Christ, so in each one of them the event is accomplished in a further degree than in the foregoing. . . . The kingdom of Christ is gradually prevailing and increasing by these several great stages of its fulfillment from the time of Christ's resurrection to the end of the world."[22]

Finally, Edwards concludes, "It may be observed that the great providences of God between these four great events are to make way for the kingdom and

16. Ibid., 350.
17. Ibid., 351.
18. Ibid.
19. Ibid.
20. Ibid., 351–52.
21. Ibid., 353.
22. Ibid., 354.

glory of Christ in the event following."[23] The time between each of the comings of Christ prepares for the next stage.

Thus, according to Edwards, the setting up of the kingdom occurs in "four successive great events, each of which is called Christ's coming in his kingdom. The whole success of Christ's redemption is thus comprehended in one word, viz. his setting up his kingdom. This is chiefly done by four great, successive dispensations of providence, and every one of them is represented in Scripture as Christ's coming."[24]

The Suffering State of the Church

Edwards describes the church during the period between Christ's ascension and the end of the work of redemption as existing in "two very different states, viz. 1. in a suffering, afflicted, persecuted state, as for the most part it is from the resurrection of Christ till the fall of Antichrist, and 2. [in] a state of peace and prosperity, which is the state that the church for the most part is to be in after the fall of Antichrist."[25]

The period of time from Constantine to the Reformation was particularly difficult. Edwards explains, "This is the darkest and most dismal day that ever the Christian church saw, and probably the darkest that it ever will see."[26] This darkness of this period was, according to Edwards, because "the two great works of the devil that he in this space of time wrought against the kingdom of Christ are his erecting his Antichristian and Mohammedan kingdoms, which have been and still are two kingdoms of great extent and strength, both together swallowing the ancient Roman empire; the kingdom of Antichrist swallowing up the western empire, and Satan's Mohammedan kingdom the eastern empire."[27]

Edwards then comes to the "fourth and last part of this space, viz. that part which is from the present time till Antichrist is fallen and Satan's visible kingdom on earth destroyed."[28] He explains that for the previous periods, Scripture history was his source but that now, "we have nothing but the prophecies of Scripture to guide us. . . . And here I would pass by those things that are only conjectural,

---

23. Ibid., 355.
24. Ibid., 351.
25. Ibid., 372.
26. Ibid., 409.
27. Ibid., 410. Like almost every other Protestant in his time, Edwards believed that the Antichrist is the papacy. On the history of this view see Bernard McGinn, *Anti-Christ: Two Thousand Years of Human Fascination with Evil* (New York: Columbia University Press, 1999).
28. Edwards, *HWR*, 456.

or that are supposed by some from those prophecies that are doubtful in their interpretation, and shall insist only on those things that are more clear and evident. We know not what particular events are to come to pass before that glorious work of God's Spirit begins by which Satan's kingdom is to be overthrown."[29] Along with "most divines," Edwards believes that "there are but few things if any of all that are foretold to be accomplished before the beginning of the glorious work of God."[30] In other words, the overthrow of the kingdom of Satan could begin at any time. Like the other stages of the kingdom, this "great work of God will be gradually wrought, though very swiftly, yet gradually. . . . This is a work that will be accomplished by means, by the preaching of the gospel, and the use of ordinary means of grace, and so shall be gradually brought to pass."[31]

The overthrow of Satan's kingdom will be accomplished by the pouring out of God's Spirit, which will be met with a "violent and mighty opposition."[32] Edwards describes it this way:

> It seems as though in this last great opposition that should be made against the church to defend the kingdom of Satan, all the forces of Antichrist, and also Mohammedanism and heathenism, should be united, all the forces of Satan's visible kingdom through the whole world of mankind. And therefore 'tis said that the "spirits of devils shall go forth unto the kings of the earth and of the whole world, to gather them together to the battle of the great day of God Almighty." And these spirits are said to come "out of the mouth of the dragon, and out [of the mouth of] the beast, [and out of the mouth of] the false prophet," i.e. there shall be the spirit of popery and the spirit of Mohammedanism and the spirit of heathenism all united. By the beast is meant Antichrist; by the dragon in this book is commonly meant the devil as he reigns in his heathen kingdom; by the false prophet in this book is

---

29. Ibid.
30. Ibid. Edwards mentions differences in interpretation of the slaying of the witnesses (Rev. 11:9) and how many of the seven vials have been poured out as matters of dispute. On the latter he concludes, "But whatever this be, it don't appear this 'tis anything that shall be accomplished before the work of God's Spirit is begun, by which it goes on Satan's visible kingdom on earth shall be utterly overthrown" (457).
31. Ibid., 458–59.
32. Ibid., 462.

sometimes meant the Pope and his clergy, but here an eye also seems to be had to Mohammed whom his followers call the great prophet of God. There will be, as it were, the dying struggles of the old serpent, a battle wherein he will fight as one that is almost desperate.[33]

Although the satanic opposition to the Spirit will be fierce, the end of this battle is not in doubt. According to Revelation 19:11–21, "Christ and his church shall in this battle obtain and complete an entire victory over their enemies; they shall be totally routed and overthrown in this their last effort."[34] Consequently, "Satan's visible kingdom on earth shall be destroyed."[35] Among the particular aspects of Satan's kingdom which will be destroyed, Edwards lists Socinianism, Arianism, Quakerism, Arminianism, and Deism.[36] But the two major kingdoms of Satan are Antichrist and Mohammed.[37] They will be "utterly overthrown."[38]

When Satan's kingdom is destroyed, "Jewish infidelity shall then be overthrown."[39] Edwards expects a mass conversion of Jews:

> However obstinate they have now been for above seventeen hundred years in their rejecting Christ, and instances of conversion of any of that nation have been so very rare ever since the destruction of Jerusalem, but they have against the plain teachings of their own prophets continued to approve of the cruelty of their forefathers in crucifying [Christ]; yet, when this day comes the thick veil that blinds their minds shall be removed, II Cor. 3:16, and divine grace shall melt and renew their hard hearts. . . . And then shall all Israel be saved. The Jews in all their dispersions shall cast away their old infidelity, and shall wonderfully have their hearts changed, and abhor themselves for their past unbelief and obstinacy; and shall flow together to the blessed Jesus, penitently, humbly, and joyfully owning him as their glorious king and only savior, and shall

---

33. Ibid., 463. The biblical quotations are from Rev. 16:13–14.
34. Ibid., 464.
35. Ibid., 466.
36. Ibid., 467.
37. Ibid., 468–69.
38. Ibid., 469.
39. Ibid.

praise with all their hearts as with one heart and voice declare his praises unto other nations.[40]

Edwards insists, "Nothing is more certainly foretold than this national conversion of the Jews in the eleventh chapter of Romans. And there are also many passages of the Old Testament that can't be interpreted in any other sense, that I can't now stand to mention."[41] Thus, Edwards sees a future for ethnic Israel in the last days, the conversion of the nation. He insists that no one can know when this will occur, "but this much we can determine by Scripture, that it will [be] before [the] glory of the Gentile part of the church shall be fully accomplished, because it is said that their coming in shall be life from the dead to the Gentiles, Rom. 11:12,15."[42]

When the kingdom of Satan is overthrown, heathenism in all its forms will be destroyed around the world. Then "the kingdom of God shall in the most strict and literal sense extend to all nations and the whole earth."[43] He explains:

> Then shall the many nations of Africa, the nations of Negroes and others—heathens that chiefly fill that quarter of the world, that now seem to be in a state but little above the beasts in many respects and as much below them in many others—be enlightened with glorious light, and delivered from all their darkness, and shall become a civil, Christian and an understanding and holy people. Then shall this vast continent of America, that now in so great part of it is covered with barbarous ignorance and cruelty, be everywhere covered with glorious gospel light and Christian love, and instead of worshipping the devil as now, they then shall serve the true God and praises shall be sung to the Lord Jesus Christ, the blessed savior of the world, everywhere. So may we expect it will be in that great and populous part of the world, the East Indies that are now mostly worshippers of the devil, and so throughout that vast country, cruel Turkey. And then the kingdom of Christ will also be established in those continents that

40. Ibid.
41. Ibid., 169–70. In the section that follows, Edwards does use "Hos. 1:11, and so in the last chapter of Hosea, and other parts of his prophecy."
42. Ibid., 470.
43. Ibid., 473.

have more lately been discovered towards the north and south poles, where now men differ very little from the wild beasts— excepting that they worship the devil and beasts do not—and in many other countries that never yet have been discovered.[44]

The Millennium

This third coming of the kingdom brings an "end to the church's suffering state, and shall be attended with their glorious and joyful praises."[45] It "puts an end to the former state of the world and introduces the everlasting kingdom of Christ."[46] This is now the "time of the kingdom of heaven upon earth . . . the principal fulfillment of all the prophecies of the Old Testament that speak of the glorious times of the gospel that shall be in the latter days."[47] This period of time will last "a long time, Rev. 20:4 . . . a thousand years."[48] Elsewhere Edwards argues that the millennium must be one thousand actual years because of the parallelism between the six days of creation followed by the Sabbath rest and the six thousand years of human history followed by the millennium. He believed the millennium would, thus, begin in 2000.[49]

In Edwards's view, Christ will not reign over the earth from the earth during the millennium. His coming prior to the millennium is not a return to the earth. Rather, he will reign over the earth during the millennium from heaven, along with the redeemed dead of all ages. Only the living saints will rule on the earth during this one thousand years. He explains that by the saints reigning on the earth "can be understood nothing but their reigning in Christ, who then shall reign; for they are united to him, and being one with him, it may very properly be said that they reign. For it is just all one as if they reigned, as the saints on earth then shall; for the saints on earth shall reign no otherwise themselves. And besides, because of their communion with the saints on earth, whereby when those reign, these do in them."[50]

---

44. Ibid., 472. Edwards explains that this spread of the kingdom will fulfill Isaiah 35:1.
45. Ibid., 476.
46. Ibid., 478.
47. Ibid., 479.
48. Ibid., 485–86.
49. See an extended discussion of Edwards and the millennium in my *Jonathan Edwards's Interpretation of Revelation 4:1–8:1* (Lanham, MD: University Press of America, 2004), 147–61.
50. Jonathan Edwards, "Miscellanies k," in Jonathan Edwards, *The "Miscellanies" (Entry Nos. a-z, aa-zz, 1–500,* vol. 13, Works of Jonathan Edwards, ed. Thomas A. Schafer (New Haven, CT: Yale University Press, 1994), 168.

Although it lasts a long time, the millennium is not the culmination of the work of redemption. The millennium will end with "a very great apostasy, wherein a great part of the world shall fall away from Christ and his church."[51] This great opposition to the church "will seem most remarkably to call for Christ's immediate appearance to judgment."[52] Edwards describes this apostasy:

> After such a happy and glorious season, such a long day of light and holiness, love and peace and joy, now it shall begin again to be a dark time; Satan shall begin to set up his dominion again in the world. This world shall again become a scene of darkness and wickedness. The bottomless pit of hell shall be opened, and devils shall come up again out of it, and a dreadful smoke shall ascend to darken the world. And the church of Christ, instead of extending to the utmost bounds of the world as it did before, shall be reduced to narrow limits again. The world of mankind being continued so long in a state of great prosperity, shall now begin to abuse their prosperity to serve their lust and corruption. . . . Thus it shall be for a little season.[53]

The Return of Christ

The ultimate and final coming of the Savior will follow the apostasy at the end of the millennium: "Christ will appear in the glory of his father with all the holy angels coming on the clouds of heaven. While the world is thus reveling in their wickedness, and compassing the holy city, about it, just ready to destroy it, and while the church is reduced to such a great strait, then shall the glorious Redeemer appear. He through whom this redemption has all along been carried on, he shall appear in the sight of the world, the light of his glory shall break forth."[54]

The effects of Christ's return will be radically different for the wicked than for the church.

> The world, that will then be very full of people most of which will be wicked men, will then be filled with dolorous shrieking

---

51. Ibid., 488. Edwards cites Revelation 20:3.
52. Ibid., 489.
53. Ibid., 488–89.
54. Ibid., 494.

and crying. . . . Where shall they hide themselves, how will the sight of that awful majesty terrify them, when taken in the midst of their wickedness? Then they shall see who he is, what kind of a person he is whom they have mocked and scoffed at and whose church they have been endeavoring to overthrow. This sight will change their voice; the voice of their laughter and singing while they are marrying and giving in marriage, and the voice of their scoffing, shall be changed into hideous, yea hellish, yellings. Their countenances shall be changed from a show of carnal mirth, haughty pride, and contempt of God's people; it shall put on a show of ghastly terror and amazement, and trembling and chattering of teeth shall seize them.[55]

In contrast, Edwards explains:

With respect to the saints, the church of Christ, it shall be a most joyful and glorious sight to them. For this sight will at once deliver them from all fear of their enemies that were before compassing them about, just ready to swallow them. Deliverance shall come in their extremity; the glorious captain of their salvation shall appear for them at a time when no other help appeared. Then shall they lift up their heads, and see their redemption drawing nigh. . . . To see their redeemer coming in the clouds of heaven will fill their hearts full of gladness. Their countenances also shall be changed, but not as the countenances of the wicked will be, but shall be changed from being sorrowful to be exceeding joyful and triumphant.[56]

The Resurrection of the Dead

The resurrection of the dead occurs at Christ's return: "The last trumpet shall sound and the dead shall be raised and the living changed."[57] Edwards stresses that the resurrection is comprehensive: "The dead shall be raised everywhere. Now the number of the dead is very great; how many has death cut down for so long as

---

55. Ibid., 495.
56. Ibid., 495–96.
57. Ibid., 496.

time as since the world has stood. . . . All these shall now rise from the dead."[58] The resurrection includes both the righteous and the wicked.

After the dead are raised, all the living will be changed. Again there will be a distinction between the wicked and the righteous: "The bodies of the wicked that shall be then living shall be so changed as to fit 'em for eternal torment without corruption, and the bodies of all the living saints shall be changed to be like Christ's glorious body."[59] Edwards concludes, "Now the Work of Redemption shall be finished in another respect, viz. that all the elect shall now be actually redeemed in body and soul. Before this the Work of Redemption as to its actual success was but incomplete and imperfect, for only the souls of the redeemed were actually saved and glorified, excepting in some few instances. But now all the bodies of all the saints shall be saved and glorified together, all the elect shall be glorified in the whole man, and the soul and body in union one with another."[60]

The Last Judgment

The resurrection is followed by judgment. "Now shall the whole church of saints be caught up in the clouds to meet the Lord in the air, and all wicked men and devils shall be arraigned before the judgment seat."[61] The judgment of the righteous will take place in the air, not on the earth and not in heaven. "They shall all mount up as with wings in the air to go and meet Christ. For it seems that Christ when he comes to judgment, won't come quite down to the ground, but his throne will be fixed in the air in the region of the clouds, whence he may be seen by all that vast multitude that shall be gathered before him. And the church of saints therefore shall be taken up off from the earth to ascend up to their savior."[62] Christ's bodily return to the earth, according to Edwards, will not bring him all the way down to the ground. Instead, he will hover above the earth and the saints will be caught up to meet him in the air.

This removal of saints from the earth is key to Edwards's eschatology. In his view, the earth is a place of judgment and death. It will not be redeemed.

> Then shall the Work of Redemption be finished in another respect: then the whole church shall be perfectly and forever delivered

---

58. Ibid.
59. Ibid., 497.
60. Ibid., 497–98.
61. Ibid., 498.
62. Ibid.

from this present evil world, forever forsake this cursed ground. They shall take their everlasting leave of this earth where they have been strangers, and that has been for the most part such a scene of their trouble and sorrow, where the devil for the most part has reigned as a god, and has greatly molested them, and which has been a scene of wickedness and abomination, where Christ their Lord has been cruelly used, and where they have been so hated, and reproached, and persecuted, from age to age through most of the ages of the world. They shall leave it under foot to go to Christ, and never shall set foot on it again. And then shall be an everlasting separation made between them and wicked men. Before they were mixed together, and now all become visible.[63]

The wicked will also be judged, but on the earth. Edwards continues,

At the same time all wicked men and devils shall be brought before the judgment seat of Christ, on the left hand, on the earth, and not in the air as the saints will be. The devil, that old serpent, shall now be dragged up out of hell. He that first procured the fall and misery of mankind, and has so set himself against his redemption, and has all along shown himself such an inveterate enemy to the Redeemer, now he shall never more have anything to do when the church of God [is gathered together. He shall not] be sufficient in the least to afflict or molest any of them anymore forever.[64]

All of Christ's enemies, everyone who has opposed the church, all of the wicked, and those who destroyed the saints will be judged. "Thus wonderfully will the face of things be altered from what used to be in the former times of the world; now will all things be coming to rights."[65]

The Eternal State

After the last judgment, the righteous and the wicked will enter their eternal home. Edwards explains, "Christ and all his church of saints and all the body of

---

63. Ibid., 498–99.
64. Ibid., 499–500.
65. Ibid., 501.

angels ministering to them shall leave this lower world and ascend up towards the highest heavens. Christ shall ascend as in great glory with all his elect church, with him glorified in both body and soul. Christ's first ascension to heaven soon after his own resurrection was very glorious. But this, his second ascension of his mystical body, his whole church, shall be far more glorious. The redeemed church shall all ascend with him in a most joyful and triumphant manner."[66] Edwards summarizes, "Thus Christ's church shall forever leave this accursed world to go into that more glorious world, the highest heavens, into the paradise of God, the kingdom that was prepared for them from the foundations of the world."[67]

In contrast, all the wicked will be "left behind on the cursed ground to be consumed."[68] Edwards explains, "This world shall be set on fire, and be turned into a great furnace, wherein all the enemies of Christ and his church shall be tormented forever and ever."[69] He continues, "When Christ and his church are ascended to a distance from this world, that miserable company of wicked shall be left behind to have their cursed future executed upon 'em here. And then some way or other this whole lower world shall be set on fire, either by fire from heaven or fire breaking out of the bowels of the earth—or both—as it was with the water in the time of the deluge; however this lower world shall be all on fire."[70] In short, the earth will be turned into hell, a place of eternal torment. The descriptive language Edwards in this section is similar to his famous sermon, "Sinners in the Hands of an Angry God," yet without the emphasis on grace found there.[71]

> How will it strike the wicked with horror when they see this fire begin to kindle, and when the fire begins to lay hold upon them, and they find no way to escape it or fly or hide from it. What shrieking and crying will there be among those many thousands of millions when they begin to enter into this great furnace,

---

66. Ibid., 505.
67. Ibid.
68. Ibid.
69. Ibid. Edwards quotes 2 Peter 3:7 in support of this claim. For another interpretation of 2 Peter and a defense of a re-creation eschatology see my "The Flood Is as Bad as It Gets: Never Again Will God Destroy the Earth," *Bibliotheca Sacra*, forthcoming.
70. Ibid., 505.
71. Jonathan Edwards, "Sinners in the Hands of an Angry God," in *The Sermons of Jonathan Edwards: A Reader*, ed. Wilson H. Kimnach, Kenneth P. Minkema, and Douglas A. Sweeney, (New Haven, CT: Yale University Press, 1999), 49–65. For a defense of the gracious nature of this sermon, see my "Sinners in the Hands of a Gracious God," *Bibliotheca Sacra* 163 (2006): 259–75.

when the whole world shall [be] a furnace of the fiercest and most raging heat. . . . And here shall all the persecutors of the church of God burn in everlasting fire, who have before burnt the saints at the stake; and shall suffer torments far beyond all that their utmost wit and malice could inflict on the saints. And here the bodies of all the wicked shall burn, and be tormented to all eternity, and never be consumed; and the wrath of God shall be poured out on their souls.[72]

Thus, the devil and the place of his evil work are joined for eternity. "And now the devil, that old serpent, shall receive his full punishment; now shall that which he before trembled for fear of be fully come upon him. This world that formerly used to be the place of his kingdom, where he set up himself as God, shall now be the place of his complete punishment, and full and everlasting torment. And in this, one design of the Work of Redemption that has been mentioned, viz. putting Christ's enemies under his feet, shall be perfectly accomplished."[73]

The saints will then "enter with Christ, their glorious Lord, into the highest heaven; and there shall enter on the state of their highest and eternal blessedness and glory. . . . The gates shall stand wide open unto them for them to enter in, and there Christ will bring them into his chambers in the highest circle; he will bring them into his Father's house, into a world not like that which they have left."[74]

The triune God's work of redemption is now complete: "And now shall Christ the great Redeemer be most perfectly glorified, and God the Father shall be glorified in him, and the Holy Ghost shall [be] most fully glorified in the perfection of his work in the hearts of all the church. And now shall that new heaven and new earth, or that renewed state of things that had been building up ever since Christ's resurrection, be completely finished after the very material frame of the old heavens and old earth are destroyed."[75]

Applications

The sermon series ends with several applications. The first is the greatness of the Work of Redemption. According to Edwards, redemption is not merely

---

72. Ibid., 505–6.
73. Ibid., 506.
74. Ibid., 506–7.
75. Ibid., 509. Edwards cites and quotes Revelation 21:1 as biblical support of this assertion.

the greatest of God's works; it is the whole of God's work: "This Work of Re-demption is so much the greatest of all the works of God, that all other works are to be looked upon either as part of it, or appendages to it, or are some way reducible to it. And so all the decrees of God do some way or other belong to that eternal covenant of redemption that was between the Father and the Son before the foundation of the world; every decree of God is some way or other reducible to that covenant. . . . The Work of Redemption is the great subject of the whole Bible."[76]

Also, Edwards explains, from the work of redemption:

> we learn how happy a society the church of Christ is for all this great work is for them. Christ undertook it for their sakes and for their sakes he carries it on from the fall of man to the end of the world. 'Tis because he has loved them with an everlasting love. For their sakes he overturns states and kingdoms, for their sakes he shakes heaven and earth. . . . Since they have been pre-cious in God's eyes, they have been honorable; and therefore he first gives the blood of his own Son to them, and then for their sakes gives the blood of all their enemies, many thousands and millions, all nations that stand in their way, as a sacrifice to their good. For their sakes he made the world, and [for] their sakes he will destroy it. For their sakes he built heaven, and for their sakes he makes his angels ministering spirits.[77]

But there is one last application. Edwards is, first and foremost, a pastor. Con-cern and compassion for people are at the center of his ministry. To the unregen-erate in his congregation, the pastor issues this plea:

> And lastly, hence all wicked men, all that are in a Christless con-dition, may see their exceeding misery. You that are such, who-ever you are, are those who have no part or lot in this manner; you are never the better for any of these things of which you have heard. Yea, your guilt is but so much the greater, and the misery you are exposed to so much the more dreadful. You are some of

76. Ibid., 514.
77. Ibid., 526.

that sort that God in the progress of this work does so dreadfully manifest his wrath against, some of those enemies which are liable to be made Christ's footstool, and to be ruled over with a rod of iron, and to be dashed [in pieces]; you are some of the seed of the serpent that it is one great design [of God to bruise the head of]. Whatever glorious things God accomplishes for his church, if you continue in the state you are in, they will not be glorious to you. . . . Let all that are in a Christless condition among us seriously consider these things, and not be like the foolish people of the old world who would not take warning when Noah told 'em that [the Lord was about to bring a flood of waters upon the earth], like the people of Sodom who would not regard it when Lot told 'em that God would destroy that place, and would not fly from the wrath to come, and so were consumed in that terrible destruction.[78]

Conclusion

Jonathan Edwards believed that God's work in the world is redemptive, that everything God does in redemption is for the sake of the church, and that in the eternal state she will be rewarded eternally in the presence of God in heaven. He looked forward to Christ establishing his kingdom successively and progressively. He anticipated the culmination of redemption in a resurrection of the dead, the wicked to spend eternity on the earth that will be lit on fire and be the place of their eternal destruction while the righteous will be caught up in the air with Jesus and ascend to heaven with him. This eschatological hope is at the center of his life and ministry and it is anchored in the person and work of Christ. Edwards concludes his sermon series with these words, and this is a fitting end to this essay: "He that testifieth these things saith, Surely I come quickly. Amen. Even so, come, Lord Jesus."[79]

---

78. Ibid., 527–28.
79. Ibid. 528. His final paragraph is a paraphrase of Revelation 22:6–20; these final words are Revelation 22:20.

The Doctrine of the Future in Baptist Theology

Kevin D. Kennedy

Years ago, while I was in high school, I memorized 1 Peter 3:15 as part of an assignment with the youth group at my church: "but sanctify Christ as Lord in your hearts, always being ready to make a defense to everyone who asks you to give an account for the hope that is in you, yet with gentleness and reverence."[1] I memorized this verse as a motivation for being ready to give a defense of my faith, but must admit that at the time I did not give much thought to some of the details in the text. Some years later I revisited this verse to test how much I had been able to remember. My memory was not as accurate as I had expected. I totally missed the reference to "hope" and had replaced it with "faith" in my memory. This caused me to look at the text again and to think carefully about what it said. Why, for example, had I thought that the word "hope" was merely an incidental detail so easily replaced with another word? What had I thought about the word "hope" when I memorized this text years before? This exercise led me to reflect more carefully on the use of the term "hope" in the Bible.

Hope, I came to realize, is not as clearly understood today as it was when Peter wrote of hope. Today, the word "hope" is viewed by many as a synonym for "wish." This can be illustrated by a curious regional phrase used in my wife's hometown. The people there often use the phrase "hope how soon," as in "Hope how soon dinner is ready," by which they mean "I wish dinner would be ready soon." Such seemingly innocent mistakes regarding the meaning of the word "hope" can actually cause us to miss out on an important element of the Christian faith. According

---

1. Unless otherwise noted, all Scripture references are from the New American Standard Bible.

to Scripture, hope is not some vague wish about mundane future events. Rather, in Scripture, hope is the believer's sure and certain expectation that God's promises regarding our future life with him are trustworthy (e.g., Col. 1:5; Titus 2:13; Heb. 6:19). God has promised us that Christ will return to claim his people, that he will raise us bodily from the dead, and that we will spend eternity with him. This expectation is certain because God has proven over and over again that he keeps his promises to his people.

In times of persecution, as in the early centuries of the church, the sure and certain expectation of a bodily resurrection and eternity spent with the Lord kept many believers from renouncing their faith when forced to choose either to abandon their faith or to die. That so many chose to die rather than to give up their faith illustrates well the kind of hope of which the Scriptures speak— a certain hope in the future deliverance by God of his people. When seen in this light, the biblical term "hope" frequently refers to elements related to what theologians have called "eschatology"—the area of theology which deals with the future hope of believers and God's plans for the future.

BAPTIST CONFESSIONS OF FAITH: MANY POINTS OF UNITY ON THE DOCTRINE OF THE FUTURE

As a Baptist theologian, I am reminded that many of our forefathers in the faith also experienced persecution because they believed in a regenerate church membership and baptism of believers only. Whether one holds that Baptists trace their roots back to the Anabaptists of the sixteenth century or to the English separatists of the early seventeenth century, it is true that both groups suffered persecution for dissenting from the state churches of their respective days. In fact, the very name "Baptist" speaks loudly of our concern for the nature of the church, that the church be viewed as a gathering of professing and baptized believers who all possess the same hope of salvation in Christ.[2]

This emphasis on a proper understanding of the church meant that when Baptists saw the need to express their beliefs in the form of confessions of faith, the nature of the church generally received the most attention. The statements dealing with other areas of doctrine, such as the future hope of believers, received

---

2. That the very name "Baptist" points to the centrality of ecclesiology in Baptist circles is also noted by Russell D. Moore and Robert E. Sagers in "The Kingdom of God and the Church: A Baptist Reassessment," *The Southern Baptist Journal of Theology,* 12 no. 1 (Spring 2008), 73.

comparatively less attention.³ For example, the Second London Baptist Confession of 1689 differs most substantially from the Presbyterian Westminster Confession of Faith (on which it was consciously based) in those sections which deal with the doctrine of the church. Those portions dealing with the future hope of believers and the eternal destiny of both believers and unbelievers differ little from the Westminster Confession. The men who drafted the 1689 London Confession were seeking to show that while their view of the church differed significantly from the framers of the Westminster Confession, they were otherwise in substantial agreement with the rest of the dissenting churches of their day in other areas of doctrine, including those areas which deal with the future hope of believers.⁴

This natural tendency for Baptists to give more attention to questions related to the nature of the church continued as Baptists wrote new confessions. One result of this propensity is an attendant tendency for later Baptist confessions of faith to display a remarkable unity with earlier confessions in some areas of doctrine, including the doctrine of the future. What was sufficient for earlier Baptists seemed sufficient for later Baptists. This general unity on the doctrine of the future in Baptist confessions also explains why the doctrine of the future, while frequently a topic of debate among Baptists, has not generally been a primary issue over which one group of Baptists would break fellowship with other groups of Baptists.

Given the fact that there is considerable unity among Baptists on many issues related to the doctrine of the future, a general introduction to Baptist beliefs on this topic would do well to start with these areas of agreement. There will be time enough to chart out the differences, but these areas of agreement are at the heart of what most Christians the world over have always affirmed about the doctrine

---

3. One of the earliest Anabaptist confessions, the Schleitheim Confession, adopted by a group of Swiss Brethren on February 24, 1527, deals only with the nature of the church, baptism, the Lord's Supper, church discipline, and issues related to the believer's relationship to the state. These are all matters proper to ecclesiology, the doctrine of the church. See William L. Lumpkin, *Baptist Confessions of Faith*, rev. ed. (Valley Forge, PA: Judson Press, 1969), 23–31.
4. The distinctly Baptist elements in the Second London Confession include the statements on the doctrines of baptism and the Lord's Supper (Lumpkin, *Baptist Confessions*, 236–38). The phrase "the rest of the dissenting churches" in the sentence above is in reference to the fact that by the time the Second London Confession was drafted, the Presbyterians themselves were out of favor in England. However, because they were so numerous, they were generally tolerated, unlike other groups like the Baptists. By basing their confession on The Westminster Confession, the Baptists were trying to emphasize their agreement with this larger, more broadly accepted group.

of the future. These points of agreement include the belief that even death cannot separate us from the love of God in Christ Jesus, the expectation of the visible return of Christ, the bodily resurrection of all the dead, and the eternal destinies of the just and the unjust. It is to these areas of agreement that we now turn.

Death Cannot Separate Us from the Love of God in Christ Jesus

In Romans 8:38–39 Paul informs us that he is "convinced that neither death, nor life, nor angels, nor principalities, nor things present, nor things to come, nor powers, nor height, nor depth, nor any other created thing, will be able to separate us from the love of God, which is in Christ Jesus our Lord." That death itself cannot separate us from Christ is a point emphasized in virtually all Baptist confessions of faith. This is an affirmation of what has traditionally been called the doctrine of the "intermediate state." This doctrine expresses the conviction that despite the death and decay of their bodies, believers will still experience conscious fellowship with the Lord while awaiting the future bodily resurrection. As chapter 31 of the Second London Confession states: "The Bodies of Men after Death return to dust, and see corruption; but their Souls (which neither die nor sleep) having an immortal subsistence, immediately return to God who gave them, the Souls of the Righteous being then made perfect in holiness, are received into paradise, where they are with *Christ*, and behold the face of *God* in light and glory; waiting for the full redemption of their bodies."[5] It is this confidence in the inseparability of the believer from Christ that gives *hope* to sick and dying believers the world over as well as those facing persecution.

The Visible Return of Christ

Not all Baptist confessions treat the return of Christ as a topic within the doctrine of the end times, but the future, visible return of Christ to earth to claim his people is affirmed nonetheless.[6] The Second London Confession, and the Philadelphia Confession that was closely based on it, address the return of Christ in the section on the doctrine of Christ. Just as Christ ascended to the right hand of the

---

5. Second London Confession, chapter 31, paragraph 1, emphasis and capitalization in original (Lumpkin, *Baptist Confessions,* 293). The Philadelphia Confession of Faith of 1742 is identical to the Second London Confession except for the addition of two articles, article XXIII on the singing of psalms and article XXXI on the laying on of hands, along with the consequent renumbering of articles XXIII through XXXIV (see Lumpkin, *Baptist Confessions*, 348–349).

6. That being said, the Abstract of Principles of 1858, included as part of the original charter of The Southern Baptist Theological Seminary, is silent on the return of Christ, although it must certainly be assumed.

Father in the same body in which he was crucified and resurrected, in the same body he "shall return to judge *Men* and *Angels* at the end of the world."[7] Other Baptist confessions place the return of Christ under the topic of "Last Things" and present Christ's return as the initial event precipitating the end times. The Baptist Faith and Message 2000 begins its presentation of the promised future by affirming that "Jesus Christ will return personally and visibly in glory to the earth."[8]

This affirmation of the future, visible return of Christ has always been a central tenet of the Christian faith.[9] That Christ will return to the earth is significant for several reasons, not least of which is the emphasis that it brings to the importance of the earth in God's plan. God created this earth and is not finished with it but is still directing it according to his purposes. Furthermore, the dead will be raised at the return of Christ, which underscores the fact that the Christian hope is not that of a disembodied, spiritual existence floating somewhere among the clouds as it is often portrayed in popular culture. Rather, it was always God's intention for his human creatures to live an embodied life in fellowship with him. This affirmation of our future physical, embodied existence naturally leads to the next topic, the resurrection from the dead.

The Bodily Resurrection of All the Dead

The bodily resurrection is not an insignificant teaching in Scripture. Jesus's own resurrection is a fundamental affirmation of Scripture, belief in which is necessary for salvation (Rom. 10:9). Additionally, Jesus's own resurrection is called the first fruits of the resurrection of the dead by the apostle Paul (1 Cor. 15:20, 23). As firstfruits, Jesus's own resurrection is the guarantee of the future *hope* of the believer's resurrection from of the dead. Furthermore, in Romans 6:4–5, Paul explains how Christian baptism actually portrays our death, burial, and resurrection with Christ. In baptism we are actually enacting this promise of a future resurrection. One purpose of baptism, then, is to help assure us of our own future bodily resurrection by having us actually portray it. Therefore, baptism is intended, at least in part, to give us *hope* of our future bodily resurrection.

---

7. Second London Confession, chapter 8, paragraph 4, emphasis in original (Lumpkin, *Baptist Confessions*, 262).
8. Baptist Faith and Message 2000, section X, available at http://www.sbc.net/bfm2000/bfm2000.asp.
9. The Apostles' Creed is one example of an early creed that affirms the return of Christ "to judge the quick and the dead." Philip Schaff, *The Creeds of Christendom*, rev. ed., vol.1, The History of Creeds (Grand Rapids: Baker, 1984), 30.

While we are on the subject, Paul's teaching in Romans chapter 6 illustrates well how Baptist ecclesiology (the doctrine of the church) converges with eschatology (the doctrine of last things). Baptists practice believers' baptism by immersion. One reason for this practice is the Baptist conviction that only believers' baptism by immersion accurately portrays this death, burial, and resurrection with Christ. This is because only those who already confess that Jesus Christ is Lord and who believe that God has raised him from the dead actually have this hope of resurrection to eternal life with Christ (Rom. 10:9). Therefore, Baptists believe that baptism should properly be reserved for believers because only believers can truly enact this death to sin in Christ and the promise of their future resurrection to eternal life in Christ.

It is not only believers who will be raised from the dead, however. Scripture teaches that unbelievers will be raised as well. While the "Principles of Faith of the Sandy Creek Association" of 1816 are very brief, this confession still contains an affirmation of this double resurrection as follows: "We believe that there will be a resurrection from the dead, and a general or universal judgment, and that the happiness of the righteous and punishment of the wicked will be eternal."[10] While both believers and unbelievers will be resurrected, their final destinies will not be the same. This brings us to our next topic.

The Eternal Destinies of the Just and the Unjust

As was stated above, a day is coming in which all the dead will be raised. However, this resurrection will not lead to the same future for everyone. Scripture clearly teaches that all of humanity will be separated into two groups with two futures (Matt. 25:31–46; John 5:28–29; Rom. 2:16). One future will mean eternal joy with the Lord for those who have believed in the gospel of Jesus Christ. The other means eternal punishment for unbelievers. The New Hampshire Confession of Faith of 1833 confesses the belief that "at the last day, Christ will descend from heaven, and raise the dead from the grave to final retribution; that a solemn separation will then take place; that the wicked will be adjudged to endless punishment, and the righteous to endless joy; and that this judgment will fix forever the final state of men in heaven or hell, on principles of righteousness."[11]

---

10. "Principles of Faith of the Sandy Creek Association," article V (Lumpkin, *Baptist Confession*, 358).
11. New Hampshire Confession of Faith, 1833, "xviii, Of the World to Come" (Lumpkin, *Baptist Confessions*, 367).

That believers will spend eternity with their Lord is essential to their future hope. It is precisely this promise that has maintained so many believers in the faith over the years when they were facing persecution. Temporary suffering is nothing in comparison to the blessing that awaits those whose hope is in Christ (Phil. 3:8–10).

On the other hand, the fact that so many will be consigned to eternal punishment should be sobering for us today. The biblical teaching that "it is appointed for men to die once and after this comes judgment" (Heb. 9:27) is something that we must affirm because it is taught in the Bible. Scripture leaves us no other alternative but to affirm the fact of eternal punishment for unbelievers. If this is true, however, that means the work of evangelism and missions is a serious endeavor. The biblical teaching on the eternal punishment of unbelievers and Jesus's command to make disciples of all nations (Matt. 28:19) are the two primary factors that have motivated Baptists over the years to take the gospel to the whole earth. Understanding the doctrine of the future is not merely an academic exercise. Nor is it merely of use to ground our own individual hope. Rather, an understanding of the doctrine of the future can be a real motivation to do the work of the ministry to which the church has been called.

THE DIVERSITY OF BAPTIST BELIEFS ON THE DOCTRINE OF THE FUTURE: THE QUESTION OF THE KINGDOM

The previous section, while necessarily selective as to which Baptist confessions were actually cited, is still an accurate presentation of the broad agreement among Baptists of different generations on several substantial areas of doctrine. The bodily resurrection of the dead, for example, is not something that has been universally affirmed in recent centuries. Baptists, however, have steadfastly affirmed this doctrine in their confessions. Nor is it popular today to affirm the eternal punishment of unbelievers. That Baptists have remained unified on such questions over the years is testimony to a considerable level of agreement on issues related to the doctrine of the future.[12]

There are, however, areas where there are disagreements within the broad topic of the doctrine of the future. At the risk of oversimplifying the situation, one might say that most of these disagreements center around the question of

---

12. While Baptist *confessions* reflect substantial unity on these topics, this is not to say that individual Baptists have not departed from time to time on some of these issues. Molly T. Marshall, for example, questions the eternal punishment of unbelievers in her work *No Salvation Outside the Church? A Critical Enquiry* (Lewiston, MD: Edwin Mellen, 1993).

how one understands the biblical concept of the kingdom of God. Is the kingdom of God present right now in the church? If it is present in the church, does the church exhaust the concept of the kingdom of God? Perhaps, instead, the church itself is in the process of creating the kingdom of God on earth. Might it be that we are mistaken in equating the kingdom of God with the church and are instead awaiting an earthly kingdom that is still wholly future? Perhaps the kingdom of God is present in an inaugurated form in the church, but the church is still waiting for the return of Christ, who will bring the full manifestation of the kingdom of God to earth when he returns. If the kingdom of God is to be understood as predominantly future, then are we to understand the kingdom as indistinguishable from the eternal state of believers with their Lord, or is this future kingdom of God a lengthy period of time prior to God ushering in the final state of the new heavens and the new earth?

Each of the above views have had adherents among Baptist theologians and lay people alike at one time or another. As the previous paragraph illustrates, the options available for interpreting the biblical teaching concerning the doctrine of the future are extensive. Trying to narrow the discussion to a manageable selection of views can be a daunting task. However, if we were to focus our attention on the three main views, and perhaps focus primarily on the interpretation of one controversial text, we might be able to narrow the discussion sufficiently so as to understand why there is so much difference of opinion on this one doctrine.

This, then, will be the task of this section: to outline the main eschatological views that one is most likely to encounter, and to do so by locating each view according to how it interprets one particular text of Scripture. The text in question is Revelation 20:4–6, a plain, straightforward reading of which describes a period of one thousand years beginning with the resurrection of the righteous dead at the return of Christ and ending with the resurrection of "the rest of the dead." During this one-thousand-year period, resurrected believers will reign on this earth with Christ prior to the ushering in of the final state of the new heavens and the new earth. Here is the text of Revelation 20:4–6:

> Then I saw thrones, and they sat on them, and judgment was given to them. And I *saw* the souls of those who had been beheaded because of their testimony of Jesus and because of the word of God, and those who had not worshiped the beast or his image, and had not received the mark on their forehead and on their hand; and they came to life and reigned with Christ

for a thousand years. The rest of the dead did not come to life until the thousand years were completed. This is the first resurrection. Blessed and holy is the one who has a part in the first resurrection; over these the second death has no power, but they will be priests of God and of Christ and will reign with Him for a thousand years.

How one interprets this particular text is a good indicator of one's overall approach to questions of the end times. Since Revelation chapter 20 is the only place in Scripture that mentions a *one-thousand-year* reign of Christ, the question becomes whether one incorporates this one-thousand-year reign into one's interpretation of the whole of Scripture, or whether one finds a way to interpret this text to fit the conclusions that one has already reached from reading the rest of Scripture.[13] The choice of one or the other of these two approaches will largely determine one's eschatological view.

There are three primary end-times approaches to how one ought to understand the one-thousand-year period mentioned in Revelation 20:4–6. These views are amillennialism, postmillennialism, and premillennialism. The negative prefix "a-" in amillennialism indicates that amillennialists teach that there will be *no* future one-thousand-year kingdom on this earth, but that at the return of Christ, all the dead will be raised for the final judgment. The final judgment will be followed immediately by transition to the final states for the righteous and the unrighteous. The "post-" in postmillennialism teaches that Christ will return *after* the church, through the transforming power of the gospel, has established the kingdom of God on earth. When Christ returns all the dead will be raised, judged, and then God will usher in the final states of both the righteous and the unrighteous. The "pre-" in premillennialism teaches that Christ will return *before*, and in order to establish, a literal one-thousand-year kingdom on this earth. The righteous dead will be raised at that time. Only after the one-thousand-year kingdom will the unrighteous dead be resurrected for judgment. Then God will usher in the new heavens and the new earth.

The text in Revelation 20:4–6, as stated above, seems to describe a future kingdom of one thousand years' duration, in which believers will reign with Christ

---

13. For a discussion of how preunderstanding can affect the reading of Scripture see Craig Blaising's chapter "Premillennialism" in *Three Views on the Millennium and Beyond*, ed. by Darrell L. Bock, Counterpoints Series, ed. Stanley N. Gundry (Grand Rapids: Zondervan, 1999), 164–65.

prior to the final, eternal state. If this text can be read in such a straightforward way, then how is it that there is so much diversity of interpretations of this kingdom? To answer that question we must examine the text in question according to how the proponents of the three views described above interpret it.

Postmillennialism

Postmillennialism will be examined first because it is by far the minority view today among Baptists. There have been influential Baptists in the past, such as Andrew Fuller, William Carey, and B. H. Carroll, who were postmillennialists.[14] However, postmillennialism has largely been eclipsed by the other two eschatological views in Baptist circles. That, however, is no reason to exclude it from consideration, especially since postmillennialism reflects concerns that are central to what it means to be a Baptist.

Postmillennialism is generally a very optimistic view of eschatology. Postmillennialists expect great success in the spread of the gospel and take seriously Jesus's promise in the Great Commission to be *with* his church as the gospel is spread to all nations (Matt. 28:20). Jesus even tied the universal preaching of the gospel to his return in Matthew 24:14, "This gospel of the kingdom shall be preached in the whole world as a testimony to all the nations, and then the end will come." If Jesus has promised to accompany his people as they fulfil the Great Commission, and if Jesus will return after the gospel has reached the whole world, then great success in this very task is assured. It is precisely this assurance of success in the preaching of the gospel that has made postmillennialism appealing to Baptists, a people who have traditionally emphasized missions and evangelism.[15]

With this brief description of postmillennialism as a starting point, it remains to be asked how the postmillennialist interprets the biblical teaching of the kingdom, especially the teaching concerning the period of time found in Revelation 20:4–6. First, the postmillennialist begins not with Revelation 20 but with Jesus's teaching on the kingdom in the Gospels. Postmillennialism emphasizes those passages in the New Testament that speak of the kingdom as already present in the preaching ministry of Jesus, as well as passages such as the

---

14. Russell D. Moore, "Personal and Cosmic Eschatology," in *A Theology for the Church*, ed. Daniel L Akin (Nashville: B&H Academic, 2007), 890.

15. Two recent developments in postmillennialism should be noted. Christian Reconstructionism, expressed by Rousas Rushdoony, goes so far as to call for the construction of a Christian social order. The other is preterism, which views the majority (or all) of the New Testament prophecies as having already come to pass with the persecution of the church and the destruction of the temple in the first century.

parables of the kingdom in Matthew 13, which speak of the slow and steady growth of the kingdom like leaven spreading through the whole loaf of bread.[16] This slow and steady growth of the kingdom through the preaching of the gospel is expected to continue until the gospel has reached every person on earth. This success of the gospel will be continual and unstoppable. When the gospel has reached the whole world, then the kingdom of God will have been established. At that time Christ will return in order to claim this kingdom that has been established by his own power through the proclamation of his church. It is for this reason that postmillennialism is characterized as being an optimistic view of the doctrine of the future. The guaranteed success of the gospel ensures the positive movement of world history toward the establishment of this kingdom.

How then does the postmillennialist interpret Revelation 20:4–6? First, it is almost universally noted by postmillennialists, and equally affirmed by everyone else, that the complex symbolism of the book of Revelation can make the interpretation of the book extremely difficult. For this reason the postmillennialist urges caution before basing an entire eschatological system on this one isolated passage in the book of Revelation. Then, with this warning stated, the postmillennialist proceeds to interpret Revelation 20 according to the pattern already established from his reading of the rest of Scripture, such as the Gospel passages mentioned above. The gradual success of the gospel over a long period of time is said to fit well with the lengthy period of Christ's reign (one thousand years) found in Revelation 20. However, the period described in this passage is interpreted to be referring to the church age at the present time rather than the time of the return of Christ. Furthermore, since it has already been more than a thousand years since the ascension of Jesus, the number "one thousand" is interpreted to be symbolic of a long period of time rather than to be taken literally. Believers reigning with Christ refers to Christ's current reign in his church. Believers' cooperation with their Lord in the spread of the gospel in this age is how they are *currently* reigning with Christ.

This description of the interpretation of Revelation 20 is by no means an exhaustive treatment of the postmillennialist interpretation of this passage. However, it is sufficient for one to grasp the general direction of the postmillennialist position on this text. The postmillennialist would not say that he is rejecting the teaching of this text. Rather, he would say that he is attempting to interpret it according to the teaching of the rest of Scripture, which he claims teaches the

16. Millard Erickson, *Christian Theology,* 3rd ed. (Grand Rapids: Baker Academic, 2013), 1108.

gradual success of the kingdom over a long period of time. It is left to the reader to judge whether his interpretation does justice to Revelation 20:4–6.

Amillennialism

Amillennialism has had many representatives among Baptists over the years. John L. Dagg, James P. Boyce, and Edgar Y. Mullins, for example, all held to this view.[17] Amillennialism is also a common view at the present time among Baptists and has been a common view among Christians of many different denominations. The primary feature that distinguishes amillennialism from postmillennialism is that amillennialism does not share the optimistic view of the future that is characteristic of postmillennialism. Other than this fact, the two positions are largely indistinguishable.[18] Amillennialists share with postmillennialists the belief that Revelation 20 does not describe a literal future kingdom with Christ reigning on this earth. Instead, this passage must be interpreted symbolically. Either it describes the reign of Christ over the church at the current time, as in the postmillennialist interpretation, or this passage describes the current condition of the righteous dead in heaven with the Lord during the intermediate state awaiting the future bodily resurrection. Both the amillennialist and the postmillennialist expect the final states of the righteous and the wicked to follow immediately after the return of Christ. Unlike the postmillennialist, the amillennialist does not expect improving conditions on the earth or a vast increase in conversions just prior to the return of Christ. In fact, there is nothing inherent in amillennialism that rules out the possibility that conditions on the earth might deteriorate considerably prior to the return of Christ.

Also like the postmillennialists, the amillennialists warn of the danger of basing one's eschatological position on a single passage found only in one book which itself is notoriously difficult to interpret. Since a *one-thousand-year* reign of Christ on earth is mentioned only in Revelation 20, it would be rather imprudent, say the amillennialists, to stake so much on such a passage. How then do the amillennialists interpret Revelation 20:4–6? This is where it actually gets complicated. Since amillennialism has been around in one form or another for such a long time, the choices for interpreting this passage are numerous. At the risk of oversimplification, two main interpretations will be presented.

---

17. Moore, "Personal and Cosmic Eschatology," 889.
18. The similarities between amillennialism and postmillennialism mean that several of the interpretations given in this section may well be applicable to postmillennialists as well. Millard Erickson mentions the fact that other than the postmillennial optimism, it is often difficult "to distinguish amillennialism from postmillennialism" (*Christian Theology*, 1112).

One interpretation of Revelation 20:4–6 takes the passage to be referring to current realities present in the church, an interpretation that reaches back all the way to Augustine in the early fifth century. The one-thousand-year reign of Christ on earth is reinterpreted to be his reign over the institutional church.[19] Prior to the year 1000 CE it would have been unproblematic to take the one thousand years mentioned in Revelation 20 literally. After the year 1000, however, it became necessary to reinterpret this number as being symbolic of a vast period of time.

What of the contrasting descriptions of conditions prior to the return of Christ, and the drastically different conditions beginning in Revelation 20? Augustine introduced the concept of *recapitulation* as a key to answering such questions and as a key to interpreting the book of Revelation as a whole. According to Augustine, the book of Revelation does not describe events sequentially but rather concurrently. Various passages in the book describe the same times and events from various perspectives, recapitulating the same events over and over again. For example, the wicked city of Babylon is not *replaced* with the glorious city of the new Jerusalem. Instead, these two cities describe two *concurrent* realities. Babylon refers to the wicked realities of this fallen world. The new Jerusalem refers to the church, where Christ is present with his people during the current age. Therefore, many of the positive elements mentioned beginning in Revelation 20 are describing current realities in the church.

What of the two resurrections mentioned in verses 4–5? Verse 4 mentions those who "came to life" at the beginning of the one thousand years. Verse 5 mentions "the rest of the dead" who "did not come to life until the thousand years were completed." A common answer to this problem was also introduced by Augustine. The reference to those who "came to life" in verse 4 is not referring to a future bodily resurrection. Instead, this "coming to life" refers to their salvation, to their regeneration to new life in Christ. Only verse 5 refers to the future resurrection of the dead. Despite the fact that the same Greek word is used in both verses, Augustine chose to give drastically different interpretations to these two verses.

The second main approach to Revelation 20:4–6 claims that these verses describe neither a future reign of Christ on earth nor Christians living today in the church, but rather they describe Christians "coming to life" in the intermediate state. The mention of "souls" and "thrones" in verse 4 are taken to be keys to interpreting this passage.[20] The setting is apparently not on earth

---

19. Blaising, "Premillennialism," 172–73.
20. Robert B. Strimple, "Amillennialism," in *Three Views on the Millennium and Beyond,* 121.

but in heaven where believers are currently "reigning" with Christ during the intermediate state, prior to their future bodily resurrection (remember they are called souls). This "first resurrection" (v. 6) is interpreted as their current experience of life and joy in the presence of the Lord, prior to the future resurrection of their bodies. The second resurrection (assumed by the use of the phrase "first resurrection") apparently includes the bodily resurrection of believers and unbelievers alike. Unbelievers do not experience the "first resurrection," the coming to life in the intermediate state. They only experience this "second resurrection" to judgment. The connection of the "second resurrection" and the "second death" in verse 6 is said to be significant. As Robert Strimple explains: "We might say that the believer in Christ will experience one death and two resurrections. . . . Unbelievers, by contrast, will experience just one resurrection—and that a resurrection to condemnation—but they will know two deaths."[21]

This all too brief survey of amillennialist interpretations of Revelation 20:4–6 has raised several questions. Are the amillennialist explanations of the one-thousand-year period mentioned in Revelation 20 compelling? Do they adequately deal with all of the data in these verses, or just some? Are the explanations of the two resurrections mentioned in the text natural to the text itself or is the interpretation forced? Amillennialists might answer by claiming that it would be imprudent to affirm a one-thousand-year earthly reign of Christ based solely on one isolated text in Scripture. Besides, argues the amillennialist, the rest of Scripture only knows the future "everlasting" kingdom of God.[22] One thousand years is far short of an "everlasting" kingdom. Furthermore, the amillennialist claims that the two "resurrections" mentioned in these verses contradict the unanimous teaching of *one* resurrection elsewhere in Scripture. This fact alone, they might say, should cause us to interpret this passage in such a way as to make it compatible with the rest of Scripture.

The amillennialist might also say that the only reason that we are even having this debate is because of the recent resurgence of premillennialism. If the premillennialists have upset the status quo so much, then they must be saying something quite different from what has been presented so far. Let us, then, see what the premillennialist position has to say about the doctrine of the future.

----

21. Ibid., 127.
22. Ibid., 100.

Premillennialism

Like the other two views already presented, premillennialism has had its share of adherents among Baptists. Charles Haddon Spurgeon, Dale Moody, W. A. Criswell, Paige Patterson, as well as Craig Blaising, to whom the current volume is dedicated, all represent the premillennialist position. As its name suggests, premillennialism teaches that Jesus Christ will return to earth *before* an actual one-thousand-year messianic reign on this earth. The time period of *one thousand* years comes directly from Revelation 20, admittedly the only place in Scripture where a period of one thousand years is mentioned. The question must be asked whether the premillennialist position is placing too much emphasis on this one text of Scripture, found in one of the most difficult biblical books to interpret. The premillennialist will answer that his position is the only position that can account for Revelation 20:4–6 *as well as the rest of Scripture's teaching on the doctrine of the future.*

The premillennialist position takes seriously a particular feature of the process of divine revelation—progressive revelation. Progressive revelation is the concept that as God gave revelation to his people over the course of history, that revelation often not only built on previous revelation but it also at times went beyond the previous revelation. As time moved forward, God disclosed greater detail to his people. When God told Abraham that all the nations of the earth would be blessed through Abraham's seed, little could God's people be expected to realize that the nations would be blessed through the one man Jesus's death on a Roman cross centuries in the future (Gen. 22:18; Gal. 3:16). The fact that revelation is *progressive* leads the premillennialist not to be surprised that a period of one thousand years is only mentioned in the final book of Scripture—the very purpose of which is to disclose God's future plans for his people as had never been disclosed before.

The concept of progressive revelation helps to clarify many issues related to the doctrine of the future in general and the interpretation of Revelation 20:4–6 specifically. It is only the revelation of the length of time, one thousand years, that is newly revealed in this passage. The idea that God's servant, the Messiah, would establish a kingdom of righteousness on this earth is a common teaching not only in the Old Testament but in the New Testament as well. The Old Testament spoke of a coming earthly kingdom when the nations of the earth would seek the Lord in Jerusalem, from which God's servant would rule the earth (e.g., Dan. 2:44; 7:12–14, 27; Isa. 2:2–4 [cf. 11:1; 9:7]; Micah 4:1–8). Jesus himself indicated that when he returned he would restore the kingdom to Israel (Acts 1:3,

6–7; 3:19–21). *That* there would be an earthly kingdom ruled by the Messiah is not something newly revealed in Revelation 20. Only the specific duration of one thousand years is newly revealed.

How do the premillennialists deal with the references to two resurrections in Revelation 20: 4–6 separated by a period of a thousand years? Simply, the premillennialists takes these as references to two resurrections separated by a period of one thousand years. The premillennialist reads the book of Revelation as the grammar and the context of the text requires. Revelation 20:4–6 is one narrative scene, introduced by the phrase "Then I saw." This is a common marker in the book indicating that a new scene in the vision is beginning.[23] Therefore, these three verses (3–6) are to be interpreted as a literary unit. This means, at least in part, that the features contained within this text should be used to help interpret the text itself. The mention of the two resurrections in the *context* of an intervening thousand-year period separating them leads the premillennialist to read this text as the narration itself demands—there will be two future resurrections separated by a period of a thousand years. Furthermore, since the same Greek term is used to describe the two instances of persons "coming to life," the text should be interpreted as referring to two instances of the *very same phenomenon*—bodily resurrection.

Perhaps the objection might be raised that the balance of the biblical revelation of the future resurrection knows of only *one* resurrection.[24] The introduction of the concept of *two* resurrections is just too much to accept. This alone should cause us to question whether we are reading Revelation 20:4–6 correctly. The premillennialist will answer by once again appealing to the concept of progressive revelation. Certainly, one would think, the Old Testament saints were expecting only one resurrection. However, since the coming of Christ we must posit *at least two* resurrections—Christ, the firstfruits (1 Cor. 15:20, 23) and our own resurrection. If progressive revelation allows for the expansion of one resurrection into two resurrections already separated by nearly two thousand years, then there is actually precedent for viewing the resurrection as coming in stages. This "expansion" of earlier revelation is not uncommon in Scripture. As Craig Blaising notes, when the Lord promised David that his son would sit on David's throne forever, it was not clear at the time that the Lord was referring to a line of kings (2 Sam 7:12–13). Nor was it clear that that line would be "interrupted and

---

23. Blaising, "Premillennialism," 215.
24. Strimple, "Amillennialism," 100–101.

the kingdom of David's son . . . be absent from the earth for a time."[25] Blaising goes on to ask: "Was it possible within the language of that promise for the kingdom to be inaugurated centuries later with the resurrection and ascension of one of David's descendants and yet be fulfilled in an everlasting sense only after a couple of millennia?"[26] This example certainly shows that it is possible for a simple promise to be fulfilled in several stages over a period of more than two millennia. Therefore, scriptural precedent itself allows for the possibility that a "simple" future resurrection of the dead might actually be fulfilled in stages separated by a period of a thousand years.

Premillennialists are actually on solid ground with their interpretation of Revelation 20:4–6. Their straightforward reading of the text fits well with the premillennialist position because they are simply taking the text as they find it. There is no obvious attempt to force the text into a preconceived prophetic pattern that they bring to the text. Also, the charge that the premillennialist is taking a risk by basing an entire eschatological position on this single text is offset by the fact that this interpretation is *consistent* with the balance of the biblical witness and is nowhere *contradicted* by the biblical witness of the doctrine of the future.

Conclusion

Baptists have a long history of preaching the message of hope to a lost world. Their confidence in the certain return of Christ, the resurrection of the dead, and the future judgment continues to motivate Baptists in the area of missions and evangelism. Despite the differences in some details relating to the doctrine of the future, Baptists have been unified in the confidence that their ministry has eternal consequences. What God has promised to his people shall come to pass. Therefore, let us all continue to bring this message of hope to a lost world.

---

25. Blaising, "A Premillennialism Response," in *Three Views on the Millennium and Beyond,* 149.
26. Ibid.

The Doctrine of the Future
and Dispensationalism

Mark L. Bailey

Dallas Theological Seminary has historically been noted as an institution that advocates a dispensational system of theology.[1] As a faculty, we believe that dispensationalism, as a system, best accounts for both the unity as well as the diversity represented in the Bible. The continuity and discontinuity of the Bible has been and continues to be the subject of great debate and discussion. The continuity of the Bible can be maintained by observing that the primary purpose of God in history is to establish his kingdom on earth and in history under a divinely appointed human representative who will rule on his behalf. Christ's righteous reign as king from Jerusalem over the whole earth will be the ultimate manifestation of the theocratic kingdom of God on earth (Isa. 9:6–7). God's anointed human representative, the Messiah, will ultimately defeat sin and death on the same earth and among mankind where the authority of God was initially challenged.

The discontinuity of the Bible is the result of the progressive revelation of God as different responsibilities have been given to different people for varying durations of time. While salvation is always by grace through faith, people have been given responsibilities that have differed according to the revelation of God given up to a particular point in the time of God's dealings with humanity. The dispensationalist elevates the glory of God as the primary unifying

---

1. I am privileged to participate in this project in honor of my friend, Craig Blaising. He is a thoughtful scholar and a respected theologian. His contributions to the understanding of biblical eschatology are deeply appreciated. He has made me a better student of the Scriptures through our ongoing interactions over the years. Craig, thanks for your friendship, fellowship, and faithfulness in the work of the kingdom!

principle that unites all the dispensations of God's economy as he works to sovereignly vindicate his right to be recognized and worshiped as the one and only true God. While the kingdom and redemptive programs of God are two strands that hold together the tapestry of the historical outworking of God's plan for the earth, the ultimate goal of history is the righteous vindication of God's glory (1 Cor. 15:20–24).[2]

Day of the Lord

Both the Old and New Testaments use the phrase "the day of the Lord" to refer to God's intervention in human history to judge or bless nations according to their response to him.[3] The prophets often telescope the near view of the present with the far view of the future in detailing the program of God (Isa. 9:6–7; 61:1–2; Zech. 10–14). While there have been times in Israel's history where the phrase may have been applicable, the primary referent of the phrase is the ultimate day of the Lord at the end of history that will take place when the Messiah himself comes in judgment and blessing. The two basic messages of the prophets were warnings of judgment for sin and disobedience and announcements of salvation and blessing for those who repent, believe, and obey (Deut. 28–30).

The time frame for the future day of the Lord is established from Paul and Peter. The beginning of the period is revealed by Paul in 2 Thessalonians 2:2–3 to be immediately following the rapture since in it are included the judgments of the tribulation and the revelation of the man of sin. Because it will come suddenly and unexpectedly (1 Thess. 5:2) during a time of apparent peace (1 Thess. 5:3), and because the "one now restraining" must be taken out of the way (2 Thess. 2:7), the day cannot begin before the rapture of the church. The end of the day of the Lord is revealed by Peter to be at the end of the millennium when the present heaven passes away with a roar and the elements will be destroyed with intense heat, and the earth and its works will be burned up (2 Pet. 3:10). With both the tribulation and the millennium being included, the great and

---

2. For a great overview of the Bible, see Stanley A. Ellisen, *Three Worlds in Conflict* (Sisters, OR: Multnomah, 1998), 17–30; J. Dwight Pentecost, *Thy Kingdom Come: Tracing God's Kingdom Program and Covenant Promises throughout History* (Grand Rapids: Kregel, 1995).

3. For a biblical theology of the day of the Lord, see Craig A Blaising, "The Day of the Lord: Theme and Pattern in Biblical Theology" in *Bibliotheca Sacra* 169, no 673 (January–March 2012): 3–19.

terrible aspects predicted by Malachi (4:5–6) are seen to be the essential components. Thus judgment and blessing are two central properties of the day of the Lord. Jesus Christ is the central character in the day of the Lord for, in reality, as Zechariah predicts, it is a day for the Lord (Zech. 14:1). He is seen to fulfill the offices of prophet (Deut. 18:15), priest (Ps. 110:4), and king (Gen. 49:10). The outcome of the day of the Lord will be the establishment of the Messianic kingdom on earth prior to its ultimate consummation in eternity (Isa. 11; 65). Such a kingdom will include a realm over which Jesus as the Messiah will reign with sovereign authority.

THE CONTRIBUTION OF DANIEL

The book of Daniel reveals the times of the Gentiles and the seventy "weeks" for Israel as the outline of God's future program for Israel. Daniel was written to explain why Israel was in captivity and how God would sovereignly use Gentile world powers to accomplish his messianic purposes for both the Jews and Jerusalem. The succession of imagery of the statue in Daniel 2 and that of the beasts of chapter 7 depict the dominant powers and the chronological order in which they will reign during what Jesus later labeled "the time of the Gentiles" (Luke 21:24-31). The prophecies of Daniel also introduce the person and work of the final Gentile ruler who will become prominent in the latter days. His wicked character and blasphemous conduct, especially toward the people of God, is graphically forecasted (Dan. 7:8, 20–26; 8:9–11, 23–25; 9:27; 11:36–39).

The book of Daniel reveals the times of the Gentiles and the seventy weeks (of years) for Israel as the broad yet specific outline of the prophetic future (Dan. 9:24–27). Six purposes can be suggested for this period of God's sovereign dealings: (1) a national purpose to fulfill his covenants with Israel; (2) a social purpose to end Israel's transgression of the law; (3) a redemptive purpose to make final atonement for sin; (4) a regal purpose to establish a kingdom of righteousness; (5) a teleological purpose to seal up or finish prophecy; and (6) a worship purpose to anoint the most holy place, which implies a future temple where God can be glorified at the second coming of Christ.

A gap of undetermined length is necessary between the sixty-ninth and the seventieth week of years, leaving the seventieth week of Daniel as yet unfulfilled and therefore yet future. According to Daniel 9 two major events were predicted to take place between the first sixty-nine weeks and the seventieth: the cutting off (death) of the Messiah and the destruction of Jerusalem

(Dan. 9:24-26). If the death of Christ took place in 33 CE and the destruction of Jerusalem occurred in 70 CE, there is a gap of at least thirty-seven years between the two events. Since the events described in Daniel 9:27 have not been completed, dispensationalists believe the seventieth week of Daniel is yet future.[4]

The Expected Future

Dispensational premillennialists believe that the prophesied future will commence with the rapture of the church and will be followed by the events of the day of the Lord. According to the biblical descriptions, the day of the Lord is both a period of time as well as a specific day when the Messiah returns to earth. As a period of time, the day of the Lord begins with the opening events of the tribulation and ends with the concluding events surrounding the end of the millennial kingdom. The specific day of the Lord will be the day the Lord returns to the earth when he will judge the nations and establish his rule in the millennium prior to eternity (Zech. 14:1–4). The day of the Lord includes both judgment and blessing—darkness and light. Therefore, dispensationalists hold to the view that there are two stages to the second coming of Jesus. He will first come for his church (rapture) and then come with his church to the earth (revelation). These two events are separated by the tribulation. While those who hold to this view maintain a distinct identity for Israel and the church throughout history, there may be similar purposes for the people of God in different eras and they may experience some overlap of blessings as they relate themselves to God in faith.

A dispensational view of the future expects a future for the nation of Israel in which Christ will reign on earth in a literal kingdom for a thousand years prior to eternity. Accordingly, a dispensationalist expects a premillennial return of Christ to the earth and a pretribulational rapture of the church prior to the tribulation. Foundational to a belief in a future for Israel is the series of unconditional covenants God made with his people. Since each of the unconditional biblical covenants—the Abrahamic, the Davidic, and the new—still has elements that are yet to be fulfilled, one can expect God to be as faithful

---

4. See Harold W. Hoehner, *Chronological Aspects of the Life of Christ* (Grand Rapids: Zondervan, 1977), 115–139; Sir Robert Anderson, *The Coming Prince*, 10th ed. (Grand Rapids: Kregel Classics, 1957); Alva J. McClain, *Daniel's Prophecy of the Seventy Weeks,* (Grand Rapids: Zondervan, 1969); Leon Wood, *A Commentary on Daniel* (Grand Rapids: Zondervan, 1973), 243–264.

with those promises as he has been with all the others.[5] One day a righteous remnant of Israel will be secured in the land God promised and will enjoy a relationship of blessing with Messiah as her king. And as God has chosen Israel to be a repository of the truth, a witness to the nations, and a channel for the Messiah, all who come to faith in Jesus Christ, the Messiah, will inherit the kingdom by virtue of their relationship with him who is the King.

A Pretribulation Rapture of the Church

Dispensational theologians are pretty unanimous that the next prophetic event will be the rapture of the church. The rapture of the church will occur before the tribulation, and the second coming will happen after the tribulation (Matt. 24:29–31). This present age will conclude with the translation of the church into the presence of the Lord for her reward and union. The word "rapture" comes from the Latin word *raptus*, which in turn is a translation of the Greek verb *harpadzo*, "caught up" found in 1 Thessalonians 4:17. The rapture will take place when the church is caught up to meet the Lord in the air. The key passages are John 14:1–3, 1 Corinthians 15:51–57, and 1 Thessalonians 4:13–17.

As an imminent event, the rapture of the church and the glorification of the body is the immediate expectation of those who have put their faith and trust in Jesus Christ. The revelation of the rapture was designed as a comfort concerning the believing dead (1 Thess. 4:13–18) and the believing living (1 Thess. 5:1–10) at the time of the Lord's return for his church. First Corinthians 15:51–52 and Philippians 3:20–21 were written to comfort living believers with the promise of the glorification of their bodies when Christ will translate Christians from this life to the next. Paul did not want the Christians to grieve over saints who have died since they have a future hope that Christ will return to take both the dead and the living in Christ to heaven to be with him.

The critical events of the rapture include the return of the Lord for his church, the resurrection of the church saints who have died before he comes, and the immediate change of body for those who are still alive when he comes.

---

5. The yet unfulfilled aspects of the unconditional covenants God has made with Israel argues for a future for Israel and hence a literal earthly kingdom to come. See Charles C. Ryrie, *The Basis of the Premillennial Faith*, 5th ed. (Neptune, NJ: Loizeaux Brothers, 1975); John F. Walvoord, *The Millennial Kingdom* (Grand Rapids: Zondervan, 1980); J. Dwight Pentecost, *Things to Come: A Study in Biblical Eschatology* (Grand Rapids: Zondervan, 1964), 65–128.

The rapture will take place instantaneously for everyone who has been a part of the church of Jesus Christ.

In 1 Thessalonians 4:15, Paul linked his discussion of the rapture of the church to the teaching of Jesus. One great possibility can be seen in John 14:1–3 and 1 Thessalonians 4:13–18, which give parallel expressions to the doctrine of Jesus returning to take (rapture) his own to be with him.

JOHN 14:1–3	1 THESSALONIANS 4:13–18
trouble	sorrow
believe	believe
God, Me (Jesus)	Jesus, God
told you	say to you
come again	coming of the Lord
receive you	caught up
to myself (Jesus)	to meet the Lord
be where I am	ever be with the Lord

The revelation of the rapture is rooted in the word of the Lord (1 Thess. 4:15). The hope of the rapture is grounded in the resurrection of Jesus himself (1 Thess. 4:14). The rapture of the church is described as occurring before the day of the Lord (2 Thess. 2:1–3). Paul and John describe what the rapture will look like when it happens. Christians will be instantly changed into the image of Jesus at the moment of the rapture (1 Cor. 15:51–53; 1 John 3:3). The result will be that the church will forever be with the Lord.

A number of reasons can be advanced for the validity of the interpretation that the church will be translated prior to the beginning of the seventieth week of Daniel.[6] First, the nature of the church as the body of Christ can be shown

---

6. Craig A. Blaising, "A Case for the Pretribulation Rapture" in *Three Views on the Rapture: Pretribulation, Prewrath, or Posttribulation,* ed. Alan Hultberg (Grand Rapids: Zondervan, 2010), 25–73; Paul D. Feinberg, "The Case for the Pretribulation Rapture Position," in *Three Views on the Rapture: Pre-, Mid-, or Post-Tribulational?,* ed. Gleason L. Archer Jr. et al. (Grand

to be distinct from the saints in the other ages (Eph. 3:1–12). The formation and community of church is a new revelation unknown in previous eras. Second, church saints are never exhorted to look for signs, the tribulation, or the Antichrist, but rather for the blessed hope of the imminent coming of the Savior (Titus 2:13). The pretribulational interpretation is the only view that fits the true concept of imminency that pervades the entire New Testament. Second, Paul revealed the church is not destined for the wrath of the tribulation or the day of the Lord (Rom. 5:9; 1 Thess. 1:9–10; 5:9; Rev. 3:10). If the rapture and the second coming were the same event, believers would have to go through the tribulation. While some see wrath as final judgment, the context is the wrath of the day of the Lord and not that of the great white throne judgment.

Revelation 3:10 contains a promise that the church of Philadelphia would be "kept from the hour" of tribulation that will come upon the whole earth.[7] The Greek preposition *ek* is best taken to mean "keep out" rather than "keep through," since it refers to a period of time designated as "the hour." In order to determine the most probable meaning of *tereo ek* in Revelation 3:10, its usage in John 17:15 must be considered. This is the only other occurrence of *tereo* with *ek* in either biblical or classical Greek. It is significant that both verses are Johannine and in both cases Jesus speaks the words. The fact that the testing will come upon the whole world shows this is not some localized pressure or disturbance. The subjects or objects of the testing are called "earth dwellers" which is a terms used eight times in Revelation for the unbelieving in the world. Revelation 3:10 does not describe the rapture *per se*. However it describes the protection of the church by keeping her out of the hour of testing. The rapture revealed elsewhere explains how, and this passage shows the results of the rapture. In light of the martyrdom in Revelation 6:9–11 and 7:14, Revelation 3:10 must refer to the protection for the church from the *time* of the tribulation because in the tribulation the saints will indeed face the wrath of the period and many will in fact die as martyrs.

Rapids: Zondervan, 1996), 46–86; John F. Walvoord, *The Rapture Question* (Grand Rapids: Zondervan, 1957); Renald Showers, *Maranatha: Our Lord Come!* (Bellmawr, NJ: The Friends of Israel Gospel Ministry, 1995).

7. David G. Winfrey, "The Great Tribulation: Kept 'Out Of' or 'Through'?" *Grace Theological Journal* 3 (Spring, 1982): 3–18; Jeffrey L. Townsend, "The Rapture in Revelation 3:10," *Bibliotheca Sacra* 137 (1980): 252–266. For a defense against a postribulational rapture position, see Thomas R. Edgar, "Robert H. Gundry and Revelation 3:10," *Grace Theological Journal* 3 (Spring 1982): 19–49; Gerald B. Stanton, *Kept from the Hour: Biblical Evidences for the Pretribulational Return of Christ* (Miami Springs, FL: Schoettle, 1991).

Third, the restraining ministry of the Holy Spirit must be removed before the manifestation of the "lawless one" can take place (2 Thess. 2:6–8). It is important to remember that an omnipresent God cannot take away his presence but that his restraining ministry can be removed. Fourth, there is a need for an interval of time between the rapture and the second coming to allow for the judgment seat of Christ before the church's return with Christ for the judgment of the nations. That this time gap must lie between the rapture and the second coming is evident in the fact that at his return rewards will already have been distributed and the marriage will already have taken place in heaven (Rev. 19:7–8). Fifth, the setting for the rapture is in the air, while the scene for the second coming is on the earth (John 14:3; 1 Thess. 4:13–18; 2 Thess. 2:1; Zech. 14:1–4; Rev. 19:11–16). Sixth, the rapture of the church is always discussed separately from the day of the Lord (1 Thess. 4:13–5:11). While they are discussed one following the other, it is clear that Paul treats them as separate and distinct events, each with the *peri de* introductory conjunction. A natural, chronological reading of the passage presents the rapture before the day of the Lord. The first is meant to comfort and the second to warn of the sudden destruction and wrath.

Seventh, the nature, scope, and purposes of the seventieth week of Daniel are distinctly Jewish (Dan. 9:24–27) and not related to the church. During the tribulation—also called "the time of trouble for Jacob" (Jer. 30:7)—God will again turn his primary attention to Israel (Rom. 11:17–31). Eighth, if the time for the rapture and the second coming were coincident, there would be no one left to inhabit and repopulate in the millennium, since according to Revelation 19:17–21 everyone who opposes Christ is destroyed. Ninth, the purpose of the tribulation is a time for Israel's refinement that implies the separate identity of Israel as apart from the church (Deut. 4:29–30; Jer. 30:4–11). Since the tribulation is called the great day of God's wrath (Rev. 6:17), and the church is promised to be saved from wrath (1 Thess. 1:19; 5:9), then the church must be raptured (removed) if it is to be spared such wrath that will come upon the earth. While the church is mentioned nineteen times in Revelation 1–3, and once in Revelation 22:16, the word is entirely absent during the description of the judgments of the tribulation in Revelation 6–18, leading to the conclusion that the church is not on earth during the tribulation and those who become believers during the tribulation are never referred to as the church. Tenth, the distinctions between the rapture and the second coming support the pretribulational viewpoint:

THE RAPTURE	THE SECOND COMING
At the rapture, believers will meet the Lord in the air and go with him to heaven (1 Thess. 4:17).	At the second coming, believers will return with Christ to reign upon the earth (Rev. 19:7, 8; 14; 20:4).
The rapture occurs before the tribulation (1 Thess. 5:9; Rev. 3:10).	The second coming occurs after the tribulation (Rev. 6–18).
The rapture will result in the removal of the believers from the earth as an act of salvation (1 Thess. 4:13–18; 5:9).	The second coming will witness the removal of the wicked as an act of judgment (Matt. 24:40–41).
The rapture will be practically invisible and instant (1 Cor. 15:5–54).	The second coming will be visible to all (Matt. 24:29–30; Rev. 1:7).
The rapture is always presented as imminent, in that it could take place at any moment (1 Thess. 4:13-18; Titus 2:13).	The second coming will not occur until the events of the tribulation, which will culminate in signs of significance (Matt. 24:15–31; 2 Thess. 2:4, 8).
At the rapture, Jesus comes from heaven and returns back to heaven (John 14:1–3; 1 Thess. 4:17).	At the second coming, Christ comes from heaven and remains to reign upon the earth (Matt. 25:31–32).
At the rapture, Jesus personally gathers his church to himself (1 Thess. 4:16–17).	Angels will gather the elect at the second coming (Matt. 24:29–31).
At the rapture the righteous are taken and the wicked are left behind (John 14:4–6; 1 Cor. 15:52; 1 Thess. 4:16–18).	At the second coming, the wicked are taken out and the righteous are left to go into the kingdom (Matt. 25:31–45).

Thus, the rapture and the revelation at the second coming are similar but separate events.[8] Both involve Jesus returning. Both are end-times events. However, it is crucially important to recognize the differences. In summary, the rapture is the return of Christ in the clouds to remove all believers from the earth before the time of God's wrath. The revelation of Christ at the second coming is the return of Christ to the earth to bring the tribulation to an end by waging a war

8. For a chart of even more comparisons between the rapture and the second coming, see H. Wayne House and Randall Price, *Charts of Bible Prophecy* (Grand Rapids: Zondervan, 2003), 98–9.

of judgment against all opposed to him, to defeat the antichrist and his evil world empire, and to establish the righteous messianic kingdom upon the earth.

THE TRIBULATION

The tribulation, the seventieth week of Daniel, is a seven-year period of time of unprecedented judgment on the earth, during which God will prepare Israel for her Messiah and will pour out judgment upon the earth because of sin (Deut. 4:30–31; Isa. 2:19; 24:19–21; 26:20–21; Jer. 30:4–7; Dan. 12:1; Joel 2:1–2; Zeph. 1:14–15, 18; Matt. 24:3–22; 1 Thess. 5:3; Rev. 6:15–17).[9] The source of the wrath may in part be traced to Satan as he unleashes his anger toward God's people (Rev. 12:12–17; 13:7), but it is ultimately to be traced to God as he brings to bear his righteous judgment against sin (Rev. 6:15–17; 11:18; 14:7, 10, 19; 15:7; 16:1).

Jesus predicted that the tribulation before his second coming would be unlike anything to happen before or after it, as far as its scope and severity are concerned (Matt. 24:21). It will be unique in that it will be a time of judgment and trouble that will be worldwide (Rev. 3:10); its severity will be such that people everywhere will believe the end of the world is near and that death will be preferable to life (Rev. 6:15–17).

The tribulation will commence with the signing of a covenant between the antichrist and the Jews that will allow the Jewish people to reestablish their worship with a temple in Jerusalem, including its rituals of sacrifice (Dan. 9:27). In the middle of the "week," the covenant will be broken and the antichrist will set himself up in the temple where he will demand the worship of the world be directed toward him (2 Thess. 2:4). Three series of seven judgments each are detailed in the book of Revelation—the seal judgments, the trumpet judgments, and the bowl judgments (Rev. 6, 8–9, 16). Each series after the first originate out of the seventh judgment of the preceding series. These judgments reinforce the important principle that all judgment prior to the final judgment is really an extension of God's grace inviting sinners to repent and believe in Jesus as the Messiah.

The length of the period will be seven years that will fulfill the "seventieth week" of Daniel (Dan. 9:24–27). The term used to describe the period are a

---

9. For an extensive treatment of the various facets of the tribulation see J. Dwight Pentecost, *Things to Come*, 259–368; Leon J. Wood, *The Bible and Future Events: An Introductory Survey of Last-Day Events* (Grand Rapids: Zondervan, 1973), 54–158; and Mark Hitchcock, *The End* (Carol Stream, IL: Tyndale, 2012), 233–379.

"week" for the entire period, in the middle of which the abomination of desolation takes place (Dan. 9:27). Half the period is identified in various texts as forty-two months (Rev. 11:2; 13:5), 1,260 days (Rev. 11:3; 12:6), and time, times, and half a time (Rev. 12:14).

Characteristics of the period include wrath, judgment, indignation, trial, trouble, destruction, darkness, desolation, and punishment. The purposes of the tribulation are to prepare Israel for salvation (Zech. 12:10; 13:1; Rev. 1:7), to pour out judgment upon the unbelieving world for sin (Isa. 26:21; Matt. 25:41–46), and to bring a great Gentile multitude to Christ (Matt. 25:31–40; Rev. 7:1–10, 13–14).

The judgments are divine judgments through human agencies that begin the time of the "seal" judgments (Rev. 6:1). The trumpet judgments are judgments of God upon both nature and people because of unrepentant sin during the second half of the tribulation period (Rev. 8–9). The bowl judgments are the climactic conclusion to the tribulation judgments that occur up until the second advent of Christ and are judgments poured out upon the beast and his worshipers (Rev. 16).

The tribulation will also be Satan's attempt to counterfeit the political and religious purposes of God for the millennial kingdom and to prevent the second coming of Christ. The beast (the antichrist) is the major personage Satan will use in the tribulation period. The false prophet will be the religious promoter of the beast (Rev. 13:3–15). Both will be judged and sent to the lake of fire when the Lord returns (Rev. 19:20).

A Premillennial Return of Christ

Hebrews 9:28 says, "So Christ also, . . .(NASB) will appear a second time for salvation without reference to sin, to those who eagerly await Him." The second coming will put an end to the tribulation and inaugurate the millennium.[10] Revelation 19:11–21 records John's vision of Christ's second coming. He comes to wage war with those who oppose him (cf. Zech. 14:3). The names of Christ associated with his return show the significance of the event. He is called Faithful and True (Rev. 19:11), the Word of God (Rev. 19:13), and the King of kings and Lord of lords (Rev. 19:16). Accompanying him will be the armies of heaven who will act as his agents of divine judgment (Rev. 15:1; 16:1). He will land on

---

10. Craig A. Blaising, "Premillennialism." in *Three Views on the Millennium and Beyond,* ed. Darrell L. Bock and Stanley N. Gundry (Grand Rapids: Zondervan, 1999), 155–227.

the Mount of Olives (Zech. 14:4), the same place from which he ascended (Acts 1:11). And while the antichrist and the nations of the earth oppose him, the battle will be brief, and Messiah will win (Rev. 19:17–20).

One of the purposes of the second coming will be to vindicate righteous justice upon all the wickedness perpetrated against God's people (2 Thess. 2:5–10). According to Revelation 19:15, the second coming of Christ has a central purpose of judging the world. The ultimate victory of righteousness over wickedness, life over death, peace over conflict, and Christ over Satan will not come until the arrival of the King who will establish his kingdom. (cf. 1 Cor. 15:20–24). The second coming of Christ will complete the judgments of the tribulation for both Israel (Ezek. 20:33–44; 37:1–14; Zech. 12:10–13:8), and the nations (Matt. 25:31–46). A remnant of Israel will be saved when they see the return of their Messiah (Zech. 12:10; Rom. 11:23). All human enemies of Christ will be destroyed (2 Thess. 1:6–9; Jude 14–15) and the beast and the false prophet will be cast into the lake of fire (Rev. 19:17–21). Old Testament and tribulational saints will be resurrected at the end of the tribulation to be rewarded and to reign with Christ (Dan. 12:2; Rev. 20:6). Two resurrections are distinguished in Revelation. The first is a resurrection to life, which includes Christ, the dead in Christ from the church, the Old Testament saints, and the saints of the tribulation and millennium. The second is after the thousand-year reign of Christ, which will be a resurrection unto a second death of judgment. Satan will be bound for one thousand years in a bottomless pit during the millennial reign of Jesus Christ (Rev. 20:1–3). The purpose of the second coming is clearly stated in 2 Thessalonians 1:7–10: to be a day of both vengeance and vindication.

The second coming of Christ is one of the most referenced events across the pages of the Bible, and therefore one of the most important. His arrival is described in Revelation 19, which entails his appearance, his names, and his judgment of the wicked regardless of the their previous position, power, or prestige (Rev. 19:11–21). The climax of judgment at this time includes the beast and the false prophet being cast into the lake of fire (Rev. 19:20).

In addition to the arguments that distinguish the revelation of Christ at his second coming to the earth and his coming in the air to take his church to heaven (rapture), dispensationalists would argue from both the Old Testament and the New Testament for a future earthly kingdom that will be established and ruled over by Jesus Christ on the earth between the judgments of the tribulation and the great white throne judgment prior to the eternal state.

The Millennium

Support for both the reality and the reasons for the millennium will frame the following discussion. First, an earthly kingdom in the future is the only adequate interpretation of the promises God made concerning the coming Messiah and the kingdom. Isaiah predicted the Messiah would establish an everlasting kingdom on the throne of David (Isa. 9:6–7). God's promises are as unshakable as the mountains (Isa. 54:10), and Israel's endurance to inherit God's promises are as permanent as the new heavens and new earth that God will create (Isa. 66:22).

Second, there is a pattern of Old Testament prophesies of judgment followed by the blessings of an established earthly kingdom. For example, in the prophecies of Isaiah 24–25, announcements of judgment necessitate a fulfillment before the blessings of the kingdom. The passage reveals the following chronology: global tribulation, the judgment, and then the kingdom. This pattern is found in other passages as well (cf. Dan. 12:1–3; Zech. 14:9). Zechariah 14:9 is important in that it shows that the Lord's kingdom comes after both a time of tribulation and the Lord's physical and visible return to earth. It is also significant because when the King reigns, he reigns "over all the earth" (Zech. 14:9).

Third, since Isaiah 65:17–25 describes the blessings of the kingdom to come with the presence of sin and death, this argues for an earthly fulfillment prior to eternity in which according to both Isaiah 25:8 and Revelation 21:4, death will be no more.

Fourth, the presence of the wicked over which Christ will rule and the presence of a rebellion after the thousand-year reign of Christ argues for a historical phase of the kingdom of God before the eternal phase (Isa. 11:4; Rev. 20:7–10).

Fifth, Zechariah 14 describes the return of Christ to Jerusalem and punishment for those who will not come to worship in Jerusalem at the appointed times (Zech. 14:16–19). Thus the kingdom envisioned in Zechariah cannot be a spiritualized kingdom in eternity, but must refer to something prior.

Sixth, a future earthly kingdom is necessary in light of Jesus's promise to the Twelve that "in the regeneration" when the Son of Man sits on his throne, they would sit on twelve thrones judging the twelve tribes of Israel (Matt. 19:28). This passage argues for a distinctly Jewish reference of a kingdom in the future, different than the experience of the disciples in the present.

Seventh, the grammar of the temporal indicators in Paul's teaching about three stages of resurrection in 1 Corinthians 15:23 and 24 is compatible with an intervening kingdom, as described in Revelation 20:1–6. Periods of time are required between Christ's resurrection, those who are his at his coming, and their resurrection, and the end when death as the last enemy is finally vanquished.

Eighth, the vision of the millennium in Revelation 20:1–6 within the literary structure of Revelation 19:11–21:8 is such that the conditions described in the kingdom do not fit the conditions of the tribulation that were described prior in the book, or the conditions after the thousand years. The events prior to and after this literary section demand a transition of events that can only be explained by the events of the section.

Ninth, the millennium described is a thousand-year imprisonment of Satan during a reign of Christ with the saints. This reign and imprisonment comes after and not before the return of Christ. The description of Satan as imprisoned for the millennial period argues for a separate period of history distinguishable from both the church and the tribulation in which Satan is described as active (Eph. 6:10–20), dangerous (1 Pet. 5:8), and even in the presence of God (Rev. 12:10) before what is described in Revelation 20:1–6. Especially telling is the reason why Satan is bound in the pit: "to keep him from deceiving the nations anymore until the thousand years were ended" (Rev. 20:3) In addition, after the thousand years, he is seen back at his old activity of deceit and destruction in the season after the millennium but before the great white throne judgment (Rev. 20:7–10, NIV).

Tenth, the visions in Revelation 19:11–21:8 are a necessary transition between that of the city of Babylon and the New Jerusalem. The New Jerusalem supersedes Babylon as the humanistic order that will be replaced by the heavenly. The opposite descriptions of character and appearance are intentional contrasts to highlight the consummation of wickedness as distinguished from the consummation of righteousness.

Eleventh, the chronological sequences introduced by "and I saw" described in Revelation 19:11–21:8 adhere most faithfully to a consistent implementation of a historical-grammatical hermeneutic. Likewise, the content of the visions argue for a logical and sequential arrangement. Six of the eight visions are contemporaneous or subsequent to the second coming of Christ. It follows that the other two are to be taken in a similar way.

Twelfth, the rebellion that follows the period of the millennium is put down differently (by fire, Rev. 20:14), as opposed to that at the coming of Christ (birds eat the flesh, Rev. 19:21).

Thirteenth, the saints who reign with Christ are described by terms that harken back to the tribulation (Rev. 6:9, 11; 12:17), which of necessity precedes the millennium. The reference to the martyrs in Revelation 20:4 identifies them as believers who suffer in the tribulation, as revealed by previous visions of John. This is confirmed by their deaths being tied to their allegiance to the testimony of Christ and the Word of God. Their resurrection qualifies and enables them to reign with Christ for the thousand years. The language of the passage picks up the terminology of Revelation 1:6 and 5:10 that promises them a reign with Christ "on the earth."

Fourteenth, John envisions a sequence of time which he calls "a thousand years" that transpires between two physical resurrections, one for the believers and one for the rest of humanity. One is a resurrection unto life, and one a resurrection unto death (cf. John 5:29). Those who are resurrected first reign for a millennium, and those in the second resurrection are raised to face a final judgment that results in being cast into the lake of fire.

In addition to the previous arguments, validation for a literal earthly reign can be supported from the purposes for which the millennium is a divine necessity. The importance of the millennium cannot be underestimated if one is to understand the kingdom and redemptive purposes of God. Just as God was faithful to literally fulfill his promises related to the first advent of his Son, so will he fulfill all that he has promised with reference to the second coming, including the promise of Christ's earthly reign of one thousand years.

The millennium will not be a monarchy ruled by man but a theocracy ruled by Christ. Hence the theocratic purposes of God for the earth will be fulfilled in this earthly kingdom ruled by his Son, the Messiah, in fulfillment of Luke 1:32: "He will be great and will be called the Son of the Most High. The Lord God will give him the throne of his father David" (NIV).

A literal millennium is necessary if God is going to fulfill his promises to the Jews. He has promised to bring together a remnant that would acknowledge Jesus as their Messiah at the end of the tribulation (Ezek. 36:22–28; Zech. 10:6–9). On that entire remnant he will pour out his Spirit without distinction (Isa. 32:15; 44:3) and expand their population as well as the area of the promised land (Ezek. 36:10–11; 48:1–29). As such Israel will be an object lesson of God's grace and mercy (Zech. 8:13). So much will they be blessed that Zechariah predicts "ten men from all the nations will grasp the garment of the Jew, saying, 'Let us go with you, for we have heard that God is with you'" (Zech. 8:23, NASB).

Another reason the millennium is important relates to the promise God has given in both the Old and New Testaments that the saints will one day reign over all people and dominions with Christ (Dan. 7:27; 2 Tim. 2:12; Rev. 2:26–27; 5:10). They will function in varying capacities of rule awarded to them by Christ for their faithfulness in previous service (Dan. 7:18, 27; Jer. 3:15; Luke 19:11–17).

A further reason for the importance of the millennium is the promises of God for the nations of the world, as well as for creation itself. God has promised a kingdom of righteousness, peace, holiness, and justice (Isa. 2:4; 11:9; Zech. 14:20–21). God has also promised to reverse the curse that has been on the earth since the beginning and release it from its bondage (Rom. 8:18–23). Examples of restoration include the change of carnivorous animals to herbivorous (Isa. 11:6), poisonous to harmless (Isa. 11:8–9), and average to bountiful (Isa. 35; Ezek. 34:25–31). So changed will be the land of Israel that people will compare it to the garden of Eden (Ezek. 36:35).

The Bible especially emphasizes the promises God has given with reference to the reign of his Son. Scriptures are replete with the promises that Jesus will return to manifest his glory, which in turn will glorify the Father (Isa. 24:23; Isa. 66:18–19; 2 Thess. 1:7–10).

A final purpose for the millennium may be to show that when left to their own devices, human hearts will still be shown to be deceitful and desperately wicked—even in a world controlled by a righteous King with immediate rule of righteousness, justice, and peace—as evidenced by the final rebellion when Satan is released, after the thousand-year rule of the Messiah (Rev. 20:7–10). Thus the need for a new heart is more important than a utopian society rooted in humanism and self-made religions of all types.

Jesus Christ will reign as the Sovereign-Savior of the world for a thousand years, demonstrating the right of God to rule the earth through God's appointed human representative. The millennial kingdom is the final form of the theocracy God will use to demonstrate himself as God over all. His reign will be from Mount Zion in Jerusalem (Isa. 2:2–4; 24:23; Zech. 14:1–9) and will extend over Israel and the rest of the world. It will be effective in that it will result in a reign of righteousness and peace. The kingdom will thus reflect the character of the King. The length of the millennium will be one thousand literal years on the earth (Rev. 20:2–7).[11]

THE GREAT WHITE THRONE JUDGMENT

The great white throne will be the scene of the final judgment of God against all unbelievers (Rev. 20:11–15). That God has delegated all judgment to the Son

---

11. Harold W. Hoehner, "Evidence from Revelation 20" in *A Case for Premillennialism: A New Consensus*, ed. Donald K. Campbell and Jeffrey L. Townsend (Chicago: Moody Press, 1992), 232–65; Robert L. Thomas, *Revelation 8–22: An Exegetical Commentary* (Chicago: Moody Press, 1995), 403–435.

is stated in a number of passages (John 5:22, 27; Acts 10:42; 17:31; 2 Tim. 4:1). Since the resurrection is what qualifies him, the judge would need to be fully human, fully divine, and to have conquered sin and death. Hence Jesus would be the only one qualified to judge.

The time will be at the close of the millennium and after a time of rebellion in which many will follow after Satan. The place of the judgment is the presence of God after the present heavens and earth pass away. The subjects of the great white throne are all of the unbelievers from all ages. They are said to be those who will be raised to judgment (Dan. 12:2; John 5:29; Acts 24:15). The bases of the judgment are the book of works that will reveal the lack of works of faith, and the Lamb's book of life that will show the absence of any unbeliever's name. The results of the judgment will be the second death in the lake of fire for all eternity. The final judgment of God upon Satan, sin, and sinners will be the final preparation for heaven (Rev. 20:7, 10). The old heaven and earth will give way to the new (cf. Isa. 65:17–19; 66:22; 2 Pet. 3:13; Rev. 21:1). The triumph of Christ as the second Adam will be seen in his delivery of the kingdom to the Father (1 Cor. 15:24–28).

The Eternal State

Eternity for the wicked will also be a place of unending punishment and death for the wicked. The place of the wicked in eternity is referred to as Gehenna, which is most often translated as hell (Matt. 18:9; Mark 9:43, 45, 47). That hell is a place is confirmed in that both the body and the soul will be housed there (Matt. 10:28). That the punishment of hell is eternal is confirmed by descriptions of "furnace of fire" (Matt. 13:42, 50), "fire and brimstone" (Rev. 19:20; 20:10, 14–15; 21:8), or the word "fire" joined with adjectives like eternal or unquenchable (Matt. 18:8–9; Mark 9:43, 47–48; Rev. 14:10–11). Hebrews 10:31 states that "It is a dreadful thing to fall into the hands of the living God" (NIV). If the result of death was only annihilation, such a statement would be superfluous. Hell will be a place of pain, ruin, and separation from all that is good and godly (2 Thess. 1:9). Perhaps that is why it is called the "second death" (Rev. 20:14; 21:8). That hell is eternal is proven by the fact that the same words used for the length of eternity for the righteous are used for the punishment of the wicked (Matt. 25:46). Hell is a place where the fire is unquenchable (Mark 9:43, 47–48) and where the worm will not die (Mark 9:48). The smoke of torment is said to "go up forever and ever" (Rev. 14:11) which is even the same phrase for the eternality of God himself (Rev. 4:9).

By contrast, the eternal state for the righteous will be the continuous enjoyment of the blissful reign of God from the New Jerusalem in the new heaven and new earth. Eternity will be a time of unending blessing in the presence of God for the righteous. Although no exact descriptions are given as to what life will be like in eternity, there are a few glimpses of its reality given. Life with God will be the experience of uninterrupted fellowship (1 Cor. 13:12; 1 John 3:2; John 14:3; Rev. 22); at home in the Father's house (John 14:2–3); in the holy city, the New Jerusalem (Rev. 3:12; 21:2, 10, Heb. 11:10, 16; 12:22–24; 13:14); eternal rest (Rev. 14:13); fullness of knowledge (1 Cor. 13:12); untarnished holiness (Rev. 21:27); fullness of joy (Rev. 21:4); privileged service (Rev. 22:3); abundant life (Rev. 21:6); glory (Col. 3:4; 2 Cor. 4:17); and last but not least, unhindered worship (Rev. 19:1; Rev. 7: 9–12).[12]

---

12. Charles U. Wagner, "Heaven and Eternity Future" in *Countdown to Armageddon: The Final Battle and Beyond*, ed. Charles C. Ryrie, Joe Jordan, and Tom Davis (Eugene, OR: Harvest House, 1999), 259–72; Mark Hitchcock, *The End*, 447–59.

THE DOCTRINE OF THE FUTURE
IN JÜRGEN MOLTMANN

Lanier Burns

T he topic "The Future in Modern Theology" is daunting not only because scholars disagree about modernity, but also because "modern
theologians" disagree about the future.[1] There are common themes,
and I have tried to point these out in the current chapter. William Hutchison pinpointed three crucial identifiers in his book *The Modernist Impulse
in American Protestantism*: "I have found, however, that when 'modernism'
finally became a common term in the early part of this century, it generally
meant three things: . . . it meant the conscious, intended adaptation of religious ideas to modern culture [elsewhere he refers to this as 'the critique of
religious language']. . . . the idea that God is imminent in human cultural
development and revealed through it . . . [and] a belief that human society is
moving toward realization (even though it may never attain the reality) of the
Kingdom of God."[2] We will attempt to show that these themes were nurtured
by the rise of science in early-modern Europe. They were cradled in reactions
against biblicism, a humanistic priority, ecumenical ideals, and pervasive concerns about justice.

---

1. My close friendship with Craig Blaising developed from our years of mutual encouragement in theological studies at Dallas Theological Seminary. Almost every day I consulted
him about the wisest courses of action. I admired his expertise in theological thinking and
his particular interest in eschatology that revitalized the subject in our classes. Recently,
he delivered insightful lectures on the subject at Dallas Seminary. According to Solomon,
"There is a friend who sticks closer than a brother." I am privileged to participate in this
volume.
2. William Hutchison, *The Modernist Impulse in American Protestantism* (Durham, NC: Duke
Univ., 1992), 2.

A working definition of modernism is only a beginning. How did various scholars envision the future? This question is admittedly impossible for present-oriented creatures like ourselves. Our subjective approach has been to trace the development of modernity from its early modern roots in Europe. Interdisciplinary perspectives about the rise of modernism have further limited the topic.

The notion of "the future" in the twentieth century resurfaced in the wake of the world wars, waves of freedom movements, and a deep-seated quest for hope out of a sense of despair. The scholar who initiated a theological recovery of hope was Jürgen Moltmann, in his influential *Theology of Hope* (1967). This chapter, accordingly, is a case study of Moltmann, from his background and method to his thesis and argument. The chapter will conclude with an assessment of his primary emphases and their bearing on the "progress and abyss" of the century.

The Development of Modernity

The twentieth century inherited conflicting impulses from the rise of modernity in Europe. On the one hand, conquests and discoveries birthed an exhilarating illusion of an ideal future which fanned imperial dreams. On the other hand, optimism in social progress collapsed in catastrophes. Moltmann labeled the impulses "progress and abyss" in his mid-twentieth-century context. The crises of abyss, in his view, portended the "final solution" of humanity. Alluding to world wars, nuclear threats, and ecological pollution, he observed, "Both of these eras are still present today—their progress and their abyss."[3]

The impulses developed from longstanding trends associated with the European hegemony and Enlightenment. The first trend was the expansion of empires across the world beginning in the sixteenth century, while a second was the seizure of power over nature by science and technology. The "age of exploration" propelled Europe from the shadows of the Ottomans, the Moguls, and the Chinese to dominance on the world stage. The Americas, for example, were molded according to the will of the European conquerors, all of whom overwhelmed the Aztec, Mayan, and Incan cultures with Christianized names and enforced languages with stereotypes like "savages" and "unclaimed lands." The expectation of these conquests was an abiding ideal of a "new world order," in which God and

---

3. Jürgen Moltmann, "Progress and Abyss: Remembrances of the Future of the Modern World," in *The Future of Hope*, ed. Miroslav Volf and William Katerberg (Grand Rapids, Cambridge: Eerdmans, 2004), 4.

gold could coexist in an undiscovered Eden or Eldorado respectively.[4] Gold was useful for enrichment and perhaps another conquest of Jerusalem—a possible synthesis of the classical "Golden Age" and the biblical millennium. Joachim of Fiore had predicted that Christ would bring the ark to Zion as the capital of his millennial reign. The Spanish Quintomonarchists—state theologians—believed that Daniel's imperial prophecies would culminate in a "Fifth Monarchy." Thus, the hope for a "new world" was baptized with messianic overtones. G. W. F. Hegel anticipated a "Third Empire of the Spirit" in which past ideals would no longer dominate the present but rather nurture dreams of a utopian future.[5]

The second development after European conquests was the progressive acquisition of power over nature by science and technology. The shift in Western thought from medieval to modern was undergirded by scientific discoveries. Exploration and conquest brought a trove of new knowledge and artifacts which exploded the comfortable boundaries of traditional European taxonomy. How were the strange objects and "primitive peoples" to be explained? A two-hundred-year struggle took place between Catholicism and emerging empiricism before the intellectual Enlightenment could flourish. Received ideas about cosmology from medieval Europe included traditional authorities like biblical revelation and Aristotle, which were revered as guides for stability and order. Nicholas Copernicus (1473–1543) challenged the church's view that the Earth was the center of the universe. Instead he held that observational evidence showed that the earth orbited the sun. In near proximity Andreas Vesalius (1514–64) wrote *De humani corporis fabrica libri septem* (1543), a brilliant anatomical presentation of the human body, which led the way for a challenge to Galen's humoral theory. Francis Bacon (1561–1626) argued for the use of experiments rather than deduction as the preferred way to increase knowledge. In 1632 Galileo Galilei (1564–1642) agreed with Copernicus, developed the telescope (with Lippershey, Janssen, and Metius), and was silenced by the Catholic Inquisition. The increase of astronomical data was matched by the development of the microscope by Antonie van Leeuwenhoek and Robert Hooke, which exposed a cellular world heretofore unknown. The scientific data matched the flood of geopolitical information that flowed from the end of empire, while institutions like the Royal Society ensured the authority of scientific advances. In the following

4. Ernest Bloch, *The Principle of Hope,* 2 vols., trans. Neville Plaice, Stephen Plaice, and Paul Knight (Cambridge, MA: MIT Press, 1986), 2.772–77.
5. G. W. F. Hegel, *Lectures on the Philosophy of World History: Introduction, Reason in History,* trans. H. N. Nisbet (Cambridge: Cambridge Univ. Press, 1975), *passim.*

generation Isaac Newton (1642–1727) advanced physics and empirical methods that influenced Enlightenment thinking. The effect of the rise of modern science was that humanity as the image of God was dethroned by the vastness of space and biological life. A steady stream of discoveries increasingly compelled nature to conform to science's agenda.[6]

Every area of academia was engulfed by the momentous changes of developing modernity. The Enlightenment in the seventeenth and eighteenth centuries was characterized by belief in the experimental method of science and a priority on reason to advance knowledge. The primary form of art was Neoclassicism, the first international style and an expression of the lofty aspirations of the period, though its symmetry was challenged by the imaginative passions of Romanticism. The period was the highest expression of modernity's movement away from medievalism's authorities and dogmatism. Science was expanding its knowledge of nature, but no longer did the justification for monarchy or the existence of God seem so clear and certain. Immanuel Kant (1724–1804), one of Enlightenment's preeminent philosophers, held that Newton's laws were shown to be true by reason ("synthetic truth" in contrast to analytic facts), and that the scientific approach could explain the phenomenal world of appearances. God, on the other hand, involved the use of faith rather than reason. His ethical ideal was a hope for a league of nations that would guarantee the "rights of man" in an age of peace. A prominent successor was Hegel (1770–1831), who sought to reconcile philosophy and history with his notion of *Geist* (the universal mind or world spirit). History progressed, he believed, through a dialectical process by which thesis and antithesis led to a greater self-consciousness: synthesis. His influence continued into the twentieth century theology. Hegel's *Geist* is thoroughly immanent to the extent that we are all part of God as we advance to know ourselves in our history.[7]

Anthropocentric education became the synthesizing hope of a better world. Gotthold Ephraim Lessing predicted that everyone could know the

---

6. Immanuel Kant, *Critique of Pure Reason*, trans. Paul Guyer and Allen Wood (Cambridge: Cambridge Univ. Press, 1998), 109: "Scientific reason has insight only into what it itself produces according to its own design by compelling nature to answer its questions."

7. In the early nineteenth century, "continental" philosophy veered toward the idealism of Hegel and later took an existentialist turn via Friedrich Nietzsche (1844-1900) and Martin Heidegger (1889–1976), Jean-Paul Sartre (1905–80), and Albert Camus (1913–60). By contrast, Anglo-American philosophers followed an empiricist and analytical emphasis from David Hume and Gottlob Frege (1848–1925), Bertrand Russell (1872–1970), and Ludwig Wittgenstein (1889–1951). There are contemporary signs of a convergence of the analytical and continental concerns.

truth for themselves without the inquisitional threats of the church. Revelation and tradition would yield to the promise of pedagogical plans for a forward-looking humanity with an increase in individual freedoms.[8] Friedrich Nietzsche (1844–1900) argued that human creativity should replace God at the center of thinking, an inevitable conclusion of modernity which had been progressively anthropocentric. Auguste Comte similarly argued that human thought had advanced to its final positive stage in which observed facts would be systematized as the basis of a better society. Charles Darwin wrote his *Origin of the Species* (1859) from his study of finches and placed naturalistic evolution at the center of scientific inquiry with his explanatory axiom "the survival of the fittest" and its implication of the common ancestry of biological life.

The nineteenth century inaugurated visions of beginnings, revolutions, and utopias. People seized the momentum of social alternatives in this world, which tended to be initiated by arms and sustained by commitment to representative government. The French Revolution promoted popular sovereignty in place of the *ancient régime* under the banner of liberty, equality, and fraternity. The *philosophes* were widely read and appealed for an unwavering allegiance to the power of reason. England's Industrial Revolution offered the possibility of general prosperity and the happiness of the greater number. The American Revolution proclaimed the self-evidence of life, liberty, and the pursuit of happiness in its Declaration of Independence, later signified by *novus ordo seclorum* ("new order of the ages") on its national seal and currency. The French Revolutionary Assembly defined natural rights as "liberty, property, security, and the right to resist oppression" in its *Declaration of the Rights of Man and Citizens* (1789). Socialist revolutions expressed a hope for a classless society built upon the industrial "realm of necessity." Claude-Henri de Rouvroy Saint-Simon (1760–1825) and Louis Blanc (1811–82) formulated the principle "from each according to his abilities, to each according to his needs." Karl Marx (1818–83) added the dimension of "economic determinism" in which exploitation would lead to a dictatorship of the proletariat. In Moltmann's words, "The hallmarks of the sixteenth through the nineteenth centuries in Europe were progress and evolution,

---

8. E. E. Lessing, *The Education of the Human Race*, trans. F. W. Robertson (London: C. K. Paul, 1881). Cf. Karl Aner, *Die Theologie der Lessingzeit* (Hildesheim: G. Olms, 1964). The emphasis is repeated by Robert Solomon, *Introducing Philosophy*, 9th ed. (New York: Oxford University Press, 2008), 16–17: "The central concern of modern philosophy is *the authority of the individual person. . . .* This stress on individual autonomy stands at the very foundation of contemporary Western thought. We might say that it is our most basic assumption."

growth and expansion, utopias, and the revolutions of hope."[9] In varying ways Lenin and Stalin carried Marxist emphases into the twentieth century with oppressions of their own in the Ukraine, as did the Cultural Revolution of Mao Zedong in agrarian China.

At the beginning of the twentieth century, the wealthy rode various engines to the ends of empire; the aristocratic foundations began to erode; the masses flocked to industrial opportunities in increasingly cosmopolitan cities; Realism and *avant garde* seem to have foreshadowed the chaos to come; the boundaries of nations and morality shifted; scientific discovery changed and preceded insights into atomic and quantum realities; and so much more in an almost inexhaustible list. Change was ubiquitous. "Modernistic" art reflected the changes in satirical expressions of anger and disillusionment (Dada and Surrealism), in its desire for exuberance and erotic experimentation, and in its desire to serve new social orders with innovative designs. A shift toward the workings of the unconscious mind was paralleled by literature's emphasis on subjective perception. The contradictory shadows of human progress veiled a deepening greed and compounding evil beneath its surface. Technological achievements were accompanied by unparalleled armaments and destructive potential.

In the First World War (1914–18), the Western powers embarked on a course of self-destruction, a war of attrition and extermination that was symbolized by the battle of Verdun on February 21, 1916. Thomas Hardy poetically quipped, "After two thousand years of mass / We've got as far as poison gas."[10] General Falkenhayn rationalized to the Kaiser that "the forces of France will bleed to death." The French even turned their machine guns on their North African allies, "firing at the backs of the fleeing men, who fell like flies" according to a witness of the bloodbath.[11] Moltmann observed, "The lights of the Enlightenment and of resplendent progress toward a better world went out too."[12]

The Second World War (1939–45) continued the self-destructive holocaust. At its end, Japan was defeated in August 1945 by two atomic bombs, which instantly killed hundreds of thousands of people. In totalitarian cults naked power, arbitrarily approved, was idolized and relentlessly pursued. The "cold war" provoked "nuclear deterrence" in which threats grew into "mutually

---

9. Moltmann, "Progress and Abyss," 12.
10. Thomas Hardy, "Christmas: 1924," in *Collected Poems* (London: Macmillan, 1930), 873.
11. Cited in Martin Gilbert, *A History of the Twentieth Century*, 3 vols. (New York: William Morrow, 1977), 1.397.
12. Moltmann, "Progress and Abyss," 15.

assured destruction," the potential annihilation of life on Earth. We should be
convinced by now that the perpetrators of chaos cannot be expected to be saviors
from evil. "Hitler and Stalin and all their willing henchmen have convinced us
that the power of radical evil is unbroken. That is why end-of-the-world scenarios, catastrophe fantasies, and *Apocalypse Now* films seem to us more realistic
than the fine, hopeful images of the nineteenth century about the golden age
and eternal peace."[13] The effects of the wars were an end to European empires,
waves of freedom movements between and within nations, and a pervasive sense
of despair in place of earlier optimism.

THE HOPE OF MOLTMANN

His Background and Method

We have defined "modernity" in this chapter as a post-medieval transition in
authorities from received traditions, ecclesial and classical, to reason and experimentation for the accumulation of knowledge and for guiding precepts in cultural
development. We have summarized this transition in terms of a vast amount of
data with altered expectations that were based on exploration and science. The
introductory "development" was very selective and dependent on how we planned
to develop "the future in modern theology" with focus on the twentieth century.
There is no single, comprehensive view of such a subject. Language is inadequate
to capture the optimistic euphoria at the end of the nineteenth century; it is inadequate to describe the earth-transforming shocks of the world wars; and it is unable
to adequately describe the monumental changes after the wars. Some intellectuals
were utopic, while others were dystopic; the Europeans were mired in existential
despair, while others such as Americans were more removed from the intensity of
conflict "over there" and more positive about recovery; science continued to develop, while theology struggled with "the death of God." Evangelical dictionaries
usually discuss the theology of the last two hundred years in terms of a liberal departure from the authority of the Scriptures and from an orthodox understanding
of Jesus Christ. As true as these rejections of historical Christianity might be, we
will attempt to examine twentieth-century eschatology "from within" in terms of
the development of modernity.

This chapter will discuss notions of the future through the lenses of Moltmann's vision for hope as an antidote to despair. He is apropos as a case study

13. Ibid.

because of his background, his eclectic theological method, and his voluminous writings. All of this means that he is representative of a number of "modernistic" theologians. Volf introduced *The Future of Theology* with the following tribute: "Perhaps no other theologian of the second half of our century has shaped theology so profoundly as Jürgen Moltmann."[14] Validating Volf's claim are Moltmann's own 1,217 writings and 1,043 books and articles about his theology. His thinking resonates with major movements in the theological academy, panentheism in process theology, and various liberation theologies.

Moltmann and his peers suffered the humiliation of World War II in their backyard. He was a prisoner of war (1945–48) and found Christianity through the ministry of English-speaking chaplains. He recalled that in his despair as a POW, he found "that comfort in the Christ who in his passion became my brother in need, and in his resurrection from the dead awakened me to a living hope."[15] Returning to Germany, he was motivated to study theology "in order to understand the power of hope to which I owed my life."[16] Thus, Christianity for him became a hopeful faith in dealing with despair, tragedy, and loss: "From first to last, and not merely in the epilogue, Christianity is eschatology, is hope, forward looking and forward moving, and therefore also revolutionizing and transforming the present. The eschatological is not one element of Christianity, but it is the medium of Christian faith as such, the key in which everything in it is set, the glow that suffuses everything here in the dawn of an expected new day."[17]

After the war he began his theological study at Göttingen. His mentors and sources were as diverse as his eclectic method. Otto Weber was his supervisor and put him in contact with Arnold van Ruler and J. C. Hoekendijk, both of whom pointed him to the importance of the kingdom of God motif. From Hans Urs von Balthasar he gained an appreciation of the beauty of creation. Ernst Wolf inspired his reflection on social ethics along with a number of liberation theologians. Hegel through Hans Joachim Iwand became the foundation of his dialectical strategy and

---

14. Miroslav Volf, "Introduction," *The Future of Theology*, 21.

15. Moltmann, *Experiences in Theology: Ways and Forms of Christian Theology*, trans. Margaret Kohl (Minneapolis: Fortress, 2000), 4. Also, Moltmann, *A Broad Place: An Autobiography*, trans. Margaret Kohl (Minneapolis: Fortress, 2008), chapter 3.

16. Moltmann, *History and the Triune God: Contributions to Trinitarian Theology*, trans. John Bowden (London: SCM, 1991), 166; also, *A Broad Place*, 30.

17. Moltmann, *Theology of Hope: On the Ground and Implications of a Christian Eschatology*, trans. James Leitch (New York: Harper and Row, 1967), 16. Moltmann was not alone in the emerging eschatological framing of theology. Douglas Meeks, *Origins of the Theology of Hope* (Philadelphia: Fortress, 1974), 1, lists Walter Kreck, Wolf-Dieter Marsch, and Johann Baptist Metz, among others.

his view of history as a movement of the Spirit. Moltmann connected Hegel's historical process of reconciliation to Christ's crucifixion and resurrection to envision a hopeful future which would demonstrate God's solidarity with those who appear godforsaken today. Isaac Luria gave him the Kabbalistic understanding of creation as God in himself that allowed for Alfred North Whitehead's panentheistic bipolarity of God's immanence and transcendence. There were many others as well, which promoted his vision of an openly structured theological dialogue among a broad constituency to point modernity toward the promises of God's kingdom.

When Moltmann moved to Wuppertal in the late 1950s, the diverse strands of his research converged with his intense reading of Ernst Bloch's *The Principle of Hope*. Bloch drew on Germany's earlier chiliasts as exemplified by Joachim of Fiore as well as Judaism's promissory themes to develop a Marxist utopian vision. Bloch was his colleague at Tübingen and especially influenced Moltmann's thought about an "anthropology of hope" and the concept of "not-yet-being."[18] Why had Christian theology neglected the theme of hope, when a century like the twentieth mandated its emphasis? If eschatology was the core of Christianity, then people are creatures of hope, constantly striving toward a future and deliverance from the crises of the present: "[Man] is a world-open creature who himself can and must everywhere build his own environment in his cultures. And yet there is an element and an environment without which he cannot live as man, and that is hope. It is the breath of life."[19] With Bloch Moltmann held that reality is dynamic, open, experimental, and processive. Unforeseen future possibilities emerge from present potentialities through dialectical processes. This process lies at the heart of God's being and his evolving kingdom, "eschatology is nothing other than faith in the Creator with eyes toward the future."[20]

Moltmann's sources helped him to work with an eclectic method that would use a symbolic, nonanalytical approach to redefine Christian theology in light of "post-critical scientific methods and ways of thinking."[21] His sources connected with large constituencies in the theological academy, especially oppressed minorities and feminine perspectives.[22] The role of method for Moltmann was to enhance

18. Moltmann, *The Experiment Hope*, trans. Douglas Meek (Philadelphia: Fortress, 2007), 20.
19. Ibid., 21.
20. Moltmann, *God in Creation: A New Theology of Creation and the Spirit of God*, trans. Margaret Kohl (Minneapolis: Fortress, 1993), 93.
21. Ibid., 4.
22. Moltmann also felt that sources should include every discipline in view of the breadth of the crises to include science, technology, and economics, which are so influential in human relationships. Because of scope, we confine ourselves to theology here.

dialogue, which contingently argued for mutual participation and a unifying sympathy to incorporate the voices of heretofore opposing populations: "Behind all of this is the conviction that, humanly speaking, truth is to be found in unhindered dialogue."[23] Christians, he believed, should be the source for change, dialogical agents, who are charged with promoting life in an imperiled world. Accordingly, method was secondary to redefining and reworking theological content in light of scientific prowess and the ecological crisis: "For me, what was important was the revision of theological issues in the light of their biblical origins, and their renewal or reworking in the challenge of the present. . . . My theological methods therefore grew up as I came to have a perception of the objects of theological thought. . . . And my attempts to walk it are of course determined by my personal biography and by the political context and historical *kairos* in which I live."[24] The implication of this "time" was that the historical symbol of hope must be expanded to a view of creation as the symbol of the new creation. Since the past represents death, the present in hope and promise takes its definition from the future resurrection of creation in God's life. "No human future," Moltmann stated, "can make good the crimes of the past, so creation must be interpreted from its eschatological future."[25] Space, by the same token, is God's world presence, "The space of the world corresponds to God's world presence, which initiates this space, limits it, and interpenetrates it."[26] Hence, space and its history is homogeneous and divine, abolishing the artificial distinction between sacred and profane in the depth of mutual dialogue.

The rise of modern sciences led to the rejection of ancient and medieval cosmologies, and biblical criticisms dismissed its narratives about origins as myths.[27] Conflicts between science and the church were severe as evidenced by

---

23. Moltmann, *The Trinity and the Kingdom: The Doctrine of God*, trans. Margaret Kohl (Philadelphia: Augsburg Fortress, 1993) xiii. In *The Coming of God: Christian Eschatology*, trans. Margaret Kohl (London: SCM, 1996), xiv, he stated, "Theological truth takes the form of dialogue, and does so essentially, not just for the purposes of entertainment."

24. Moltmann, *Experiences in Theology*, xiv–xv. Richard Bauckham, ed., *God Will Be All in All: The Eschatology of Jürgen Moltmann* (Minneapolis: Fortress, 2001), 36, similarly stated: "Someone who, ultimately speaking, lives consciously in his own time never does theology in the form of abstractions for all times; he pursues it as a contemporary for contemporaries, specifically, contextually, and in relation to its *kairos*."

25. Moltmann, "Progress and Abyss," 17. He does not intend for us to understand chronological time in his eschatology, since the future already has been present from the beginning and in messianic resurrection.

26. Moltmann, *God in Creation*, 157.

27. A similar emphasis is advanced by Keith Ward, *The Big Questions in Science and Religion* (West Conshohocken, PA: Templeton Foundation, 2008): "Religious beliefs cannot remain what they were before the rise of modern science any more than ancient scientific beliefs can. . . .

the trials of Bruno and Galileo and subsequent reactions against Darwin and Freud. There could be no reconciliation, he held, when the sciences naturalized the world and neutralized traditional theology's anthropocentrism. Biblicism tried to render as absolute archaic testimonies about nature and render all further research superfluous.[28] It disregarded the wealth of mutual relationships in its static cosmos. In light of this unfortunate position, Moltmann mandates that theology must "start again . . . if it is to comprehend creation and God's activity in the world in a new way, in the framework of today's knowledge about nature and evolution, and if it is to make the world as creation—and its history as God's activity—comprehensible to scientific reason also. If this is to be our purpose, we must first of all be critical, and must get rid of the bias and narrowness which have taken root in the Christian doctrine of creation in the wake of polemic against the theory of evolution."[29] The problem was that evolution had demoted Christians and Europeans alike, who in the name of God had understood themselves as the masters of nature. The theory undermined the anthropocentric view of the world by reducing it to a small link in a vast sequence and expanse whose end cannot be determined. Church and civic communities overreacted because evolution threatened their justification for conquest of the world and exploitation of nature. This ideology, Moltmann asserts, is neither biblical nor Christian. Even the "Social Darwinism" of T. H. Huxley politicized evolution to justify European colonialism, racism, patriarchy, and class conflict.

Science, too, has its problems. It objectifies creation with language that separates subject and object, so "we must try to get away from analytical thinking with its distinctions between subject and object, and must strive to learn a new, communicative, and integrating way of thought. . . . We no longer desire to know in order to dominate or analyze and reduce in order to reconstruct. Our purpose is now to perceive in order to participate, and to enter into the mutual relationships of the living things."[30] Existence can only become a home if the relationship

---

This leads to the conclusion that the unprecedented and revolutionary changes in scientific knowledge of our age will involve a new formulation of ancient religious beliefs." This call for change points to the modern trend of redefining theology according to scientific assumptions and language. Moltmann belongs to a long modernist procession that has reacted against biblicism.

28. Moltmann, *God in Creation*, 192–93: "So it is not merely possible to relate the biblical testimonies about creation and God's history with his creation, to new insights about nature, and new theories about the interpretation of these insights; it is actually necessary to make this connection and to reformulate the biblical testimonies in the light of these things."

29. Ibid.

30. Ibid., 2–3.

between human beings is without stresses and strains—if it can be described in terms of reconciliation, peace, and a viable symbiosis. The indwelling of human beings in the natural system of the earth corresponds to the indwelling of the Spirit in the soul and body of the human being, which puts an end to the alienation of human beings from themselves. In other words, his view of humanity flows from his Trinitarian history of nature.

His Thesis and Argument

Moltmann pursued his "impossible possibility" of hope in two trilogies, advocating a "dialectic of reconciliation." His first trilogy argued for hope with a christological focus.[31] The cross and resurrection were his dialectical "opposites": The resurrection was God's promise of his presence for all humanity and creation (*Theology of Hope*), while the cross demonstrated God's solidarity with the godlessness of the world (*The Crucified God*). The cross must be interpreted with themes of divine compassion and fellow-suffering. The outcast Son of Man, who died between oppressed wretches, cried, "My God, My God, why have you forsaken me?" So, God was dialectically present in his own contradiction to lovingly deliver his creation from sin and suffering as well as to express love within himself. The cross was not meant to solve the problem of suffering but to embrace it with voluntary fellow-suffering, that is, to move from the particularity of Jesus to the inherently universal dimensions of the gospel. On the other hand, "The distinctive element of the Christian possibility of hope rests in the fact that it is born of the memory of the raising up of the crucified Son of Man." The contradiction between hope and despair, and life and death respectively, was reconciled in the person of Christ. Through the dialectic of hope a person is "embedded" in the comprehensive hope of the cosmos in its Creator. The cross pointed to a Trinitarian and messianic history in which God reciprocally related to the world, being both affecting and affected as a community of divine persons who have included creation comprehensively in their love. The Spirit has resolved the dialectic by indwelling creation and transformatively moving it in resurrectional hope toward the new creation, when God's presence will fully indwell all of reality (*The Church in the Power of the Spirit*). Moltmann identified this central theme of his Trinitarian history as "immanent transcendence,"

---

31. The first trilogy was *Theology of Hope* (1964), *The Crucified God* (1972), and *The Church in the Power of the Spirit* (1975). See also, Moltmann, *Jesus Christ for Today's World*, trans. Margaret Kohl (Minneapolis: Fortress, 1994), chaps. 5–6.

a concept that is akin to Schleiermacher's "common spirit" that coheres reality.[32] The new creation, we must note, will not merely be a fulfillment of present possibilities but also a radically new life and glory and is the basis for our hope in every historical present: "Man attains to knowledge of himself by discovering the discrepancy between the divine mission and his own being, by learning what he is, and what he is yet to be, and yet himself cannot be."[33] Like the Trinity "the quest of humanity is not concerned with an immutable ontology but rather with an awareness of our present journey with a view to who we will become."[34]

Theology of Hope prompted a desire in Moltmann to write a new approach to creation. *God in Creation* was the result, which appeared in his second trilogy, after *The Trinity and the Kingdom: The Doctrine of God* (1980) and *The Way of Jesus Christ* (1989). We have noted that the new approach to creation involved a rejection of the Christian past. The issue, for Moltmann, was reconciliation toward the future culmination of Trinitarian and messianic history. And the future of creation is accomplished by the Spirit in a universal, sabbatarian community. To develop this notion of creational transformation toward resurrectional glory, he advances three correctives to replace the one-sided perversions of the past: from biblicism to *zimsum*, from monotheistic causation to panentheistic Trinitarianism, and from anthropological dominance to communitarian indwelling.

First, in place of the biblical account, Moltmann used the Kabbalistic teaching of *zimsum* as "the only serious attempt ever made to think through the idea of 'creation out of nothing' in a truly theological way."[35] The *zimsum* principle is that God must act inwardly before he can act outwardly, "It is only as *causa sui* that God can be *causa mundi*."[36] God determined to concentrate and contract himself, a withdrawing into himself, to create nothingness for creation. That is, he continually and simultaneously creates inwardly and outwardly. He uses the symbols of

---

32. The meristic, all-encompassing phrase has been characteristic of modern theology's humanistic focus in various expressions such as the "infinite depth" of personal consciousness and similar notions. See Moltmann, *The Spirit of Life: A Universal Proclamation*, trans. Margaret Kohl (London: SCM, 1992), 31–38.
33. Moltmann, *Theology of Hope*, 285.
34. Moltmann, *The Way of Jesus Christ*, trans. Margaret Kohl (London: SCM, 1990) 55–63, where he discusses at length the problem of the alienated self.
35. *The Trinity and the Kingdom*, 108. Kabbalah in Jewish mysticism is a "way of transformation." Eliahu Klein, *Kabbalah of Creation: The Mysticism of Isaac Luria, Founder of Modern Kabbalah* (Berkeley, CA: North Atlantic, 2005) may be used to compare Luria's and Moltmann's views of transformation.
36. Moltmann, *God in Creation*, 100. On page 86 he also notes, "In order to create a world 'outside' himself [in creation, incarnation, and redemption], the infinite God must have made room beforehand for a finitude in himself."

"great World Mother" and "Mother Earth" to support his principle of nurturing life: "From the symbol of the World Mother to the symbol of the redeeming cosmic human being, Christ is the panentheistic understanding of the world as the sheltering and nurturing divine environment for everything living."[37]

The *nihil* (nothingness) is a negation of divine being, literally "God-forsakenness, hell, absolute death."[38] Moltmann believes that divine negation becomes annihilating nothingness (German *verniehtanden Nichts*) in God's encounter with sin. As the divine act of self-humiliating, creative love is the initiation of God's kenotic interrelationship with the world: "Through his self-emptying he creates liberation, through his self-humiliation he exalts, and through his vicarious suffering the redemption of sinners is achieved."[39] This allows for a change from "creative making" in masculine terms to a loving process in feminine terms: "Creation as God's act in Nothingness and as God's order in chaos is a male, engendering notion. Creation as God's act in God and out of God must rather be called a feminine concept, a bringing-forth. God creates the world by letting his world become and be in *himself*. Let it be!"[40] In summary, God enters the annihilating nothingness and "becomes omnipresent," gathering *nihil* into his being and giving creation a part of his eternal life. The crucified Son, in turn, becomes the foundation of the kingdom of glory, which begins with his resurrection and glorification.

Second, the feminine process means that panentheistic Trinitarianism must replace monotheistic causation. Monotheism had led to differentiation within the Trinity, distinction between God and the world, and human domination over nature. God's paternal transcendence had objectified nature as his immanent domain; as a consequence "nature is stripped of her divinity, politics becomes profane, history is divested of fate."[41] We must stop thinking that creating the world is causing it. Instead we must think of a creative web of interrelationships, a cosmic community of being between God the Spirit and all created beings. We must stop trying to understand God monotheistically as the one absolute subject, but instead see him in a Trinitarian sense as the perichoretic unity of the Father, the Son, and the Spirit. We can no longer con-

---

37. Ibid., 300.
38. Ibid., 87.
39. Ibid., 89. "Liberation, for him, is a central concept in his theology and is broader than egalitarian movements in the mid-twentieth century, though it includes them. It refers to freedom from situations that alienate and oppress people as well as freedom to take responsibility for their world. It is God's invitation to move into the 'broad place' of perichoretic living."
40. Moltmann, *The Trinity and the Kingdom*, 109.
41. Moltmann, *God in Creation*, 13.

ceive of his relationship to the world as a one-sided relationship of dominion. In the operation and indwelling of the Spirit, the creation of the Father and the reconciliation of the world through the Son arrive at their goal. "All the works of God end in the presence of the Spirit."[42] Ecology and pneumatology converge in the symbolism of creation as home, analogous to the Kabbalistic view of Shekinah. The notion of home with feminist undertones means that creation is an evolving openness toward a future sabbatical world community. It will involve a finitude that embraces infinity, in which "everything will not be in God, but God will be in everything."[43]

Moltmann connected his "new thinking about God" with panentheistic theology.[44] Its central tenet is the recognition of the presence of God in the world and the presence of the world in God. In his words, God creates the world and manifests himself through its being: "Everything exalts, lives, and moves *in others* . . . in the cosmic interrelationships of the divine Spirit."[45] The Creator of the world is the Spirit of the universe, "its total cohesion, its structure, its information, its energy . . . The evolution and the catastrophes of the universe are also movements and experiences of the Spirit of creation."[46] "The Trinity is no self-contained group in heaven, but an eschatological process open for men on earth, which stems from the cross of Christ."[47] He so identifies the Spirit with creation that he includes all of history in the divine experience, which means that the human spirit is largely unconscious in a multilayered life system, "Spirit is the quintessence of the human being's self-organization, and his self-transcendence, his inner and outward symbioses."[48] Through the Spirit people are bound, socially and culturally, with all living things in a spiritual ecosystem.

---

42. Ibid., 96. Concerning the goal of history, Moltmann identified himself with "eschatological millenarianism," not historical millenarianism. He comments, "Christian eschatology—eschatology, that is, which is messianic, healing, and saving—is millenarian eschatology," *The Coming of God*, 23.
43. Moltmann, "The World in God or God in the World?," in Richard Bauckham, *God Will Be All in All*, 37, 40.
44. Moltmann, *God in Creation*, xi. In twentieth-century theology, the desire to reconcile the naturalism of science and its method with theology usually resulted in some form of panentheism, an identification of the presence of God with the powers of nature. Traditional understanding of the incommunicable attributes of God will not allow for finite testing and verification. Moltmann is no exception.
45. Ibid., 11.
46. Ibid., 16.
47. Moltmann, *The Crucified God: The Cross of Christ as the Foundation and Criticism of Christian Theology*, trans. R. A. Wilson and John Bowden (Minneapolis: Fortress, 1993), 249.
48. Ibid., 18.

In the process of transformation, the Spirit of creation (cosmic Spirit) must be distinguished from the Holy Spirit, but they eventually merge: "The Holy Spirit does not supercede the Spirit of creation but transforms it. The Holy Spirit therefore lays hold of the whole human being embracing his feelings and his body as well as his soul and reason."[49] His principle of "mutual interpenetration" implies that "all relationships are analogous to God and reflect the primal, reciprocal indwelling and interpenetration of the Trinitarian perichoresis: God *in* the world and the world *in* God."[50] The imperative, therefore, is to expand personal consciousness to embrace self-transcendence to social, ecological, cosmic, and divine realms.

We should not be surprised that Moltmann seeks to distinguish his panentheism from pantheism. He notes that the philosophical root of evolution is Neoplatonic pantheism and quotes Ernst Haekel as saying, "Pantheism is *the world-system of the modern scientist*."[51] He also refers to Heinrich Heine's rejection of pantheism because it translates into indifference.[52] The indifference refers to the inevitable consequence of equating God with the godlessness of the world. If God is godlessness, then there is no force for transformation toward the future; that is, bipolarity is reduced to a single polar reality. Future glory would be relegated to a perpetually hopeless chaos. He also rejects Heine's "differentiated panentheism," because it cannot link God's immanence in the world with his transcendent relation to it: "Without the difference between Creator and creature, creation cannot be conceived of at all; that this difference is embraced and comprehended by the greater truth . . . the truth that God is all in all. This does not imply a pantheistic dissolution of creation in God; it means that the final form which creation is to find in God."[53] In effect, Moltmann presses God's initial self-limitation to a future-delimited pantheistic oneness. The problem is

---

49. Ibid., 263.
50. Ibid., 17. In his *Science and Wisdom*, trans. Margaret Kohl (Minneapolis: Fortress, 2003), 123, Moltmann explains the mutual indwelling as follows: "This is a reciprocal indwelling of the unlike, not the like. The world lives in God in a world-like way, and God lives in the world in a God-like way. They interpenetrate each other without destroying each other." The distinction is so blurred ("interpenetration"?) that it begs for clarity. How can personal consciousness (i.e., finitude) "self-transcend" to cosmic and divine realms? Nevertheless, he notes in *The Experiment Hope*, 53, that he spoke of a "coming God" rather than a "becoming God."
51. Ibid., 194, 341.
52. Ibid., 103, 336.
53. Ibid., 203. In describing the Parousia, he appeals to Luria's Kabbalistic thought again to say that "God de-restricts himself and manifests his glory so that in the transfigured creation he may be 'all in all,'" *The Way of Jesus Christ*, 329.

that the future is resident in the present, so that he has already identified God with all dimensions of time. The burden remains for Moltmann to demonstrate that he is not trying to argue both ways, for he cannot deny analysis by his readers as he idiosyncratically appealed to symbolic coherence.

Third, the feminine process of panentheistic Trinitarianism means that communitarian equality must replace anthropological dominance. Moltmann blamed "the ecological crisis" on the fact that "modern European anthropology uncritically took the modern anthropocentric world picture as its premise," which necessarily entailed the modern abuse of nature.[54] The "crown of creation is not the human being; it is the Sabbath."[55] The sabbatarian mandate is an anticipation of the world's redemption: "The Sabbath is the prefiguration of the world to come. So when we present creation in the light of the future—'the glory of God,' 'existence as home,' and 'the general sympathy of all things'—then we are developing *a Sabbath doctrine of creation*."[56] That is, when God is all in all, then all of creation becomes an egalitarian community in the Spirit.

The sabbatarian doctrine of dethroned humanity introduces his view of an evolving humanity that is questing for a humane world rather than self-knowledge. Humanity must be understood in terms of the wholeness of existence with three dimensions: the original designation (*imago Dei*), the messianic calling (*imago Christi*), and the sabbatical, eschatological glorification (*gloria Dei est homo*). The original divine resolve was the culminating work that honored humanity in community with creation, which in turn pointed to Christ as the promise of holistic kingdom. Sexually differentiated humanity brings community to the forefront and means that people are social in a perichoretic sense: "The isolated individual and the solitary subject are deficient modes of being human, because they fall short of likeness to God."[57] The *imago trinitatis* means that the Trinity is "the archetype of true human community."[58] The Augustinian-Thomist view of one divine being with sovereignty must be changed to accord with the Orthodox understanding of the social doctrine of human likeness in a theology of the open Trinity to the extent that the human family becomes a community of generations over space and time.

---

54. Moltmann, *God in Creation*, 185.
55. Ibid., 31.
56. Ibid., 6.
57. Ibid., 223.
58. Ibid., 234. On page 241 he similarly states, "In their various communities, human beings are to be understood not merely as the image of God's rule over creation but also as the image of his inward nature."

The original designation looked forward to the *imago Christi*. Christology must be understood as the fulfillment of anthropology. The biblical account democratized the image to the extent that all people and every human being reflects and represents the divine presence in creation. Humanity's transformation into the image of Christ is a reciprocal growth in cross and resurrection, an open dialectic of reconciliation in God's freedom to love which can only be resolved in the glorification of all things. So, true humanity is identity with Christ's solidarity with the broken world in opposition to its power structures.

The present dilemma is that we have to think about human beings as God's image and sinners at the same time. Sin fractures relationships with God and others, an alienation that perverts creation but never cancels it, so that even idolatry is a form of the image: "It is only as God's image that human beings exercise divinely legitimated rule; and in the context of creation that means only as whole human beings, only as equal human beings, and only in the community of human beings—not at the price of dividing human beings into ruler and ruled—not at the price of dividing mankind into different classes."[59] People love the honor of rule, but they become wretched when they forget the trust and use their position to accumulate power and destroy nature. *Imago Dei*, properly understood, cuts the ground from under the feet of oppression and exploitation.

Social perversion indicates inward alienation. The wholeness of the human person has been compromised by Western theology; the soul has been differentiated and separated from the body in the interests of egotism and exploitation. The older traditions like the patristic and medieval theologians used the hierarchical model to preserve ordered relationships. Modern developments discarded the "higher-lower" dichotomy as irrelevant for a scientific, technological civilization. Moltmann observes that "a world with an 'order' of this kind [hierarchy] can hardly be called a peaceful one."[60] Modern theologians must discard the self-alienated person and restore the oneness of body and soul. In accord with the Old Testament, we must view "the soul and body, the core of the inner life, and the outward mental horizon . . . as existing in reciprocal relation and mutual interpenetration."[61] Moltmann projects the oneness of a person to the embodiment of God's promises for all living things in his kingdom, a reversal of the traditional emphasis on the

59. Ibid., 225.
60. Ibid., 255.
61. Ibid., 257.

dominance of the soul. Central to the evolving process is an inalienable human dignity, which is God's creational claim on humanity in his image and is expressed in human rights: "Human dignity requires human rights for its embodiment, protection and full flowering. Human rights are the concrete, indefeasible claim of human dignity."[62] His goal was to make churches aware of their political ties and to "Christianize" their political existence. This was grounded in humanity's right to God's future; the right and duty to reconcile communities that point to the approach of God's kingdom.

CONCLUSION

In summary, Moltmann attempted to confront twentieth-century crises with hope by developing a christological center for an eschatological orientation in his theology. His central dialectic is between the cross and the resurrection; the cross symbolizing God's solidarity with his godless world and the resurrection symbolizing his eschatological presence with his creation. The Spirit has been resolving the dialectic by transforming present darkness toward a glorious presence in kingdom. The problem involves how we view humanity as *imago Dei* and sinner at the same time. Human sinners usurped divinity in the accumulation of power to oppress people and to destroy nature. In his development of hope from past abuses, Moltmann advanced three themes in two trilogies as corrections to traditional Christianity; *zimsum*, panentheism, and communitarian equality. Through his kenotic self-limitation God liberates, exalts, and redeems creation into a single community of hope. The process is feminine; God births creation by letting it become eternal in his omnipresence. Consequently, eschatology is redefined as faith in the Creator as we serve his future in the intricate web of interrelationships in his cosmic community.

We need to reemphasize the extent to which Moltmann represents the concerns of modern theologians in the abyss of the twentieth century. These concerns must be examined under three questions. First, can modern methods redefine Christianity without the loss of its identity? Second, can God be marinated

---

62. Douglas Meeks, "Introduction," in Moltmann, *On Human Dignity: Political Theology and Ethics*, trans. Douglas Meeks (Philadelphia: Fortress, 1984), xi. Again, Moltmann placed himself at the center of the theological academy's dialogue about the postwar role of religion. Human rights emerged in the mid-twentieth century as the "concrete" focus of ecumenical dialogue in which Moltmann was deeply involved. It was accompanied by collaborative dialogue surrounding the "Universal Declaration of Human Rights" (1948).

in a panentheistic process without dissolving in the acids of pantheism? Third, does Moltmann in particular, and modern theology in general, offer hope to a catastrophe-prone world?

First, we recall that Moltmann mandated that theology must start again, if it is to comprehend God's activity in the world in a new way. A foundational premise of his redefinition of Christian beliefs is that they must conform to the naturalistic boundaries of the modern scientific method. We must, in brief, get rid of archaic biases of the Christian past. His self-evaluation in *The Coming of God* reflects his method in general, "For me theology is not church dogmatics, and not a doctrine of faith. It is *imagination for the kingdom of God* in the world."[63] An obvious response to his methodological changes is, "How much redefinition is possible before Christianity loses its identity?" The question surfaces the many ways that people understand their Christian identity: culture, tradition, sources, and beliefs among other authorities. No one disputes the right of modernists to define life as they wish, but can the Christian faith be divorced from its sources without becoming something else? Of these authorities, historical sources and beliefs are most definitive for our purposes. To begin with, Moltmann substituted general revelation and history for salvation history and special revelation: "The distinction between 'natural theology' and 'revealed theology' is misleading. There are not two different theologies. There is only one, because God is one."[64] Of course, the "universal dimension of the gospel" becomes more than an implication with this change. One must ask if monotheism is to blame "for stripping nature of her divinity, profaning politics, and divesting history of its fate"? His rejection of premodernistic beliefs, notably patristic theologians, conciliar conclusions, and medievalists, reduces them to the vanity of a perverted past. Did Moltmann not speak to himself when he argues, "It always causes misunderstanding when biblical texts are torn out of their proper context in the biblical tradition and are used to legitimate other concerns."[65] Biblical causation, which he decries, was argued by Paul in Acts 17:24–27 as the basis for one of his oft-cited verses, "For in him we live and move and have our being" (17:28). Even more alarming, Jesus himself is changed:

---

63. Moltmann, *The Coming of God*, xiv.
64. Moltmann, *God in Creation*, 59.
65. Ibid., 30.

> Whereas in the ancient church the dispute about the relation-
> ship of the two natures of Christ was always a dispute about
> physical redemption as well, and the idea of the real incarna-
> tion of God was always associated with the deification of man
> (*theosis*) which made it possible, the dispute at the present time
> about the true humanity of Jesus, his awareness of God, his "in-
> ner life" and his freedom finds its basis in the demand for true
> humanity, authentic life, inner identity, and liberation. The
> point of reference and purpose of the questions have changed,
> and Jesus is accordingly manifested in a different way and must
> supply a different answer.[66]

In other words, when Jesus is redefined, the identity of the One to be followed
is changed as well. So, we must conclude that modernistic redefinitions of the
Christian faith, like Moltmann's, have lost their claim to be identified as Christian. No doubt, the perversions of Christianity in historical crimes and injustices,
sometimes nightmarish, are inexcusable and horrifying. But such aberrations do
not warrant voiding the doctrines that condemn such behavior.

Second, can God be involved panentheistically in world processes without
slipping into pantheistic indifference? Panentheism is a frequent theological
cover for scientific acceptability. In Moltmann's case, the Spirit is "the total cohesion, structure, information, and energy" of the universe to the extent that
"its movements and experiences are his as well."[67] He attempts to reserve God's
"de-restriction" (or de-limitation) to a future pantheistic oneness. But the future
is already present through the resurrection, so that the total identification of
God and creation has been made. "Christ is the panentheistic understanding
of the world as the sheltering and nurturing divine environment for everything
living."[68] Of course, analysis is not allowed in his new thinking, so his symbolics
absorbs the "impossible possibility" of a new Christianity.

Third, does Moltmann in particular, and modern theology in general, offer
hope in a fallen world, when evil relates to "the practical and specific and social
conflicts of people who have never received justice, and people who are themselves unjust"?[69] He rejects the Pauline and Protestant doctrine of "universal sin,"

---

66. Moltmann, *Crucified God*, 93.
67. Moltmann, *God in Creation*, 16. Also, *Spirit of Life*, 274–78, on the "formative metaphors."
68. Ibid., 300.
69. Moltmann, *Spirit of Life*, 128.

because "collective guilt of this kind makes people blind to specific, practical guilt . . . The universality of sin leads to a universal night in which everything is equally black, and even to use weapons of mass extermination is no longer special."[70] This claim is simply wrong. Who would equate petty crimes, which can be horrible in themselves, with holocausts and genocides? How can Moltmann correctly perceive the ecological extinctions of the twentieth century and ignore the underlying godlessness which led to them? "Collective guilt" does not excuse "specific sins," regardless of how horrible they may be, nor does it trivialize or obscure degrees of evil in the world. Instead, the world wars and unspeakable horrors of the century should remind us of our need for divine grace.

Does Moltmann offer the modern world hope? Biblical hope resonates with confident expectation, "being sure of what we hope for . . . a city whose architect and builder is God" (Heb. 11:1, 10). By faith believers through millennia have lived in light of God's promises (v. 39). Christianity is about faith in God's revealed word as well as community that is shaped by dialogue. We should dialogue with as many people as we can. But are we supposed to hope that people who have created the problems are going to correct their addictions to power and exploitation? Are we to hope that the agents of mass destruction are going to change their elemental fears and violent behavior in behalf of "an intricate web of interrelationships," as desirable an ideal as that may be? Hebrews 12 points us to "the author and perfecter of our faith, who is the same yesterday and today and forever" as the object of our hope (vv. 2, 13:8). Instead, Moltmann offers us hope in a God, who "because of the restriction of his omniscience cannot foresee how those he has created will decide, and how they will develop. He leaves them time, and opens for them an unforeseeable future. . . . He is curious about the path they will take, for they are his future. He learns from them."[71] He has traded the Parousia of the biblical Messiah for an evolutionary process that has been mired in sin for millennia under its struggling gods. Has he given us hope or exposed our embedded hopelessness?

---

70. Ibid., 126.
71. Moltmann, *Science and Wisdom*, 120.

The Doctrine of the Future
in Contemporary European Theology

Friedhelm Jung and Eduard Friesen

I n Western European theology there are three major branches: liberal theology, Catholic theology, and evangelical theology. Liberal theology is predominantly a product of Protestant theologians and is normally taught by the Protestant faculties of the universities; some theologians in denominations which were formerly evangelical, such as the Methodists and the Baptists, have also become increasingly liberal and teach "higher criticism" in their seminaries. Catholic theology is also taught in the universities of Germany as well as in Catholic seminaries. Catholic theology is moderately liberal; but Catholics are bound by the official teachings of their church and are not allowed to teach opinions which are contrary to the catechism of the Catholic Church. Consequently, theologians in the Catholic Church must always be very careful when they teach or write. Evangelical theology is by definition conservative. It is taught at evangelical seminaries, which can be found in almost every European country. Some of these seminaries belong to free churches and some are nondenominational. In some of these seminaries, the faculty members believe in the inerrancy and infallibility of Scripture; in others they do not, although they acknowledge that the Bible not only contains the word of God but is the Word of God. These seminaries teach that all "theological" teaching of Scripture is inerrant, but that historical or geographical information in the Bible may contain errors.

Officially, liberal theological faculties of the German universities are required to teach what the Bible and the creeds say. Lutheran theologians, for example, are required to teach what the Augsburg Confession teaches, and Reformed theologians must conform to what the Heidelberg Catechism and the Second Helvetic Confession teach. For example, Question 57 of the Heidelberg Catechism reads:

Q: In what way does the resurrection of the body comfort you?

A: That, after this life, not only my soul will come to Christ, but that also my body will be raised by the power of Christ, and will be joined with my soul and will be conformed to the sacred body of Christ.[1]

Like the Heidelberg Catechism and the Augsburg Confession, the creeds of the Reformation teach biblical eschatology: We have an immortal soul; after death the soul of the believer goes to be with Christ in paradise; the soul of the unbeliever goes to Hades to await judgment; in the future there will be a resurrection of the body, and a reunification of the new body with the soul; unbelievers will go to eternal punishment, and believers will enjoy everlasting life in the presence of Christ.[2]

At one point the Reformers had problems with a literal interpretation of biblical eschatological teachings: They rejected the idea of a literal millennium. Negative experiences with some Anabaptist theologians in the early sixteenth century produced a deep aversion to a literal understanding of the biblical teaching of the millennium.[3]

For two hundred years, beginning with the period of the Enlightenment, many theologians have had difficulties in accepting the creeds and the teachings of the Bible. For example, Rudolf Bultmann (1884-1976), longtime professor of New Testament at the University of Marburg in Germany, rejected a literal understanding of biblical eschatology. He could not believe that Jesus is the Son of God, born of the virgin Mary, crucified for our sins, resurrected by the power of God, exalted to the right hand of the Father and ready to come back to overcome all satanic power. For Bultmann these biblical teachings are only myths. He wrote, "Christianity has always held to the belief that the rule of God would come in the near future, although it has waited in vain. This hope, which Jesus and the early church shared, was not fulfilled. The same world continues to exist and history moves on. The course of history has disproved these myths. The conception of the rule of God is in fact mythological, just as the idea of the end times is mythological."[4]

Although Bultmann was Protestant, his theology has influenced both Lutheran and Catholic faculties and has spread not only on the European conti-

---

1. *Bekenntnisse der Kirche. Bekenntnistexte aus 20 Jahrhunderten*, 2. Taschenbuchaufl. Wuppertal: Brockhaus Verlag, 1997, 142.
2. CA, Artikel XVII, und Confessio Helvetica Posterior, chapter 11.
3. CA, Artikel XVII.
4. Rudolf Bultmann, *Jesus Christ and Mythology*, (London: SCM Press, 2013), 10.

nent but all over the world. Many seminaries, even in Asia and America, have been influenced by his ideas. Today, almost all theological faculties in the German universities are liberal. Many students have lost their faith in Christ, and professors who still believe in a literal interpretation of the supernatural elements in the Bible are rare and have a difficult time.[5]

Liberal theologians in the tradition of Bultmann do not believe in the rapture and don't believe that Christ will return to establish the millennium. They interpret all eschatological terms in the Bible in an existential manner. This position is called "existentialist eschatology."[6] After we have focused on the evangelical position, we will learn more about the liberal positions.

EVANGELICAL ESCHATOLOGY

Evangelicals still believe what all Protestants should believe but have rejected since the period of the Enlightenment. Evangelicals are Protestants, but to distinguish them from the liberal Protestant wing, we call them "conservative Protestants" or "evangelicals." In Germany, liberal Protestants are in the majority. Among the twenty-five million German Protestants, there are only about 1.3 million evangelicals. Half of them belong to the Lutheran church, the other half to free churches such as Baptists, Mennonites, Evangelical Free churches, charismatic churches, etc. The situation is similar throughout the rest of Europe.

Almost all evangelicals agree concerning the major eschatological teachings of the Bible: the rapture, Christ's return, the millennium, the last judgment, a new heaven and earth. But if you take a closer look you will find some differences.

One segment of evangelicals believes that the rapture will take place before the tribulation. They teach that according to 1 Thessalonians 4 Christ will come to take the Christians to heaven. Christians who have died will be raised, Christians who are alive at that time will be transformed, both will meet Christ in the air, and the Lord will take them to heaven (1 Thess. 4:16–17). According to these evangelicals, the rapture will take place at the beginning of the great tribulation.[7] Born-again Christians will not have to suffer in the times of the antichrist who will reign during the great tribula-

---

5. Klaus Berger, "Das Elend der kritischen Theologe," in: *idea-spektrum 22/2013*, 15–18.
6. Heinrich Ott, *Die Antwort des Glaubens. Systematische Theologie in 50 Artikeln*, 3. (Aufl. Stuttgart: Kreuz Verlag, 1981), 483f.
7. René Pache, *The Return of Jesus Christ* (Chicago: Moody Press, 1976), 92ff.; Erich Mauerhofer, *Biblische Dogmatik*, Band 2 (Nürnberg: VTR, 2011), 839f.

tion. At the end of this dark time Christ will return, defeat the antichrist, enlighten the Jews so that they understand that Jesus is the Messiah, and establish the millennium; Israel will then be the leading nation on the earth for one thousand years. Evangelicals who hold this position are sometimes called "dispensationalists." They are found especially among the Plymouth Brethren Churches, whose founder was John Nelson Darby.[8] The *Scofield Reference Bible* has spread these ideas to many churches. It has also introduced premillennial theology, which teaches that Christ will return before the millennium. For this reason the position is often called "dispensational premillennialism" or "pretribulational premillennialism."

A second segment of evangelicals believes that there is no chronological gap between the rapture and the return of Christ. According to this interpretation Christ will return at the end of the great tribulation, defeat the antichrist, and establish the millennium where Christians and converted Jews will reign together with Christ.[9] This position is called "classical premillennialism." Indeed, this viewpoint is not very pleasant for Christians, as they would have to suffer through the great tribulation.[10]

A third but small segment of evangelicals believes that Christ will come after the millennium and that we are today already living in the millennium. According to this interpretation the influence of Christianity will influence pagan society with increasing success. Wars and crime will decrease and the people of all nations (including the Jews) will adopt Christian values. At the end of this time Christ will return and the eternal state will commence.[11] This viewpoint is called "postmillennialism," because Christ is said to come after the millennium.

A fourth and also small segment of evangelicals believes that there has never been, and never will be, a literal millennium on earth. Israel as a nation does not have a special position in God's plan for the future of the world—the church has taken Israel's place. All of the promises and prophecies in the Old Testament no

---

8. Frank S. Mead, *Handbook of Denominations in the United States* (Nashville: Abingdon Press, 1995), 244–246.

9. Jacob Thiessen, *Biblische Glaubenslehre* (Nürnberg: VTR, 2004), p. 194ff.; Friedhelm Jung, *Glaube kompakt. Grundzüge biblischer Dogmatik* (Aufl. Lage: Lichtzeichen, 2013), 146f.

10. Some evangelical scholars teach that Christians will have to suffer a certain time but not for the whole duration of the great tribulation. See Karl Baral, *Handbuch der biblischen Glaubenslehre* (Neuhausen-Stuttgart: Hänssler, 1994), 208.

11. Jacob Thiessen, *Biblische Glaubenslehre* (Nürnberg: VTR, 2004), 202; Friedhelm Jung, *Glaube kompakt. Grundzüge biblischer Dogmatik* (Aufl. Lage: Lichtzeichen, 2013), 149f.

longer relate to Israel, but to the church. Eternity will start after Christ's return. This position is called "amillennialism."[12]

It is very difficult to say how many supporters the different positions have. One can only say that evangelicals in the free churches (like Plymouth Brethren, Baptists, Mennonites, and Pentecostals) have a strong tendency to adopt either the first or the second position. Lutheran evangelicals tend to prefer either the second or the fourth position. The third position can be found among a small number of evangelicals who may be members either of free churches or of the Reformed and Lutheran churches.[13]

Catholic Eschatology

In the last fifty years there has been an increase of liberal Catholic theologians who do not believe in the reliability of the Bible. Hans Küng, Eugen Drewermann, and Uta Ranke-Heinemann are representatives of the liberal wing of the Catholic Church. All of them have been influenced by liberal Protestant theologians like Rudolf Bultmann.

Although these liberal Catholic theologians do not believe in a literal interpretation of eschatology, the mainstream Catholic Church remains close to the Scriptures. Catholic theology is defined in the *Enchiridion Symbolorum*[14] and in the *Catechism of the Catholic Church*,[15] and no Catholic Christian is allowed to teach opinions opposing these documents.

Official Catholic eschatology is not far removed from the "classical premillennial" position: Before Christ comes back the church will experience a time of tribulation. There will be persecution and many heresies, and the antichrist will reign on earth.[16] Then Jesus will come back and the last judgment will take place. After the judgment God will create a new heaven and a new earth. (The rapture has no place in Catholic theology.) Israel will recognize that Jesus is the Messiah and will live together with the church in the kingdom of Christ.[17]

---

12. Thomas Schirrmacher, "Sechs evangelikale Modelle der Endzeit im Vergleich," in *Wahrheit und Erfahrung—Themenbuch zur Systematischen Theologie,* vol. 3, ed. Christian Herrmann (Wuppertal: R. Brockhaus, 2006), 396f.

13. Ibid., 393.

14. Heinrich Denzinger, *Enchiridion Symbolorum: A Compendium of Creeds, Definitions, and Declarations of the Catholic Church* (San Francisco: Ignatius Press, 2012).

15. *Catechism of the Catholic Church* (New York: Random House, 2003).

16. Ibid., 194.

17. Ibid., 207.

Catholics avoid speaking about a millennium. This term has negative connotations for Catholic theologians because of historical misunderstandings.[18] They believe that the "Church Age" is the millennium.

Important in Catholic eschatology is the concept of the immortality of the soul. When a member of the Catholic Church—having the forgiveness of all sins—dies, his soul goes directly into the presence of the Lord in heaven.[19] Those members of the Catholic Church who don't have the forgiveness of all sins in the hour of their death must first go to purgatory to gain complete purification. Purgatory differs from eternal punishment. Eternal punishment is for nonbelievers. Purgatory is for believers who do not die in a state of sanctification. Catholics pray for those who died in order to shorten their time in purgatory. They justify these prayers from 2 Maccabees 12:45ff.[20]

Because Catholics do not believe in a literal millennium on the earth after Christ's return, they place the last judgment just after the second coming of Jesus. The order is therefore: the great tribulation, Christ's return and the last judgment, and the creation of a new heavens and a new earth.[21]

Catholics believe in heaven and hell. Those who reject Christ and remain in unbelief until their death will be separated from God for eternity. Hell is a place of great pain and suffering. The most severe pain is to be excluded from fellowship with the triune God, the angels, and redeemed Christians.[22]

One of the most prominent Catholic theologians of the last decades is the German Joseph Ratzinger, who was pope from 2005–2013. Ratzinger published his eschatological views in 1977 when he was archbishop in Munich-Freising. In response to Moltmann's "theology of hope," he felt it was urgent to stress that hope does not necessitate a task for mankind to change and improve the world in order to bring in the kingdom of God. Rather, it was the somewhat passive expectation of God's coming and acting in history. Ratzinger stressed that the future is a creative act of God, not of man, and that the kingdom is likewise God's work and not man's. Even though faith, combined with hope, is never passive, it is nevertheless necessary to distinguish human responsibility for works of love from the divine promise of *God's* coming and *his* work of renewal. The acts of God in the future give meaning and continuity to the actions of men in the present time.

---

18. Ibid., 207f.
19. Ibid., 292f.
20. Ibid., 294.
21. Ibid., 297.
22. Ibid., 295.

The recognition of the priority of the acts of God should prevent theology from becoming merely a part of a political agenda. Ratzinger felt it necessary to place eschatological thinking firmly in the realm of the church and theology rather than in the realm of politics and society.

A second correction by Ratzinger concerned the concept of the immortality of the soul. After Vatican II the Roman Catholic Church experienced a crisis in having to deal with doubt regarding its tradition. The tendency, said Ratzinger, was that theologians were striving to define their thinking carefully according to the teachings of Scripture. The result was the discovery that the Scriptures speak only of the hope of resurrection, but not of the immortality of the soul. The concept of the immortality of the soul was, at that time, in danger of being dismissed as a platonic substitute for the hope of resurrection. It leads to an understanding of eternity as timeless existence into which people pass through their natural death. Ratzinger affirmed that the traditional terms of "body" and "soul" used in the Council of Vienne (DH 902) are in harmony with the varied biblical concepts and terminologies.

This created a dispute in which Ratzinger was charged with simply defending the traditional platonic concepts of the Catholic Church. In the sixth edition of Ratzinger's theology, published in 2007 after being elevated to the office of pope, he restated his position with explanatory nuances in an appendix. Starting with the argument between Jesus and the Sadducees in Mark 12:26–27, Ratzinger argued that Jesus defended the eternal existence of humans on the basis that God remained Jacob's God even after his death. This theological understanding is further based on the "dialogue" between man and God. Ratzinger defines "soul" as nothing other than "man's capacity for relatedness with truth, with love eternal."[23] This relatedness occurs in the body of Christ, his incarnation, and the believer's participation in it. The believer belongs to Christ's body, and is in this sense attached to his future. The believer will never be in a disembodied state (soul without the body) since Christ also retains his body in eternity. The correction Ratzinger introduces does not revert to a traditional understanding of the soul as viewed by its critics. Rather it seeks its foundation in the person of Christ, the life-giver, and the place of dialogue between the believer and God: "It is important to me that what we say about the human person must be entirely theological and christological."[24]

---

23. Joseph Ratzinger, *Eschatology: Death and Eternal Life* (Washington, DC: Catholic University of America Press, 1988), 3.
24. Ibid.

LIBERAL ESCHATOLOGY

The Ethical Model

Nineteenth-century Protestant eschatology was characterized by its emphasis on the ethical dimension in the here and now. Following Albrecht Ritschl, the kingdom of God came to be viewed as a community of faith and love that would be expanded here on earth through mankind's application of the ethics of Jesus.[25] This was the consequence of liberal theology following the naturalistic pattern of critical thinking. The "ethical model" would not have to explain the transcendent dimension of the Christian faith, such as the existence of heaven, the physical and visible return of Christ, the final judgment and the final state (heaven or hell).

The Consistent Eschatology Model

The "history of religions school" attempted to view the meaning of eschatology in light of Jewish apocalyptic literature. Johannes Weiss, Richard Kabisch, and Albert Schweitzer viewed the message of Jesus as being consistent with contemporary Jewish thought. The end of the world would usher in a new kingdom that would be in stark contrast to present life on this earth. Jesus himself would be the judge and ruler in that future kingdom, and he would take his followers to that new kingdom. The kingdom of God would be a future but imminent reality, not an ethical concept or fellowship. This understanding was linked with the expectation of its imminent fulfillment. Since Jesus's promises were not literally fulfilled, the disciples had to redefine his death, not as a failure, but as a part of the meaning of his life. In addition, they created the legend of the physical resurrection, attempting to perpetuate Jesus's ministry. This model was called "consistent eschatology" because of its consistent application of Jewish hopes in the teaching, expectation, and ministry of Jesus.

The "Redemptive History" Model

Oscar Cullmann[26] proposed in his "redemptive history model" a concept that would stress both the ethical implications of the kingdom of God and its relation to real time and real history. He stressed that both the current relevance of eschatology with the expectation of its imminent fulfillment, and the transcen-

---

25. Albrecht Ritschl, *Unterricht in der christlichen Religion*, I. in Die Lehre vom Reiche Gottes, Hrsg. Gerhard Ruhbach (Gütersloh: Gütersloher Verlagshaus Mohn, 1966), 15–33.
26. Oscar Cullmann, *Christ and Time* (Philadelphia: Westminster Press, 1964).

dent character of its delayed fulfillment can be held in balance. He divided history from a biblical perspective into three time periods: time before creation, the time period from creation to the Parousia, and time after the Parousia. The most decisive event in human history, then, is the death of Christ, combined with his resurrection, which divides human history into two periods after his passion. These give us a firm basis for future eschatology. The imminent expectation of the kingdom of God is partially fulfilled in the faith community of believers. The future fulfillment is delayed but guaranteed through the cross and resurrection of Christ, which constitutes the breaking in of eternity into time; it is the appearance of the eschaton and the beginning of the unraveling and fulfillment of future hope. Cullmann illustrated the succession of events with the analogy of D-day and V-day. The decisive battle had been won through the resurrection. Thus it was only a matter of time—not whether, but when—until V-day.

Realized Eschatology (C.H. Dodd and Rudolf Bultmann)

Rudolf Bultmann moved even further in the direction of realized eschatology in the here and now.[27] Under the influence of Heidegger's existentialism, he interpreted the gospel of John and the writings of Paul as locating the eschaton in the personal encounter of humans with Jesus. In his view these biblical authors do not speak of the future as historical events at the end of world history but rather as events that shape men and women in their present existence. The simple futuristic approach was termed by Bultmann as "historical" (German *historisch*), whereas the existential event without any reference to time and history was referred to as "historic" (German *geschichtlich*).[28] Eschatology understood this way would focus on the decision of the individual and his or her experience of eternal life in the here and now. With this decision the individual would step into an otherworldly experience and reject the world. The one-sidedness in this approach is seen in the fact that any future historical expectations are omitted from this view of eschatology.

---

27. Rudolf Bultmann, *Geschichte und Eschatologie* (Tübingen: Mohr & Siebeck, 1958).
28. "Während die Geschichte des Volkes und der Welt an Interesse verliert, wird jetzt ein anderes Phänomen entdeckt: die echte Geschichtlichkeit des menschlichen Seins. Die entscheidende Geschichte ist nicht die Weltgeschichte, die Geschichte Israels und der anderen Völker, sondern die Geschichte, die jeder Einzelne selbst erfährt. Für diese Geschichte ist die Begegnung mit Christus das entscheidende Ereignis, ja, in Wahrheit das Ereignis, durch das der Einzelne beginnt, wirklich geschichtlich zu existieren, weil er beginnt, eschatologisch zu existieren." Rudolf Bultmann, "Geschichte und Eschatologie im Neuen Testament," in *Glauben und Verstehen,* vol. 3 (Tübingen: Mohr & Siebeck, 1954), 102.

Futuristic Eschatological Concepts

The latter part of the twentieth century witnessed a necessary eschatological correction. Both Wolfhart Pannenberg and Jürgen Moltmann restored the future hope as the core element in eschatology. Placing eschatology solely in the heart of man through an existential encounter (as with Bultmann) did not satisfy their understanding of biblical eschatology.

Wolfhart Pannenberg. Following the views of Cullmann, Wolfhart Pannenberg developed his own understanding of the relationship between time, history, and eschatology. He viewed history from the end, from its final consummation.[29] The cross and resurrection of Jesus Christ are precursors of the consummation. Christ's historical resurrection then becomes the assurance of the final eschatological resurrection of believers. Realized eschatology is woven into the fabric of a futuristic eschatology. The inward choice for Christ is neatly united with the historical trajectory of eschatological fulfillment. Because of the connection between the inward choice for Christ and eternal salvation, this view is widely affirmed by evangelicals today.

Jürgen Moltmann. Jürgen Moltmann opposed the transcendental approaches of realized eschatology which were so popular in his day.[30] He brought eschatological fulfillment back into history and into the world. To his thinking realized eschatology reduced the future promises of God with their ethical implications to a *"kairos"* moment of making a choice for Christ. His *"eschatologia crucis"* emphasizes that the cross and resurrection of Christ redefined history. The uniqueness of the historical work of Christ becomes the foundation for the believer's hope for his own future and the future of this world. This hope then implies that the church will participate in changing society. But the final transformation will occur through God's coming into the world, not by human means. Thus "eschaton" is not timeless eternity in the believer's heart, nor simply the historical future as described in end-time scenarios, but "the coming of God"—the title of his 1995 eschatological treatise.

"Apokatastasis Panton"

Karl Barth, the prominent Swiss theologian, has sometimes been classified as a universalist. Applying double predestination to the person of Christ in death

---

29. Wolfhart Pannenberg, *Theology and the Kingdom of God* (Philadelphia: Westminster Press, 1969).
30. Jürgen Moltmann, *Theology of Hope* (Minneapolis: Fortress, 1993); *The Coming of God: Christian Eschatology*, Margaret Kohl, trans. (Minneapolis: Fortress, 1996).

and resurrection, Barth understood that God is free to apply the outcome of Christ's work to mankind. Predestination then is not linked to individuals who are predetermined for heaven or hell, but to the suffering and glory of Christ.

Barth insisted on God's freedom to grant grace. A system of universalism would limit that freedom and force grace into a straitjacket. But to teach hell as an individual judgment would also limit God's freedom. "The proclamation of the Church must make allowance for this freedom of grace. *Apokatastasis Panton?* No, for a grace which automatically would ultimately have to embrace each and everyone would certainly not be free grace. It surely would not be God's grace. But would it be God's free grace if we could absolutely deny that it could do that? Has Christ been sacrificed only for our sins? Has he not ... been sacrificed for the whole world? . . . [Thus] the freedom of grace is preserved on both these sides."[31]

Current Protestant theology is much more open to universalism. A somewhat typical representation can be found in Wilfried Härle, professor for Systematic Theology at the University of Heidelberg. He argues against the traditional understanding of a final judgment with heaven and hell as eternal consequences. To him the criterion of judgment—faith that is manifested in works—seems to be fluid and uncertain. He questions whether the nature of faith is such that it can be used as a criterion for judgment, where its presence is rewarded with eternal life or its lack is punished with eternal damnation. Further, if one were to admit the possibility that the gospel does not speak to every person and encourage him or her to believe, would these people be punished for something they did not deserve? Furthermore, faith in this life is always a struggling faith, because it is constantly questioned and doubted. How then can the alternative of belief and unbelief be a criterion for the eternal fate of men and women troubled by mistrust and doubt? Finally, since faith is defined as trust in God whose nature is love, does this not imply that it also includes those who are unable or unwilling to believe? Härle sees the danger of saving trust becoming trust in its own belief rather than trust in God.[32]

Härle maintains that implications for the doctrine of God are relevant to this matter. The first implication concerns the power and the scope of divine love. The dual outcome of judgment stands in contradiction to the omnipotence of God as the omnipotence of love in its convincing and winning work that moves the believer toward God without the use of coercion or force. For Härle, a complete reliance on the omnipotence of God is brought into question

31. Karl Barth, *Church Dogmatics*, IV/3 (Peabody MA: Hendrickson Publishers), 477–78.
32. Wilfried Härle, *Dogmatik* (Berlin: de Gruyter, 1995), 614–15.

and limited by the acknowledgment that God does not reach his goal with all of mankind. These ideas weaken the essence of the Christian doctrine of God. He cannot be described as omnipotent without further qualification. Since the power and scope of divine love are questioned, this would necessarily be true for its uniqueness as well. The doctrine of a dual outcome would imply the eternal existence of sin and evil in competition with the eternal God. This would also compromise the eschatological sovereignty of God. The difference between human love (which is imperfect, intermingled with the desire for reciprocation, etc.) and divine love is seen in the person of Christ. This divine love would not be compatible with eternal punishment for its creatures.

The solution that best fits the proclamation of Christ is, according to Härle, a universal participation of all men in eternal life. He arrives at a slightly modified version of Schleiermacher's universalism, which spoke of the universal restitution of all human souls.[33] The final resurrection then would be part of the cleansing of mankind in order for men and women to participate in eternal life. This should not exclude the relevance of lifetime decisions and actions. The final judgment would reveal these actions and decisions and would uncover the truth of a life lived in faith or in unbelief. A life lived without the love of God would be, for Härle, not worthy of punishment, but merely be declared as a futile, meaningless, lost life. The uncovering of truth in the final judgment would do what repentance would have done during one's lifetime: It would deliver the person from the prison of sin, by breaking sin's power through its public revelation. This deliverance would then be an act of benevolence and healing for the sinner.

A further aspect of Härle's universalism is seen in the personification of the final judgment. Jesus Christ is to judge the living and the dead. Since this Judge is the Savior of the world, who himself wrought salvation on the cross, no other criterion than the saving love of God would be applicable in court. His verdict as a judge would sound accordingly "your sins are forgiven" (Mark 2:5) or "I don't condemn you either" (John 8:11).[34]

What difference would a life of faith or a life in unbelief then make? Härle seeks to strengthen his view of a universal salvation by avoiding the idea that the manner of life has no consequences. At this point he turns to Paul's description in 1 Corinthians 3:11–15. The common distinction between a judgment according to faith (for salvation or final judgment) and a judgment according

33. Ibid., 625.
34. Ibid., 643.

to works (for rewards for believers) is not convincing to him. The foundation of this judgment is not faith, but the person of Jesus Christ. The text does not speak of plural "works" but four times of "work."

Thus Härle sees no distinction in this text between faith and works. In addition, he asserts that the New Testament does not mention a judgment according to faith and a judgment according to works. The judgment in 1 Corinthians 3 then speaks of the faith that is visible in loving works. The lack of faith and love meet the anger of God and burn. The person perishes, but is being saved.

Summary

Contemporary viewpoints in Europe concerning eschatology are quite varied, but may be generally classified as liberal, Catholic, or evangelical. To a large measure, the outcome of the various viewpoints are determined by: (1) the degree to which the theologians accept the complete inerrancy of the Scriptures, (2) whether or not they adhere to a basically literal interpretation of prophecy, and (3) if they are willing to accept the negative as well as the positive aspects of biblical eschatology.

Liberal theology, as represented by Wilfried Härle, advocates a universalistic eschatology through a rationalization of clear biblical teachings concerning eternal judgment. However, a one-sided emphasis on the love of God marginalizes the importance of the holiness, justice, and sovereignty of God. Catholic eschatology recognizes more clearly the biblical teachings of hell as well as those of heaven, but adds to the biblical teachings a time of cleansing in purgatory.

Most evangelical theologians understand the importance of a literal hermeneutic and accept the teachings of Christ and the biblical writers and recognize that eternal suffering in hell for the lost is just as clearly revealed in the Scriptures as is eternal joy in heaven for those who are saved through the merits and substitutionary death of Christ. The faithful preaching and teaching of biblical eschatology gives warning of eternal loss to the unsaved and the assurance of eternal blessing, as well as motivations for godly living, for those who believe.

The Doctrine of the Future: Millennialism in Contemporary Evangelical Theology

David S. Dockery

One day the trumpet will sound for His coming;
One day the skies with His glories will shine;
Wonderful day my beloved One bringing;
Glorious Savior, this Jesus is mine! . . .
One day He's coming—O glorious day![1]

The words of this great hymn communicate well the longing of many evangelical Christians throughout the ages and reflect the desire of Jesus's disciples for restoration.[2] Just before Jesus ascended to heaven, his disciples asked, "Is it at this time you are restoring the kingdom of Israel?" (Acts 1:6). They were seeking to put together some pieces that didn't seem to fit. They seemed to be asking: "Is it time to complete what you came to do?" Without consensus, the evangelical community over the past generations has sought answers to these questions. One of the outstanding contributions that Craig Blaising has made to the field of evangelical theology has been the thoughtful proposals in the area of eschatology, seeking to build a consensus around what he has called "progressive dispensationalism."[3] The following essay tries to locate the role progressive dispensationalism might play in building an evangelical consensus on the doctrine of the future.

---

1. J. Wilber Chapman, "One Day," No. 170 in *The Hymnal* (Nashville: Word Music, 1986).
2. It is a privilege to contribute this chapter in honor of my good friend, Craig Blaising.
3. See Darrell L. Bock and Craig A. Blaising, *Progressive Dispensationalism* (Grand Rapids: Baker, 1993).

ESCHATOLOGICAL PERSPECTIVES IN HISTORY

The interest in eschatology within the evangelical community is not just a recent phenomenon; it has been a focus of the church in numerous periods of its history. The teaching of the early church leaders was characterized by an expectation of a series of dramatic events.[4] The church looked for the supernatural intervention of God in human history to conquer evil and establish his kingdom. Such an outlook brought great comfort and encouragement to Christians who suffered at the hand of imperial Rome.

The expectation that Jesus would return to establish his kingdom on earth was the prevailing teaching during the first centuries of the Christian era and is found in the works of Irenaeus (130–200), Justin Martyr (100–165), and Lactantius (240–320), among others. Faith in the nearness of Christ's second coming and the establishment of his reign of glory on earth undoubtedly was a strong emphasis in the primitive Christian church. Several church historians have noted that the most striking point about the teaching of the church prior to the Council of Nicea (325) was the belief in a visible reign of Christ in glory on earth with the saints for a thousand years. There was a clear consensus in the church's early centuries regarding the expectations and establishment of the coming kingdom.[5] The expectancy for a future kingdom, however, took on a more "here-and-now" interpretation with the conversion of the emperor Constantine the Great and the adoption of Christianity as a favored imperial religion.

The "here-and-now" interpretation was given theological articulation by Augustine, Bishop of Hippo (354–430). For Augustine, no victory was imminent in the struggle with evil in the world. Yet, even for Augustine, there was a future expectation. Throughout the Middle Ages and the Reformation period, Augustine's teaching dominated.

The Reformers declared that those who engaged in calculations based on the apocalyptic portions of Scripture were uninformed. Yet, they did look forward to Christ's coming, believing that Christ would appear in the ineffable glory of his kingdom. Indeed, it was the Reformers' insistence on a straightforward, literal reading of Scripture, as opposed to a spiritualizing or allegorical reading, that led to a renewed expectation of the coming of Christ's kingdom, and which

---

4. See George E. Ladd, *Jesus and the Kingdom* (New York: Harper, 1964).
5. See Robert Saucy, *The Case for Progressive Dispensationalism* (Grand Rapids: Zondervan, 1993).

continues to influence evangelicals in the twenty-first century. The literal reading of Scripture, coupled with an emphasis on Bible prophecy, opened the door
for the eschatological focus that evangelicals have maintained for the past two
hundred years, especially in America.[6]

At different times and to different degrees, American evangelicals have ad-
hered to a wide range of approaches to the subject of eschatological hopes. At
times, these hopes have been directly tied to America itself. Some evangelical
groups have even seen America as the location of the future golden age, or at
least a crucial instrument of its appearing somewhere else. Some have turned
kingdom expectations into secular ideas and applied them to American expansion and human progress, while others have used millennial expectations
to predict America's doom.[7] Kingdom hopes were so intermingled with the
American dream that eschatological expectations were employed to explain
Manifest Destiny, the Mexican War, the North's victory over the South in the
Civil War, the treatment of Native Americans, and growing American imperialistic perspectives.

Aberrations of kingdom expectations and differences of opinion regarding
eschatological perspectives within the evangelical movement have sometimes
created intense divisions. The intensity of these differences has been known to
drive away other believers, as well as unbelievers, from the scriptural teaching
and practical implications of the second coming of Christ.

Few subjects arouse both curiosity and contention like the subject of eschatology.[8] Progressive dispensationalism offers a position that is neither indifferent
nor fanatical about the return or reign of Christ. Whether one agrees or not with
the particulars of progressive dispensationalism, I would like to suggest that this
position offers a balance on these matters that has been extremely helpful for all
of us, as we seek to live with the hope that Christ's return could be soon, while
recognizing it has been two thousand years since Christ's ascension, and that it
could be two thousand years more before Christ returns.[9]

---

6. See the helpful surveys in Robert G. Clouse, *The Meaning of the Millennium* (Downers Grove,
   IL: InterVarsity, 1977), and Stanley J. Grenz, *The Millennial Maze* (Downers Grove, IL: InterVarsity, 1992).
7. Ibid.; also Timothy P. Weber, *On the Road to Armageddon* (Grand Rapids: Baker, 204).
8. See J. Barton Payne, *Encyclopedia of Biblical Prophecy* (New York: Harper, 1973); also see
   Kent E. Brower and Mark W. Elliott, *Eschatology in Bible and Theology* (Downers Grove, IL:
   InterVarsity, 1997).
9. See Craig A. Blaising, "Contemporary Dispensationalism." *Southwestern Journal of Theology*
   36 (1994) 5–13.

A Biblical Overview

The New Testament affirms the return of Christ, or his second coming. For those who await the return of Christ with expectancy, there is a sense of both anticipation and comfort. For those who do not expect, understand, or believe in his return, there is irritation, confusion, or fear. Some make fun of such teaching, often depicting people to be out of touch with the real world.

The expectation of Christ's return can be seen throughout the New Testament, with nearly one out of every twenty verses in the New Testament pointing to this theme. Of the 216 chapters in the New Testament, there are well over three hundred references to the return of Jesus Christ. Strictly speaking, the New Testament does not use the term "second coming" or "return of Christ," though Hebrews 9:28 comes very close. This passage says: "So Christ . . . shall appear a second time for salvation . . . to those who eagerly await him." The New Testament, rather, employs the language of an "arrival," "appearance," or "revelation" of Christ in the future.

The New Testament makes a clear distinction between Christ's first coming in humility as a suffering servant and his return in glory as a judge of all humankind. Thus, it does not seem inappropriate to use the traditional language of "second coming" or "return of Christ," even though the terms themselves do not appear in the New Testament. The emphasis on Christ's second coming does not imply Christ's absence in this interim period, nor does it deny that in a real sense he comes continually in grace to men and women in their times of need.

This distinction helps us to understand that Christ's presence now is spiritual and invisible. At the first coming, he inaugurated his kingdom; at his second coming, he will consummate his kingdom. The return of Christ will be physical and personal, as was Christ's resurrection and ascension. At that time, he will bring this age to a close, pass judgment on the lives of men and women, and gather his people into God's final kingdom.

The predicted second coming of Christ is implied in hundreds of Old Testament prophecies concerning future judgment on the world and a coming kingdom of righteousness. The Old Testament presents a mingled picture of the first and second coming of Christ, often combining both comings in the same context. The apostle Peter described these differences in 1 Peter 1:10–12:

> As to this salvation, the prophets who prophesied of the grace that would come to you made careful searches and inquiries, seeking to know what person or time the Spirit of

Christ within them was indicating as He predicted the sufferings of Christ and the glories to follow. It was revealed to
them that they were not serving themselves, but you, in these
things which now have been announced to you through those
who preached the gospel to you by the Holy Spirit sent from
heaven—things into which angels long to look (NASB).

The prophets frequently pointed to the age of salvation that lies on the far side
of judgment. It will be the age in which God's will shall prevail, characterized
by peace and justice (Isa. 2:2–4). The prophets looked for a time when the Davidic King would rule Israel and the nations as God's representative (see Isa. 9:6;
Micah 5:2–4; Zech. 9:9–10). This principal feature centers Israel's hope in the
Lord's coming rule of righteousness. It points to a time of both judgment and
salvation (Mal. 3:1–5). In the Old Testament, the two comings of the Messiah
are often combined, without a clear distinction between the two. Only in the
New Testament is the revelation clear enough for the two to be distinguished,
primarily because the first coming had already occurred.

The New Testament amplifies these Old Testament themes. Jesus is seen as
the fulfillment of these Old Testament pictures and prophecies. Jesus, in Luke
4:18–19, returned to his hometown of Nazareth. When he was asked to read in
the synagogue, he read Isaiah 61:1–3. After he finished the reading, he sat down
in the synagogue and amazingly proclaimed, "Today this Scripture has been
fulfilled in your hearing" (Luke 4:21, NASB). Jesus is described as "the coming
one" with reference both to his first coming (see Matt. 21:9; Luke 7:19) and to
his second (see 2 Thess. 1:10; Rev. 1:7; 22:7). The New Testament writers also
looked forward to Christ's second coming as further fulfillment of prophecy to
bring God's saving purpose to its consummation.

There was great emphasis in Jesus's teaching on the life here and now in the
inaugurated kingdom of God. He focused on the fulfillment of Old Testament
teaching in his life and mission. From the beginning Jesus taught that "the kingdom of God is at hand" (Mark 1:15). Yet, Jesus certainly looked forward to a
future coming when this world would exist no more and a new world would be
ushered in according to God's plan. Jesus warned that anyone ashamed of him
and his teachings at that time would find the Son of Man ashamed of him "when
He comes in the glory of His Father with the holy angels" (Mark 8:38, NASB).

Jesus maintained that the second coming will be sudden and unexpected
(Matt. 25:13; Luke 12:40), but when it happens, it will be like lightning for

all to see (see Matt. 24:27; Luke 17:24). Jesus said that his coming will occur unexpectedly; thus his call for watchfulness is significant, for it indicates that the coming of the Son of Man has decisive importance (Matt. 24:36-51). When the Son of Man returns, all believers will account for their use of talents and of the opportunities that he provided.

The New Testament consistently places an emphasis on judgment at the time of Jesus's return. This is seen first in the separation of saved from the lost (see Matt. 24:37–41; 25:31–46). Also, it will be observed by the mourning of all the nations when they see the Son of Man revealed (see Matt. 24:30; Luke 17:30). The point of these sayings is that people on earth, particularly unbelievers, will be carrying on their usual activities without awareness of Christ's second coming. In these teachings, thoughts of final judgment and human accountability are clearly present. The teachings urge the followers of Christ to be watchful while waiting.

The New Testament uses four terms to refer to Christ's return: *parousia* (appearing), *apokalupsis* (revelation), *epiphaneia* (manifestation), and *erchesthai* (coming). At times, the words are used in combination, but, in general, they are synonymous, pointing to the great day of his return. *Parousia* is the most frequently used of the four terms. It is employed in 1 Thessalonians 4:15 to designate Christ's coming to raise the righteous dead and to catch up believers to be with him. This "appearing" will also result in the destruction of the man of lawlessness, the antichrist (see 2 Thess. 2:8).

Apokalupsis literally means "revelation." Paul speaks of waiting for the revelation of our Lord Jesus Christ (1 Cor. 1:7; 2 Thess. 1:6–7; 1 Peter 4:13). *Epiphaneia* and *erchesthai* point to Christ's "coming manifestation." Believers place their hope in this "coming" as the time of the completion of their salvation (see 1 Tim. 6:14; 2 Tim. 4:8; Titus 2:13–14).[10]

Evangelical Christians through the years have differed over the details of how the Bible's teaching on this subject is to be understood. Various systems have been articulated, expanded, and defended by various evangelical scholars, preachers, denominations, organizations, and communities. While all maintain that the return of Christ is a foundational doctrine, the differences in biblical interpretation and systematic formation at times evidence much variety. At this point, it will be

---

10. Much of this material has been taken from George E. Ladd, *Blessed Hope* (Grand Rapids: Eerdmans, 1979) and Anthony Hoekema, *The Bible and the Future* (Grand Rapids: Eerdmans, 1979), as well as the two volumes noted in note 6 above.

helpful to look at these different approaches before our concluding focus on the contributions of progressive dispensationalism.[11]

ESCHATOLOGICAL SYSTEMS

How one interprets the Bible's eschatological teachings often depends greatly on their understanding of the "one thousand years" mentioned in Revelation 20. While the interpretation of this phrase is far more complex than whether or not this phrase is to be understood literally or symbolically, the basic differences in eschatological systems as explained in evangelical pulpits focuses on the question of whether the second coming of Christ will take place before or after the thousand years.

The return of Christ seems to be described in Revelation 19 when the rider on the white horse comes with his armies to destroy the forces of evil. Amillennialists and postmillennialists suggest that the coming described in Revelation 19 is the triumph of the testimony of Jesus in the world. Postmillennialists believe the millennial age will be established by the proclamation of the gospel. Amillennialists believe the millennium is another way to describe the age in which we now live and in which Jesus reigns as Lord by virtue of his resurrection and ascension. Consequently, the amillennial view is, in many ways, a variation of postmillennialism. Let's look more closely and in greater detail at the various systems.

Postmillennialism: The Preaching of the Gospel and the Reign of Christ

The interpretation of Revelation 20 that developed into postmillennialism has its roots in the great Christian thinker Augustine. According to this view, the age of the church flows into the millennial kingdom. Augustine took the figure "one thousand years" to be symbolic, not the actual length of time.

By the seventeenth century, the system that we know as postmillennialism had been fully developed. The millennium, as an extended period of peace and righteousness, would come about through Spirit-empowered preaching resulting in the conversion of the world. This expectation served as a powerful motivation for preaching during that period.

---

11. See Bruce A. Ware, "Eschatology," in *New Dimensions in Evangelical Thought: Essays in Honor of Millard J. Erickson*, ed. David S. Dockery (Downers Grove, IL: InterVarsity, 1998), 354–65; also Millard J. Erickson, *Contemporary Options in Eschatology* (Grand Rapids: Baker, 1977).

Postmillennialism might attract the loyalties of only a small percentage of evangelicals today, but it nevertheless is a system with several commendable strengths. For postmillennialists, the kingdom is not a territorial realm over which the Lord reigns. Wherever people believe in Jesus Christ, commit themselves to him, and obey him, the kingdom is present; it is not something to be introduced at some future time. At the heart of postmillennialism is a trust in the primacy and effectiveness of the preached word to change lives and bring conversion to the nations.

Such accomplishment is not because of an optimistic spirit or human progressivism, but by the divine enablement and empowerment of the Holy Spirit. Postmillennialists expect the preaching of the gospel to transform the world, resulting in a long period of earthly peace and righteousness. Not only will conflict cease among the nations, but also prejudice between races, disputes among social classes, and jealousies, turmoil, and competition among Christians.

For postmillennialists, it is difficult to determine the beginning point of the millennium. Thus, like the growth of the mustard seed (see Matthew 13:31–32), the kingdom will expand and spread over the years. They believe the end of the millennium will conclude with a time of apostasy, and the end will come with the personal, bodily return of Christ.

The strength of postmillennialism is its confidence in the power of the gospel and its belief in the primacy of preaching. Much of the impetus for the seventeenth-century Puritan movements and the eighteenth-century awakenings came from their confidence that God would bless their preaching, which was informed and shaped by their postmillennial eschatology. Thus, some have called for a modern-day renewal of postmillennialism. Several important evangelical theologians (like Donald Bloesch) have expressed openness to postmillennial beliefs and others, including John Jefferson Davis and Lorraine Boettner, to name two, have attempted to revive the postmillennial teachings of Jonathan Edwards, A. A. Hodge, A. H. Strong, and B. H. Carroll.[12] This approach also points the church to a belief that Christian truth can and will transform our culture and the entities of society, thus reminding us that the reign of God is in one sense a present reality. Postmillennialism, therefore, emphasizes that God's kingdom resources are available to the church. Christ's lordship is exercised to and through the church as it takes its mission mandate to the world.

---

12. See Donald G. Bloesch, *The Last Things: Resurrection, Judgment, Glory* (Downers Grove, IL: InterVarsity, 2004); John Jefferson Davis, *Christ's Victorious Kingdom: Postmillennialism Reconsidered* (Grand Rapids: Baker, 1986); and Lorraine Boetner, *The Millennium* (Philadelphia: Presbyterian & Reformed, 1966).

Though the source of revival motivation in Puritan times, postmillennial-ism has had difficulty maintaining a thoroughgoing supernaturalism. As the reign of God is seen in every aspect of society, some have failed to discern the differences between good and evil. The biblical distinction between the holy kingdom of God, which will be present only when Jesus Christ personally returns, and the sphere of evil, with which God's kingdom is always in conflict prior to Christ's return, is diminished (also, the progress and development, apart from the power of the gospel). Though these weaknesses are evident, let us pray for what we sing, "that Christ's great kingdom shall come on earth, the kingdom of love and light."[13]

Amillennialism: A Coherent System

Amillennialists believe there will be no literal thousand-year reign of Christ with his followers on earth. Simply stated, amillennialists believe in the literal return of Christ that will be followed by the general resurrection of both the righteous and wicked, the last judgment, and the passage into the eternal state.[14]

Amillennialists believe that Revelation 20:1–10 portrays the current time in which we live. During this time, the gospel is to be preached to the whole world. Believers who have died and are already reigning with Christ in heaven are those pictured in Revelation 20 as the ones who are said to be reigning with Christ for a thousand years. Of course, Christ's reign must be understood as a spiritual reign rather than a bodily reign. This spiritual reign fulfills the words and promise of the Great Commission in Matthew 28:18–20.

Amillennialists hold that the "thousand years" of Revelation 20 is simply a metaphor representing a long period of time, during which God's will is accomplished. Advocates of this system look forward to a literal bodily return of Christ, at which time there will be both a resurrection of believers and unbelievers. Those who have not placed their faith in Christ will be raised to face judgment and eternal punishment. The bodies of believers will be raised for all eternity.

Amillennialism has been taught by a large sector of those who have influenced the evangelical movement since the time of the Reformation, including the major Reformers themselves, as well as a variety of Lutherans, Presbyterians, Anglicans, Baptists, and Methodists.

---

13. H. Ernest Nichol, "We've a Story to Tell to the Nations," No. 296, *The Hymnal* (Nashville: Word Music, 1986).

14. See G. C. Berkouwer, *The Return of Christ* (Grand Rapids: Eerdmans, 1972); also Sam Storms, *Kingdom Come: The Amillennial Alternative* (Ross-shire, Scotland: Mentor, 2013).

Amillennialism is a coherent system of the end times, which recognizes that biblical prophecy and books like Daniel and Revelation utilize a great deal of symbolism. Amillennialism maintains a realistic approach to history. There is flexibility within the system that allows for either an improvement of conditions (often associated with postmillennialism) or a deterioration of trends (usually associated with premillennialism). Amillennialism teaches neither that the entire world will be converted prior to Christ's return (postmillennialism), nor that the world conditions will inevitably grow worse (premillennialism).[15]

Progressive dispensationalists have remained respectful of both amillennial and postmillennial approaches, and have offered constructive responses to each. However, they have proposed a premillennial model as the most promising option for the evangelical community.

Premillennialism: The Promise of Progressive Dispensationalism

Many evangelicals believe that the premillennial system interprets the biblical materials in a more coherent and systematic fashion than the other two options. Premillennialism teaches that Christ will return prior to the establishment of Christ's kingdom reign on the earth, which may or may not be understood as a literal thousand-year reign of Christ. Premillennialists differ among themselves over the timing of Christ's return in relation to the tribulation period that precedes the millennium.[16] In many ways, progressive dispensationalism is an attempt to bridge that divide.[17] Craig Blaising, in particular, has emphasized the need for dependence on God for illumination accompanied by a profound respect and tolerance for other evangelical Christians who have arrived at different understandings of eschatology. The issue is our hope in Christ. If discussion of these different positions among evangelicals distracts us from this focus, then these things are not helpful or beneficial for us.[18]

Given the differences among evangelical communities through the centuries, it is easy for some to dismiss the question of the millennial reign as having little importance. It is certainly the case that we cannot know for sure about future matters, but these matters are of significant consequences for serious Christian

---

15. Hoekema, *The Bible and the Future*.
16. See John Walvoord, *The Millennial Kingdom* (Grand Rapids: Zondervan, 1959); Robert H. Gundry, *The Church and the Tribulation* (Grand Rapids: Zondervan, 1973).
17. See Craig A. Blaising, "Changing Patterns in American Dispensational Theology," *Wesleyan Theological Journal* 29 (1994) 149–64.
18. See Craig A. Blaising, "Spiritual Formation in the Early Church," in *The Christian Educator's Handbook on Spiritual Formation* (Wheaton, IL: Victor, 1994).

thinking concerning the climax of human history, understood in terms of God's intention for creation. The subject of eschatology, while clearly a matter over which evangelical Christians disagree, should not be a topic of quarreling among fellow believers who have acknowledged Jesus as Lord.[19]

Let us hold our convictions with humility, recognizing various strengths in other viewpoints. More importantly, let us draw encouragement, comfort, and hope from knowing that God's plan will not be thwarted in any way. The Bible presents God's plan for a redeemed people within a redeemed creation.

God's plan for history is meaningful in that it is directed toward the reign of God over the earth. This plan forms the center of the Lord's model prayer: "Your kingdom come, your will be done, on earth as it is in heaven" (Matt. 6:10). The future world order pictured at the conclusion of the book of Revelation will be the completion of God's redemptive plan for human history and for all of God's creation. This plan of God is bigger and broader than eternal life for individual believers, as important as that is. Evangelical eschatology focuses on corporate human history, the fulfillment of God's plan for his people.

Eschatology, rightly understood, leads not to division but to doxology. The one who is coming again to rule and reign (Rev. 19–20) is the one, also, who created all things (Col. 1:15–17) and reconciled all things to God (Col. 1:18–20). This one, the Lord Jesus Christ, is worthy to be praised because he was slain, because he purchased men and woman for God, and because he made them a kingdom and priests. The theological significance of this majestic portrait of Christ should not be lost, for here we find a lofty and exalted Christology that shapes and informs our understanding of eschatology.

The praise of Christ should not be reserved only for the church's future, however, but should be central to the church as presented in the New Testament. The ultimate purpose of the church is the worship and praise of the one who called it into being and who purchased redemption by his blood (Eph. 1:7). To worship the crucified, risen, and exalted Christ is to ascribe to him the supreme worth that he alone is worthy to receive.[20]

To think that the purpose of Christ's return is to satisfy our curiosity or our own agenda is to miss the mark. Christ will return to consummate God's plan, to display his glory and his victory, and to restore the richness of fellowship

---

19. See Craig A. Blaising, Kenneth L. Gentry, and Robert B. Strimple, *Three Views on the Millennium* (Grand Rapids: Zondervan, 1999).
20. See David S. Dockery, "Worthy Is the Lamb," in *The Cosmic Battle for Planet Earth*, ed. Ron duPreez and Jiri Moskala (Berrien Springs, MI: Andrews University Press, 2003), 409–14.

among his people. Evangelicals should continue to study and reflect upon the importance of the Bible's eschatological teachings. For only as we understand God's purposes for his future plan, do we understand his will for our lives in the present. As the evangelical community further understands God's plan and reflects on his purposes, the darkness that we now see (1 Cor. 13:12) will be removed by the power and light of God's Word. Let us give thanks together that the hope of the return of Christ is a powerful reality to direct and shape our lives.

Part 4:

THE DOCTRINE OF THE FUTURE
AND CHRISTIAN MINISTRY

The Doctrine of the Future and Pastoral Care

J. Denny Autrey

> Because the Lamb who is at the center of the throne *will shepherd them*; He will guide them to springs of living waters, and God will wipe away every tear from their eyes.
> —Revelation 7:17

F rom an in-depth study of the pages of Holy Scripture, to a review of the classic ministers of church history, the true model for effective pastoral care is reflected in the person and work of Jesus Christ. Even with respect to the future events of eschatology, the passage above reflects the reality that the pastoral ministry of the "Lamb" will continue as he "shepherds" the people of God. Thus, questions arise. What is pastoral care, and what does it mean to shepherd the people of God? How does the doctrine of the future impact the role of the evangelical pastor for ministry in the twenty-first century? How does a pastor integrate the study of the doctrine of eschatology into the practical aspects of everyday pastoral care? Is the doctrine of the future really relevant for the work of the pastor in the contemporary setting of the church, or should that subject of doctrinal teaching be relegated to the classroom for only those students preparing for some form of ministry? If such a doctrinal study of eschatology and future things is necessary, then how can the study of the doctrine of the future translate to the practice of the local pastor of First Baptist Church, County Seat, USA?

The answers to such questions are of vital importance and can only be affirmed if one takes seriously the call to minister. How one incorporates the doctrine of the future and its implications into the everyday pastoral care and concern of the evangelical minister is essential. The twenty-first-century pastor who models his shepherding ministry after that expressed by Jesus Christ in the New Testament will be concerned with a comprehensive approach that involves preaching, teaching, and words of counsel offered to those experiencing the difficulties and the uncertainties of life and death. The comfort of the eternal hope of a returning Lord is the reality that life is worth living now, because of the finished work of the Shepherd-Savior who will once again return for his own. As Stephen Kuhrt states, "Hope for the future is something that clearly lies at the heart of faith in Jesus Christ."[1] Most, if not all, Christians within the culture of the modern west would affirm this statement. Yet, in his argument Kuhrt declares that for the average churchgoer, the reality of the doctrine of the future is more often oriented toward the personal comfort that awaits the believer after death rather than setting the agenda and direction for the contemporary church. His assertion, to shift away from an escapist mentality of eschatology toward a more biblical approach, will have significant implications in terms of the church's ministry and mission.

Thus, more questions arise. How does the truth of the doctrine of the future impact pastoral care? Or how does the minister of the gospel incorporate eschatology within the fabric of his life of service to the church? How does the doctrine of the future impact pastoral care?

Pastoral care occurs within the context of the church, and yet it takes place within a vision that looks toward history's end. Therefore, a proper understanding of pastoral ministry and a true biblical pattern for such care should be derived from a study of both the Old and New Testaments. A review of pastoral care as modeled throughout church history will add further insight into the task of pastoral service. It will also be necessary to examine the terms used to communicate what the practice of pastoral theology is and how it is expressed in the service of the church.[2]

An examination of historic definitions explaining pastoral theology and its description of pastoral care along with a brief review from pastors throughout church history who maintained strong biblical perspectives concerning the pastorate are compared to the contemporary definitions being touted as the new norms for pastoral care in conjunction with that which has been modeled from a New Testament perspective and presented in the person of Jesus Christ.

---

1. Stephen Kuhrt. "The Importance of Being Eschatological: Providing Clarity and Direction for the Local Church," *The Bible in Transmission* (Winter 2013): 8–10.
2. Thomas C. Oden, *Pastoral Theology, Essentials of Ministry* (San Francisco: Harper & Row, 1983), x.

With these specific insights, the informed theologian will be able to formulate a framework for ministry incorporating the doctrine of the future in a well-rounded practical approach for the contemporary church.

With a renewed emphasis on the doctrine of the future, "rather than being 'escapist,' biblical eschatology and the Christian hope is thus revealed to be radical, practical, and completely reinvigorating the twenty-first century through the clarity and purpose that it provides for its mission and ministry."[3] The doctrine of the future must be an integral part of effective pastoral care for the twenty-first-century minister.

What Is Pastoral Theology?

Pastoral theology is that branch of Christian theology dealing with the office and function of the pastor.[4] Pastoral theology is expressed as the art of pastoral care through the life of the pastor-servant. It is eloquently defined by Thomas Oden, "Pastoral theology is a special form of practical theology because it focuses on the practice of ministry with particular attention to the systematic definition of the pastoral office and its function. Pastoral theology is also a form of systematic theology because it attempts a systematic, consistent reflection on the offices and gifts of ministry and their integral relationship with the practice of the tasks of ministry."[5] Oden further acknowledges, "As theology, pastoral theology is attentive to that knowledge of God as revealed through the witness of Scripture, mediated through tradition, expressed in systematic reasoning, and embodied in personal and social experience."[6]

Carroll A. Wise adds to the understanding of pastoral care in his definition: "Pastoral care is the art of communicating the inner meaning of the gospel to persons at the point of their need. Pastoral care is more of a function than an activity, more a living relationship than a theory or interpretation, more a matter of being than doing. It is the manifestation in the relationship between pastor and persons, either individually or in groups, of a quality of love which points to, and gives a basis in experience for, the realization of the love of God."[7] This exact depiction of the biblical motif of shepherding expresses such a relationship

---

3. Kuhrt, "The Importance of Being Eschatological," 9.
4. Oden, *Pastoral Theology*, x.
5. Ibid.
6. Ibid.
7. Carroll A. Wise, *The Meaning of Pastoral Care* (New York: Harper & Row, Publishers, 1966), 8.

of care and consolation. Throughout the biblical narrative, from the Old Testament to the New, pastoral care is often expressed in the metaphor of shepherding. Beginning with Abel in Genesis 4 through the shepherd boy, David, who became king reflected in Psalm 23, the care of God's people has been compared to shepherding. Jesus took the image of the shepherd as the major profile to represent his own self-expression as the good shepherd of John 10. John promises in the book of Revelation that Jesus will continue that ministry throughout eternity.[8] Since Jesus is described as the "Good Shepherd" (John 10:14), the "Great Shepherd" (Heb. 13:20), and the "Chief Shepherd" (1 Peter 5:4), those who serve in his name are often referred to as "under-shepherds" who offer care in his name. The common Greek term for "shepherd" is *poimén*, and is derived from the Latin term *pastus* for a person who is a pastor.

Within the plethora of literature on pastoral theology, entire volumes have been devoted to the shepherd theme of pastoral care. The shepherd symbolism pervades the imagery of the Scriptures.[9] As the shepherd of his people, Jehovah God is seen as the one who leads, feeds, disciplines, and protects his people. Thus, those who labor in his name should reflect the same nurturing character as the Great Shepherd of the people. Recorded by the psalmist as the proper mode for leadership, King David "shepherded them with a pure heart and guided them with his skillful hands" (Ps. 78:72).

A Biblical Perspective on Pastoral Care

The Old Testament Concept. The scriptural basis for the proper definition of pastoral care is derived from an examination of both the Old and New Testaments. As expressed briefly above, any study of pastoral ministry must begin in the Old Testament with the motif of God as the shepherd of his people. Thus, the Old Testament provides the foundational concept for understanding the office and function of the pastor. The image of the shepherd not only demonstrates God's care, love, mercy, discipline, compassion, protection, and provision, but also reveals God's authority and faithfulness to meeting the needs of his sheep. Included in the imagery of the shepherding concept is the necessity and implications of the mandate of obedience to the master of the flock. Without pressing

---

8. David Stancil, "The Ministry of Shepherding," *Preparing for Christian Ministry, An Evangelical Approach*, ed. David P. Gushee and Walter C. Jackson (Grand Rapids: Baker, 1998), 205.

9. C. W. Brister, *Pastoral Care in the Church* (New York: Harper & Row, 1977), 19.

the imagery to extreme measures reveals the reality that no human servant leader could ever mirror the perfection of the Chief Shepherd. God has chosen to implement his sovereign plan throughout human history by utilizing both the strengths and weaknesses of his servant leaders to accomplish his purposes.

The New Testament Concept. With the Old Testament as the chief building block, the New Testament builds on this foundation of shepherding as revealed in the writings of the apostles Peter and John, as well as the writer of the book of Hebrews. Each casts the image of Christ Jesus as "shepherd" in declaring him as the Good Shepherd who gives his life in service for the sheep (John 10:11, 14); as the Great Shepherd who seals the eternal covenant in his blood (Heb. 13:25, 1 Peter 2:25); and the Chief Shepherd as the model for all shepherds who serve the people of God's flock (1 Peter 5:4). John recalls the image of Christ as shepherd in Revelation 7:17 where it is the "Lamb in the midst of the throne" who will be the "shepherd" of those who have survived the tribulation. In context the shepherd's care involves washing their robes, providing sustenance, shelter, and comfort. Revelation 19:15 depicts Christ's shepherding of "the nations" who oppose him in a very different light. He is said to "rule (Greek *poimanei*) them with a rod of iron." In this context the shepherd will "strike down" with the sword from his mouth and "tread the winepress of the fury of the wrath of God the Almighty."

Numerous biblical terms are employed to describe the role and duties of the pastor in following the example of Christ as shepherd. These defined terms are the basis for the biblical ministry of the pastor, and are expressed by numerous pastors throughout history in demonstrating the biblical pattern that was established in the first century. Five distinct terms have emerged from the Scriptures reflecting the work of pastoral care; they are: (1) "elder" (*presbyteros*), a recognized leader among Jews in the administration and spiritual care of the church (Acts 15:6, 1 Tim. 5:17, 1 Peter 5:1–4); (2) "bishop" or "overseer" (*episkopos*), a recognized leader among Gentiles in the oversight of the church (Acts 20:28, 1 Tim. 3:2–5, Titus 1:7); (3) "shepherd" or "pastor" (*poimen*), a place of authority (Acts 20:28–31, Eph. 4:11, 1 Peter 2:25; 5:2–3); (4) "preacher" (*kerux*), one noted for the proclamation of the gospel to the flock (1 Tim. 2:7, 2 Tim. 1:11); (5) "teacher" (*didaskalos*), one gifted in the instruction of the Scriptures (1 Tim. 2:7). The combination of these titles has been established as the basis for the biblical concept of pastoral care. The following will identify specific examples which reflect the biblical pattern for ministry from the scriptural truths gleaned from the Old and New Testaments.

A Biblical Pattern for Pastoral Care from Church History

A proper summary of the development of pastoral theology throughout church history is beyond the scope of this essay. Therefore, specific individuals have been selected and highlighted as expressing the proper methods for pastoral ministry. In the study of the history of the church, it is interesting to note that those who held a high view of Scripture also placed a premium on the importance of preaching, which resulted in effective pastoral care. When the proclamation of the Word of God is strong, the influence of the church is strong, and when proclamation is weak, the impact of the church is weak. Thus, those who hold a high view of Scripture and adhere to the biblical mandate for ministry bring the practice of the biblical truths to life in their ministries.

From the second century through the fifth century, the spontaneous simplicity of the early church began to succumb to the complexity of a more institutional structure with the development of sacerdotalism and the elevation of the clergy to priests, resulting in the minister becoming the one who participates with God in the conferring of grace to any individual.[10] Sacerdotalism has been defined in this manner: "The priestly Order is required for the valid administration of Penance and Extreme Unction. As to the Eucharist, those only who have priestly Orders can consecrate, i.e., change bread and wine into the Body and Blood of Christ. Consecration presupposed, anyone can distribute the Eucharist species but outside of very extraordinary circumstances this can be lawfully done by bishops, priests, or (in some cases) deacons."[11] Yet, several rejected this trend in favor of the biblical model that had been set forth by the apostles.

Listed below are some who held the Holy Scriptures as the basis for their pastoral care. As the development of the institutionalized church progressed, they held forth a model for pastors to follow.

Polycarp (70–155). Polycarp, perhaps the apostle John's most well-known disciple, writes:

> And the presbyters (elders) also must be compassionate, merciful towards all men, turning back the sheep that are gone astray,

---

10. James F. Stitzinger, "Pastoral Ministry in History," in *Rediscovering Pastoral Ministry, Shaping Contemporary Ministry with Biblical Mandates*, ed. John MacArthur Jr. (Dallas: Word, 1995), 34–63.

11. Daniel Kennedy, "Sacraments." *The Catholic Encyclopedia*, vol. 13 (New York: Robert Appleton, 1912); http://www.newadvent.org/cathen/ 13295a.htm (accessed April 28, 2014).

visiting all the infirm, not neglecting a widow or an orphan or
a poor man: but providing always for that which is honorable
in the sight of God and of all men. . . . Therefore if we ask the
Lord to forgive us, then we ourselves ought to forgive, for we
are in full view of the eyes of the Lord and God, and we must
"all stand before the judgment seat of Christ," and "each one
must give an account of himself." Let us therefore so serve Him
with fear and all reverence, as He himself gave commandment
and the apostles who preached the gospel to us and the prophets who proclaimed beforehand the coming of the Lord.[12]

Polycarp reminds presbyters of a future judgment of their ministry. They are expected to practice what they preach, and to preach as the apostles and prophets
did by pointing to the gospel and the coming of the Lord.

Clement of Alexandria (155–220). Another early church father drawing on the
imagery of shepherding was Clement of Alexandria. He emphasized, "Ministers
are those chosen to serve the Lord, who moderate their passions, who are obedient to superiors, and who teach and care for the sheep as a shepherd."[13]

John Chrysostom (347–407). John of Antioch was born the son of a Roman soldier
who died while he was yet an infant. His mother, Authusa, who was widowed in
her early twenties, committed herself to raising her son with a Christian education.[14]
He was trained by the noted scholar of rhetoric Libanius, who was disappointed
when his prodigy refused to succeed him as professor of rhetoric, choosing rather
to devote his life to the ministry.[15] Under the tutelage of Diodorus, who rejected
the Alexandrian method of interpretation by allegory as established in the homilies
of Origen, Chrysostom held to a more literal and historical method of interpretation as espoused by the Antiochene School.[16] "The Antiochene School placed a

---

12. Polycarp, "Epistle of Polycarp to the Philippians," in *The Apostolic Fathers*, ed. J. B. Lightfoot,
(London: MacMillan, 1926), 179.
13. Clement of Alexandria, "The Stromata, or Miscellanies," in *The Ante-Nicene Fathers*, ed. Alexander Roberts and James Donaldson (Grand Rapids: Eerdmans, 1983), 2:535.
14. Robert A. Krupp, "Golden Tongue & Iron Will," *Christian History* 13, no. 44 (1994): 6–11.
15. Clyde E. Fant Jr. and William M. Pinson, *20 Centuries of Great Preaching: An Encyclopedia of
Preaching* (Waco, TX: Word, 1971), 53–54.
16. Carl A. Volz, "The Genius of Chrysostom's Preaching," *Christian History* 13, no. 44 (1994):
24–26.

high value on the authority of the Word of God, and their basis and method for interpreting Scripture was often called the grammatical-historical method."[17] "It developed as a reaction against the School of Alexandria established by Origen in Alexandria, Egypt, during the early to mid-second century. Origen was untrained in classic rhetoric, but approached his preaching as a trained grammarian and, thus, was known as the 'first major exegete in the history of the church and the originator of the sermon structure known as the "homily."[18]

The most powerful preacher, some say in the history of the church—graced with the title "Golden Mouth" nearly one hundred years after his death—John Chrysostom was also known for his commitment to the priesthood as established by the Lord Jesus and the apostles. He wrote extensively on the role and responsibilities of those who were to serve in the priesthood. In his "Treaties Concerning the Christian Priesthood," he describes the character traits and qualities of those that are called to serve in the priesthood, "For the pastor of sheep has his flock following him, wherever he may lead them: and if any should stray out of the straight path, and deserting the good pasture, feed in unproductive or rugged places, a loud shout suffices to collect them and bring them back to the fold those who have been parted from it: but if a human being wanders away from the right faith, great exertion, perseverance and patience are required. The pastor therefore ought to be of a noble spirit, so as not to despond, or to despair of the salvation of wanderers from the fold."[19]

> Consider, then, what kind of man he (the priest) ought to be who is to hold out against such a tempest, and to manage skillfully such great hindrances to the common welfare; for he ought to be dignified yet free from arrogance, formidable yet kind, apt to command yet sociable, impartial yet courteous, humble yet not servile, strong yet gentle, in order that he may contend successfully against all these difficulties. And he ought to bring forward with great authority the man who is properly qualified for the office, even if all should oppose him, and with the same

---

17. Hughes Oliphant Old, *The Patristic Age*, Reading and Preaching of the Scriptures in the Worship of the Christian Church, vol. 2 (Grand Rapids: Eerdmans, 1998), 168.
18. O. C. Edwards, *A History of Preaching* (Nashville: Abingdon, 2004), 34.
19. *Sacerdot.* 2.4, in "Treaties Concerning the Christian Priesthood," in *A Select Library of the Christian Church, Nicene and Post-Nicene Fathers,* vol. 9, ed. Philip Schaff (Peabody, MA: Hendrickson, 1994).

authority to reject the man who is not so qualified, even if all should conspire in his favor, and to keep one aim in view, the building up of the Church, . . . for without this a man would be a destroyer rather than a protector, a wolf rather than a shepherd.[20]

Augustine of Hippo (354–430). Augustine was another major spokesman from the early church who took great care in shepherding the flock, based on his salvation experience and his late call to the ministry. After experiencing in his early years a life of vice and anarchy, from the time of his conversion at age thirty-three, "Augustine was greatly concerned with the life of the preacher. He contended that there were two ways a preacher can gain the confidence of his hearers: he must be wise (in the Scriptures) and he must be pious."[21] Therefore, "Augustine was not so much concerned with producing great human literature as he was with the exposition of the Word of God. It was God's Word which fascinated him."[22] This adherence to a strict interpretation of the Scriptures by a vocal minority kept the early church tied to a biblical pattern for pastoral care.

The Medieval Period and Pastoral Care

With the death of Augustine in 430 and the abdication of the last Roman Emperor in 476, the Roman Empire was officially over, and the period known as the early medieval period had begun. The period of history from 500 to 1000 has been referred to as the "Dark Ages, under the illusion that it was a period of intellectual stagnation."[23] Fant and Pinson describe the same era as the "Dark Age of Preaching."[24] Once again it can be seen that when expository preaching is strong, then more effective and fervent pastoral care is portrayed among those in ministry.

The period from the mid-fourteenth century to the early sixteenth century brought a revival of learning in many areas and a reinstitution of the importance of the role and function of the pastor. The period from 1361–1572 is known as the "Reformatory Period" and is divided into two distinct sections: (1) the Renaissance (1361–1499); and (2) the Reformation (1500–1572).[25] Without question,

20. *Sacerdot.* 3.16.
21. Fant and Pinson, *20 Centuries of Great Preaching*, 1:118.
22. Old, *Patristic Age*, 2:345.
23. Edwards, *History of Preaching*, 125.
24. Fant and Pinson, *20 Centuries of Great Preaching*, 1:v.
25. This timeframe has been suggested by numerous historians as an awakening of artistic and literary forms that brought profound change to the thought of the day that affected attitudes in almost every area of life including that of religion.

those early voices of the pre-reformers such as John Wycliffe, John Huss, and William Tyndale were willing to herald forth a mandate calling for a return to the biblical pattern for ministers. For some this was a commitment unto death.

One of the leading scholars of the Renaissance period and one of Oxford's finest, John Wycliffe, issued some of the boldest statements reminiscent of Augustine's convictions concerning the importance of preaching the entire counsel of God's Word. In his treatise, *On the Pastoral Office*, he declares, "There are two things that pertain to the status of pastor: the holiness of the pastor and the wholesomeness of his teaching. He ought to be holy, so strong in every sort of virtue that he would rather desert every kind of human intercourse, all the temporal things of this world, even mortal life itself, before he would sinfully depart from the truth of Christ. . . . Secondly, the pastor ought to be resplendent with righteousness of doctrine before his sheep."[26]

Wycliffe's style set a new tone for the preaching of his day, which is why he is referred to as the "Morning Star of the Reformation." His open attacks on the corruptions of the Roman Catholic Church in doctrine and practice, with his appeal to Scripture as his sole authority, set his preaching apart from most of his contemporaries.[27] In summarizing the work of Wycliffe and his Lollards, Dargan puts their reform preaching in proper prospective as he notes: "The spirit of the true reformer is not that of the satirist who sees evil and derides it, nor that of the pessimist who sees it only to despair; nor that of the pious mystic, who flees before it to the withdrawn and introspective life; but that of the leader of men, who combines whatever is good in all these ways of regarding evil and adds to them the courage to attack and hope to overcome, or at least, to abate the ills of his time."[28]

The Reformation Period and Pastoral Care

The Reformation was built on the centrality of the Bible. The principles on which the Reformers launched their call for change were simple: *Sola Deo Gloria* ("glory to God alone"), *Sola Gratia* ("by grace alone"), and of course, *Sola Scriptura* ("the Scriptures alone"). All stemmed from their study and teaching of the Word. *Sola Scriptura* indicates "the freedom of Scripture to rule as God's Word in the church, disentangled from papal and ecclesiastical magisterium and

---

26. John Wycliffe, "On the Pastoral Office," in *Library of Christian Classics: Advocates of Reform*, ed. Matthew Spinks (London: SCM, 1953), 32, 40.
27. Edwin Charles Dargan, *A History of Preaching: From the Apostlic Fathers to the Great Reformers AD 70–1572*, vol. 1 (Grand Rapids: Baker, 1954), 310.
28. Ibid.

tradition."[29] The emphasis on the Scriptures brought about a continuing charge concerning the importance of pastoral care in the church.

Martin Luther (1483–1546). Martin Luther inspired many by bringing the preaching event back to center stage for worship. Through a reexamination of the sermons of John Chrysostom, by men like Ulrich Zwingli and John Oecolampadius, many of the Reformers turned from the allegorical method, which was still the common practice of interpretation, to the more literal, historical-grammatical approach of hermeneutic interpretation.

Yet as Robert Kolb describes, the crisis of pastoral care, and not simply an exercise in academic thought, brought Luther to the forefront,

> The fundamental appeal of Luther's Reformation sprang from its effective address of the crisis in pastoral care which plagued the Western church at the end of the Middle Ages. During the fifteenth century European Christians had become increasingly active in expressing their piety in traditional ways. At the same time many had found increasing frustration because the old system of caring for Christians souls did not seem to be working. Priests had failed to be good pastors. Luther was propelled to center stage in the Western church by events that arose out of his deep personal concern for what the abuse of the indulgence trade was doing to the piety of the parishioners of Wittenberg. His was a Reformation, a revolution, of pastoral care.[30]

Luther had not tackled the theological questions concerning his theology of justification by faith, but he had already recognized that the care of souls was being deeply undermined by the treachery of indulgences as portrayed by the uncaring priests of the church. As related to the work of the pastor, Luther says, "Men who hold the office of the ministry should have the heart of a mother toward the church; for if they have no such heart, they soon become lazy and disgusted, and suffering, in particular, will find them unwilling. . . . Unless your heart toward

---

29. David F. Wright, "Protestantism," in *Evangelical Dictionary of Theology*, ed. Walter A. Elwell, (Grand Rapids: Baker, 1984), 889.

30. Robert Kolb, "The Doctrine of Ministry in Martin Luther and the Lutheran Confessions," in *The Reformation in Medieval Perspective*, ed. Steven E. Ozment (Chicago: Quadrangle, 1971), 50–75.

the sheep is like that of a mother toward her children—a mother, who walks through fire to save her children—you will not be fit to be a preacher. . . all kinds of suffering will meet you in this office. If, then, the mother heart, the great love, is not there to drive the preachers, the sheep will be poorly served."[31]

John Calvin (1509–1564). This type of love for the sheep permeated the hearts of the Reformers concerning their biblical responsibility for the care of the local flock. Known more for his theology and exegetical work, "of all the Reformers, John Calvin, was the theologian" who was also known for his pastoral ministry.[32] The following comment reflects the importance of that reality for Calvin:

> We who have charge to teach the people . . . we must mark also, that it is not enough for a man who is a shepherd in the Church of God, to preach, and cast abroad the word into the air, we must have private admonitions also. And this is a point that many deceive themselves in. For they think that the order of the Church was made for no other end and purpose but that they should come to Church one hour in the week, or on certain days, and there hear a man speak, and when he has come out of the pulpit, he should hold his peace. Those who think so, show themselves sufficiently, that they never knew, either what Christianity, or God's order, meant.[33]

Calvin, and the other Reformers like him, were not aloof preachers simply dispensing information. They were shepherds involved in the everyday lives of their people, seeing it as their task to help the people know God, pray, worship God, persevere, and one day die well with the hope of the resurrection. They did not glean this simply from the study of the Scriptures and a reexamination of the early church fathers, but it was modeled to them by many who were their mentors.

As has been stated, with a renewed emphasis on the preaching of the Word of God and a mind toward hope of resurrection, the responsibilities for

---

31. Martin Luther, "Ministers," in *What Luther Says: A Practical In-home Anthology for the Active Christian*, ed. Ewald M. Plass (St. Louis: Concordia, 1959), 932.

32. Hughes Oliphant Old, *The Age of the Reformation*, Reading and Preaching of the Scriptures in the Christian Church, vol. 4 (Grand Rapids: Eerdmans, 2002), 91.

33. Des Gallars, "The Pastoral Emphasis of Calvin's Ministry," *The Counsel of Chalcedon* (March/April 1997): 12.

pastoral ministry continued to expand in the hearts and minds of each suc-
ceeding generation of pastors.

The Puritans and Pastoral Care

During the years leading into the seventeenth century, those within the An-
glican Church who were drawn more to the Reformed elements of worship and
theology became known as the Puritans.

Williams Perkins (1558–1602). With regard to their understanding of pastoral
care, the individual often referred to as the most prominent Puritan theologian
was William Perkins.[34] Perkins was largely responsible for reigniting a belief in
the centrality and importance of preaching in ministry. A man uniquely gifted,
Perkins has been described as "the Puritan theologian of Tudor times."[35] Known
primarily for his preaching and for producing what many believe to be one of
the first works on homiletics, *The Art of Prophesying*, Perkins produced a second
work dealing with the importance of the ministry. It was entitled *The Calling of
the Ministry.* First published in 1605, it addresses what God calls ministers to do
and to be. Perkins's disciple William Crashaw recorded it, as Perkins expounded
Job 33:23–34 and Isaiah 6.[36] Perkins used the comparison of the minister as the
"angel of God"; as such, "the messenger of God" was to pay close attention not
only to the high calling he had received, but also to the high privilege in which
he was to speak to the people for God. The timeless truths of his message need
to be translated into a fresh understanding of the duties and dignities for the
contemporary minister of the twenty-first century. The following reveals Perkins's challenge to the minister: "Ministers must confer with their people and
also visit, admonish and rebuke them in private. Most of all they must preach,
and do so in such a manner and with such diligence that they may redeem souls.
Winning souls is the goal they must have in view."[37]

Richard Baxter (1615–1691). Another well-known Puritan following in the
footsteps of Perkins was Richard Baxter, who is remembered for the pastoral
care and counsel he rendered during his nearly two decades as pastor in Kid-

---

34. Jonathan Long, "William Perkins: Apostle of Practical Divinity," *Churchman* 103 (1989):
    12–18.
35. M. M. Knappen, *Tudor Puritanism* (Chicago: Eerdmans, 1939), 375.
36. William Perkins, *The Art of Prophesying* (Edinburgh: Banner of Truth, 2002), xiii.
37. Ibid., 116.

derminister, England. With great concern for his flock and his fellow ministers, he penned his most famous work, *The Reformed Pastor*, in 1656. Taking as his text Acts 20:28, "Take heed therefore unto yourselves, and to all the flock, over the which the Holy Ghost hath made you overseers, to feed the church of God, which he hath purchased with his own blood," Baxter developed his complete model for ministry based on this scriptural admonition clarifying the minister's responsibilities to God and his people. Additionally, he took the passage literally by committing private times of weekly discipleship to every family within his flock over his nineteen-year tenure at the church. He understood and accepted the call to shepherd the sheep entrusted to him by God.

Thus, throughout the history of the church, there are those who have given themselves to the biblical pattern for pastoral care. Additionally, to build upon their examples, the doctrine of the future must be included in all pastoral care if that care is to be considered a biblically based ministry. The following reflects how a pastor should incorporate the aspects of this truth into his ministry.

The Doctrine of the Future and Its Implications for Pastoral Care

With regard to the doctrine of the future, this writer concurs with the authors of this volume in their explanation and presentation of eschatological truth. As declared by Craig A. Blaising in his work *Progressive Dispensationalism*, "the Bible is the sole inerrant verbal revelation of God available to the church today and that it provides a sure foundation for Christian life and faith. They (Dispensationalists) believe that dispensational ideas and interpretations help people understand the Bible and help make the Scripture more intelligible to them, allowing them to more knowledgeably appropriate it in their everyday lives."[38] Blaising further states, "The word *dispensation* refers to a particular arrangement by which God regulates the way human beings relate to Him. Dispensationalism believes that God has planned a succession of different dispensations throughout history, both past, present, and future. Furthermore, dispensationalists believe that these dispensations are revealed in Scripture, in both biblical history and prophecy. Understanding these dispensations, these

---

38. Craig A. Blaising and Darrell L. Bock, *Progressive Dispensationalism* (Grand Rapids: Bridgepoint, 2000), 14.

different relationships God has had and will have with humanity, is crucial for comprehending the teaching and message of the Bible."[39]

Even if not dispensationalists, most evangelicals view the impact of eschatology and the doctrine of the future with regard to biblical pastoral care. A proper view of future events and the return of Christ and the coming of the kingdom should impact the tasks and methods whereby ministers bring hope and healing to those struggling through this sojourn of life.

From their work of over fifty years ago, Clebsch and Jaekle reflected such a view in their definition of pastoral care, "The ministry of the cure of souls, or pastoral care, consists of helping acts, done by representative Christian persons, directed toward the healing, sustaining, guiding, and reconciling of troubled persons whose troubles arise in the context of ultimate meanings and concerns."[40] It was from Seward Hiltner's explanation of pastoral ministry as "healing, sustaining, and guiding" that their addition of the aspect of "reconciling" brought a fresh understanding to the importance of pastoral care.

Life is lived in a complex world where questions concerning "ultimate meanings and concerns" must be answered from a biblical perspective. Questions and concerns of such nature are best answered by those representing a Christian perspective on life and the future. Their concept of "reconciling, seeks to reestablish broken relationships between persons and between persons and God. Reconciliation is the antithesis of alienation and may be seen to be the ultimate purpose of God (Eph. 3:10–11)."[41] With this overview, the ministry of pastoral care becomes a nurturing ministry, but how is such a nurturing ministry fleshed out, and how should the doctrine of the future be incorporated into the life of the church?

The Nurturing Ministry of Pastoral Care

An effective nurturing ministry of pastoral care adequately declares that the doctrine of the future will be expressed both internally to the local body of believers, as well as externally through the practical expression of biblical truth

---

39. Ibid.
40. William A. Clebsch and Charles R. Jaekle, *Pastoral Care in Historical Perspective: An Essay with Exhibits* (Englewood Cliffs, NJ: Prentice Hall, 1964), 4. Seward Hiltner was the first to identify the functions of "healing," "sustaining," and "guiding." Clebsch and Jaekle added "reconciling" to the list. In his assessment of pastoral care, David Stancil stated that, taken together, each of these elements of pastoral care is involved in developing a proper "ministry of nurturing."
41. Stancil, "Ministry of Shepherding," 211.

to the contemporary society at large. Internally, the pastor's responsibility for equipping the people of God most often is related to his pulpit ministry and the weekly exposition of the Scriptures.

A second internal expression of pastoral care will be provided during everyday occurrences and the circumstances of life. These events will arise from times of grief and sorrow, sickness and bereavement, and thus, will open the door for biblical counsel and personal interaction. Since the purpose of the church is the expression of the gospel message, then all preaching and teaching should be the proclamation of truth that produces the conversion of a lost soul with a God-given desire for holiness and maturity in knowing and growing in Christ that is only produced by a true conversion experience. The external expression of such truth will be a reality, as Craig Blaising affirms:

> [We] would do well to explore the internal social holiness of the church as a form of witness to the external society. In other words, if we as the community of Christ worked on creating our community as a model of social justice and peace, then we really would have some suggestions to make for social reform in our cities and nations. And we could do it as Gospel because the message, the suggestions, even the external social work would be based in a call to Christ in whom individual and social conversion go hand in hand. . . . Understanding the church as a present form of the future eschatological kingdom should lead us to see that multicultural phenomenon is precisely what God intends. The future kingdom will encompass all nations. The church today is a Spirit-united communion of Jews and all kinds of Gentiles.[42]

Therefore, effective pastoral care will be incomplete without the inclusion of biblical preaching, teaching, and counsel on the doctrine of the future. In the following, each aspect of such a nurturing ministry of pastoral care is summarized.

The Exposition of the Word. The pastor's primary platform for imparting biblical truth has been his weekly pulpit ministry. Traditionally, the normal pulpit ministry has consisted of one and, in some cases, as many as three opportunities to preach or teach God's Word to the flock. In most evangelical pulpits, a

---

42. Blaising and Bock, *Progressive Dispensationalism*, 288–89, 291.

combination of expository or topical/textual sermons will be delivered. Even though many definitions abound for expository preaching, John R. W. Stott declares the essence of what true biblical exposition should be:

> Properly speaking, "exposition" has a much broader meaning. It refers to the content of the sermon (biblical truth) rather than its style (a running commentary). To expound Scripture is to bring out of the text what is there and expose it to view. The expositor pries open what appears to be closed, makes plain what is obscure, unravels what is knotted and unfolds what is tightly packed. The opposite of exposition is "imposition," which is to impose on the text what is not there. But the "text" in question could be a verse, or a sentence, or even a single word. It could be a verse, or a paragraph, or a chapter, or a whole book. The size of the text is immaterial, so long as it is biblical. What matters is what we do with it.[43]

Applying proper hermeneutic principles to the doctrine of the future will enable the pastor not only to bring encouragement in the present, but also to bring hope for the future, as well as the proper motivation for service under the authority of God's Word. When a pastor approaches his task of heralding forth the truth, expository preaching will require the pastor to deal with the issues of eschatology as he works his way through the entire counsel of God rather than selecting specific portions of the text to preach. Most of the Old Testament prophecies, along with every book of the New Testament, present some aspect of eschatological truth that will give the faithful expositor the opportunity to incorporate the doctrine of the future into his normal preaching schedule.

Through the Counsel of the Word. The ministry of comfort is an important part of pastoral care. If the church is to be a true fellowship of care and nurture where believers minister to one another as the reciprocal commands expect, then the counsel that the fellowship presents to the brokenhearted will be filled with opportunities to incorporate the message of the future hope of God's kingdom. The occasions that most offer the message of future hope and

---

43. John R. W. Stott, *Between Two Worlds, The Art of Preaching in the Twentieth Century* (Grand Rapids: Eerdmans, 1982), 125-26.

restoration will be at times of sickness, chaos, and deep despair over a tragic event or the loss of a loved one. At times such as these, the message of the gospel will bring the reality of forgiveness, acceptance, guidance, and purpose that can only be found through belonging to the body of Christ, the church. If the message of the church is to be relevant within contemporary culture, then evangelical pastors "have to become more serious about what the Bible says about the Christian hope and bring their eschatological perspective more in line with the everyday realities of life."[44]

Rather than an eschatological view that espouses the biblical theology of the future to be employed as simply an escape from the real world or the judgment to come, the effective pastor must teach that salvation is not only a rebirth in this life and a hope for the life to come, but that such a life and eschatological view is designed for a clearer understanding that the church is to be a place of conversion and renewal in a world of heartache, pain, and loss today. Through this perspective, any sense of escapism is eliminated from people's perception of Christianity, and the call to conversion is presented as exciting and challenging not only to live with purpose in the present, but that one's eschatological hope becomes the mission of the contemporary church. With this understanding of the mission of the church, the doctrine of the future presented through the pulpit and counsel of the pastor becomes a vital tool for doing ministry internally to the church and externally in the community.

CONCLUSION

The pastoral care ministry of the church is built week by week, but it is tested in the laboratory of life on a daily basis. In the regular course of his ministry, the pastor must build his people through a steady diet of expository preaching and help prepare them for crisis, uncertainty, and death through the counsel of the Scriptures. Incorporating the doctrine of the future within a systematic study of God's Word must be the goal of every pastor. In doing so, he will not only unite the congregation in a fellowship of caring, but will equip and motivate them to take the redeeming and empowering message of eternal hope to a world that is filled with doubt and despair.

As pastoral care has been briefly summarized, effective pastoral ministry is most impactful when the exposition of the Scriptures, includes the

---

44. Kuhrt, "Importance of Being Eschatological," 8.

proclamation of eschatology. A general rule is that as it goes with the pulpit, so it goes with people. Thus, the importance of the doctrine of the future must be incorporated through consistent preaching, encouraging counsel, and active ministry within the context of the church and that of contemporary society. "It holds the key to so many of our current problems and beyond that of equipping the church for its ministry and mission. It is time to rediscover the importance of being eschatological."[45]

---

45. Ibid., 10.

The Doctrine of the Future and Contemporary Challenges

R. Albert Mohler, Jr.

Christian eschatology has often been treated as the theological "appendix" to the Christian worldview. Placed at the end of our volumes on systematic theology and often riddled with speculative interpretations of prophetic texts, evangelical approaches to eschatology regularly fail to integrate the importance of eschatology into the Christian life. Yet as the Bible and the church's rich theological heritage bear witness, eschatology is vitally important not only for how Christians are called to live their day-to-day lives, but also for their engagement with the public sphere. In this light, Christians must learn to ask and answer the question. How does a Christian eschatology shape our present lives in terms of our engagement with the culture? I hope to respond to this question with a uniquely and unashamedly Augustinian proposal.

Augustine and the Two Cities

Augustine, the great bishop in North Africa, is a theologian of almost inestimable importance to the intellectual life of the church. His voice was uniquely needed in his own day, and in some respects, it is just as urgently needed today. Whether in his oppositions to Manicheanism or Pelagianism, Augustine's theology set the church on a doctrinal trajectory that would shape it in almost every era of its existence. Without the Bishop of Hippo, the church would look radically different than it does today.

Furthermore, Augustine, serving as a bishop (a pastor of pastors), helped the early church theologically grapple with perhaps the most significant historical and cultural challenge it faced—the collapse of the Roman Empire.

Many Christians viewed the Roman Empire as the one great societal and cultural foundation without which the church could not exist. In fact, at least a few thought that the church had been rescued from its early perils by the conversion of Emperor Constantine. For many, the Christianization of the Roman Empire explained the power of the church. When the empire was at its height, the church's close association with the empire assured its protection. Thus, a collapse of the empire meant a collapse of every assurance of life and liberty according to the human economy. The fall of the empire raised monumental practical and theological questions for the church.

The first question, of course, was: How could Rome fall? The self-evident rectitude of Rome and its principles were obvious to all.[1] Its military power and economic might were unmatched over the course of centuries. How could this great empire be brought low, particularly in light of its imperial reach? The importance and magnitude of the question cannot be overstated. In fact, the question is of such importance that even modern historians still obsess over uncovering all the reasons Rome fell.

What we do know is that Rome did fall. Rome was a fact, until it was a fact no more. The collapse of Rome left a gaping cultural and intellectual hole in the human experience that demanded some form of explanation. Enter Augustine of Hippo. It is critical to remember that Augustine was doing theology not as a detached, ivory tower theologian unconcerned with the world around him. Augustine was doing public theology and negotiating ministry within the tumult of the fall of Rome. In light of this, Augustine was very much engaged in public theology. One of his primary tasks was to consider the relationship of the church to the public square, particularly now that the church was no longer the center of that public square.[2]

On the heels of that question was another important theological issue: To what degree should the church care about the fall of Rome? Or does this ultimately teach us that politics does not matter? Is this in any way related to the church's gospel witness? Augustine's answer to these questions was profoundly *eschatological*.[3]

---

1. *Ciu.* 1.3 in Augustine, *The City of God against the Pagans*, ed. R.W. Dyson (New York: Cambridge University Press, 1998), 6–8.
2. *Ciu.* 1.1.
3. E.g., the last five books of *The City of God* deal explicitly with eschatological matters, however throughout the work the city of God is viewed as a "pilgrim" (*ciu.* 1.35), "preparing through her present humiliation for her future exaltation" (*ciu.* 18.49).

His chief work in this regard was *The City of God*. Augustine employed the metaphor of a city—a *polis*—to describe the kingdom of God and the kingdoms of this world. Building theologically out of Jesus's teaching about the first and the second greatest commandment (Matt. 22:36–40), Augustine suggested that the Christian must understand that there are two cities in the world. The first city is the city of God. This city is God's not merely because he resides there but because God's character and authority define the city. In that city, God's sovereign authority is unmitigated and unconditioned. It is ordered according to the rule and reign of the law of God demonstrating simultaneously and in equal proportion his justice, righteousness, mercy, and holiness. Thus in the city of God everything is exactly as God would have it to be. The longing of every Christian is to live in that city.

By God's grace and the power of the gospel, Paul indicates, we have already been made citizens of the city of God (Phil. 3:20). This citizenship is given to us by divine promise, though we do not yet reside there. In fact, every Christian alive now lives in and experiences quite a different city—the city of man. The church recognizes that Jesus Christ is Lord and ultimately sovereign. Yet that sovereignty is conditioned by his forbearance and allowance for human beings to exercise moral responsibility. Unlike the city of God, the city of man is not as it should be.

With regard to each city, Augustine posited that we must understand that the city of God is a coming thing never to pass away while the city of man is a passing thing. The city of man is a temporary city, both conditioned and created. The city of man does not exist on its own terms. However, as Paul makes clear in Romans 1, the city of man refuses to acknowledge its creaturely and dependent status. In light of these truths, Augustine warned the church not to be fooled into seeing the coming thing (the city of God) as a passing thing and the passing thing (the city of man) as a coming thing. The warning remains just as vital for the church today.

Augustine also argued that both cities are characterized by a primary love. The love of man animates the city of man, even as the love of God animates the city of God. The problem with the city of man then is apparent when compared with Jesus's teachings on the first and second greatest commandments in Matthew 22. The love of man is not a self-reifying love; it does not exist on its own. In other words, on this side of Genesis 3, we are naturally inclined toward loving one another, but we do so as those in the line of Cain. We love those of our tribe, clan, family, and nation. Yet as Genesis 4 shows us, in the city of man even love for our own kin will be dispensed if no longer expedient.

As far as Rome exemplified the city of man, Augustine's words proved true before the church's very eyes. Augustine reminded the church that even while Rome was at its height, it was already crumbling, because it was built on the wrong kind of love. Failing to see this reality is ultimately due to the fact that humans tend to see the passing thing as a coming thing and the coming thing as a passing thing. In other words, even at the height of its earthly glory, Rome was already rotted from within.[4]

Re-engaging with Augustine and Christian Eschatology in the Twenty-First Century

Modern American evangelicals have often failed to think theologically about the church's relation to the public square until they are forced to do so. When Christianity is culturally mainstream and exercises significant cultural influence, the church rarely reflects on the Christian character of cultural engagement. Furthermore, when the church has addressed the issue of cultural engagement, it has often fallen into extremist theological positions.

For example, one wrong approach to cultural engagement is to assert that the church must dominate the culture until the culture is forced to agree with the Christian worldview. Another wrong approach is to withdraw from the culture, out of the conviction that the culture is ultimately a lost cause because it will never agree with the Christian worldview. Of course, there are different calibrations of each of these proposals but both fall short of Jesus's commission in Matthew 22 to give ultimate allegiance and love to God, while yet remaining *in* the world *loving* our neighbor.

As already seen, a robust understanding of the Great Commandment solves many of the problems associated with these two wrong theological proposals. However, something else is also needed for a right theology of Christian engagement with the culture: Christian eschatology. Christians and pastors need to reclaim the centrality of eschatology in the Biblical worldview. This does not mean we need a return to overly detailed and speculative prophecy charts. Rather, Christians must meditate on an eschatology defined by the biblical categories of the arrival of God's kingdom and the blessed hope of consummation and new creation.

---

4. The same reality regularly shows up in our own world. For example, the 2007 recession hit in the middle of what economists called an economic bubble. In other words, healthy economic growth occurred until the bubble "popped."

A Christian eschatology of this kind has monumental implications for the Christian life. First, as Augustine himself noted, a Christian eschatology endows the church with a patience that the world does not have. A purely secular worldview must view the immediate with a sense of urgency—an urgency that is relativized in a Christian eschatology.

Second, a biblical eschatology preserves Christians from the notion that they must find ultimate satisfaction in this life, whether in terms of our own personal pursuits or in the public sphere in matters such as social justice. Of course, this does not mean that Christians do not pursue the public good and justice in this life. Instead, it means that in the face of the world's insurmountable problems and injustices, we ultimately entrust ourselves and the world to the judge who will one day make all things right. The Bible's future resurrection hope put an end to utopian pretensions. Christians must recognize that ultimately this world is not our final home. If it is, then we are of all people most to be pitied (1 Cor. 15:19).

Finally, a Christian eschatology dignifies our current historical moment. A providential understanding of history recognizes that our time and culture is not here by accident. Our historical moment is part of the sovereign plan of God as revealed by the fact that the Lord has tarried. The church militant is still on mission and must continue to carry out that mission with fidelity. In other words, the waiting is for the witnessing.

What about the Church?

The Augustinian paradigm of two cities immediately raises an important question: Where is the church in all this? Thankfully, Scripture has spoken to this very issue. The consistent testimony of the biblical authors (and of Paul in particular) is that the church is in both cities at the same time—but it is secure in only one of those cities, the city of God. The ultimate security of the church in the city of God is rooted biblically in the notion that the covenant of redemption precedes the creation of the world. In other words, the eschatological church was designed and determined by our atemporal God before laying the foundations of creation. The church therefore is eternally secure in the city of God.

Why then would the church be left in the city of man after, through Christ, God accomplished all things necessary for the reclamation of those whom he predestined to eschatological glory? More simply, why is the church still here? The church ultimately belongs to the city of God, yet at the same time the church on earth has the responsibility of bearing witness to the gospel of Jesus Christ in the city of man so that the inhabitants of this city may become the inhabitants of the city of God and thereby show the glory of God in a fallen world. The fact that the church is in this world, while its citizenship is ultimately in that other world, makes our citizenship in this world meaningful. The church must therefore relate to the world in order to show the glory of God, in order to demonstrate the power the gospel, and in order to present the gospel that people may hear, believe, and be saved.

The fact that the church experiences this tension of residing in both cities should preserve it from falling to the temptation of believing that the church can bring society into total alignment with the purposes of God. Essentially, this type of theology, classically embodied in postmillennialism, is the error of mistaking this world for the kingdom. Postmillennialism has posited that God's will for the church was to bring this world into eventual submission to his will and to his word such that the city of man becomes the city of God.

The problem with postmillennial theology (aside from the fact that it does not do justice to the teaching of Scripture) is that the church begins to perceive its task as creating a culture that is "Christian-ish." In other words, postmillennialism assumes that as long as the culture is moving in the right direction, the problems of the city of man can eventually be solved. *This* world can become *that* world.

Augustinian eschatology also nullifies the isolationist and retreatist approaches to cultural engagement. It is an insult to the King to suggest that he has left us in the city of man for no purpose, or that his purpose is merely that the church ought to learn some set of valuable lessons that will ultimately be useful in the city to come.

Eschatological Preaching as Cultural Engagement

Given Augustine's paradigm of the two cities, we see that the church has a public responsibility because it is a public fact. Cultural engagement will happen. It is at just this point that the early church provides another incredibly helpful insight: Preaching the arrival of God's kingdom in the person of Jesus Christ (i.e., eschatological preaching) will get you in trouble. The first problem the church faced was not secularism but religious pluralism. More specifically, the message of the kingdom of God was in direct confrontation with the emperor worship of the Roman cult. To declare "Jesus Christ is Lord" is to declare that Caesar is not. Thus to preach the kingdom is to do public theology, particularly in the eyes of Caesar. This Christian commitment to the lordship of Christ in the arrival of God's eschatological kingdom was thus the primary reason Christians were persecuted and put to death. Christians were considered subversive and traitorous because they could not join the imperial cult or accept the deity of Caesar.

The church has witnessed the same phenomenon in other periods of its history. For example, in Germany in 1922, public Christianity was the norm. A so-called "cultural Protestantism" (German *Kulturprotestantismus*) reigned in the collective social conscience and in the idiom of public discourse. Yet by 1942, the Nazi regime had supplanted the old cultural Christianity with a new religion: the German Evangelical Church (emphasis on *German*) under the oversight of the "Reich bishops." This new state church, controlled by and therefore in support of the Nazi regime, recognized the statement "Jesus is Lord" as subversive to the state. Again, to declare Jesus is Lord is to say Hitler is not. Believers in the Confessing Church could find themselves on a train to Flossenbürg for such treason.

The rapid disappearance of cultural Christianity in our own time will mean that Christians may soon find themselves in a situation similar to that of the early church in Rome. Preaching the lordship of Christ and biblical eschatology rooted in the arrival of God's kingdom will be considered culturally and politically subversive. Proclaiming a biblical eschatology that heralds the message "Jesus Christ is Lord" will lead to direct confrontation with the culture.

While the disappearance of cultural Christianity is a cultural disaster, it is also a theological gain. It is disastrous for society because it will destroy a worldview most conducive to human flourishing. A post-Christian culture will be a very inconvenient place to raise your children, minister the gospel, or speak in the public square. Yet, at the same time, the evaporation of cultural Christianity may prove a theological gain for the church. Our lives and beliefs will only make sense if indeed Jesus Christ is Lord and our hope is not bound up in the city of man, but in a city to come. From a gospel-witness perspective, that is a very convenient place to be.

The Doctrine of the Future
and the Marketplace

Stephen N. Blaising

O n September 15, 2008, the world changed. Lehman Brothers filed for chapter 11 bankruptcy protection, and in the hours and days that followed "there was a virtual breakdown of the global financial system."[1] The unthinkable occurred when Henry Paulson, Secretary of the Treasury, and Ben Bernanke, Chairman of the Federal Reserve, walked stoically across Capitol Hill for a meeting with every senior legislator in the US Congress at Nancy Pelosi's office. The strongest economy in the world, the United States of America, was on the brink of melting down. Without fanfare or hype, Paulson and Bernanke said they needed $700 billion immediately to unfreeze the credit markets. Paulson minced no words about the gravity of the crises by warning earlier in the day that "the market is ready to collapse."[2] Bernanke added, "It is a matter of days before there is a meltdown in the global financial system."[3]

I was in Austin for an upcoming University of Texas football game at the time. While football activities unfolded as usual, I sat in a hotel toom, watching a televised press conference; Senator Christopher Dodd described the meeting as so tense that "you could hear the air leave the room."[4] What was I doing at a football game, when the known financial world was coming to an end? The

1. Alan Greenspan, "How to Avoid Another Global Financial Crisis," *The Journal of the American Enterprise Institute,* http://www1.realclearmarkets.com/2014/03/06/how_to_avoid_another_global_financial_crisis_151194 (accessed March 13, 2014).
2. Henry M. Paulson Jr., *On the Brink: Inside the Race to Stop the Collapse of the Global Financial System* (New York: Business Plus, 2010), 254.
3. Ibid., 259.
4. Ibid.

foundation of capitalism, the US economy, was on the brink of melting down in hours, and poised to bring down the world economy with it.

Like pinecones in a campfire, contagion and fear ignited throughout through the markets. Credit lines vanished worldwide. Financial institutions desperate for cash were locked out. The stock market plunged. Home equity was eviscerated. No asset was untouched by the calamities of 2008.

The concern today is that the Federal Reserve and central banks around the world frequently use a strategy of recovery that could set the stage for the same meltdown again.[5] The technique of recovery from the 2008 financial implosion is known as Quantitative Easing (QE), which simply put, means the printing of money to pay debt, increasing government debt at a torrid pace. Even if QE ends, the fact is that it is now a major policy option for central banks around the world. On top of this, the ever-deeper-in-debt US government is the one guaranteeing the majority of home mortgage loans. Henry Paulson explains why this is not good: "From my first days at the U.S. Treasury, I had sought to reduce the role and strengthen the regulation of Fannie Mae and Freddie Mac, which owned or guaranteed about half of America's residential mortgages. . . . Today fully 90 percent of new residential mortgages are government guaranteed. Our addiction to government subsidies, and not just in housing, may actually sow the seeds of the next crises."[6] The outstanding national debt of the United States is soaring. It has increased seventy percent in five years.[7] Timothy Geithner, in a 2012 *Wall Street Journal* opinion column, stated that one of the main causes of the 2008 crises was that "a large shadow banking system had developed without meaningful regulation, using trillions of dollars in short-term debt to fund inherently risky activity."[8] In other words, there are large unregulated credit markets funding high-risk activity. He said, "We cannot afford to forget the lessons of the crises . . . amnesia is what causes financial crises."[9]

---

5. Carmen M. Reinhart and Kenneth S. Rogoff, "Financial and Sovereign Debt Crises: Some Lessons Learned and Those Forgotten," IMF Working Paper WP/13/266, 3, 12–16. Here is a discussion of how current policymakers risk misleading the public's expectations about how debt will be excused. Policymakers also have amnesia about the catastrophic consequence of how the World War I debt to the United States was absolved. One of the consequences was the Great Depression.

6. Paulson Jr., *On the Brink*, xix–xx.

7. "Monthly Statement of the Public Debt of the United States," www.treasurydirect.gov/govt/reports/pd/mspd/2013/opds102013.pdf, last modified October 31, 2013 (accessed November 26, 2013).

8. Timothy Geithner, "Financial Crisis Amnesia," http://online.wsj.com/news/articles/SB10001424052970203986604577253272042239982 (accessed January 18, 2014).

9. Ibid.

Perhaps greed is the cause of amnesia. When financial markets are unregulated like the shadow banking entities throughout the world, greed can spread like wildfire. This greed is fed twenty-four hours a day by social media, which sells its wares at high speed, by appealing to the reptilian instinct of the public. Purchases are based more on current cost as a monthly payment than the total cost of a final debt. Greed easily accelerates debt because it fails to calculate, or in many cases ignores, the final cost. Greed is focused on the appetite of the moment. Credit cards and mortgages are the servants of people's appetites. QE and budget deficits are the servants of political appetites. Unfortunately, the cost is often not counted until it is too late. The market meltdown of 2008 vividly illustrates how quickly material wealth vanishes when massive debt comes due. The mirage of this world is that security is primarily an abundance of material wealth. The problem with that view is that the valuation of all forms of material wealth is held captive by many more multiples of debt. Values vanish instantly in chaotic events like market shocks. No one is spared loss. Real estate, currencies, stocks, bonds and commodities are valued against a worldwide landscape of individual and national debt. Debt is holding the world captive.

The doctrine of the future (eschatology) makes no apology for significant changes that take place quickly. It simply advises that trouble and volatility will increase in the last days and that one should prepare wisely. Chaotic events, by definition, are volatile and sudden. Economic volatility and market disruption will increase as the world sinks deeper in debt. This chapter focuses on how eschatology informs Christians to survive and thrive in their business, financial and marketing decisions, practices, policies, and relationships, as worldwide debt and volatility swirl at breakneck speed.

Early Decisions as Strategy

Much is at stake in the first decision on any new job or business venture. The first decision will command most of the time, energy, and resources down the line. The entire direction of life or business follows the lead of the first decision. Decisions determine direction. Making a new decision can initiate a change of direction. However, the lead decision sets anchors that are hard to remove.

Jesus Christ affirmed the importance of the early decision. His illustrations of the man finding treasure in a field and a man searching for fine pearls in

Matthew 13 demonstrate the value of the kingdom of heaven.[10] Above and beyond any investment or purchase one could ever make, the first decision one
should make is to seek the kingdom of heaven. "The kingdom of heaven is like
treasure hidden in a field. When a man found it, he hid it again, and then in his
joy went and sold all he had and bought that field. Again, the kingdom of heav-
en is like a merchant looking for fine pearls. When he found one of great value,
he went away and sold everything he had and bought it" (Matt. 13:44–46, NIV).

A potent benefit to members of the kingdom of heaven is the unlimited
potential of faith.[11] Jesus's seven words spoken to a desperate father are liberat-
ing: "Everything is possible for him who believes" (Mark 9:23, NIV). He didn't
say everything is probable. He didn't say everything is likely. He said everything
is possible for him who believes. That is all the father needed to know in a hor-
ribly impossible and frightening situation. It is all the disciples needed to know
about this circumstance where the father's son was consumed by powerful forces,
such that Jesus explained the problem as "this kind can only come out by prayer"
(Mark 9:29, NIV). Another impossible scenario was presented to Jesus regarding
the difficulty for anyone to be saved. "With man this is impossible, but not with
God; all things are possible with God" (Mark 10:27, NIV). Rudolf Schnackenburg referred to Jesus's miracles as "the kingdom of God in action."[12] The kingdom is "connected with his [Jesus's] person and his work."[13] The gospel authors
present an action-packed drama of Jesus quieting storms, reversing ills, changing
misfortune, defeating evil, healing diseases, and raising others from the dead,
before presenting himself alive after his own death "over a period of forty days"
(Acts 1:3, NIV). Forget about the highly acclaimed principles of diversification
such as those found in Modern Portfolio theory.[14] The Nobel Prize–winning
theory argues that risk can be minimized and returns increased by diversifying
across a variety of investments. Jesus, on the other hand, presents a different
view. "What good will it be for someone to gain the whole world, yet forfeit

---

10. Progressive dispensationalists "make no substantive distinction between the terms kingdom of
    heaven and kingdom of God. And they see Christ's present relationship to the church today
    as a form of the eschatological kingdom," Craig A. Blaising and Darrell L. Bock, *Progressive
    Dispensationalism* (Wheaton, IL: BridgePoint, 1993), 54.
11. J. Dwight Pentecost clarifies that "entrance into the kingdom is based on the new birth" (John
    3:5). J. Dwight Pentecost, *The Parables of Jesus* (Grand Rapids: Zondervan, 1982), 60.
12. Rudolf Schnackenburg, "Jesus and the Kingdom of God," *Dictionary of Jesus and the Gospels*,
    ed. Joel B. Green and Scot McKnight (Leicester: InterVarsity, 1992), 422.
13. Ibid.
14. Harry Markowitz, "Portfolio Selection," *Journal of Finance*, Vol. 7, No. 1 (1952): 77.

their soul . . . or what can anyone give in exchange for their soul?" (Matt. 16:26, NIV) Before making decisions on all the important matters of life and business, make a decision first for Jesus Christ.

The decision to join the kingdom adds spiritual resources that uniquely enable the Christian in all of his or her activities in the marketplace. Christians live in this world as "a temple of the living God" (2 Cor. 6:16, NIV). They are forgiven all sin (Col. 2:13, NIV), granted eternal life (John 3:14–16, NIV), given access to God the Father (Eph. 2:18, NIV), blessed with an inheritance (1 Pet. 1:4), "dearly loved" (Col. 3:12, NIV), "strengthened with all power" (Col. 1:11; Eph. 3:16, NIV), and equipped to endure hardship (1 Cor. 15:57, Rom. 8:37, 1 John 5:4, NIV). A member of the kingdom of heaven is a transformed human being. As Paul said, "It is no longer I who live, but Christ who lives in me" (Gal. 2:20, NIV). All of these benefits provide powerful endurance, strength, and joy while living in the marketplace. Prayers are heard and answered (John 16:24, NIV). Loneliness is only an emotion and not a fact anymore, because the "Spirit of Him who raised Jesus from the dead is living in you" (Rom. 8: 11, NIV). The eternal presence of the Holy Spirit is the powerful presence of God in a Christian's life (1 Cor. 3:16, NIV). He is with the Christian always, whether a bad health diagnosis is given, money is lost, an attack ensues, trouble explodes, or death strikes. Investing one's life in the kingdom of heaven is entrusting one's life and soul to the one and only person who demonstrated reversal of all the ills that plague mankind.[15] With a relationship to God "sealed for the day of redemption" (Eph. 4:30, NIV), one is powerfully enabled to face market complexities with courage and confidence.

Profound Simplicity as Strategy

Navigating an increasingly complex marketplace calls for decision-making skills that break through obstacles. Our Lord advocated a strategy of profound simplicity. "Suppose one of you wants to build a tower. Won't you first sit down and estimate the cost to see if you have enough money to complete it? For if you lay the foundation and are not able to finish it, everyone who sees it will ridicule you, saying, 'This person began to build and wasn't able to finish'"

---

15. Paul Hertig, "The Jubilee Mission of Jesus in the Gospel of Luke: Reversal of Fortunes," *Missiology: An International Review* 25, no. 2 (1998): 173–177. A full discussion of the reversal theme announced at the beginning of Jesus's ministry (Luke 4:18–19) is developed in light of the messianic text in Isaiah 61:1–2.

(Luke 14:28–30, NIV). Simplicity counters complexity. Simplicity breaks a strategy down into basic components. Technology is rapidly changing the way every product and service is produced, priced, and sold in the marketplace. Zeroing in on what is absolutely necessary is the clearest way to make decisions, solve problems, and achieve goals in an era whose business practices are being propelled at high speeds by the Internet. The age of the microchip speeds up our lives with our inboxes loading, our calendars filling, and our Facebook updates changing even while we sleep—if we sleep. Along with more TV channels, shampoo, blue jeans, radio stations, and sporting events are more choices at increasing speed. The omnipresent nature of smartphones screaming for attention has shortened the timeframe in which decisions are made. Hence, they are often made quickly and therefore prone to error. Decisions made without clear calculations lead to disaster, as Jesus illustrated in his parable of the tower. More intended destinations would be reached if thoughtful calculations were made. Fewer detours with explosive consequences would follow.

To enhance better calculations, ask the question that makes better futures. If I proceed down this road, choose this person, or deploy this capital, how will this play out three years from now? Three years is far enough into the future to imagine what the likely outcome will be. Jesus's premise is that when time is considered and a scenario projected, some towers are better left unbuilt. Some roads are better left untraveled. Solomon reminds us that "the prudent see danger and take refuge, but the simple keep going and pay the penalty" (Prov. 22:3). Anticipating these traps brings prudence into decision making. This is contrary to the snap decisions we are prone to make in the Internet age. Daniel Kahneman argues that in many areas of life people make decisions primarily based on feelings "in which the answer to an easy question 'how do I feel about it?' serves as an answer to a much harder question 'what do I think about it?'"[16] Counting the cost is a form of thinking slowly and strategically. Mistakes can be avoided, and destinations reached with careful deliberation. Think about how decisions today look three years from now.

OPPORTUNITY IN DYNAMIC PRACTICES

The doctrine of the future advises Christians to use their time expecting change to come quickly in business and in life (James 4:13–14). But the speed of today's

---

16. Daniel Kahneman, *Thinking Fast and Slow* (New York: Farrar, Straus and Giroux, 2011), 139.

information can be used as an advantage through dynamic practices. There is no need to be submissive to the speed of change. The doctrine of the future implores members of the kingdom to be at pace with the changes. Like a pace car at the Indianapolis 500, one can be in front of change by welcoming its arrival, not by competing with its speed. With warnings like "be sober" (1 Thess. 5:8, NIV), "be on the alert" (Matt. 24:42, NIV), "be ready" (Matt. 24:44, NIV), "pay attention" (2 Peter 1: 19, NIV), "be very careful" (1 Cor. 3:10, NIV), "we urge you" (1 Thess. 4:10, NIV), "contend earnestly" (Jude 1:3, NIV), "win" (1 Cor. 9:19, NIV), and "lead" (1 Thess. 4:11, NIV), the doctrine of the future urges Christians to lead an expectant life of vision and anticipation.[17] The time in this present age should be used productively with no thought or design of ever reaching a point of being idle.[18] Time is short for many reasons. Time is short because Christ can return at any moment. Time is short because health can change. Time is short because technology is making jobs obsolete. Time is short because markets are closing niche businesses every day. Many jobs in the clerical, retail, and manufacturing sectors are being replaced through the Internet or with robotic technology. This same deflating trend is also happening in professions such as law and medicine.[19] There is no guarantee that a planned job, skill, or license will carry you through the marketplace. Therefore, time at each point in a career can dramatically change for any reason and at any moment.[20]

Making the most of every opportunity captures fleeting time. This can be enhanced through a practice I will call *flow*. This is a clever business practice that recognizes how creative ideas and solutions are spawned through movement. Flow is the opposite of idleness. Flow is expectant movement. Flow recognizes that people, information, ideas, and solutions are in constant motion. Flow is not mindless movement or unplanned purpose. Flow recognizes that there is a treasure of information to be found in creative collisions. This treasure cannot be found by being idle, sitting tight, or even using the same resources over and

---

17. A constant upbeat outlook even during troubling times is supported by the Christian hope of complete redemption and salvation after death from all of the weaknesses and limitations of the human body and for receipt of an inheritance "that can never perish, spoil or fade, kept in heaven for you, who through faith are shielded by God's power for the coming of the salvation that is ready to be revealed in the last time" (1 Pet 1:4–5, NIV).
18. This can be seen in the parable of the Ten Minas in Luke 19:13 where Jesus illustrates business activity as a way of being productive until He returns. See also 2 Thess. 3:6-7, 11; Eph. 4:28.
19. Erik Brynjolffsson and Andrew McAfee, *Race against The Machine* (Lexington, MA: Digital Frontier Press, 2011), 51.
20. Andrew S. Grove, *Only the Paranoid Survive* (New York: Crown Publishing, 1999), 188.

over again. Using the same methods or the same resources will yield the same results. Flow recognizes that there is no wasted time because every moment is significant, including the moments we suffer. Even trouble can only exist in the present moment (2 Cor. 4:17). Moments fly by quickly so that the next moment may lead to the solution, the breakthrough, or the relief that leads the way.

Flow is on display in the dramatic story of an entourage of wealthy astrologers following a star to see "the newborn king" (Matt. 2:1–12, NIV). Everyone who made it to the first Christmas was a traveler. Most intriguing about the astrologers or magi mentioned in Matthew is that even though they likely had the most money compared to the other attendees, they had the most trouble. But they embraced flow to solve problems and find solutions when they pulled into Jerusalem. The magi saw the star initially and had enough information to arrive in Jerusalem. As often happens, it appeared to be a dead end. But they start asking questions. "Where is the one who has been born king of the Jews?" (Matt. 2:2, NIV). They had no idea this question would lead to an audience with Herod the Great, which was likely an unpleasant experience.[21] Unplanned, the magi find a key piece of information directly from a creative collision with the king. Here is the sequence of flow: (1) Arrive in Jerusalem; (2) dead end; (3) start asking questions; (4) talk to a lot of people; (5) find critical information from an unexpected meeting with Herod the Great. After all, the magi were not headed to Bethlehem until they were summoned by Herod for a secret meeting (Matt. 2:8–9). As Darrell Bock has noted, "what is clear is that their initiative stands in contrast to the indifference or secret hostility of Israel's leaders."[22]

Indifference is the opposite of flow. Indifference quits early. Indifference does not care. Indifference has tunnel vision. Indifference does not recognize, much less seek, opportunity in unexpected encounters. Herod had resources the magi didn't have, such as the religious leaders who tell him that the Messiah will be born in Bethlehem. Herod tells the magi to go to Bethlehem, and indeed they do and are rewarded. Flow is being alert and attentive to erratic encounters with people or events that yield unsought discoveries. Flow doesn't quit too early. But close-minded tunnel vision can easily miss the one opportunity or the one piece

---

21. Harold Hoehner, "Herodian Dynasty," in *Dictionary of Jesus and the Gospels* (Leicester: Inter-Varsity, 1992), 317–326. Herod was not someone anyone would like to confront or have a disagreement with, especially involving the news of a potential threat to his rule. He executed many of his political enemies—as well as his first wife, mother-in-law, and brother-in-law—long before Jesus was born.
22. Darrell L. Bock, *Jesus according to Scripture* (Grand Rapids: Baker Academic, 2002), 70.

of information that leads to treasure, finds the solution, or opens the door. It is in the asking, looking, and seeking in the erratic developments of life and business that treasures are found. This is the habit of flow.

Surplus

The doctrine of the future is clear that believers should design life to be content, free from the love of money, and free from debt (Phil. 4:12, Heb. 13:5, Rom. 13:8–9). Immediately before his mention of the rapture in 1 Thessalonians 4:13–18, Paul implores the church "to make it your ambition to lead a quiet life: you should mind your own business and work with your hands, just as we told you, so that your daily life may win the respect of outsiders and so that you will not be dependent on anybody" (1 Thess. 4:11–12, NIV). The word for "content" in Philippians 4:12 is αὐτάρκης, which Thayer defines as "sufficient for oneself, strong enough or possessing enough to need no aid or support; independent of external circumstances."[23] Contentment is a component of surplus because it recognizes and stops within limits. Contentment does not create excessive debt because it recognizes needs and is not controlled by wants. It doesn't pursue wealth for the sake of riches (1 Tim. 6:6). Contentment pursues a relationship with God first and then others. The by-product of contentment is surplus. Surplus is "the amount that remains when use or need is satisfied."[24] This kind of freedom is rare in a world where most nations are drowning in debt. Contrary to surplus, the financial health for governments today is defined by the price of debt, not the amount. Debt is understood. Excessive debt is the norm. A nation is considered healthy if it has ample "fiscal space."[25] Fiscal space is how much more debt a government can stack atop existing debt and still operate. Lack of fiscal space is when lenders stop buying a country's bonds. Fiscal space skates on the edge of a cliff. Debt is serviced and extended for government operations through bond sales and printing money. This works as long as the marketplace functions. But as debt levels increase, the marketplace is more vulnerable to shocks like wars and credit meltdowns.[26] Room for error has vanished.

---

23. James Henry Thayer, *Greek-English Lexicon of the New Testament* (Grand Rapids: Zondervan, 1962), 85.
24. *Merriam-Webster Collegiate Dictionary*, 11th ed., s.v. "surplus."
25. Simon Johnson and James Kwak, *White House Burning* (New York: Vintage Books, 2013), 158.
26. Ibid., 159–160.

Surplus is fiscal freedom. Surplus of a relationship with God is what Jesus valued most (Luke 12:21). He also recognized surplus as a skill well deployed in the marketplace. "If you have not been trustworthy in handling worldly wealth, who will trust you with true riches?" (Luke 16:11, NIV). Surplus is a by-product of skillful habits. Surplus is lauded in two parables of Jesus—Matthew 25:14–30 and Luke 19:11–27.[27] In Matthew, the master responds to the servants who doubled his money, "Well done, good and faithful servant! You have been faithful with a few things; I will put you in charge of many things. Come and share your master's happiness!" (Matt. 25:21, NIV). A similar response is given in Luke to the servants who had doubled the master's money. "I tell you that to everyone who has, more will be given, but as for the one who has nothing, even what they have will be taken away" (Luke 19:26, NIV). Clearly, there is affirmation at the highest level when one's work in the market place achieves compounded results.

With employment tight, competition intense, and deflationary forces in play, imagination will be vital to solving problems and overcoming obstacles.[28] Jesus commends the imagination of the manager in Luke 16:1–13. The manager is told by his boss to give a final accounting, and after that he will lose his job. This is a common problem today. He doesn't have much time and so he must act quickly. In a clever move, he renegotiates the debt of each customer in the business while he has the authority. Each debt is restructured to match their ability to pay. His boss and the clients are pleased and impressed. When bad news arrives, people tend to panic or shut down, but waiting for all of the violent and sudden emotion of the bad news to subside allows one to see the next step. Versatility is an astute survival skill. Restating a problem or analyzing an obstacle in simpler terms and focusing on what's available as opposed to what's missing turns unsolvable problems into solvable ones. The manager used his remaining time on the job to creatively meet the needs of his clients which confirmed and strengthened relationships that could help him later.

The next link in the chain to surplus is setting limits. Cost-cutting is the tool that widens surplus within limits. Surplus in scary times results from a personal or corporate culture that is budget minded. As stated earlier, the future promises increasing disruption in financial markets. This is due to the exponential growth of

---

27. Craig S. Keener, *The IVP Bible Background Commentary* (Downers Grove, IL: InterVarsity Press, 1993), 117, 241. Keener provides a concise rendition on the background of monetary units in first-century Judea.
28. Paul Krugman, "Can Deflation Be Prevented?", http://web.mit.edu/krugman/www/deflator.html (accessed July 7, 2013).

debt. When turbulence results in dramatic losses such as the real estate and stock market crashes in 1987, 2001, and 2008, the people and businesses that have made cost-cutting the cornerstone of their financial policy can be at peace and less susceptible to the threat of implosion. They have "margin."[29] They have a safety gap between their income and their expenses. They are prepared.

Like a fruitful vineyard, surplus grows in a weeded garden. The laws of the vineyard illustrate that decisions, practices, and policies in the marketplace should be planned and adjusted over time. There is no last-minute prep for an exam in the vineyard. The seed must be planted in the spring, watered in the summer, weeded throughout the year, and harvested with a watchful farmer present at all times. The antithesis to vigilance is neglect as captured in this proverb. "I went past the field of a sluggard, past the vineyard of someone who has no sense; thorns had come up everywhere, the ground was covered with weeds, and the stone wall was in ruins. I applied my heart to what I observed and learned a lesson from what I saw. A little sleep, a little slumber, a little folding of the hands to rest and poverty will come on you like a thief and scarcity like an armed man" (Prov. 24:30–34, NIV). Thorns and weeds in this ancient proverb represent neglect. The stone wall was a boundary to wild animals and is in shambles. Properly farmed, the vineyard has a boundary with no weeds or thorns and a fruitful crop. Setting the size of the vineyard is the wise guideline of modern business policy. The early decision as presented at the beginning of this chapter defines the business purpose, the project, the ministry, or the goal. Business practices support the business policy. Practices that endorse a culture of creativity, openness, and curiosity to pursue the second, third, or fourth option will thrive in a volatile and uncertain marketplace. Surplus sets the limits needed to price the product or the service. The goal of business, as Jesus lauded the shrewd manager, is to find the right balance in producing what the customer is willing to pay for at a price that is distinctive from all others. Fit the distinctiveness of the product or service to what the customer will pay for. Do not produce what the customer is not willing to pay for. Customers and clients are not helped by building unwanted bells and whistles into products and services that raise the prices they must pay. Entrepreneurs naturally add all the goodies that make for distinction. A farmer mentality needs to be present side by side with the entrepreneur, looking for all the thorns and weeds the customer doesn't want. If little attention is paid to reducing unnecessary parts of a product or service that customers do not want, then overhead creeps in and chokes profitability. This includes

---

29. Richard A. Swenson, *Margin* (Colorado Springs: NavPress, 1992), 91–92.

excessive office space, office equipment, supplies, and components and materials. These are the thorns and weeds that choke a fruitful vineyard. But if the farmer mentality is disciplined to design products and services for what the customer will pay, then demand will naturally reward this preparation with the consequence of a good harvest. Good farmers never stop weeding the vineyard. Never stop cutting unnecessary costs.

The doctrine of the future states that a final day of accounting is coming (1 Pet. 4:17). This final accounting will confirm the success or failure of the choices men and women have made while living in the marketplace (1 Cor. 3:10–15, Heb. 4:13). There are exhortations throughout the New Testament to seize the opportunities of each moment by being faithful, productive, and wise with the time, talent and resources one is entrusted with, "because the days are evil" (Eph. 5:16, NIV).

BREAKFAST ON THE BEACH

No marketing team has been as empowered and successful as the one that assembled for a breakfast meeting on a beach in Galilee in John 21. It was exactly the opposite of a death-bed gathering, when the room is darkened by sorrow over endings. This was an out-of-this-world event marking new beginnings, new hope, new vision, and new expectations for a kingdom that will ultimately reverse all of the sorrow, suffering, pain, and misfortune its members have ever experienced. A successful launch of this marketing campaign required personal encounters with the risen Messiah that not only confirmed the "imminent fulfillment of the eschatological kingdom" with the presence of the King but would also impact and inspire the promoters and their potential customers until the end of time.[30]

Great marketing strives for a visual that people never get out of their mind, emotion, or appetite. Super Bowl advertisements are an example. Who can forget the Coca Cola commercial of Mean Joe Greene tossing a can of soda to a young boy, "Hey kid! Catch!"?[31] Or the Apple Macintosh ad directed by Ridley Scott in 1984?[32] Vision-casting must be as distinct for a business as it is for potential customers. In this case, a loving figure the disciples see but don't recognize is waiting for them after a night-long fishing trip. He reverses their fruitless

---

30. Blaising and Bock, *Progressive Dispensationalism*, 232.
31. Vicki Hyman, "Top 10 Super Bowl Commercials Ever Made," *The Star Ledger*, http://www.nj.com/super-bowl/index.ssf/2014/02/top_10_super_bowl_ads_all-time.html, last modified February 2, 2014 (accessed March 26, 2014).
32. Ibid.

night of fishing with a haul they can barely control. John recognizes Jesus, Peter plunges into the lake, and when they get to shore, they can see a campfire. Before their eyes, noses, and ears is the crackling smell of early cooking and the recreated physical body of the Son of God saying, "come and have breakfast" (John 21:12, NIV). Come and have breakfast. After all the loss of hope, loss of dreams, loss of life, and fear of losing their own life, here is the Son of Man cooking their breakfast. No hurry, no worry, no fear. Be still. Come and have breakfast. The best times in our lives are waking up in the morning to the smell of breakfast and someone who loves us is cooking.

Demonstrating the new creation in his resurrected body, Jesus empowered his disciples with love and forgiveness at the beach. The fact that Jesus is alive and cooking breakfast is a mind-blowing and circuit-breaking development. This is an encounter they needed for final verification of their mission. Through the striking presence of his resurrected body, these disciples had a final glimpse of the kingdom indelibly cooked into their senses. Breakfast was a demonstration by Jesus of love, forgiveness, and restoration.[33] Forgiveness is the state of being clear of all accusation. It is the state in which one has been "let go" or set free (Acts 13:39, NIV).[34] Restoration is a return to belonging. It is a return to full relationship. These seven men must have recalled Philip asking Jesus days before his crucifixion to "show us the Father and that will be enough for us." Jesus said to him, "He who has seen me has seen the Father'" (John 14:8–9, NIV). Who is the Father? What is God like? Look at Jesus. Here is the King, the God of the Ages cooking and serving breakfast on a beach to a group of seven tired men who deserted him at his time of greatest trial (Matt. 26:56).

One of the great gifts of Christian faith is the possibility of cooperation through forgiveness. Since God clears us of all bitterness, anger, revenge, malice, and everything else that equates to sin, we should forgive and clear others. This allows peace and unity to prevail (Col. 3:12–15). Being clear in relationships frees up energy to perform at the highest level. Jesus put this on sharp dis-

---

33. The good news of the gospel is that all are invited to be permanently restored in their relationship with God through faith in his Son's atonement for sin. This is illustrated in the parable of the prodigal son, whose return to his father is an image of restoration. The marketplace application is the priority and reward for operating as a unified team whose chief qualities are cooperation, humility, and big vision.

34. The work on ἀφίημι by Bultmann points out the New Testament usage for the meaning "let go" such as Mark 1:20 as well as forgiveness given through faith in the redeeming act of Jesus Christ such as Acts 13:38. Rudolf Bultmann, ἀφίημι, in *Theological Dictionary of the New Testament*, vol. 1, ed. Gerhard Kittel (Grand Rapids: Eerdmans, 1977), 509.

play at breakfast. Instead of their failures, Jesus focused on their potential (John 21:15–17). He sent a message that in order to be at peace, one must forgive. The opposite of forgiveness is to blame other people or blame circumstances. Organizations are pools of relationships that need to be nurtured for the common vision upon which they were formed. Cooking breakfast is an unforgettable image to model for relationships in the marketplace. When management and team members concentrate on empowering each other through their unique gifts, then the atmosphere of the organization is ripe for growing success. The impact of forgiveness for Peter shows up in his performance in the marketplace when he appears on a big stage in Caesarea. He is summoned by a prominent centurion of the Italian Regiment along with "his relatives," "his close friends," and "a large gathering of people" (Acts 10:24, 27, NIV). Peter presents the message of "the good news of peace through Jesus Christ" (Acts 10:36, NIV) and then recalls the impact of breakfast with Jesus "by us who ate and drank with him after he rose from the dead" (Acts 10:41, NIV).

Gratitude and humility are fruits of forgiveness. Gratitude allows one to focus on the strengths of others while letting go of their weaknesses. Humility spawns a gracious viewpoint that many others are involved in the sum total of reasons that success in a project or mission is achieved. Others include fellow entrepreneurs, supervisors, employees, suppliers, and providers. The marketplace is connected. Declining sales or results in the marketplace means at some point the others playing a role in that success were ignored or underappreciated.

Jesus gave these men enormous responsibility: "feed my lambs," "take care of my sheep," "tend my sheep" (John 21:15–17, NIV). Here is the Son of Man empowering his marketing team and asking for their help all at the same time. These unified men would establish and launch his worldwide enterprise: the church.

Storms and Rainbows

"Unequaled distress" (Matt. 24:21, NIV) that has never been seen or will ever be seen again is in the future. This period of distress is the great tribulation prophesied by Daniel (Dan. 12:1) and Jesus (Matt. 24:21). Signs that precede the end of the age and signal the second coming of Christ are presented in Matthew 24:15–31.[35] Only God, the Father, knows the exact time when the Son of Man

---

35. Elliott Johnson, "The Gospels," unpublished class notes for BE105 (Dallas Theological Seminary, Spring Semester, 2011), 53.

will return to the earth (Matt. 24:36). Volatility in markets is increasing and pressure against economic growth will intensify as nations are surrounded by accelerating debt, but those who have placed their life in trust to Jesus Christ can be prepared by making wise decisions, embracing dynamic practices, exercising the keys to fruitful relationships, and employing the habits of surplus.

On April 3, 2012, I was driving to Dallas after visiting my parents, when quickly the sky and everything around me grew dark. It was lunchtime. Weather reports indicated storms were in the area but not anything like I encountered. Darkness overtook the light. A few cars crept in front of me, their drivers wondering what to do next. They pulled over and so did I. Wind speed suddenly changed and I was face to face with an EF-2 tornado in the middle of Interstate 35. There was no time to do anything but run to the ditch and pray. The tornado threw twelve-thousand-pound tractor trailers like Tonka trucks hundreds of feet into the air. I felt like Dorothy in the Wizard of Oz. I wanted to go home. Fortunately, the tornado slowly moved east instead of due south toward my ditch.

On the other side of the storm is the rainbow. John saw a rainbow wrapped around the throne in heaven during his vision for the book of Revelation (Rev. 4:3). Ezekiel, in his vision, saw a rainbow which he said was "the appearance of the likeness of the glory of the Lord" (Ezek. 1:28, NIV). Treasure, fine pearls, breakfast, and a rainbow are some of the images we see in this review of the doctrine of the future and the marketplace. Take them with you all the way home.